CHESTER B. HIMES

ALSO BY LAWRENCE P. JACKSON

My Father's Name:
A Black Virginia Family after the Civil War

The Indignant Generation:
A Narrative History of African American Writers and Critics,
1934–1960

Ralph Ellison:
Emergence of Genius

CHESTER B. HIMES

A BIOGRAPHY

Lawrence P. Jackson

W. W. NORTON & COMPANY

INDEPENDENT PUBLISHERS SINCE 1923

NEW YORK   LONDON

For information about permission to reproduce selections from this book,
write to Permissions, W. W. Norton & Company, Inc.,
500 Fifth Avenue, New York, NY 10110

For information about special discounts for bulk purchases, please contact
W. W. Norton Special Sales at specialsales@wwnorton.com or 800-233-4830

Manufacturing by Quad Graphics, Fairfield
Book design by Daniel Lagin
Production manager: Julia Druskin

ISBN 978-0-393-06389-9

W. W. Norton & Company, Inc.
500 Fifth Avenue, New York, N.Y. 10110
www.wwnorton.com

W. W. Norton & Company Ltd.
15 Carlisle Street, London W1D 3BS

1 2 3 4 5 6 7 8 9 0

This book is dedicated to my mother, Verna M. Jackson; my sister, Lynn S. Jackson; my grandmothers, Eleanor Christine Macklin Mitchell and Virginia Jefferson Jackson Rowe; my children, Katani, Nathaniel, and Mitchell; and the women who bring us forth:

Sarah Farrar	Barbara Dugger	Martha Allen
Francis Jones	Gennifer Dugger	Irvina Mallory
Amanda Jones	Jackie Martin	Elise Mason
Maude J. Macklin	Anne Taylor	Carol Carter
Betsey Maclin	Carol Taylor	Carrie Dorom
Frances Maclin	Veronica Norwood	Marylin Washington
Daisy M. Mitchell	Dr. Jeanette Dates	Edna Mae Greer
Luvenia Daughtery	Doris Brunot	Thelma Jackson
Sandra Daugherty	Kay Drayton	Rosie Hutchinson
Grace Macklin	Jewell Campbell	Gwynn Tartar
Grace Gee	Barbara Golden	Ada Lovick
Harriet Macklin	Juanita Wilson	Nancy Barrick
Marsha M. Thomas	Betty Nunn	Bernice Beaird
Vera Macklin	Jean Smith	Ella Edemy
Sally Macklin	Shirley Anderson	Olivia Dixon
Teresa Hutchinson	Bertha Blow	Candace Simms
Deanne Hutchinson	Mary Holman	Camay C. Murphy
Doris Mitchell	Alicia Allen	Phyllis Alston
Clara Mitchell	Carol Miller	Eliza Johnson
Sally Breedlove	Janette Hopkins	Rosalee Smith
Dicey Lee Waller	Carolyn Tubman	Jacquelyn Jackson
Alice Jefferson	Twilah Grant	Reba Robinson
Morning Hundley	Phyllis Shelton	Ruby Fuller
Celestia H. Jackson	Dianne Claiborne	Gladys Despaigne
Jennie Dickerson	Dr. Nina Rawlings	Delores Lewis
Mary J. Kesee	Helen Bentley	Naomi McGadney
Martha J. Womack	Eula Gray	Regine Jackson
Marnice Tolber	Patricia Jessamy	Marie Ostine
Elizabeth Mills	Sarah Taylor	Patricia D. Ouisley

For all angel is not'ing more dan de shark well goberned.

—OLD FLEECE, *MOBY-DICK*

Contents

Prologue

In the spring of 1934 a young prisoner in Ohio's maximum security penitentiary sat in a raw dormitory near an open latrine with a typewriter purchased from his gambling winnings. For three years, he had plunked away at short stories, one after another, dozens of them, mailing them out to newspapers in Chicago and Atlanta. Slowly he had mastered his craft while reading everything that the prison trustee had in the cart, from glossy magazines and detective stories, to Omar Khayyám and the latest by John O'Hara. He studied the writings of Ernest Hemingway. Five years into his sentence, the twenty-four-year-old had known some minor literary successes, but in that year he would have some major ones. Although it wasn't unheard of for an Ohio convict to achieve literary fame—O. Henry had walked the same yard—there was a difference. Chester Himes was black.

If race has reasserted its powerful relevance in the twenty-first century, in the early 1930s it had fully evolved into what the sociologist and writer W. E. B. Du Bois forecast in 1903 as "the problem of the Twentieth Century . . . the problem of the color line." Up to 1934 there had been one black professional writer of regular national reach, the short-lived poet and novelist Paul Laurence Dunbar, who was best known for poetry in black "dialect," what he himself was prone to dismiss as a "jingle in a broken tongue." Others had tried and abandoned the job, moving on to steadier work. For most people whose parents or grandparents had reached adulthood as chattel slaves, it was thought improvident and foolhardy, if not genuinely odd, to pursue a career exclusively as a professional writer of fiction.

This was certainly true for Chester Himes. At the beginning, he ignored, denied, erased, or felt ashamed of much of what is understood today as racial ancestry or racial identity. He knew mainly that blackness had helped him pull a twenty-year-sentence for an armed robbery, a punishment he received at nineteen after he threw himself on the mercy of the court and confessed. A broken back was the only reason he had the leisure to write in the segregated prison and, unlike the other black convicts, wasn't shoveling coal all day, everyday.

But to look at Chester Himes in 1934 was not, however, to be overwhelmed by something that mattered little to him. Light-skinned and slightly built, he exuded boyish, almost feminine charm. He had chipped teeth and several prominent scars, the main one on his chin, but they were the result of an accident, not street fights. For all of his life he would strive to appear tougher than what he felt inside, and writing helped him steel himself emotionally. He often compared the literary life to prizefighting and he accepted the discipline of training, punishment, and rejection, saying that "a fighter fights, and a writer writes."

What he would accomplish in gray dungarees on the gray bunk surrounded by the clamor of unruly men suffering through the winter of their confinement would land him in a national magazine in 1934, repeatedly, alongside the best American writers, Ernest Hemingway and Langston Hughes, another young black man from Ohio attempting to make a career in writing stick. Within ten years, after an early parole, Chester Himes fulfilled all of his youthful promise, and published a fiery first novel with America's largest press, Doubleday. Not even two years after that, and with arguably America's best literary publisher, Knopf, he completed the book that would define his career, *Lonely Crusade*. But although he was acclaimed—"if he is not the greatest writer of fiction among contemporary American Negroes, there is none greater"—by the American impresario of modern art Carl Van Vechten, Himes fled the United States as soon as he could, in 1953, returning in contrite humiliation for ten months in 1955, then happily abandoning America forever. In France, Chester Himes became a writer of international renown and shaped the attitudes of the next generation. He did it by living in an unbending style and pioneering black stories in a new genre: detective fiction.

Himes was driven to expose racial injustice, especially its sub-liminal and libidinal dimensions, and all of his work was that of a bold man struggling to survive by the writer's discipline. His candid, revealing books shamed other writers and always repulsed and offended parts of his audience. Early on, his publishers considered him unique "for sheer intensity of feeling, for conveying utter frus-tration, the heart-breaking effect of constant defeat, and fear that can be dissolved only by violence." But he insisted on taking his fight not simply to the most obvious sources of racial cruelty in Ameri-can society, but to the doorstep of progressive liberals congratulating themselves for their altruism and kindness. He specialized in biting the hand that fed him, and he earned that reputation by accusing the presses that acquired him of perfidy. His first book, *If He Hollers Let Him Go*, made one of his editors at Doubleday remark that he "nause-ated her," which led Himes to develop a critique, which he made over and over, that the company sabotaged and cheated him. Doubleday's editor in chief once responded testily, "We are not accustomed to having our word questioned the way you question it in that letter, Chester." The editor would be joined by virtually everyone who ever published Chester Himes. Chester worked both sides of that street.

He was the rare black writer to earn official condemnation from the NAACP.

Chester Himes soldiered on, writing books with a vulnerable honesty that left him wounded when the works floundered, typically on account of the claim that the author was too bitter, too graphic, and ignoring the progress in U.S. race relations after the 1954 *Brown* decision. He became, midway through his career, a scapegoat, the black writer unwilling to accept that the United States had become a blameless, functioning multiracial democracy. He was outcast for his blunt unwillingness to herald a Pollyannish future of healthy racial integration and economic justice. History has borne out some of his vinegary judgments.

In an America that was enjoying *Amos 'n' Andy*, Himes wrote about black men lusting after white women, crippling skin-color prejudice, and the difficulty of combat against the power of corporate industrialists. Himes might have been considered a prophet if he had not begun a career in the era when Richard Wright was the recognized black writer exploring the arc of race relations, Willard Motley the best-selling author who had completely eschewed the race problem, and Ralph Ellison the shining artist-intellectual who transcended race and wrote because he loved his craft.

Although Chester wrote about Harlem and black workers struggling to get ahead, he was reared in the Deep South and Cleveland, the middle-class child of college teachers. He was the first twentieth-century black American to walk the path of petty criminal and convict turned dynamic writer that would later make celebrities out of Malcolm X, Claude Brown, Eldridge Cleaver, Robert Beck, Nathan McCall, and several others. Himes's early novels—*If He Hollers Let Him Go* (1945), *Lonely Crusade* (1947), *The Third Generation* (1953), and *The Primitive* (1955)—revealed a fundamentally racist American society less inclined to lynch blacks but preferring to dismantle them psychologically. In his French detective series starring Gravedigger

Jones and Coffin Ed Johnson, he reversed gear, discarding the exposure of corruption and ethical hypocrisy and instead exaggerating the gross carnival created by slavery and segregation. Himes resolved the pain and indignation of his life by revealing the humor in it and by acknowledging the absurdity of western humanity and the inextricability of black people from any vision of America. His vernacular tales gained wide appeal and were turned into films. The generation who became writers after the assassination of Malcolm X, proudly calling themselves "black," defining their identities in the storm of left-wing politics and black nationalist aesthetics, considered him their forebear. Their respect and admiration was unsurprising. During his lifetime, Chester Himes published seventeen novels, a book combining a major playscript along with several short stories, and a two-volume autobiography: he left a decisive archive and a legacy that endures.

CHESTER B. HIMES

Chapter One
OLD SCHOOL NEGRO
1909-1914

Chester Bomar Himes was born on July 29, 1909, in a comfortable white two-story, three-bedroom cottage at 710 Lafayette Street on the corner of Dunklin Street in Jefferson City, Missouri. In the late 1920s, the poet Sterling Brown and his wife, Daisy, would occupy the same house. On the other side of Lafayette from the house stood the limestone pillars and wrought-iron main gates of the campus of Lincoln Institute. The school's elaborate brick buildings towered on the hill opposite the house, and the students could be seen scrimmaging at football on the school grounds below. Chester was born into a family, on both parents' sides, of professors teaching in America's Negro higher education system. The last of three sons, Chester was named by his mother, Estelle, to honor her father Elias Bomar, who was known to his family and friends by his middle name, Chester.

An exacting, slight woman in adulthood, Estelle Himes was proud of her family and ancestry. Both of Estelle's parents had been born into slavery in Spartanburg, South Carolina, in the 1830s and emancipated as adults after the Civil War. While they were light complexioned enough to pass as not being black (exasperating and befuddling to the Dalton, Georgia, census numerator), they were hardly considered white. Born after legal chattel slavery, Estelle belonged to a generation of African Americans who heard rumors about the identity of some of their grandparents. South Carolina, especially its coastal parts, also had a tradition of using the terms "turks" and "brass ankles" to include mulattoes among whites in times of need or to palliate ardent natives refusing enslavement and black codes. But wistful Estelle pondered about her forebears, and she developed elaborate genealogical and romantic myths, linking herself at every turn to aristocrats. Estelle liked to describe her mother as the offspring of a "pedigreed Englishman," an Irish trader, and a woman whose mother was an "African princess." She proudly described her father's father as "a direct descendent from an English noble family."

The truth was a bit messier than the family legends she raised her younger sons, Joseph and Chester, to admire. Estelle's mother, Malinda Cleveland, had grown up a prize possession of Jesse Cleveland, a prosperous Spartanburg merchant, whose father had distinguished himself as a Revolutionary War captain at the Battle of King's Mountain. Hardy and independent, Cleveland conducted his business in dry goods and slaves overland by wagon train to ports in Baltimore and Philadelphia to elude the import taxes applied to the goods shipped by boat from Charleston's harbor. He claimed title to much of the original land that became the town of Spartanburg and, by 1835, was named a trustee of the Spartanburg Male Academy, along with another prominent citizen, Elisha Bomar. In his will, Cleveland donated his cow pasture, or the land west of the courthouse, to what is today's Wofford College.

When Cleveland died in December 1851, Malinda was a young girl of about twelve, and she was valued at $700. Apparently a striking child, Malinda looked like a mixture of Irish or English with Native American and African, a common outcome of the sexual relations that slaveholders forced upon enslaved women and girls. Malinda was moved to the town household of Cleveland's middle son, Robert, in the northwest part of the village. A silver-tongued graduate of Charleston Medical College, Robert Easley Cleveland was a well-liked doctor in his thirties specializing in typhoid cases. By 1860 the younger Cleveland was wealthy and owned $39,000 worth of "personal property," mainly enslaved mixed-race people. Although her mother's presence nearby may have helped her put off the pressures of concubinage for a time, in her late teens Malinda found herself in a sexual relationship with a white man, probably Cleveland. By 1867, when she was in her late twenties, she had four children: eight-year-old Maggie, six-year-old Thomas, two-year-old Phillis, and newborn Charles. Phillis seems to have been the last Cleveland child, and Maggie seems to have been the first. While the other children were probably fathered by Elias Bomar, there is no way of knowing with certainty.

At some point during this period, Malinda fell in love with the spirited and dashing young groom and mason Elias Bomar. As a child she had had the opportunity to first meet Elias, who was quite difficult to distinguish physically from a white man, when Robert Cleveland married Elizabeth Bomar in Spartanburg in 1844. Elizabeth was the oldest daughter of John Bomar Jr. and the marriage united two of the town's prominent white families. The Bomars descended from Whig Englishmen who had settled in Halifax County, Virginia, fought the British and then trekked down to South Carolina after the surrender at Yorktown. Elisha Bomar was the local patriarch, who married Amaryllis Earle in 1823 and, like Jesse Cleveland, sent his children into the professions. His son John Earle Bomar was born July 29, 1827.

Technically, Estelle Himes's father, Elias, was never owned by any Bomar. Theron Earle, a relative of Amaryllis, owned the title to the man, and in 1840, before Elias was ten, his estimated value was $550. In piecemeal notes about her father written at the end of her own life, Estelle described him as the son of an "octoroon" and a "white Englishman." Earlier, during Chester's childhood, she told her sons that she was the granddaughter of Elisha Bomar from Spartanburg, which is possible. Elisha Bomar might have visited Theron Earle's farm at some point in the 1830s and conceived a son who came under his control during later years. After Earle's death in 1841, roughly three-year-old Elias seems to have been entrusted to Elisha and Amaryllis Bomar, and became the valet to their fourteen-year-old son John.

The slavery that Elias knew at the hands of the Bomar family was unique. Like other Southerners with pretensions, the family preferred the term "servant" to "slave," and they built sturdy brick dwellings on their grounds for slave houses. Bomar children weren't permitted to slough off their chores onto the servants. Elias's main job, along with walking the cows to pasture, was probably as a groom. When John attended the famed Charleston military academy The Citadel (he did not graduate) and then took classes at Erskine College (again without finishing a degree), Elias probably accompanied him. John then found his true vocation, working as the editor of the two-sheet Spartanburg paper the *Carolina Spartan*, where it was claimed that, "no one ever wielded a more graceful pen." Bomar became county clerk, or intendant, before the war, and he amassed a large library stocked with works by Alexander Pope, Samuel Taylor Coleridge, and Walter Scott, along with a complete set of Charles Dickens, which he enjoyed reading aloud. In the wake of the master's professional climb—the colleges, newspapers and books—Elias learned how to read. His second daughter, Estelle, would have a son named after her father who shared a birthday with his grandfather's slave master John Earle Bomar who had wanted to become a writer.

Journalist Bomar was also a master mason who had lain the corner stone of the town's courthouse. He passed on the trade to his servant, and by the end of the 1850s Elias had become a skilled mason. Then came the century's and the nation's defining crisis, the Civil War. Genteel slaveholder that he may have been, Bomar gathered together local men into the Holcombe Legion and was elected captain of Company C. Groom Elias Bomar, tall, "white looking," and with "a long blond beard," accompanied his master to war. The Holcombe Legion participated in optimistic skirmishes in early March 1862, where individual valor seemed important. By June, however, immediately after the Battle of Seven Pines, it had become immersed in the massive slaughter for which the Civil War was to be known, the inauguration of horrifying modern warfare. After only a few months the Confederate army discharged John Earle Bomar because of ill health, and he returned home with Elias while his unit fought on until Appomattox. By 1864, even Spartanburg natives were dismayed by the bedraggled Holcombe Legion, saying that it was "seldom" to find "a worse heartbroken, low-spirited, set of chaps."

After the end of the Civil War, Elias and Malinda decided, like many freedmen, to marry and make their emancipation genuine by leaving South Carolina. The Bomars tried Dalton, Georgia, a town still "vivid" in "devastation wrought by war," and thus needed to have all of its brick buildings rebuilt or repaired. By 1871 Elias had prospered enough to pay $125 for a lot to build a house on E. Morris Street near the railroad. Estelle, her mother's seventh child, was born on February 23, 1874. Her birth occurred as her own family fortunes sank, forcing them to sell their home at a loss and become renters in the "Gate City"—Atlanta—where Malinda had to take in wash. But Estelle would carry only sketchy memories of her Georgia girlhood. Her family left their Atlanta residence on Foundry Street when her father's health was broken by consumption (the term used then for tuberculosis), and by 1878 the Bomars had returned to Spartanburg, the place Estelle thought of as home.

When the Bomars returned to Spartanburg, Elias's brother Charles was prospering as a grocer, an undertaker, a realtor, and a landlord. Both Bomar brothers got in on the ground floor of the spurting Spartanburg economy before the end of the 1870s. On November

15, 1878, O. P. Earle, serving as the executor for Elias's former owner
Theron Earle, accepted $103 from Elias and Charles for 5½ acres of land
on the "Gap" road off Howard Street, about two miles west of downtown. The brothers built houses in the shadow of the construction of
the gigantic Spartan Mills cotton factory, the largest cotton mill of its
kind in the South. Elias and his son and stepsons helped to construct
the sprawling cotton warehouses and tenements for workers and profit
as landowners putting up houses to rent. Soon the Bomars could claim
membership in Spartanburg's African American bourgeoisie: teachers,
clergy, builders, merchants, two doctors, and one journalist.

Estelle's brother Thomas genuinely flourished, securing contracts to erect many of Spartanburg's downtown brick buildings. A
gifted architect, a meticulous craftsman and a swift deal maker, he
purchased multiple shares of stock in the leading companies he saw
popping up around him, like the Spartanburg Savings Bank and the
Saxon Mills cotton manufacturer. Thomas would eventually own
twenty-seven shares of stock in the Spartan Mills manufacturing
campus. The only nonwhite man elected to the town council, Thomas
was Spartanburg's principal black citizen.

Perhaps because of ill health, Elias Bomar became increasingly
devout. He claimed a founding membership at the Westminster Presbyterian Church, a single-story gable-roofed wooden building just
north of the courthouse square. The white Bomars were Baptists, but
not their ex-slaves. The Presbyterians were known for fair dealings
with blacks and setting up schools for freedmen. Thus the Bomar girls
were sent and dutifully thrived at the Presbyterian college for black
women, Scotia Seminary, in Concord, North Carolina, about one
hundred miles northeast on the rail line. A school of three hundred
students and twenty teachers founded in 1867, Scotia's catalogs carried
the slogan of its New England mission: "We must make this institution the Mount Holyoke for the African people." Scotia offered two
tracks: a four-year grammar program, including English, arithmetic,

algebra, geography, science, history, and literature; and a three-year normal and scientific program, including geometry, astronomy, physics, chemistry, history, Latin, and rhetoric. The industrial department taught cooking and sewing, but for its era Scotia offered a strong liberal arts curriculum. Cultured refinement, appropriate diction, dress and manners were emphasized as strenuously as the course work. Music teachers like Ida Cathcart not only taught the piano but also provided poorer students with shoes and undergarments.

In the nineteenth century the administration of black education after grade school was exclusively white, but at Scotia the school faculty was racially mixed. Despite the fact that there were not many black Presbyterians, the church always had a large number—three-fifths—of black teachers at their schools and a few had graduated from liberal arts colleges like Oberlin. The president of the school during most of the years that the Bomar girls attended was David Junkin Satterfield, a Princeton alumnus. Satterfield tried to bridge the racial divide, disdaining to use the common logic that segregated the races into "you people" and the white majority. He was also a severe theology teacher who demanded that the young women "know the Book from cover to cover and their Catechism word for word." Estelle admired him and specialized in music.

Estelle's older sister, Hattie, achieved early success and became a young member of the Scotia faculty in the 1890s. Teenagers like future college founder and U.S. presidential adviser Mary McLeod (later Bethune), brimming with pluck and ambition, but straight from the South Carolina cotton rows, stood in awe of Hattie Bomar. McLeod, who graduated a year before Estelle, explained that Hattie Bomar "gave me my very first vision of the culture and ability of Negro women." Like some of the other girls, McLeod had never before met young black women who combined the qualities of erudition, cultural refinement, and chastity, or had eaten at a table set with linen and flatware.

Naturally the conspicuous refinement served a very practical purpose: it was impossible to be further from the cotton furrow, the musky animals, the huts with dirt floors, the offal, and the households with children who shared no common paternal ancestry. Even liberals from the North, like Harvard educator Albert Bushnell Hart, who toured North Carolina in the 1890s, were dismissive of "the greater part of the [Negro] race," living in a "nether world of great ignorance and greater degradation." Hart did more than just describe conditions; he passed a judgment. "The long continuance of slavery is not wholly responsible for this degradation," he suggested, advancing a view shared by many whites, "it is a defect in the character of the race." The Scotia women felt personally bound to disprove him. McLeod's elegant manners and Estelle Bomar's competent Chopin études and sonnet writing, as well as the gourmet aestheticism that the school cultivated, strode against the "nether world."

Inspired with commitment after her education, Mary McLeod decided to become a missionary and go to Africa; Estelle was content, like her older sister, Hattie, to continue teaching the children of freedmen. Although Estelle spent a couple of summers in the 1890s receiving musical training in Philadelphia, she readied herself to become a public school teacher in Spartanburg. By the time she was seventeen she earned a first-class certificate on her teaching exam, placing second (behind a Scotia upperclasswoman), and was on her way to professional standing. For several years in the 1890s Estelle divided her time between Spartanburg schools and working at Scotia, alongside Hattie. The center of black education in Spartanburg was the graded school on 239 North Dean Street, headed in 1891 by principal C. C. Scott and later in the decade by R. M. Alexander. At the Dean Street School, the Bomar girls began their teaching careers.

The man Estelle would marry, Joseph Sandy Himes, was born on February 2, in 1873 or 1874, in the middle of Georgia, near Tennille, his father's birthplace. He spent his adolescence in Newberry, South

Carolina, some forty miles southeast of Spartanburg. He and Estelle had a great deal in common, beginning with the fact that both of them were born in Georgia but raised in relative prosperity in South Carolina's Up Country. Black people in the highlands had known hard slavery, but theirs was not the total slave society of the low-lying rice-cultivation country in the coastal areas around Charleston. Newberry was a prosperous, stylish village, with federal-style brick buildings lining the downtown along Pratt Street between the Newberry Opera House and College Street, an attractiveness that later earned it the designation as America's "most charming" small town.

Joseph had grown up the fourth child of a blacksmith also named Joseph Sandy Himes, known for the first half of his life as Sandy Neely. His mother was Anna Robinson Himes and she may have grown up on the farm of the Washington County, Georgia, planter Samuel Robinson. Sandy Neely was almost certainly enslaved nearby. Down the road from the Robinson place lived Elizabeth Hines, who in 1860 owned several men in their twenties and a large farm. Better known than Elizabeth though was the most noted farmer in antebellum Washington County and the owner of the celebrated Whitehall Plantation, Joseph Henry Hines. This line of the Hines name in Georgia had originated with a 1650 Virginia immigrant named John William Hines, who came from Londonderry, Ireland. The original name there was O'Heyne, or O'hEidhin. The Hines name was connected to remarkable wealth in Tennille and surrounding Washington County. Strong Southern accents parsed little distinction between "Hines" and "Himes," and for years Chester and his father would have their surnames spelled either way on official records.

Born around 1847, Sandy Neely was rather admired himself. Rumored to have had an "ungovernable temper," he was thought to have killed an overseer after slavery had ended, the sort of violent, racially charged event that was not uncommon among the fifteen thousand citizens of Washington County, where blacks outnumbered whites. But Sandy Neely was known better for his prominence at the forge; he was the unusual skilled freedman with a business large enough to employ fellow blacks. In 1874, he ran a carriage-making and blacksmithing shop in Tennille, and he owned personal goods worth almost two hundred dollars. Whites in the town accorded him the sort of respect that they denied virtually all other black Americans. Continuing in the spirit of slavery, the postbellum Washington County tax lists were segregated by race and enumerated freedmen under the names of their employers, in a separate register at the end of the district account. Neely was the only African American in the county registered under his own name.

Once he left Tennille and switched his name to be nearly the same as the most prominent man he had come across, Joseph Sandy Himes settled in Newberry, South Carolina in 1880, and, along with his thirty-three-year-old wife, was the parent of six children. Thirteen-year-old Leah was oldest. She excelled at school and would go on to study at Hampton Institute in Virginia, perhaps the most famous school for freedmen in the South. Thomas was eleven, Bennie nine, Sandy seven, Wesley five, and Andrew only a year. All but Andrew had been born in Georgia.

The Himeses lived in a section of Newberry with shops and Negro tenements called Amasoka, close to the railroad line, where merchants, the railroad supervisor, machinists, laborers, and cooks kept busy in wooden stores clustered together on Caldwell Avenue. Newberry provided a singular advantage to African Americans: nearby to Amasoka was the Hoge School for freedmen. Even five-year-old Wesley was enrolled for study, the great fulfillment of the promise of emancipation. In the middle of September 1885, mother Anna Himes died, and Joseph married again, to a woman named Mary. They had a child named Fannie in 1886.

Not four years after Fannie's birth, on February 29, 1890, Sandy died, leaving his large family the mechanics shop and half-acre parcel of land by Vincent Street. By then, the "well known and highly honored" Himeses could boast of Leah, who had graduated from Hampton, earned a first-grade South Carolina teaching certificate, and taught school in Newberry. On February 4, 1891, a diminutive and shy Leah married a schoolteacher named Rodney Moon. Moon was from just beyond the city limits in Mendenhall, and he had stayed in state for his education, attending Claflin University. In the fall of 1890, it had been to Claflin too, that Leah's bright younger brother Joseph Sandy Himes went.

Short, pigeon-toed, dark-skinned and blue-eyed, and called Sandy like his father, Joseph Sandy Himes entered the first-year normal school class in blacksmithing in 1890 at Claflin University, in Orangeburg, eighty miles southeast of Newberry. The school carried the name of an abolitionist governor of Massachusetts. Young Sandy possessed the qualities necessary for admission to the Claflin normal department—"a good moral character" and the ability "to read and write well." He faced the world without great means, but with a confidence that endeared him to men and women alike. His son would describe him as a "magnificent actor," who could "dissemble" and "pose" "with validity." Joseph and his sister Leah would become the best educated and the most distinguished of their family, leading very different lives and affording their children vastly different opportunities than could their brothers and one other sister, who spent their lives as hotel waiters, porters, and hairdressers. Joseph's matriculation to college must have fulfilled a dream of his slave-born father. The son belonged to a generation who would turn a handcraft into a white-collar job.

Nearly one hundred other sons of freedmen joined Joseph at Claflin in the field that he had first learned at the Vincent Street shop. Claflin was "fully committed to Industrial Education" and made the promise demonstrative. Shortly before Joseph arrived at the school gates, a new large blacksmith shop had been completed, and steam fans drove eight billowing forges. There were even courses in steam engineering. Claflin boasted impressive young men, like recent black-smithing graduate and teaching assistant Wilson Cooke, who spent summers at Massachusetts Institute of Technology and went on to design buildings for the federal government. Cooke was living proof that, followed as one track, the industrial arts were gateways to professions like engineering and architecture.

At Claflin Joseph witnessed the sharp tensions and occasional, violent conflicts over the direction of black schools. White Claflin professors sometimes directly attacked their black colleagues. Students resented bigoted white professors and they resisted the mounting Jim Crow protocols emerging in the South. But even while he acknowledged the right to black self-determination, white founding school president Lorenzo Dutton derided the leadership ability of the poor children of ex-slaves: "not one in 1,000 has enough executive ability to manage the concerns of his own household successfully." Unlike many of the students who had known only rural hardship, Joseph put his years in his father's shop to use and succeeded admirably well. He finished the three-year course in blacksmithing and mechanical drawing with marks good enough to land a job at Georgia State Industrial College for Colored Youth in Savannah. Starting in 1893, he taught a standard curriculum on how to design, care for, and use a blacksmith forge, to file, chip, and anneal metal, and to make tools.

Its ornate public squares of English-style gardens made the port city of Savannah one of the most attractive destinations in Georgia and, until nearly 1880, the state's most densely populated town. Cosmopolitan and richer than the South Carolina Up Country, it had liberal origins as a debtors' colony that had outlawed slavery. Savannah was home to a population that included several comfortable and well-educated African Americans. At the turn of the century, more than 28,000 of Savannah's 55,268 residents were African American. Much of their optimism centered on the Georgia State Industrial College for Colored Youth.

Set on an eighty-one-acre farm, Georgia State Industrial had been founded in 1891 as a result of an 1890 amendment to the Morrill Act, which had created the land-grant colleges in the United States in the 1860s. That amendment required states to make provisions for Negro Americans. The school had gotten under way with four professors and forty students, most of the instruction and living occurring, at first, in Boggs Hall, an old plantation mansion. Parsons Hall, the dormitory for students, had been erected with money from the sale of the last gang of African captives sold into Georgia in 1859. In 1896 the school opened Meldrim Hall, a two-story wooden-frame industrial arts building, with an eight-hundred-seat chapel on the second floor, a building put up with Joseph Himes's help.

The college was led by erudite Richard R. Wright, who became one of the paramount black educators of his generation. When the one-armed Union general Oliver Otis Howard, later Freedman's Bureau head and founder of Howard University, had stopped in Atlanta to meet with Georgia freedmen and asked a crowd of begrimed ex-slaves what message to carry to the North about their condition, an illiterate twelve-year-old Wright had sturdily replied, "Massa, tell 'em we are rising." He lived up to his legendary reply by graduating from Atlanta University as valedictorian in its first college class, and was known far and wide as "We'se a-risin Wright."

To win that achievement Wright had become an expert classicist and Francophile and he stocked his library with books emphasizing the African role in the life of the mind and the creation of art. Thus for Joseph Himes, boarding at the school was another kind of education. Few blacks had ever seen as many books before dealing with the black condition (Claflin's library held fourteen hundred volumes). In the college president's personal collection were "huge encyclopedias—*Britannica*, *Chambers's*; reference books; Bible commentaries; groups of books on the history of the nations, of religion, of philosophy; books on economics, politics, etc. and every available book written by a Negro-American." Among Wright's prized volumes was the abolitionist work *An Enquiry Concerning the Intellectual and Moral Faculties, and Literature of Negroes*. Written by Henri Gregoire, a prominent French philosopher who'd corresponded with Thomas Jefferson, the translation presented the lives of distinguished blacks in science and the arts in order to dispute claims of racial inferiority. In Boggs Hall—where the president, his family, and college faculty (including Joseph) lived—the discussion regularly centered on Hebrew and Greek literature, Shakespeare, Milton, Dante, Emerson, Whittier, Longfellow, and other favorites of Wright's. Accordingly, Joseph built a library resembling the president's.

But what the black teachers learned about African contributions to the world could not stave off the mounting pressure of racism. At the commencement exercises, the white school commissioner and Savannah mayor Peter Meldrim would have no problem telling the black crowd, "I do not believe in educating you people to want things you can never get. We must educate the Niggra to be the best possible Niggra and not a bad imitation of a white man." To effect his prescription for a caste society where blacks would not reasonably aspire to citizenship, Meldrim spied on faculty and students at the school, getting reports on their conversations from the black groundskeeper—who, although uneducated, openly aspired to become the college president. The students and the faculty who recognized the liberal arts curriculum as the most direct route for the black elite to gain parity with whites found themselves in opposition to instructors who were beholden to the state legislature for the wherewithal to keep the college open. Ten years earlier it had been different. At Claflin commencement, speakers like African Methodist Episcopal Bishop William Arnett had encouraged the students to resist by every means, including their feet. "Get up and go!" he had exhorted, spurring westward migration. "Go, take your family with you." Not willing to become western "exodusters" yet, Joseph and his friends had thrown themselves into work that proved or developed their competence, trying to balance what the black editor and novelist Pauline Hopkins called the "contending forces."

By 1900, when he was still in his twenties, Joseph Himes was elevated from his position as instructor of blacksmithing to director of the industrial department, which contained agriculture, wheelwrighting, mechanical drawing, blacksmithing, carpentry, shoemaking, bricklaying, and painting. He reorganized the unit into two branches, one of manual training and the other of trades. The promotion showed Wright's faith and Joseph's ability to mount the administrative ladder. While the black intelligentsia strategized to combat Jim Crow, Joseph added a practical dimension to his classroom work. He ran a commercial blacksmithing and wheelwrighting shop at 309 Hall Street, specializing in horseshoeing and probably joined with his friend E. D. Bulkley in the National Negro Business League. With his higher salary and managerial self-confidence, he felt ready to consider marriage.

His colleague, masonry department chief Lewis B. Thompson, married President Wright's daughter Essie, securing his future. Joseph turned his attention to the young Bomar women of Spartanburg, first courting Gertrude Bomar before focusing his attention on her older sister Estelle. For her part, Estelle was old enough to fear being left behind by her married sisters. She had lived and worked in Spartanburg for half a dozen years and she liked that Savannah was a well-groomed small city boasting a prominent educational institution. She saw in Joseph a young department head who could reasonably expect future leadership roles of greater importance.

And he appealed to her mildly baroque sensibility. He courted her with devotion and romanticism, bringing her fresh-cut flowers and other touches of refined grace. Estelle visited Joseph for "Violet Teas," garden parties, and the "Yellow Buffet." The faculty entertained the young couple lavishly, and soon Estelle and Joseph were engaged.

An amenable Joseph spent Christmas 1900 with the Bomar family in Spartanburg and in his rich baritone voice he spun dreams of even more dramatic success and distinction in the years ahead.

Estelle and Joseph married on June 27, 1901, at Westminster Church in Spartanburg. Reverend Satterfield from Scotia had even agreed to perform the ceremony for a young lady who had been a distinguished pupil. That kind of symbolism for the new segregated American century was extraordinary: a white minister and college president marrying two Negroes and then socializing with them afterward. But, at the eleventh hour, Satterfield canceled his appearance and Westminster's regular pastor, Hydar Stinson, administered the vows. Gertrude Bomar was maid of honor and Dr. E. D. Bulkley, who lived in New York, served as best man. Estelle had the church decorated in ferns and more extravagant flowers, and after the ceremony the "popular" young couple returned to the Gap Road house for an "elaborate reception" that included musical selections and refreshments. They stayed in Spartanburg until September, when school started. The Himeses soon started a family. Surrounded by family and friends at her mother's house back in Spartanburg, Estelle delivered a healthy boy named Edward on May 26, 1902. When Estelle returned to Savannah, Joseph's baby sister, Fannie, came to live with them to help care for Edward and keep house.

The newlyweds pressed ahead but the atmosphere in Georgia became ever more difficult. Mayor Meldrim hobbled the college's liberal arts curriculum, trying to eliminate Latin, Greek, and calculus. The tools for imagining a world beyond, for abstraction, for uncovering sources, would be withheld. The students resisted strongly, and white visitors to the campus were greeted with deep suspicion.

Not surprisingly, there was a radical streak among the blacks in town, spearheaded by the college faculty and called the Savannah Sunday Men's Club, a debate forum with a strong civil rights agenda that met at the Masonic Hall. The club, founded by Monroe N. Work,

a University of Chicago MA and a researcher assisting W. E. B. Du
Bois in his case studies at Atlanta University, was an explicit offshoot of the Niagara Movement, which would become the National
Association for the Advancement of Colored People. It is likely that
Joseph attended the meetings, as did his intellectual colleagues like
mathematician Emanuel W. Houston. Monroe Work would go on to
more lasting fame as the leader of his own studies on African Americans at Tuskegee. An adept journalist, Houston galvanized support
to criticize the politically apathetic well-to-do members of Savannah's
black community in his *Savannah Tribune* columns under the pseudonym "Nuff-Sed."

In October 1904, Estelle's brother Thomas Bomar died unexpectedly, leaving a large estate. Thomas and his wife, Carrie, did not
have any children and the estate was divided by his wife and siblings
into equal shares. In November the court granted Estelle one-tenth,
$752.04, or roughly $44,700 in 2015 dollars. When summonsed by the
state, she signed her name "Estelle Hymes," the only document carrying this spelling of the name, and perhaps indicating that she did
not wish her husband, in business on his own, to have ready access to
the money.

Around this time, the harmonious early seasons of their marriage
had ended; Estelle and Joseph were beginning cycles of deep marital
discord. It may have had to do with the fact that Joseph's ascent had
stalled. He had reached thirty and seemed content. The next step up
for Joseph would have been joining the faculty at a larger school, such
as Tuskegee or Hampton. His shop in downtown Savannah may have
been one of their early conflicts. Estelle hoped that Joseph would find
less satisfaction in the anvil in favor of administrative duties. Instead,
he wanted to have his own business and to take satisfaction in horseshoeing, "promptly and satisfactorily done."

The state's climate curdled too. In spite of a comforting visit from
national hero Booker T. Washington to deliver the Georgia State

Industrial commencement address in 1905, the year 1906 saw even more of the "ignorant and narrow-minded" discord that Washington had railed against. Candidate Hoke Smith ran for the Georgia statehouse on a "reform" movement ticket, which proposed regulations excluding blacks from politics and proscribing interracial social contact. The movement swept Georgia and culminated in cruelties against blacks in Atlanta in September 1906. During the violence, marauding white mobs scoured the downtown Five Points intersection, Brownsville, and the Fourth Ward, and "chased negroes, stoned and shot them to death, and boarded trolley cars, snatching off negroes and beat them to death with clubs and sticks." At least twenty-five African Americans lost their lives. Estelle was familiar with the neighborhoods that had been attacked. Wholesale racial murder also demanded that people like Estelle who could pass for white pick sides with their family, neighbors, and friends who bore the brunt of the mob enmity. Future NAACP secretary Walter White, who became famous and beloved because he used his white appearance to investigate lynchings, was barely a teenager but had to shoulder a rifle during the riot to help protect his family.

In Savannah racial oppression was not as lethal but it was comprehensive nonetheless. The new laws were sure to pique a sensitive and intelligent woman like Estelle, whose marriage to a dark brown-skinned man away from where she was raised was taking on complications. The local board of education began requiring teachers to use a racially derogatory paraphrase of the song "Dixie" during regular classroom recitals, blacks were fined for "jeering" at whites, and could be expelled from the courthouse for sitting in "white folk's seat." A Jim Crow law officially passed in Savannah on September 12, 1906, segregating the streetcars, and introducing a series of insulting signs there, with chains stretching across the car to reserve a portion for whites. Black Savannah citizens boycotted the trolley cars, walking and taking buckboards and hacks driven by blacks wherever they needed to go. But the clock's hands were turning backward. Nationally, President Theodore Roosevelt summarily dismissed, without so much as an investigation and against the advice of Booker T. Washington, three companies of black troops for defending fellow soldiers set upon by white civilians in Brownsville, Texas.

The college teachers insulated themselves where they could, but among many of them, particularly the Savannah Sunday Club members, the commitment to resistance was strong. R. E. Cobb, a mathematics professor, ran afoul of white sentiment on a streetcar when he dodged out of the way of an elderly white passenger who tried to "correct" him with a cane. Cobb was chased by a mob to the campus and his life threatened; it took soothing efforts by Wright, white patron Meldrim, and the Savannah sheriff to prevent an angry crowd from dragging him by the neck from the school grounds. At his trial, the sheriff tried to get Cobb to plea-bargain to a year on chain gang. A white attorney won the black academic's freedom by arguing that "the Negro was emotional and like a beast was not controlled by reason," and having Cobb pay a $250 fine. In Augusta, white mobs killed blacks for attempting to defend themselves after being attacked and beaten. Accepting the exodusters' counsel from the 1880s, black Americans began talking up migration to the west. Missouri, alongside Kansas and Oklahoma at the turn of the century, seemed a potential western refuge for blacks leaving the traditional cotton belt and its thickening climate of hate.

Joseph's buddy the competently trained classicist Benjamin F. Allen had already anticipated the ugliness of twentieth-century Savannah in the wake of the Atlanta riot and left. Previously, he had graduated from Atlanta University (as a classmate of the poet James Weldon Johnson) in 1894, and taken a job at Lincoln Institute in Jefferson City, Missouri, as a professor of ancient languages. Allen had extensive interests in psychology and ethics and held a doctorate of law degree. An impeccably dressed, well-fed, light-complexioned man, with an imposing mustache that set off his completely bald head, Allen swaggered around his campus staring through a pince-nez. In the fall of 1902 Allen returned to Lincoln to take the helm as the school president.

Joseph had gotten the chance to know Allen during the spring semester of the 1902 academic year. The men socialized and had parties, which were noticed in the press together in the company of Joseph's dentist friend Bulkley, other faculty, and President Wright. Perhaps responding to anxious feelers sent out by his old comrade, on August 27, 1907, Allen got his trustee board to authorize the post "blacksmith in the industrial department" for Joseph. The pay was seventy dollars per month.

Grasping after the possibility of better times, Joseph took his wife and son to the capital of the Gateway State. The move out west to their own white house, to a place where they already had friends— away from Estelle's family and away from Georgia, where black opportunity was more and more choked off—probably helped restore the marriage. Estelle delivered another son on August 4, 1908, and in what seems a conciliatory gesture on Estelle's part to her husband, they agreed to name him Joseph Sandy. After Estelle successfully delivered Joseph Jr., she probably did not imagine that she would conceive again quickly. But ten weeks later, sometime in October 1908, thirty-four-year-old Estelle Himes was pregnant.

Chester's earliest years took place on a campus of 535 students enrolled mainly in the secondary and the lower schools. If Joseph's new school did not have the strongest college preparatory curriculum of the black institutions, it had a particular claim for pride. Black Civil War veterans of the Sixty-Second and Sixty-Fifth Regiments of the United States Colored Troops had founded the Lincoln Institute in 1866. In the months after the war the ex-slaves turned fighting men had managed to equip a permanent school to educate other Missouri freed people. At Lincoln, named after the Great Emancipator, the "fundamental idea shall be to combine study with labor, so that the old habits of those who have always labored, but never studied, shall not be thereby changed and that the emancipated slaves, who have neither capital to spend nor time to lose, may obtain an education." By 1879 the state had taken over Lincoln in an effort to develop a normal school to train qualified teachers. The school's inaugural president was Inman Page, the first African American to graduate from Brown University. A true exoduster, Page served twice as Lincoln's president and went on to found secondary schools with strong liberal arts curriculums in Missouri and Oklahoma.

The impressive brick buildings on Lincoln's campus outshone the world that the Himeses had been most intimately familiar with before. Twenty broad limestone steps led to the main arched entranceway of redbrick, castlelike Memorial Hall, Lincoln's administrative and main building. The young men's dormitory and Barnes-Krekel Hall, a twelve-classroom building, followed a similar splendid pattern. President Allen occupied an ornate, three-story Queen Anne style brick mansion. Estelle's father had been a mason and she had seen buildings going up all of her life, but Lincoln's cathedralesque brick marvels were of another scale.

It was the industrial curriculum in tailoring, shoemaking, carpentry, wood turning, machinery and blacksmithing that took up the majority of the faculty lines and school resources. Housed in four-story Chinn Hall, the artisan departments had a major practical significance: they enabled the institution to be self-sufficient and literally sustained the physical structure of school life. These teachers and their students designed and built the buildings, grew much of the food, sewed the clothes, and made the shoes. The black "college" was really a full-service, all-black town.

Joseph must have felt a certain fulfillment by 1910. He was father to three healthy sons, husband in a renewed marriage, and blacksmith of good reputation in Lincoln and Jefferson City. He had a modern, whitewashed brick shop to work in, with built-in ventilation, giant metal exhausts over the forges and bellows, and enormous floor-to-ceiling bands to run the grinders they used to shape the metal. An "artist at the forge," Joseph Himes was now highly skilled. He crafted Christmas toys that were the envy of the neighborhood and superior to any from a catalog or town craft shop: little replica wagons with spoke wheels and iron tires and springboard seats, miniature garden tools and sleds with iron runners. Joseph Himes was, at heart, a contented and modest artisan.

Estelle was not so easily satisfied. Her ambition for a world of refinement and equal rights was similar to the vision of another black woman she knew at Lincoln. Between 1906 and 1910 the most prestigious figure on campus was the slave-born celebrity academic Anna Julia Cooper. A veteran classicist pushed out of the principal-ship of the M Street High School in Washington, D.C., Cooper was an articulate advocate of the liberal arts and she spoke regularly at festivals and academic and religious institutions in Missouri. Estelle had probably had exposure to Latin at Scotia, but not even Georgia Industrial's erudite Richard R. Wright would have rivaled the scope of a commanding intellectual like Cooper, a graduate of Oberlin College. Like many of her privileged peers, Cooper worked strenuously to include black people in a vision of grand American possibility. She echoed Theodore Roosevelt when she argued that "fresh and vigorous" American society was "synonymous with all that is progressive, elevating and inspiring." When it came to "modern civilization," Cooper approved of the "European bud and the American flower."

If the romance of Anglo-Saxon imperialism seems odd a century later, Cooper presumed to include African Americans within the narrative of American exceptionalism in a more forceful manner than Booker T. Washington was then doing. She argued in her speeches that a uniquely valuable destiny was at hand for blacks in North America. "Here in America," she predicted to her audiences, "is the arena in which the next triumph of civilization is to be won." While at Lincoln, in between mounting scenes from the *Aeneid* that depicted Dido Queen of Carthage, prepping the Olive Branch female debate society, the Ruskin Literary Society and the Shakespeare Club, Cooper patrolled the dormitories and tried to inculcate students with "the vivifying touch of ideas and ideals."

Black students at Lincoln shared Cooper's view regarding the value of an American nationality in a world of escalating European rivalry. "It is necessary for us who are by birth already Americans," a student leader wrote, "not to throw down our birth right, and with contemptible folly, to back down to the alien gods which our forefathers have forsaken." If they favored being Americans over Africans, they were conscious of not wanting to be Europeans either. Young women, togged in mandatory mortarboards, were convincing themselves that "to be a first class American is much better than to be a first class imitator of a Frenchman or an Englishman."

This sort of Cooper-inspired blend of smarts, maturity, patriotism, polish, and worldliness certainly would have appealed to Estelle during the middle of her journey in Missouri. Dainty and fastidious, Estelle resented the shabbiness of everyday life and people who didn't try to improve themselves. She disapproved of her neighbors, the Cains, who lived in a house next door, and she refused to let Joe and Chester play with their children because they spoke what she termed "bad English" and used "vulgar" words. She preferred to have her sons play tamely with President Allen's daughter Julia, who was the same age as Chester, on the other side of street, up at the top of the hill.

Her prim demeanor and expectation of refined treatment created the perception that Estelle Himes was "color struck," or inclined strongly toward the society of lighter-skin blacks like herself. Possibly she did express a preference for her own kind, but there was a significant social-class dimension to the prejudices she displayed. Estelle celebrated blacks who had partial descent from the Southern aristocracy. But in an episode as a toddler that Chester Himes remembered all of his years, he and his brother Joe had found an open can of paint around the house on Lafayette Street. Chester delightedly smeared paint throughout his never-cut hair. To clean them up, Joseph Himes shaved his sons' heads and Chester's hair grew back as kinky as his father's. Estelle considered the loss of Chester's softly curled hair—which emphasized his complex racial ancestry and delicate upbringing—a minor tragedy.

If Estelle Himes indeed possessed a bias against the man she married and darker-skinned people generally, it was a view she mainly kept to herself. To have done otherwise would have been to open herself to being reminded of her own mother's trials and misfortunes during slavery. And while she might have sought out light-skinned blacks, they were not in the majority in the places she lived. Also, if, in South Carolina or coastal Georgia, the skills learned from working in wealthy white households and literacy gave obviously mixed-race African Americans a kind of prestige, in places like Scotia and Georgia Industrial, such persons were not conspicuously prominent among faculty or students.

Nor did their presence easily translate into fawning attitudes toward white people generally. At Lincoln, Anna Julia Cooper expressed disdain for her slave-master father. Leah Himes's husband Roddy Moon, a dark-skinned man six years older than Joseph and Estelle, seems to have had his sister-in-law in mind when he made some observations about skin color and appearance. After graduating from Claflin University, Moon had been a school principal in South Carolina with his wife. He developed the habit of appearing verbally impressive, as well as the habit of projecting himself as well-prepared and left the educational field. By 1904 he had been appointed to the federal bureau of agriculture as a meat inspector. He started that career in St. Joseph, Missouri, moving to Cleveland in 1906. When he made friends he observed an upheaval in social caste. "All the leading Negroes are black or dark brown. I have not seen but one bright skin professional man." One woman's skin was so light that "you cannot tell her from a white woman to save your life." Another person, Carriou, was less unusual "about Sisters color." Roddy Moon mentioned Estelle when writing to his wife, Leah, who had remained in Ohio. Joe's "bleached" wife Estelle was a little different from them, certainly, but not unusual, and not the kind of person who "you cannot tell from a white woman to save your life."

The Himeses found a new dragon that westward movement had not slain, the national upheaval over industrialization and black schools and which seems to have contributed to the souring of the relationship between Joseph and President Allen. The transition from the horse-and-buggy era and subsequent curricular transformations coincided at Lincoln with other messy politics. Traveling to other black schools to recruit professors, Allen returned in the spring of 1913 to find roughly a quarter of his teaching staff in what he treated like revolt. To consolidate his power, he dismantled his faculty. Allen docked salaries of Fannie Moten in elocution, Frederick Parker in shoemaking, and Grace Hammond and O. W. Ferguson, all of them punished for what he used military language to describe, being "absent without leave." Over the next several months he made moves to replace the entire industrial department. Allen replaced the wood-turning and mechanical drawing instructor and the shoemaker.

In August 1913, after the trustees had restocked the machine shop with fresh lathes and new tools that they bought at a St. Louis symposium and as they prepared for courses in auto mechanics, Allen fired his old friend Joseph Himes. It was just as well. "The automobile has replaced the wagon and buggy to a great extent," admitted the school bulletin a few years later. The blacksmithing course remained necessary only "to do the work connected with auto repairs." By 1914 there was a student revolt, quashed when the board of trustees dismissed all of the signatories to a protest letter, and resulting with not a single student enrolled in the college preparatory curriculum the next fall.

Joseph and Estelle hauled the children to Joseph's sister Leah Moon in Cleveland. The summer bled into the fall, and all of the Himes children enrolled in school, which meant kindergarten for Chester. The Moons had as many children as the Himeses, but theirs were older: Joe, a twenty-one-year-old house painter who also worked in hotels, fourteen-year-old Ellen, and eleven-year-old Henry Lee. The Moons were also determined to outmaneuver Jim Crow, as Roddy's job with the federal government indicated. They were the rare migrant black family living on a main street with German, Swiss, English, and other white American neighbors, which might have seemed refreshing to Joe Sr. and Estelle, whose lives had been spent in the South.

Less pleasant, though, were the cramped quarters with the Moons and the recently married, new mother Fannie Himes Wiggins, whose son Gerald was one year old. Estelle's high-strung manners now rattled Fannie, pressing hair for a living, and who had done the housework and child care for her sister-in-law in Savannah as a teenager. The crowded household and clashing temperaments were sowing the seeds of future discord.

Chapter Two

THE SOUTHERN CROSSES
THE YELLOW DOG
1914–1925

Harried in the search for a new post, Chester's father secured work in a place where nineteenth-century industrial education seemed on sure footing. He became the new blacksmith professor at Alcorn College in the rural hamlet of Lorman, Mississippi, about thirty miles south of Vicksburg. Eerie, isolated, and serene, Alcorn was located along a series of rolling hills dipping into ravines, shaped by the mighty mile-wide Mississippi River to the west, the ridges of rich soil yielding forests of sweetgum, red oak, water oak, and magnolia trees draped with Spanish moss. At one time vast expanses of Claiborne County had been cleared and planted in cotton, but the boll weevil infestation of the 1890s had wiped out the cash crop, and scraggly low-grade timber was returning the land to a condition before the plantation era. The closest town to the school was nearby Port Gibson, from 1918 on the home of the Rabbit Foot Minstrels. That company's notable members included two of the most original blues singers of all time, Ida Cox and Gertrude "Ma" Rainey. The accent that Chester had for the rest of his life was the soft Southern speech of Mississippi. He referred to it as his "lazy

Missouri accent," because that was where he had been born, but his speech habits were stamped in Lorman. When Chester revisited his images of childhood security and satisfying innocence, the mental reflections that he conjured were of the family's roughly seven-year stretch in Mississippi.

Founded as Oakland College in 1828 by Southern Presbyterians and sold in 1871 to the state for the education of "Negro citizens," Alcorn College bore the name of Mississippi's Reconstruction-era governor James A. Alcorn. A man who had favored gradual emancipation and the use of black Confederate troops during the Civil War, Alcorn had suggested a future for Negroes in Mississippi that it would take more than a century to achieve, "protected in all their rights of person and property." Hiram Revels, the first elected Negro senator in United States history, had served as Alcorn College's earliest president. For Estelle and Joseph Himes, Mississippi could be uncomfortable like Georgia, but, on the other hand, the remote campus was a cocoon that "shielded" the boys from "the harshness of race relations."

When the Himes family arrived in 1914, the school flaunted some signs of modest prosperity, like a new three-story brick dormitory for boys called Mississippi Hall. Relatively austere in comparison with the extravagance of Lincoln, the campus still had some elements of antebellum architectural charm. Alcorn had two historic buildings on the campus, holdouts from the Oakland College days, the Old Chapel and the Belles Lettres Building. The elaborately detailed seventeen-step iron staircase of the Old Chapel had been dismantled from the ruins of a nearby plantation called Windsor Castle and reinstalled intact at Alcorn, a minor engineering feat. The chapel, the president's mansion, the dormitories and the academic buildings, were grouped in a horseshoe around a grove of magnolia, pine, and oak trees.

With an enrollment comparable to Lincoln, Alcorn had only a quarter of its students in the college department. The tuition was free to Mississippi natives and room and board stood at $17.50. When

Joseph Himes arrived with his family, the ailing mathematician John A. Martin was president of the school. He would die in 1915, and Levi Rowan, the head of the English department and a former president who had fallen off the log in a difficult balancing act with the board of trustees, resumed his role as president. Rowan—who, on one occasion as president, turned away a hundred female students because he had no dormitory space—faced fundamental problems, like providing clean drinking water for the college. Only a few years older than Joseph, Rowan's English department conducted an elementary mission, to "give the students a thorough mastery of the mother tongue in order that they may better be able to comprehend the instructions given in the other Departments." The local *Woodville Republican* would report the state education superintendent as voicing more precise fears that "the negro dialect and foreign tongues is [sic] contaminating the speech of pupils." If for different reasons, Chester's mother and father concurred heartily with this sentiment; at the threshold of their door they drew a line for the sake of grammatically correct English: "ain't" was "absolutely prohibited." Estelle would also prohibit Joseph Jr. and Chester from attending the local grammar school, preferring to teach them at home.

As the director of the "Blacksmithing, Horse Shoeing and Wheelwrighting Department," Joseph supported his family on the same salary that he had drawn in Missouri, and he instructed about fifty male students. Alcorn was not attempting to train the intellectual vanguard. Every student in the college department ultimately had to select a trade—carpentry, blacksmithing, laundry, or agriculture for the men; sewing, nursing, and domestic science for the women. Outfitted with electric lighting and a furnace, the single-story Mechanical Building, where Joseph Himes took the reins, was the only modern structure on campus.

But in spite of Alcorn's seeming commitment to the trades, the credentials necessary for the faculty to advance had dramatically increased.

Of the twenty-six teachers, every teacher had a college degree, and fifteen had completed college degrees in the academic subjects. President Rowan had even completed a doctorate. As the Himeses approached middle age, the mounting academic qualifications for genuine leadership among "New Negroes" threatened to leave them behind.

It was also increasingly difficult to ignore that after twenty years, Joseph Himes's craft was outmoded. Even for Mississippians, the long-standing aim, "to train practical blacksmiths," decreased every year. At first, between 1913 and 1915, about five Alcorn graduates each year finished in blacksmithing; but by 1916 and 1917, the department was only producing one graduate annually. Henry Ford's Model T assembly-line factory in Michigan was eliminating the rationale for the horse-and-buggy equipment and piecework metal crafts; the aftermath of World War I would make industrial-scale metal manufacture standard.

Dissatisfaction had pressed Estelle from the beginning. Settled in a simple, whitewashed two-story frame house, one of the seventeen plain wooden-frame structures allotted to the teaching staff along a white-picket fence lane, the Himeses had little refinement. Their lot included a square backyard of baked clay, complete with an outhouse, a shed, a water well, and a chicken coop. In the winter a damp chill seeped through every crack in the wall of their thinly insulated cottage. Joseph and Estelle planted crops on the nine-acre field behind the house, but the unattended front yard went wild, and the children copied the locals and started walking barefoot. The seasons in western Mississippi seemed distinct only in terms of the peculiar force of the elements. In the summer clouds of red dust were sandwiched by sheets of rain that quickly turned the land into a floodplain and rutted the roads. The ubiquitous sight of cornfields and pine forests, as well as the pungent odor of manure, mud, and draft animals, barely concealed the distance from insidious plantation slavery. Estelle stiffly told her husband that the move to backwater Lorman was "a comedown."

Even leisure lost its innocence. In an episode that Chester reproduced in his autobiography and in the novel *The Third Generation*, he remembered witnessing an early moment of horror. As a small boy, he had enjoyed watching the Alcorn men pull a wagon full of young women from the school's gates to the dorm in an elaborate annual display of strength. But during the merriment one year, a girl fell and slipped underneath the full weight of the wagon wheels and was crushed to death. The macabre sight of the jet of dark blood from the young coed's mouth shocked Chester as if the wheels were crushing him, as if he too "had been hurt." He fainted and had to be carried home and given medical attention. The trauma haunted him, foreshadowing his own immense personal suffering.

His disappointed mother was also tough-minded, willful, and independent, and she showed her mounting dissatisfaction in the fall of 1915 by accepting a position as a music instructor at Haines Normal and Industrial School in Augusta, Georgia. Her son Joseph would characterize the year in eastern Georgia as an "escape safari." Augusta was an "escape" from Mississippi, but to Joe, the experience was odd enough to remain a voyage into the wild. Considering the gruesome August public murder of pregnant Mary Turner—hanged, shot, set afire, and her fetus cut out and then stomped by a mob because she had threatened to expose her husband's lynchers—Georgia certainly evoked wildness. But it was mainly a chance at family for Estelle. Her young nieces Mabel and Margaret Bomar, "very fair girls with brown wavy hair," were teaching at Haines and would bolster her spirits.

Haines Institute had been chartered by the remarkable ex-slave Lucy Laney. Begun in the basement of a Presbyterian church in 1883, by 1915 twenty-six teachers and 694 students crowded two large three-story brick academic buildings. The iron-willed Laney had been born in Macon, Georgia, in 1854 to an enslaved mother and a free black father. Stocky and dark-skinned, the young Ms. Laney had been known in Macon for her ability to translate Latin with ease. She graduated from Atlanta University alongside Richard R. Wright and the famous classicist William Scarborough, the first black member of the Modern Language Association.

Chester did not recall the founder's ease in handling the classics, but rather, the contrast between her and his mother. He wrote that he and his brother were "shocked by the sight of the big, black ox-like woman who greeted them in a deep, gruff voice." Like Joseph, Chester imagined them to be in a foreign, mildly feral land. When he met Laney, she was past sixty, a taskmaster applauded by President William Howard Taft who hoped to inspire her students and deserved the reputation of one of the premier educators of the era. Resilience and determination were necessary traits for Laney, who operated in a state that did not provide public high schools for Negroes. But even the success of the Haines School could only do so much to soften the rough edges of the crowded shanty neighborhood and the folkways that made Estelle especially uncomfortable. The children at Haines spoke a version of black dialect called Gullah, which made the idiom of the Mississippi normal school's enrollees seem to be a model of English enunciation by comparison. Chester always recalled a locally born student, mourning the loss of the school mascot, by heralding "de goat done dead."

At once their Georgia schoolmates nicknamed Joe "Goat," for his prominent nose, narrow face, and slender, plodding style, and Chester "Cat," for his feline quickness and sly attractiveness, his easy charm, and his hysterical squabbling. And Chester found reason for crying there. He well remembered that when he disobeyed Lucy Laney she dropped his pants and hit him with an oaken paddle with holes in it.

Much greater calamity hallmarked Chester's time in Augusta. On March 22, 1916, an apocalyptic fire, complete with bursting gas pipes shooting flames fifty feet into the air and pillars of smoke overwhelming the skies, destroyed two miles of the downtown business district. Augusta's "Cotton Row" of filled warehouses, its skyscrapers and newspaper offices were ruined, and three thousand people were left homeless. The Haines School was a mile from the flames and no one was killed, although citizens fled the residential areas, stacking their belongings in the street. At the end of the school year, perhaps due to the calamity, Estelle and her children returned to Mississippi.

More feisty than disconsolate, Estelle used her writing to bring Lorman up to her standard. She proved to the small faculty her view on class and bearing in a way that made her husband proud. By 1918 Estelle had written "Alcorn Ode," a celebratory poem that remains the school song.

> Beneath the shade of giant trees,
> Fanned by a balmy southern breeze,
> Thy classic walls have dared to stand—
> A giant thou in learning's band;
>   O, Alcorn dear, our mother, hear
>   Thy name we praise, thy name we sing
> Thy name thy sons have honored far;
> A crown of gems thy daughters are;
> When country called, her flag to bear,
> The Gold and Purple answered, "Here."
>   O, Alcorn dear, our mother, hear
>   Thy name we praise, thy name we sing
> Far as our race thy claim shall need—
> So far to progress thou shalt lead
> Thy sons, with clashing arms of trades
> In useful arts, full garbed, thy maids;
>   O, Alcorn dear, we proudly bear
>   Thy standard on to victory.

"These were the moments he lived for," Chester later wrote about his father, married to a woman who, when she chose, was quite capable of impressing President Rowan and the college-educated faculty.

Estelle's ode reinforced the patriotic ethos of Anna J. Cooper and seems to have echoed the popular July 1918 editorial in *The Crisis* written by W. E. B. Du Bois. "Forget our special grievances," was Du Bois's famous counsel, "and close ranks with our own fellow citizens and the allied nations that are fighting for democracy." Closing ranks was not easy. In theory at least, Alcorn faculty would be dismissed for reading northern periodicals like *The Crisis* that engaged the race question. But the Du Bois lines showed that even the professionally radical were patriotic during that peak summer of American involvement in the war in France. Military necessity aside, in composing her poem Estelle managed to champion her husband's craft in the phrases "clashing arms of trades" and "useful arts," and she included her particular embarrassment in Mississippi, her hope that the "maids" would be "full garbed."

One dramatic incident of rural shamelessness concerned Estelle. The Himeses paid a Sunday visit to a student's family in the Delta and attended a country church there. At the climax of the sermon, while singing and dancing, women did more than bare just their souls to God. Chester wrote the scene down in *The Third Generation*.

> Women were standing in the pews, eyes glazed, tearing the riotous colored clothes from their strong dark bodies, shouting to their God.
>
> "Ah is pure. Look on me, God. Ah is pure."
>
> Raising strong black arms to heaven, full black breasts lifting, buxom black bodies tautening, their shocking black buttocks bare as at birth.

Believing the naked expressions of religious frenzy inappropriate, Estelle reacted with more than distaste and hustled her sons out of the church.

To keep her youngest away from other children who came to Alcorn straight from the wooden shacks that were the area's version of primary schools and the raw version of black Christianity that emphasized passion without restraint and propriety, Estelle Himes invested a great deal of energy in teaching her young boys at home. With the exception of the Haines year, she instructed them personally from about 1914 to 1922, carrying over her Scotia liberal arts preparation, and imparting "high levels of expectation" in the process. But Estelle's declaration of the unfitness of the local public schools for blacks caused her to cloister Joe and Chester. She discouraged play even with the children of faculty. Instead of gaining friends and a peer group, Chester would rely upon his mother and father, but especially his brother. "We were a small, close-knit family," Joseph Jr. later recalled, and the central activity of that unit was reading. Chester saw the home library as a place of "security and happiness."

At Christmas, Estelle wrote original stories for her boys. She strongly encouraged reading but also would have to discipline precocious Chester, who was always overstepping well-known family rules. When Chester was reading Edgar Allan Poe's "The Raven," he exclaimed the word "damn" in the living room where his family sat, each engrossed in a book or magazine. Of course this deed required punishment. Estelle also put her musical training to use, insisting that the boys hear "good" music, and she played the piano for their education, for entertainment, and to overcome her own isolation. Chester loved to hear her at the piano for hours at a time playing Chopin's "Fantaisie Impromptu" and Beethoven's "Moonlight Sonata." The Himeses bought a phonograph and spun 78-rpm recordings of Enrico Caruso, Fritz Kreisler, and John Philip Sousa. Chester loved Caruso's arias and Kreisler's version of "Flight of the Bumblebee," but when his mother played Sousa's version of the second act of Verdi's *Il Trovatore*—"The Anvil Chorus"—she brought the house down. During the climactic moment when the chorus chants the lyrics "*Chi del gitano i giorni abbella? La zingarella,*" Chester and Joseph Jr. shouted and hammered in accompaniment with the percussion players.

Estelle's deliberate efforts to make Verdi counteract the nude church amazons and to prevent the consumption of the chitterlings that her husband loved, had a hand in dismantling what she was fighting to keep together: her marriage. Increasingly she seemed inclined to push outward into the world, whatever the cost. In her early forties, she began to resist the protocols of racial segregation. Estelle instructed her small sons in a kind of catechism that she imagined as her most powerful safeguard against the low self-esteem and low expectations that Jim Crow ingrained. "You mustn't think of yourself as colored," she told Joe and Chester with a spooky intensity. "Your mother is as white as anyone. You both have white blood—fine white blood—in your veins. And never forget it." Her recitation of the creed of mixed bloodlines seems to have begun around the time that Eddie, her eldest son, entered the junior preparatory class at Alcorn in 1915. Her earnest sincerity must have struck the boys as poignant, but over time her children found the claims uncomfortable and bizarre.

Edward was on the verge of leaving the family, and he would, of the three sons, accept the least direction from his mother. By the fall of 1920, he had begun the college preparatory curriculum at Atlanta University. But his years at Alcorn did not stand him well. He returned to Atlanta in his second year, still a freshman. After that academic trial, he apparently withdrew from the university and never completed his degree. The combination of embarrassment and stung pride would drive a wedge between him and his parents, and he never again lived for a long period with his family.

Nothing better captured the growing distance between the two spouses than Joseph Sr.'s relish for life on the Mississippi, and apparently even for Governor Theodore Bilbo, the official president of the board of trustees at Alcorn, and a regular visitor to the school. When the governor, who had served under the malicious James Vardaman who encouraged lynching, conducted the commencement exercises, Joseph Himes joked with him in the odd idiom of familiarity allowed blacks and whites within the caste system. Years later, Chester grumbled that such affinity was possible because "my father was born and raised in the tradition of the Southern Uncle Tom," which was nothing more than "an inherited slave mentality." The irony of Chester's view was that Joseph Sr. did not inherit the submissive mentality from his own rebellious and independent father, who actually had been enslaved.

If the flattery and camaraderie with the powerful—done within accepted Jim Crow avenues for adult behavior—gratified Joseph Himes, it did nothing to make his wife more satisfied. The marriage only grew more openly rancorous, and the children took front-row seats. "Mother kept chopping him down to size because what he did wasn't like anything he boasted about," thought Joseph Jr. As Estelle kept at him, her husband "got to be dissatisfied with her nagging" and simply came to believe that his wife possessed "a quarrelsome nature."

The home life of bickering and tense silence between mother and father was made more difficult because Joseph was a hero to his children, nearly like a figure out of the Greek and Roman myths that Estelle read to them at night. His sons admired him as a thoughtful man's man. A leather apron over his white shirt and vest, Joseph combined precise mathematical knowledge, physical strength, and craftsmanship, in a sphere well regarded by rural men of the era. Powerful when it called for it, he was a man who held a horse's leg between his knees, used planes and chisels on wood, and taught students to melt iron and drive steel.

But the heroic myths never spent their poetry on the inner workings of a modern marriage. With their heads shaved and dressed in overalls, Chester and Joseph looked more and more like the country black boys who populated the grammar school at Alcorn. The boys got chicken pox, and the severity of that common disease was magnified in a countryside with few doctors. But particularly troubling was the worldwide influenza epidemic, which began devastating Clai-

borne County. In November 1918 the public schools closed and by the
next month thirty-two people were dead from the dreaded illness.
By the time the outbreak reached its highest proportions in the area,
in February 1920, Estelle had enough leverage to insist on a change.

In the summer of 1920, the Himeses left Mississippi for St.
Louis, Missouri, where they owned an investment property at 4525
Garfield Avenue, at the corner of Taylor Street. By that fall, Joseph
made arrangements for a new position in Pine Bluff, Arkansas, at
Branch Normal, Arkansas's state-supported secondary institute for
Negroes. (In 1922, the school would change its name to Arkansas
Agricultural, Mechanical and Normal, and became a division of the
University of Arkansas.) The family, minus Edward, who was by
then enrolled full-time at Atlanta University, joined a wartime surge
of blacks to the cotton-rich soil on the western bank of the Mississippi north of Louisiana.

For black Americans it was a difficult time, defined by the so-
called Red Summer of 1919 and extending for many years, from
Rosewood, Florida, to Tulsa, Oklahoma. When black soldiers began
returning from overseas duty, warlike racial riots broke out in more
than twenty-six cities across the United States; they left scores of
African Americans dead. Chicago was the site of the deadliest urban
riot, which resembled the 1906 Atlanta debacle in its violence. Elaine,
Arkansas, in the Mississippi Delta about one hundred miles east of
Pine Bluff, was the site of the estimated largest loss of black lives in
the country: in late September 1919, unionizing black sharecroppers
of Phillips County found themselves at the mercy of large numbers
of armed whites, joined by regular Army soldiers, who committed
atrocities. Hundreds of Africans Americans are believed to have lost
their lives.

In addition to the turmoil of those years, Joseph stepped into
the most contentious teaching post he had yet known. In 1911, the
trustees at Branch Normal had removed its director, Isaac Fisher, for

trying to implement industrial education. Local blacks were suspicious of industrial education because whites supported it. The year before Fisher was removed, the entire senior class had their diplomas rescinded after the state demanded an evaluation and none of the graduates passed. Jefferson Ish, a mathematician, was superintendent in 1920, and the school itself was moving academically in the direction of a junior college degree—the pride of the administration.

Still more changes in leadership occurred. Charles Smith, also a mathematician, became superintendent on an interim basis at the end of the Himeses' first year in Pine Bluff. In 1922 Robert Malone replaced Smith. Malone was junior to Joseph Himes by ten years, and, in spite of the fact that cotton prices were still high from war contracts, resulting in students wearing fine clothes and driving new automobiles, the situation for the middle-aged Joseph Sr. was tottering. Branch Normal represented the last grasp at family life and professional success for the Himeses.

The humble campus, two blocks away from a branch of the Arkansas River, had as its showpiece two-story Corbin Hall, the home to the academic classes. Twelve-year-old Joe and eleven-year-old Chester began their formal educations in the six classrooms on the ground floor. Assemblies capable of seating four hundred were held on the second floor of the building. The girls' dormitory, where some of the unmarried female professors lived, was an old military barracks. A boys' dormitory, a trades buildings for both sexes, and the Training School Building completed the campus.

At first the Himes family boarded downtown with a forty-year-old widow named Lillie Grotia at 519 W. Sixth Street, near a Catholic church. Later they settled more permanently in a plain frame house at 2020 W. Tenth Street in an expansion neighborhood about a mile south of the campus. Sitting on an unpaved road, the Himes neighborhood catered to workers from the lumber mill; only one or two blacks of the professional class lived in their midst. On their walk

down Tenth Street to school, Chester and Joe skirted avenues of black
women lolling and bantering provocatively with men.

Decidedly more reliable than Chester, Joe became a drugstore
porter making bicycle deliveries. They were both growing up "where
the Southern crosses the Yellow Dog," a blues song lyric describing
the intersection of the two large railroads in Pine Bluff. Estelle tried
giving them piano lessons, but the neighborhood, the locomotive
switch engines, and the bustle ignited a new curiosity in her sons.
Nervy and energetic, Chester practiced jumping aboard the cars and
leaping off before the trains got out of town. A bookish lad in the
backwoods of Alcorn, Chester had tended to measure himself against
heroes in search of the golden fleece; now, in the clanging world of the
larger town of Pine Bluff, the boundaries between adventurousness
and foolhardiness came close together.

In September 1920, the superintendent and his staff examined
the new matriculates. The Himes boys were placed in the first section of the second year of the normal department—the tenth grade—
alongside about seventy other students. That level was very close to
the limit of what was being taught at Branch Normal. There were
roughly eighteen professors on the faculty, but, as elsewhere in the
region, they were heavily weighted toward trades. However, most of
the traditional college preparatory courses were taught: pedagogy,
psychology, mathematics, biology, chemistry, history, civics, English,
geography, music, and history. The academic department took advantage of the new professor Joseph Himes Sr., bringing him into its
ranks as history teacher.

For Chester, the pubescent struggle for school-age belonging had
begun. In a school that had a great many teenagers, Chester and Joe
had their classes in the upper division with the school's older teens.
The boys were thoughtful and academically advanced but, having
been schooled at home, less comfortable in a classroom. Their classmates were usually between sixteen and eighteen, the age today of

students in the last stage of high school; Chester and Joe were closer to the age of students entering junior high school, with Chester being the youngest student enrolled. Thirty U.S. Army veterans rounded out the student population.

The Himes boys' adjustment to school included dispiriting moments that characterized the inelegance of the serve-all segregated institution, which catered to the needs of adults and children in the same classroom. Noting the naïveté of the bright youngest member of his class, an older student played a rough joke. He bade Chester to report his absence during the morning roll by telling the professor that he had "gone to Memphis chasing whores." Although not every schoolboy would have been unfamiliar with that term, Chester was. He could only parse out that "'hoers' were always needed to hoe cotton and chop corn." When the class resumed a day later and the roll was called, Chester repeated the message word for word. The professor called him to the front of the class and attempted to paddle him, but now Chester fought back. The teacher threw him to the ground, and his brother Joe leaped up, both children tussling against the instructor in front of the roaring class of older students. "It caused," Chester remembered dryly, "quite a scandal in the school." And the next day he learned, of course, what the scandal was about, and it changed his walk along the avenues.

The bright spot at Branch Normal was the stand-out English teacher, Ernestine Copeland. Using a textbook called *Composition and Rhetoric*, she taught the simple foundation and construction of the English language, diagramming sentences and conjugating verbs. Copeland's was a strong, up-to-date academic class. She even brought into the classroom the iconoclastic New York magazine *The Independent*, which sometimes carried book reviews that throttled the "sentimentality and hypocrisy" coating discussions of race mixing in the "mongrel South." By 1923 she had provided Chester with his initial exposure to *Hamlet, Macbeth*, and *The Canterbury*

Tales and allowed "theme" essays to be drawn from her students' personal experience. Chester "ate that stuff up!" remembered his brother. Copeland's class was the singular academic experience in Chester's educational career.

Equally inspirational, Chester's father began to offer a one-of-a-kind class in black history. The normal school department considered it important to require "History of the Negro," a course that would "acquaint the student with the facts as they are in order that he may find his place without friction and perform most efficiently his part in the social welfare." Beginning with literary critic Benjamin Brawley's 1913 book *A Short History of the American Negro*, Chester's father strove to make students understand "the origin of the more harsh system of chattel slavery in the New World." To prepare his lectures, Joseph pored over his copy of the twenty-volume *Encyclopedia Britannica*, which would have emphasized the value of hard work, discipline, and talented individuals triumphing against overwhelming odds. Inside the classroom, Chester's father used Carter G. Woodson's *The Negro in Our History*, a comprehensive volume by the champion black historian of the twentieth century. Woodson's red-covered book, just off the press, was among "a number of textbooks and reference books on Negro history which I have never seen since," Chester recalled. For Joseph Sr.'s sons, reading about the achievements of blacks in the past was "a thrilling and eye-opening experience."

Chester also picked up an education from the trade departments at Branch Normal, where he learned to drive a tractor and automobile. It was because of this foundation that, during the Second World War, Chester would be able to make the claim "I could read blueprints; I understood, at least partially, most of the necessary skills of building construction—carpentry, plumbing, electric wiring, bricklaying, roofing; I understood the fundamentals of combustion engines; I could operate a number of machine tools—turret lathes, drills, milling machines, etc." For the young Chester, these were mildly thrilling, empowering experiences that connected him to his father and built a sense of masculine self-confidence.

Chemistry was perhaps the most intriguing subject for the Himes brothers. They spent their "happiest hours" unsupervised in the chapel basement with Bunsen burners and mortar and pestle, melting crystals, heating mixtures, and grinding solids. The singular achievement was the combination of three chemicals—saltpeter, charcoal, and sulfur—to make gunpowder. When they added potassium chlorate and ground glass, the mixture would detonate itself. "A delicate and dangerous performance," Chester adjudged.

Branch Normal's commencement week exercises were under way on May 23, 1923, when Joe and Chester were scheduled to make a chemistry presentation in Corbin Hall to an assemblage of parents, students, and other guests. At the time for the presentation, Joseph Jr. went onto the stage by himself. Throughout the remainder of his life, Chester would mull over the events that happened that evening. He wrote that his mother had prevented him from participating because he had broken one of her many rules. He had been "naughty" and thrown an explosive compound against the house and defied her by talking back instead of apologizing and acting contrite. Confirming the breach between the two siblings that was about to occur, Joseph maintained that Chester simply refused to perform the experiment. Whatever the case, when Joseph mixed the last elements onstage for the famous gunpowder demonstration, he miscalculated the ingredients and the mixture erupted prematurely. In a loud puffing flash, a smoke cloud the size of a gallon jug engulfed him; ground glass had been driven into his eyes. Horrified, Chester and his parents watched as the ghastly haze enveloped Joe.

They rushed the injured boy to Davis Hospital, the largest medical facility in Pine Bluff. There, the doctors summarily declined to treat him because he was black. Joseph Sr. pleaded, as did Branch Normal principal Robert Malone, but to no avail. When they

returned to the Stutz touring car, Chester's father was weeping. The
family went next to Lucy Memorial Hospital, where, instead of surgeons attempting to remove the glass from Joe Jr.'s eyes, doctors could
only dress and bandage his wounds, in preparation for a future trip
to a hospital in a different city that might offer a higher level of care
for black Americans. In the following days, Estelle traveled with Joe
to St. Louis, to Barnes Hospital, which was available to all citizens
"without distinction of creed."

Because he would need long-term care, Joseph and his mother
took lodging in St. Louis. Back home, Chester and his father moved
to one or two rooms close to the entrance of the campus. The family
had begun unraveling earlier than this, but now the drama of dissolution took on the dimensions of epic tragedy. When the oldest
Himes son, Edward, had gone out on his own, his loss to the family
did not seem permanent or evidence of a mark against them. After
Joe's accident, however, Chester's parents began reinterpreting
family history, seeing the crises as a series of inexorable calamities
marking Estelle and Joseph Sr. for special punishment, their come-
uppance for overambition.

During this summer of separation, Joseph Sr. also served as acting
president over the small Branch faculty. Chester, now taller than his
father at age fourteen, had completed the high school course. He
played tennis, drove the school tractor around the grounds, and developed a crush on one of the young teachers from the summer school.
At the church picnics and youth gatherings, he learned graphically
about sex—at least as a voyeur. The country girls wanted to seduce
him and the willing boys proved their mannish conquests by dis-
playing to one another their vaginally slickened genitals. The mating,
the public parade of intimacy, the braggadocio of the boys and girls,
equally attracted and distressed Chester. Chaste and self-conscious,
Chester preferred to walk with girls his age to the state fair, saying to
one that she was "Penelope and I was Ulysses returning home from

twenty years of wandering." A youngster who inhabited a world of mythic quest literature more comfortably than he did one of a stray, behind-the-shed groping at sex, melancholy Chester was a boy whose valiant romantic ideal was clashing with the reality of shabby black town life.

Considering the opportunities to continue his profession, Joseph Sr. made the rash decision that fall to reunite with Joe and Estelle in St. Louis, then a city of nearly 800,000. The family moved into the historic and crowded black neighborhood called the Ville, eventually settling on Belle Glade Avenue, a quiet street of one- and two-story brick tenement houses with built-in gardens on the median strip. The house was a few minutes' walk from Chester's new school.

They lived near the downtown heart of the sprawling, wealthy, and sometimes angry metropolis of wide paved streets and tall brick and stone buildings, like the recently built and massive City Hall and unsegregated main library. But while the streetcars did not require segregation, St. Louis was no haven for blacks. Six years earlier, in July 1917, labor unrest and black migration had unleashed an orgy of white violence that had left an estimated fifty people dead and 240 buildings burned down across the river in East St. Louis.

The decision to stake the entire fortunes of the family on the slender possibility of recuperation of one of its members was a tricky gamble. Joe had fleeting sight in one eye, enabling him to distinguish print a few inches away and shapes and sunlight at a distance. The other eye was useless. Bright and dutiful, Joe began instruction in Braille at the integrated Missouri School for the Blind. Certainly it would have been better for Chester if they had remained in Arkansas.

Without a faculty job lined up, Joseph Sr. joined the ranks of black porters and laborers. Chester later captured the shrunken man that his father became after they moved. "He was a pathetic figure coming home from work; a small black man hunched over and frowning, shambling in a tired-footed walk, crushed old cap pulled down over

his tired, glazed eyes, a cigarette dangling from loose lips." Bereft of
a prestige occupation and fearing that his middle child and namesake
might become an invalid, Joseph Sr. steadily lost his authority and his
will to correct his youngest child.

In the fall of 1923 Chester attended Charles Sumner High School.
Named after the famed abolitionist senator from Massachusetts,
Sumner was the first black secondary school west of the Mississippi.
For the first time in his life, Chester was not known to adults on
account of the stature of his father. He knew that his parents owned
and rented some property, but he was embarrassed to admit that his
father worked as an unskilled laborer, a problem at Sumner where it
mattered a great deal who your parents were. Modern, competitive,
and the only post for black educated elites, Sumner boasted nine professors teaching English, seven teaching math, and several of them
held master's degrees. The highly skilled faculty, headed by George
Brantley, demeaned the work Chester had completed at Branch
Normal, and his teachers belittled him when he insisted that Branch
had a college division that he had attended. They dropped Chester
in with his rough age group; at fourteen he started the tenth grade.
Again. He smoldered with resentment.

Chester was hoping to please his mother and become a medical doctor, and he took the "scientific" curriculum. For a full year he
specialized in algebra I and II, geometry, chemistry, biology, physics, English, and German. He passed his classes with above average
marks, but he never made As. Without Joe in class beside him, and
having no rank on account of his surname, Chester was unsure of
himself.

The emotional pain connected to experiencing the reduced social
esteem of his brother, his father, and himself in such a short span
invented Chester's famed quicksilver rage at circumstances beyond
his control. He "hated" Sumner, finding his fellow black students
"cheap-smart," "city-dirty," "preoccupied with themselves," and "quick

to ostracize and condescend." He disliked the rituals and rhythm of the scholastic team sports, instead favoring rough-and-tumble games with working-class boys at Tandy Park, during which he scarred his ear and battered a shoulder blade. But grueling, unregulated contests were preferable to the classroom of black strivers and their mentors. Struggling to come to grips with the devastation of his family, he had found a convenient, lifelong scapegoat: the blacks of the middle class and their pretentiousness.

By the fall of 1924, restoring Joe's sight was making little progress. The Himeses clutched after family support and, as they had done before, retreated to Cleveland. Chester, dislodged again, would not even be allowed to finish out a complete academic year in St. Louis.

Chapter Three

BANQUETS AND COCAINE BALLS

1925–1928

At the hinge of downtown Cleveland stands the Cuyahoga County Soldiers' and Sailors' Monument, a 140-ton granite column 125 feet high. Dedicated in 1894, the stolid Civil War monument depicts life-size bronze figures during four engagements of the conflict. Perhaps the most riveting scene shows a black man straining to fit a cannonball into an artillery piece. Equipped with an ample interior gallery, the monument's northern inside wall contained a bronze frieze of Abraham Lincoln holding broken handcuffs and a freedman bracing himself on one knee and holding on to a rifle and cartridge box extended by Lincoln: the militant moment of emancipation. After a childhood in towns anchored around public monuments to the Confederacy, Chester, who had become preoccupied by a portrait his father had once shown him of black prisoners biting Confederate dogs, was now living in the northern United States.

The city of Cleveland curved along the edge of Lake Erie, one of the five Great Lakes. A place of hot summers and cold, snow-filled winters, "Lake City" relied on its great heavy industries in steel and natural energy to fuel its boom during the 1920s. In 1920 Cleveland was America's fifth-largest city. Densely populated by immigrants from Poland, Italy, Hungary, and Germany, as well as Jews who grouped together in a neighborhood called Glenville, Cleveland contrasted sharply with St. Louis, Pine Bluff, and rural Mississippi.

Chester Himes's family arrived piecemeal, and they faced their greatest challenge with dwindling resources. Joseph Sr. and Chester came first, in February 1925, and Estelle and Joseph Jr. followed in July. As in St. Louis, Joseph Sr. was reduced to manual labor. He advertised himself as a carpenter, and he tried to make a living in the building trades. Fannie Wiggins, the youngest of the Himes siblings, gave them quarters in her seven-room house at 1711 E. Sixty-Eighth Place. Chester's older brother Edward had spent summers and perhaps a year at the home. Joseph Sr.'s brother Andrew, who worked in Cleveland as a waiter, seems to have lived there much of his adult life. Joseph Sr., Chester, and Joseph Jr. would live in the house off and on over the next fifteen years. The family ties were strong, as were the privileges that the Himes men expected and received from Fannie.

By marrying a man fifteen years her senior from Seneca, South Carolina, Fannie had somewhat narrowed the gulf in experience between herself and her siblings. Her husband, Wade Hampton Wiggins, was named after a famous Confederate guerrilla fighter and worked as a "stationary engineer" for Standard Oil, shoveling coal in the boilers at the offices and warehouses. A gentle, tall, dark man whose shaved head accented an imposing physique, Wiggins was profligate. He owned a car he could not drive and rented a home. He had one serious concern in his house: consuming his rations in quantity, enough so that—be it simple fare like beef lungs and rice—it had to be served on a turkey platter. Chester's aunt Fannie was not as simply or regularly pleased. When she could, she affected the air of a dapper stylish woman. Fannie hoped for cultivation beyond her means.

By the time Joseph Sr. moved his family to his sister's, the hub of black life was at the intersection of Central Avenue and Fifty-Fifth

Street. The Wiggins house on Sixty-Eighth Place, a black side street, had initially put them up against better-off white neighbors on the large boulevards, most of whom were northern European immigrants: Danes, Germans, and English. But in the mid-1920s, all of this was changing, as the slum quarters near the shipyard docks, manufacturing plants, and railroad depots crept outward along the rail lines. Unskilled black workers, often brought in temporarily and unused to urban living, spread into neighborhoods along transport routes and cheap housing and the once white boulevards became all black. From the later 1910s to the late 1920s, nearby Hough Avenue at the corner of E. Sixty-Eighth Street would become as solidly African American as Fifty-Fifth and Central. By 1930, Seventy-Ninth Street was the racial dividing line, which pushed beyond Ninety-Third Street a decade later.

As black migrants poured in and faced a closed housing market, the glamour of the city soon gave way to grime. Chester's most regular memory of life on the shores of Lake Erie was of soot raining down upon the plowed snow lining the street curbs, creating a blackened slush, the airborne residue of companies like Otis and Corrigan-McKinney Steel.

Joseph's sister Leah Moon and her husband, Roddy, had seemingly leapfrogged the problem of encroaching poverty. In 1915 they purchased a two-story home in Glenville on Bryant Avenue, several miles east of their relatives. Roddy Moon had become the extraordinary man in his community. If Moon got his initial government appointment on the basis of conservative political leanings connected to the Booker T. Washington machine, in 1912 he had turned in another direction and founded the Cleveland branch of the NAACP. For twenty years he headed the local black fight for equal treatment under the law.

Pious, rigid, and ever mindful of appearing the confident educated American, Moon dominated his household. He introduced his youngest child, Henry Lee, to classic Victorian era writers, including Victor Hugo, Dunbar, Dumas fils, Dickens, and Browning. Leah Moon, a devoted cook, was best known for tending an immaculate, prize-winning garden, but she was also a friend of Mary McLeod Bethune, Estelle's Scotia classmate. The Moons were model members of the black minority in Glenville. The family had not just adapted to successful careers in the North, they had transformed themselves and shucked off the misery of the past. Although Leah and Roddy had been born and bred in small South Carolina towns and the children had spent their early years in the South, none of the Moons retained a Southern accent. The glaring difference between the middling Wigginses and the starched Moons was obvious and put the freeloading Himeses in the middle.

Chester believed his aunts and uncles exacerbated the escalating marital tensions between his parents. In his later years, he wrote, "My father's people suspected my mother of looking down on them because they were black. Maybe she did. They hated her. She hated them." Joseph Jr. felt similarly. Both of them oversimplified the family crisis. Estelle was almost certainly snooty toward the grade-school-educated Wigginses and Andrew Himes, even though she was relying upon their goodwill, if not their outright charity. But Estelle neither lived with nor had achieved enough to look down upon Leah and Roddy Moon. If she disliked something about them, it was that they were inclined to flatter themselves and look down upon her.

Chester correctly identified the clash of wills between Estelle and Fannie Wiggins, who had worked in Estelle's house back in Savannah, who did not know her own father well, and who did not have the same mother as her older siblings. Her education had probably been curtailed after her father died and the children had divided his estate. Fannie would have greeted her sister-in-law and her two hearty-eating boys with more than reluctance. In the novel *The Third Generation*, Chester condensed the crisis of his family, as they tried to get their footing in the North and his parents struggled to repair their marriage, into a classic battle between his youngest aunt and his mother.

"You don't like black people but soon's you get down and out you come running to us."

"I married a black man who happens to be your brother."

"Yes, you married him 'cause you thought he was gonna make you a great lady."

"I'll not discuss it."

"You're in no position to say what you'll discuss, sister. This is my house. I pay taxes on it."

"If Mr. Taylor hadn't spent all of his money sending you and your sister here from the South he'd have something of his own."

"You dragged him down yourself, don't go blaming it on us. If you'd made him a good wife instead of always nagging at him, he'd be president of a college today."

Comfortable with the pattern of providing for herself and Joseph Jr., Estelle responded after a short time to the strife in the Wiggins household by removing herself and her disabled son to another neighborhood, effectively walking out of the marriage while claiming it was for her blind son's health. Joe thought he was "infantilized" in the process. Chester, as usual now, was an afterthought, and almost from the time they arrived in the city, he would seek a haven outside of the emotionally charged house.

During his two semesters there, he was unable to achieve a refuge at East High School. One thousand students strong, East High was one of Cleveland's strong academic public schools. Chester began his scholastic year in February 1925 alongside seven other black boys and girls. Unlike the black Cleveland poet Langston Hughes, a popular student when he graduated from rival Central High in 1920, Chester had a difficult time socially jumping into the final year. Without any history with the faculty or fellow students, and his brother now fully a year behind him in course work, Chester became ever more disinclined to prove his academic worth. The end-of-the-year chemistry experiments included explosives demonstrations, which must have made vivid Joe's terrible mishap. If Chester had dominated the classroom in Pine Bluff and been able to disregard it but still succeed tolerably well in St. Louis, at East High School he could do neither. In a white classroom where students were considering the leading American colleges, pupils maneuvered to display skill. One young woman teased him when he made errors, and, in what he had now established as a pattern of rebellion, he became a show-off in the cafeteria and kept classroom activities at arm's length.

Nor did Chester warm to the organized exclusive social activities, like the Friday Frolics, afternoon dances held in the gymnasium, the Atheneum Literary Society, or the football games that East High lost every single time that season. Fifteen years old and fresh from St. Louis, he was "anxious to prove I was an all right guy." This meant smoking cigarettes and telling the baseball crowd that he had the slugging power of Babe Ruth, then ditching entire afternoons of class and jogging over to play the Catholic school boys at Rockefeller Park. But Chester was no Sultan of Swat. One afternoon he foul-tipped a ball into his own eye and the ballplayers razzed him for a couple of days, but for a brief period of time he felt included.

By his second term, in the fall of 1925, the final semester he needed to graduate, the college prep curriculum at East High was a maddening chore for Chester. The public schools in Cleveland organized classes according to student scores on IQ tests, part of the classification rage after the First World War. Chester's strong score balanced his miserable classroom performances and made him egotistical, the misunderstood genius. Complicating matters, Joe entered the East High School junior class that fall, speedily made the honor roll, and then kept a 90 average. Chester was not even competing with his brother, who was more or less blind, and he quietly resented his mother's focus on Joe, their movement from city to city in search of doctors and schools.

Meanwhile, on October 8, 1925, his parents bought a three-story colonial revival at 10713 Everton Avenue. Constructed in 1918, the spacious five-bedroom was, as Joseph Himes recalled, "the nicest house we ever lived in." Chester rejoiced in the new home, which erased the shame of their frequent moves, dip into poverty, and family quarrels—the Thursday the Himeses bought it would be the brightest day in his life for the next ten years. The four Himeses were also trailblazers. The block they moved on was completely white, and Estelle could have the satisfaction of living even farther away from the ever-widening black slums than even her sister-in-law Leah. The ample house and the address in Glenville gave both sons elite standing in black Cleveland.

Chester beamed at the new status and the possibility that his parents' troubled marriage was on the mend. He gravitated to a new group of young people, accommodating himself to mastering the complex Charleston dance and slicking his hair down with Vaseline and black goo to achieve the Pomp, the imitation of the Rudolph Valentino hairdo from the popular 1921 film *The Sheik*. But possibly by then the ragtag pilgrimage had taken its toll on him. The requirement of submitting to the discipline of a pioneering family like the Moons—who responded to the requirement of being the "first" blacks on their street as if awakening to a trumpet blast—was uncomfortable. Unprepared to cope with the slights, the shouts of "colored boy" and "nigger" from neighbors and schoolmates, such as his cousin Henry had already endured, Chester was less inclined to leap the hurdles required to win friends and impress adults.

East High School's winter commencement exercises were on Thursday, January 28, 1926. The eager students sang and gave orations, but the moment was bittersweet for Chester, who had been asked to return to school to repeat a course. In error, one of the Latin teachers had written "86" on his report card in place of the 56 that he had earned; he was awarded his diploma by clerical mistake. Adopting a belligerence that he would never fully discard, Chester felt, of course, that he had, by then, graduated three times from high school: from Branch Normal, from Sumner in St. Louis, and from East High.

Prideful, he decided to attend Ohio State University along with dozens of other members of the class, telling people that he would become a medical doctor. He would have received firsthand information from his cousin Henry about the opportunity for a quality education available in Columbus at the flagship university for the state. Henry Lee Moon had gone to Howard University as an undergraduate, pledging the Omega fraternity there, and then completed a master's degree in journalism at Ohio State, to his father's satisfaction. Despite that accomplishment, Chester's Aunt Leah then tried to push her younger son into the medical field, advising him on a creed she undoubtedly shared with her nephew: "Our people need more doctors; besides you'll be your own man and will not have to take tips and orders from any white man." Tuition for Ohio residents was only $10, although fees, including room and board, were estimated at another $658. If the Himes family had a real discussion at home about where Chester ought to go to school—Joseph likely supporting a Southern Negro college and Estelle advocating for anything but—the decision might easily have revolved around Estelle's willingness to help foot the cost of fees. Their eldest son Eddie's difficulty when at Atlanta University wouldn't have helped Joseph's case for the potential of all-black schools. Chester, who had limped away from East High, decided he would try to outdo his older cousin Henry: he would become a doctor in six or seven years and do all of the work at Ohio State.

Following his winter graduation, Chester's father got him a job through a church connection at the luxurious Wade Park Manor, an extended-stay hotel off Wade Park, one of Cleveland's planned public squares and gardens. Constructed in Gilded Age grandeur, the twelve-story hotel overlooked a lake and was staffed by black busboys, waiters, and maids. "No matter what your aim is in life, waiting tables is a good profession to know. Many of our most prominent men got their start waiting table," Chester was told. The opposite was true too, as he knew and his mother and Aunt Leah certainly forewarned: the Moon family were convinced that their older boy, Joe, had been "ruined" after a season as a bellman at the Cleveland Athletic Club. By getting used to accepting gratuities from the rich, a black man could permanently lose his dignity and willpower.

If Joseph Sr. feared he was leading his son down the path of his brother Andrew or his nephew he did not let on, but supported the basic position of value in honest work. Showing off, Chester had already wrecked the Wiggins automobile, and the accident had encouraged his father to believe that steady labor was the most important quality that Chester yet needed. But Joseph Sr. was unsuccessful at bending his youngest son to the value of a work ethic, saving, and ambition. With his hotel salary and exposure to the older men's locker room talk, and two flirtatious white girls at the hotel check counter, Chester took five dollars from his earnings to an establishment in the red-light district on Scovil Avenue to lose his virginity.

Himes wrote more than one version of this coming-of-age moment, and in one, he acquainted himself with the scarred, run-down wooden tenements and abandoned cars of Scovil at the height of winter. In his memoir, he writes that he impetuously began his sexual initiation in this area known as the "Bucket of Blood," a young cad making his way "to an old fat ugly whore sitting on a stool outside her hovel."

What fascinated him in his adulthood about the Cleveland tenderloin was that the prostitution had grown out of the forces of the American race dynamic. Steel industrialists in the Cuyahoga River valley had imported male laborers from Romania, Hungary, Yugo-slavia, and Czechoslovakia. These men were herded into ghettos and, with the money that they earned, were able to employ black women as cooks and laundresses. Sexual unions for pay, pleasure, and romance began at the same time. Black men locked out of the labor market began procuring women for the lonely foreigners. By the 1920s, black female prostitution was very nearly an industrial commodity itself, and a hardened lot of women earned a living along Scovil Avenue.

However, Chester's sexual triumph was short-lived. He had been at work about two weeks when, in the middle of February, not looking while chatting with the young white girls who scrutinized the dinner trays headed up to the hotel patrons, he stepped backward through open elevator doors. Although the doors to the elevator parted, the carriage had already passed to a floor above. He fell two stories down the shaft, shattering his chin and jaw, his left arm, which he used to break his fall, his pelvis, and three vertebrae. Chester likened the sensation of hitting the steel plate at the elevator shaft bottom to "spattering open like a ripe watermelon." Gurgling blood and spitting out teeth, he was rushed to the hospital.

Near the hotel was the brand-new and technically advanced University Hospitals of Cleveland. Doctors there turned him away on account of space constraints, after first giving him an injection of morphine. Inevitably the scene reminded him of Joseph's rejection in Arkansas by a whites-only facility. Accepted at the homeopathic-friendly Huron Road Hospital for charity cases, about two miles from the scene of his accident, he was given a room on a crowded ward with patients who were terminally ill. Ohio Industrial Commission physicians placed sixteen-year-old Chester in a complete body cast. A few hours later and under emergency conditions they inserted a tube in his bladder to substitute for a ruptured urethra. Chester had smoked cigarettes before and he had experimented with booze, but the injections he began receiving to deal with the pain of his injuries opened him to a new range of psychic moods. The reality of his wounds and pains, the distancing from his own paralyzed body, and the likelihood of his permanent injury led him to a place of brittle irony with others, and self-pity with himself.

After an investigation presented findings of hotel negligence, the newly established workman's compensation fund began paying Chester seventy-five dollars a month; Ward Park Manor also continued his salary. Estelle Himes wanted to sue the hotel. Joseph Sr., astounded by the existence of state laws regulating the workplace—which meant the hospital bills were paid and that Chester would get the same salary his father had earned for the best years of his working life, even if the boy seemed as if he might never walk again—encouraged Chester to sign away legal liability for the accident, which he did. The arguments between his parents deepened in their rancor, also carrying the strong symbolism of an ideological conflict. Chester's white-looking mother was acting as the rebellious dissenter while his dark-skinned father played the obsequious Uncle Tom. In short order, Estelle and Joseph's putative reunion in the new house began to sputter.

The catastrophe also tore Chester's relationship with his mother. He had identified something in her, a kind of "incontinent vanity," the indulgent prickly side of her willful intention to ignore racial barriers and proclaim as true her fantasy heritage. When Estelle visited him at the hospital and berated the hotel, he recoiled. "Mother," his character Charles Taylor groans through his bandages in the novel *The Third Generation*, "will you please-please-please shut up!" Thinking of his family's vagabond trail along Southern outposts, and the loss of her affection to blinded Joe, Chester re-created the scene by having the wounded boy strike out savagely, "You're as much to blame as anyone."

Dropping weight from an already slender frame, Chester managed to heal over four months, and, once his wrist had mended and he could wiggle his toes, he willed himself to stand and take tentative new steps. But the experience was more complicated than regaining strength. Before he could walk, he watched two men die on his ward, a confrontation with tragedy and doom that opened full his new window on despair. With the beds aligned in rows within a hall, the intimate lives of his neighbors were unavoidable. The man beside him recited the Lord's Prayer for eight hours before dying, giving Chester ample time to recall the image of the young girl in Alcorn beneath the wagon wheel. To his personality now came an edge of fatalism.

On July 3, 1926, Chester left the hospital to return home. A conscientious commission-appointed dentist canalled, filled, and crowned his broken teeth. Chester was nearly an invalid, learning how to walk again, and encumbered by a leather-and-steel back brace that fastened underneath his groin and that Estelle helped him attach. His mother was also angry, and she defied Joseph Sr. and continued to argue the case at the hotel, which she claimed had taken advantage of teenaged Chester. The only result was the suspension of his monthly salary of fifty dollars and renewed outbursts at home. It was a final rough passage in a marriage, where she had doted affection on her sons in lieu of her husband. She was again caring for Chester, whom she adored, he would later believe, because he was the lightest-colored of her children and perhaps the least outwardly masculine. But in response, Chester left the house and found another woman.

In one version of his life, Chester wrote about spending the post-convalescent end of July and August on Cedar Avenue in the arms of a prostitute. If the encounters took place as he wrote them in the 1953 autobiographical novel *The Third Generation,* they occurred habitually not just because he had the temerity to venture into the red-light blocks, but because of the pension from his accident. The relationship, which required the sex worker to refasten him into his back brace after intercourse, began a period when sensual joy and ecstasy would always be inflected by deep feelings of shame, humiliation, embarrassment, and the need for secrecy. The experience also disabused him of his boyhood romantic ideal. Chester was quick-witted enough to grasp the ancient hierarchy of the street, which put the "trick" in the sex trade at the bottom, the "whore" in the middle, and the "pimp" or "madam" at the top. At the end of his adolescence, Chester subconsciously connected sexual desire, pleasure, and fulfillment with using people and expecting to be used in return.

The summer trysts twined the violation of his parents' and the state's rules with a healthy growth beyond his family. He learned to drink white mule—a highly potent alcoholic beverage of Prohibition—and edged toward more serious illegal behavior. The Eighteenth Amendment, prohibiting the sale of intoxicating beverages and enforced by the 1919 Volstead Act, had the effect in cities like Cleveland of dramatically building up organized crime and urban criminal zones. Chester's classmates wrote short stories about Cleveland's pistol-wielding bandits (and comic, fearful black menials) in the high school paper.

In September, with money from workman's compensation and without telling his parents, Chester bought a beat-up Model T and left Cleveland for college in Columbus. A state-sponsored land-grant university designed at its outset to train farmers and mechanics, Ohio State University enrolled 8693 in 1926 and had blossomed into the largest institution for higher education in Ohio. Student life for freshmen got under way with an orientation week that included placement examinations and physicals at the gymnasium. Still gamely wishing for distinction, but without the day-to-day discipline instilled by his mother, Chester signed up for a premedical curriculum, with an emphasis on chemistry. But the summer spent recovering from the accident, his parents' troubled marriage, drinking, and visiting prostitutes colored his September arrival. What should have been memorable was anticlimactic.

The cornerstone of his academic career that fall was the advanced chemistry class, the gateway to premed. The class was broken up into an hour-long lecture, followed a day later by an hour-long recitation, and completed by two three-hour laboratory sessions. Students sat in assigned seats and attendance was habitually taken by the graduate teaching assistants who conducted the labs. Chester's other courses met daily for an hour and included elementary German and introduction to American literature, which focused on the nineteenth century, with "a brief survey of recent literature." (Ernest Hemingway's daring hit novel *The Sun Also Rises* was published in late October.) The academic program for the quarter included a mandatory one-credit course with William Henderson, the dean of the college, sharing his wisdom on picking classes, study habits, and campus rules.

After fifty successful years, the sprawling university was a miniature city, with late-Victorian-style academic buildings clustered around an enormous oval. Off to the southwest of the library was large Mirror Lake, where freshmen and sophomores engaged in a ritual tug-of-war battle that ended that fall with the frosh being pulled into the water. On October 2, when the freshmen went to the psychology department to take IQ tests, Chester placed an impressive fourth. The joyfully frivolous opening days of school, called "Know Ohio Week," were precisely the ritual dramas of belonging he had missed in high school. Toward the end of October the physical education and military science departments "permanently excused" Chester from drill and exercise, required of all freshmen, because of the disabilities from his fall. He ditched the beanie hat required of frosh, and strutted the campus in the blazer worn by the most ardent of school boosters, with broad vertical red and gray stripes. By mid-fall, with his Model T nearby, he had assumed the pose of an upperclassman.

African American students had begun attending Ohio State in 1892. By the fall of 1926, more than two hundred blacks were enrolled. Black Ohioans also saw themselves with a key stake in the school and had successfully petitioned the university president to prohibit professors in the departments of history and anatomy from using racial epithets like "nigger" and "coon" in the classroom. As for those professors who performed an annual minstrel show, there was less they could do. In 1926 a single African American participated in intercollegiate athletics, on the track and cross-country team. (Track star Jesse Owens would arrive on campus in 1930.) No blacks were permitted to join the white fraternities or eating clubs, effectively sealing them off from campus life. A family named Harrison ran a popular rooming house for African Americans at 236 E. Eleventh Street, where Chester's friend Oscar Stanton De Priest, the communications major, lived. With his ample budget, Chester took a private room in a large house at 1389 Summit Street, about four blocks east of the main campus. Despite being so ubiquitous as to appear normal, the obtrusive, steady racial prejudice was jarring. "He dreaded the classes where no one spoke to him, he hated the clubs he couldn't join, he scorned the restaurants in which he couldn't eat," Himes would later write. The psychological impact on the black students was perhaps also indicated by their attrition rate. Only fifteen graduated in 1926, and rarely more than thirty in any year. As for the official attitude toward racial segregation, school president W. O. Thompson thought that "colored people should not undertake to force that issue, and if it came about I should ask them not do it."

In response, the black students created a segregated playland on the black east side of Columbus. The boys took their dates to Long Street dances at the Crystal Slipper Ballroom and home-brew and whiskey joints there crowded onto "the Block." At the Empress Theater, the Columbus version of the famed Apollo in Harlem, emcees and announcers sang and strutted to engage the young coeds who copied the performers' manners. The artistic excellence and sensuality of musicals like *Runnin' Wild* featuring Ethel Waters or Josephine Baker blended with street-corner brawls and violence. Brassfield's Restaurant satisfied their appetites and then Lincoln Park afforded the students a secluded wooded reprieve for romance.

Chester later realized that the frantic pace of the social activities was partly designed to shield the black coeds from the oddity of segregation, the tenuousness of their membership in the college community. His own attitude during the period was "slightly hysterical," by which he meant frantic, enthusiastic, uneasy, and garrulous about private matters. Chester worked overtime to commit himself socially, enjoying the brash self-confidence of the group that Howard University philosopher Alain Locke was calling the New Negroes. Swiftly, Chester joined forty-four other black boys as Sphinxmen pledges for Alpha Phi Alpha—a leader in the fraternity system of the New Negroes that had begun at places like Cornell and Indiana University. Fellow pledge Jesse Jackson was his closest friend. With his pension, Chester could masquerade as one of the carelessly affluent. He palled around with some of the black upper crust, including Stanton De Priest of Chicago, whose father Oscar would in 1929 become the only African American serving in the U.S. House of Representatives. Always there was a sense of the possibility of extraordinary success given hard work and some luck; always there was the poison of maddening and numbing slights.

During early 1925, when he had lived at his aunt's house, he had felt the sting of skin-color divisions among African Americans. Chester now found at the university considerable proof for Aunt Fannie's disgust: "Light-complexioned blacks were more prejudiced toward darker blacks than were many white people." In his childhood Chester had accepted simply the complex dimensions of the slave descent of his parents: white-looking valets and concubines and dark-skinned artisans and field workers. His experience and heritage caused him to recoil against the skin-color snobbery: "I despised the in-group class distinctions based on color and the degree of white blood in one's veins." At this crucial moment of making the transition from adolescence to adulthood, he wanted to show that he was fully a black man, someone who accepted his ancestry and was not attempting to pull off a white imitation.

But the manner of his showing his black preference was not balanced. Instead of trying to romance one of his peers, he ditched the campus belles and took his libidinal urges to the Columbus brothels. In a move of risky defiance, he took up with a good-looking prostitute named Rose. At first, it was difficult to believe that a "young and beautiful," seemingly healthy woman would make herself available sexually. Rose encouraged him with faint praise, "You got an awful lot of steam for a li'l boy."

His newfound pleasures cost him quite a bit. Around Thanksgiving, Chester began to experience the painful urination and pus discharge indicating gonorrhea. Ashamed to admit the symptoms to a physician on campus, he went to a private doctor, who prescribed a solution of silver mercury, which Chester injected into the meatus of his glans to rid himself of the disease. The fall quarter examinations took place between December 18 and 22, and their outcome verified where Chester had passed his ten weeks. He turned in a blank form for the German final, and pulled a D. English was the high mark, with a satisfactory grade. He hadn't bothered to attend the course taught by Dean Henderson and took home another D. He failed chemistry outright. Following a fistfight with one of the graduate students who ran the laboratory portion of the chemistry class, he had simply stopped attending. Those marks ended the beginning of Chester Himes, M.D.

Chester hobbled back to Cleveland a few days before Christmas 1926. His collegiate misadventures seem to have helped accelerate the final dissolution of his parents' marriage. His father sympathized with Chester, blaming his son's failure on the uncertainty of their lives in Cleveland, the disaster of the parents' marriage, the ravages of the elevator accident, and his own shaky employment.

During the two-week break, Chester discovered the fullness of the black ghetto at Cedar Avenue and Fifty-Fifth Street by way of the cabaret at the Improved Benevolent Protective Order of Elks. At the Elks lodge Bud Jenkins's Virginia Ravers played "Bugle Blues," and, at least to Chester, Cleveland's black domestics responded as had the women in the remote church in Mississippi. In descriptions of his youth that always tripped over themselves with sex, he wrote that the women "leaped atop tables and pulled up their dresses showing strong black legs and black pussies as though on the slave block." Chester Himes recorded the moment in the classic mixed-metaphor idiom that he made his own, combining the voluntary expression of intimate desire with sexual coercion. But the image of women exhibiting themselves, not so much for the pleasure of men as for their own exhibitionist fantasy and congress with the music, emphasizes the sexual abandon that swept portions of America during the "roaring" 1920s and which Chester always felt coursing through black slums. "Practically every night during the holidays," Himes remembered, "I wound up with some black woman in the Majestic Hotel." The Majestic Hotel was down the street from the Elks Cabaret, and Chester believed that he had perhaps graduated from paying for sex to being able to initiate reciprocal sensual relationships. Light-skinned Chester was also "sweetmeat" for the domestics who had carefree moments on their days off.

When he returned to Columbus in January to begin the winter quarter, his academic standing was perilous. Freshmen who failed two-thirds of their academic load were placed on probation. Demonstrating his worldliness to his fellow pledges and their dates at a stiff, invitation-only dance, Chester led the group to the parlor of the brothel where he had kept his assignations with Rose. The man who operated the house told Chester that Rose was asleep. When the coeds began slow dancing, Rose awoke and stumbled upon a scene that included Chester in the arms of a proper, middle-class young woman. Possessive of Chester, Rose exploded, breaking phonograph records. The couples fled in fright and Rose glared at Chester with contempt. "I fixed your little red wagon, you snotty little motherfucker!" Then the proprietor of the house beat her for her tirade. Hapless, Chester slunk away. A few days later, he was summoned to the office of Dean Henderson, who had received a report from one of the young women. The dean allowed him to save face: on Valentine's Day 1927, Chester withdrew from school on account of "ill health and failing grades." Embarrassed about what had happened, he hung around Columbus for another six weeks until the examinations began, then returned to Cleveland. Still only seventeen, Chester had concluded his formal education.

Feckless, he appeased his family by playing up the elevator accident and keeping abed until the weather brightened. At the start of the summer he revived a bit and began seeing Maude, a woman he described as "one of those soft, pleasing, flat-featured mulatto women with big cushiony mouths, bedroom eyes and a thick caressing voice." She was an easygoing Georgia girl temporarily living with her married sister, who herself was sleeping with one of Chester's buddies on the side. Maude is the only woman whom he ever admitted to impregnating. Chester claimed that she presented him with the fact of his paternity at the end of the summer. On both sides of Chester's family, pregnancy and marriage went together, and, barely eighteen, Chester believed that the early marriage to an unaccomplished woman would forever ruin his relationship with his ambitious mother. He evaded Maude, who left Cleveland, he believed, to have the baby. His abandonment of her, and his difficulty distinguishing between romantic attachment and sexual pleasure, inclined Chester to attempt outwardly to harden his emotions. But he was arcing swiftly toward an emotional crisis. He tried to redeem himself from the episode thirty years later by concluding his novel *The Third Generation* with the protagonist, Charles Taylor, looking for the mother of his child. But this was not what he did in real life.

In a case of dubious charity, one of the busboys at Wade Park Manor took Chester to a sporting house on Cedar Avenue, on a respectable stretch of the road up by Ninety-Fifth Street. The gambling house was run by a man from Arkansas who knew what to do if a casual girlfriend got pregnant. His sporting name was "Bunch Boy," but Chester, who admired him, got to know him as Gus Smith, a "small, dried up looking, light-complexioned man with straight hair, strange washed-out blue eyes, and a cynical expression." Smith was in his early fifties, lived on an exclusive street near Rockefeller Park, and dressed the part of the hustler, togged in "silk shirts, English-tailored suits, and Stacy Adams shoes." Chester was enthralled by Bunch Boy's forbidden world. Smith called Chester "Little Katzi," from the popular Katzenjammer Kids comic strip. With his expensive Packard Coupe, Smith took on a paternal role for Chester. Chester's own father was pushing a broom at a joint called the Sixty Club from midnight to eight in the morning. The tragedy of the black college teacher whose son could not finish a quarter in good academic standing and was imitating local gangsters was complete.

At Bunch Boy's there were two regular games, craps and blackjack. Both of the games had professional dealers or referees, and Chester became intrigued by blackjack and befriended the gentlemanly operator of the game, Johnny Perry. Other than Perry, there were no guards, and the seductively quiet operation of the house did not advertise itself as breaking the law. Most of the patrons held steady jobs "in service," the euphemism for black domestic work, and Perry himself was "soft-spoken, handsome and married, a pleasant-appearing man with a soft voice and a superficial air of culture." From Smith, Perry, and the card-game lookout named Val, Chester began an education in the streets. In the novel *Lonely Crusade*, Himes described the emotional link between a character very much like himself as a young man and an older crook, "that peculiar, almost virgin love that the Negro hustler and criminal sometimes feels for the young, ambitious, educated Negro with sense enough to know the score—a sort of inverted hero worship that led them on to back these youths in what they did, as if it would make themselves bigger, more important men." Chester warmed to his fast-life tutors and the ambience of Negro decadence.

After a time he learned that the black men were not really in charge. In Cleveland the Sicilian Mafia, with ties to Al Capone in Chicago and the large families in New York, controlled liquor and gambling. The syndicate bosses were Italians and Jews, and the largest, "Big" Joe Lonardo and Joe Porello, operated a legitimate business as sugar wholesalers to the distillers who then stocked the speakeasies and private clientele with liquor. Operating around the Italian lower East Side neighborhood, the large crime families of Lonardo and Porello operated by supplying the distillers—bootleggers—with sugar and in turn assisting with the distribution of the prohibited alcohol products, colloquially known as "white lightning" and "white mule." The mobsters were generally known as the Mayfield Road Gang. The violence connected to these figures and the price of doing illegal business in liquor was changing the nature of crime in Cleveland. Gruesome killings in public of over one hundred bootleggers occurred in the city during the thirteen years of Prohibition. Crime boss Joe Lonardo was gunned down at a barbershop at the so-called Bloody Corner, E. 110th Street and Woodland Avenue, in October 1927. Twenty months later Angelo Lonardo killed his father's assassin, enabling Angelo to become the head of the Cleveland Mafia.

Using his workman's compensation income as his stake, Chester avidly played cards at Smith's, frequently opening the games. His initiation led to other things, and soon he was across the street, accompanied by his busboy friend, to shoot craps with a high rolling and violent crowd at Hot Stuff Johnson's. Craps was a large, standing dice game, where a dice thrower rolls to hit seven or eleven or to match the number he rolls the very first time. Chester was now in a place where an armed man kept the door and searched everyone who entered the premises, removing weapons of all kinds, including pistols. At the green baize table, a dog chain stretching over the center, Chester met the pillars of Cleveland's gambling set: gray-haired Abie the Jew, who bet the dice to win or lose, a pimp named Chink Charlie, and professional gamblers Dummy, Red Johnny, and Four-Four, whom he featured in his first detective fiction in 1957, *For Love of Imabelle*. The idiom that Chester accustomed himself to now would shape the rest of his writing life. In his first novel, in 1945, he would revisit the lingo that became a part of him: "'Unchain 'em in the big corral,' the boys used to say in Hot Stuff's crap game back in Cleveland."

The card club on Cedar became so successful that Smith opened a new location farther downtown on Central Avenue, in the true ghetto, with a rougher, more freely spending crowd and the new game that was thriving in Chicago, policy. Without the steadying influence of the chic underworld manager, Chester was influenced by less restrained men like Perry and Val, the card sharpie who tried to sexually exploit Chester to hard-edged madams who ran the brothels on Central Avenue. Their discussions were less about cards than the Italian mob in Cleveland, the numbers and policy syndicates, different Midwestern pawnshop and store owners who might expertly dispense stolen goods, and the prized getaways if anyone ever made a bonanza. To escape the scrutiny of his parents, he told his mother that he worked as a night waiter at the Gilsy Hotel and was saving money to return to college.

Between gambling and drinking with his demimonde pals, Chester met a professional thief named Benny Barnett, "a big-framed, light-brown-skinned, simpleminded boy," who befriended him and took him farther into the alleys off of Cleveland's slum streets. Twenty-one and on his own, Barnett introduced Chester to automobile theft and hard drugs. "But where he got his real kick," Chester wrote about a character like himself in an early short story, "his mind leaping afar, was out gambling or sitting around with a bunch of pretty molls 'sniffing' cocaine. Cocaine!" Thrilled by gambling, sex, and narcotics, Chester had fully forgotten Maude, college, and his parents.

He had a moment of sobriety in August when he accompanied Joe Jr. to Oberlin College. Years earlier Chester had lost whatever distinction he'd felt as the favorite within his own family. The Himeses had taken up residence in Cleveland on account of their middle son, who was now proving the value of his parents' trust, having graduated with the highest overall grade average in the history of East High, in spite of his disability, and been awarded a full academic scholarship to college. Joe's accomplishment gained notice in national newspapers and East High principal Daniel Lothman proclaimed Joe a "genius" to the press. With determined effort, Joseph embarked on a career where he attained academic distinction every semester. Within six months of starting at Oberlin, the school president, Ernest Wilkins, would write him "hearty congratulations on your excellent standing." Throughout the 1930s Joe's accomplishments would mount. Joe was the herald of the Himes family, and now the son for whom Estelle would make every sacrifice. Chester's mannish behavior helped intensify the arguments between his parents so much that by August his mother had moved into a spare bedroom.

Chester sought thrills in more dangerous paths. A few weeks after Joe left, he and Benny stole a car and drove to Columbus, returning to his old haunts for a weekend of partying. Arrogant and high, on September 26, 1927, Chester committed a series of bungling confidence scams and wound up in jail in Columbus, charged with fraud. He had stolen a university identification card that belonged to Phillip J. Dann Jr. and cashed a bogus thirty-five-dollar check drawn from the Cleveland Trust Company at one of the men's clothing stores near the university. At the beginning of the year he'd been a student at Ohio State; nine months later he was an inmate at the nearby Franklin County jail.

His parents were notified and the embarrassment of a jailed child of the middle class was the equivalent to their unusual step that fall, divorce. Chester's loss of moral compass had as its source the collapse of his immediate family. He witnessed his father's professional ruin coupled with the mounting and sticky paranoia of his mother, which all culminated in his parents' court battle during an era when divorce was infrequent. On November 16, 1927, Estelle pushed her brinksmanship to the edge, unexpectedly filing for alimony and "an absolute divorce from the Plaintiff" even while she and Joseph Sr. remained in the same house. She went to the courts to compel her husband to support her, claiming that he had "failed and willfully neglected to provide her with the common necessaries of life" and had on more than one occasion "desert[ed] and abandon[ed] her." Just three days later, on November 19 the couple had a violent fight, Estelle throwing whatever she could get her hands on and both of them cursing and impugning each other with candid vigor. Joseph Sr. temporarily left the Everton Avenue home, dismissing a reconciliation with Estelle on terms not to his liking. Not long after that, she moved permanently to another part of town.

The battlefield shifted to their joint property. In 1925 when they had bought the house, the Himeses had paid $3700 up front. Now Estelle claimed that she had contributed $2200 of that down payment; Joseph countered that he had paid every penny. Estelle pursued Joseph for increases in alimony while the divorce was in process, and she had Joseph in court on December 6, arguing that with his monthly income of eighty dollars and odd jobs as a carpenter and mechanic he could more than afford to pay her between five and ten dollars per week. She had the county sheriff summon Joseph to court multiple times in 1927 and 1928 for alimony relief. On December 20, 1927, they sold the Everton Avenue house to Marrilla and William Jackson. Chester would not live in a home with the Himes name on the deed for forty years.

The next month, on January 23, Joseph Himes Sr. came to Columbus for Chester's plea agreement before Judge Robert P. Duncan. Chester changed his plea to guilty in exchange for a suspended sentence and a supervised probation. Joseph Sr. took his

eighteen-year-old home with him to Cleveland. A boy who had now
spent several months in the Franklin County jail, Chester was officially an embarrassment to his mother and father, as well as to his
father's family. Angry, confused, and with his nuclear family now
torn apart, Chester faced life in a seedy rented room with his father
on the East Side, near a block of Cedar called "the Avenue," "a congested area of vice and destitution." Joseph Himes was as dispirited
as his son, and almost certainly the profit from the sale of the home
went to Chester's legal fees.

Hardened by the season in jail and wild and unsupervised after
the separation of his parents, Chester began working as a bellhop
at the Gilsy Hotel on E. Ninth Street near Euclid Avenue. A flea-
bag hotel with $1.50 rooms, the Gilsy exposed him to well-organized
prostitution, bootlegging, and racketeering. "Home" was little better.
Partly to escape the dank quarters with his father, Chester resumed
his friendships with Benny Barnett and Harry Plater, another young
petty criminal.

At a party at Benny's two-room basement flat on Cedar Avenue,
he was introduced to a provocative sixteen-year-old named Jean
Lucinda Johnson. Enjoying the all-night parties of booze and dope
with the young gamblers, Jean was breaking off from her poor family.
Good-looking, brown-skinned, and nearly as tall as Chester in her
bare feet, Jean turned heads with her grown-up body. She had not yet
finished high school when she took over one of the rooms in Barnett's
apartment and allowed Chester to live with her. Some nights they
ambled out together, getting drunk, and he left her alone to fend for
herself. However, Jean clung hard to Chester, the light-skinned ex-
college boy from a good family.

With a desirable girlfriend to defend, Chester started carrying a
pistol, an owl's head .32 revolver. Even Bunch, Chester's patron, hoped
to take Jean to Detroit and lure her into the sex trade. But shooting the moderate-caliber pistol made only a slight impression on the

neighborhood thugs, and Chester had to upgrade to a .44 caliber Colt. All of his running partners carried guns.

On June 18 Chester had an especially anguished moment: his father's attorney subpoenaed him to testify in the divorce case. Roddy Moon and Fannie Wiggins, among others, were also conscripted on Joseph Sr.'s behalf, but Chester did not wish to have to choose between parents, to go on record in a way that might forever wound his mother. Nor, as his own forays into the underworld expanded, had he any desire to participate in a courtroom proceeding. At a June 20 hearing, Estelle completed the divorce from Joseph Himes, winning $7 per week in alimony; $300 for the maintenance of her blind son, Joseph; $811.23, half of the proceeds from sale of the Everton Avenue house; and her attorney's costs. His family shattered and feeling as if he had to pick sides, Chester gave himself more fully to his girlfriend, Jean, and the more dangerous places to hang out on Cedar Avenue and then over to the sketchy part of Scovil Avenue, the "Bucket of Blood."

By the end of the summer he was out of control. Possibly Jean was pregnant or believed herself pregnant and asked him to marry her. If so, for the second time in twelve months, Chester was faced with what seemed a permanent tie to a woman and a child whom he would be obligated to support financially for the foreseeable future. He did not want to face the considerable, vigorous objection from his mother, and he could also picture a future of being unhappily married, like his father. It was too much. In his emotionally revealing novel *Yesterday Will Make You Cry* appears a scene that had its basis in truth:

> She told him she thought she was going to have a baby. . . .
> Then he said, "I know a swell guy in the pool room here who's just crazy about you, Joan. I'm going in and get him and send him out. Marry him, Joan. I'm sorry, but I can't."
>
> . . . .

He closed the door behind him and sent Eddie out to her.
She married Eddie.

That tiny, oblique narrative, buried in the first novel he wrote, is
important because it is all that sheds light on one of the cloudiest
moments in Chester's life. On September 12, 1928, Harry Plater married Chester's seventeen-year-old girlfriend Jean, who raised her age
on the certificate to nineteen.

Exactly two weeks later, Chester, Benny Barnett, and Cornalee
Thatch, an auto mechanic who captained the heist, robbed the Ohio
National Guard Armory on Cedar Avenue of a cache of .45 automatic
pistols. Next, the men kicked in the window of a furrier and drove
to Warren, Ohio, to sell all of the loot to steel mill hands. But the
amateurs botched the escapade: the police arrested them on October
9 and returned them to Cleveland.

When Chester had had his sentence suspended in Columbus in
January, the court believed that he was "not likely to engage in an
offensive course of conduct and that the public good does not demand
that he be immediately sentenced." His October arrest signaled otherwise. However, the weapons and fur coats were recovered, and Barnett and Thatch pleaded guilty. Thatch went to the Atlanta Federal
Penitentiary for eighteen months. A wise attorney provided by his
parents used Chester's youth to have his case heard before a sympathetic female judge at the municipal court, who listened attentively
to the Himes family saga and, undoubtedly impressed by the formidable public success of Joe Jr. and shy, boyish-acting Chester, who
wore knickers instead of long pants to the trial, paroled him "over the
vehement protests" of the prosecuting attorney. Neither contrite nor
steadied in the days that followed, Chester began minor assaults in
restaurants and swilled liquor in the Cedar Avenue dives. His sullen
distemper was evident to anyone who wanted to see it. One night at
Bunch's gambling club he heard a light-skinned chauffeur bragging

about the riches of his employer, and Chester, convinced now that he ought to escape Cleveland, decided upon an impulsive course.

On November 25, he stole a car and drove to the wealthy home of Mr. and Mrs. Samuel Miller in Cleveland's Fairmount Heights neighborhood, the one their chauffeur had described at Bunch Boy's. The maid, a suspicious black woman, refused to let him in and called the police. Chester hid from the patrolmen, then waited in the garage while trying steel his nerves to commit a major crime alone. The Millers returned to the house about 1:30 A.M. and went inside; then Mr. Miller returned to the garage, where Chester had secreted himself. This time, Chester emerged from the cars, produced a handgun, and demanded entry. Samuel Miller let him in and apparently tried to satisfy Chester with the contents of his wife's purse, but Chester directed them to the bedroom wall safe, hidden in a closet, alerting them to the fact that he had informed knowledge of their home. He had been led to believe that the couple had quantities of cash on hand; when the safe was opened, it held less than a few hundred dollars. Chester, knowing it was foolhardy, stole four rings worth about five thousand dollars and fled in a snowstorm in their Cadillac. The couple must have been amazed by the ferocity of the sensitive-faced boy with even white teeth and manicured hands, who hadn't yet put a razor to his face. Chester was telling himself that he would flee to Mexico.

Chester showed cunning and nervy execution when he hopped a passenger train early in the morning and hightailed it to Chicago to sell the jewels. But after one night as a criminal mastermind, the next day he was arrested in a pawnshop trying to sell the jewelry, taken to a nearby police precinct, and hung upside down and beaten on his testicles until he confessed.

A Cleveland detective named Gill Frabel escorted him back home and on November 27 a Cuyahoga County grand jury indicted him for the robbery. On December 4 he entered a plea of not guilty and had his bond fixed at $20,000. His distraught parents had no more resources to cope with this new bout of lawlessness. The state-appointed public defender encouraged him to plead guilty to lessen the severity of the sentence. Chester was told he could expect six months at the state reformatory. Two days later he appeared again before the court and entered his guilty plea. Chester said later that all he could recall of the December weeks in prison was a loud argument he had with a guard, and the combination of flared tempers and the shifting pleas for the very young man seemed to have made the court sympathetic. Initially it assigned his case to the probation department, requiring an examination by Dr. George H. Reeves, a state-appointed psychiatrist.

On December 19, 1928, after three weeks in the county jail, Chester was brought before the Common Pleas Judge Walter McMahon, a heavyset man in his fifties who looked not unlike Herbert Hoover. Stern and unforgiving, McMahon astonished the defendant by describing Chester's impulsive night out with a pistol as "one of the boldest and most cautiously plotted robberies in the history of Greater Cleveland." Nineteen-year-old Chester had thrown himself on the mercy of the court in hopes of leniency, but quite obviously now the state reformatory was out of the question. Instead, undoubtedly noting that Chester had already received probation for forgery and robbery, the judge drew down the hardest penalty levied against any person he saw that day. In a crushing blow, McMahon sentenced Chester to a minimum of twenty years in prison, with a maximum of twenty-five years. Chester would not be eligible for parole until 1948. It was his turn to whip Joe in the bout for local headlines: "Robber Gets 20 Years: Youth Sent in Pen for Holdup in Heights."

Chapter Four

GRAY CITY
OF EXILED MEN
1928–1936

After the heavy sentence fell in Cleveland, Chester clambered aboard a guarded train with other manacled convicts destined for the state penitentiary in Columbus. He entered the prison two days after Christmas, alongside white and colored men in their late twenties, men convicted of burglary and robbery, writing bad checks and swindling the unaware. None of the "fish"—prison slang for a newcomer—had drawn as severe a sentence as Chester. The number 59623 was stenciled to his underwear. He could count on not being released before he was thirty-nine years old. He was numbly devastated.

An imposing thirty-foot-high wall of brick and stone enclosed the nearly century-old penitentiary complex in downtown Columbus. The four-story administration building, prison cell blocks, chapel and honor dormitories made a large L that stretched for a block on Spring Street and a portion on West Street. Heading east, the prison's wall and intermittent guard towers stretched back toward the rail yards. Inside the walls, the main yard was dominated by a 100,000-gallon steel water tower and the two-story dining hall and kitchen. In the square between the moorings for the water tower, the Protestant chapel, and the interior entrance to the administration building were several plots of manicured grass with pruned trees and a fountain.

During Chester's first winter inside, the penitentiary was jammed with about forty-two hundred convicts, almost three times as many men as it had been designed to contain. The prisoners themselves worked steadily to build new dormitories to ease the overcrowding and that winter cell block L and the Honor Dormitory were under construction. The Annex Building in the southeast corner of the yard, a small one-story brick carriage house, was brand-new when Chester arrived. It housed the penitentiary's regularly used electric chair.

Prison life in the 1920s was designed to break the will of incorrigible men. The inmates were required to work hard, to submit to iron discipline, and to suffer nature's elements. They marched in crisp lines and the guards forbade speaking, or else they thwacked the inmates with clubs. Death or permanent injury was not uncommon for prisoners. The inmates were assigned to companies for their daylong work assignments at the coal mill, power plant, tin shop, machine shop, woolen mill, knitting mill, print shop, auto tag shop, or shirt shop, which in turn dictated the cell blocks that they lived in. The outdoor work of the coal company, which required the men to shovel coal from a pile into a nonstop flow of wheelbarrows marched to a crusher and then to the furnace, was thought the dirtiest and most physically demanding job. Any job inside working as a porter was understood as a reward, or light duty. Housing as many as eight hundred men apiece, the alphabetically arranged cell blocks had six tiers. Black men and white men, wearing identical gray pants, coats, and caps, and hickory-striped shirts and allowed to bathe once per week, crowded the cafeteria tables, two thousand at a time, for their meals.

Racial segregation was enforced in the penitentiary. Black prisoners received permanent labor assignments in the coal company and as janitors cleaning latrines and hallways. The black men stood at the end of lines for guest visits, the commissary, recreation, and medical treatment, although the mess hall did not require strict segregation. In the dormitories black prisoners predominated in so-called black bottom sections, and cells were typically occupied by men of the same race. As overcrowding increased, however, Ohio's penitentiary ended up less segregated than Ohio State University, particularly at dinner and chapel.

African Americans made up barely 5 percent of the Ohio population in the early 1930s, but constituted more than a quarter of the inmates at the state penitentiary. Among the black prisoners, most of the men, like Chester, had been born in the South, and many had come to Ohio in search of work. In all of Chester's prison writing, the black characters are set off by strong accents, which was probably true of men he knew like the forty-six-year-old Kentuckian Flo Wallace, whom he bunked beside, or another dormitory mate, sixty-eight-year-old Georgian Simon Stevens, who had been born in slavery. When he entered the prison, Chester was able to accept other black Americans who he felt were like himself—bright and talented, or worldly and attracted to the fast life. Judging by his earliest fiction, however, he felt contemptuously uneasy about being grouped with the African American peasantry. (When his father mailed him a sack of flour, he threw it away.) Jaunty and guileful, Chester was partly a city boy who understood uneducated African Americans with Southern accents as comic stereotypes, undeserving of compassion or serious consideration.

Chester's three teenage years scudding through the dice parlors, cabarets, speakeasies, and brothels had not earned him associates from Cleveland to help him adjust to penitentiary life. However, in the early weeks in prison he could certainly have been comforted by the simple fact that Cleveland's Cuyahoga County sent the lion's share of convicts to the state penitentiary. But beyond the fact of having a hometown in common with so many of the prisoners, Chester was unusual in nearly every dimension. There were 1645 new arrivals to the prison in 1929. Only about fifty of the other prisoners had ever set foot inside of a college classroom. Singling him out even more, only twenty of the newly admitted inmates were as young as he was; large numbers of men entered prison in their late twenties or early thirties, required to serve only a year or two. And of course the most obvious marker was time. Only twenty-five men were sentenced to twenty years or more. "He hadn't ever had a chance to live, not really live," remarked a character in an early short story, capturing Chester's exact doomed sentiments upon arrival.

During the first weeks of his incarceration, Chester found the cell block on the top tier so cold that he had to sleep fully clothed. After the induction, including IQ testing, he was sent to the large dormitory housing the two hundred members of the coal company. The first thing to be overcome was his initial fear. "Every one of them looked big and tough," his trepidation-filled character Jimmy Monroe reflects when he steps out into the dormitory. Crude cardboard signs regulating prisoners' behavior hung from the naked lightbulbs dotting the large dormitory in the main part of the cell block where he slept: Spitting on the floor and wall forbidden. No running water after dinner. No sleeping naked in summer. No sweaters in the winter. No tailoring of the prison uniform. Then the unvarying prison routine began: up at six, line up for breakfast at seven, work, dinner at eleven, back to the dormitory, supper at three, lights out by nine. The men tramped by company in a line, adorned in identical threadbare caps, jackets, and brogans.

Chester complained about the rough wintertime assignment. The guards punished him for speaking up at all by sending him to "the hole"—the darkened isolation chamber of the prison—but he was transferred and became a porter. Finally, and possibly after some letter writing and wrangling by his mother, on account of his physical infirmity he gained an assignment to the "cripple" company, a large dormitory for the physically disabled lodged on a cell-block ground floor. This designation was sought after because the men couldn't be forced to work; as for the convicts with disabilities themselves, Chester learned that they were a "treacherous" lot.

Chester's minor privileges may not have been extraordinary at all. Jacob Nesbitt, convicted of second-degree spousal murder, and a former fraternity brother of the son of Warden Preston E. Thomas, was reputed to have been "free to roam the city," eating in local restaurants and visiting the university campus, during his time in prison. After the initial adjustment to the routine of prison life, the reality that this terrible punishment would cost Chester his youth settled in painfully. Still dreaming that he was waiting for girls outside of the chemistry building at the university across town, he was learning to become a convict.

Attractive, slender, and with his face unmarked, Chester was vulnerable as a teenager and as a reflective person. The first episode that he recorded in both versions of his long prison works *Cast the First Stone* (1952) and *Yesterday Will Make You Cry* (first published posthumously, in 1998) began with an effeminate convict trying to seduce a twenty-year-old protagonist sentenced to twenty years for armed robbery. Initially, Chester greeted the predatorial sexuality in prison with disgust. Sodomy itself was regarded by prison officials, as well as by many of the men practicing it, as a descent into the realm of animal behavior, hence the classificatory term used by prison officials, "degeneracy." Men were in fact committed to the penitentiary for sodomy, like prison newspaper writer Joseph Kerwin, who was sentenced to a minimum of five years for that crime, two months before Chester arrived. Like most of heterosexual society, Chester believed homosexuals were perverted. Disoriented and big-eyed when he arrived, Chester was like Jimmy Monroe in *Cast the First Stone*, "half afraid that every big tough-looking convict might try to rape me." If he could avoid the strong-arm tactics of the wolves, he thought it would be a straightforward matter to also avoid homosexual contact.

The bleak prison monotony, the gray uniforms, the gray days, inside the gray barred walls of the gray city, gave over to electric moments of excitement and horror. Many of the convicts, and especially the men sentenced to life terms, were desperate and prepared to risk death for the possibility of even brief freedom. Opportunities to escape were regarded seriously. Pat McDermott, a murderer considered one of the most dangerous inmates, scaled the walls with two other murderers and two armed robbers. They were at large for several weeks during Chester's second month in prison. Later on, the guards in the yard shot and killed a black convict during a scuffle, and prisoners briefly overcame the guards in a recreation room and held them at gunpoint, until one fearless captain restored order, clubbing some men into submission and emptying a revolver into others. Then, on February 28, 1930, Dr. James Howard Snook, an Ohio State professor and gold medalist at the 1920 Olympics, was electrocuted for the murder of a coed. The men yelled obscenities at the professor as he passed on his way to "the cooker," as the convicts dubbed the electric chair. During the five full years that Chester stayed in the penitentiary in downtown Columbus, the death house and its "lightning ride" was the final destination for about forty-five men.

The guards attempted to enforce extensive rules—no whistling, no talking in line, no talking after lights out—to regulate behavior and demonstrate their control of the yard, but they were outnumbered by the often unruly men. All the myriad rules were negotiated and renegotiated. Prisoners feared deadly violence from one another more than from the guards. Typically each imprisoned man armed himself with a homemade knife called a "chiv," and other assorted blades and clubs. The convicts ridiculed the warden and his staff, the prison doctors, and the chaplain, sometimes appropriately so, as men unfit for life outside of the prison. The professionals were flawed and unable to operate in the legitimate corporate or government world; the guards were too inept to perform as policemen or soldiers. The authority of the guards—themselves only a step beyond poverty—and other employees of the prison lay as much in coercion as it did in willful submission and cooperation. They were known to use the extralegal tactics at their disposal: prevarication, theft, brutality, and murder. But they also urged on friendships and cultivated relationships with prisoners. All were given the honorific title "captain."

The warden of more than fifteen years, Preston Thomas, liked telling the men during the chapel services "in these hands I hold your destinies." He struck the bulk of the convicts as corrupt, a profiteer from narcotics trafficking who allowed men like Toledo gangster Thomas Licavoli to run the prison. Chester described the warden as an addling big man wearing on his ring finger a diamond as big as a robin's egg to make plain which side of the law he believed in. It would require the governor sending the National Guard to the prison to make Thomas finally resign in 1934.

Chester's attitude after his first year and a half was still one of furious adjustment and depression. When the 1930 census was taken, for example, he claimed ignorance of the state his father had been born in, and he told the census enumerator that his mother hailed from Missouri. He spoke his name so that it was written "Hines." He amused himself with the nonstop gambling games; the colored men's favorite was Georgia Skin. The game went on all day and night in the Black Bottom part of the dormitories. Good with cards, Chester saw himself as a distinctive, educated man among hoi polloi, who gave him his due. The men flattered him and he enjoyed receiving it. "I didn't get anything but what I had always wanted most in life, and that was adulation," remarked Jimmy Monroe, the main protagonist created from his prison experience.

However, having little in common with the foreshortened aspirations and poverty of so many of the men, Chester was lonely. In prison the saying went that after the lies swapped in the halls during the day, "the night's for crying." Being half afraid of his fellow inmates and terrified of showing any weakness didn't help. Chester took the point of view that it was nearly always safer to defy the guards than the convicts; men were killed in the dorms over petty arguments and minor discourtesies. A middleweight and not noted for his physical power, Chester walked the prison ranges and yard with a six-inch "deterrent" blade. After having been sent to the hole a number of times by a deputy, he back-talked to one of the range guards and was hit in the back of his head with a "loaded stick and the concrete range came up and touched my nose." Surviving imprisonment would require incredible poise and no small degree of luck.

Shortly after the evening meal on April 21, 1930, Himes and his comrades in the dormitory above the barbershop and bathhouse, a narrow, long brick building with a wooden roof north of the chapel, heard shouts of the men in the G and H cell-block tiers. When they looked outside, they saw smoke. A fire had broken out right beside the scaffolding being used to construct more new cell blocks. The vaulted ceiling of the upper ranges of that building, constructed in slate over top of wooden timbers, had ignited. The guards, not realizing the urgency of the moment, only released prisoners haphazardly; some guards, believing that it was hazardous to release any prisoners, resisted efforts to open the cells. When the correctional officers finally understood the dangerous extent of the fire, they began unlocking the cell blocks of the bottom ranges first. By the time turnkeys had reached the third and fourth tiers, the heat and smoke were unbearable, except to a few intrepid convicts, who had begun wetting blankets and racing along the ranges with hammers to smash the locks so as to free the men. Doomed, screaming men rammed their heads into the toilets in a futile attempt to escape asphyxiation and death by fire. But the upper-range rescue efforts were not even piecemeal; the fifth and sixth tiers of the G and H cell blocks were completely incinerated. Adding to the overall sense that the prisoners were willfully sacrificed, Warden Thomas patrolled the locked gates outside of the prison with a shotgun, preparing to fire on the first convict daring to climb over the walls.

After the city fire department used high-pressure hoses to extinguish the blaze, the entire roof structure and top tier of the G and H cell blocks collapsed into a pile of charred rafters, joists, and heat-twisted metal bars. In the two-hour span before the fire was extinguished, 322 convicts perished. By nightfall, stiffened black-faced corpses with twelve inches of green vomit stretching from their teeth to their chests littered the prison yard. The Ohio Penitentiary prison fire would rank among the greatest incidents of death by fire in U.S. history. With seven of every fifty prisoners dying in the conflagration, the clerk made up a special stamp for the prison ledger. He used it to fill in the column "When and How Discharged": "DIED in FIRE APRIL 21, 1930."

Radio networks set up stations outside of the yard and gave prisoners a chance to tell their stories, like prisoner 46812, who produced such a vivid account he received a check of $500 from the head of CBS. That night and the next, prison discipline did not exist inside the walls. High on diluted ether purloined from the penitentiary hospital, the men refused to be locked in their cells. They had sex, shot dice, and played Cab Calloway on the organ in the chapel. On the fifth tier of cell block C a convict named Broadway Rose staged lewd shows and set up a red-curtained bordello.

The day after the fire khaki-clad troopers from the 166th Regiment of the Ohio National Guard began to arrive outside the prison, relieving the hastily called in and weary police. But after the phantasmagoric night of "bitchery and abomination" and leveling the power of the guards, the men declined to return to their work companies. More than a thousand convicts elected a "Forty for Facts" Committee and initiated a "passive resistance" campaign to enact an agenda of prison reform, including the removal of Warden Thomas. Cries of "down with the pig" percolated throughout the yard. On April

28, Warden Thomas brought into the main yard hundreds of heavily armed riot squads with ring-handle .45s and machine guns to quell the protesting men. One thousand men continued their calls for the removal of the warden in the white painted cells of the A, B, C, and D blocks, a section known as "White City." The prisoners, termed "belligerent" by the warden, sabotaged the lights and fought guards for thirty-six hours; some of the men took the opportunity to begin seriously digging to try to escape.

On May 1, the National Guard took over the prison, routing the belligerent prisoners from the hovels of White City and herding them into the yard. The renegades were searched and stockaded in tents on the ball field, enclosed by a hastily assembled chain-link fence topped by barbed wire. A week later, on May 7, the stockaded men burned the tents; Warden Thomas declined to use any firefighting equipment, and punished 150 of those determined responsible with lockdown in White City and bread and water rations. The rest of the men remaining in the stockade slept on the ground. Around 6 A.M. the next morning, a guardsman accidentally squeezed the trigger of a Browning water-cooled heavy machine gun, releasing several 30.06 rounds into the heads of two convicts, one a Cleveland black named Albert Freeman who was working in a dormitory on the other side of the prison yard. The commandant of the 166th gave only the slightest notice to the killings. The gruesome deaths touched a deep nerve in Chester, pensive and maddened after surviving the apocalyptic fire, only to be confronted anew with random, purposeless death once more. Guard units manned machine-gun posts in squares around the stockade until May 27.

Perceiving himself the scapegoat for the public relations nightmare of state malfeasance, corruption, and overcrowding, Warden Thomas turned his attention to the "small rebellious army" of prisoners and began a plan of reclassifications, transfers, and sending the leaders of the resistance to the hole. By the middle of May the prisoners were reassigned and soon twenty-five hundred men were lined up in the yard, rolling gravel all day. A year later two prisoners would receive life sentences after pleading guilty to second-degree murder, confessing that they had rigged the roof fire in an attempt at escape. Ultimately, they committed suicide.

The bustle of construction, new concrete ceilings for the cell blocks, and state-sponsored reform commissions occupied much of the Ohio inmates' interest for the duration of 1930. Shortly after the fire detritus had been cleaned up, in June executions began again, ending the lives of seventeen-year-old Lee Akers and of George Williams, both black and from Cleveland, each convicted of killing a police officer. Surrounded by death and ruin, Chester yet had no idea if it was possible to wager on the future.

The Negro inmates were the recognized heroes of the calamity, and individual blacks were credited with saving dozens of inmates from the flames. But in 1930 Chester did not draw from his racial background as a source of unique strength, pride, or identity. For him, the baffling terror of the deadly night magnified his loneliness and childlike vulnerability. Hardly imperturbable, he used two words over and over again to describe his new feeling: "queer" and "hysteric."

Chester's writing career seems to have its impetus in the fire and his attempt to cope with the trauma he had witnessed and his internal feelings of horrifying shame. The 1934 short story "To What Red Hell" and the two novels drawn from the same manuscript—*Cast the First Stone* and *Yesterday Will Make You Cry*—position a main character, a surrogate for Chester named Jimmy Monroe, in the laundry-and-barbershop dormitory, a two-story brick building separated by the chapel from the main cell blocks that were on fire. In these tales the protagonist wanders the yard, observing the spectacle of the dead and dying, the heroic and the indifferent. Chester's character Jimmy, a young, attractive boy serving a twenty-year sentence for armed robbery, has a stark awakening while witnessing the men dying in the fire and gaining the brief freedom available during the chaos. He tells of being unable to bring himself to rescue anyone, and he sees himself as morally feeble and emotionally distressed, unable to contain a desire he considered perverse, thrust into a world of "grotesque fantasy." But if the inferno of horrifying death was imminent and likely, what value should he attach to noble behavior and restraint?

In *Cast the First Stone*, Jimmy Monroe insists that a dormitory mate accept a passionate kiss and then tells him, "I want you for my woman." If Chester, like Jimmy, had once thought "I haven't got to the place where I can do that yet," after a year and a half of prison and a devastating fire, he could have Jimmy say that homosexual acts did not "even shock me anymore." The deadly prison fire loosed a homoerotic impulse in Chester that marked the middle period of his prison experience, and in his later detective fiction he would frequently remark upon the conjunction between eroticism and death. When writing his memoirs he allowed that "no one tried to rape me," but what shifted in him internally following the fire was far different than relief at escaping attacks from predatorial convicts. The fiery explosion and his deep need for emotional contact certainly corresponded to Joe Jr.'s blinding and the loss of his brother and ultimately his mother as confidants. But clearly Chester no longer found the homosexual practices objectionable on principle. Instead he considered uncoerced situational homosexuality in prison a compensatory and human reflex to the despair of life behind bars. But this acceptance was difficult to handle.

Writing was one activity that helped him overcome lonely isolation and puzzle through the welter of emotions after the fire. Chester started putting pencil to paper on the ground floor of the E and H cell block in the crippled company. His efforts to deal with the personal tragedy of incarceration, loneliness, physical vulnerability, the conflict of homosexual desire, and the gruesome slush of human entrails in the yard during the long night of April 21 launched his writing career. The prison fire itself served as the imaginative ground for the best of his

earliest successes, "To What Red Hell," which in turn served as the
bedrock for his first full manuscript, *Black Sheep*. He must have begun
drafting the short story soon after the fire to preserve the sharp details
of the event, but considering it was apprentice work, it is also polished
and sophisticated. As Estelle the sonneteer's precocious son, Chester
had experimented with composition before, but even the trauma he
had known—the trampled young girl in Alcorn, his brother's blinding, the multiple arrests, the pregnant girlfriends he had abandoned,
even the prisoners he had seen gunned down by guards—did not
inspire him in the manner of listening to the shrieks of the dying,
stumbling through the gore of two cell block tiers' worth of burned
alive men, and living in its aftermath. He had the seed of a searing
emotional experience to drive his ambition.

Twelve months after the fire, Chester found another reason to
ready himself for a life beyond bars. In April 1931, the Ohio legislature
passed three laws expediting parole by reducing sentences for good
behavior and applying the relief retroactively, thus addressing prison
overcrowding. "Under the provisions of the parole law every inmate of
a state penal or reformatory institution automatically becomes eligible
for a hearing before the Board of Parole at a specified time, determined by the statute under which he was convicted and his prison
record, except, of course, those convicted of treason or murder in the
first degree," read the warden's annual report to the governor, reflecting the new legislation. All of a sudden, Chester's twenty-year minimum had dropped to six years and five months. The night the word of
the law's change was announced, the prisoners' ebullient cries could
be heard all over downtown. By the middle of September, the penitentiary newspaper counseled the overanxious, bellyaching inmates to
"take it easy," predicting that the newly enlarged parole board would
start meeting in a week and begin paroling men.

Chester celebrated too early. On September 17, 1931, he was taken
before a prison court and punished by having fifteen days added to his

original sentence. Although Chester was silent about this infraction, technically men could have their sentence extended for infractions as simple as talking out loud, although most were simply punished on the spot, demoted from a work assignment, or sent to the hole. Still, he had no cause to lose optimism at the end of that summer. Surviving the fire, and then having the sentence shortened by two-thirds, revived his pursuit of distinction. Upon hearing that his sentence has been dramatically reduced, Chester's character Jimmy Monroe thinks, "having stared so long into the gray opaqueness of those solid twenty years, it seemed as if I could look right through them and see the end; see freedom in all its glory, standing there." Now Chester would discipline himself for a new life.

His initial determination to begin ordering his life through writing also had support from his family, some of it inadvertent. His back seized up on him, and the remedy was a partial body cast, an impossible solution in a prison with dilapidated mattresses and irregular convalescent care. Finding a rusty nail discarded on the hospital ward floor, Chester hacked off the plaster cast, infuriating the ward doctor. Fearful of reprisals, he begged Estelle to return to Ohio from a furlough in South Carolina to look after him, which she did. His workman's compensation money allowed him to help his parents as the Depression worsened. Joseph Himes, looking thin and gray, paid a lone visit and moaned plaintively "if I just had my life to live over." In fact, he would do just that. In May 1932, Chester's father remarried, to a woman almost half his age, an entertainer from Baltimore named Agnes Rowe. The thirty-one-year-old singer of the Harmonique Five, who made her living in the clubs Chester had patronized in his street odyssey, had been divorced for only nine months. Rowe was glitzy enough to have the *Chicago Defender* carry news of the nuptials. Chester forked over four hundred dollars of his savings to his father.

Chester's brother Joe was eclipsing him. Despite his loss of vision, he graduated Phi Beta Kappa from Oberlin, draped in national medals, and had been asked to work toward a master's degree in the fall. His successes were admired all over the nation. In 1932 Joe left Ohio altogether, to begin his career teaching modern languages at Shorter Junior College in Arkansas. The next year he went to Austin, Texas, to Samuel Houston College. He was fulfilling his parents' dream of a responsible teaching career. Estelle accompanied Joseph Jr. proudly, prepared to keep house and carry on surrogate reading and typing duties. Chester would remain in the penitentiary and have to rely exclusively on his own resources.

The Ohio Penitentiary had groomed a few writers, notably the embezzler turned master of the short story William Sydney Porter—O. Henry—whom it was impossible not to hear about, and whose stories Chester devoured while in prison. Writing was held in no little esteem by numbers of the incarcerated men. The weekly prison paper, distributed Saturday afternoon and mainly staffed by men serving long sentences, contained considerable literary banter during Chester's confinement. The *Penitentiary News* battled against the loudmouths who shouted from the tiers during all hours and ruined the concentration of the more cerebral prisoners. The paper trumpeted the writers' creed, quoting Jack London: "There is one rule that I rigidly observe. Nothing must interfere. I write fifteen hundred words a day. I may do more, but never less. When I say 'a day' I mean every day, seven days per week, 365 days per year." There were enough men around for Chester to think of writing, fiction in particular, as serious work, meriting his strongest effort. In *Cast the First Stone*, Chester wrote that the prison newspaper editor approached Jimmy about contributing, to which he responded, wise-guy style, "'I asked him was there anything in it for me.'" But the novel Chester wrote was from the point of view of a white protagonist, and it is not at all clear that a black writer at any level of talent would have been able to participate on the *Penitentiary News*.

Inward-looking and aloof, Chester began cobbling together his own short stories. In his autobiography, he described the disregard with which his fellow convicts greeted his work. But he admitted to having met one "black murderer of great intelligence," a jeweler. In *Cast the First Stone*, it is this convict, called Metz in the novel, who sits on his bunk with a "textbook on short-story writing," and persuades Jimmy to study the craft with him: 'I'm going to take you up on that writing course,' I said. 'I'd like to know something about writing.'"

With gambling winnings and his steady income, Chester secured a typewriter. Remington portables and Underwoods were sold among the convicts for sums between fifteen and forty dollars. The clerklike function of typing and the example of solitary intellectual activity made the guards look favorably upon writing, since it eased the inevitable tension of holding so many able-bodied men in prison. Chester's relationship with the prison officials changed; he now counted several among them as friends. At twenty-two, the age his brother had finished college, Chester devoted himself to acquiring a refined skill.

A torrent of short stories poured out of him in different styles. Perusing magazines like *Collier's*, *Black Mask* (where he read a serialized version of *The Maltese Falcon*), *Liberty*, *Cosmopolitan*, *Redbook*, and the *Saturday Evening Post*, Chester began writing romances and crime thrillers for the black press, including the *Atlanta Daily World* and *Abbott's Monthly*, where his first short story "His Last Day" was published in November 1932. That story featured a condemned black convict awaiting his trip to the electric chair, a theme Chester continued in another story, 1936's "The Night's for Crying." Significantly his formal writing career began by creating men modeled physically on his uncle Wade Wiggins and spiritually on the toughs of Scovil and Cedar Avenues. Chester evolved these early portraits into one of his finest characters, Luther McGregor of *Lonely Crusade*, his most important novel. His early concern had an obvious origin: Chester wrote about the intimidators within prison, men who held the yardstick to his own manhood. "Most of the black convicts in the Ohio State Penitentiary were dull-witted, stupid, uneducated, practically illiterate, slightly above animals," he recalled surly in his autobiography *The Quality of Hurt*. But he had to give them respect. He had to orchestrate carefully his actions to share the cell block with such men and retain his own pride; it makes sense that his earliest work reflects his attempts to understand black murderers from the street-corner bar.

Condemned for killing a policeman, Spats Wilson of "His Last Day," a "dark brown skin" man with a "large, powerful body" and "jungle strength and animal cunning," wants to appear carefree and fearless on his way to the electric chair. "I'll be smiling when the juice is turned on," he yells after the reporters, "I'm a man." While the clumsier elements of the stereotype seem to stand in the way of the full development of a character named for his attire, Chester wanted the reader to grapple with the emotional complexity of a violent black convict who struts across the yard to the death house, while "in his eyes there was the subtle hint of utter fear." Similarly, in "The Night's for Crying," the hero, Black Boy, crimps the edges of a stereotype by "crying softly" in his prison cell after his girlfriend has visited. With early characters like Spats and Big Blue from "A Cup of Tea," Chester exposed the softer side of statuesque black men, and worked to render their voices in the argot of the black street.

Of course he drew the stories of condemned men from the more than 1400 African American prisoners at the Ohio Penitentiary, 263 of them serving life sentences by 1935. Chester was inspired to write "His Last Day" in the wake of the execution of two brothers, Walter and Blanton Ralls, put to death in 1931 for the murder of the Crawford County sheriff. Six months later, four men, three of them black, who were members of a gang, were executed within a few days of one another. Walker Brown, one of the gang, was twenty-four, about Chester's age. In March 1933 Athay Brown was electrocuted for murdering a woman in Cleveland. Five months later, brothers James and Joseph Murphy were both executed, on August 14, and prior to their meeting with the electric chair, they delivered rehearsed public testimonials protesting the barbarism of the death penalty. Another black man, Merrill Chandler, died in the electric chair that November, for killing a guard.

Throughout 1933, Chester sent the lion's share of his work, about half a dozen short stories, to *Abbott's Monthly*, the entertaining brainchild of *Chicago Defender* founder Robert Sengstacke Abbott. In the first part of that year, Chester's work was published in every single issue. A magazine of about one hundred illustrated pages that cost a quarter and featured a close-up drawing of a bobbed sepia beauty, *Abbott's Monthly* specialized in "true confession" fiction, and reached a circulation of around 100,000 before it closed at the end of that year. Two other young African American Midwestern writers published in *Abbott's Monthly* as well. The first African American to make his living exclusively from writing, Langston Hughes, best known by then for his collections of Jazz Age, racial uplift poetry and the novel *Not Without Laughter*, published in the magazine between 1932 and 1933 and was from Cleveland. Chester's first cousin Henry Lee Moon was a buddy of Hughes. Chester, who might have heard specific details about Hughes's career from his cousin, imitated several of Hughes's publishing moves in the 1930s. The other *Abbott's Monthly* writer was a Chicago man breaking into print for the first time who was almost Chester's exact age: Richard Nathaniel Wright. Although later other magazines would claim to have nurtured his talent, Chester was a direct product of the literary black press of Chicago.

Chester mailed his stories to Abbott in bundles. They were accepted and published as the editor saw fit and had space. Chester, missing girlfriends and parties, and wondering about the kind of life that awaited him after he left prison, also scribbled glitzy tales like "Her Whole Existence" and "A Modern Marriage" about gangsters and molls, flirtatious chippies, and independent sexually curious young women who might romantically commit themselves to men of the criminal class.

After perhaps eighteen months, Chester outgrew the genre sto-ries. Around the end of 1932 or beginning of 1933, he had crafted a formidable short story, the twenty-thousand-word "Prison Mass," which appeared in *Abbott's Monthly* in three successive issues, March through May 1933. Mature and deep, the story drew its characters from his own life. This important and slightly autobiographical long story served as the proving ground for the manuscript that became the 1952 novel *Cast the First Stone*. "Prison Mass" offers three black convicts, named Kid, Brightlights, and Signifier, attending Catholic mass as a commentary on the dilemma of prison life, the propensity toward evil, and the foundation of hopeful transformation. Signifier is a career criminal in middle age who is cynical, suspicious, and super-ficial. The Kid is an idealist, who unwittingly accepts a life sentence for a murder that he didn't commit. His purity makes him capable of strong emotional responses, from the sentimental to the violent. And in a move that made him personally vulnerable, Himes wrote from autobiographical experience when he created the twenty-five-year-old man serving a twenty-year sentence for armed robbery named Bright-lights, "put in the 'cripple' company because he had a fractured verte-bra and wore a steel back support." Of course, all of the men shared portions of Chester's experience. Signifier, a professional thief, recalls a woman named Jean who was "simply nuts about him."

"Prison Mass" shows Chester leaping ahead with confidence and agility as a storyteller. He shifted the point of view from character to character without any transition, collapsing the distance in conscious-ness, so that, in the course of the religious service, the three troubled men reach a kind of joint revelation. The key epiphanic moment is held by Kid, an Achilles-like sacrificial man whose mother is dying and who will never gain release from prison. Chester was showing the capacity to encounter subjects of personal disinterest without denying their importance. "I might not have believed in all of that tommy-rot that the ministers were trying to cram down my throat," thinks the character Brightlights, "but I respected their belief and their honest endeavors to teach others to believe, and I sure as hell didn't mock it."

While the men sit in a row in three shades of blackness from dark to "the whiteness of Swiss cheese," little racial prejudice intrudes on the story. Nonetheless, Brightlights muses that "people were more religiously inclined when they were ignorant and afraid than when they were intelligent and courageous. That was true among his people especially, or at least that was the impression he had received." Chester was not the race militant he would become; he was still picking through what he had learned around the dinner table at home, the homily of Booker T. Washington.

If Chester connected easily and naturally to a black audience, he also chafed in a basic and fundamental way against the Jim Crow society, an acrimony that never required an ideology to shore up. Whatever histrionics were connected to Estelle's rendering of their complex racial origins, she had instilled in Chester and Joseph Jr. a sense of fierce competitiveness and an expansive horizon of possibility. "He wanted to do something worthwhile, but it had to be something that would bring fame. That was the secret reason he had taken up writing, he admitted to himself. He had wanted the renown more than the money; wanted to see his name." In 1932 with some effort, but not perhaps as much effort as it would have taken for him to complete college, he found success, his name on the byline in a newspaper. It was an experience that he would have, as a young man behind bars, over and over again in 1933 and 1934. Not even midway through 1933, Chester's gambler's instincts told him that he might reach a large audience who wished to read what he had to say.

While he showed signs early on of wanting to explore a complex, artistically provocative style, Chester wrote energetically for a commercial audience. He pursued dozens of publications, winning acceptance in several, from Chicago, Atlanta, and New York. In 1933 and 1934 he had had accepted the short stories "A Cup of Tea" by the *Atlanta Daily World* and "The Black Man Has Red Blood" by the *Chicago Defender.* "A Cup of Tea" featured Big Blue, who starts punching furiously when he is served tea. The resulting fights lead to a riot in which guards machine-gun prisoners, making it gallows entertainment for the *Atlanta Daily World* readers. In the more explicitly race-conscious *Chicago Defender,* he wrote of a black butler charged with rape and murder who, in spite of his imminent lynching, preserves the innocence of his young white charge. The short story asked a painfully brilliant rhetorical question, one that posed a question that was uniquely Chester's: "What right had a 'nigger' to a white man's nobility?"

In the middle of the Depression, Chester had an edge over some of his competitors: a roof overhead, three daily meals, and plenty of time. The prison conditions were the opposite of ideal, to be sure, but the advantages couldn't be denied, an ironic condition captured in this Black Bottom ditty of dormitory life: "we ate our good-doin' bread and called it punk, slept on our good-doin' bed and called it bunk."

Chester became friends in 1933 with a man who encouraged his talent, a twenty-four-year-old convict named Prince Rico, who sometimes fancied himself with the nom de plume of Auber LaCarlton Williams. Sentenced to ten years for a robbery in Columbus, Rico entered the penitentiary on June 27, 1933, and was assigned to the cripple company on account of damaged knees. Theatrical, flamboyant, and tough, Rico had been born in Georgia and grown up in California. He had spent a nomadic youth wandering the country, working in circuses, and learning the musician's trade and gaining a professional interest in black folklore and lyrics. He tramped around the dormitory with a ukulele attached by shoestrings to his neck.

There were dramatic differences in background between the two men and, having heard of Chester's success in the literary world, Rico openly admired him. He was also sexually attracted to Chester, who reciprocated his feelings, while, apparently, still struggling with a desire that he understood as degenerate and which, if discovered by prison authorities, could lengthen his sentence. In a 1952 letter to Carl Van Vechten, the photographer and booster of black art, Chester admitted that Rico "was the boy in the story [*Cast the First Stone*], entire and absolute, and I was in love with him more, perhaps, than I have ever been in love with anyone before or since." Fifteen years after prison Himes could cautiously admit some details about the relationship to a man like Van Vechten, a dear friend who was known to have homosexual affairs.

At the end of the spring 1934 academic term, Joseph Jr. and Estelle Himes returned from Texas to Columbus, to 49 E. Eleventh Street, and Joseph began the course work toward a doctorate in sociology. His acceptance in the graduate program again won newspaper acclaim. Joseph was the darling of his class, the student who had already mastered the theoretical positions that his peers were scurrying to adopt. Even though the brothers would never resume the intimacy of their youth in Mississippi and Arkansas, their successes weighed on each other. Chester's budding victories in 1932 had turned into bona fide professional success by late 1934. Joseph countered by researching and writing an eighty-four page dissertation entitled "The Negro Delinquent in Columbus, 1935." Estelle's regular visits to Chester resumed and, in Joseph's mildly begrudging view, it was her influence that single-handedly enabled Chester to launch a writing career. "I think Mother talked with the prison Administrator and persuaded him that because of his injuries, Chester could not work in the shops," Joseph Jr. recalled years later. But Joe, who neither wrote to nor visited Chester in prison, made an unreliable claim; in 1932 and 1933 Estelle had lived with Joe so that he could begin his career. Chester's earliest push was internal and had come earlier.

It is within the context of his friendship with Prince Rico that Chester's ambition grew, almost as if an intensifier had been added to his literary skill. Chester pursued the next step as a writer in two directions, perhaps equally obvious. First, he wanted to get beyond the short story and require more of himself than being a sepia O. Henry. There was, however, an element of O. Henry's success that Chester did want. Apparently the labile nature of race relations in northern and middle Ohio, as well as the absence of absolute segregation in high school, college, and prison, encouraged him to think squarely of success on the grandest—and most commercial—terms. Since he accepted black Americans as a minor ethnic group sullied by slavery, it made perfect sense to Chester to begin writing stories headed by white characters. As a man who was, on account of his prison term, completely déclassé himself, Chester did not consider first what the black bourgeoisie into which he had been born thought of him. He knew that American whites wished to read about themselves as forceful decision makers and that they understood black Americans as passive subordinates, distinctly lesser beings. If he was at all unsure on his course of action, he had only to look at the success of Ernest Hemingway, a Michigan-reared man who had lived abroad and whose early work—like *The Sun Also Rises,* "The Killers," and "Fifty Grand"—deliberately attempted to project churlish and belittling racial attitudes. Captivated by Hemingway's success and mystique, Chester would write stories of white life.

If "Prison Mass" was his breakthrough in theme and symbolism, the shift to white characters enabled him to land before a larger audience. In 1934, Chester wrote and published his best stories about prison life, featuring white protagonists, in a brand-new magazine shifting the terms of American masculinity, *Esquire.* Founded in October 1933 by Arnold Gingrich, a smart young graduate from the University of Michigan, *Esquire* was a men's magazine first appearing at nearly the precise moment of the repeal of Prohibition.

Promoting sport, commercialism, and sex, *Esquire* was also very nearly a magazine crafted around Ernest Hemingway, who appeared in the inaugural issue with John Dos Passos, Erskine Caldwell, and

Dashiell Hammett. Hemingway wrote for the magazine every other month in its first couple of years and always received top billing when he did. Promised a mere $250 per short story, Hemingway started out sending sporting letters from Bimini and Cuba; then, in August 1936 he published one of his finest short works there, "The Snows of Kilimanjaro." In its early years *Esquire* also published F. Scott Fitzgerald, Maksim Gorky, Thomas Wolfe, Ring Lardner, and Langston Hughes. In September 1934, *Esquire* had a newsstand circulation of 121,812; in two years circulation was seven times that figure. The magazine quickly became a bellwether for American literary taste.

Gingrich had bragged to Hemingway that the new rag would have "ample hair on its chest, to say nothing of cojones," and he incorporated another modern version of America in it as well. A bargain hunter for talent, he didn't draw the color line, as long as the material didn't reveal "any trace of any kind of accent" or ethnic badge. For practical commercial reasons Gingrich was initially reluctant to address American racial relations. Thus, the first issue, of 124 pages, contained 27 pages of drawings from a "fantastically talented colored kid" named E. Simms Campbell, who also designed the *Esquire* logo. Campbell's drawings never revealed his African American ancestry.

By January 1934 Gingrich changed his mind, realizing that controversy was superb advertising. On his editorial page he announced to his readers his intention to publish a Langston Hughes short story about a wealthy New Yorker with a fetish for black chorus girls. In the next month, he printed all of the replies, and he joked that the commentaries indicated either "compulsory and universal miscegenation" or the "resumption of the Civil War." Gingrich learned that the animus was genuine. One reader said, "If you print the story by the negro author, Langston Hughes, I shall not only cancel my subscription to your magazine, but shall discontinue any further business with Jacob Reed's Sons, due to the fact that they recommend your magazine." Another subscriber from Tulsa, a bigot who was still dismayed by the numbers of blacks "it took the city incinerator days to burn" after the infamous 1921 massacre, wrote, "Don't you think having the only nigger in Congress is enough of an embarrassment to the administration without Chicago starting something that it may cost men and millions to stop?"

The clashing energy and affirming voices—"By all means shoot through the 'high yaller' story," and "your readers would appreciate a little dash of spice"—were precisely the sort of titillated yelp that Gingrich needed for the young magazine. In April Hughes had his *Esquire* launch with "A Good Job Gone," a tale of a wealthy banker, college-educated black butler, and oversexed chippie, "one of these golden brown's, like an Alabama moon," who emitted a "nigger laugh—one of ours. So deep and pretty." A month later *Esquire* published Hughes's "The Folks at Home," a conventional racial-uplift story about the lynching of a black man whose elegant taste has taken him far away from his rural Southern roots.

Chester charmed his way into the magazine and "through correspondence, I came to know Arnold Gingrich well." For his submissions to *Esquire,* Chester adhered to Gingrich's initial wariness toward the ethnic trace and abandoned black protagonists and narrators and themes of racial uplift. At the same time he would send the magazine some of its coarsest material, sharply contesting Victorian mores that stressed restraint, moral uprightness and courage. Instead, Chester showed violent, cynical, emotionally overwrought men about to dissolve.

He was paid seventy-five dollars for his initial short story, and Gingrich bought two at once, "Crazy in Stir" and "To What Red Hell." Chester debuted in the August issue, which included lead articles by Hemingway and Leon Trotsky and poetry by Ezra Pound. *Esquire* introduced Chester as "a long-term prisoner in a state penitentiary." "Crazy in Stir"—"the first convict writing to appear in our pages," *Esquire* boasted—tried to take the reader inside of the madness of a hard-boiled convict named Red whose confinement leads him to the brink of psychosis. Chester's truculent inmate reflected the burgeoning classificatory system of the prison, which adjudged from a sample of 862 men 347 as "psychopathic" and 157 "psychotic."

While Red was a popular name, one used among African Americans to note anyone light enough in color that he could be seen to blush, a convict named John "Red" Downing, electrocuted on March 10, 1933, had achieved a notoriety at the Ohio Penitentiary. He had killed the wife of Danile Bonzo, the chief record clerk. Chester's character patrols the aisles of a bunk-filled dormitory, similar to Chester's, raging at the cage he inhabits and the denizens of its corridors, from the tedious cretin trying to barter oranges for nickels to the Negro inmates singing and dancing near the latrine at the Black Bottom. Like a Hemingway hero, Red sharply disparages black Americans. "He would see what the hell they were doing, the black, stolid animals. . . . The days passed and they didn't know it. Time meant nothing to them."

When Red sees two colored men on a bunk praying, he thinks "singing to a white man's idea of God." Here Chester's hard-bitten white protagonist cynically canceled out the agnostic religious position of "Prison Mass." While Red shares common prejudices about black people—theirs is a life limited to sensation and corporality—in his tense parade through the barracks, he finds himself reluctantly drawn again and again to the Black Bottom, to its music and song, to "the anguish of a race that has learned to suffer." Chester was penetrating the interior of a hurt man, by using description and dialogue, and he was pulling back from the heavy-handed narration that had limited some of his earlier works. He was also deftly alluding to complex racial dynamics in American life.

Publishing "Crazy in Stir" in a trendsetting magazine landed Chester on the front page of the Columbus newspaper. In a short time he was lauded for his powerful short story in the New York newspaper the *Amsterdam News*, where his cousin Henry had taken a position.

The *Amsterdam News* even included him as a geographically distant member of the Negro Writers Guild and the Harlem Renaissance. "A 'new O. Henry' in the person of inmate Chester Himes (colored), is in the budding," informed the paper.

Despite being incarcerated, from the reality of a cement-floor cell block and an open latrine, his prospects, in fact, looked amazing. With his second short story in *Esquire*, Chester actually began to make the difficult transition to novel writing, and he was putting together a longer work that rang out with fully convincing tragic intensity. If Chester had started with heroes similar to Hemingway's, "To What Red Hell," published in Gingrich's magazine in October, presented another kind of man. Himes turned the mordant prison-fire episode into an absurdity-tinged quest for the personal salvation of a squeamish World War I veteran named Blackie, who struggles to withstand his baptism by fire. Like a tactician depicting the scene of battle, Chester shows the inferno, the grotesque array of dead, and the heroic black giants hauling men to safety.

Blackie has a "queer feeling" and shrinks from the rescue, unable to "lend a hand." He assures himself that his lame response—"No can do"—is not based on fear. Instead of heroic martyrdom, he stakes out the ground of the prison, which duplicates the symbolic grid of western civilization's response to the human crisis, including religion, science, and liberal humanism. Blackie ambles from the Protestant chapel, where a convict plays Handel's "Death March," to the hospital where convicts rob the corpses, over to a group in darkness advocating a passive-resistance prison reform movement, which he scorns. Blackie finds the tawdry homosexuality of prison life breaking into the open on the evening of the fire: a "big blonde guy kissing a nice-looking, brunette youth" and a "tall, black boy called Beautiful Slim" crying, "'Oh Lawd, ma man's dead.'" When he spots Beautiful Slim rifling a corpse's pockets, Blackie tries to hit Slim and regain his ethical standing but, unlike the traditional hero, he falls instead into the muck of charred entrails. Thinking of a Kate Chopin short story, "Dead Men's Shoes," which is set on an old plantation, Blackie advances to another house of worship, the Catholic chapel, where he generates an alternative creed of American nihilism: "I believe in the power of the press, maker of laws, the almighty dollar, political pull, a Colt's .45." After seeing a fireman shoot an arsonist, Blackie passes the death house, then the commissary and cafeteria, exposing the entire underbelly of the prison and its engines of condemnation, recrimination, and specious justice.

Chester used this short story to collapse the racial distance, gaping wide now after thirty-eight years of legally enforceable Jim Crow. First, the entire symbolic apparatus of the deadly fire erases racial identity. The white protagonist called Blackie notes that the dead all suffer the same "smoke-blackened flesh." Blackie identifies a similar chiaroscuro melding among the living convicts, the "White faces, gleaming with sweat, streaked with soot" and the "White teeth in sweaty black faces." Chester also presents notable blacks: a "big Negro called Eastern Bill" saving men from burning alive, the "tall, black boy called Beautiful Slim," and Dangerous Blue, a scarred "wide-mouthed Negro standing on the kitchen range with a six-inch dirk in his hand." While Chester did not ennoble all of these portraits, the black characters were distinct and remarkable; in a mainstream publication avoiding racial-uplift politics he had successfully moved black men beyond villains or comic menials. After Chester was out of prison, Meyer Levin, Gingrich's astute literary assistant, would write to him saying that the short story "received the greatest 'curtain call' of any short story published in *Esquire* during its first years of publication."

Chester had a rare perspective on black life from American society's utter margin, one that he never relinquished. He managed to impose standards of artistic discipline and to cultivate his imagination. That he had done so—without artistic instruction and literary friendships, and in rejection of a code of social and racial improvement—while on a Negro convict's bunk with a folding table next to a urinal was more than surprising. It was distinguished.

Undoubtedly, having a collaborator or artistic coconspirator, cerebral as well as sensual, helped Chester as he prepared his short stories. But his affection for Prince Rico also attracted unwanted attention. On August 2, 1934, both Chester and Rico had two months added to their sentences, likely for being caught in a sex act. While the novel *Cast the First Stone* has the men punished but specifically makes the relationship chaste, Chester revealed to Van Vechten that he and Rico "had a full and complete and very touching love affair, and fulfilled each other emotionally, and spiritually and physically."

The punishment was offset by the Prince Rico's deep friendship and admiration, which played a role in inspiring Chester during the extraordinary working twelve months between the publication of the final installment of "Prison Mass" in May 1933 and the acceptance of his *Esquire* stories. In spite of the penalty of extra time, Chester still managed a transfer to the London Prison Farm on September 21, 1934. As he concluded in the novel *Cast the First Stone*, "the farm was the way to freedom."

London Prison Farm was a large working farm used to reward model prisoners and produce food for the other state institutions. During Chester's time there, the population fluctuated between 1163 and 1561 men, monitored by a small number of guards. At "the Farm," the "better class" of inmates remained incarcerated, but not behind bars. Of course, it was still prison: dreary, banal, and on the brink of violence.

In Chester's earliest extant letter, written to the London Prison Farm censor Alice Armine, Warden William Armine's daughter, he asked for permission to explore the unseemly side of penitentiary life. Calling his works in progress "script[s]," Chester testified to having received "so many upbraidings from the different officers of this institution" that he was weary. He had arrived at the London Prison Farm already preparing to send out versions of stories and chapters loosely based on his prison time. Chester confided to the prison censor that he labored on "a story that deals with the growth of affection between two convicts" with "the implication in one of the character's thoughts of sex perversion—*but not the statement.*" He seems never to have considered writing that regretted the reality of his experience.

Chester's final eighteen months serving his sentence would have reminded him of the rural life he had known slightly as a child in Lorman and then briefly driving the tractor in Pine Bluff, Arkansas. He lived on the farm throughout 1935, and while it could be tranquil, deadly violence was never far off even among men near parole. On May 16, one prisoner stabbed another to death with a guard standing only twenty feet away. Men perished regularly from tuberculosis and botched surgeries by prison doctors. If there was slightly less incentive for nearly released men to escape, the ease with which it could be done still enticed them regularly. Seven walked off at the end of August 1935. With only minimal educational facilities, boredom and idleness were severe, and the deputy warden added to Chester's unease by glowering at him as he filed out of the mess hall.

In the winter of 1936, when Chester's parole date was announced, it made news back at the Columbus prison. Prince Rico wrote to him from the coal company, two weeks before Chester's release. "Glad you're through with the long road," the letter began. Rico was at work sending out short stories for prison anthologies "plugging hard at the writing game, and music." While Chester concluded *Cast the First Stone* with Duke Dido's suicide, real-life Prince Rico was thanking Chester for his help. "Working with you has done everything for me and my writing," he admitted, in the midst of asking Chester for his radio once he was released. Rico's emotional letter showed him balanced and still somewhat infatuated, in the manner in which Chester would show the denouement of their friendship in the novel. "I'm flattered and glad no end you think I was able to give you anything of value," Prince Rico wrote, still referring to Chester as "Puggy Wuggy," the endearment the men cribbed from O. Henry stories. Rico had taken out an annual subscription to *Esquire* and the former burglar praised Chester, who would publish another short story in the magazine that spring and again late in the summer. "I've learned to think, treat people as people, and use good judgment," he wrote. The friends promised to meet again in Los Angeles, a promise that Chester would keep. Recalling the artists that they had discussed, like Langston Hughes and black cartoonist E. Simms Campbell, Rico's letter also provided the first evidence of Chester having systematically looked at a modern novel—Hemingway's *A Farewell to Arms.*

Even though Chester had sought an odd dance of restraint and intimacy with Rico, for much of 1934 he had at least found a fellow prisoner with whom he could exchange ideas and test out his knowledge. Rico had begun by serving as a literary secretary, retyping the stories for him, but he also became an artist in his own right. By the beginning of 1935, Prince Rico would be lauded in the press for trying to write an opera, based on black convict and farmhand work chants, very close to what the trained African American composers Nathaniel Dett and William L. Dawson (of Hampton and Tuskegee Institute, respectively) were trying to do. He had also made contact with playwright and screenwriter Jonathan Finn, the author behind the films *Chalked Out* and *Jailbreak*, in hope of getting his work anthologized.

Chester and Prince Rico had created a literary society together, and Chester had written and published strong work during their poignant friendship. For the remainder of his career, Chester required an intimate connection as a kind of daily ignition for writing. With

Rico he had had the gift of being able to convince someone of the validity of his ambition, and he had matured beyond the callow youth of his most troubled years. "You'll write great things because it is expected of you—by all of us," Prince Rico wrote to him. Chester took that prophecy with him when his parole was finally granted on April 1, 1936.

Chapter Five

WHITE FOLKS
AND THE DAYS
1936–1941

O n April 1, 1936, Chester took a bus back to his mother's house on Miami Avenue in Columbus. In the tragic, slightly absurd short story "On Dreams and Reality," which owed something to Gogol's "The Overcoat," Chester described a prisoner's ragged coming home to mother and brother in Columbus after eight years of incarceration. It was a grim, deeply shattering event. Reassuring himself during his imprisonment with golden dreams of life on the outside, he had overlooked the Depression's lacerating impact on his family. His narrator gasps, "'This can't be *my* home,'" as he takes in the "unkempt yard" where "dirty paper lay limp in the rain" and then treads the "worn, wooden steps" of a "bilious green" frame house.

A slip of paper tacked to the door-frame to his right held the notice, *Bell out of order, please knock.* Below were the names of his mother and brother. He laughed suddenly. What was the matter with him? he asked himself. Sure, it'd be all right here. It had to be.

He knocked and waited. The door cracked open and a haggard, gray-haired woman peered from a darkened room.

"Mother!" he exclaimed, his laugh choking off. "Mother!"

"James, my baby! James!" she sobbed, clinging to him.

He almost asked, "Oh, mother, what has happened to you?" but caught himself and said instead, "Gee, mother, it's swell to be home." . . . He followed her through the gloomy parlour, side-stepped the jutting edge of a cane rocker, and entered the central room, feeling deflated. His first impression was that of squalor; it hit him a solid blow below the belt.

Recalling his mother's elaborate oyster luncheons spread out in the prison dayroom to revive his spirits, Chester now found it unnerving when Estelle said, "We'll put the big pot in the little one and make hash out of the dish rag." Another defeat was in store when he learned that the Ohio Industrial Commission was eliminating his workman's compensation; he had no income for the first time since 1926.

Adding a psychological dimension to the pressing economic circumstances, Chester would find himself begrudging his mother's devotion to Joe, who had just completed his course work and campus residency requirement toward his PhD. In June, Joe would begin work as the director of research for the Urban League, completing his doctorate two years later. Estelle loudly blamed Joseph Sr. for his failure to help speed Chester's release from prison. The absence of a governor's commutation record for Chester's final parole from London Prison Farm strongly suggests that Chester served out the maximum sentence under the new laws and found no favoritism whatsoever, despite any wrangling or proceedings initiated by lawyers on his behalf. Meanwhile Chester, "more hysterical than I had ever been before," after seven years and five months in prison, was trying to relieve himself of the memory of degradation of life behind bars, which meant also the personal shame of having homosexual relations there.

Although he swung into the routine of attending church with his mother and Joe, he knew that to woo successfully any of the young women of the black middle class would take a lifetime of reassembling the respectability he had lost to prison. So he crept along the underside of black Columbus for adult pleasures. With an eye on prestige, he satisfied his sexual longing by courting the white prostitutes working the ghetto and eluding their pimps. "Several times landlords had to intervene to keep me from being shot." His peccadilloes escalating, he lined up with other ex-cons to "Georgia" a black girl—which meant to promise payment for sex and then renege on her fee—then stepped back when his turn came. One Sunday following church, he wandered up to Warren Street, where one of his hooligan friends turned him onto "gage"—marijuana—which made him hallucinate, prompting Estelle to summon a physician.

Mother and son argued forcefully about his conduct in matches that required Joe Jr. to step in and referee. Believing that Chester's antics might jeopardize his brother's career, his mother turned over control of his parole to his father. The move signaled the end of their kinship; Estelle had given up on him.

Returning to his father's in Cleveland meant Aunt Fannie's house and bussing tables at Wade Park Manor, where he'd nearly been crippled. This was a move as miserable as being berated by his mother. Joseph Sr. had been making ends meet with odd jobs and work teaching trades at the Woodland Center Neighborhood House, a community center lodged in a refurbished church that ran programs in music and vocational training. Now in his early sixties, he was still married to Agnes Rowe but had never been able to purchase another home. His younger sister probably needed her brother at the time. Fannie's husband, Wade, by then was living with extraordinary pain from passing gallstones in his urine; he would die of hypertrophy of the prostate in ten months.

In Glenville aunt Leah and uncle Roddy Moon prepared a celebratory dinner for Chester's first Sunday back in Cleveland. Glad to hear he had finished "with the past kind of living," his staid older relatives tried to "make him feel as though nothing has ever happened." Roddy Moon was "anxious to see him make good." They meant well for him, in a general sense, but they insisted on a straitjacket of propriety. Another disaster on Chester's part would bode ill for all his relatives, especially those like the Moons who lived on streets with white neighbors and whose thriving relied upon impeccable appearance and good relations. Roddy Moon was so strict that he had prevented his daughter, Ella, from marrying a man he considered beneath her, destroying his daughter's confidence, health, and career in the process. Despite his dinner-table attempts at probity and telling everyone that he had written a novel and was working at the hotel, Chester, in the elder Moon's eyes, "looks well but [is] somewhat downcast."

That summer, Chester met Cleveland's most famous writer, Langston Hughes, who had traveled to the Soviet Union with Henry to make a film in 1932. Hughes, the original black trailblazer in *Esquire,* was living with his mother on E. Eighty-Sixth Street, and was tightening his musical comedy *Little Ham* at the Karamu House, Cleveland's local experimental black theater. In the fall at Karamu, the Gilpin Players would present Hughes's *Troubled Island*, the first play about Jean-Jacques Dessalines and the successful revolt of the enslaved in Haiti. Fun to be around and easygoing in his manner, Hughes was not complacent or tepid. Although he was less black-looking than Chester, Hughes always asserted his racial identity with pride, something that Chester had waffled over in his early work. Hughes also argued forcefully on behalf of economic and political justice in those years, "because I am both a Negro and poor," he told the press. Nor did he turn up his nose at Chester because of the stretch in the penitentiary; Hughes was in fact giving lectures at middle-class teas titled "Cowards in Our Colleges." Hughes epitomized the socially conscious artist, and when he left Cleveland in 1937, it would be to use his talents as a journalist in war-torn Madrid. Chester now had an obvious model for a literary career.

But that goal was at odds with the job at Wade Park Manor Hotel, which lasted Chester through his first couple of check-ins with his probation officer. Clearing dinner tables and pushing dish carts weren't the same as when he had been a rising freshman at Ohio State, keen on a career in medicine. After nearly eight years of prison and bunking with his father, who had known nothing other than demotions for almost thirty working years, service work probably struck Chester as a painful symbol of the likelihood of being a permanent member of the laboring class. In the same way that he had learned to be a convict, now he was learning to be a black servant without prospects for advance.

He did, however, gain a mature sensibility on the black head-waiter who hired him, the subject of a short story emphasizing the generation gap called "A Salute to the Passing." An elegiac testament, Chester's story revealed the obvious value of the old caste relations. Immaculately comported Dick Small has thrived in his role as head-waiter, "America's principal servant," "pampered protégé of millionaires and royalty among his own people." But Chester endorsed the men of his father's generation, who understood that the people whom he served "were his life," with a significant caveat; whatever public achievements on behalf of racial progress they attained, the benefits were doled out as personal favors, not because of any real power.

Chester's work for *Esquire* continued to sustain his identity as a writer. Gingrich published "The Night's for Crying," the story detailing Cleveland's tough streets, in January 1937, and he probably bought another 1937 story, "Every Opportunity," a lighthearted and facetious romp through Cedar Avenue poolrooms and gin parlors as a convict's appetites lead him back to prison. That September *Esquire* published one of his better hard-boiled tales of prison life, "The Visiting Hour," an exploration of a white inmate receiving his young wife in the prison visitors' room, while trying to contain his anger at the slow and corrupt process of parole. In that same issue, *Esquire* announced Chester's racial identity by printing a woodcut of him based on an unsmiling, mildly gangsterish photograph shot after his release. Although Chester was the lightest in color among his brothers, anyone who cared to pay attention would have noticed he was black.

With his son back at home, Joseph Senior attempted to secure new lodgings, a rented room or two in a frame house crowded with tenants on E. Ninety-Third Street. Chester described the tension of the little place in a letter to a friend, recalling "I had it hard." Although his father's second wife seems to have lived only intermittently with the men, Chester claimed that his father "had very little money" and that, like the moll in "The Visiting Hour," Agnes "was taking that." The house was shouting distance from the major crime and vice block on Cedar Avenue.

The broad suffering of the Depression at least made Chester feel that it wasn't exclusively his family that was failing. When asked his occupation for the city directory, Chester tried to put on a confident mien and called himself a "businessman," which must have seemed more prosperous to people like his aunt and uncle than "writer." He wasn't quite sure that "writer" was it, but Gingrich, apparently seduced by Chester's regular correspondence, increased his fee to one hundred dollars per story. However, the well was drying up. He had outlived some of his usefulness for *Esquire*: his special conceit of being a "long term penitentiary insider" had ended.

From the Ninety-Third Street room Chester rekindled the romance with Jean, who lived a couple of blocks away. When Chester was released from prison in 1936, Jean was living with her brother-in-law Philip Plater. No longer a brash teenager, Jean claimed that the drunken Harry Plater had abandoned her not six months into the marriage. Chester believed that she used men to live, but her interest in Chester, the boy with long eyelashes and tender manners, was earnest. Whatever the complex nature of her living situation when he arrived, he latched on to Jean like a person drowning: "I grew to love her too, desperately and completely."

Inexperienced in romance, Chester asked Jean to marry him not long after getting to Cleveland, which was made difficult by the fact that she was still married. In November, Jean issued a summons and posted public notices in the *Daily Legal News* alerting Harry that she planned to petition for divorce, claiming abandonment. In March Jean's attorney brought her case into the court of common pleas and cited Plater for "gross neglect of duty." Plater had been only a few miles away but never appeared at any court proceedings. The court granted her petition and dissolved the marriage. A justice of the peace married Chester and Jean on Tuesday, July 13, 1937.

Born in Texas, Jean worked as a domestic when she could get work, but she was attractive and young, and housecleaning and caretaking—occupations that left women especially vulnerable to sexual assault—were humiliating to someone who could glimpse into the world of black women who had been to college, like Chester's mother or his aunt Leah Moon. Both of them agreed that, rather than having Jean work as a maid, Chester should support the two of them. His reward, in a sense, was the appearance of being in charge.

He was frank with Jean regarding what precisely had taken place in the summer of 1934 in prison. In a complex dynamic within his own personality, Chester sought absolution for the homosexual desires he had indulged in prison through merciless candor. If the honesty was good medicine psychologically, what he did not understand immediately was that there would be other hills for him to climb connected to his masculinity. The difficulty to maintain a standard of living that would allow Jean to stay at home would take not one-time courageous revelations but much more: tedious, dull consistency and self-control.

Marrying Jean did more than absolve him of the "degeneracy" he had experienced in prison. He had tried to show himself a tough during the intense months of their 1928 courtship, actions that led to his dangerous robberies. She of course had her own secrets to divulge, her years with Harry and other men while he was locked up. For Chester, by marrying Jean, a humbly educated woman several shades browner in color than himself, he was also forcibly discarding his mother's ideals of betterment and domestic progress. Jean, however, was welcomed by his father, the Moons, and the Wigginses as a cheerful, agreeable relative.

After tiring of hotel work, Chester turned to the whites-only Cleveland country club circuit going out to the suburb of Shaker Heights. The country club work required one quality above all others: submissiveness. He was exhausted trying to smile at the racist chortle that bubbled up when the members drank. Nightly, Chester had to persuade himself that the tips justified his playing small, his acting to "just be a nigger."

For seven years he had focused his attention so sharply on release from prison that it was with difficulty that he faced the new realization: that he was black in America. "Until then there had been nothing racial about my hurt, unbelievable as this may seem," he wrote in his autobiography. Married life, however, made "a difference." The tattered rented rooms the couple could afford—skimping on heat and other necessities—galled Chester, as did his humbling employment. Jean's divorce was made possible by accusing Harry Plater of abandoning and failing to support her, but inside the house he was doing little better.

In the time away from the mops and steam trays, he probed the magazines for publishing opportunities. Disappointed, Chester grumbled to Henry Lee Moon that he had been shut out of the moneyed magazines that were home to Hemingway: *Scribner's* and *Collier's*. "They have all admired my work, in fact they have requested to see some of it," he assured his cousin, "but they all say the same thing— they can't use it." To put him over in New York, Chester had engaged

Thomas Uzzell, part fiction editor, part literary charlatan, an agent who advertised himself as "the leading American teacher on the short story and novel." Uzzell advertised pamphlets and by-mail seminars in the *New York Times Book Review*, and it was not surprising that Chester, who paid him twenty dollars upfront to place ten short stories, had no success. One of the short stories was probably "Did You Ever Catch a Moon," which Chester retitled "A Nigger," and gave itself over to the frank treatment of the love triangle or quadrangle with Jean before his arrest. To someone with better connections like Henry, a story about a kept woman and a contract with an unscrupulous literary agent seemed inexpert. The upside was that Chester wasn't backing off from a career even if he was making a misstep. He maintained to Henry that the prison novel was "outlined in my mind" and "only needs writing." At the end of 1937 Chester poured himself into the penitentiary tale, tentatively called *Day After Day*.

The irony of being financially better off and more successful as a short story writer while an inmate was easy to see but hard to accept. Chester's only publication for 1938 was "Every Opportunity," which *Esquire* had acquired earlier. In February 1938, he sold another story of a bewildered convict to *Bachelor*, a new men's magazine for the "discerning cosmopolite" whose "ambition has been stifled by monotony." Chester's tale "Scram!," an insider's look at the isolation cell, was wearing gimmicks thin to bind an audience to the story, which was narrated in the second person. He grunted with the slang and prejudice of his implied white readers with lines like "You call out to the Negro on sudden impulse and ask him, 'Say, shine, do you hear that guy saying "scram!"?'" But neither the writing nor the shared terrain with Hemingway (whose narrator used the word "nigger" eighteen times on the first page in the famous February 1936 *Esquire* short story "The Trademan's Return") was distinguished.

In March 1938 his brother crowned himself the winner of their sibling rivalry. Joe completed his doctorate in sociology and "enjoy[ed] the recognition" available to him in Columbus. He had not limited himself to academic success. Somehow Joe had managed to pledge Alpha Phi Alpha, the fraternity to which Chester had never completed his initiation, and a few years later he would marry a college-educated French-language teacher who had served as one of his readers. A well-connected sorority woman who finished a master's degree at Ohio State, Theresa Estelle Jones was the granddaughter of the man who owned the land on which Tuskegee Institute was built. Everyone called her Estelle, just like Joe's mother. Joe was a glimmering success.

Cousin Henry Lee Moon was having a career liftoff too. After writing for the *New York Times* on black voting power, the progress of antilynching law, public housing in Harlem, Liberia, and even the illegal "policy" lottery game, Moon accepted a position in the federal government serving Assistant Secretary of Housing Robert Weaver. He joined a group organized by the Himes and Bomar family friend Mary McLeod Bethune, now a college president (the Negro newspapers called her the convener of the "Black Cabinet" to President Franklin Roosevelt). Moon worked as secretary and public relations man for Weaver, a black wunderkind raised in Washington, D.C., who had completed a PhD in economics at Harvard by the time he was twenty-six. In August 1938, Henry wed his longtime confidante and girlfriend, Mollie Lewis.

Inspired by the splashy victories of Joe and Henry in regional and national affairs, Chester tried to press the case locally with the Cleveland dailies. Louis Seltzer at the *Cleveland Press* brusquely dismissed him. "I could not hire you if you were Jesus Christ reincarnated," Seltzer growled, by which he implied that the rejection had nothing to do with race. Chester kept at the typewriter. By the spring of 1938, Chester had amassed portions of a novel about his prison experience and a bundle of short stories. When Henry saw the "pile of manuscripts," he envied the power and work ethic that his young cousin had shown, proudly noting that Chester had "got the stuff already."

Chester had also secured a better agent, Gideon Kishur of the International Literary Bureau. Kishur sent out several of Chester's stories to the most esteemed glossy magazines and got a comment back from Kenneth Littauer at *Collier's*, who rejected one story because it was "rather depressing as an entertainment." Chester hit upon the idea to write a feel-good narrative about Joe's extraordinary success. But after *American Magazine* turned the story down, his country-club-experience-induced paranoia got the best of Chester. He wrote *American Magazine* politely to ask if they were racists. "I hope I am not presumptuous in this, my effort to ascertain your policy on this, a subject that may or may not be a ticklish one, but since I am not in a position to know, I must ask." "This" was, of course, whether or not the editors had any use for profiles on American Negroes. U.S. magazine customs were changing, but slowly. When they upheld the rejection at the end of May, Chester found only that his tenderfooting had caused the staff to smother him with graciousness. "We were very much interested to read of the splendid record," his rejection began, before plateauing with "we're sorry we cannot cooperate with you on your friendly suggestion" but "many thanks for keeping us in mind." Chester knew all he needed to know and abandoned the story about the professional triumphs of disabled Negro intellectuals.

He feared that his career might be over before it had begun properly. Five years later, he would describe the agony of trying to live from his writing after prison as a conflict between his white identification and his black lived experience: "It does not occur to him that now he is trying to write 'white' out of a subconscious store of Negro knowledge, Negro incident, language, emotion, reaction, motivation, obstruction, culmination, and such, imposed on him by his condition of living 'black.'" Instead, he became convinced that the editors knew that he was a Negro, and that they rejected him on account of it. Chester was growing "bitterly resentful [of] that fate" which "identified him with the Negro race," more or less the spirit of his brittle and caustic mother Estelle.

Splitting his time between Washington, D.C., and New York, Henry Moon made an important assist. He discussed Chester's work over lunch with Sterling Brown, a Howard University English professor, an esteemed poet, and the director of Negro affairs for the Works Progress Administration (WPA). After the meeting, Brown, who already knew about Chester's writing from *Esquire*, fired off a brief letter of advice to him. It couldn't have come at a better time. Chester admired Brown's work—his poetry collection *Southern Road* bore, arguably for the first time, the robust and soulful personality of black workers who had evolved a magnificent cultural tradition in the face of an often bleak situation. As much as any other writer of the time, Brown had seemed to resolve the dilemma of wanting the best that exclusive white America had to offer without denigrating one iota of black language, culture, or people. Developing Brown as a friend, Chester asked for critical feedback on his stories. Brown had not encountered a black writer like Chester before, astute but honest, humorous, admiring of the laconic, matter-of-fact tradition of Hemingway, but with squishy emotions, which Himes's short stories meditated upon figuratively and literally, and prone toward a tragic theme. Admitting that he was missing being published by a hair, Chester had the humility—and confidence—to ask for help. "I am happy to know of your interest in my work. Perhaps after reading one or two you may be able to drop me a helpful hint."

A genuine dean of African American literature and culture in the 1930s, Brown went much further. Brown had schooled at the famous black academy the M Street High School of Anna Julia Cooper. He'd gone on to distinction at Williams College and got his MA in English at Harvard University; then he'd started teaching at Lincoln Institute and lived in the house where Chester was born. Having spent several years as the regular literary critic at the Urban League journal *Opportunity*, Brown was writing on his signature ideas about the prevalence of black stereotypes in white American literature. In the late fall of 1938 he sent concerned suggestions to Chester, who showed the aplomb and seriousness to weather a professor's scrutiny. Glowing with appreciation, Chester admitted that the responses were "the first clear, pointed and understandable criticism which I have received during the six years which I have been trying to write."

Brown counseled Chester to be wary of overwriting—the flaw of adornment—and to examine his tendency toward tragic themes and desperate acts. He told him that the hard-boiled style then in vogue was already on its way to being a cliché. In language that was gentle and brotherly, Brown explained the tastes of the American reading public—especially the decision-making magazine editors— as fundamentally biased away from black truth in favor of stereo-typed shenanigans. Chester had already exploited this vein and pushed at its limits, presenting the stereotype to get closer to the human being underneath.

Approaching thirty, Chester understood, in spite of Brown's rare gift of criticism, that he had his own lights to follow. His long prison years, the grisly fire, the added months on his sentence with Rico and then resurrecting himself with Jean, for better or for worse, had made him a writer. "What seems 'tragically desperate' to you," he countered, "—and the editors and the reading public—is just a matter of course to me." Still beside his prison years, Chester wouldn't apologize for his brutish view of the world and the language he insisted upon to describe it. "If I have one 'bastard' kill another 'bastard' in a story, it's just one dead bastard and another one electric-chair bound as far as I am concerned," he wrote back. "I am indifferent, unsympathetic, and can see nothing shocking, unusual, or repulsive about any of it." But if Chester held tight to his point of view, he did not flatter him-self about the jejune short tales. He decided in his considerate reply to Brown, "I can mark them down to apprenticeship served and go ahead to better work."

Chester did not reveal all of what he was about to Brown. If the magazines didn't take his shorts, he continued to hammer away at his first-person novel, an effort 650 pages long by that May. Chester thrived off of the madcap defiance of what he was attempting—a sympathetic portrait of a convict's years inside the penitentiary replete with graphic depictions of violent and homosexual acts. He built the book by the episode and let the structure take care of itself. By "packing in a maze of essentials," he believed that he had achieved a tone that was "brusk [sic], to the point, and unsentimental," but revealing "every phase" of the prison insider's life. Shielding nothing, Chester described himself as "stating the facts as best I can and letting the explanations and psychoanalyzing go."

With no publisher in sight for this magnum opus of uninhibited material, for the more immediate task of survival he turned to the WPA. Although Chester applied for the Ohio branch of the Federal Writers Project (FWP), he was added to Cleveland's 78,000 WPA workers as a ditchdigger, the kind of work he hadn't even been forced to do in prison. For $60.50 per month the men labored in the snow and slush, building roads, sewers, drains, parks, cultural gardens and recreation areas throughout the city. The ideal of freedom in the Cuyahoga County WPA was utterly hypocritical. No African American was employed in white-collar work: no state staff people, no executive or administrative personnel, not even any clerks. Taking his own publication career seriously, Chester wrote letters to local officials insisting on a desk job.

He followed in a tradition. In the spring of 1938, black Cleveland—led by Assistant State's Attorney Perry B. Jackson, city councilmen Harold Gassaway and Lawrence Payne, and Reverend Sylvester Williams—began to demand the inclusion of blacks in more diverse employment than unskilled labor. Initially they were inelegantly rebuffed, but they made enough noise to receive minor adjustments. Using his own contact with the upper-level national administration, Sterling Brown himself, Chester complained that May about the racism in Cleveland that required him to shovel, even though he was a nationally published writer and merited appointment to the state FWP.

If racism abounded, the WPA jobs were precarious anyway: supervisors evaluated positions month to month and dismissed workers at whim; congressional authorizations sometimes flagged, forcing massive, nationwide layoffs. Chester's jolting experience inspired a new formulation; he found that the horror of death and the problem of confinement had a counterpart in the world of daily work in the Depression. Chester worked the dread into "With Malice Toward None," a new short story:

> He filled with a recurrence of the numb, cold fear which had haunted him ever since he went to work on the W.P.A. No one would realize how scared one stayed in that living from hand to mouth, from one check to another, he reflected bitterly. It wouldn't be so bad if they'd tell a man he had so many months to work and that was all, but to keep him like this, on pins and needles, never knowing when the layoff would come and no work open, it was worse in a way than downright starvation. It kept a man scared all the time.
>
> As a relief he worked up an intense resentment toward his wife.

The formulation of fear compounded by externally directed loathing, drawn from his own life certainly but transmuted into literary expression, was a signal and essential observation of Himes's literary art. And also a bright flare commenting that his marriage was in trouble.

The local black newspaper, the *Cleveland Call and Post*, took a lead role in exposing Jim Crow in the Cuyahoga County WPA, especially the practice of demoting foremen and allowing local supervisors to fire workers at will. The mood of black Clevelanders was stiffening against Jim Crow employment policies generally. The black radical organization the Future Outlook League directed militant attempts at white businesses to force them to employ blacks and started publishing a journal recording their victories in the fall of 1937. (In 1939 the local clamor against the WPA would initiate a federal investigation, resulting in Charles Dickinson being appointed a labor investigator and becoming the top ranked black in the state.) Chester lobbied vigorously by mail for a position as a writer on the FWP, and in the process started to associate with men like Urban League director Sidney Williams, and Grant Reynolds, minister of the important Mt. Zion Congregational Church on Cedar Avenue. After Chester's contentions reached the desk of the state FWP director, Ohio State University professor Harlan Hatcher, and probably with a note of support from Sterling Brown, he was granted a transfer to the writers' project. Before the end of June 1938, Chester was making a "favorable impression" as a research assistant and writer for the Cleveland Public Library Project. His monthly pay jumped to $95.

Writers on the Ohio FWP worked out of the imposing five-story main branch of the Cleveland Public Library. Opened in 1925, the heavy marble, French Renaissance style library helped to renew his dignity and properly reinforced the gravity of his work. Typically, the FWP writers worked anonymously to construct large single-volume state guidebooks; in New York and Chicago, a few elite writers worked on their own manuscripts. Surprised by his credentials and admiring his typing speed, the FWP put Chester to work writing vocational bulletins. As the Congress of Industrial Organizations (CIO) tried to unionize the library workers, he showed interest and started to contribute articles to their local organ, the *Cleveland Union Leader*. Chester received another promotion to "professional" status and drew assignments writing on little-known aspects of Cleveland history. He warmed to the challenge. All that survives of the Cleveland project writing is a thirty-page essay on the history of Cleveland in the *Ohio Guide*. The essay pointed to a unique criterion for Cleveland's national distinction: "one of the most racially diversified communities in the United States." As for the value of the legacy of black people to the city, the guidebook was unsure.

> Most of Cleveland's Negroes, who came in during the labor famine of the World War and immediately after, live in the slum area extending from the fringes of the business section to East 105th Street and south of Carnegie Avenue. The few who became affluent move to other sections of the city, but the birth rate of those who remain has created a serious housing problem.

Politically undecided, groomed by gangsters, and having been reared in a Tuskegee-friendly home, Chester was certainly capable of presenting poor black Americans as a drain on society. He was aggrieved by humiliating segregation but disinclined to make common cause with the black poor. He could accept himself as black and ghetto-built, but he easily blamed black people for the misery that they faced. He had little critique of a modern political economy, which Joe and Henry were studying seriously. "While on the Writers' Project," he judged at a later date, "I did not feel the racial hurt so much." When Chester felt comfortable, he had the capacity to forget his race, in the way that a "hincty," or snobbish person, might. But if he couldn't have started with the assumption that he shared the same fundamental attitudes as his white classmates from East High, he wouldn't have been able to imagine an audience for his fiction.

In a room where project writers worked on the library's third floor, Chester got to know Ruth Seid, a young assured woman who, since she was the child of immigrant Polish Jews, published under the name Jo Sinclair. Chester immediately charmed Ruth. He had also begun blaming Jean for his difficulties in getting work and publishing and was on the lookout for something that hinted of more than friendship. The attraction was mutual, but Seid left the sex alone. They chatted about films, music, theater, and politics. She told him about a new book she had read and its author, who had won the $500 *Story* magazine prize: *Uncle Tom's Children* by Richard Wright. Surprised that Chester didn't know about the latest black writing sensation, Seid underestimated him, which he disliked but tolerated, wishing not to repeat the failures of high school and college. Like Chester, she too had a slender understanding of the economic structure of racial discrimination. When they talked about local politics, she found Chester bitter and cynical regarding antidiscrimination groups.

Chester introduced Ruth to Jean and the three of them whiled away hours together. Ruth thought him mannerly at first, then, after a few rounds of whiskey and reefer, she believed him loud and egotistical. Once, he took them to a ghetto dive after the nightclubs had closed. Chester's parole requirements forbade his association with known criminals; blue laws forbade gatherings after hours. On cue, the police raided the house, and Ruth's active imagination was considering the iniquity of the women's bull pen at the city jail. Chester showed himself adequate to the occasion, remarking to Ruth as he ushered her to safety, "This'll be good for you as a writer." Nor was the range of contacts limited to the dives off Cedar Avenue. Pearl Moody, the pair's supervisor and a professional librarian, invited Chester, Jean, and Ruth to her home in the exclusive suburb of Shaker Heights many times, an unusually bold gathering in the 1930s.

Like Chester, Seid began her short story career publishing in *Esquire*, in February 1938. She continued to find success in some of Gingrich's later projects, like the arts monthly *Coronet* and the more politically dense and uncompromising *Ken*. In the December 1938 issue of *Ken*, she made her friendship with Chester pay dividends. The article, "Cleveland's Negro Problem," embarrassed Chester later, and showed the caustic skepticism that consumed him in the years immediately after he'd left prison. Seid described with suspicion and misgiving the Future Outlook League's organized pickets against employment discrimination, a technique of resistance growing increasingly popular in the North. In March 1938 the U.S. Supreme Court had levied a favorable decision emboldening picket lines, in a determination that race discrimination in employment was akin to discrimination on the basis of union affiliation. But what his cousin Henry had praised in the pages of the *New York Times* as "an effective campaign for jobs," Seid had decided, apparently with Chester's goading, was simple extortion.

In sympathy with the Jewish shop-owning class in the Negro slum areas against which the protests had been mounted, she opened her essay in *Ken* with the lines "Sam Katz opened a wine store on Central Avenue. All of a sudden wine was popular with the colored people; they were drinking it like water." Her information from the black street came from "a Cleveland negro writer . . . an intelligent, thinking young man," obviously Chester. Her anonymous source inferred that the Future Outlook League, "located in the heart of the racket district," was twisting public perception to hide an illegal reality. But the story of Sam Katz concluded with a vintage observation by Chester: "If the undernourished and absolutely powerless are suddenly given a bit of power, they may well lose a little balance in the process. You know how it is. But look out for possible race riots, I say!" Chester wanted to help out a new friend but, only sure of the likelihood of conflict, his language was bombastic. When he recalled the piece a few years later, he would find Seid guilty of "insidious Jewish chauvinism." She continued to draw on their friendship, using Chester's life as the source of inspiration for the character Aaron Wright in her unpublished "They Gave Us Jobs," written in 1940.

The summer of hard, rewarding work on the "Cleveland Guide" and his novel did not keep the wolf from the door. Chester had a working knowledge of carpentry, plumbing, and auto mechanics, but he badly mismanaged household affairs, always living beyond his means. He wanted the privilege of drinking or entertaining when he chose, and the result always left a gnawing deficit "to catch up on financially" and no savings. By August 1938, he and Jean were shuffling along a circuit of coarse rooms just east of Rockefeller Park, a nomadic search for decency and a tawdry limping away from bad debts. Chester penned the forlorn short stories "With Malice Toward None," "Looking Down the Street," and "All God's Chillun Got Pride," during their summer and fall wanderings. Probably toward the end of fall, *Opportunity* took the restaurant maitre d' story, "A Salute to the Passing."

By winter, they had returned to E. Ninety-Third Street, to a room at the home of Mary Reese, a forty-seven-year-old domestic who put down their talk of New York by claiming that when she had visited Manhattan, the Savoy Ballroom and Small's Paradise Inn failed to surpass the dance halls and juke joints on Cedar Avenue. Chester's writing and his $900 annual salary on the FWP did provide something more coveted than decent quarters. The great boost to his confidence that year was a successful petition to Ohio governor John Bricker that would in 1939 restore Chester's full citizenship rights. For the first time in his life, he would be able to vote.

Reconsidering his strategy to reach the national magazines, Chester published with the locals. Through Langston Hughes, Chester met Rowena Jellife, the founder of Karamu House. Rowena and her husband, Russell, were 1910 Oberlin graduates and almost certainly knew of Joe's successes there. Rowena Jellife served on the editorial board of a new Cleveland literary venture called *Crossroad*, a "medium for creative talent in every field." *Crossroad* featured left-wing short stories and modernist visual art, including abstract impressionist prints, suitable for "mounting and framing." Cleveland's white liberal crowd, including associate editors at the *Cleveland Plain Dealer*, Milton Fox

of the Cleveland Art Museum, and music professors from Case Western Reserve University all participated; Dan Levin, a young Communist and Western Reserve graduate, recruited the local artists.
Contributing three short stories to the magazine during its first year,
Chester got through his rough patch of literary rejection and financial
hardship in the pages of *Crossroad.*

The inaugural issue in April carried Chester's "With Malice
Toward None," the story of Chick, a boozy Negro who works in the
library copying old records for the WPA. (Jean nicknamed Chester "Chess" and "Chet.") *Crossroad* had declined into a quarterly
by summer but, never lacking a manuscript, Chester gave them "A
Modern Fable—Of Mr. Slaughter, Mr. McDull, and the American
Scene," his earliest unambiguous wading into the political crisis of
relief. The story was a lumbering allegory that contrasted the positions
of the conservative and unprincipled Republican senator Harold A.
McDull with those of an unemployed worker named Henry Slaughter. Chester showed the culpability of the senator, who, after voting
to end WPA appropriations to the poor, tells the press, "My God,
politics isn't fatal, it isn't a matter of life or death!" Slaughter attempts
to assassinate the senator and is taken to an asylum; the reader is playfully counseled to ignore the imminent class war.

Chester was making a turn in the direction of class friction and
local politics, only to have the pace of world events overtake him.
After a tense series of standoffs, annexations, negotiations, and international bickering, Nazi Germany and the Soviet Union invaded
Poland on September 1, 1939. France and Great Britain declared war
against Germany two days later.

With calamitous world events under way, the Depression and
racial discrimination appeared more solvable. Chester had kept up
talks—pleas, really—with the Cleveland press, and with Louis Seltzer in particular, through the summer of 1939. Fearing the end of his
job on the WPA, Chester encouraged Jean to start searching for a job

as a nanny, which they upgraded to a "governess." Needing something that didn't exist, Chester approached the *Chicago Defender* with some ideas for a serious national Negro magazine, "which would inspire Negro art and literature and give it an outlet," a resource that would "serve the Negro race as much so as a contribution to a school or church fund." But the newspaper couldn't find the money. Chester resolved to apply for a job in Cleveland's mushrooming defense industry, which would grow from sales of $15 million in parts in 1939 to $120 million a year later.

Private industry, however, was comfortable with a high level of racial discrimination. Instead of joining the market of skilled laborers, Chester earned an education in "what racial prejudice is like," an experience which left him teetering on the edge of violence. Queuing for jobs at the tool company Warner & Swasey, American Steel & Wire, and the Aluminum Company of America was an exercise in futility. Whenever his turn came, he learned that the employment directors lunched between 11:30 A.M. and 3 P.M., the plants weren't hiring, or that he hadn't apprenticed; other times, after several hours in line, he simply trudged away, finally accepting the implausibility of getting a job as the lone black man alongside a hundred white men. Any redress at all was impossible until President Roosevelt issued an executive order in June 1941 outlawing racial discrimination by industries with government contracts and establishing the Fair Employment Practices Commission. But the FEPC was only an investigative body that heard charges brought before it, not a council issuing orders and levying fines. In Cleveland, very little changed; even highly qualified black applicants found themselves "shunted away" from skilled heavy industry "by means of evasions, excuses, and at times through the use of deliberate lies." Chester's writing was increasingly fueled by the impotent rage he felt at the mountain of freshly created racial discrimination in the defense industry.

With his full citizenship restored, his temperature boiling, and Jean seriously pursuing work caretaking white children, Chester began to look elsewhere for opportunity. When Henry Moon popped up for a visit in February 1940, Chester drank down his conversation like a "tonic." Cleveland sapped his energy and he hadn't been able to write but Henry's tales of mingling with national leaders in Washington and celebrities in New York, shook off his gloom. His straitlaced cousin—now earning $3200 a year, and married to a woman who spoke German and had lived in Berlin—was a minor marvel. Well aware that his versatility as a writer might be the difference between success and burial in Cleveland, Chester closely modeled himself after his older cousin. He got a copy of Henry's 1938 article "Negroes Win Help in Fight for Jobs," and interviewed Future Outlook League president John O. Holly, hoping to submit a piece to Seltzer's *Cleveland Press*. Pondering the successful application of boycotts and pickets to change the employment picture for blacks in Harlem, he jotted down a few articles about the WPA for the CIO's newspaper, the *Union Leader*; Chester turned these into an examination of race and class in the arena of heavy industry. He also wrote the text of the *Future Outlook League Second Anniversary Yearbook*. By summer of 1940, Chester was putting his weight behind a combination of bold black nationalism and union organizing.

He had a minor success that spring with an encore in *Esquire* called "Marihuana and a Pistol," showing a jilted criminal planning a bank robbery to win back his girl but getting high and winding up butchering a confectionery store owner instead. The nugget of the story partly reflected on the episode that had propelled him to leave Estelle's house in Columbus. Chester was warning American audiences of the next stage in mood-altering substances after the legalization of alcohol. Perhaps concerned to demonstrate in print the pristine quality of his own citizenship, he brought the jazz musician's "tea" and "gage" into view as a social menace; the "jag" of inebriation would spur outlaws to violence. His story culminated in a bloody shooting sure to please *Esquire*'s readers. This winning story would result in the magazine's acceptance of an inferior mobster story, "Strictly Business," for more money, later that summer.

As the Nazi Army raced across the Low Countries and overran France, "Looking Down the Street: A Story of Import and Bitterness," appeared in *Crossroad*'s pages. It was another dirge about Cleveland Depression life without heat or food, where the protagonist urges on war to speed the end to a decade of grinding poverty. He now fully linked his work to the local scene. Mayor Harold Burton had ended food subsidies for thousands at the end of 1939 and the palpable signs of cruel deprivation lingered throughout the city, especially so in the black ghetto strip bounded by Fourteenth and 105th Streets along Cedar and Central Avenues, where 90 percent of Cleveland's 84,000 blacks lived in barely passable housing.

More intoxicating than anything that had happened to his writing career was an event in New York, the publication of a novel about a young man not quite dissimilar to Chester and written by someone whose early career arc had, up to then, so sharply resembled his own. The novel was *Native Son*, written by Richard Wright. Chester read it shortly after hearing his and Wright's mutual friend Langston Hughes appear at the end of April to speak at Cleveland's Lane Metropolitan Church about the sensational book. At the time, Chester was "attacking *Esquire* with wave after wave of manuscripts," hoping to regain his national reach. About the novel that would sell hundreds of thousands of copies as a Book-of-the-Month Club selection and change the commercial expectations of all black writers, Chester gasped, "*Native Son*—some book! It got me."

Native Son was so pungent that it demanded something new from Chester—a literary review—and in a new place, *New Masses*, the Communist cultural journal. There, he defended the book, which Wright, then a Communist Party member, was being chastised for on the far left for failing to show a successful solution to racism and poverty and, on the right, for his ingratitude. Wright's chief Communist detractor was silver-tongued, pedigreed Ben Davis, a Harvard-educated black lawyer whose father had edited an Atlanta newspaper. Although Davis was friends with Henry Moon, Chester would never feel at home with the pretentious banter, from conservative or ultra-liberal, of the black elites. In touch with the depth of his ugly life experience, Chester "felt called" to enter the national debate and "to express the feelings" that *Native Son* "inspired in me."

He sent in an essay too long to print. His opening sentence revealed a novelist's sense of what Wright was doing: "Bigger Thomas came alive to me when he stood on the street in front of the pool-room and got a sudden glimpse of life, feeling it push down inside of him through his shell of hard indifference which was his only defense against it."

For the rest of his life, Chester would admire Wright and his vision, at least partly because the characters from *Native Son* on— oppressed black young men cut off from their peers—put onto paper so many dimensions of his life before Chester had reached middle age. *Native Son* gave Chester back to himself as a man not simply flawed but also oppressed, as someone not merely capable of explosive violence as a partial response to segregation, but also one who could use it as a serious-minded act of rebellion for full inclusion. Wright had redeemed him. "When a person can see and feel the beauty and importance of the vast, eternal, changing mystery of life, and yearn to be part of it, no one can truthfully say that person is a bad nigger with all the degradation which the chauvinist term implies," he argued. As for the controversial parts of the book, the murders of a white girl and a black girl, they were "inexorable." While, with the exception of *Cast the First Stone*, Chester was too embarrassed to ever structure a novel around a criminal protagonist, he knew the terrain of Wright's creation—more so than any of the writers of the coming generation—and he reminded the leftist audience of the American citizens Wright called forth that had eluded their imagination.

By then Chester had achieved a kind of poor black man's literary celebrity in Cleveland. A Karamu-sponsored production, *Pre-vue Worlds Fair Concert*, on June 21 at the House of Wills on E. Fifty-Fifth Street, flattered him by including his work. Chester was indisposed and missed the event, but an elegant, voluptuous, and confident Jean Himes read one of her husband's short stories. When she finished she was "quite swept away by the reception."

At that time, a wily New York literary agent named Jacques Chambrun wrote to Chester offering his services. Chambrun had read the anthology *The Best Short Stories 1940*, edited by Edward O'Brien, and found Chester's "A Salute to the Passing" saluted with two asterisks—O'Brien's designation of the work as a distinguished short story. Chester's work hadn't been reprinted, an honor reserved for the likes of Hemingway and Katherine Anne Porter, but he was the only Negro whose work was honorably noted, and, sensing another *Native Son*, Chambrun looked him up. By the end of the month, Chester and Jean decided they would go east to D.C. and to New York, "what with Hitler looking westward." Who knew but that like Augusta and the cell blocks, it would all be in flames shortly?

Chester and Jean vacationed east during early July, as the Germans began their systematic bombing campaign of England, having already conquered France in six weeks. The Himeses went to New York first, where they roomed at the renowned Theresa Hotel, were squired about by Henry's wife, Mollie, and looked up Chester's long lost brother Eddie. Then they took the train to Washington, D.C., where they were entertained Midwestern style by Henry, with Carstairs beer and Vienna sausage canapés. In D.C. they drank toasts alongside Sterling Brown and housing advisor Robert Weaver. A professional social worker, Henry's wife, Mollie, struck Chester as a babbling, haughty parvenu, even if she was gentle with her husband. Chester began to note her personal traits, especially what she ate and her figure; he would remember her habits and mannerisms at best with sarcasm, at worst with outright contempt. The Himeses left on Tuesday, July 9 for home.

Back in Cleveland, some leftover grants allowed Chester to continue his FWP career on a subsidiary renamed the Ohio Writers' Project. He had been transferred after a series of promotions and demotions, which Chester now thought were explicitly racist. At this new project, he received his assignments from a "big fat mannish woman who wrote detective stories." She told him he had been sent to her to be quietly fired; instead she chose to route to him the tasks of the entire division, working him to the height of his capacity. Chester accepted the challenge and the legend of his work ethic was born. He would claim to have crafted "the entire history of Cleveland by myself," but that manuscript, a volume he identified as the "Cleveland Guide," has never been located.

Another project supervisor was Ted Robinson, an editor at the *Plain Dealer* newspaper. Chester wrote a seventy-eight-page book on *Recreational Opportunities in Cleveland* and was told that he might begin collecting material for a larger campaign fleshing out the history of the Negro in Cleveland—that is, if he could produce a list of two or three thousand subscribers. The *Ohio Guide*, which he most certainly worked on, was published in 1940. "I found the job of editing the whole thing wished on me," he carped to Henry, and by the fall it was "driving me nuts." The work was bringing him in contact with journalists and professors working at Cleveland College and Western Reserve and Chester took their measure. He came to accept the fact that, in spite of his lost years and mangled education, he could hold his own.

At the end of 1940, he would be kicked off the WPA, now not so much the victim of Congress as a technicality: he had exhausted his eighteen consecutive months on relief. With polished chapters from the prison manuscript, Chester approached Nathaniel Howard, the white editor of the *Cleveland News*, to write him a recommendation letter for an Alfred A. Knopf publishing fellowship, which Howard agreed to do. A tall, slender Oberlin graduate, Howard sported bow ties, served on the Karamu House capital campaign board, and played the blues piano in his spare time. A person who had covered the 1930 prison fire, Howard felt a connection to Chester and, eleven years his senior, offered valuable words of consolation. "Chester, you have paid the penalty for your crime against society," Howard told him, "now forget about it." A humble, friendly man who confessed his own errors, Howard engaged in discussions about race with Chester that must have made him pause at the knee-jerk racist stereotypes his hard-boiled white men, flesh of the flesh of Hemingway's Harry Morgan, had so consistently articulated. Howard kept the conversation open with Chester and brightened his outlook. They would discuss the work of William Faulkner, a novelist who was growing, it seemed, more aggressively liberal and complicated on the race issue, and Richard Wright's *Uncle Tom's Children* and *Native Son*. Chester considered Howard one of his "best friends" in Cleveland.

Impressed by Chester's ability and noting the difficulty for serious black writers, Howard offered Chester an arrangement where he could contribute regularly to the newspaper. The sprightly, local-color, 150-word vignettes of Cleveland's street corners would appear under the header "This Cleveland" in the back pages. Chester regarded the opportunity with pleasure and, since he perceived that whites on the staff would protest if his race were known, he agreed to sign the columns simply "C.H." Howard paid a dollar a try, and starting on November 6, 1940, fifteen of Chester's prose poems appeared through the end of that month. He began as an expressionist, detailing local sites—"The Mall, from Rockwell," and "Playhouse Square"—until one of the columns "drew blood." "E.55th–Central" exposed the cross-road of black Cleveland:

> People coming from the drug store at the corner, from the bar next door where the good fellows get together, from the church on the corner where they're having a revival meeting, from the undertaker's where they are having a tea, from the doctor's, the dentist's, the dice game up the alley, the pawnshops, barber shops, beauty shops, butcher shops. Black people. Brown people. Yellow people. Waiters. Porters. WPA laborers. Number writers. Racket boys in long, green, shiny cars. With long, tan, shiny shoes. Transients, looking for the place where the long green grows. Must be somewhere where the long green grows. This is a paradox. This poverty, squalor, and huge sums of cash. This is drunkenness, wantonness, and a struggle to see the light. But above all, this is a pure and simple faith in the white folks and the days.

The "boys down there blew their tops," he explained to Henry, referring to the crack he made of black people putting their "faith in the white folks." He also knew that references to "poverty, squalor" made few friends. But Chester had found something that he enjoyed, putting his thumb in the eye of prigs too squeamish to admit any moral dirtiness. He continued writing on class politics when he nosed around the old Central Market to record the abomination of steel mill sprawl. In "Shaker Square," a vignette on the upper-middle-class suburb, he levied a quieter accusation: "is there not a little of disappointment, of frustration, and hopes that have gone astray." But the legwork, haunting cold street corners for a couple of hours to get the atmosphere, seemed to keep him from the novel, so he quit writing these "prose poems."

Chester took a job with Weil Coffee and Tea Importers, biding his time and hoping for the Knopf fellowship, or a plum such as when *Mademoiselle* editor Marion Ives showed her pleasure at his work and almost took a story. Chester continued to labor on the prison manuscript that winter, "struggling to inject continuity" into his 200,000-word "sociological novel." But the glimmer of success—if his survival as a writer could be called that—was upon him. On December 14, his friends the Jellifes entertained a man who would be helpful in arranging Chester's future beyond Ohio: William Converse Haygood, director of the fellowship division of the Julius Rosenwald Fund.

The Rosenwald Fund was a large endowment left by Julius Rosenwald, one of the principal managers of Sears, Roebuck. Guided by Booker T. Washington, Rosenwald had started building schools and libraries in the South to improve conditions, but race prejudice was so thick that by the early 1930s the fund directors, led by President Edwin Embree, were extending individual grants to cultivate creative and intellectual talents. By the time the fund exhausted its principal in 1948, roughly fifteen hundred individual awards would be made. Chester, alongside virtually every talented black or white artist in his cohort with a curiosity about race in America, would receive one. William Haygood, an Atlantan who completed an advance degree in library science at the University of Chicago, doled out the money. "Grand" and "enthusiastic," Haygood encouraged the Jellifes to submit a few applications to advance Karamu House's work. There is good reason to believe that the Jellifes praised the local short story sensation Himes to Haygood. Excepting the well-known and intermittently present Langston Hughes (dividing his time between Los Angeles and Carmel by 1940), Chester Himes was the stand-out writer of the "Colored Belt"—the neighborhood around the Karamu House.

The Jellifes also introduced Chester to Louis Bromfield, Ohio's best-known popular writer. An early Pulitzer Prize winner, who had served in the ambulance corps during World War I alongside

Dos Passos and Hemingway, Bromfield was an imposing man who saw the world through a blend of arrogance and fulsome American pride. Sometimes the critics chided him as the "poor man's [Somerset] Maugham." Tall and vigorous, he had lived for more than a dozen years just north of Paris, returning to the United States in 1939 to live near the town of his birth, Mansfield, Ohio. Bromfield had a quality of vitality that was reflected by the energy he could command at the writing table: in thirty-four years as a working novelist he wrote thirty-seven books. But in 1939 he divided that energy in a variety of ways. First, he worked for Hollywood, where he commanded sums of $50,000 to $60,000 for the rights to his own books and where, for $5000 per week, he worked on the screenplay of Ernest Hemingway's *For Whom the Bell Tolls*. Accordingly, Bromfield was cozy with celebrities—Lauren Bacall and Humphrey Bogart would marry at his Ohio home in 1945. More demandingly, he had taken on a side career as not merely a gentleman farmer, but as an agricultural priest, a prophet of soil conservation and independent, government-regulation-free farming. He lived in a thirty-room house on a six-hundred-acre estate called Malabar Farm in Lucas, Ohio.

Chester admired a success, and Bromfield, then at work on a novel describing the occupation of New Orleans by federal troops during the Civil War, was nothing if not that. Booming and profane in conversation, he could turn on charm as if from a tap and humor people he imagined beneath him when it suited him. Bromfield, who had also lived in India, was tickled by the Negro ex-convict whose parents had graduated college and who had written a coming-of-age novel while in Ohio's grim prison. After a brief parley, Bromfield invited Chester to join the household at Malabar, ostensibly to revise his prison novel. In exchange, Chester would perform seasonal chores. Sensing opportunity and believing in Bromfield, Chester agreed to leave Cleveland for Malabar in the late spring of 1941. Deliriously excited about their good fortune, he and Jean crammed their apartment with credit-bought furniture, but, in a never-ending pattern of profligacy, in a few weeks the bounty of merchandise was repossessed.

In February the *Esquire* offshoot *Coronet* published his "Face in the Moonlight," a second-person account of the "queer nonsense" that occurs during prison isolation. The magazine still introduced him as an outlaw: "Chester B. Himes writes with authority about the locale of his story: he spent seven years behind grey walls for robbery." But the venue had reach and publishers like Doubleday and Dodd Mead started sending Chester query letters. Another prison story, "The Things You Do," lifted straight out of the novel manuscript, went to *Opportunity.* Chester was cutting and rewriting and trying to respond as best he was able during "one of those periods of frustration that undermines the confidence." The quandary was the problem of specialty: would he fit into the narrow groove of a prison writer or this new idea that was tugging at him, the black writer of social justice?

Reinventing his relationship to his mother would help him answer the question. In "The Things You Do" he sentimentally exposed the tortured encounters with Estelle on visiting days, emphasizing the way that the pain of his sentence had aged her. But at the same time he was acknowledging the grief and destruction he had caused, he observed that his mother's zealous righteousness was too crowded with white supremacist bigotry. In the winter of 1941, he worried that she might be moving from Columbus to Cleveland, something he didn't want. "I'd hate to see mother come up here for she hasn't changed any and she never will," he lamented to his cousin Henry. Estelle's paranoid rattling about slights and conspiracies "to harm her" seemed too strongly rooted in the isolation she imposed upon herself on account of her appearance. For years Chester had only censored her "mentally for her attitude," but he no longer could face her in close quarters and discard her influence. Chester was compassionate and loving and he had just acknowledged the real pain he knew himself to have caused his mother. But he also was recognizing the accumulated damage of racism and the manner that it warped the personalities of people like Estelle. If he allowed the warping to distort his artistic vision before publishing a major work, he might never become an independent artist.

Chester didn't recoil only against the possibility of conflict with his mother as he tried to hone his prison manuscript. He wanted space to consider unashamedly his prison experience, as well as the skewer of racial oppression that leaped out to him from Wright's new book. It was hard to do that while scraping by for work and relying on the charity of family, who were "half ashamed" that he wrote about prison, poverty, or being black at all. What he remembered of the moment before he went to Louis Bromfield's farm was "I had the story *Yesterday Will Make You Cry* and then let it get away by yielding to personal pressures and such." By leaving Cleveland, the city he had roared through as a wild teenager from a disintegrating family, and then submitted to as an adult, a married man putting felonious life behind, Chester would find himself.

Chapter Six

RUIN OF THE GOLDEN DREAM

1941–1944

C hester and Jean arrived at Louis Bromfield's Malabar Farm on June 5, 1941, and stayed the summer. At first Chester thought the pastoral retreat would refresh his writing. The squalor of Central Avenue, parsing through the intrigues of black labor organizing, and the timid caution of his relatives had been stifling. He put it in slang when he confided to Henry, "I had to give up Cleveland because the colored people there were jiving me." An unhurried summer at the idyllic "museum piece" estate of one of America's best-known writers seemed like the antidote.

Busy Malabar Farm was recognized by most of its visitors as an arcadia. The grounds contained the sprawling clapboard manor, known as the Big House, sustained by a thicket of outbuildings, including barns and a brick smokehouse, all sharing identical copper roofs. Bromfield's six-hundred-acre village in the Ohio foothills was of beauty scenic enough that when Chester laid eyes on it he fancied, "I would be content to remain here the rest of my life."

Bromfield employed a professional staff including Ray Smith, a uniformed black chauffeur from Cleveland, and Reba Williams, a black cook. Chester found the staff was fully needed because Malabar was more a hotel than a working farm. From April to New Year's Day, Malabar averaged twenty overnight visitors daily, with the kitchen serving guests three full meals. The arrangement, poorly conceived, was for Chester to serve as butler and Jean to help out in the kitchen. Jointly they were paid $120 a month, and they had Sunday afternoons and every other Thursday off. Chester would write, apparently, like Bromfield himself, in daily two-hour bursts of vitality between more callousing labors. Bromfield dashed off his sentences "until I'm numb," he liked to brag, "then I go out and plow." When he wasn't doing either, he exhorted his servants and guests to pitch in, and his young daughter Ellen fondly remembered the admonition delivered by the squire who had never known anything other than ample board. "Them that works, eats," he said, repeatedly, loudly, obnoxiously. Fights between spirited guests and Bromfield himself were known to break out on account of the demanding regimen, but Bromfield thrived off of the rippling currents in his household. He always had another intense spectacle on the rise. In July, Bromfield hosted a Malabar carnival, an extravaganza of flower shows, garden parties, dances, Monte Carlo games, and musical entertainment. Instead of serenity, Chester was up to his eyeballs in service.

Bromfield encouraged everyone, including his family, to call him "the Boss" and he expected hirelings to double up on chores. As butler, Chester worked close to the Boss and his live-in secretary, George Hawkins. After a fortnight, Chester found the job "exceedingly hard, the hours exceedingly long." He told Henry, "The main reason for coming down here was that I thought Bromfield might give me a lift." But the lift went down and not up. Chester was too exhausted to write anything. "All I get out of it is a lot of work from 7 A.M. to 8 P.M., which is too goddamned much." Beguiled at first by the authority he respected from his mother and which had been imposed on him by the state, Chester began swiftly to chafe against it.

Rewriting *Black Sheep*, the novel of a Mississippi white boy's experience in an Ohio prison, would have been onerous regardless of the burden of service work at Malabar. The editors at Doubleday got back to him with a report that flattered and floored him all at once. Chester wrote "extremely well and vividly" but the world he described—his no-holds-barred account of American prison life—was "perhaps too vivid." "Frankly," Doubleday's representative admitted, "we do not feel that we can sell a book as grim as this one." He couldn't understand the rejection as biased when Edward Dodd, from Dodd Mead, shared a similar written estimate. While Chester could "write so well I'd hate to let him go," and the book itself was "unusually powerful," the "morbid" and dyspeptic theme was "strong meat for public consumption." Touching on the abundant reference to degeneracy in prison life, one of the readers had suggested, "I should think he could soft pedal one element of it." With praise for his writing but no contract for the rough novel, he was facing adversity now that reminded him of censorship in prison. But by making all of the main characters white, he could at least imagine that the color barrier was not holding him down.

As for Bromfield and his wife, Mary, "despise" was the adjective that characterized Chester's emotions by the third week of toting and hefting. He determined to leave after the first payday, and he did little to hide his enmity toward Bromfield. However, according to Chester, his employer disliked being thought ill of by subordinates. Bromfield responded to Chester's sour mood by offering to take his *Black Sheep* manuscript to Hollywood film producers. In August Bromfield would make three trips from Ohio to Los Angeles to work on screenplays and negotiate contracts. Bromfield also promised his new butler that he would heartily recommend the prison manuscript on his October trip to New York, and get *Black Sheep* over the hump with cautious publishers. Urging Chester to go west, the Boss held out the tantalizing dream of big-time publication and Hollywood success.

The source of Bromfield's kindness had something to do with the

Jellifes in Cleveland, but probably even more with Bromfield's good friend Edna Ferber, the author of *Show Boat*. When that novel was adapted for Broadway, it had helped to make Paul Robeson famous with the hit song "Old Man River." To her credit, Ferber had helped educate the important black novelist Waters Turpin, the son of her maid. Bromfield would go Ferber one better by launching a man farther down, a black ex-con.

Chester and Jean began planning to relocate to Los Angeles, where he had been assured he could find work writing screenplays and serving as a consultant on Hollywood movies with prison themes. The studios had brought out three such films in 1940, *Castle on the Hudson, Millionaires in Prison*, and *Johnny Apollo*, and they were casting or planning *City Without Men, Prison Mutiny*, and *Escape from Crime* that fall.

Nevertheless, Chester regarded the friendly gesture as an example of liberal guilt. While he hoped to use Bromfield's leverage, Chester retained his contempt toward the man. Five years later, when he drafted the novel *Lonely Crusade*, Chester would depict Louis Bromfield as the fictional Louis Foster, the "tall, gangling man in plaid woolen shirt and old corduroy trousers," an industrialist and aircraft company executive, and the novel's fascist villain. That novel would be one of the best books probing the overlapping realms of race, class, and sexuality after the Second World War. Instead of cherishing Bromfield's liberalism—Bromfield had begun as a New Dealer, until the government started regulating farms—Chester would forever point to America's self-made aristocrats as haughty, spoiled bullies.

"There is no place like America," Foster said, and the emotion in his voice was genuine because the opportunity for betterment afforded by America was his special love. He was convinced that any American (except women, whom he did not consider men's equal; Negroes, whom he did not consider as men; Jews, whom he did not consider as Americans; and the foreign born, whom he did not consider at all), possessed of ingenuity, aggressiveness, and blessed with good fortune, could pull himself up by his bootstraps to become one of the most wealthy and influential men in the nation—even President. The fact that neither he nor his associates had been faced with this necessity had no bearing on his conviction. Like other fables of the American legend, the truth made little difference—as long as he believed, just as he now believed that there was no other place on earth where a Negro son of servant parents could achieve a college education. "No place like America," he repeated.

Not content merely to smear Bromfield and what he represented, Chester was capably examining his own complicity, which made both Bromfield's swagger and his own obsequiousness possible. With their authority so unequal, he admitted his own "compulsion to agree, flatter, serve the vanity of this great white man." As an obsequious man, he understood perfectly well that Jean would lose respect for him, a difference in sphere but not in kind from what he had witnessed in his own household as a child. At Malabar Farm, comparing himself with a cocksure white writer who had attained wealth beyond all that he and Jean hoped to achieve and who was in the process of accumulating more . . . well, that comparison was deeply unflattering.

Chester visited his father in Cleveland and consulted with him about the possible excursion west. He encouraged Joseph Sr. to tag along. Chester believed he might be on the verge of making it big, and his father had always supported his youngest son, even when he had not provided practical guidance. Joseph Sr. told him he would consider the relocation. At a going-away party their Cleveland relatives wished the couple well. Jean's folks presented them with a black horsehide suitcase, while Chester's Aunt Leah presumed he was headed for more flittering and foundering. "I hope that they will soon find themselves? They don't seem to know what they want to do" was her general observation about the couple. Chester then went down on his own to Columbus to see his mother and Joe Jr. When Jean met him there, about the first week of October, they boarded a Greyhound bus for Los Angeles.

Chester and Jean arrived in a West Coast metropolis that was a migrant's beacon but becoming increasingly like the American South. Exodusters from Oklahoma and Arkansas flooded California at the end of the 1930s, fleeing the Depression and drought that ravaged their farms. Barely 63,000 of L.A.'s 1.5 million people were black in 1941, but by 1944 that figure would jump to 118,000. Chester viewed goodly portions of the 448-square-mile city as "a drab panorama of one-storied, stuccoed buildings unfolded in monotonous repetition." With "no place for Negroes to live" in Hollywood or Beverly Hills, where there was domestic work, he and Jean had to find lodging in a corridor that Langston Hughes called the "remote districts," an area south of downtown, in the central part of the city.

In a show of extravagance, the Himeses booked rooms at the posh Erskine Apartments at 1464 Central Avenue, close to the Twelfth Street streetcar line and the bustling crossroads of black Los Angeles, fondly called "the Harlem of the West." Central Avenue, nicknamed the "Great Black Way," was the mighty river for Southern California's African American community, connecting downtown to the southern suburb of Watts. At Forty-First Street and Central lay the key strip with bars, lounges, jazz clubs, and nightclubs, like the Club Alabam, the Downbeat Club, and the cocktail lounge at the Dunbar Hotel (the first luxury hotel for African Americans), while the Lincoln Theater at Twenty-Third Street and the Plantation Club farther up Central rounded out the nightlife. The high-paying aircraft and shipbuilding industries were an automobile ride away at the docks of San Pedro near Long Beach. African American film celebrities and jazz musicians flocked to Los Angeles, some working on big-budget productions like *The Green Pastures* (1936). Celluloid minstrel Eddie "Rochester" Anderson had a house with a fabulous swimming pool and garage at Thirty-Sixth Street and Western Boulevard, so dubbed "Rochester Lane." If perhaps the main draw was yet the opulence of the Hollywood film industry, all of L.A.'s parts helped to sustain an atmosphere of carefree stylishness along the palm-tree-lined streets.

Sunny Los Angeles had elements of a dreamworld in the early fall of 1941 for the young Midwesterners, used to the sooty pall of an industrial city frozen for half of the year. But 1941 L.A. was not progressive. Even after the Second World War, crowds would balk at interracial bands, like the combo led by Dizzy Gillespie and Charlie Parker, and not merely on account of racism, but inadequate cultural antennae. "California," remembered Gillespie's drummer Stan Levey, "was in those days ten or fifteen years behind the times." Gillespie himself put a more pointed racial marker on the people in Los Angeles: "Man, it's a whole lotta 'Toms' and musical nothings and all that." In even more stark terms, a specific meanness kept Chester and Jean alert. If Jean walked down Central or Vernon Avenue alone, "ten, fifteen, or twenty" cars would sidle up to the curb, driven by white men, soliciting.

Bromfield had topped off their pay with a $100 bonus, so the Himeses had a small stake of perhaps $300. They needed to find work—and success—immediately. Chester quickly secured a job with the California Sanitary Canning Company, who hired him as a labeling machine helper. If it was unskilled labor, at least it wasn't pushing a broom or swinging a mop. Buoyed up by the employment and getting used to clutching Jean by the arm as they traveled, Chester softened his opinion on L.A. a bit, writing to Langston Hughes in mid-October that he and Jean liked "the city a little better than we did at first." But the favorable impression was fleeting. After a short time Chester quit the job, claiming racial discrimination, and he did so with enough public theater to be remembered by the foreman. The unfair labor conditions forced Chester to conclude that "black people were treated much the same as [in] an industrial city in the South." Yet, L.A.'s whites seemed to want blacks to understand that they were receiving deluxe treatment for which they should be conspicuously pleased.

Generous and gracious, Langston Hughes sent Chester a full roster of contacts, directing him to the black literati of Los Angeles, especially those on the left: his comrade the civil rights attorney Loren Miller, the bright youngsters Welford Wilson and John Kinloch, policeman Jess Kimbrough, and his old friend and sometime nemesis, novelist and folklorist Zora Neale Hurston. A week later, when Hughes was asked to preside over a League of American Writers dinner for L.A.'s black scribblers, he put Chester's name first on his list of invitees for the early November event. A supportive Hughes then approached Blanche Knopf in New York directly about publishing Chester's prison novel. Chester took the lists of introduction and tried to wend his way into professional circles.

Some of the people were inaccessible. The recent winner of the Anisfield Wolf Prize for race relations, the well-known Hurston had secluded herself to work on a novel and on an opera with composer William Grant Still. But Chester received a hearty response from Welford Wilson. An orator and former track star at City College in New York who had been a leader in opposing Jim Crow at athletic events in the mid-1930s, Wilson worked for the U.S. Employment Agency and was also a budding novelist. Wilson had known Hughes since the end of the 1920s, and Hughes recommended him for the Communist-backed League of American Writers School in Los Angeles. Energetic, bright, and invested in radical politics, Wilson too was newly arrived to Los Angeles. Heavily involved in Communist Party organizing, he tried to recruit Chester. "I was given the works," Chester remembered, recalling their attendance at cell meetings, social affairs, lectures, dinner parties, and interviews in the fall of 1940.

Chester went with Wilson as he spoke or hobnobbed with ambitious young California blacks like the Reverend Clayton Russell, the young minister of the three-thousand-strong congregation of the Independent Church of Christ. Flamboyant and nervy, Russell had just returned from a trip to Europe and had visited several of the capitals prior to their fall to the Nazis. Chester also met two Los Angeles black veterans of the Abraham Lincoln Brigade, Edward Carter and Eluard McDaniel, who had fought heroically in Spain. On account of his contacts and devoted politics, Wilson had "a great influence" over Chester in those early months in L.A.

In the course of his meanderings, Chester was introduced to Dalton Trumbo and John Howard Lawson, Hollywood's leading Communist screenwriters; more than a quarter of the screenwriters were thought to belong to the Party in the early 1940s. Trumbo especially had the career that Chester wanted. He had published the novel *Johnny Got His Gun* and then been hired by Warner Bros. for sixty dollars a week and raced up the writing ladder with speed. In spite of his wealth and success, Trumbo was a principled antiracist. When FBI agents visited him, under the pretense of examining pro-fascist mail he received, but grilling him more closely for his leftist politics, he pivoted back, "Are you anti-Semitic? anti-Catholic? anti-Negro?"

Lawson was the dean of the Communist writers. It was said that at Lawson's parties he invited guests into his elegant, spacious home and proclaimed, "Welcome to the Communist Party." Lawson was a mover and shaker in the California chapter of the League of American Writers, fundamentally an offshoot of the Party's John Reed Clubs from the early 1930s, but still functioning as a broad organization that bonded creative artists, leftists, New Dealers, and antifascists of all stripes. Both Lawson and Trumbo were known for helping novice writers, especially by critiquing their work. Chester never fully thawed the big shots like Trumbo and Lawson, who invited him in for a drink, but always informally, in the kitchen.

Chester was more at home among the local black left-wing intelligentsia, a group that included *California Eagle* publisher Charlotta Bass and her nephew and managing editor John Kinloch, a member of the Screen Writers Guild who was hoping to develop an African American film production company, and a member of Clayton Russell's church. At the center of the circle was Loren Miller, Hughes's good friend who had gone on the ill-fated film trip to Russia in 1932 with Henry Moon. A biracial self-described cynic, Miller was then hard at work on developing a legal means to defy restrictive real estate covenants and thinking of running for Congress. He would go on to write most of the NAACP brief for perhaps the most consequential Supreme Court case of the twentieth century, *Brown v. Board of Education*. Unconcerned to be among those openly connected to Communist organizations and journals, Miller sat on the fence between Communist proselytizer and comfortable bourgeois attorney. By the early 1940s, Henry Lee Moon was finding Miller using the word "duplicity" to discuss the Party and its relationship with black Americans, but at very least Miller was a strong believer in Marxist principles. He was also a literary man, who had joined the League of American Writers in 1939, wrote literary and cultural criticism, and offered analyses of the creative work of his friends, like the white screenwriter John Bright. He advocated the study of black literature as a part of the whole American culture, hoping to evaluate black writing "realistically" and in the context of its "social history." Probably what Chester enjoyed about him best was his tendency to satirize mercilessly and use his wit to "burn holes in the toughest skin." In Miller's company, Chester met men like Clarence Johnson, the national field representative for Negro employment and training for the War Production Board. Miller and Johnson steeped Chester in a dense factual overview about the state of black migration, race relations, the legal structure, and the possibilities for organized labor to wear down corporate managers.

For a short time Chester's best friend from prison, Prince Rico, regularly visited the couple. Rico had always admired him, and Chester had continued to build on the literary promise that set him apart in prison. About the intimate connection that the two men had forged, Chester later wrote, "I don't know when it got over, but when it got over, it was completely over." In the career that Chester was embarking upon, he would refer to homosexuality from time to time, most explicitly in his prison manuscript, sometimes scornfully to belittle a fiction character, and sometimes playfully, as evidence of an exotic desire. At nearly the end of his writing career, in the novel *Blind Man with a Pistol*, he wrote about homosexuality as an ordinary part of human life. But in terms of his sexual preference, Chester seems to have ended his same-sex desire in prison.

A small olive branch from the slick magazines came when Chester met *Collier's* editor Kenneth Littauer, who was visiting Beverly Hills and who encouraged him to keep sending fiction treatments to the magazine. Littauer assured Chester of the popularity and value of his *Esquire* stories. The pep talk was followed by a chat with Meyer Levin, his old *Esquire* editor, who was then working at Columbia Pictures, and Chester felt more optimistic about his chances to work on scripts. Levin mentioned Zora Neale Hurston's being retained by Paramount as an expert on Haiti; surely Himes could do the same, maybe for Columbia's *City Without Men*. During this time an agent for Warner Bros. read over Chester's prison manuscript, probably considering whether to use him as an advisor for director Ross Lederman's *Escape from Crime*. But Chester "got to feeling funny about it"—perhaps he thought he would be ripped off—and he raced over to the studio asking for the return of his material. Then *Esquire* sent what seemed an acceptance letter followed by a crisp rejection from Gingrich personally the next week. With nothing to eat but smiles and promises, it seemed as if Chester had been foolish to venture to Los Angeles even while gleaming success seemed to be at hand if he pushed hard enough. The ambivalence left him feeling "jittery."

Shortly after *Esquire*'s reneging on the story, he confessed that "things are getting a little pressing." The familiar wretchedness he had known in Cleveland had returned. Straitened circumstances had Chester and Jean camped out at Welford Wilson's small one-story bungalow on Crocker Street. Wilson's wife, Juanita, had recently arrived from New York and the Party helped him secure a bigger place. Chester made up his mind to forsake Los Angeles and search for work, but he wasn't sure where to go. Then on Sunday, December 7, Japanese naval aircraft attacked the U.S. Seventh Fleet based in Pearl Harbor, in the American territory of Hawaii. The next day Franklin Roosevelt addressed Congress, which then passed a declaration of war. Instantly there was a palpable escalation in racial tension in Los Angeles. "This town is getting too hot for me," Chester thought, and he headed for San Francisco, where he found a job in the Henry J. Kaiser No. 1 Shipyard in Richmond, just north of Oakland. He apprenticed as a shipfitter trainee, preparing the ten-day-wonders of resupply, the so-called Liberty ships. But the labor situation was exactly the same as in Los Angeles.

While he tried to use a blowtorch and a rivet for Allied victory against Japan and Germany, Chester heard the news of the gruesome January 25, 1942, lynching of a man named Cleo Wright in Missouri. *Pittsburgh Courier* columnist Arthur Huff Fausett welcomed the outpouring of letters and telegrams from disgusted black Americans, who now fashioned lapel emblems making a double V, to signify victory against fascism abroad and lynchers and racists at home. Referring to lapel emblems, Fausett wrote, "I think the suggestion that Negroes should wear a Double V for Double Victory, is a brilliant one." The slogan became the nationwide trademark of nearly two million readers of the black press. The motto was taken so seriously by some black servicemen that they burned the logo onto their skin.

The northern California hiatus ended when Hall Johnson, the renowned black arranger and composer whose choirs had integrated Hollywood sound tracks and film scores, sent Chester an urgent message about possible publicity work at M-G-M. The cast for the film version of *Cabin in the Sky* was set and Johnson, a technical director for the production, believed that additional blacks were to be hired on the other side of the camera. Scholarly and gentle, Johnson had gotten his start as a violinist in the orchestra of the Broadway musical *Shuffle Along*. He then arranged Georgia slave songs for a trained choir and brought it successfully to the stage in Marc Connelly's *Green Pastures*. In 1935 he introduced the choir to California, where the choir debuted in the film version of the musical; it subsequently appeared in dozens of Hollywood films.

Chester returned to L.A. in the spring of 1942, but the job was put on hold. Closer than before to Hollywood stars, he pitched a Lena Horne profile to *Collier's*. The magazine took him seriously but decided the piece was too big for an amateur and assigned it to a regular feature writer.

Nosing around the studios, Chester talked to Johnson about screen treatments and met several talented entertainers. He hit it off with Charles Holland, who sang in the choir. A tenor with a voice like Roland Hayes, Holland had wowed radio audiences and gone on to win a role in the 1940 M-G-M feature *Hullabaloo*. Classically trained and hoping for opera auditions, Holland resented the prohibitions restricting his talent in the same manner as Chester had sounded off against the Federal Writers Project in Cleveland. The two men would remain lifelong friends.

While they did not go so far as to hire black writers, Hollywood studios did get pressure to build black morale from the federal government's Office of War Information, and in the persons of NAACP

Secretary Walter White and his friend Wendell Willkie, the 1940 Republican Party presidential nominee. At a luncheon hosted by producer Darryl F. Zanuck at Twentieth Century–Fox, White told those gathered that the "restriction of Negroes to roles with rolling eyes . . . [and] none too bright servants . . . perpetuates a stereotype which is doing the Negro infinite harm." Simply put, the Hollywood film's "mentally inferior" stereotypes, which made wealthy actors of Stepin Fetchit (né Lincoln Perry) and Eddie "Rochester" Anderson, were key "reasons for the denial to the Negro of opportunity."

Chester remained to the left of the NAACP. To help his chances in films, he joined a group called Hollywood Writers Mobilization, whose members included the screenwriting crowd who were among some of the most committed leftists, and also got a scholarship to the League of American Writers School. News bulletins like *Communiqué*, created by rank-and-file members of the Screen Writers Guild like Ring Lardner Jr., attempted to change the attitudes of the industry from within. Lardner exposed the long-standing complicity of the screenwriters in perpetuating stereotypes. "We've been discriminating as surely as, and probably more effectively than any Klu-Kluxer [sic]." For his stands against discrimination—used as evidence to prove his Communist ties—Lardner Jr. would eventually be blacklisted and shut out of Hollywood.

However, in Tinseltown some black actors feared that if screenplays eliminated minstrel roles and featured light-complexioned beauties like Lena Horne, dark-skinned performers would vanish from the screen altogether. Hattie McDaniel, Warners' contract black star, seemed to both curry favor with the executives and preserve her livelihood when she told the press in August, "I don't believe we will gain by rushing or attempting to force studios to do anything they are not readily inclined to do."

So the barriers remained on both sides of the camera. Chester went to Warner Bros. and met the head of the reading department.

He was asked to write the synopsis for *The Magic Bow*, a well-known book about the Italian violinist Niccolò Paganini, entry-level work. On the basis of his written report, a low-level studio factotum offered him a job. But within days he was perplexed; the bias at the studios was no different from that of the aircraft unions. Studio head Jack Warner barked to Chester's supervisor, "I don't want no niggers on this lot."

Waylaid by the attitudes of studio executives, Chester hoped for help from Hall Johnson. He learned that M-G-M would hire an African American to cover publicity for *Cabin in the Sky*, to tap into the segregated American media networks. He hustled over to the studio only to find that Phil Carter, a young black from New York, had already landed the job. Then Chester noted that Carter's office was not really in the studio publicity department; he had been secreted at the very end of a corridor of abandoned dressing rooms. Meanwhile, the *Chicago Defender* heralded the appointment in an article called "Phil Carter, Harlem Scribe, in Film Job," noting that Carter "has his own office." Chester was disgusted and amused. He enjoyed the point of view of Leon Washington, the maverick publisher of the local *Los Angeles Sentinel*, who believed that *Cabin in the Sky* was "degrading" and also a cattle call "so that the employed Negroes would use pressure to hush up the militant Negroes."

Disgruntled by race prejudice in the war services industries, from Los Angeles to San Francisco, rejected by the studios for work he was qualified to do, and having to eke out a living in an expensive city where he needed a car, Chester fell into the steady orbit of the Communist Party in 1942. He hoped to work as a screenwriter or expert consultant for Hollywood, but it was mainly through the informal Communist Party networks that he rubbed shoulders in Hollywood at all. In none of Chester's writings in 1942 and 1943 did he dramatize an attempt to integrate the studios. Instead, he focused on what he knew best, and what he presumed his friends wanted and needed to read:

stories about blacks and whites working together on the political left to overcome segregation and desegregate the war services industries.

Los Angeles was also racially redrawing itself. By mid-February President Roosevelt signed an executive order to create exclusion zones that effectively allowed for the removal of anyone of Japanese ancestry from the Pacific Coast. The next month, in Los Angeles, Japanese citizens were removed to a way station at the Santa Anita racetrack. By May 8, the *Los Angeles Times* estimated that only 4000 Japanese remained in the city, down from a prewar population of 50,000. Little Tokyo, which began at the downtown dock of Central Avenue extending toward the Los Angeles River and had housed 30,000 Japanese Americans, became Bronzeville, which soon spilled over with 80,000 blacks. In Boyle Heights and City Terrace, the neighborhoods due east of Little Tokyo, For Rent signs sprouted.

Understanding the linked fates between the nonwhite Americans—Japanese and blacks—Chester noted with dismay the families herded onto busses and trucks for the internment camps. Some of his literary comrades were among the victims. Probably when the fledgling writer Mary Oyama Mittwer and her husband, Frederick, and their son, Rickey, were sent off on "unforgettable" May 9, Chester and Jean took over their prize bungalow at 120 E. Second Street for a portion of 1942. But in 1942, the Himeses also rented a house in City Terrace on North De Garmo Drive, overlooking downtown L.A. With a yard to grow carrots, beans, cabbage, and beets, the house was a symbol of true prosperity. Their neighbors were white and Latino, and for a while Chester scratched along with a forklift job at a warehouse for $22.50 a week. At first, Jean did only a little better earning $24 per week working the four-to-midnight shift at a defense plant, and resigning herself to a four-hour daily commute.

Chester abandoned the forklift job to devote himself more fully to writing fiction cognizant of the problems of organizing the black laborer. In the spring of 1942, Chester had gotten to know a similarly committed writer, also on Langston Hughes's list, an old-time, rock-hard black police officer named Jess Kimbrough. Chester was always ready to talk crime, and the playful "Strictly Business," his Cleveland syndicate hit man story, had appeared in *Esquire* that February. Originally from Texas, the forty-nine-year-old Kimbrough had joined the department in the early 1920s and reached the rank of detective lieutenant at the Newtown Station. He was precisely the kind of police officer that Chester was lucky not to have encountered during his youthful sprees of lawlessness. Like his partner Charles Broady (who retired that spring after a battle that left another officer dead), Kimbrough had excelled on the basis of his unforgiving manner toward suspected black criminals; other black officers on the force were notorious for shooting and killing unarmed black teens. The lethal antics of these policemen lodged in the recesses of Chester's imagination, and he learned enough about their reputations to call them "pitiless bastards."

Surprising to some, Kimbrough was a member of the Communist Party. He wrote short stories for the International Writers Union magazine *International Literature*. When he met Chester, Kimbrough had just published a play called *Georgia Sundown*, about a militant black World War I veteran who gives his life to defeat white supremacy. Philosophical about the contradiction between his work as a lawman defending white property and people and his pro-black socialist convictions, Kimbrough puzzled to no end "how I managed to carry out a sworn duty and preserve my dreams." Chester marveled at the balancing act as well, finding Kimbrough a "much better writer" than those accepted by Sterling Brown's new anthology *Negro Caravan*, which reprinted his own story "The Night's for Crying."

Chester was concerned that the prison manuscript and indeed his own criminal past were sinking him. Louis Bromfield had dropped out of contact, and Chester wrote to Sterling Brown requesting that any reference to his prison record be removed from his author biography for *Negro Caravan*. His new agent in New York, Lurton Blassingame, a forty-two-year-old from Alabama who liked pulp fiction and had success by selling a novel called *Chicken Every Sunday,* was proving unable to help him crack the literary market. But Blassingame had little to work with. Given the difficulty of finding a suitable place to work and live, Chester had not produced anything as complex and layered as the early prison short stories "To What Red Hell," "Prison Mass," and "Crazy in Stir." Even the racial-uplift journals *Opportunity* and *The Crisis,* which paid only a nominal fee for fiction and had limited audience reach, had said they were unable to use his material. "I have just about come to the conclusion that my destiny lies in hard work building up to one final everlasting explosion," he admitted with exasperation.

No direction he turned to seemed fully satisfying. If the Communist Party opened for him a door of interracial collegiality and radical ideas, there was also the mechanistic bureaucracy connected to the organization's national position, what was known as the "Party line." Weeks before Germany had invaded Poland, the Soviets signed a pact with the Nazis. Earl Browder, the American Communist Party's head, accordingly pressed for nonintervention in the war by the United States. That policy had plenty of benefits for black Americans, particularly loud advocacy of civil rights and antisegregation maneuvers. But after the Nazi invasion of the USSR in June 1941, the line shifted, and the Party's black arguments decreased in volume, to the extreme point of countenancing segregated blood banks.

The fifteen hundred or so members of the Los Angeles chapter were led by an African American named Pettis Perry, a spectacled, scholarly man who reminded Chester of his cousin Henry Moon. With an organizational structure duplicating the electoral political divisions, the Los Angeles Communist Party grouped most black Angelenos into the Fourteenth Congressional District; the district "organizer" or head was another African American, Lou Rosser.

Nationally, Communist activity was dominated by what culminated in a meeting in Tehran among Stalin, Churchill, and Roosevelt in December 1943: the "Tehran line," with its antistrike pledges, was designed to keep war industries open.

Locally, however, the Los Angeles Communist Party had a dynamic policy shaped by activists like Dorothy Healey, who pushed the chapter's attention toward issues like Loren Miller's fight against the real estate covenants that kept blacks from living in white areas, police brutality, and the NAACP's work against Hollywood stereotypes. Chester himself burned shoe leather to test racist hiring practices, by systematically answering in person news advertisements for positions for which he was qualified—that is, until the employers saw his face. That experience proved to him once and for all that L.A. was "as Jim-Crowed as Atlanta, Georgia." For him, the new allies and new foes produced feelings difficult to contain and channel. He found the "mental corrosion of race prejudice" was leaving him "bitter and saturated with hate," an inner roiling that worked its way into his fiction.

He befriended thirty-year-old Eluard McDaniel, who had published in *Story* magazine, and visited Hollywood on clothing drives for the Spanish refugees and on employment campaigns testing segregation laws. The jaunts on behalf of the refugees netted the men opulent cast-off wardrobes from Hollywood directors and producers. Dark-skinned, proud, and revered among the veterans from the Abraham Lincoln Brigade for his ability to pitch grenades, McDaniel was a colorful man who had left Mississippi at ten and traveled the nation, arriving at San Francisco at eighteen. There, he attracted the attention of an innovative photographer twice his age, Consuela Kanaga, a white woman who enjoyed erotic photographic play by manipulating skin color and light. She helped McDaniel gain an education and in her company he entered circles of radical politics and high art. Chester would immortalize him as Luther Macgregor in the novel *Lonely Crusade*.

After a late summer political rally, featuring Charlotta Bass and members of the Indian National Congress, Chester wrote for the West Coast Communist newspaper the *People's Daily World*. In wooden-sounding prose, Chester connected support for Indian nationalists like Jawaharlal Nehru to the Party goal of opening up a second military front. While the latter was a key plank of the Soviet agenda of 1942, the former, immediate decolonization, was not. Chester was feeling his way and he felt compelled to reveal his own irrevocable proletariat standing—an utterly dispossessed industrial worker and an ex-convict. And yet, in his moment of peak fellow traveling, as unofficial Communist membership was then called in America, he wouldn't choose class over race, writing that "regardless of the capitalist politics to split the unity of the people," India deserved its independence from Britain. Chester was a double V internationalist.

Within a few weeks, he had worked through his position on the domestic colonial front. In a call to arms in *Opportunity* entitled "Now Is the Time! Here Is the Place!," he recommended a dynamic plan: victory for the so-called United Nations (a collective term then used by progressives that included Africa, Asia, and Latin America in the fight against fascism) required black victory over segregation at home. He wrote, "Now, in the year 1942, is the time, here, in the United States of America, is the place for 13,000,000 Negro Americans to make their fight for freedom . . . to engage and overcome our most persistent enemies: Our native American fascists." The turning point of the Second World War, the Nazi defeat at Stalingrad, was in the distance. At the moment when German Panzers were within a hundred miles of taking the Soviet capital of Moscow, Chester didn't want to be labeled strategically naïve. But for Chester, without a home front victory, the future could hold only a major or minor version of Nazism.

He began his article with an apology to his past: "the character of this writer is vulnerable, open to attack, easy to be smeared." In the Urban League's house journal, Chester explored, using euphemisms for the word "Communist," the Party's backpedaling on black rights, as well as the credulity gap between what committed socialists argued was realistically necessary to defeat the Nazis and what was idealistically necessary in the future to implement socialism in the United States. He described this two-step dance as the "fight to preserve and make strong a form of government which will never serve the purpose for which one fights, and as a consequence, after the victory for its continuance is attained, must be overthrown and replaced by another form of government." Chester suggested such a doctrine was incomprehensible.

After the article came out, Chester would begin to trust his own vision, shorn of bourgeois propriety and Party politics. His best short story in several years went also to *Opportunity*, where, in a sense, he was remaking his name. Increasingly he wanted to find the backbone of white liberal motive. "In the Night" dramatized an interracial Communist cell in Los Angeles, where the black worker Sonny Wilson faces the unwavering force of racial discrimination in the aircraft industry, a shut door that threatens his capacity to have congenial relationships with whites at all. Although Sonny studied for several months and passed the necessary examination, he can't earn a skilled position. (At Lockheed's Los Angeles plant, the International Association of Machinists included in their induction ritual a decree to pledge only "qualified white mechanics.") Sonny's white Communist comrades have to understand the motivation that got them beyond bigotry and into a radical movement. Chester's fiction explained that unconscious libidinal desire prodded the whites to join. A white Communist named Carol needs to fulfill maternal drives: "she would mother the entire Negro race; or, if not that, give birth from her own deep love to an entire new social order." A man named Andy has a "queer sympathy for the underdog, sensual in its development." What all of the young Communists lack is toughness, the quality that might elevate their convictions beyond a self-serving affection for the downtrodden to the will to transform a nation.

The principal voice in Chester's short story belonged to Cal, a black Communist who distinguishes himself generationally from twenty-year-old Sonny with a curious atavistic quality. He tells his comrades that when push comes to shove, his skill as an old-time Negro will rescue him: "I can revert. I can go raggedy . . . somebody will have to take care of me. I can walk down the street and whistle. I can stop in front of a joint where the juke box's playing and cut a step of off-time boogie and listen to the white folks say, 'Look at that nigger dance.'" Sonny, who silently observes the discussion, is the modern black citizen, incapable of Uncle Tomming. Himes ends the story by implying that without this younger, more virtuous, tougher man, "the revolution had never seemed so far away."

As evidence of his own distance from "revolution," Chester exclusively published in the NAACP's *Crisis* in 1943, even if the journal was an excellent place to counter stereotypes and caricatures. Founded by W. E. B. Du Bois in 1910, the magazine was edited by Roy Wilkins. Sterling Brown sat on the advisory board. *The Crisis* kept Chester's name and salty approach to life before Henry and Mollie Moon's set of liberal reformers, a connection that would soon pay dividends. Humorous and slightly farcical, Chester's "Lunching at the Ritzmore" joked about the scientific reluctance to concede to the reality of racial discrimination, which could be overcome by a combined mass movement.

"Two Soldiers," a short story of a black martyr whose heroism reforms the abject racism of a southern white soldier, was published in January 1943. Two months later, Chester published a folk allegory of the generational conflict called "Heaven Has Changed." Instead of heaven as a place where race strife and hard labor have ended, Jim Crow reigns unabated. The short story seemed shaped by conversations Chester had had with his father, who was more

Theodore than Franklin Roosevelt, stoutly religious, pro-business, pro–Booker T. Washington, and reluctant to protest publicly against racial discrimination. Chester reflected on the problems of material and aesthetic differences between the generations, from the picket protest against the "little God" Jim Crow to the fight between enthusiasts of spirituals and the children of hot jazz. "Led by Uncle Tom's son, they threw down their sacks and rebelled and organized a procession and marched toward the big manor house where the Big God lived." Although the resolution of the story was indecisive, his ear to reproduce speech, tell a joke, and identify black divisiveness had grown sharper.

Chester worked hard at home in 1943, and Jean alone seems to have carried the financial load. In fact, they were on completely different employment trajectories. Loren Miller's wife, Juanita, was a consulting supervisor for the city housing authority and through her influence Jean soon secured a white-collar job as a civilian war aide and community services director at a large, racially integrated housing project at Pueblo del Rio. On Jean's initiative the community center strengthened its curriculum with a ceramics class, taught by a University of Southern California professor, that attracted the attention of the press and the Los Angeles Museum of Fine Arts. While Jean had always excelled in the role as Chester's adoring fan, as a professional making decisions in the workplace, she reached a milestone in development unconnected to him. In some portions of their lives together, she had represented herself as helpless and devoted, which inspired Chester's masculinity. But when she began to trump his prestige regularly in the nine-to-five world, insecurity began to gnaw at him. Chester was irked because Jean was "respected and included" by her white coworkers, and now clubby with "well-to-do blacks of the Los Angeles middle class who wouldn't touch me with a ten foot pole." Chester almost certainly meant finely mannered Juanita Miller, a slender, light-skinned USC graduate, with an advanced degree in social work, and a charter member of the USC Delta Sigma Theta chapter.

Simmering on the inside about his marriage, Chester was even edgier as he noticed the neighbors around him. From their De Garmo Drive retreat, Chester observed a new phenomenon—whites living down the hill looking up at him with what he took to be envy. Like other disgruntled black Americans, especially in the cities, a part of him savored every Japanese victory and the sight of humiliated, frightened white people. Chester put aside his prison manuscript and started thinking about a new short story, something that showed white fear.

The tension within the city that spring—as eager black and white Southern migrants poured into defense industries, and the Japanese military was keeping the U.S. Navy at bay in the Pacific—created new problems for the artist. First, on May 19, Los Angeles's stolid, unimaginative Mayor Fletcher Bowron addressed the city over the radio and kindled racist hysteria. "When the war is over," he told Southern Californians, "some legal method may be worked out to deprive the native-born Japanese of citizenship." He continued even more worrisomely, "The Japanese can never be assimilated. . . . They are a race apart."

Animosity to other ethnic groups was cresting as well. During the first week of June 1943, initially dozens, then hundreds, and ultimately thousands of uniformed white servicemen descended on L.A.'s Mexican and black neighborhoods, stripping and beating so-called zoot suiters and anyone else who got in their way. The sailors—members of the U.S. military branch that still proudly prohibited blacks from any other job than servant—marched on Central Avenue for a week, pulling men and boys out of theaters and restaurants, thrashing and terrifying them. Not only did the Los Angeles police refuse to intervene, they were observed using nightsticks on disabled Latino men and on Latina women carrying infants in their arms. The conflagration, at a hot spot at Twelfth and Central, seemed eerily similar to the race war promised by the Nazis. Surprisingly no one was reported raped or killed.

In an article for *The Crisis,* Chester, an "eye-witness of the recent riots in Los Angeles," schooled the NAACP's audience on the West Coast violence, which was framed by the mainstream media as juvenile delinquency suitably corrected. Less compromising than before, he defined the brutality as a home-grown Kristallnacht, characterized by "the birth of the storm troopers." Down the hill from Chester's home in City Terrace was the Belvedere neighborhood; after getting off the "P" streetcar there, Chester often waited at Rowan Street to catch a cab for a quarter ride up the hill. The cabstand had become a flashpoint for the attacks. Chester believed that the police, corralled briefly after the Sleepy Lagoon case, a recent murder investigation in which they were found to have coerced confessions from young Chicanos, wanted badly to harm the Latinos, but instead "got the sailors to do it for them." While the rioting flared, Chester sat on his steps with a Winchester rifle, looking down into Belvedere, waiting to see if his white neighbors below would make good on their threats.

But his rifle always deferred to his typewriter. Charlotta Bass's *California Eagle* caught up to him, proud of Chester's legendary absorption, his unwillingness to allow "aimless bridge games, barstools and telephone sessions" to derail the solitary task of writing. More and more now, he gave his mind over to the possibility of the ugliest racial violence breaking out. He eased his fears by toying with an idea for a story that amused him, "the compulsion making a Negro kill white people, most of whom he didn't know and had never seen, simply because they were white." There were few writers or intellectuals he knew to whom he could describe such a plot. To his NAACP friends, he said he was working on a novel about the growth of a black writer.

As Chester achieved more recognition from the black middle class, he became friends with Bill Smith, a roustabout newspaperman from Kansas City. White-looking and belligerent, Smith had roughed around, managed to complete three years at the University of Kansas, and landed in Los Angeles in his late thirties still seeking his fortune. He carried a heavy chip on his shoulder. Like Chester, as a young man he had turned his back on respectability, squandering the chance to join his stepfather as physician on the staff of a hospital that he directed. But by the mid-1940s Smith had turned in the direction of propriety and married Helen Chappel, a Wilberforce University graduate and sorority president, who wrote for the *California Eagle* and had been appointed to the Los Angeles Youth Commission.

Helen had probably met fellow Ohioan Jean through the network of city recreation centers and learned that she was married to the man who wrote for *Esquire* and *The Crisis*. A "beautifully brown" professional woman like Jean, but one who did not cook, Helen invited the Himeses over for dinner. When they arrived she told them about her husband Bill's lengthy manuscript, abandoned in the garage.

Bill Smith too had been shocked and outraged by the Japanese internment, which struck him as "the ruin of a golden dream." Smith admired Chester's pluck, the fact that he had "refused to be stopped" as a bold writer when up against "cultural segregation." He recalled, "For years I had pulled back," but Chester had "stubbornly shoved ahead." Finally Chester had a colleague with whom to discuss the accumulated rage he felt. They argued about the best method to advance racial equality and publish unrestrained prose. Smith thought of Chester as a combatant, a person who believed that "you had to slug until something gave." Not faint of heart when it came to slugging, Smith felt that he had reached a point where public combat was unfair to the well-being of his wife and two children. "What's the matter . . . scared?" Chester sometimes taunted him. "Perhaps," answered Smith honestly. Childless and married to a woman who had known something of street-corner life, Chester didn't have the same problem and became known as the person always edging the discussion toward "thunder." Chester paid back the compliment of his high personal regard for Smith by writing "he was that type of mulatto black who will shoot a white man on sight."

By the middle of the summer, Chester's thoughts drifted to the likelihood of having to serve in the segregated military, even though he had still not been called by the draft board. He let out the most generous and romantic elements of his imagination in the short story "So Softly Smiling," a depiction of a nerve-frazzled veteran of North Africa falling in love and committing to Roosevelt's version of social-ism, the "Four Freedoms": freedom of speech, freedom of worship, freedom from want, and freedom from fear. "I—I don't know just when it started, but I got to feeling that I was fighting for the Four Freedoms," Chester's character sputtered, finding his way. "Maybe I had to feel it; maybe I had to feel that it was a bigger fight than just to keep the same old thing we've always had. But it got to be big in my mind—bigger than just fighting a war. It got to be more like building, well, building security for peace and freedom for everyone." Chester continued the homily of freedom and double V in two more short stories, one of them a humorously odd and slightly ghoulish set piece of black brutalization called "All He Needs Is Feet," and the other, a throwback to his Cleveland WPA penury, "All God's Chil-lun Got Pride." Shifting away from the hard-bitten convict writer, he was solidifying a minor place now as the house wit for the black bourgeoisie, sometimes drawn to the far left, and often pulling in the direction of racial integration.

While Chester made solid his position with the NAACP, his cousin Henry gained more influence in the powerful circles of govern-ment policy advisors, and was courted by the likes of Walter White and his efficient deputy Roy Wilkins. Mollie Moon had left her career as a social worker and had begun running an auxiliary organization for the Urban League, the Urban League Guild. There she created an annual Beaux Arts Ball, an interracial extravaganza of gaudy cos-tumes, feasting, and music that brought out New York's black elites and their white supporters and raised loads of cash for the Urban League. Mollie was also excellent friends with such influential whites as Edwin R. Embree, the director of the Julius Rosenwald Fund. Additionally, the fund's managers and advisors overlapped with the Urban League and prominent national interracial committees, granting Mollie much coveted social access to influential people.

In Chicago in August 1943, Mollie attended a party with painter Charles White and Edwin Embree at Vandi Haygood's home. Twenty-eight-year-old Vandi, a native of small-town Montana, was married to William Converse Haygood. When Haygood was drafted, Embree promoted Vandi to serve as acting director of the fellowship division of the Rosenwald Fund. She excelled in the position and became chummy with many prominent African Americans, like Horace Cayton, the director of Chicago's Parkway Community House. In her circle of well-educated black and white liberal elites, Haygood was known for her sexual promiscuity and her heavy drinking. The same was said about Mollie Moon, with the addition of her appetite for good food. "Here I sit over at Vandy's [sic]—both of us recovering from hangovers but mine not quite as bad as hers," Mollie wrote to her husband about the Chicago visit. Then, insinuating the possibility of an affair with the black painter, Moon wrote, "I told her to ask for Charlie White and she did."

In November Chester applied for a Rosenwald fellowship, putting Henry's name in the opening sentence of the letter addressed to Vandi Haygood. In pursuing the $1500 fellowship, which would give him the leisure and the confidence to write, he fully embraced his new identity as a racial uplifter. "During the past couple of years I have been writing short stories and essays for *Opportunity* (A Journal of Negro Life), and *The Crisis*," he wrote to Haygood. Chester's core impulse as a mature novelist was autobiographical and in the proposal he stated that he wanted to use fiction to examine his own life during the Depression and the early war years. He would give himself a break and erase his prison time, but the rest of the book, by and large, would depict his years in Cleveland and Los Angeles, as well as the stint at Malabar Farm.

The novel would reveal the social evolution of Joe Wolf, a writer who happens to be Negro, but who becomes a Negro writer. At first Joe publishes short stories without black characters, desiring simply "success as an individual, not equality as a Negro." Turned down as a reporter and hating his toil on a farm for a wealthy writer, Joe goes to Los Angeles, where black Communists befriend him and overcome his initial skepticism. However, after Pearl Harbor (not the invasion of the Soviet Union), Joe finds the Communists fully supporting seg-regationist management and he ends his fellow traveling. Joe learns "the hard way that there are no 'unusual' Negroes." Then, following the riots in the middle of 1943, Joe becomes "dangerous, explosive," "convinced that minority group problems will become worse before they become better." Chester concluded the synopsis on an unusually bold stroke that would in fact become his signature.

> He knows that the Negro problem will never be solved until the problem of democracy is solved—until the white people of the nation decide whether or not they want democracy.
>
> And now what he wants is to know how to force this decision—*one way or another.*

Chester believed in thunder, the efficacy of organized violence in the struggle to gain constitutionally guaranteed rights.

Providing recommendations for Chester's "strong and shrewd" project were Roy Wilkins, Nat Howard of the *Cleveland Daily News*, Arnold Gingrich, and Chester's first cousin Henry Lee Moon. Henry claimed that if Chester could avoid the fallacy of excessive modernism—a tendency toward overerudite stream of consciousness—he might write "a dynamic and comprehensive story of Negro life." In February 1944 Henry would also telegraph the fund on Chester's behalf. Henry's letter of recommendation was the most in-depth and supportive, perhaps because he had mercifully been left out of the story. Both Nat Howard and Arnold Gingrich recognized themselves in Chester's synopsis. In his letter, Howard hoped to divert Chester from "consideration of his own opinions and emotions exclusively." Roy Wilkins, cranky and overcautious after obviously having learned that Chester had served time, endorsed his newest writer with an extended caveat: "We have never met him personally. We have never seen his picture. We have never met anyone who knew him personally. All our business has been by correspondence."

Wilkins and Himes were not quite an odd pair. Alongside other major black newsmen, Wilkins had been called before the War Department's Office of Facts and Figures (the predecessor of the Office of War Information) in June 1942 and prodded to boost the morale of black servicemen. The assembled black editors were made to understand that continued editorials in support of double V and reports exposing discrimination and brutality could be considered sedition. Defiant in a way, Wilkins defended his editorial choices at the meeting, saying, "The Negro has been psychologically demobilized in this war." Chester, the least compromising writer that Wilkins published, would remain a "valued contributor."

Not long after the application was sent in, *The Crisis* published Chester's "All He Needs Is Feet." Set in Rome, Georgia, this short story invoked the infamous July 1942 beating of the internationally renowned black tenor Roland Hayes, who was accosted by police and local whites after his wife said, "Hitler ought to get you" to a rude clerk in a segregationist shoe store. Chester re-created the scene by making the violence more grotesque. For calling a tormentor "Hitler," a black man named Ward has to defend his life with a knife, an act for which he has his feet set on fire. The story concludes with an Arkansas white man beating a feetless Ward in Chicago because he fails to stand for the national anthem.

In the last months of 1943 Chester had a regular column in a union magazine called *War Worker*. He introduced himself as a man-about-town, able to get quotes and insider's information about race relations from New York magazines and Hollywood honchos. Chester was taking advantage of every contact he had, and all of them—Gingrich, Wendell Willkie—were in favor of racial advances in Hollywood films. Chester attended a two-day writers' congress organized by the Hollywood Writers Mobilization and held at UCLA, which opened on October 2. The participants included Walter White, Marc Connelly, military officials, and university professors. James Cagney and Theodore Dreiser also put in appearances. Lawyer and historian Carey McWilliams, who got to know Chester at the conference, emphasized the importance of removing racist laws from immigration and naturalization. At a panel discussion on minority groups in American films, Dalton Trumbo delivered a stern rebuke. Hollywood made "tarts of the Negro's daughters, crap shooters of his sons, obsequious Uncle Toms of his fathers, superstitious and grotesque crones of his mothers, strutting peacocks of his successful men, psalm-singing mountebanks of his priests, and Barnum and Bailey side-shows of his religion," Trumbo charged. The black film star and *Chicago Defender* columnist Clarence Muse then stood up and exclaimed, "Here I am—exhibit A of the stereotype of the Negro! I'm glad to learn that as an actor I will soon return as a human being!" The audience roared in approval. With the praise of the battling USSR in the news, the radical movement regained some of its standing. In December, Trumbo would officially join the Communist Party. By 1944 *Cabin in the Sky* star Rex Ingram had too.

Chester tried to raise awareness for the interned Japanese Americans. He obtained and published portions of an internee's diary in

War Worker, probably letters from his friend Mary Oyama Mittwer, to show the possibility of sedition among the multitudes "who have never been permitted to share the rights, privilege, and opportunities which make this nation magnificent." He excerpted from the diary, "It is hard to feel loyal, or patriotic, sincere to the land of our birth when prejudice rears its ignorant head, or when we are dismissed as a 'bunch of yellow Japs.'" But what made Chester's work stand out, apart from the touching empathy he showed he was capable of for Japanese Americans, was his Swiftian satire at the conclusion: "If, after reading these excerpts from this Nisei's diary all of us are consumed by our relentless hate for them, let's not quibble, investigate, and vituperate"; instead, "let's take them out and shoot them."

A visibly angry Chester waited on his Rosenwald application, prepared to abandon writing for politics once and for all. The segregation in the war industries in Los Angeles continued to be sharp and robust, and he took and abandoned menial tasks rather than investing himself emotionally in the fights to obtain good jobs at a place like the Kaiser-Hughes Aircraft Company. The Army called him up for a physical on February 15, 1944. He had told Jean that he would be shot before serving in a segregated military, but Chester did not have to make a decision. The physician examining him discovered a fractured vertebrae, an injury from the elevator shaft calamity of 1926, and classified him as 4-F, thus writing him out of the war.

The same week as his physical, Chester impatiently watched *Sweet-and-Hot*, a flat-footed musical on Central Avenue, and he no longer brooked his disgust at such a piss-poor cultural stew. In the pages of Bass's *California Eagle*, he cataloged the faults of black American pop culture: an inadequate "appeal to carnality"; "absolute unintelligence"; and lastly, abject imitation of "a white show." If black entertainers themselves did not have the "courage of a Bert Williams, a Florence Mills, a Paul Robeson," there could be no progress. In

addition, "the white folks," Chester wagged, "are now taking sides."
He vented in his unique hard-boiled idiom,

> Those that are on the other side are not going to support a
> Negro show even if we gave them a seven-course spread of
> Hollywood mammies. And those who are on our side want us
> to come out with the best we got, hard, fast and timely; they
> expect us to speak up, to voice our desires and protests in songs,
> demo[onstration]s and otherwise.

He extended his literary contacts by agreeing to serve on the
editorial board of *Negro Story,* Alice Browning's new black magazine out of Chicago, but the hard-edged critic still struggled to hold
down a job. In March he successfully applied for a job at the Los
Angeles Shipbuilding and Dry Dock Company in the San Pedro
harbor, becoming shipworker 35436. He was assigned a skilled job—
as a sheet metal helper installing a ventilation system—only to quit a
week later, faulting his back impairment. Himes later said he left for
"domestic reasons." Despite the contestatory ending of his position—
whether Chester had to labor below his skill rating or if he had a
bad row with Jean—the job had one tangible benefit: the dry dock
company in San Pedro would become the setting of his novel *If He
Hollers Let Him Go.*

On April 24, a mild day in a week threatening rain, Chester
received a letter from the Rosenwald Fund's Vandi Haygood, a life
buoy to an artist at sea. He had won a yearlong, $1500 fellowship.
Although not war wages by any means, the regular monthly checks
would be comfortable steady pay, roughly twice what a domestic in
Cleveland earned. He aimed well beyond one of his least substantial
Esquire prison stories, which came out in April, "Money Don't Spend
in Stir," a humorous vehicle for a quick $100. In a florid tone, unusual

to direct at someone he had not met, he explained to Vandi Haygood what the Rosenwald fellowship meant to him.

> It is difficult to express just how much this means to me. It is more than the actual award of the $1500. It is the confidence expressed by the Committee in my ability. Serious creative writing is an uphill grind against indifference, disapproval, antagonisms, and even destitution. Encouragement is seldom had from any source.
>
> I can truthfully say that this is my first "break" in fourteen years of writing. I hope I will never look back.

For the first time since prison, he could devote himself uninterruptedly to a novel.

Before he had known whether he would receive the fellowship, he had put his resolute if desperate logic about the struggle between the races into a jeremiad, published in *The Crisis* that May. In "Negro Martyrs Are Needed," Chester wandered into the field of comparative political theory. *The Crisis* proclaimed "our author argues brilliantly for revolution and leaders in the tradition of Gabriel and Nat Turner," but the essay was actually an odd mash. Moving between Crispus Attucks and Lenin, Chester wanted to encourage martyrs to sacrifice themselves in public acts of legal defiance to create the media spectacles necessary to stimulate a sociopolitical revolution. The revolutionary aim, however, was only "the enforcement of the Constitution of the United States." While Chester believed that the Bill of Rights and the Constitution's plan for representative government constituted the best "way of existence," the revolution he hoped to inspire would undoubtedly "bring about the overthrow of our present form of government." Not until the second page did he begin to identify his real target: the black middle class, prone to abandon its leaders and mistake social acceptance for democratic equality. "We have not achieved equality by week-ending with our white friends and drinking their liquor or flirting with their wives," he complained. The black middle class was vain, soft, and unprincipled.

Even though "Negro Martyrs" had equated communism to dictatorship, the Communications Section of the Federal Bureau of Investigation flagged him. On June 13, his Bureau file began with a memo from the Criminal Division of the Justice Department to Director J. Edgar Hoover and Assistant Attorney General Tom C. Clark. "You will note that the article recommends revolutionary action on the part of the colored people and for that reason I thought it should be brought to your attention," wrote the lead investigator. Initially, the agents were trying to figure out whether the Chester Himes writing in *The Crisis* was the same man their informants had fingered in Los Angeles as "an adherent or supporter or perhaps a member of the Communist Party or other organizations reported to be in sympathy with the Communist Party." They learned it was indeed the same man. Since "Negro Martyrs" coincided with a May directive from Hoover to address the "Negro Plan of Revolution," the Bureau began a fuller investigation in July. Not "desirous of having an investigation of the publication, *The Crisis*, carried out," the Justice Department asked "that this inquiry . . . be conducted as discreetly as possible."

Having received his grant, Chester dug into his proposed project, but that journey was unrewarding. He was riding along the surface of his own life since he had been released from prison and the findings were messy and difficult for an audience to identify with. For *The Crisis* he wrote "All God's Chillun Got Pride," the Cleveland part of his story, where his hero, Keith Richards, works as the only black research assistant in a public library. The narrative is an exploration of a black man's total fear: "every morning that he lived, he awakened scared." Keith worries that he will be crushed by the stereotype "of being a black beast in white America." If that discouraging account wasn't enough, he echoed the horrifying possibility of extermination he had insisted upon in his Nisei diary article. "After he had seen the truth sheared of all falseness of tradition and ideology, there would have been nothing to have done with that 'nigger' but to have taken him out and shot him."

However, Chester had achieved one new conceit, borrowed from the "encouraging" spirit of L.A.'s black migrants, and which remained a part of his work. For the Rosenwald-funded novel, he had described a feeling of belonging and black identity. "He is proud of their independence, their defiance which they carry on their shoulders like chips. He receives courage from their numbers. His people. For some strange reason, among them he feels as if he has come home." In spite of its general gloom, for his *Crisis* story he had created a protagonist "well-groomed," "handsome" and whose "complexion was black [with] features like an African prince. . . . When he forgot his scowl and accidentally laughed, he came on like bright lights." Chester had become proud of his racial background. Related to his ennobling brown-skinned male characters, he was no longer wedded to the black middle-class ideal of feminine beauty and success, sorority women who looked like pinups of Lena Horne and dripped with affluence and academic titles, women like Juanita Miller. Few people could understand why he was so angry, critical toward established customs, and dejected about the prospects of racial justice and employment during the war's final twelve months.

America then had the highest employment levels in its history and the Depression conditions of "All God's Chillun Got Pride" seemed fully over. After only marginally successful attacks in North Africa and Italy, on June 6, the second front was launched in France by the colossal invading D-day force of American and Allied troops. Delighted by the turn in military events, U.S. Communists, under the leadership of Earl Browder, downgraded themselves from a revolutionary party to a political association, sending the strong signal that

American capital and American labor had no fundamental disagreements. Since the Japanese losses at Midway and Guadalcanal in 1942,
the Pacific war had slowly begun to favor the Americans, even if to
eyes like Chester's it appeared as if a race war were under way in Asia,
with the rigidly segregated U.S. Navy and Marines fighting on terms
similar to the "zoot suit" battles of 1943.

Meanwhile, Jean Himes's career revealed evidence of racial and
gender barriers giving way under the pressure of wartime labor short-
ages. Vivacious and cordial, she had flourished developing recreational
programs at Pueblo Del Rio and by the summer of 1944 had joined
the United Service Organizations (USO), the private charity partner-
ing with the War and Navy Department to provide leisure activities
and relaxation for members of the armed forces. Jean now worked
closely with white regional directors and she caught the eye of the
press. With regular radio programs, film events, and maneuvering
celebrities to different troop camps and local centers, the job enabled
her to glow in public and in the eyes of black Angelenos.

In short order Jean became the high-placed coordinator for wom-
en's activities for the Los Angeles USO. But Chester's wife's continued white-collar successes undermined him psychologically, in spite
of the Rosenwald fellowship. He described her managerial success
and public notice as starting "the dissolution of our marriage." When
Jean said in an interview with the Baltimore-based newspaper the
Afro-American, "I gave up my good job with the City of Cleveland
and we went traipsing off to California," she caused Chester to moan
about the nature of American labor exploitation that promoted black
women and not black men. "It hurt for my wife to have a better job
than I did." Jean's success stung too because a deep part of Chester required her inertia, her never-ending adoration and subordinate
standing, and the "adulation" he had craved in prison. So Chester
blamed her and pitied himself. "I was no longer a husband to my wife;

I was her pimp. She didn't mind and that hurt all the more." He eased his mind by drinking heavily.

The battle with his wife's success and the forty painful hours at the shipyard in March stuck in his craw as he abandoned the Cleveland novel based on his own life. "Shattered" by the "mental corrosion of race prejudice in Los Angeles," Chester persuaded Henry Moon to host him in New York, and in September he went there. Either unwilling to accompany him, or discouraged from doing so, Jean remained in L.A. He channeled his feelings about the war, black opportunity, and Jean's prospects at work into the redirected novel, a frantic and brilliant exploration of black labor conditions and American sexuality that he wrote "defiantly," and "without thought of it being published." After years of coyly shielding his audience from his thunderous rage, he would force the reader to confront implacable fury.

Chapter Seven

TRYING TO WIN A HOME
1944–1945

By the time Chester arrived in New York, he had set out on a full-scale drunken bender. He arrived at his cousin's three-bedroom apartment at 940 St. Nicholas Avenue. From the window of the spare bedroom, where he slept, he could see lower Harlem, the East River, and Yankee Stadium in the Bronx. But the real view was his perch in Harlem's most elegant neighborhood, Sugar Hill. "Harlem's most talked about men and women in law, sports, civil liberties, music, medicine, painting, business and literature live on Sugar Hill," declared *Ebony* magazine. Chester had arrived at the playground of "the moneyed, the talented, the socially prominent, the intellectually distinguished, the fast crowd." And in that crowd Henry's wife, Mollie, might have claimed the crown as the most socially prominent. Part of the allure of the Moons was the whiskey that seemed to run from the tap and which kept Chester going. People introduced to him at this period would begin future inquiries about him asking simply, "Was Chester drunk?"

The cross street for the Moon building was 157th Street, an easy stroll away from 409 Edgecombe Avenue and the famous fourteen-story building where W. E. B. Du Bois, Walter White, and the painter Aaron Douglas lived, the "tallest and best kept apartment for blacks" that Chester had ever laid eyes on. Chester had arrived in the neighborhood in the city where a leading minister was called a "matinee idol in the pulpit" and was divorcing one beautiful showgirl wife for an even more beautiful, more talented star. Two blocks down St. Nicholas Avenue was Chester's favorite neighborhood haunt, the Fat Man's Bar-and-Grill, a hangout for jazz musicians and film celebrities. Eddie's Chicken Shack, as well as the other bars, the barbershops, and fronts for numbers houses, provided down-home pleasures. At 145th Street and a few blocks east was Harlem's Seventh Avenue, "the land of dreams," where a hard drinking and good-looking man or woman need never be lonely. The Renaissance Ballroom, Small's Paradise Inn, and Dickie Well's Restaurant all featured fine dining, dancing, and big bands. There was no shortage of glamour.

Despite the binge drinking, Chester was able to hold his own at the typewriter. With the assured income from his fellowship, he swiftly amassed chapters of a manuscript about the destruction of a favored black shipyard foreman and readied himself to sell his book in New York. Probably, as Chester boasted to the *Chicago Defender* that October, he had already drafted the novel he was calling, apparently because he was immersed in Tolstoy, *Race, Sex and War*. Writing at Mollie and Henry's wasn't easy, however; he landed at his cousin's during a time of bedlam. Henry and Mollie were fully devoted to the extraordinary campaign to reelect Franklin Roosevelt when Chester arrived. In April 1944 Henry had left his federal job with the housing agency to join the Congress of Industrial Organizations' Political Action Committee. Sidney Hillman, the director of war production, a dapper Lithuanian immigrant who had made a name for himself as an organizer in the garment industry and from 1914 as president of Amalgamated Clothing Workers of America, headed this committee; Mary McLeod Bethune, Robert Weaver, the theologian Reinhold

Niebuhr, and Howard University Law School dean William Hastie sat on its board. Henry would lend his talents as a journalist and public relations expert to organize and inform black members of the union, registering them to vote and educating them about politics.

Even though the group was theoretically nonpartisan, by May it had declared for Roosevelt and "progressive" liberal legislators. Hillman told audiences that "all of labor's gains and all progress made by minority groups during the past twelve years will be endangered if we do not elect progressive congressmen and a liberal president." The committee, which paid Henry a comfortable salary of $250 per month, was funded by CIO dues. While his work on the Political Action Committee focused on the election cycle, Henry also hoped to keep black industrial employment at high levels following the war, and he advocated a permanent Fair Employment Practices Commission to protect gains. However, by the summer's end, important supporters like Hastie resigned from the CIO committee, disappointed that they were in the process of delivering a black vote for no new tangible gains.

Several prominent black Communist artists—including Paul Robeson, Langston Hughes, and poet, professor, and journalist Melvin B. Tolson—also joined a Hillman-led offshoot called the National Citizens Political Action Committee during the summer. Whether Henry was in or out of town, everyone headed over to his apartment, where he and Mollie hosted almost nightly celebrations, supper parties, get-togethers, and toasts, in the process creating one of America's earliest genuinely interracial salons. The white Americans included Winthrop Rockefeller, the young vagabond son of the oil billionaire, Commission on Interracial Cooperation head Will W. Alexander, and Doubleday editor Bucklin Moon. The African Americans were the bright lights of the striving middle class, most of them hoping to finally break the back of segregation in some reputable field: NAACP lawyer Thurgood Marshall, Walter White, Richard Wright,

Abyssinian Baptist Church minister Adam Clayton Powell Jr., Illinois congressman William Dawson, and *Crisis* editor Roy Wilkins.

While Chester had known elites of the black world in Cleveland and Los Angeles, the sight of all of these New Yorkers together putting their efforts on the Roosevelt campaign was powerful and overwhelming. Years later, when he looked back on that fall, he decided that the nightly socializing to get a Democrat elected took on the "strangely religious" elements of a primitive ritual. To Chester it was sometimes pompous and sometimes preposterous. When Chester joined Mollie, her boon companion Polly Johnson, and others in fêting Winthrop Rockefeller at the grill at the Theresa Hotel, Johnson, tears of gratitude in her eyes, told the table of cosmopolitan elites, "This is social equality." Whether or not racial barriers in housing, education, or employment would ever trickle down from Sugar Hill seemed a minor concern.

A nightly guest to the Moon household was a young woman from Cincinnati named Ann Mason, who headed the Women's Division at the CIO Political Action Committee office. "Brilliant and charming," Ann was an attractive, ninety-pound divorcée, a year older than Chester. A former public schoolteacher and *Pittsburgh Courier* writer, Mason was another new arrival to New York. Touting the fact that women would cast 60 percent of the vote in 1944, Mason concentrated her efforts on recruiting black women in the CIO to the polls, where they could apply "the weapon most useful to the Negro." Sometimes with Henry, she barnstormed heavily populated California, Texas, Illinois, New York, Ohio, Michigan, and Pennsylvania, building caucuses of black women among the industrial workers, echoing the value of voting rights and the ballot.

At the soirees on St. Nicholas Avenue, Ann and Chester began an affair. "I lost myself in sex and drunkenness" was Chester's memory of the fall of 1944, a maze of adultery and flirtation. Even such public models of respectability like NAACP secretary Walter White, whose

marriage to his wife, Gladys, according to the biographer Kenneth
Janken, "had been a charade" for several decades, apparently escorted
his flame, white socialite Poppy Cannon, to Mollie Moon's shindigs.
Other guests—such as singer Paul Robeson and his wife, Essie—were
known to have an open marriage, and pursue multiple love interests.
The sexual double standard that allowed indulgence for the affluent
and sacrifice and condemnation for the commoner was on full display.

In some corner of his mind Chester resented his cousin's wife for
her role as hostess to the erotic buffet. Witnessing the viciousness of
the race rioting of 1943 in L.A. had dealt a powerful blow to his ideal
of American democracy. Life in New York in the last year of the
war among the Talented Tenth bruised too his ideal of middle-class
marriage. When he tried to explain himself in a forum that he knew
Jean would have access to, he described what he indulged in as "the
decadent, rotten sense of freedom that comes with being absolved of
the responsibility of trying any longer to be a man in a world that will
not accept you." As he had written about while in Los Angeles, he
was disgusted by the substitution of specious sexual kicks for genuine
political freedom. Chester was internally pained by the black promiscuity of New York, even as he participated in it.

Among the white partygoers to Mollie's was the tall, formida-
bly built, and open-minded Doubleday editor Bucklin Moon. Buck
Moon enjoyed the stimulating conversations and soaked in the moody
atmosphere, "sometimes one of frustration and rage" but also "barbed
with a bitter and almost sardonic humor." Originally from Minnesota, Buck had gone to college in Winter Park, Florida, where he had
befriended Zora Neale Hurston from nearby Eatonville. Moon had
joined Doubleday in August 1940 and worked his way up to the editorial staff after a couple of months managing one of the firm's New
York bookshops. Recognizing the uphill battles and sacrifices necessary to render just portraits of black Americans in the field of letters,
Moon had gone into publishing "with a feeling akin to someone about

to enter the clergy." A lifelong stutterer and legendary drinker, he was steadied by his belief that "one of the greatest stories to come from the Negro in America is in the migrations from the South to the North," and in fact he wrote a 1943 novel on that topic, *The Darker Brother*.

Buck Moon scouted black literary talent at Henry and Mollie's, signing Walter White to a contract for *A Rising Wind*, his investigation of the attitudes of black soldiers and British colonial subjects. While undeniably more fond of Negroes than most American whites, Moon believed he had to publish upbeat, original voices. He had "strong feeling[s]" by the fall of 1944 that "too many negative novels with a race background" had made their way into print, some of them as "standardized as the slick magazine serial." Chester's novel set in Los Angeles certainly seemed unique, if Moon tended to look at Chester's stories and political commentaries as overly bright reflections on a future without racism. To tempt Chester, Moon promised him the inaugural George Washington Carver Book Award, a new Doubleday promotional tool awarding $2500 for the best book "that deals with American Negroes." Black writers like Ann Petry and Roi Ottley had been celebrated for winning Houghton Mifflin pre-publishing prizes before, but the award in Carver's name seemed earmarked for a young black writer like Chester. Looking rather favorably on Chester's novel exploring racism in the West Coast war industry from the vantage of a middle-class striver, on October 19, 1944, Moon signed Chester to a contract with Doubleday, the country's largest publisher.

Asserting himself with more political writing, Chester hit the liberal New York Four Freedoms crowd that fall with a piece called "Democracy Is for the Unafraid" for the interracial amity magazine *Common Ground*. In this article Chester explored some of the recent material on the foundation of race prejudice and the authoritarian personality. Chester now embraced the point of view that modern man committed his most heinous acts because of fear. White supremacy, however, was doubly deadly because, in his view, when its purveyors became conscious of their fear, they reacted with renewed violence against nonwhites. "What frightens me most today," he began, were not the cruel stereotypes against black people, the race riots, the economic pressures, or the internment of the Japanese "(whose loyalty to the ideology of white supremacy is doubted)." Instead, Chester exposed the problem of "the white man's sudden consciousness of his own fear of other races." Chester's impersonal, academic position on the race problem—that it belonged to whites and was rooted in their insecurity—won esteem from his new friends. Bucklin Moon liked the piece so well that he reprinted it in an anthology he had under way called *Primer for White Folks*.

To celebrate her cousin's book contract, on Thursday, November 2, 1944, Mollie threw Chester one of her "famed get-togethers," a drunken bash attended by Alta Douglas, wife of the painter Aaron Douglas; Mrs. Edward Matthews, wife of the highly regarded concert baritone; white Gladys Ottley, the wife of Roi Ottley, who was reporting from the European war zone; Horace Sheffield, national representative of the United Auto Workers–CIO; Lewis Fairclough, chief of oral surgery at Harlem Hospital, and his spouse; Bucklin Moon; and Ann Mason. Nearly all of the attendees would be caricatured in Chester's novel *Pinktoes*.

Perhaps the most intriguing guest was Chester's old acquaintance from Cleveland, Reverend Grant Reynolds, former pastor of Mt. Zion Congregational Church. Reynolds had risen to the rank of captain as a chaplain in the Army and had supervised Jean's brother Andrew before being discharged for protesting too boisterously against discrimination. Like Chester, Reynolds was impatient with segregation and not reluctant to combine acts of intrepidness with publicity seeking. Two weeks before the party, Reynolds had resigned from the NAACP to found his own organization, the Non Partisan Council for the Abolition of Discrimination in Military and Veterans Affairs; he now proclaimed he was voting against Roosevelt "for the debase-

ment he has allowed to befall Negro men in uniform." Reynolds
and Henry Moon were fraternity buddies, and Reynolds would run,
unsuccessfully, as a Republican against Adam Clayton Powell Jr. for
Congress in 1946. Having just begun law school at Columbia, Reynolds crackled with energy, studiousness, and righteous indignation.

Although Chester could bluster through these crowds, he did not
prefer them. Almost certainly he concealed his prison record when
he was among them, as he did when he got his first press in the *Chicago Defender* and facetiously told a reporter that his stories in *Abbott's
Monthly* turned his "career from medicine to writing by accepting
his first short stories." The campaign for Roosevelt and liberal democratic equality seemed superficial and insincere when he sobered up,
so he worked on not doing that. That week and the next, he was so
drunk and disillusioned that he missed voting in the election. He even
resented the sex. As he waded through "white women who wanted to
give me their bodies," a voice inside Chester insisted that Mollie was
to blame. To Chester, Mollie was a black person of obviously common
origin who had somehow maneuvered into a gilded world of plenty
and could paw over rich and influential blacks and whites. But what
was worse than whatever she did was her shameless talking about it,
which Chester, "a puritan all my life," disliked hearing.

His distaste for Mollie was becoming attached to his yearning for
a partner endowed beyond what Jean, who was eerily becoming like
Juanita Miller (but without her polished background), had to offer.
With the final breakthrough—the fellowship in the spring and the
book contract by the fall—he started to envision a future that wasn't
ever shaped by the collapse of his family and the stain of prison. Partly
insecure and partly ungrateful, Chester drew fictional characters close
enough to real-life people so that the resemblance stung. In several of
his fictions, Mollie and Jean appeared. But in his first novel, he rendered a complex but still unflattering portrait of a kind of saccharine
black female professional, closely modeled on Juanita, the acme of a

type of light-skinned affluent success. He would begin the separation from his wife by tearing down the ideal Jean seemed to be striving for.

After the elections, Chester's investigation by FBI agents shifted into a higher gear. Special Agent in Charge R. B. Hood was making the rounds in Los Angeles, tracking down Chester's contributions to left-wing periodicals, adding his prison record to the file, and noting his friendships and sympathies with Communists, although he was "not known to be a member or active therein himself." Observing his NAACP membership and not wishing to attract untoward notice, the Bureau applied customary discretion to see whether his book had been published and could then be examined for "seditious or revolutionary material."

Chester made his own allies at confidential parties held at the Moon apartment when Mollie was away. He befriended Constance H. Curtis, the regular book reviewer for the *Amsterdam News*, who singled out the majesty of Melvin B. Tolson's *Rendezvous with America*, and who had challenged her audience to read books that "deal with life in direct terms and direct language." Chester's ambitions suited Curtis's scheme to win foundation support for black writers who could devote themselves to "a real literature which concerns itself with our people." Langston Hughes, the best-known black writer connecting to "our people," partied too. He lived farther down St. Nicholas Avenue and was spending that fall reading his poetry at black high schools. Tireless Hughes was also the lead writer, black or white, for *Common Ground*. In January 1943 he had launched in the pages of his *Chicago Defender* column an enduringly popular character called "My Simple Minded Friend," later shortened to just "Simple." He and Chester met for drinks at the Theresa Hotel bar.

Constance Curtis brought to Chester's parties a bookish young man originally from Oklahoma City. Thirty-one-year-old Ralph Ellison was the most talked about unknown black writer in New York. The same height as Chester but losing his hair, Ellison was reprinting his apprentice pieces alongside Chester's Negro troop-morale builders in *Negro Story* that year, while also serving on that magazine's editorial board. A concert-trained trumpeter who had gone to school at Tuskegee, Ellison was cycling away from the Communist Party, in which he had been heavily involved since 1937, to the point of preparing to fight in Spain. An editor at the Communist *New Masses* but a ghost in the world of the well-to-do black elite, Ellison lived down the hill from the Moons' fashionable digs. Chester, who knew the Urban League's Lester Granger, might also have noticed Ralph speaking at an event sponsored by that group at the East and West Association with crusading author Pearl Buck on October 24. In spite of his poverty and obscurity, Ellison was rapidly becoming the black literary intellectual of his age, and he had one most attractive calling card for Chester: he was perhaps the closest friend and confidant of Richard Wright.

Ellison had spent a good portion of his summer proclaiming and defending Wright's work, whose two-part article "I Tried to Be a Communist" caused a sensation when it appeared in *Atlantic Monthly*. Both Ellison and Himes had gone through periods of infatuation, reliance, and dissatisfaction with the Communist movement, though Chester's significant mainstream success early in his career had prevented a strong attachment from forming with the hard left. Ellison, on the other hand, had begun writing at the suggestion of Hughes and Wright, and had all of his early publications in Communist magazines. He had reached, however, a turning point in his career. That September Ellison had secured a deal at publisher Reynal and Hitchcock similar to Chester's at Doubleday. With brand new short stories like "King of the Bingo Game" and "Flying Home," Ellison had started to write a new, intellectual, symbol-laden style of fiction that was attracting the eye of the critics. In 1944 he would successfully apply for a Rosenwald fellowship and Bucklin Moon, Himes's editor, would support Ellison with letters of recommendation.

The men liked each other. Although he was in the process of developing a legendary intolerance for sentimentality in discussions of race relations, art, or politics, Ellison was "congenial and attentive" in those early encounters with Himes. They had contrasting styles. Chester hung out regularly in bars swapping lies about the black folklore character Signifying Monkey with GIs, while Ellison, sifting through Communist Party maneuvers and Marxist philosophy in spirited discussions with literary friends, was more worried about the draft and being sent overseas. The men were often in each other's company, most memorably at Ralph's 147th Street apartment for a mess of pressure-cooked pig feet and rice, where Chester consumed more trotters than anybody.

An historic gathering of black writers took place a month after the election. Langston Hughes threw a gala party on Sunday, December 10, that brought the black intelligentsia to the two-room apartment he shared with Toi and Emerson Harper. The guests included Cuban writer Jose Antonio Fernandez de Castro, W. E. B. Du Bois, Mollie and Henry, Owen Dodson, Alta Douglas, Nora Holt, Alice Browning, Dan Burley, Richard Wright, Ralph Ellison and Fanny Buford, Charles Holland, and Oliver Harrington and his Norwegian wife. Hughes gave the party to honor Loren Miller, visiting from Los Angeles with Juanita. Chester had established himself so well in Los Angeles, and now impressively gotten a book contract in New York, that Miller took the occasion to thank him and remind him that L.A. was his "home town." When Chester's book appeared the next year, he would become the first nationally published Los Angeles–based black novelist.

The party's most impressive guest to Chester was Wright, then editing the galleys of his next book. Accompanied by a juvenile delinquency expert, Wright arrived to the cramped party where Du Bois was "reigning in the place of honor," a phenomenon that stoked Wright's own private disgust about his relationship to members of the black educated elite—a feeling he and Chester would share. Chester remembered Wright's mood as "antagonistic and resentful." A few days before the party Wright had learned that his attempts to place a reasonable program of black family life on the radio had been thwarted by a "very small and prejudiced minority" of "so-called Negro leaders that I've had to deal with ever since I've been writing." Wright connected Mollie's crowd of "middle-class matrons," represented by Alta Douglas, Nora Holt, and visitor Juanita Miller, to those trying to snub him.

The other significant attendee to the party was Jean, who had rejoined Chester for what was at first a traumatic reunion. According to Chester, Jean arrived in Harlem and "found me deeply involved in so many affairs that she tried to take her own life." Jean drank heavily alongside Chester and in that condition might easily have made a melodramatic flourish in a desperate hour; certainly a fain theatricality had become a part of her manner. Friends remembered a drunk Chester carrying passed-out Jean back up St. Nicholas Avenue, and an ungallant Chester threatening meek rivals over imaginary slights. For New Year's the Moons invited Vandi Haygood to the apartment, undoubtedly increasing the degree of drinking and bawdiness in closed quarters. In a short story he was working on, punningly titled "A Night of New Roses," published at the end of 1945, Chester summed up a disposition that reflected his practical approach to life in the war years: "I spent half my time thinking about murdering white men. The other half of the time taking my spite out in having white women. And in between, protesting, bellyaching, crying."

After the German offensive operations ended following the Battle of the Bulge, it was merely a question of time before the collapse of the Nazi regime and the end of the war in Europe. The prime literary event in the early winter of 1945 was the arrival of Richard Wright's fourth book, *Black Boy*. This autobiography, his second selection by the Book-of-the-Month Club, was a rare best-selling work of nonfiction that didn't deal with the war. Wright proved that racism need not impair the commercial success of a black writer. Setting new standards for himself, Chester worked hard on his manuscript.

In the years following *Native Son*, alert commentators had picked up on the fact that the symbolic interaction between Bigger Thomas and Mary Dalton had a sexual component. In his novel, now called *If He Hollers Let Him Go*, Chester reversed the symbols and used the sexual tension between a black male and a white female as the center of the novel. His black hero was middle-class and upwardly mobile, and his white villain was a dissipated cracker biddy. *If He Hollers Let Him Go* supplies an adrenaline-filled five days in the life of Bob Jones, a charismatic young black man with two years of college who is the lone black "leaderman" at a California shipyard. The novel begins with its hero at the height of prosperity. He owns a car, is nearly engaged to a glamorous, white-looking social worker, the daughter of a local black physician. By the end of the novel Jones has been arrested for the attempted rape of a washed-out blowsy white Mississippi welder's helper, mainly because, in the published version, after a series of intense dalliances, he refuses to have sex with her. All of Jones's tangible symbols of success are gone: job, fiancée, car, and draft deferment. The racial, environmental, and biological tensions of the naturalistic world prove steadily ruinous, but the psychology of internalized racial oppression is the novel's prime focus. *If He Hollers* concludes with Jones physically broken and being mustered into the Army, which for a black soldier meant at least a long drink of humiliation during basic training at a Southern camp. The book's title came from the children's counting rhyme, "Eeny, meeny, miny, moe / Catch a nigger by the toe / If he hollers let him go / Eeny, meeny, miny, moe."

The arc of the published plot was quite tame in comparison with the sex-and-profanity-laced manuscript that Chester submitted to Bucklin Moon in the spring of 1945. The mild-mannered editor found Chester's imaginative world quite different from the one he had glimpsed bantering over cocktails at Mollie's. Buck Moon was taken aback and understood that the manuscript was a professional precipice from which "there was no way out." He would have to stand his ground with the Doubleday higher-ups to get the book published at all. He could admire the value of Chester's "memorable" project, which trumpeted "the psychological lynchings which every Negro suffers almost daily," but he didn't prefer the caustic tone or the pessimistic ending.

The book was remarkable. Chester deliberately speared conventional good taste, writing with the confidence of a man whose own personal life would seem to have lifted him beyond reproach. In early drafts Chester even used the word "fuck," which was outlawed in 1944. But the rib-breaking punch he sought to deliver lay in the depictions of raw interracial sex and rape. He seemed determined to force American readers to recognize that on their own terms Negro men had slept with white women, a violation of not just the great American taboo, but a great many enforced laws. Furthermore, in his original draft, it is not clear that Bob Jones does not rape Madge.

"I'm gonna have you or we're gonna fight all night," I panted.

"You nigger, nigger, nigger," she grated.

"Call me what you want," I said. "You don't hurt me baby."

"Get up then, goddamnit," she said. "You can't do nothing like this."

I got back on my knees, ready to pounce if she made a false move. She clutched her robe, flung it open. "Here." She didn't have on a nightgown, *and her big white body spread out on the dark robe like the one that had every nigger lynched.*

I had her right there on the floor, fully dressed, and out of breath, panting like a dog. She started gasping "Nigger, nigger, nigger," and she almost screamed it, and that was it.

Chester had written a graphic account of rape as a calculated act of retribution for racism. But he was living in a completely different world, one where white men raped with impunity, black women suffered assault and degradation, and black men could be easily killed.

In December the CIO's Political Action Committee was helping to organize the Committee for Equal Justice for Recy Taylor, an effort to investigate the gang rape of Mrs. Taylor, a black woman abducted and brutalized as she walked home from church in Alabama that September. Chester's book would not simply be banned, but might serve as a legal resource verifying black bestiality, exposing Chester himself as well as other black Americans to assault. Not even Thomas Dixon's 1905 novel *The Clansman* had rendered so controversial an account of interracial sex.

Chester thought it important to explain what had taken place, graphically, at a later point when the two principal characters are again skin to skin. He wanted to, in a single document, modernize race relations by revealing the libidinal underside of prejudice, upheld legally by fear-filled white men and women, who secretly desired intimacy with blacks. At the same time, he wasn't seeking to fall into the trap of producing black saviors who, like Harriet Beecher Stowe's Uncle Tom, redeem white barbarity by way of their saintliness. His hero would have ample sex desire, fused with explicit black rage.

"You can't insult me, nigger," she told me. "You'd die for these fine white thighs of mine, you can't fool me."

"Die in 'em," I grinned, peeling off my clothes.

She lay on the bed beside me, looking at the ceiling. "There's something about a nigger screwing you that gets in your blood. I can just think about you raping me last night and wet all over myself. Gotdoggit, it ain't—." She broke off suddenly and asked me, "You ever been to Chicago?"

"Sure, plenty of times," I said. "I know some fine white chicks in Chicago."

"They tell me niggers is married to white women in Chicago and nobody does anything about it," she said.

"Hell, that happens everywhere," I said.

"Let's go to Chicago and get married," she said.

We both rolled over to face each other at the same time. I wanted to see if she was kidding. I don't know what she wanted to see, but I thought it was a good time to hurt her if I could, so I said, "If I was going to marry a white woman I wouldn't marry a slut like you."

Her whole body began twitching and her face was like a square red bar. "You know what I'm going to do with you, nigger. I'm gonna make you screw me then I'm gonna get you lynched. I'll be the last white woman you ever screw."

I began pawing at her. "Take off your gown, goddammit," I said impatiently.

She peeled off her clothes, her big white body spreading out on the bed like the grandmother of all the whores in the world. I tried to win a home. She went through her rigmarole of, "Nigger, rape me; oh, rape me, nigger!" as she had done the night before. Her face was flushed bright crimson and her eyes threw off weird sparks. But she didn't fight.

When we had finished we lay there a while and she said harshly, "Gawdddd-damnnnn, a nigger just sets me on fire. I wanna run through the fields and get raped by every nigger in Texas."

I lit a cigaret and became analytical, lying there, puffing. "You're just like all the other southern white women," I said. "You're frustrated and inhibited. If it wasn't all this business about race, you probably wouldn't even think about colored men."

Himes topped off his draft by including a graphic lesbian scene involving Bob Jones's middle-class society girlfriend, Alice.

Doubleday would not publish it.

Bucklin Moon was not prudish; in his own novel the heroine works as a streetwalker to support herself. But she was black. And, in December 1944 Buck Moon submitted "Slack's Blues" to Alice Browning's *Negro Story*; it was a deeply sensitive and historically revealing portrait of a blues-playing piano man from Alabama making it in New York, a guy who knew how to handle himself. Moon reworked some of the materials from the famous jazz club scene in *The Sun Also Rises,* where the black drummer is the potent masculine comrade to Brett Ashley (James Baldwin, Moon's young protégé, would, in a dozen years, take a similar story to even further heights). But Moon had met Chester in the company of civil rights lobbyists, and he expected that the material would not explode in his hands. He wanted at least a slight portrait of black heroism and keeping Bob Jones chaste in the novel and having Madge falsely accuse him of rape at the conclusion would help. Even within those limitations, the novel could still carry the scorpion's sting of sex and race.

So Chester and his editor settled on rough, sexually charged interactions, nudity, and sexual frustration. Himes gave his archetypal description of the dissolute white welder from Texas, Madge Perkins, in chapter 17:

> Her blonde hair, dark at the roots, was done up in metal curlers tight to her head. Without lipstick or make-up she looked older; there were deep blue circles underneath her eyes and blue hollows on each side of the bridge of her nose. Tiny crow's-feet spread out from the outer corners of her eyes and hard slanting lines calipered obliquely from her nostrils. . . .
>
> She looked like hell. She was really a beat biddy, trampish-looking and pure rebbish. . . .

She had a big mature body with large sagging breasts and brownish-pink nipples the size of silver dollars. Her stomach was soft and puffy and there were bulges at the top of her big wide thighs.

As his manuscript went through editing, Chester dashed off pro-Roosevelt racial-uplift stories. One, "Let Me at the Enemy—an' George Brown," was a black language experiment in the jive idiom that was becoming an increasingly accepted part of American life by way of Dan Burley's *Original Handbook of Harlem Jive,* Cab Calloway's performances, and radio disc jockeys all over the nation. He also dealt with the shifting gender expectations after women joined the war industry. In two stories set in California—"The Song Says 'Keep on Smiling,'" which appeared in April in *The Crisis,* and "Make with a Shape," which followed later in the summer in *Negro Story*—Chester wrote about contemporary married life. A tongue-in-cheek set piece, "Make with a Shape," expresses dismay at the remade, wartime spouse, "so industrialized and athletic and self reliant." The story after all was not just a hyperbolic allegory of his own life. Jean had rallied from her disappointment at his affairs and was conducting "a tour of inspection" of USO facilities in Philadelphia, and handing out quotes to the press.

Chester sent his revised draft to Moon, who then put the manuscript into production, sending it to the copy editor. By March 1945 Chester was "roughly in the middle" of a new novel and asking his acquaintance Vandi Haygood at the foundation to extend his award so that he could continue writing. Chester needed to return to Los Angeles to concentrate and sober up. He and Jean told the press that they were leaving to avoid the "many social obligations they would have in New York City [that] would take too much time from writing." The Julius Rosenwald Fund extended his fellowship, with a new grant of $500. Jean returned to L.A. by April and Chester followed

the next month, to a house at 1717½ W. Thirty-Seventh Street, in the
crowded Central Avenue neighborhood. The FBI was now "pretext"-
calling his house to determine his whereabouts and using its resources
to take a look at his manuscript.

Chester traveled to California in the aftermath of the European
war, as a mushrooming euphoria swept the United States. When the
train stopped in Chicago, he took the opportunity to drop by the
Ellis Avenue headquarters of the Rosenwald Fund, in Hyde Park,
just north of the University of Chicago, and meet the staff. He visited
Vandi Haygood, who had approved his fellowship as "a good bet,"
but who also didn't "like Himes' project much." The layover became a
torrid affair, "a wild, drunken week of sexual extravagance." Precisely
what he meant at first to Haygood is unclear. Some white women who
had a taste for black men did find him elegant, graceful, and "very put
together," but Chester also initially struck people as "meek mannered,"
effusively polite, and speaking with a mild speech impediment (perhaps only his Mississippi twang). With Vandi, Chester could palaver
with a graduate of the University of Chicago about the highbrow publishing world, literature, and the arts, and also receive her sympathy
on account of the day-to-day racism and poverty he endured. Whatever the impetus for the liaison, in Vandi Haygood Chester found
a feminine ideal—attractive, sure of herself, and with the means to
provide.

Back in L.A. and still hoping to crack the fortunes of Hollywood
screenwriting, Chester accepted an invitation from the Actors' Lab,
a collective touting the "very progressive" and "very political" training that steeped young migrants to Hollywood in the Stanislavsky
method and other exercises to heighten concentration. But L.A. was
still the kind of place where columnist Hedda Hopper believed that
"dancing between Whites and Negroes" at the Actors' Lab was "the
sort of thing that leads to race riots." So with some wariness, Chester
agreed to meet Marc Connelly there and discuss a new project on

George Washington Carver, the famous black Tuskegee scientist who pioneered peanut production. Connelly had also secured the services of Arna Bontemps, a novelist and the librarian at Fisk University; he was "summoned" to Los Angeles in mid-May on an expenses-paid trip by M-G-M to see whether the play *St. Louis Woman* could be transformed into a screen-ready musical. Bontemps was talking to Lena Horne, whom he hoped to interest in the starring role. He had also just served on the Rosenwald Fund committee that had decided to extend Chester's grant. Even-tempered and a literary man to the core, Bontemps loved writing and black culture and was best friends with Langston Hughes, but kept his family life at center stage and never established a big name.

Bontemps and Himes had quite a bit to chat about. Bontemps and his white friend Jack Conroy were nearing publication of their Doubleday book about black migration, *They Seek a City*; they too had worked with Bucklin Moon and also had been promised the Carver Award. By the mid-1940s, Bontemps was pragmatic about literary deals and publishing companies. He did not open himself to sorrow on account of the way the business trendily picked up and then discarded black writers or black themes.

Connelly, understood as one of the great liberal voices in American film and theater as the creator of *The Green Pastures*, began his meeting with Chester and Bontemps by declaring that all he was certain of was the opening to the film. "Dr. Carver was a very humble man, and he always ironed his own shirts. So when we start this film on Dr. Carver, he goes into the kitchen and irons his shirt." Insulted, Chester stood up and walked out. Bontemps, who lived in Nashville, could swallow quite a bit more than that. Writing Bucklin Moon, he attributed all the dramatics to Chester's anxiety about the publication of his first novel. "I think he is too excited about his immediately forthcoming novel to make the headway he would like on his second one, but he'll calm down and get in stride presently."

But Chester would have to do more than exit a room in outrage to preserve his artistic vision. Before the summer began, he received unnerving news. *Publishers Weekly* announced on June 9 that the Carver Award, a prize of $2500 that came with a handsome amount of publicity, had gone to Fannie Cook's *Mrs. Palmer's Honey,* a novel about a black domestic voting for Roosevelt. The *New York Times* remarked later that "it seems a little grotesque to honor as undistinguished a book as *Mrs. Palmer's Honey.*" Chester, who believed that Bucklin Moon had promised him the award to launch *If He Hollers,* felt betrayed.

The situation was actually worse than not getting the award. Moon had been out of the office the entire spring, preparing his anthology *Primer for White Folks* and writing a new novel. Around the middle of July, he guardedly conveyed to Himes that *If He Hollers Let Him Go* was in trouble at Doubleday; this was followed by official misgivings about the manuscript from the legal department. Apparently fearing that Chester would take the removal of major portions of his novel personally, Moon attributed the corrections to an anonymous editor and kept the person's identity secret, except for her sex. "One of the women executives said that the book made her sick at the stomach," he informed Chester. Even with the dramatic adjustments to the manuscript, Chester learned from his editor that he had a real foe at the publisher. Moon told Chester that if this highly placed woman "had known what [the novel] was like she would have fought its acceptance." The editor disinclined to publish *If He Hollers Let Him Go* and strong enough to make her dissent meaningful could only have been Clara Claasen. Chester never learned her identity.

As he had done when he thought he was wrongfully treated on the writers' project in Cleveland, a frantic Chester started writing letters. Fit to be tied, he explained to heartthrob Vandi Haygood the new problems with the revisions and scrambled back to New York to his cousin's apartment on July 19. By then, the manuscript had been set into type and galleys were ready for him to read.

Aside from any possible vendetta held by Claasen, Doubleday attorneys had gone over the manuscript because of concerns with two issues. First, had Chester written any scenes that might be considered obscene? Lillian Smith's 1944 novel *Strange Fruit* had just caused an uproar and launched a legal case on account of profanity, an allusion to the rape of a black woman by a white man, and a suggestion of lesbianism. In chapter 17 of Chester's novel, the hero, Bob Jones, goes to the hotel room of the white female antagonist and tries to rape her; in another chapter Bob slums at an erotic party with his girlfriend and several lesbians. The legal department would also have considered the point of view of the four-year-old Council on Books in Wartime, whose executive board included two Doubleday executives. The council was responsible for getting reprints to servicemen, keeping up their morale, and bolstering emotional confidence on the home front. Chester's book emphatically climaxed with Bob Jones's defeat, a vanquishing symbolized by his being railroaded into the military. Chester's combination of raw sexuality and rejection of military duty must have tested the Doubleday legal team. A conservative judge might easily have placed a ban on the book.

For Chester, the occasion of examining the galleys proved a minor scandal in a writing career that would involve legendarily bitter accusations levied at publishers. Responding to a secretary's telephone call, Chester arrived in the late afternoon at the Doubleday office at Rockefeller Center. Bucklin Moon was out of town and it seemed to Chester as if the staff were questioning his identity. He couldn't be sure if he was only unfamiliar or if they were automatically dismissive because he was black. An employee asked him to read the galleys in Moon's office before their editorial suite closed for the day at five o'clock. Chester loudly insisted on his right to take the galleys home.

That night, when Himes finished reading them, it became clear that the manuscript had not been just edited: it had been ransacked.

He and Moon had already toned down chapter 17, but now it had been completely eliminated. The furor over the accepted manuscript and the considerations from the legal department had apparently led to the unusual step of re-editing without any notice to the author. Chester telephoned Vandi Haygood, searching for a sympathetic ear. Then, dealing with Bucklin Moon, also apparently by telephone, Chester became adamant and fought skillfully enough to have the hotel room tempest between Bob and Madge restored. Through Moon he learned that a company vice president and the legal department had required the re-editing. If being outspoken was enabling some victories like the restored chapter, he was also earning the label of troublemaker.

Jean joined him from California in September. Knowing his vulnerability and tendency toward debauchery, they wisely left the Henry Moon apartment and sought their own place to live. But even in the outer boroughs, racism and the postwar population surge was making it impossible to find an apartment. They wound up taking a room with a young, cheerful schoolteacher at 121 Bainbridge Street in Bedford-Stuyvesant in Brooklyn. Mollie Moon continued to dutifully invite them to her choice gatherings, which she managed to schedule around her own appearances at Café Society, Broadway premieres, and NAACP showdowns between Walter White and Countee Cullen over the musical *St. Louis Woman*. Mollie had befriended Hollywood now, and was boosting screenwriter John Bright, who also became friends with Chester. But she was showing weariness at having to deal with her "crazy cousins," who were known to overstep, and maybe now more so that Henry was always on the road building coalitions for the CIO's Political Action Committee. When she had her crowd over on Sunday, September 16, she wrote to Henry that "everyone had a nice time, including the Himeses, whom I kept sober."

On September 30 Chester got devastating news from Ohio: his seventy-one-year-old mother had died of a cerebral hemorrhage. He cried hysterically, despite their long emotional separation. With the Rosenwald money long gone, Chester had to scrounge around for train fare. He traveled alone to Columbus, where Estelle had been living with Joe Jr. and his wife. The day before his mother was cremated, on October 2, his aunt Fannie Wiggins died at fifty-eight in Cleveland. Estelle's sister-in-law and nemesis was buried three days after Estelle. A week later, Henry's father, Roddy Moon, had a serious illness that required medical attention. The generation born in the aftermath of slavery was giving way.

Estelle's death hurt Chester more because she had not lived long enough to see him praised and redeemed in the way he had dreamed of when he was in prison. He was reconsidering her contumacious personality, which had defied his father, his father's employers, and the strictures of white society at large, dominating his household and driving him into the streets. Compared with other adults, he thought of Estelle as "a woman of iron will and ruthless determination and burning ambition." But her death allowed him to glimpse a new, softer quality: "my mother had been innocent." He was recognizing that he knew little of the struggles of her life. He did know that she would have been disappointed by a novel like *If He Hollers Let Him Go*, with its rough language, obsession with sexuality and interracial conflict, and its contempt for upper-class light-skinned blacks. For the rest of his life, Chester derived strength by explicitly repudiating some of Estelle's cherished values, while he escaped having to confront her about his own choices. But the chance of his having misjudged her and needing something that she had lavished upon him remained.

His bereavement roughly coincided with the earliest advertisements for his book. In the weeks before Estelle's death, Doubleday ran two ads in *Publishers Weekly*, which showed the cover and referred to Himes's book as "a tough, controversial novel, loaded with dynamite, built around the racial tension inherent in a West Coast shipyard." The second ad, appearing in the next issue, was a full page that presented the novel as a thriller: "A Real Shocker! Dynamite! Tough! Fast Paced! Reading as Gripping as *The Postman Always Rings Twice*." Doubleday's ads used graffiti-style letters for the book title. The publication of *If He Hollers Let Him Go* was set for November 1.

In the final days of October, a "surprised" Chester saw the first copy of the book, "very much discouraged by the jacket and preface." Himes could not have liked the dust-jacket language, which praised his realism by belittling his creative skill: "what he writes comes from firsthand information rather than from a fertile imagination." Nowhere was his mastery of craft, his journeyman years with *Esquire* and the racial-uplift magazines, or his Rosenwald fellowship mentioned. A week before publication, he learned that Doubleday had no biographical portfolio on him, and that metropolitan dailies and literary people in Cleveland and Los Angeles who knew Chester personally had not been targeted. Seeking to rescue his book, Chester prepared lists of names to be sent press releases and review copies. But his mood was prickly, defensive, and accusatory.

Reading Bucklin Moon's *Primer for White Folks* while in Detroit at the end of October, Henry Moon was excited for his cousin Chester, after so much recent raw pain in the family, including the death of Henry's older brother, Joe Hubbard Moon, in 1944. In spite of the hiccoughs in their relationship, Henry was giddy on the eve of publication and asked his wife to "remember me kindly to Jean and to him." At the same time Bucklin Moon requested that Henry and Mollie throw the official Doubleday book party for Chester at their home. The white junior editor might have considered the request thoroughly ordinary, since Henry and Mollie gave smashing interracial parties to the smart set in New York and could generate publicity with easy flair. They agreed to hold the event at their apartment on November 2.

Chester interpreted the gesture quite differently. Doubleday threw parties for white authors like Earl Wilson at the Copacabana and Elizabeth Janeway at the Rainbow Room. In a couple of weeks a rival press would debut first-time black writer Ann Petry at the Hotel Biltmore to two hundred guests. Added to the Carver Award betrayal, Himes now felt small-timed and Jim Crowed by his publisher.

Chester reacted to his publisher's slight and his mother's death in a battle of words with Mollie a few days before the book launch. He brought her to tears. Weary and wounded "deeply," she called Henry, who responded with uncharacteristic anger. "I don't like it one bit and will let him know when I see him," Henry threatened. Containing his disfavor, Henry encouraged Mollie to carry on with the celebration, giving her painstaking advice on the invitations, and asking her to include all of the "in" crowd: Richard Wright, Langston Hughes, Walter White, Roy Wilkins, P. L. Prattis of the *Pittsburgh Courier*, George Schuyler, Doxey Wilkerson, Dan Burley, John Bright, William Attaway, Countee Cullen, and Ralph Ellison.

Chester had a reason to be happy. In spite of what he understood as his publisher's bungling, the day before the party the book had received a lengthy review in the *New York Times*. While hardly an endorsement of Chester as an artist, the review signaled that he had indeed struck the nerve he was after. The *Times* decreed *If He Hollers* "a mixture of polemics and melodrama," but it did not ignore the gauntlet Chester threw down with full force: "Bob is forever wanting to kill someone."

Chester "took his bow" that Friday evening "amid the clinking of many glasses and the shaking of many hands." Unperturbed, Mollie grinned and hammed it up at the party. Pictures show Chester looking genuinely happy, shaking hands with John Bright while Owen Dodson cheers him. A head taller than everyone else, Sterling Brown (who was teaching at Vassar that year) and Bucklin Moon look down approvingly. Jean beamed at everyone who had a good word for Chester. Referring to two of the revered black brainiacs from the Harlem Renaissance, *Amsterdam News* gossip columnist Dan Burley thought that the convivial creative spirit of the 1920s had been revived: "'Twas like years ago in the days of [Rudolph] Fisher, Wallace Thurman et. al. eh, Ted Poston?"

Dour about the event retrospectively, Chester would write dismissively, "I consented to go to the party, which I thought was a flop." Flop or not, he wouldn't have another book party like it for almost thirty years. The aftermath of the party also cut family ties. Henry returned to New York sick and in a bad mood, considering the "nerve-wracking" tension of his job, worrying about his father and "Chester's reaction." After whatever confrontation occurred between the two men, the former camaraderie and coaching were permanently ended. Chester never again stayed at the apartment and rationalized his spiteful ingratitude by deciding that cautious, bookish Henry, wrapped around his "Mollishka," would no longer be useful. The original title to *If He Hollers* had been *Breakout*, and now that Chester had battled his publishers, friends, family, and censors in his passage to becoming a novelist, breaking out was what he wanted to do.

On November 10, Chester gave a "Meet the Author" talk at the George Washington Carver School on 125th Street, an adult education bureau run by the poet Gwendolyn Bennett with heavy Communist support. A Harlem Renaissance belle, the Marxist Bennett approved of Himes's novel for "presenting a true picture" of white prejudice and black psychological response. On the flyers, he was presented as "Chester Himes, author of the forthcoming George Washington Carver Memorial Award novel," an error that was a source of embarrassment and resentment for him. Meanwhile, he received a self-described "fan letter" from his old Cleveland friend Ruth Seid. It was a compliment wrapped in barbed wire. While she "enjoyed" *If He Hollers* "very much," she emphasized that she knew as much about writing as he did: "I'm more eager to see the next book.

ABOVE: Chester Himes's birth home, Jefferson City, Missouri. *(© Lawrence Jackson)*

BOTTOM, LEFT: Himes family, ca. 1911. From left, standing, Joseph, Edward, Estelle. From left, seated, Joseph Jr. and Chester. *(Used with permission of Lesley Packard Himes)*

BOTTOM, RIGHT: Brothers Chester, Edward, and Joseph Himes Jr., ca. 1910. *(Chester Himes Papers, Amistad Research Center, New Orleans, Louisiana)*

Lincoln Institute, ca. 1910. *(Lincoln University Picture Collection, Page Library, Jefferson City, Missouri)*

LEFT: Joseph Himes, Lincoln Institute blacksmith shop, ca. 1911. *(Lincoln University Picture Collection, Page Library, Jefferson City, Missouri)* RIGHT: Downtown Cleveland, Ohio, in the 1920s. *(Cleveland Public Library Photograph Collection)*

Himes's uncle Roddy, aunt Leah, and cousin Ella Moon. *(Courtesy of Western Reserve Historical Society, Cleveland, Ohio)*

Himes's Cleveland home. *(© Lawrence Jackson)*

Home of Mr. and Mrs. Samuel Miller.

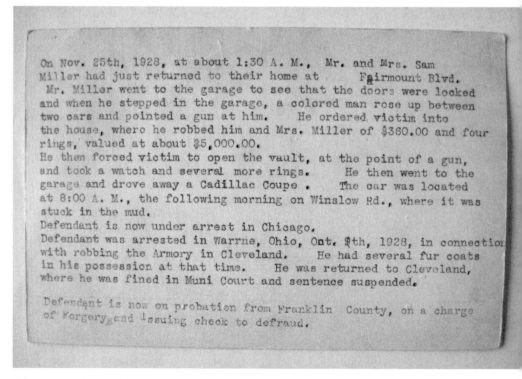

CCP 24-5M-2166-27

CRIMINAL RECORD DEPARTMENT
405 OLD COURT HOUSE

No. 35051   **Name** Himes, Chester   **Alias**

Offense Robbery   **Sec. G. C.** 12432

Arrested by Frabel, Gill   **Arrest Date**

Residence 2254 E. 100th St., Chicago, Ill.   **File No.** Cleve.Hts.

Occupation Chauffeur

Nativity U. S.   **Married** No   **Sex** M   **Race** C   **Age** 22   **Bail**

Accomplices

B. O. Cleve.Hts. **G. J.** 11/27 **Indt.** 11/27 **Argmt.** 12/4 No **Trial** 12/6 **Prob.** 12/7

Blotter ✓   **Index** ✓   **Report**   **Record**   **Comp.**

Disposition Change plea to guilty   O. Pen. 20 years   22

   Paroled 4-1-36

Judge Mc Mahon   **Date** 12/19/28
   Photo-32729   Inst.59623.

RECORD

On Nov. 25th, 1928, at about 1:30 A. M., Mr. and Mrs. Sam
Miller had just returned to their home at   Fairmount Blvd.
  Mr. Miller went to the garage to see that the doors were locked
and when he stepped in the garage, a colored man rose up between
two cars and pointed a gun at him.   He ordered victim into
the house, where he robbed him and Mrs. Miller of $360.00 and four
rings, valued at about $5,000.00.
He then forced victim to open the vault, at the point of a gun,
and took a watch and several more rings.   He then went to the
garage and drove away a Cadillac Coupe .   The car was located
at 8:00 A. M., the following morning on Winslow Rd., where it was
stuck in the mud.
Defendant is now under arrest in Chicago.
Defendant was arrested in Warrne, Ohio, Oct. 9th, 1928, in connection
with robbing the Armory in Cleveland.   He had several fur coats
in his possession at that time.   He was returned to Cleveland,
where he was fined in Muni Court and sentence suspended.

Defendant is now on probation from Franklin County, on a charge
of Forgery, and Issuing check to defraud.

Ohio criminal record for Chester Himes.

LEFT: Spring Street entrance, Ohio State Penitentiary, ca. 1929. *(Courtesy of the Ohio History Connection)*

BELOW, LEFT: Penitentiary cellblock fire, April 21, 1930. *(Courtesy of the Ohio History Connection)*

BELOW, RIGHT: Prisoners marching, spring 1930. *(Courtesy of the Ohio History Connection)*

BOTTOM: Convicts at dinner, ca. 1930. *(Courtesy of the Ohio History Connection)*

VICTS AT DINNER OHIO PENITENTIARY

RIGHT: Himes, ca. 1926. *(Chester Himes Papers, Amistad Research Center, New Orleans, Louisiana)* **BELOW:** Cousin Henry Lee Moon and his wife-to-be Mollie Lewis, ca. 1938. *(Courtesy of Western Reserve Historical Society, Cleveland, Ohio)*

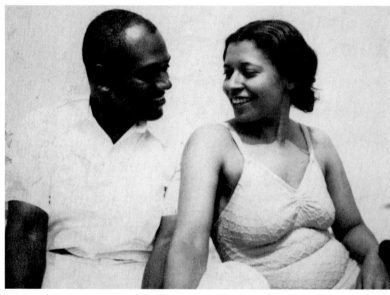

Lewis Bromfield's Malabar Farm. *(© Lawrence Jackson)*

Himes, ca. 1936. *(Courtesy of Western Reserve Historical Society, Cleveland, Ohio)*

Himes and Jean with unidentified couple, ca. 1944. *(Used with permission of Lesley Packard Himes)*

Jean and Chester Himes, fall 1945. (Afro *Newspaper / Gado / Getty Images*)

The Himes's Los Angeles residence. (© *Lawrence Jackson*)

ABOVE: The Himes brothers. From left, Joseph Jr., Chester, and Edward, ca. 1945. (*Chester Himes Papers, Amistad Research Center, New Orleans, Louisiana*) **LEFT, TOP**: Himes, 1943. (*Fisk University, John Hope and Aurelia E. Franklin Library, Special Collections, Julius Rosenwald Fund Collection*) **LEFT, BOTTOM**: Himes's mother, Estelle, ca. 1930. (*Chester Himes Papers, Amistad Research Center, New Orleans, Louisiana*)

I suspect that it will be less purely bitter, or if as bitter, then more focused."

A week later, he had a satisfying role on a panel at the New York Public Library's Schomburg branch on 135th Street with sociologist Horace Cayton and anthropologist St. Clair Drake. The two social scientists had just completed *Negro Metropolis,* an enormous study of black-belt Chicago. Richard Wright had helped the men get a trade contract for the book and had written the introduction. A man with a perpetual curiosity regarding the social psychology of race relations, Cayton had fallen in love with *If He Hollers Let Him Go.* Before he left Chicago for New York, he wrote to Richard Wright, "very much excited about this book . . . I've gone all out for it." Cayton, whose father had graduated from Alcorn, admired the book in his columns in the *Chicago Sun* and *Pittsburgh Courier.* A social reformer, Cayton prized the exposure of "the paralyzing fear and hatred which Negroes have developed toward their white suppressors" and encouraged his readers to buy the "courageous and strong book . . . a great piece of literature."

The momentum of the reviews picked up. In Cleveland, Ted Robinson, the *Plain Dealer*'s reviewer, certified *If He Hollers* as "the ticket-of-admission of Chester B. Himes to the limited company of our top-flight novelists." In New York Chester's buddy Constance Curtis praised him for showing "the calculated castration of prejudice," and, unlike the *Times,* glimpsed that the real problem was that "Bob had too much of the desire for unequivocal equality. That was his mistake." Even in the pages of the more staid *Crisis,* editor Roy Wilkins admitted that Chester "tells so accurately how Negroes feel about the countless humiliations heaped upon them hour after hour."

But to Chester the most important praise came from Richard Wright. Wright had approached the alternative left-leaning newspaper *PM* to examine *If He Hollers Let Him Go* alongside a new book by Arthur Miller. Wright delivered the review on November 25, beginning his article with a quote from Karl Marx and calling the two books "fairly competently executed novels." Then Wright zeroed in on Chester's book:

> Jerky in pace, *If He Hollers Let Him Go* has been compared with the novels of James M. Cain, but there is more honest passion in 20 pages of Himes than in the whole of Cain. Tough-minded Himes has no illusions: I doubt if he has ever had any. He sees too clearly to be fooled by the symbolic guises in which Negro behavior tries to hide, and he traces the transformations by which sex is expressed in equations of race pride, murder in the language of personal redemption and love in terms of hate.
>
> To read Himes conventionally is to miss the significance of the (to coin a phrase) bio-social level of his writing. Bob Jones is so charged with elementary passion that he ceases to be a personality and becomes a man reacting only with nerves, blood and motor responses.
>
> Ironically, the several dreams that head each chapter do not really come off. Indeed, Himes' brutal prose is more authentically dreamlike than his consciously contrived dreams. And that is as it should be.
>
> In this, his first novel, Himes establishes himself not as what has quaintly been called a New Negro, but as a new kind of writing man.

Chester and Wright became men of shared vision. Recuperating at home from a bad cold, Wright received Chester on December 14. Having their boyhoods in Mississippi in common—Himes in Lorman near Vicksburg and Wright seventy-five miles north in Jackson—the two men bonded easily and warmly. Chester confided to Wright about his youthful criminal rebellion, and his nearly eight years in jail— this was of great interest to Wright, who that spring had completed a novel about juvenile gangs and crime he was calling *The Jackal* (it would be published after his death as *Rite of Passage*). Unlike the literary men whose work came exclusively from the library, Chester had known and survived deadly, torturous adversity. After recounting the adventures and punishments, he told Wright, "Nothing can hurt me." Chester's prison experience impressed and thrilled Wright, a mild-mannered man, as the verification of a kind of machismo. Nevertheless, at about the same time that Chester's relationship collapsed with Henry Moon, a guiding force for him for eight years, Chester befriended and was befriended by Richard Wright, the most famous living black writer.

A couple of days after their get-together Chester sent Wright a note of "appreciation." "The manner in which Horace Cayton, you, Ralph Ellison have come forward with such good will and interest," the letter began warmly, "is indicative of a new day on the literary front." Chester thought Wright able and mature, beyond the "petty jealousies, snipings, bickerings, animosities that have plagued Negro writers." He proudly enrolled himself "in this new school which it has fallen your responsibility to head." A day later they arranged a morning rendezvous so that the Himeses and the Wrights could meet. Chester and Jean later had "a wonderful time" at the Wrights' Christmas Eve party. On other occasions they met over West Indian food at a restaurant called Connie's in Greenwich Village. When Joseph Himes Jr. came to town for New Year's, Chester and Jean invited the Wrights to their party. In turn, Wright took Himes to meet some of the staff at the Book-of-the-Month Club, and publicist Vivian Wolfert helped Chester draw out a new strategy to advertise *If He Hollers*. They continued getting together at the Wrights' Washington Square apartment with Wright's inner circle of friends, including Ellison, Horace Cayton, St. Clair Drake, C. L. R. James, and his companion, the professional model and socialist Constance Webb. While the good times were genuine, sometimes serious tensions flared up. At one of the parties, according to Webb, Wright teased Ralph Ellison about his novel in progress so persistently that a frustrated Ellison drew a knife and Himes intervened to disarm him. Wright would sometimes exaggerate to his other friends that Chester had committed murder.

Chester almost certainly mentioned to Wright his relationship to Ruth Seid. Before Seid's *The Wasteland* was published in 1946, Wright reviewed the galleys of the book, a novel he liked because it helped him understand the narrow racial prejudice of his mother-in-law, an immigrant Jew from Poland. But that circle of acquaintance was too small for Chester. He put some distance between himself and the next star alum of Cleveland's Writers' Project. If Seid thought his character's emotion overblown, he declared that she "used to pump frustration through me almost as intense as that suffered by Bob—only I, being inhibited by the numerous restraints of life, never quite showed the depth of my resentment." Chester wanted her to understand that she had no right to presume any familiarity. He had been out of sorts, more or less at every stage in his life, and had finally found peers. He was now anxious to keep others at bay.

The year 1945 for Chester was a watershed, like 1928: the book publication and his mother's death, the survival of the marriage to Jean—or her forceful claim to it, in spite of his drunken infidelities—and the cutting of his ties with his influential cousin, in favor of two of the twentieth century's most influential American novelists. In the process, Chester had become a national figure. Near year's end, he gave an interview to Earl Conrad of the *Chicago Defender*. Conrad's article, complete with a large photograph of Chester, corralled him, Ralph Ellison, and Richard Wright into a "blues school of writers" who were "trying to show what the inexplorable caste system can do to the human being." Chester offered a series of polite, highly temperate responses and he revealed to Conrad that while he worked on the WPA, "I developed a hatred of the ruling class of whites." But

Conrad regarded Chester as having internalized racism and turned negrophobia on its head. He wrote of Chester and his mates as "literary projections of the social type they portray—Bigger Thomas." If they were not driven to murder in their confrontation with racial discrimination, the "blues school" men were "highly sensitized, nervous, jittery, ultra-critical, cynical." Chester's cynicism and rejection of ideology were palpable to all, and they paid at least one tangible dividend. In December 1945, deciding that he made poor material for the Communists, the special agent in charge from Los Angeles requested that the director of the FBI shutter Himes's file.

Chapter Eight

MONKEY AN' THE LION

1946–1948

Unnamed in the *Chicago Defender* interview was the intellectual leader of the "blues school" of black postwar thought, E. Franklin Frazier. During the first week of January 1946, Chester convened "the upper IQ brackets" for a party: the Schomburg librarian Laurence Dunbar Reddick (who would also write the first serious biography of Martin Luther King Jr.), Horace Cayton, and Frazier, chairman of the sociology department at Howard University. Richard Wright, Ralph Ellison, and Trinidadian Marxist C. L. R. James probably also attended. Taken all together, it was an extraordinary informal convention of black humanists and social scientists.

Chester was finding distinctive import in the views of the fifty-one-year-old Frazier, whom he knew from Mollie and Henry's. Born in 1894 and a University of Chicago graduate, Frazier had become the most celebrated black academic of his era, a gutsy infighter who confronted bigotry and injustice and published leading studies on the condition of the black family—books that innovatively tapped the work of novelists like Rudolph Fisher and Langston Hughes—

all while achieving the highest honors and positions of leadership in spite of segregation. Wary of Frazier's commitment to ordinary black people, his Howard University colleague Ralph Bunche called him a "crazy racialist." Chester gravitated toward the commanding view of Frazier in one key area: the Negro family. Frazier believed that black Americans needed a firmly patriarchal family structure to compete for resources in the United States; and when he examined the past, he didn't see one in evidence. As disgruntled as Chester, Frazier sensed that the situation of black Americans had not yet reached the threshold of even subordinate caste relations. "It is not a question of the Negro being all right in *his place* but rather that there is *no place* for the Negro," Frazier wrote that year. The absence of patriarchal models was part of the "no place" problem.

This meeting with these intellectual heavies confirmed in early 1946 that Chester had secured a niche. He received $2000 in fat royalties from Doubleday in January, and then, after a minor delay, $2700 more came in March. Having accumulated within three months a sum equal to what he was used to living on for two years, Chester felt like this was the dawn of financial success. The reviews of *If He Hollers Let Him Go* continued to compliment him. Highbrow liberal magazines like *New Republic* treated him respectfully, even when pointing to the narrow range of the characters' choices, between the hammer of "limited opportunities as a Negro" and the anvil of "suicidal . . . militancy." Only one review, in the *Cleveland Call and Post*, mentioned that Chester had gone to prison, where his blemish became "the one clouded spot in the young writer's life, an unfortunate experience indulged in by a youngster." Walter White, smeared in *If He Hollers* ("If he asked me if I knew Walter Somebody-or-other I was subject to tell him to go to hell," snaps the hero), quibbled a bit in the *Chicago Defender* before deciding Chester had made a "contribution to American literature and American racial thinking of no small distinction."

Arthur P. Davis, a Howard University colleague of Frazier, called

If He Hollers a "stout weapon" with a "powerful message." Davis understood that the black middle class would reject the novel's literary naturalism and its portrayal of unrefined blacks. But he believed in Chester's vision, partly because a "writer like Himes, who has worked in the factories and the shipyards, knows the masses: he has seen the effects of discrimination, bad sanitation, and malnutrition in the shocking speech and low morals of these people and he puts down what he sees and hears. But he also puts down a whole lot more and that redeems the work for me."

In the Communist-controlled organ of the National Negro Congress, the *Congress View*, New Yorker Ruth Jett mouthed the hoary Party line used against *Native Son*; while "powerful" the book had failed to "see the progress made in Negro-white relations through the progressive section of American labor." Then an odd, minor miracle occurred. In the Communist *Daily Worker*, writer Eugene Gordon unreservedly praised the book, even though it had criticized the Communist wartime line that racial grievances should be subordinated for the sake of the war effort. "Communists should read the book, so that they may be reminded of much we forgot in the past period," Gordon told the rank and file. *If He Hollers* would "shock" because, unknown to the Party faithful, "there is a hell of a lot of work to be done among the Negro and white masses." A black Communist like Gordon was in a good position to critique Party politics in the months following the removal of leader Earl Browder, which was a time of "self-flagellation." Curious about the *Daily Worker* endorsement, Richard Wright, who had had his own falling-out with the Communist Party, telephoned Chester to warn about "maneuvering." But Himes hoped to harness the Communist energy to give the book a push. "The thing I have been trying to do is promote book sales," he wrote, "since my company doesn't seem to give a damn about it."

After the remarkable season of reviews for *If He Hollers Let Him*

Go, Chester was right to feel slighted by Doubleday's handling of the book. In 1945 and 1946 it skimped on his novel, which made the press uncomfortable, and went all out for Fannie Cook's *Mrs. Palmer's Honey.* Written by a white woman, what was obviously valuable about the book was its pointing to a "brighter future." From the beginning of its advertising campaign to booksellers in January 1946, Doubleday deliberately seemed to contrast Chester's book with Fannie Cook's. The publisher ran a full-page advertisement dominated by a black maid, a representation of the main character, Honey. The text of the ad explained, "*Mrs. Palmer's Honey* is a book which you can sell to any reader. It is an honest, intelligent novel, devoid of lynching, mixed love affairs, and profanity. Shunning the sensational, Fannie Cook has written a fine, sincere novel. . . ." Doubleday seemed to disparage *If He Hollers* by suggesting that blacks were too emotional to know with certainty whether or not they were being oppressed; the firm also dismissed Chester's book as being without appeal to white readers. Bucklin Moon, the editor of both novels, made recommendations about the advertising campaigns but shared little of his decisions and strategies with Chester.

By February a storm had erupted that mimicked the jeering the *New York Times* initiated when Cook received the Carver Award. In an advertisement in *Saturday Review of Literature,* written to seem like the commentary on a published book review, Doubleday tried to temper the appearance of ill will, by emphasizing its credentials as publishers of black writers.

> [*Mrs. Palmer's Honey*] is a novel which has a social conscience, and yet is "devoid of lynchings, mixed love affairs, and profanity"; a novel which eases its points along with good reading rather than a series of sledge-hammer speeches punctuated by spit; a novel which was chosen only after we had considered books by Walter White, Arna Bontemps, Chester Himes, and many others.

Still shielding Cook's white identity, the advertisement nonetheless manages to score all black authors as writing venomous and unworthy tracts. Jack Conroy, the white man who wrote *They Seek a City* with Arna Bontemps, was curiously spared inclusion. The circulation of these sullied mea culpas incensed Chester, who began his redress with his Doubleday editor. Bucklin Moon told Chester that he was imagining conspiracies and making "unreasonable" complaints. The two men would more or less fall out over the ads and the handling of *If He Hollers*. In desperation, Chester mailed a clipping of the ad to Ken McCormick, the editor in chief, protesting "the veiled references to my book and the use of my name" to market *Mrs. Palmer's Honey*. McCormick reportedly responded with a ten-line telegram of apology.

The situation with Doubleday became ugly after Chester stormed the publisher's Manhattan headquarters, armed with letters from Cleveland, North Carolina, and Los Angeles attesting to the fact that books were unavailable in markets where he would be sought out. Going upstairs, he griped to Hilda Simms, the beautiful star of the Broadway play *Anna Lucasta*, who also happened to be in the elevator. But Chester was overheard by a freelancer in advertising, who rushed ahead of him and alerted the staff. Chester was determined to be heard. He revealed his suspicion that a Doubleday editor or vice president had disrupted the print run, then he turned to McCormick himself. Chester accused him of appointing Buck Moon to preside over a "black corner" at Doubleday, a Jim Crow section that held books written by African Americans to a quota. Then, he insisted that "someone in the firm was against the book." After a few minutes of "bad words," he left the company president's office, finished, in the near term, at Doubleday. "I believe conclusively that my book was sabotaged by some one in the company," he wrote a few months later, still seething.

Despite the fireworks, it's unlikely that Chester was making a bad situation worse. Even mild-mannered Arna Bontemps agreed with him, having already written several months previously that Doubleday "treated us like stepchildren" and that the powers in control there planned to sell "10,000 copies of this title—and no more!"

However, one element of Chester's new prestige as a nationally reviewed novelist was the ability to hit back. On February 26, three weeks following the unflattering advertisement in *Saturday Review*, Chester had his druthers in the magazine. He insisted that *If He Hollers Let Him Go* presented "a tiny facet of the frustrations inherent in the lives of present day Americans" and the resulting "compulsive behavior." Chester struck out against the public and his own publisher's presumption that because he had the nerve to broach the issue of racial discord he had to be a civil rights problem-solver. He refused to back down about the raw materials in his book:

> the only change I would consider would be to restore some of the passages that were deleted from the script for fear of offending the delicate sensitivities of the American public. . . . Certainly I would not attempt to offer a solution for the "Negro problem." . . . Nor would I saddle an underprivileged, uneducated, poverty stricken, oppressed racial group with this responsibility (and I have nothing but antipathy for those who do).

Eight years later, Chester declared that the "New York Critics have never forgiven me" for this tart article, a most stinging cry against whites for black artistic freedom during the 1940s.

In the black press Chester was more easygoing. He sent a letter to Walter White, agreeing that black writers should construct Negro heroes such as Cook had done with her political volunteers in *Mrs. Palmer's Honey*. Chester suggested that "the bitter cries of a suppressed people" was actually a stimulant for white bigots, a chemical that purged "the slovenliness from their ambitions and impels them to drive on to great white supremacy." Since it was really black pain and torture that fueled white Americans' strength, "there are very few white people, including most white liberals, who sincerely want to hear of Negro heroes," he ventured. But he would keep pitching until something stuck. He told White, "However, if you give us a chance, we'll get some Negro heroes in—I, personally will make you that promise."

The solid reviews and the Doubleday mishandling left him in the gap between artistic notoriety and full-fledged success. He would learn eventually that part of his debut's greatest value was its timing and its ability to cadge reviews at all, but his career might never have continued if Chester had known that this first book would remain his best-known novel in a long career. During its year and a half of hardcover sales, Doubleday sold 13,211 hardcovers. In 1949, the reprint rights were sold to New American Library for $5461, and they then sold, over two decades, more than 450,000 paperback copies. The book was translated into French by a man named Marcel Duhamel and published in 1949 by Albin Michel. Chester's commitment to bringing the contemporary speech rhythm and experience of black urban life to print would have long-term impact. His hardcover sales were respectable and suggested that he might create at least a coterie following. The problem was that to cut that narrow slice he would have to top Richard Wright. Underscoring the growth he'd need to show to go beyond Wright's achievements, *Esquire* brought out one of Chester's stories that had likely been purchased in 1941, "The Something in a Colored Man." The piece was a "coffin caper" story told in "jive" and set on L.A.'s Central Avenue. With the delayed appearance of this early work, Chester was regrettably back in national magazines as a stereotype of himself in prison learning to write.

There were also competitors vying to top Wright's high mark of achievement. During the winter of 1945–1946, Chester was familiarly dropping by Wright's house in the company of his buddy Ralph Ellison. As the three men gathered to "beat that boy"—Ellison's preferred

term for a discussion of race relations—Himes lapped up the chance
to discuss literature, politics, and American race problems with brainy,
courageous comrades.

Wright certainly was not slowing down. By March, he was putting in his passport application, determined to exchange Greenwich
Village for the Latin Quarter, hoping that Paris would have the
enchantment and wonder for him that it had had for Americans from
the time of Benjamin Franklin. Wright had met Jean-Paul Sartre a
year earlier when the guru of the existentialist philosophy arrived in
New York. He had also taken up a literary correspondence with Gertrude Stein. In the subsequent year he had been building himself up
on the existentialist movement, conferring with Hannah Arendt and
Paul Tillich, and in April he would consult with a visiting Albert
Camus. But Wright downplayed all of the scurrying and parlaying
to Chester, a subterfuge done partly because of political difficulties
Wright anticipated around obtaining his passport. However, Chester
also discerned another quality. Although they were the same age and
Wright was generous, he sometimes acted bored with Chester.

One way that Wright seemed to put Chester in a notch below
was by keeping "the important people to himself." Nevertheless, in
March 1946 Chester accompanied him on a trip that proved invalu-
able. The occasion was an appointment at the posh Central Park West
apartment of the famously bucktoothed white cultural critic, novelist,
and photographer Carl Van Vechten. Now sixty-five, the foppish Van
Vechten had introduced American audiences to Stravinsky's sympho-
nies, Marcel Duchamp's *Nude Descending a Staircase No. 2*, modern
dance, and Gertrude Stein. Van Vechten had also done as much as
anyone to trounce the barriers of racial apartheid in American social
life. His special affinity for black people and jazz had begun during
his student days at the University of Chicago, when he would crash
all-black parties and be "invariably taken for a coon." He called jazz
music not the last hope or the best hope of America: "it is the only

hope." In New York he was known as "the undisputed downtown authority on uptown night life," and as a good buddy of Langston Hughes, whom he helped to launch at the same time as Paul Robeson. When Chester met him, Van Vechten had started collecting manuscripts from African American writers and personally photographing as many black artists, singers, and published writers as he could get to pose. Wright's papers would one day find their way into the collection Van Vechten established in James Weldon Johnson's name at Yale.

Chester found the scene comic. Wright was uncomfortable around Van Vechten and masked his discomfort by being "pompous." Wright's artifice made Chester "hysterical" with laughter, and Van Vechten shared a few bemused glances with Chester in confidence. "Intrigued" by Himes and unable to forget his loud guffaws, Van Vechten opened the door to a warm, crucial friendship for Chester. He invited Chester back for his own series of photographs the next day; afterward, Van Vechten wrote to suggest that Chester, like Richard Wright and other black authors, send him manuscripts of his published novels for preservation at the Yale Library. In their discussions over the years, Chester would find the "calm and serene" older man a steadying force—even if Chester always catered to Van Vechten in soothing tones of fidelity.

Revisiting his promise to Walter White, Chester partnered with his brother Joe to deliver a short story about discrimination in the war industries called "The Boiling Point" in the pages of the *Afro-American* on March 9. Openly discriminated against at the war plants, the main character, Impetuous Brown, is sued for claiming discrimination, then bribed. On March 16, Chester returned to the New York Public Library on 135th Street where the Schomburg Collection of Negro History and Literature was held and Laurence Reddick the librarian. Chester described his work on a panel with Carey McWilliams, the Los Angeles writer and labor lawyer. At the event Chester worked hard to generate support from liberals like McWilliams for his career beyond Clevelanders and racial uplifters.

Chester had written in his *Saturday Review* article that the only criticism he would accept from the self-appointed apostles of black writing would be in the area of technique. This was untrue; he took the criticisms of political content to heart. In the novel he was writing during the period when *If He Hollers Let Him Go* was garnering reviews, Chester looked fondly at the CIO and organizations like its Political Action Committee as broad solutions to racial and economic injustice (as his competitor Fannie Cook had). Chester kept the self-searching quest cited in his original Rosenwald fellowship application in his new book, but he redirected its punch by nodding toward these two groups (without naming either) as a means to destroy segregation in heavy industry. The hero of the book would be a union organizer, an intellectual whose job was to educate and unionize black industrial workers. The novel would itself explore the abundant tension facing a black intellectual, from interactions with black Southern migrants at work, union bosses, politicos like the Communists, and in the bedroom with his spouse. Chester had darts to throw at every category, but he was not anti-Communist. He still believed that, in terms of political freedom for blacks, "citizens of the communist-dominated socialist state of the U.S.S.R. have come closest." Chester's hero, now called Lee Gordon, would combine the aims of the CIO and its Political Action Committee, and also come to terms with the Communist Party. Using the revolutionary martyr he had described in his "Negro Martyrs Are Needed" program, the novel concluded with the evolution of the left-wing political movement, consisting of labor, Communists, and blacks. Chester's approach to the political scene was widely shared by many Americans, indicated by the groundswell that would later coalesce behind the alternative political candidate for president in 1947–1948, former vice president Henry A. Wallace.

Despite his difficulties at Doubleday, Chester felt potent as a writer and in good spirits. He roared into the new novel, sometimes pulling forty pages from the typewriter in a day. On the side, he worked on a review of Ann Petry's first book, *The Street*, a naturalistic treatment of a black woman's downfall in Harlem. Chester applauded almost everything about that book, save its retinue of black men who abused and exploited black women and refused to support their families. If he believed himself committed to the male duties neglected by Petry's characters, racist New York made some of them impossible. Despite the cash windfall he'd drawn, he remained unable to rent a decent apartment in New York.

Out of sorts and tired of looking for a place in crowded, segregated New York, Chester and Jean decided upon a sabbatical in California, this time to the northern part of the state, where her brother owned property. They bought a Mercury Coupe and, because the Klan was active and lynchings were surging, a .303 Savage rifle for "security." Shouldering the firearm was done for the same reason "other Negroes own long-bladed knives," Chester joked, half serious. After a final colloquy with Wright, who would sail for Paris on May 1, and a hurried telephone call to Ralph Ellison, Chester left New York with Jean about April 18, coasting comfortably along America's first cross-country national road, the Lincoln Highway.

Their route would take them through Ohio. In Cleveland Chester checked on his father; invited his brother Joe Jr. and his wife, Estelle, to spend a portion of the summer in California with them; and chatted with Ruth Seid. Ruth was now famous, having won a $10,000 literary prize from Harper's at the beginning of the year for her unsparing novel *The Wasteland*. When they talked, Ruth mentioned that she disliked the lesbian scene in *If He Hollers Let Him Go*; Chester blamed the cuts to the book and told her to get the original manuscript from Wright, which probably would have rankled her further. But he looked in vain in the shops for *If He Hollers*.

Before leaving Ohio, he and Jean went to Malabar Farm. He

wanted badly to prove to Louis Bromfield that, after five years, he was more than capable of handling his career himself. The experience backfired. Bromfield hustled them in through the front door of the Big House and offered them neither seats nor refreshment, seeming unimpressed that his former servant had won a Rosenwald fellowship and achieved national reviews and good sales for his novel. Instead, only Bromfield sat down, "chatted with us then took us back to the kitchen to meet the help and let us out the back door."

Bromfield had prepared them for the rest of journey. After the Himeses left Illinois and until they got to California, they found "no place" where they could "sit down to a table and have a meal." During the thirty hours of driving that it took between Denver and Reno, Nevada, they would not be able to purchase any food at all. Unsurprised by mean bigotry in the United States during the 1940s, even Chester found it difficult to endure "brutal and vicious . . . American race prejudice in the North." When he wrote Van Vechten, he was noting the wisdom of Wright's exodus: "I hope to be following him within a year."

Chester and Jean reached California at the end of April. They drove over to Oakland for Jean's older brother, Hugo Johnson, a forty-five-year-old noncommissioned officer who had served more than half of his life in the Navy. He was working in San Francisco as chief of the shore patrol at the Embarcadero. With Jean's blunt, muscular, and humorless brother, they drove 350 miles to a ranch in Milford, California, arriving on May 7. Johnson owned a ten-thousand-acre farm, most of it barren, between the dried-out, ten-mile-wide Honey Lake and the six-thousand-foot peaks of the snowcapped Sierra Nevada.

Although they rented their place from a black man, Hugo Johnson's tenants had left when they learned a Negro couple were coming to spend the summer there. A malnourished, lewd squatter family had taken the opportunity to camp out in the dilapidated two-story house that served as the main dwelling, a hovel so unseemly that Chester repaired and painted another building on the property, a "modern version of a sharecropper's shanty," for living quarters. He and Jean lived in a three-room shack, sitting fifty yards from the road, and separated from the tottering main house by a grove of fruit trees. And although he and Hugo hunted a deer that summer, Chester used the rifle mainly to shoot rattlesnakes coming out of hibernation. In the pristine Sierra wilderness in the shack besieged by rats, lizards, and snakes, Himes would put in some of the finest writing days of his career. He recalled, "I remember that summer as one of the most pleasant of our life."

Despite the travails at Doubleday imperiling his young career, his editor, Bucklin Moon, was telling the black American public in the pages of *Negro Digest* that the publishing climate for black-themed books was fantastic. Happy about such progress, Moon acknowledged that ten years earlier "no publisher would have touched" a book as "bitter" and "explosive" as *If He Hollers Let Him Go* and praised Chester for having "power and rare insight." But Moon continued to defend Doubleday and white liberalism. He insisted that the only negative sentiment against Chester's book was "from a Negro who felt that writers like Richard Wright and Chester Himes . . . were setting back race relations fifty years!"

Chester couldn't have disagreed more. In the first week of June he wrote Doubleday requesting "a better relationship with them or a release." His hope now went out to Carl Van Vechten, who had a keen friendship with publisher Blanche Knopf. He wanted Knopf to buy out the Doubleday contract and pay him an additional $500. He admitted that he was "a spendthrift," and the car and the trip had already consumed all the royalties received to date. Alert to the books that Van Vechten had written with gay themes, Chester introduced his three-part prison story, calling it partly "a homo-sexual love story." The book was now called *Yesterday Will Make You Cry*. Thinking that the "homo-sexual story seems to have killed it," Chester mailed the manuscript. Van Vechten, working on an introduction for Gertrude Stein's new book, took the time to read it and became a permanent supporter and fan of Chester's, the Howells to his Dunbar. Meanwhile, the pictures that Van Vechten had taken of Chester earlier that year had been forwarded to California. Chester disliked the photographer's prettying touch, preferring the "blemishes, marks, scars, and lines of the face to show, even at the risk of appearing like a thug."

A week later, Chester wrote Ken McCormick at Doubleday, seeking to draw further royalties. The reply shocked him. Claiming an accounting error, McCormick wrote that Chester owed the company more than one thousand dollars. Sensing mistreatment, Chester asked formally to be released from the contract for his new book and McCormick reputedly sent him a long saga about Doubleday's attempts to sign black authors and place black books. But they assented, and three weeks into June, Doubleday agreed to release Chester if he repaid about two thousand dollars (and, ultimately, if he purchased 2400 remaindered copies). He was beginning a long career of what he perceived as métayage to publishers, a relationship where, as he saw it, he was mysteriously overadvanced and then ever tied to his publisher until someone bought his debt, shackling him to a new boss.

By the time of the discussions to leave Doubleday, Chester had a rough draft of three hundred pages of his new novel about the union organizer, what he thought was about two-thirds of the book. His agent, Lurton Blassingame, and Knopf conferred in mid-July. Knopf awaited the manuscript before making a final decision. Now the pages came more slowly to Chester "as it nears the end." Four weeks after that, in early August, he had a completed draft of a new novel. He was scared that the book might be rejected by Knopf as amateurish, even as he felt the emotional loss connected to completing a massive project

Weakened by "absolute exhaustion," he suffered extremely when news reached him of his father's costly operation in a Cleveland hospital, followed by the death of his puppy, hit by a car. The anxieties about the new book and the personal traumas came pouring out in a message to Van Vechten: "Few things that ever happened to me hurt me so, not even when I was sentenced to twenty years in prison," he wrote from the lodge in the Sierras. Ostensibly about his dog, the message was referring to his anxiety about all of his writing. Badly needing affirmation, Chester airmailed the newly finished manuscript to Van Vechten to provide a "general evaluation." Van Vechten read the long manuscript and sent back a letter of reassurance. Van Vechten's main caution was for the future; he noticed that, like Ernest Hemingway, Himes was using the same "quick-tempered but charming" protagonists. But the writer whose novel *Nigger Heaven* had stirred controversy during the Harlem Renaissance deemed *Lonely Crusade,* as the book had been renamed, "tremendous and powerful."

In another serious misfortune, Hugo Johnson had an accident in August, fully disabling the Mercury Coupe. Chester and Hugo searched futilely at the local Ford dealer for parts to repair the vehicle. When they returned home, Jean was missing. After searching by torchlight, they found Jean three miles away from the ranch, stumbling and sobbing in the desert. Chester assumed the worst: that she had been raped. But Jean had not been assaulted; she was distraught after reading the manuscript of *Lonely Crusade.* Jean believed that she served as the model for Ruth, the wife of the protagonist Lee Gordon, a character who "felt a sense of inferiority because her skin was brown." In the novel, Chester has Ruth smearing white powder on her face after concluding that her husband is having an affair with a white woman. Ruth's feet of clay were on much greater display in her depiction as a manipulative social climber, whose appearance called to mind "that beaten, whorish look of so many other Negro women." Few wives would not have been disturbed by the neurotic, unappealing character resembling themselves physically and written by their husbands. Hugo calmed his sister by reminding her that the next bus out of Susanville, the nearest town, wasn't for another twelve hours.

As before in New York, Jean went home to Chester. But she "hated" the novel. Jean was right to perceive that the depiction of Ruth was a more direct severing of their tie. Chester would only ever go as far as admitting, "I often wondered if I had drawn a true picture of which I was not consciously aware." Chester would dedicate the book to Hugo.

Jean's outcry was a suitable finale to the summer. With the car destroyed, the Himeses had no way to get provisions and had to surrender California. In September Chester sent the manuscript off to Blassingame, who then delivered it to Knopf on October 7, 1946. Chester and Jean took a bus to Reno and then a train to New York. They checked in at the Theresa Hotel, the Harlem crossroads, on October 14.

Chester and Jean reconciled in the midst of interesting a better publisher for his next book. Again Chester appeared on the verge of significant achievement. As *Ebony* magazine described him that year, he was "no great shakes as a success story," yet "a good prospect" to become one. To fulfill that hopeful mandate meant continuing to live in style. By mid-October Chester had secured quarters in Wading River, Long Island, about seventy-five miles from Manhattan. The Himeses lived on the second floor in a small four-room carriage house on a nine-acre beachfront estate owned by Columbia University neurologist Frank Safford. Safford had the estate set up as a writers' colony during the summer, usually hosting the *New Yorker* staff. The Saffords' large wooden home, occupied by a caretaker, sat near the beach, and a wooded hillside was stippled with small cottages. Except for when the Saffords, a family of five, came out for Christmas 1946, Chester and Jean passed the fall by themselves, with the sea and the small upper-crust town of Wading River, where the white residents were "too well-heeled and secure to worry about a black couple in their neighborhood." He sounded confident in a message to Langston Hughes about their new lodging, where he could put the "finishing touches" on his book.

The staff at Alfred A. Knopf was impressed by what he had done. Knopf reader Clinton Simpson understood immediately that Himes had written something of an existentialist novel, since it used Marxist material and economic critiques, alongside modern concerns about sexuality and unconscious drives, concluding with hard-fought personal affirmations of liberty and choice. Himes's protagonist was considered to have "become a free man in a sense that he is finally free of the fear which has oppressed him all his life." Knopf's Milton Rugoff noted that the "raw and fiery" book compared favorably with Wright's *Native Son* and carried real depth: "sheer intensity of feeling" and "the heartbreaking effect of constant defeat, and fear that can be dissolved only by violence." Knopf agreed to publish the book and it took an option for an exclusive look at his next. As Simpson had written when he encouraged Knopf to take on the project, "He doesn't strike me as likely ever to write best sellers, but he might become, if he is not already, one of the finest Negro novelists." Chester signed the contract on November 6, 1946.

Boutique-size, patrician Knopf, the firm founded in 1915 by the married business partners Blanche and Alfred A. Knopf, was for Chester a bright improvement over Doubleday. Then in her early fifties, Blanche Knopf typically vetted and edited the fiction list of about one hundred titles per year. Van Vechten and the influential journalist H. L. Mencken were two of her closest friends. She had, through Van Vechten, published Langston Hughes's first book, *The Weary Blues*, in 1926, and she worked with other hard-boiled writers to whom Chester was or would be compared, such as James M. Cain, Raymond Chandler, and Dashiell Hammett. Like her editorial team, Blanche Knopf believed that Chester was writing "one of the most dramatic and striking stories of Negro life."

His old colleagues learned of his good news. Bucklin Moon was admitting now, in the pages of *New Republic,* that "southern liberals" and "a great many white readers in the North" hadn't been ready for

Chester's first book. Convinced that Himes was at least a budding star, Moon considered it a milestone to have worked with Chester, the new master of the "psychological lynching."

Despite signing the new contract, money remained a problem. After Doubleday had been repaid to release him from his contract, he had only a few hundred dollars up front, and a monthly allotment from Knopf of perhaps one hundred dollars to last through the winter. Chester hatched a new plan. He returned to the Julius Rosenwald Fund, hoping to follow Wright out of the United States. Chester knew that having a contract with Knopf would help, but his project was dreamy and lacking strong purpose. He wanted to "travel abroad for a year—England, France, Russia, India, and China—to broaden my knowledge of the cultures of the world, and thereby add depth and objectivity to my potential contribution towards a better world." As he had since his experience on the Cleveland Writers' Project, Chester sought reprieve from "the immediate influence of American racial oppression." During Christmas he hoped to pitch the travel idea to William Haygood, Vandi's husband, who had returned home from the Army to resume his work at the Rosenwald Fund.

At Thanksgiving weekend, a recently wedded Fanny and Ralph Ellison shared the carriage house, delighting in "the good food, the marvelous talk, the long walk on the beach and in the woods." Chester was pleased to spend time with Ellison, who had become more opinionated since Wright left the United States. Before the couple arrived, Chester wrote to Ellison asking to borrow "Lenin's Principles of Marxism or any of Lenin's discussions on dialectical materialism in pamphlet or booklet form." Ellison almost certainly shared the materials, which then made their way into Chester's novel, in the form of speeches and lectures between principal characters. Ellison also brought Bucklin Moon's *New Republic* article touting the strength of *If He Hollers Let Him Go*.

Chester and Ellison hunted and drank and, by and large, the

outing was pleasant and affectionate. Ellison had spent a good portion of the previous spring and summer camped out in a cabin in Quogue, southeast of Wading River, and he was working on a new topic, different from the bitter novel of a downed black airman that he had shared with Chester in the fall of 1944. However, their more intense discussions now had an increasingly competitive edge. Thirty-seven-year-old Chester and the thirty-three-year-old Ellison tussled over who was most politically astute, who best understood the nature of black life in America, which literary techniques and literary masters were the most important, and who was capable of surpassing the achievement of Richard Wright.

By 1946, Ellison was becoming a sought-after cultural analyst of growing importance. He had reached his largest national audience in *Saturday Review* that summer, and that fall he was drafting an essay for *Survey Graphic*, slated to appear side by side with Chester's older academic friends E. Franklin Frazier and Sterling Brown. Ellison believed that the tradition of white American writing, from Herman Melville to Ernest Hemingway, created empty shadows of black people and this practice had hallowed out the country's democratic ideals. Taking the view that black people were completely healthy when properly recognized, Ellison was distancing himself from his black friends who were fully committed to the idea that racism had damaged and made black people—men in particular—fearful. Speaking more like a college professor—he had given lectures at Bennington that fall—Ellison now sharply critiqued Horace Cayton's pet idea of a "fear-hate-fear" complex operating in the mind of black men. During a meeting that summer, he pointed out to Cayton that while he had accurately determined "certain general aspects of Negro personality," he "underplay[ed] the subjective element," which was completely necessary to understand individual black people as well as a work of art.

Instead of the problem of fear, Ellison valued "the blues," for him an artistic kit that solved a variety of life's dilemmas, in a manner similar to the way that Albert Camus was pushing for "the absurd" in his *Myth of Sisyphus*, "the certainty of a crushing fate, without the resignation." Ellison thought that the musical art form emanating from the Mississippi Delta had the capacity to "transcend" the "jagged grain" of experience "not by consolation of philosophy but by squeezing from it a near-tragic, near-comic lyricism." And while Richard Wright himself had been suspicious of Ellison's concept of "the blues" as an explanatory device to unpack Wright's memoir *Black Boy*, Ellison in turn rejected the Earl Conrad creation of the "blues school," which Cayton had echoed in a column.

In the discussion with Chester, Ellison, who had been raised, for the most part, by a single mother, insisted that the black family had a matriarchal cast. Although this was one of E. Franklin Frazier's points, Chester was disgusted that his erudite friend would so easily concede what was then considered an admission of the immorality of black women or the uncivilized nature of black people. Chester accurately reproduced Ellison's arguments in *Lonely Crusade*. The point was to show Ellison's arrogance and embarrass him, the hector who "for three hours" propounded "learnedly and vehemently that the Negro family unit was matriarchal." Chester wrote in the novel, "It was like tearing the heart out of reason to learn of the Negro scholar who not only was convinced, himself, of his own inferiority, but went to great scholastic lengths to prove why it was so." To Chester, black matriarchy and black women's white-collar financial success were prime evidence of general African American dishonor under segregation. If winning a place among white elites meant admitting base facts about black people, Chester would remain the outsider.

Although the diverging styles of the two writers, the composer and the counterpuncher, did not ruin the weekend—one that the Ellisons pleasurably recalled as "one of our best times"—Ralph and Fanny could also be prickly, such as when a book they had lent that week wasn't returned promptly. Jean, gracious and glamorous in dealings with Fanny, yet another black professional woman with an advanced degree from a white university, tried to smooth it over, sending a note: "Hope it didn't cause any troubles or apologies." Not long after the encounter with Ellison, Chester lost interest in discussing his work with anyone during composition. "I am intolerant of all opinions but my own and do not want to hear any others and am greatly disturbed and distracted by them," he decided.

For Chester, the period from Thanksgiving to well after Christmas was an occasion for toil, "long and steadily without a day's letup," to correct his manuscript. There were also a couple of occasions of pathos. On December 21, Chester's first cousin Gerald Wiggins walked up to his girlfriend, Mattie Muldrew, while she waited for a Cleveland streetcar and gunned her down. He then fled a short distance to a parked car and turned the weapon on himself. Gerald died and Mattie survived. Somehow Joseph Senior's hospital bill from his emergency surgery wound up with Chester, a whopping $977. The basic rationale of his Rosenwald application, "I want to go to Europe so I can see America better," did not appropriately distinguish him. One dramatic difference between his applications of 1943 and 1946 was in his support team, now all white: UCLA sociologist Leonard Bloom, English novelist Jack Aistrop, Carl Van Vechten, Carey McWilliams, and Blanche Knopf. Though considerable, the support could lift up the underwhelming project only so far. "I wish that I could have been more convincing," lamented Chester to William Haygood.

Chester resubmitted the revised manuscript to Knopf in sections, beginning with a 425-page batch on January 13, 1947, and delivering all the pages not long after. The final report on *Lonely Crusade* came back to him on February 10. Knopf's in-house reviewers applauded his efforts. "Himes has done everything we could expect," they decided, "in smoothing out and tightening this manuscript." Now, after having yielded to the process of writing and revising for two years, Chester was face-to-face with himself. He awaited the galley proofs "experiencing a sense of letdown, tired and broke and wish to hell I was out in California with a coupla thousand bucks." Chester recognized by then how badly he desired respectability, but he also realized that "the circle of restraint" weakened him as a writer. As for what he had accomplished, he was hopeful but circumspect. The novel had run to 540 manuscript pages, and Chester knew it was an opus at least; perhaps it was a masterpiece, a life's work.

Once the manuscript was off, Chester and Jean returned from Wading River and again billeted at the twelve-story Theresa Hotel, the "Waldorf of Harlem." Despite its nickname, the costly hotel was drab, run-down, and gloomy inside, a crumbling edifice of segregation that exploited black Americans who had no first-class options. At the Theresa he comported himself as a sport and started putting himself in a deep financial hole. Combined with the flashy intemperance he'd acquired as a Cleveland dandy, Chester also succumbed to bouts of heavy drinking to bridge the gaps between major projects. Soon strapped for cash, Chester had started to tinker with his prison novel, hoping that Knopf might also take that book. Then he drew on his "secret understanding" with Richard Wright, who had returned from France that month. Wright picked up the telephone and Chester got $500 in a few hours from the Authors League. On February 1, the Himeses settled into better rooms at 421 W. 147th Street, in the artsy Hamilton Heights neighborhood, between Convent and St. Nicholas Avenues.

To address more directly their economic predicament, Jean took a job as recreational director for Girls Camp, a residential facility on Welfare Island, off Manhattan, where delinquent girls were detained before trial in the youth court, and, if necessary, treated with psychiatric therapy. The teenage Billie Holiday had been confined there in the late 1920s. Jean was the consummate professional in this demanding job and, again, she impressed her colleagues and supervisors and made friends. Feeling pinched and his ego bruised, Chester started casting about for more money. Rashly, he asked Lurton Blassingame, his agent, to pursue a book contract for the prison novel *Yesterday Will Make You Cry* with Knopf. When Van Vechten found out, he scolded Chester for behaving like an amateur. "No publisher is likely to be interested in two books at once," he counseled. Besides, the topic of that novel hadn't changed from when it had been rejected years earlier. To be published at all, reminded a loyal Van Vechten, it needed "some preparation and explanation in the right quarters before it is read." Shifting gears, Chester pressed his agent to return to Knopf with a new proposal, *Immortal Mammy*, a novel about a black woman raised in a white neighborhood as the exceptional black child.

Chester worked hard drafting the outline for this next project and staying abreast of new material on race relations, for instance through the winter issue of *Survey Graphic*. When edited by Alain Locke twenty-three years earlier, *Survey* had inaugurated the Harlem Renaissance. Now, Thomas Sancton, a provocative young crusading journalist from New Orleans, was continuing the special-issue tradition. Chester was tickled by the "artistic flow of language" and logic in Sancton's essay, and by the sociologist E. Franklin Frazier's "blunt attack." He also learned that the article Ellison had been working hard on for that issue, later published as "Twentieth Century Fiction and the Black Mask of Humanity," had been rejected.

Chester, on the other hand, was feeling quite well liked across racial lines. His friend William Haygood told him to drop by the New Yorker Hotel on March 13 to talk about art and fellowships; a few days later, Van Vechten had a group to his home for a small photography exhibit, as well as a piano recital by black critic George Schuyler's talented daughter Phillipa.

Then Blanche Knopf offered a contract for *Immortal Mammy*. Blassingame requested a $2000 advance, with $350 on signing and the rest paid out in monthly installments. This was an improvement beyond the $500 advance that Chester seems to have received for *Lonely Crusade*. Chester thought the terms of the contract could be improved and he debated whether or not he ought to sign it, not knowing how well *Lonely Crusade* might do and after the bad experience of indebtedness with Doubleday. He rushed off a letter to Haygood, trying to sniff out his chances for the Rosenwald fellowship, which would not be announced until May. Haygood wired him to accept the Knopf contract.

He did. On April 30 Knopf sent out the paperwork and he returned it to them on May 5. If *Lonely Crusade* did well, perhaps he could go into hibernation again and spend the demanding twelve-hour days writing another strong work. But Chester's exceptional work habits in 1946 would be battered by the difficulties of his life. After finishing proofs of the galleys, which had arrived in late May, he found himself needing to get away from New York as well as from the burden of the image of himself he had concocted, the hard-drinking, candid black cynic. "We simply must get away from here," he confessed to Van Vechten, "both for morale and health."

Chester and Jean escaped Manhattan in early June, taking off for several days to Westford, Vermont, to the home of his friends from Los Angeles Helen and Bill Smith. Agreeing with Chester's assessment of the corrosive dimension of race relations in Los Angeles, the Smiths had moved to Vermont in October. Eight months later the Smiths weren't quite sure that they had not made a tragic mistake; initially they had considered relocating to Haiti. Vermont had won out because of the access to Boston and New York, its legendary history as a stop on the Underground Railroad, and the easy route to Canada. Bill Smith was "riding out another recurrence of doubt and depression" about his abode and his career when Chester and Jean arrived. He had submitted the manuscript of a book called *God Is for White*

Folks to publishers under the pseudonym Will Thomas and been told, in essence, that he belonged to a lesser breed of humanity. One editor had replied, "I do not see a very promising future for a writer who would probably continue to base his writings upon Negro more than human situations and problems." In Smith's kitchen, he and Chester consoled each other over pipes filled with marijuana.

Chester returned to New York after a week, to strategize his way forward with Carl Van Vechten, who recommended that he try a brief stay at the writers' colony at Yaddo in Saratoga Springs, New York. At first, Chester rejected the idea but Van Vechten took the additional step of broaching the matter with Langston Hughes, the first African American invited to Yaddo. "You know: give us the answers!" Van Vechten rattled to Hughes. However Hughes, who had done no less for Chester than he had for so many other black writers, was growing increasingly unsure about his Cleveland homeboy. "I expect by now that Yaddo has perhaps filled its quota for the coming summer," Hughes replied accurately, but brusquely. Three months later, Hughes would turn down Blanche Knopf directly when she asked him to endorse Chester's new book. "Most of the people in it just do not seem to me to have good sense or be in their right minds, they behave so badly which makes it difficult to care very much what happens to any of them," he explained. Chester was now fully in the process of exchanging racial bases of support, as his recommendation letters for the Rosenwald fellowship indicated. He would cater to the tastes of the white vanguard more so than the franchise among black Americans.

Blanche Knopf also thought it imperative that Chester receive an endorsement from Richard Wright. Chester sent the galleys to Wright, working at one of the Safford cottages in Wading River and pondering a return to France. Wright responded warmly with a statement to the publisher on June 5. Noting the plot's concern with the internal decision making of the American Communist Party, Wright initially understood *Lonely Crusade* as exclusively a novel of politics.

"What he has to say will take the Communist Party of America twenty-five years to answer," he fired off in praise.

At first, Chester was pleased by "this fine statement," since he understood how central Communist politics were to Wright's life and work. But then Carl Van Vechten threw a party and invited Chester, Wright, Blanche Knopf, and the latest black writer of national note, Willard Motley, whose novel about an Italian American juvenile delinquent, *Knock on Any Door*, became a best seller. About Chester's age, dapper, and self-controlled, Motley seemed to have the world in his hands that June; the reviews of his naturalistically drawn Chicago were strongly positive. Despite its being a story of reform school, slums, pederasty, and petty crime, Motley's book was being described as "beautifully written." The apparent secret of Motley's likable book was that, like Chester's best *Esquire* stories, it had no central African American characters.

Chester spent his time huddled with Wright and his new business partner, the bob-wearing, chain-smoking aesthete Blanche Knopf. His book was scheduled for September publication. Chester begged Wright to revise his comment on *Lonely Crusade*, to one that emphasized "marital conflict and the Jewish-Negro angle." Actually, he wanted Wright to recommend the book not only for more than its critique of communism, but for its "literary merit." Not wishing to seem ungrateful, Chester added pleasantly that if Wright demurred, "it will in no way affect my great admiration for you and your achievement." He was also remembering his unrepaid Authors League loan. Wright supplied another blurb in ten days:

Chester Himes' *Lonely Crusade* chalks up another significant literary victory for Negro prose expression in America. His hard, biting, functional style reveals the truth about a marital situation never before depicted in novels of Negro life. Lee Gordon's tense and tragic search for integrity cuts deeper into our consciousness than piles of academic volumes of sociology and psychology. Himes stands in the front ranks of literary truth-tellers in our nation.

Long live Chester Himes!

This statement represented approval, as well as being an act of friendship, but the groove was definitely narrow. Wright had succeeded because he was bright and worked hard, but he liked to fit friends into categories, which was perhaps the somewhat mechanical way that he understood the world. Chester, an ex-convict, served Wright as an example of a person who had transformed from the apotheosis of sin to civilized reform. But Wright would never consider him an artist.

After the hot months spent readying the novel to appear, Chester and Jean moved to Welfare Island, at first to a studio apartment, and then for three weeks in a two-room flat. The apartments were salvaged out of an old, condemned eighty-one-room mansion, renovated by the city and large, but still indelicate. Chester and Jean lived on the side of the island that faced Queens, enjoying the cool evenings and the relative quiet. Welfare Island was accessible only by ferry. Defending the choice of his hard-to-get-to residence, Chester stammered to Van Vechten, "Honestly, it is rather nice."

By August Chester's other supporters came through for him. Horace Cayton told Knopf that *Lonely Crusade* rivaled *A Passage to India* and that it was "a great work of art." Carl Van Vechten surpassed everybody in applause, declaring "this novel boasts such power of expression and such subtlety of treatment, the author possesses so sensitive a command of character and incident the culmination is so reasonably magnificent, that I, for one, am not afraid to call this book *great*." Chester was wooed by competing book publishers: William Targ, a writer for the *Cleveland News*, and Ben Zevin, the president of World Publishers, also located in Cleveland, took Chester and Jean to the Algonquin Hotel, the watering hole of the *New Yorker* staff and writer John O'Hara, for lunch. An interview with the *New York Times* went so well that Chester allowed himself to say that he retained "happy memories" of the South. If they slightly misrepresented him on that point, when Chester said that his favorite writers were Wright and Faulkner, whose bizarre accounts of twined black and white life gave him hope, they had it correct. In a piece in the newsmagazine *Newsweek*, which appeared a week before publication, he found himself lauded as "among the most promising of younger negro writers," and his book "brilliantly introspective" and "forthright and compassionate." *Negro Digest* contracted to run the third chapter of the novel, which revealed the early years of Ruth and Lee Gordon's marriage and exposed the Communist shift away from protesting against racial discrimination, in its December issue. Meanwhile, a mended Joseph Sr. traveled from Cleveland to be with Chester on the triumphant publication day in New York. All the signals indicated that enduring commercial and critical success was at hand.

An array of publicity ventures had been arranged in advance by Knopf, in contrast to the Doubleday scrambling and errors. On Sunday, September 7, 1947, Chester recorded a segment for the WCBS program *This Is New York*, to be broadcast a week later. Early Monday morning, Chester was scheduled to appear at Macy's bookstore for a pep talk with booksellers. For that afternoon Knopf publicity director William Cole also scheduled a live WNBC radio interview with the fashionable Mary Margaret McBride to coincide with the book's release.

But on Monday morning, a warm day with a sprinkling of clouds, the best laid plans began to unravel. *This Is New York* went ahead with their broadcast, despite their promise to air later. McBride's secretary heard the interview at 9:15 A.M. and angrily telephoned Cole, canceling the afternoon program, because their contract to exclusively launch the book had been violated. Then, even though Chester was on the early ferry to Manhattan, the boat broke down, delaying him by forty-five minutes. When he arrived at Macy's at ten o'clock, his audience of book clerks was already hard at work. He collared a few from the fiction department, but rushed back to the Seventy-Ninth Street dock to get Jean and his father for the McBride interview. Another ferry ride later he arrived and Jean told him the appointment had been canceled, kindling a desperate "fustle and bustle." Chester felt bad and showed it. Joseph Himes tried to console his youngest child, who had known so much anguish and grief. "Remember, son, New York is not the only city that has skyscrapers," he sputtered. "We have one on the new Union Station in Cleveland."

After this opening fumble, there were some minor recoveries, courtesy of his friends. In the *Amsterdam News,* Constance Curtis approved of his "tightly constructed . . . good novel." For the *New York Herald Tribune,* Arna Bontemps reviewed the book he thought a bit long, deciding that "the story has power" and provides "excitement quite out of the ordinary." In Atlanta, reviewer Marian Sims, who liked the book particularly well for its attacks against Communists, thought that Himes had imbued it with the "terrible and tragic ring of authenticity." Another fan, John Farrelly at *New Republic,* gave Chester his due: "The victim is the classic modern hero; undefined, pervasive fear, emotional and physical insecurity, sexual neuroses, the abnegation of beliefs, the loss of values, a general cynicism and brutality; these are universal disasters." Farrelly agreed with Chester's skepticism about "the healing aspects of an equality which is as much a problem for the white man as the Negro."

However, one of the dissenting reviews injured him personally. Willard Motley wrote him "regretfully," five days before publication, to warn Chester that he would review the book for the *Chicago Sun.* "I didn't like *Lonely Crusade,*" he began, "I react violently to it—my ideas and opinions are so different from yours." Repudiated by a writer who described expertly the meanness of the modern city and its destructiveness to human beings, Chester wasn't sure how to respond. He had regaled Motley's *Knock on Any Door* and identified personally with the story of choirboy Nick Romano's trip to the electric chair, calling the book "wonderful." As Nick gets his taste of life behind bars in the boys' reformatory, Motley explored the world of cruising gay men exploiting children and teens in the slums. Chester knew of few other published books that put a contextual perspective on the "degenerate" episodes of his own life, books lifting him out of isolation and providing language to unpack his own complex experience in prison. Before reading Motley's review, Chester tried to patch up their differences in a letter. While he did "regret exceedingly" Motley's dislike of *Lonely Crusade*, he wanted to keep him as a friend: "Please do not feel that I would ever have you do otherwise than be honest to yourself."

But then the *Chicago Sun* piece appeared. Borderline calumny, Motley's review was a series of oversimplifications, which worked quite well in the pithy format of a newspaper. In a critique that refused to distinguish between the novelist and his chief character and ignored the novel's sophisticated political dimensions, Motley decided that since Lee Gordon was a graduate of UCLA, he would have shared the experiences of its star black athletes: "We learn early that Lee hates all white people (at least men) though he must have met some decent men of different color in the University of California at Los Angeles. Kennie Washington, All American football player, and Jackie Robinson, Brooklyn Dodger first basemen, did."

Himes had clumsily but directly responded to Motley's chief critique at the end of the book. Bright and perceptive in the midst of his own doom, Lee decides that "some white people must have been his friends right down the line from slavery. All of them could not have been his hateful enemies." Motley's suggestions that Lee Gordon's life "pivot[s] on race or nationality" and "through bitterness or pride he turns his back on the people as a whole" made Chester consider the review "a vicious personal attack." He never spoke to Motley again.

Even though some black college graduates out of Chicago thought

Motley was "closer to the ofays than he was to the Brothers," this review demonstrated what was at stake for the middle class. (Motley's uncle Archibald, a celebrated painter, had famously done a series of portraits extolling light-skinned black beauty at the expense of darker-skinned women.) In the pages of *Ebony*, where he had been celebrated a short time before, Chester found personal slander: "Gordon—and his creator Himes—are infected with a psychosis that distorts their thinking and influences their every action." In New York's *The People's Voice* he received the same diagnosis, but this time from the black left, which was also solidly middle-class, educated, biracial, and married across the color line. "It has been rumored that this novel is largely autobiographical. If this is true, then Himes should repair to the nearest clinic before writing another novel. For he is a mighty sick man." These critiques showed the unwillingness of African Americans with public voices to push loudly against racism or to prick the weaknesses of postwar white liberalism. Timid black reviewers convinced themselves that they were risking black progress by mounting vigorous critiques a year before American armed forces were formally desegregated. Nor were they comfortable in admitting to personal feelings of enmity toward whites, a standing taboo for the black professional class. So they assailed Chester as neurotic.

Further to the left, he was declared insufficiently working-class. The Socialist Workers Party sheet *The Militant*, ridiculed Chester as "a Negro intellectual," which meant being bourgeois. "He does not know the worker, and least of all the Negro worker," the article charged. "Mr. Himes has fought with his typewriter alone in his room."

The newly reorganized U.S. Communist Party took a turn. Chester had written bon mots such as "It was not that the Communist Party lacked integrity; it simply did not recognize it." Lloyd Brown, a new African American reviewer for *New Masses*, was assigned Chester's book, which was probably the most detailed fictional exploration of blacks in the Communist Party. He promptly called it a "literary lynching" and then decided, "I cannot recall ever having read a worse book on the Negro theme."

These were what the *Cleveland Press*'s Emerson Price had in mind when he noted that "extreme leftists" had delivered a "really serious beating" to the novel and made "grave charges" against Chester personally. So Chester's ground became ever more narrow, when the highbrow press belittled him both as a middlebrow hack and as a heretic to the faith of postwar American antiracist zeitgeist. *Atlantic Monthly* reviewer Stoyan Christowe offered this memorable quote: "Hatred reeks through his pages like yellow bile." Honest about the attitude of an audience wanting to see discontent smoothed over, *Forum* derided the book because it was "bound to stir up animosity rather than sympathetic understanding." In the highly charged Red Scare political atmosphere of loyalty oaths and Communist purges, *Lonely Crusade* was opposed for spearing the hypocrisy of two warring, unequal sides.

If his portrait of whites like the aircraft company executive Louis Foster and Jackie Forks, the Communist dilettante, maligned the middle class, Chester had not so much made a sharp critique of the left as he had exposed some of its social world, and particularly the roles of blacks and Jews in it. But the big question of black industrial employment after the Second World War—enfolding the key issues of migration, home ownership, and college education connected to the GI Bill—would wind up defining much of the second half of twentieth-century American domestic politics. Chester dramatized the barriers in practice and thought that prevented the integration of the labor force in heavy industry and caused the emergence of the ghetto as the central locale of black urban life.

As he had done two years before with *If He Hollers Let Him Go*, he attempted to direct the novel's reception, a rare duty presumed by a black novelist for their own work. When Milton Klonsky, the reviewer for *Commentary*, dismissed the novel with "Such writing, no matter how well intentioned, and the graffiti in the men's rooms are part of the same debased culture," Chester took the time to rebut him in Klonsky's own magazine. In a March 1948 letter to *Commentary's* editor, Chester blamed the graffiti comment on Klonsky's "sub conscious disturbances," and his "prejudices." Believing himself "fulsomely condemned" by "learned colored people" like black critic J. Saunders Redding, he addressed Redding in his own column in the *Afro-American*. He insisted that one fictional character "is one colored person, not all colored people" and "Lee Gordon is presented as mentally ill. The author does not imply that all colored people are mentally ill."

Amid the messy reviews Chester was also losing a friend, Ralph Ellison, who saw in Himes's career an example of what not to do. Like a seminarian, Ellison had once committed himself to the Communist Party. Later, feeling more at home with the ideas of the midcentury critic Kenneth Burke, he moved to the philosophy of art and literary technique. He disproved of Chester's freewheeling compositional style, which in *Lonely Crusade* involved the addition of material from the press, oral poetry heard in bars, the problems that his brother Joe and cousin Henry had written about, and what seemed to Ellison the transmutation of whole portions of the Lenin pamphlets he himself had supplied to Chester. Ellison faulted his buddy for making Communist arguments seem frivolous.

Ellison could not, however, get around the fact that *Lonely Crusade* was the most important novel written by an African American in the seven years since *Native Son*. So he chatted the book up with his white friends, feeling them out while making up his own mind. He had been excited to recommend the book to his main patron, Ida Guggenheimer, a wealthy sponsor of the Communist Party. Now he was sour. "For the most part I didn't like it, especially not his attempts at political criticism," Ellison decided a year after publication. He described the novel as "unclear" and worse, called Himes's "motives questionable" for publishing the book. Guggenheimer, to whom the novel *Invisible Man* would be dedicated, agreed with his estimate, judging *Lonely Crusade* "very poor stuff." A friend Ellison cherished, Stanley Edgar Hyman, a literary critic and college professor who also wrote for *The New Yorker,* dismissed Himes as well. Hyman was just getting around to reading *If He Hollers* and wrote Ellison to levy the negative verdict: "I read the old Himes book, just about the time the new one came out and didn't think it came to much." Hyman would be the prime critical voice in Ellison's ear as he wrote *Invisible Man.*

A few months later and in a move that signified the impossibility of Ellison's ever sharing intimacy again with Himes, he tore the book apart in a letter to Richard Wright. "Personally I was disappointed," he began. "I found it dishonest in its pseudo-intellectuality, and as false as Cayton's 'fear-hate-fear complex' in its psychology." For Ellison, Himes made tawdry intellectual and artistic missteps and then dared to tell people he had written a best seller. Ellison had been told by a Knopf editor that although the publisher "eagerly put money behind the book it laid an egg."

At the end of 1947, Chester called Ellison about a holiday party and sent a Christmas card, but Ellison had written him off as a "mixed-up guy" and an opportunist. And while Earl Conrad believed that Ellison, Cayton, Wright, and Himes all had the personality of Bigger Thomas, for Ellison the joke was on Himes. Cocky and feeling superior, Ellison mused about Chester's wounded feelings. "Could he fear that I might put him in *my* book?" he noted to Wright before making a *Native Son* reference. "If so, he should forget it; *you* put him in a book seven years ago."

Chester Himes always maintained that the overall response to *Lonely Crusade* ruined his literary reputation in the United States. "It was then that I decided to leave the United States forever if I got the chance. . . . I felt like a man without a country, which in fact I was." Certainly it was true that some former allies were now pointing to him as fearful, vindictive, and ignorant. But Chester held on to his desire to write the stories that had both come out of his prison past and relied upon what he had learned in California—his critique of the evolution of racism in the United States and the creation of the modern integrated industrial workforce. Unlike Wright's *Native Son,* which produced a Communist defense attorney to deliver the work's lacerating social critique, or Ann Petry's *The Street,* which needed its narrator and a series of male villains to make plain the argument of the racist urban environment of the North, or Motley's *Knock on Any Door,* which reproduced Wright's courtroom melodrama and made explicit the environment-as-culprit theme, Chester had relied upon a dramatic narrative lodged in concrete historical circumstances to identify the contesting pressures wrecking the mass movement for peaceful social transformation. He exposed all comers, from the black family under segregation to the autocratic ultrapatriots, and the quixotic left-wing movement itself. None of his characters were improbable cutouts. But even more significant than crafting the book's uncompromising, smart originality, Chester had exposed the crisis of industrial work as the postwar national woe. "I will never change on the book," he wrote five years later about *Lonely Crusade,* "with all its faults it still tells the truth as I saw it then and see it now."

Chapter Nine

INFLICTING A WOUND UPON HIMSELF

1948–1952

B y February 1948 *Lonely Crusade* was a certified flop. The hardcover sales petered out at thirty-five hundred copies and Chester's greatest book was never considered for a paperback reprint edition because of the heavy pile of remaindered surplus. *Lonely Crusade* would pass quickly into obscurity, as if the book had not been written at all. And if Knopf did not deliberately sacrifice the book as Doubleday had *If He Hollers Let Him Go*, they did not overadvance authors whose books were not doing well. Chester earned only $1701.89 from book sales after *Lonely Crusade* had been out a month, not enough to recoup his initial $2000 advance. Before the end of 1947, Knopf accountants had started billing his *Immortal Mammy* advance for all fees and expenses against *Lonely Crusade*, which by then showed "a debit balance." That December Knopf had docked him $123.78, reducing that month's stipend to around $28. Even his agent, Lurton Blassingame, was surprised by the unusually harsh accounting practices. "Advances against royalties paid to finance the writing of a new work have never, in my experience, been subject to charges held over from a previous work," Blassingame lobbied the publisher, requesting that Chester's final money be remitted intact. The last $150 *Immortal* advance payment was paid in full at the end of March. Downcast about *Lonely Crusade*'s failing and feeling punished again by a publisher, Chester was hard-pressed and "needed support badly."

But the more difficult task of writing was intolerable while he and Jean resided in a cramped apartment with the dandyish Caribbean bandleader Eddie Bonelli on Franklin Avenue in the Bronx. "It is a great self punishment," Chester concluded about their comedown after leaving Welfare Island, "to write a book while living in a small room in someone else's house."

To relieve himself from the tiny room and the bleak disappointment connected to the reception of *Lonely Crusade,* Chester violated one of his better principles. In February he applied for two months' residency at the artists' colony at Yaddo. A billet there would not bring relief financially—all that Yaddo provided was room and board—and, since Jean would not be allowed to live with him there, he would still have to sell stories to contribute to their room rent. But he was hoping that intangibles like scenic beauty, prestige, and a crew of new backers could inspire him and prove therapeutic. The first small victory was to be admitted.

For the application he pitched *Immortal Mammy*, the story of the black girl in the all-white world that would feature the "psychological processes of an 'exceptional' member of an oppressed group." He planned for the novel to be a semibiographical piece, probably drawn from some of the episodes attributed to the popular and beloved singer Billie Holiday, who was released from federal penitentiary after serving nine months for narcotics possession, and performed at Carnegie Hall that March. He considered using a first-person narrator and exploring the life of the blues singer using the environs of Cleveland, Los Angeles, and New York.

His friend Horace Cayton, supervisor of the Parkway Community House, tried to lift Chester up a bit, inviting him to Chicago to lecture in May. Chester was working up treatments of articles for the slick magazines and hoping that the new book "won't take me long . . . when I get going."

While struggling to draft *Immortal Mammy* and dealing with "a siege of virus X" shared with Jean, Chester renewed his political ties. He lent his talents that winter to Grant Reynolds, who had joined forces with union leader Asa Philip Randolph and created the Committee Against Jim Crow in the Military. In March, the committee started issuing press releases, threatening Gandhian civil disobedience against the Universal Military Training and Selective Service Acts being debated in Congress. At the beginning of April, Randolph and Reynolds conveyed their demands for desegregation to President Harry Truman and the Senate Armed Services Committee. Although ultimately successful, their spring of 1948 stand went against the growing anti-Communist hysteria that sought to quash all dissent to government policies.

Like the hero Lee Gordon in his novel *Lonely Crusade*, Chester shared that outspoken commitment to ending Jim Crow wherever it appeared. By April he was writing newspaper editors in Cleveland and Chicago to advance the Randolph–Reynolds campaign in favor of "mass civil disobedience" if segregation in the armed forces was not summarily abolished. To the movement he also contributed a short story, called "These People Never Die," published in the *Amsterdam News*, about a courageous black draftee who accepts prison instead of serving as a "sugar boy" in the Jim Crow army. But while Chester was suggesting that prison was more dignified than stooping to federal law, he was growing increasingly doubtful of the existence of a public that wanted to read *Immortal Mammy*, the manuscript of which was due to Knopf on May 1. With the sales of *Lonely Crusade* what they were, Chester admitted that "I don't have any great enthusiasm for another racial novel."

What he also meant was that he was losing his taste for writing literature that engaged the politics of American social class, a true disappointment on account of two brilliant character portraits from *Lonely Crusade*. The *New Leader*'s reviewer, twenty-three-year-old James Baldwin, had immediately recognized Chester's Luther McGregor as a nefarious and significant character in African American literature. Chester perhaps slightly mishandled Luther by repeatedly emphasizing his likeness to an ape. However, it is smooth-talking Luther McGregor who quotes the epic Signifying Monkey rhyme in its entirety, and thus introduces a syncretic version of African rural folk culture into an urban American setting. Luther also delivers the Hamlet-like "I is a nigger first" soliloquy, a moment when black fear and violent reprisal are transformed into twentieth-century ethnically rooted national citizenship.

Another prime distinction in *Lonely Crusade* was the portrait of Louis Foster, and the character, though drawn from Louis Bromfield, quite brilliantly and accurately modeled the beliefs of several powerful Americans whose oligarchic attitudes consistently not only imperiled civil rights and democracy in the United States but threatened to bring on atomic war and global catastrophe. Henry Luce, the propaganda-producing publisher of the newsmagazine *Time*, which was described in the 1940s and '50s as "misinformation trimmed with insults," and his friend, General Douglas MacArthur, who consistently defied President Truman and brought the United States to the brink of all-out war with China and the Soviet Union, were both eerily similar personalities to Foster. Chester was really the first black writer to wrestle onto the page a psychological portrait of a righteous plutocrat from the atomic bomb era.

In early April Chester heard from Yaddo administrator Elizabeth Ames that he had made the "guest list" for the coming season at the artists' colony. Guests, as the admitted artists were termed, stayed for short stints in the spring and summer, typically six or eight weeks.

Chester arrived by afternoon train at Saratoga Springs on May 10, 1948, and took a cab to the six-hundred-acre estate on Union Street, once the home of financier Spencer Trask and his wife, Sylvia. Yaddo featured gothic revival buildings, slender lakes, and lush sculpted grounds. The principal building was the Mansion, a hewn granite structure of twenty-seven rooms, closed when Chester first arrived. Artists had studios for their work and the writers too went out to ateliers every day. A heavy garage housed some of the studios and Chester had a bedroom in a two-story clapboard manor called West House. Elizabeth Ames's office was in a stucco building called East House. A statue-lined rose garden covered what, in the early nineteenth century, had been slave quarters. The only uncomfortable part of the arrangement was that Saratoga Springs, New York, a resort famed for its racetrack and its mineral springs, was like Atlantic City, a Jim Crow town.

The nearly deaf, prominently leftist Ames was the original director of the artist's colony and her vision guided the place for fifty years. When Chester met her, she had just left the hospital, having spent three weeks convalescing after an eye operation. Unsure of whether or not he would encounter racial prejudice, he tried to befriend Ames by gushing to her about Van Vechten, whom she knew. Although Ames was admired by her "colonists," she was also punctilious and officious, a morally rigid woman who left typed admonitory notes for guests on the escritoire in the great hall, where they took their meals. Liberal, like the members of her admissions committee—Malcolm Cowley, Granville Hicks, and Newton Arvin—but averse to risk, Ames admitted that Negroes "should have come before" the racial barrier fell in 1941. Then, she had had to defy at least one Yaddo trustee who resigned when she and Arvin resolved to start admitting black artists. Ames tried to break segregation down by small, safe degrees.

In the first season of black guests, she confided to Malcolm Cowley that integration seemed to have spawned "one or two weird things," likely a sobriquet for sex and drunkenness. One of her apparent responses was to henpeck black Yaddoites. On the grounds they were not to be overloud or create large phone bills; in Saratoga Springs, they were not to run up bar tabs or be in debt. She did not want them carousing drunkenly or lecherously, activities that reached legendary proportion among all who went to Yaddo. As one Yaddo researcher suspects, "the formal integration of Yaddo was subtly undermined by 'well-intentioned' inquiries about the behavior of African American guests." Eventually Jim Crow Saratoga Springs made certain grudging exceptions. When asked specifically by Ames if he would object to Langston Hughes being served at the New Worden restaurant, proprietor Edward Sweeney relented, somewhat. "I do not object to Langston Hughes, the colored writer, coming in our bar as long as he is in the company of someone else from Yaddo."

Not all black guests accepted Ames's grooming. The year before Chester arrived, hard-drinking Horace Cayton had frightened Ames with his behavior. Even fifteen years later, Cayton's loud escapades were clearly recalled. Despite Cayton's genuine attraction to Yaddo, his requests for readmission were refused by Ames, who explained to Malcolm Cowley, "we have decided that an alcoholic is too sick a person to be invited to Yaddo." She would be looking closely at Chester.

At first, Chester marveled at the new level of splendor. "It is an ideal place to work," he bragged to Van Vechten about his room, which had four windows and a view of the manicured grounds. His basic needs were catered to. Guests could count on a buffet for breakfast and lunch packed in a black tin box at noon. Yaddo even had quiet hours—no visiting or public talking from 9:00 A.M. to 4:00 P.M.—that were enforced. The dinners were grand jacket-and-tie affairs, known for the rich quality of the food and turning the guests into "beaming Sybarites waddling out from the groaning board," in the words of the writer Eleanor Clark.

The retreat catered to both the already famous and young prodigies. Unknown Flannery O'Connor, a young, sheltered, "thirteenth century" Catholic girl from Georgia, arrived on June 1. Chester had prepared himself for elevated literary discussions with the Yaddo crowd, and he brought with him Joyce's *Finnegans Wake,* Faulkner's *Light in August,* and a translation of Rimbaud's *A Season in Hell.* But what O'Connor found with annoyance, and that Chester must have been amused by, was dining-room table banter about the latest vogue that kept Billie Holiday in the news: narcotics.

In Chester's session the white wunderkind was twenty-six-year-old Patricia Highsmith, who awoke to a breakfast of liquor and biblical passages. Yaddo stimulated and deranged her; she was "a coiled Spring" and "happy like a battery chicken." Slender and tall, the dark-haired Barnard graduate hailed from a Texas slaveholding family and consistently tried to tackle Chester on his own turf: evil and sexuality. Their rooms were across the hall from each other, and at the end of May they went into town, found Jimmy's, a bar on Congress Street, and drank themselves into a stupor. Then Highsmith followed Chester into his room, where he attempted to consummate rather perfunctorily what seemed to be unfolding. When Chester tried to kiss her, Highsmith, free-spirited and sexually libertine during her eight weeks at Yaddo, withdrew. She camouflaged the episode of interracial hanky-panky by writing about it in German in her notebook, but it was vivid. As she wrote to him dryly after almost twenty years, "Maybe you remember me from Yaddo. Anyway, I remember you."

Highsmith's seeming dismissal of sex with Chester and, what's more, a writer's friendship, is curious. She was hatching the well-received novel *Strangers on a Train,* which became famous when turned into a film by Alfred Hitchcock. When Highsmith completed the important *"raison d'être"* murder scene in her novel that summer, she wrote in her diary, "I feel I have grown older, completely adult." At Yaddo, Chester was the hands-down expert in crime and murder, but mainly Highsmith remembered him talking about his car. In the 1960s, after she had become comfortably wealthy and reviewed Chester's novel *Cotton Comes to Harlem* for London's *Times Literary Supplement*, Highsmith received a letter from Chester, asking what he never found out from the hallmate he drunkenly tried to seduce. "I was sitting here, wondering, when the postman brought your letter, how your life has brought you the intimate and detailed knowledge required to write such a realistic and living story." Underneath Chester's polite question was the thinly veiled accusation that, like many other writers, she had taken something from him without acknowledgment.

Another obvious tie between the two writers was Highsmith's ache over her sexual preference. Chester had written a book on the subject: he had his prison manuscript with him, and he was, around this time, separating out the competing plot strands from the book. One part, "Stool Pigeon," would deal with the prison fire and have a reptilian black preacher as its protagonist. The other story, "Yesterday Will Make You Cry," would present "the boy's development of homosexuality." Highsmith should have been a natural comrade, but perhaps the simple fact is that a talented young white woman sowing her oats would be wary of a Negro ex-con from Cleveland, Knopf novelist or not.

Chester broke off from the excitement at West House and caught a train to be at the University of Chicago on May 18. Sponsored by the Creative Writing Forum, his evening lecture was advertised as "The Individual in Our Writing World," but Chester was speaking nearly exclusively about "the dilemma of the Negro artist." He had emphasized to a reporter in advance of the talk that *Lonely Crusade* "was more concerned with Lee Gordon's search for the meaning of manhood than with any lengthy condemnation of prejudice as such." He also quoted at length from Horace Cayton's essay "Race Conflict in Modern Society." From the stage Chester told his audience of postwar collegians that writing was about intellectual and emotional experience, and then, even more philosophically, that "the essential necessity of humanity is to find justification for existence. . . . We are maintained at our level of nobility by our incessant search for ourselves." But the inner journey of self-definition led him to an abyss in terms of creativity. Ignoble himself, he had been "brutalized, restricted, degraded" and his "soul" was "pulverized by oppression." As a result, he could not but succumb to "bitterness, fear, hatred, protest." Chester supposed that an honest reflection by a black writer on the black way of life in the United States would "be like inflicting a wound upon himself." The reward for integrity was being reviled.

He accused those of his peers who had achieved polite acclaim of "a trenchant sort of dishonesty, an elaborate and highly convincing technique of modern uncle-tomism," and gave out some dazzling turns of logic which probably seemed like a con man's spiel to everyone but Cayton: "Any American Negro's racial experience, be they psychotic or not, are [sic] typical of all Negroes' racial experience for the simple reason that the source is not the Negro but oppression." The fact that he was right made him more doomed. As for the "guiltless" liberals in the audience, they were told bluntly that they "abhor . . . the revelations of Negroes' personalities." He insisted, making the crowd uncomfortable, "What sort of idiocy is it that reasons American Negroes don't hate American whites?" He concluded that "the whole Negro race in America, as a result of centuries of oppression, is sick at soul." Chester, who had fortified himself before he took the podium with champagne, topped off by capsules of the stimulant Benzedrine, noted sadly that "a dead silence" followed his remarks.

After attempting to forget his Chicago audience's disbelief by way of binge drinking and philandering, Chester staggered back to Yaddo, where he continued the pageant of self-indulgence and self-pity. "Until the period of my visit expired," he recalled, "I was drunk every day." As he described himself to another writer in 1952, "although I might not be the wittiest person I do think of myself as being jolly, especially when I have had a great deal to drink, which is one of my favorite hobbies." Others among Yaddo's guests joined him in debauchery. During one evening spectacle a high-spirited female artist slapped a man down and then broke some of the Mansion's windows. When Elizabeth Ames reflected upon the cohort whose eight-week stay ended in July, she confessed to Malcolm Cowley that "there has been a lot of very rowdy drinking."

Chester conducted his heaviest drinking downtown, at Jimmy's, which was a hangout for the Yaddo crowd, and at afterhours dives for the black cooks and waiters who worked in town, like Glenn Finley's Blind Pig, where they served barbecue and Chester could drink until five in the morning. Chester described himself at the all-black joints as "a man going home after a shipwreck." But recuperating at the bar with his kinfolk meant that the experience with the white artsy crowd was equivalent to drowning at sea. A sentence from his 1955 novel *The Primitive* (which punningly used Skidoo for Yaddo) uncovered his bewilderment and anger, "Some day he'd have to sit down and discover why he hated Skiddoo and all the artists there."

One element of the discontentment was Chester's realization about himself. In 1948, Chester wrote a moving short story based on the Saratoga Springs artists' retreat. "Da-Da-Dee" took its title from an onomatopoetic transcription of Ella Fitzgerald scat-singing "I'll Get By—As Long as I Have You." The maudlin tale centered on Jethro, "a famous writer of two racial novels," who has been invited to an artists' colony to "work on a novel called *Stool Pigeon*." The short story exposed two places of rot: first, the protagonist could no longer escape the fact that his life was governed by his race; second, drinking, the salve he used to endure the first problem, was destroying him. Forty-one-year-old Jethro scats and drinks in the all-black Saratoga Springs bars until he discovers "how much of the street was in himself and how much of himself was in the street." In an epiphany, he realizes that "the street" was simply ordinary, low-ceilinged black life. Instead of nobly writing to resolve the race problem and to inspire individual triumph, a fitful Chester, revealing his innermost feelings later, in *The Primitive*, "felt more like just lying in the gutter and never getting up."

To make matters worse, by June 8 he was broke. Chester pushed back from the bar long enough to dash down to New York, in a "desperate need to raise some money." Predictably he went first to Carl Van Vechten. Chester claimed that he needed $100 to defray expenses before Jean started a new job as a recreational director for federally funded housing projects in New York on July 1. Van Vechten seems to have resisted being dunned, because the next day Chester wrote Blanche Knopf, telling her that Jean was "ill and our need urgent." Confronted by "the bare and irreducible problem of expenses which I have been unable to relieve," Chester requested $100 from his publisher, who was already heartily disinclined to advance him money. Blanche Knopf told him so on June 14: "This is a rather unusual request of yours, which I know you realize, in view of the advance paid on the next book and the bad position we too are in on *Lonely Crusade*." But because Chester had invoked the helpless tragedy of his wife, Blanche Knopf was "of course sending your wife a check immediately."

Chester returned to Yaddo and continued his sport. Befriending the Iowa mural painter Francis White, who used the term "atom-alypse" to describe the contemporary geopolitical moment, Chester tried to reassert his pride by recommending White's work in a letter to Knopf. But having failed to submit the *Immortal Mammy* manuscript, which he seems to have abandoned completely by the end of June, or to repay the money to Blanche Knopf, from roughly that point forward the firm considered his every communiqué importunate.

The disaffection that grew between Chester, prestigious publishers like Knopf, and the artistic circles Yaddo represented was apparently mutual. By the time he left Yaddo in July, Elizabeth Ames was not likely to invite him back. If she believed in the summer of 1948 that "a good many now here are mistakes," she almost certainly counted Chester as one of the people who "have very not definite objectives in work." Facing increasingly desperate circumstances in subsequent years, Chester would try to rejoin the guest list, but he would never be invited to revisit Saratoga Springs, which, more than anything, probably shaped his unflattering portraits of "Skiddoo" in 1955 and in his memoir in 1972.

Back in the Bronx, without a finished book and depressed, he edged toward ragged dissolution. His marriage to Jean had been brokered on his determined effort to appear masculine and in command, in spite of the vulnerabilities of his characters and his willingness to write about homosexuality. But he was too tattered and feeble to uphold the front of prowess and control any longer. Even Jean, whose past life and lack of erudition sometimes embarrassed him, "felt truly sorry for me then."

A shriveled Chester sobered up at the end of the summer, when budget cuts eliminated Jean's position. "The support of the family reverted to me, and I had to take my position as the man and the husband," he reported in his memoir. The solution for their well-being was to work as off-season caretakers at summer resorts, and Chester cast about, placing an advertisement in the *Times* and facing a few anxious weeks of interviews. "If I can spend this winter in some isolated camp or summer colony or estate I will be able to come up next spring with another complete book," he wrote Van Vechten, the strongest of his allies.

By October he at least knew where he would live for the following six months: Andover, New Jersey. Chester signed on as caretaker at Sussex Village, a former German American Bund parade ground and resort owned by Frank Bucino, a Hoboken real-estate broker. Chester thought Bucino, who claimed to be Frank Sinatra's godfather, had seen Edward G. Robinson in *Little Caesar* too many times. The one-eyed man certainly looked the part of a gangster, from his "voluptuous" wife to his street-fighting bodyguards and Lincoln Continental. Bucino paid $150 a month, the same as Chester's literary advances, and he supplied plenty to eat and drink. With dogs for company and three upstairs rooms of their own in an old tavern, Chester and Jean agreed to look after thirty-six bungalows surrounding Clearwater Lake.

Even though the first month involved quite a bit of drudgery—such as painting and repairs—the Himeses wanted for little. The cozy, rustic life of walking in snow-filled woods suited them. He pored over novels like Hiram Haydn's *The Time Is Noon,* John O'Hara's *Butterfield 8,* Budd Schulberg's *What Makes Sammy Run,* and Horace McCoy's *They Shoot Horses, Don't They?* Horace Cayton visited for a week in December with his new wife, Ruby, whom he had just married on Yaddo's grounds. Flamboyant but manic-depressive, Cayton had tried to get off alcohol the previous year, but when Chester met him in Chicago at the Creative Writing Forum he had returned to heavy drinking. Now Cayton was in free fall. Burly, but always dignified in manner, he had previously divorced two white women and was now with a former showgirl. This marriage wouldn't last long and the visit was a drunken folly. After spending a week together Chester couldn't recall a "moment of lucidity" with the Caytons, other than lengthy rambles from Horace about his sessions with psychiatrists. Then, instead of working on *Immortal Mammy,* Chester focused instead on preparing a stage adaptation of *If He Hollers Let Him Go.* Just before Christmas he had completed 140 pages, consisting of two acts and three scenes. In an unguardedly optimistic moment, he reflected that "I think in many ways [it] is better than the book."

Chester would never find his métier with the stage, although he did write another play, *Baby Sister,* in 1961. While he sat out the fall and winter, he applied for a Guggenheim fellowship hoping to work on a book called *An Uncle Tom You Never Knew,* and he thought that if American audiences were so misinformed about the prison-house of race and class, that he might take upon himself, "an autobiographical novel til the time I went to prison."

In late January 1949, Chester wanted to send his play to Margot Johnson, the same agent used by Willard Motley and Patricia Highsmith. Since the connection was through Van Vechten, he sent the script, which has since been lost, to his patron first. Van Vechten disliked the "smutty and profane" adaptation of *If He Hollers*, causing Chester to apologize and admit, "I got lost in the character and forgot about the stage." But what was holding him back was his everlasting resistance to a world that did not have a place for a black artist who didn't emphasize the value of assimilation. "What I have done will be repugnant to those Negroes who define their progress in terms of their similarity to upper class whites," he wrote in justification of his ribald play. The real worry was Van Vechten's dimming enthusiasm.

By March Chester learned that he had not received a Guggenheim. He was feeling pressure about the unwritten novel and his missed deadline with Knopf. "I know what I have to do" and "have it all in my head" were how he tried to persuade Van Vechten, saying it more to himself. No new writing had occurred since the play. All he knew was that "it will take a little time." But the six months in New Jersey were up, and on April 2, 1949, Chester and Jean returned to their small room at Eddie Bonelli's in the Bronx.

Instead of producing a new manuscript, Chester had actually been rewriting *Black Sheep*. Circumventing his agent and the wilting relationship at Knopf, on March 1 he had presented his latest version to editor Bill Raney at Rinehart. Raney had a reputation for giving contracts to incorrigible geniuses. He had been involved, toward the end, with the fight to have Norman Mailer's *The Naked and the Dead* published, and he left Rinehart in April for another job. Raney asked Chester to withdraw the book from Rinehart and resubmit it at his new employer, Henry Holt. Chester agreed.

Chester's formidable coming-of-age novel *Black Sheep* never featured black main characters, probably because at the beginning of his career Chester had reasoned that success with American editors and audiences meant white protagonists. Notwithstanding the white cast, Chester had again broken convention and cut a path by writing about the misery and brutality of life inside prison. Chester's novel combined the development of his protagonist's homosexuality with a hard-boiled exposé of the penitentiary that had never appeared in an American novel. He was blazing a trail on two issues, but he elected not to blaze a third, on race relations.

Homosexuality was still taboo in the 1940s but a shift was under way. New studies by researchers like Indiana University sexologist Alfred Kinsey had appeared throughout the decade, greatly complicating the portrayal and range of what was considered "normal" male sexuality. By the 1948 publication of *Sexual Behavior in the Human Male*, Kinsey would suggest that 37 percent of American men had had at least one homosexual experience. Truman Capote's *Other Voices, Other Rooms*, with an adolescent gay protagonist and an adult gay transvestite as a key character, had been well received in 1948. Also published this year, and more graphic than Capote's book, was Gore Vidal's *The City and the Pillar*, featuring the gay love life of an adult man. As arguments for tolerance and civility, other postwar novels about gay men tended to explore the theme tragically, like the novels about the cruelty of racism.

Chester's first-person novel depicted a young man coming of age in prison under physically and emotionally grueling conditions. It concluded with the protagonist, Jimmy Monroe, demanding in a self-sacrificial gesture that he be charged with violating the prison regulation against "sex perversion," forsaking an opportunity for a commuted sentence. Jimmy's self-awareness occurs at this decisive moment: "I had done it to be a man. And if I had lost freedom by doing it, I'd never had freedom. . . . I had done a lot of time and I could do plenty more. But I couldn't be a man later. I couldn't wait." Chester revealed much of his own story throughout; the last third of the book offered a candid sketch of his yearlong relationship with Prince Rico.

While *Black Sheep* was not precisely a "gay" novel, in that ultimately it did not have as its central concern Jimmy's coming to terms with homosexual desire or even homosexual romance as its central plot, it was certainly a "queer" novel, a word used repeatedly throughout the book. Duke Dido, the character in love with Jimmy Monroe, explains "queer" when he tells Jimmy about Hollywood.

> "Everyone else seems to think a lot of them are rather queer."
>
> "Queer? That's a funny word."
>
> "I mean sexually."
>
> He looked at me strangely. "There's really nothing lost when a physical change is made unless you feel that it's wrong. It's the feeling that it's wrong that makes it queer."
>
> "How did you feel?" I couldn't help but ask.
>
> "It never came to that," he said again. I didn't know why I needed to be reassured so often.
>
> "Do you think queerness in prison is right?" I pressed.
>
> "That's an odd question—" he began.
>
> "Why is it odd?"
>
> "Do you?" he countered.
>
> "Not particularly so," I said.

Provocative and searing, *Black Sheep* cautiously approached portraying sex acts. However, Jimmy was undeniably queer.

Chester's instincts for survival were tearing him in different directions: toward what he was driven to narrate on the basis of the life that he knew and toward what he was told incessantly his audience wanted to hear. For the latter, he published "Journey Out of Fear" in

June 1949 in the journal *Tomorrow*. In the essay, Chester revisited the experience of driving out to California, rifle in hand, buffeted by the slights of Jim Crow and expecting the worst from his white fellow citizens. He wrote that he and Jean, after living in the foothills of the Sierra Nevada, had overcome bitterness and fear and finally achieved "inclusion in the social and community life of the neighborhood." He put in the buzzwords that might have come from the mouth of his Louis Foster, his *Lonely Crusade* plant owner. "Most important of all," he concludes, "we lost all consciousness of race . . . and were welcomed not as Negroes but as individuals." The final flourish signaled not real depth but dishonesty. "I managed to recapture a feeling I had left behind when I grew out of early childhood—the happy, secure feeling of being wanted."

Chester was either lying to himself or to others on his views of being black in America. If it later seemed to Chester that his autobiographical *The Third Generation*, a new novel he was working on in 1949, was "a subtly dishonest book, made dishonest deliberately," then "Journey Out of Fear" marked the beginning of the deceit. He managed a similar kind of fake performance in a stilted boyhood morality tale set in the Deep South called "Mama's Missionary Money," which would be published in *The Crisis* that November, after *Collier's* accepted and then rejected it.

Worse than being reduced to a writer who soft-pedaled the race problem was being reminded of what the world considered his labor was worth and the kind of labor which best suited him. Chester had salvaged himself from 1948 through mid-1949 with the caretaker job in New Jersey, which enabled him to appear like a competent husband in his marriage, so essential to his mind-set. For the next four years he would perform similar off-season custodial work on what he called the "Borscht circuit" in New York and New Jersey, resorts for Italians and Jews that were "like the Bronx set down in hot rural terrain." When the seasonal jobs ended, Chester and Jean took refuge where they could in overcrowded New York, in the Bronx at Bonelli's or in Bedford-Stuyvesant in Brooklyn. To make ends meet between the caretaker posts, he had to serve as a bellhop, porter, or janitor, where he was reminded how basely the white world considered black servant men.

In the spring of 1950, another caretaker assignment presented itself, for a Madison Avenue attorney who owned a Thoroughbred horse farm near Stamford, Connecticut. Chester and Jean had light duties, though they were required to cook, serve, and clean for their proprietors when the couple arrived with their personal maid and a gigot of mutton on the weekend. Otherwise, he and Jean had a Jeep, a sedan, unlimited gas, and food at their disposal. They could travel to New York City or head up to Vermont to visit Bill and Helen Smith, as they wished. "Life there was like something in a Hollywood film," Chester recalled.

In June 1950 a still enthusiastic Bill Raney contacted Chester about making changes to the manuscript. Always ready to please, Chester accepted the recommendations, apparently removing Jimmy Monroe's background story and orchestrating Duke Dido's suicide. He simply needed a book contract.

Chester's brother Joe, by then a tenured professor of sociology in North Carolina, provided the highlight of that summer: Chester gave a series of lectures and seminars in Durham at North Carolina College for Negroes. When Chester let it be known that he would be quitting the Stamford job to return to full-time writing, "there was a bit of unpleasantness." "I was somewhat surprised," mused Chester, that a wealthy Madison Avenue attorney "held such a low opinion of black writers." Imagining a third successfully published, adult-theme novel with a high-end publisher, a feat that no other postwar black writer had accomplished in 1950, Chester was deluding himself. The conversation to terminate his and Jean's employment brought him back down to earth.

At midcentury an African American could really be no closer to the ground in the United States than to live in the still acrimoniously segregated Southern states, with their offensive public signs and deadly customs, like the refusal of emergency medical care. And yet, Joe had gone on to a notable if not prominent career as a sociologist in the segregated college system. He and his wife, Estelle, lived walking distance from the campus in a comfortable stucco home with a Spanish-tile roof. The tidy black Durham neighborhoods, with well-kept bungalows full of the latest conveniences, seemed to epitomize the consequences of efficacious racial segregation. Many black Americans worked in the tobacco factory; others managed their own insurance company with a handsome three-story brick office in the downtown. They were as proud as whites of the heavy stone buildings on Duke University's campus, despite not being able to attend college there, and blind Joe was treated courteously in nearby Chapel Hill, when he used the facilities at the state's flagship university. A measure of public respect could be maintained if black North Carolinians subscribed to infinitesimal political gradualism.

Chester opened his public lectures with fire on Sunday, July 9, returning to his liberal politics stump speech from 1944, "Democracy Is for the Unafraid." "Believers in democracy must have the courage to advocate equality of opportunity for all citizens," he told the interracial audience, politely ruffling a few feathers. The next afternoon Chester spoke to an all-black college audience with the lecture "Lonely Crusade: The Composition and the Philosophy." To inform his remarks, Chester had written publishing contacts, including Blanche Knopf, asking them point-blank whether there was a color bar among the mainstream publishers and editors. Invariably, each person responded with the "no good book goes unpublished" mantra, an axiom believed by some blacks but not by Chester.

Chester was particularly tickled to have his sessions featured in the pages of the local white dailies, the *Durham Herald* and *Durham*

Sun, alongside coverage of the "test" discrimination case of Harold Epps, a black man who was trying to win admission to law school at the University of North Carolina. Chester noted that somber-looking Thurgood Marshall, whom he knew from Mollie Moon's Harlem parties, was in Durham during the fortnight of lectures, before deciding to drop the Epps case. In his spare time in North Carolina, when Chester wasn't visiting his mother's relatives in the countryside and eating roast ham and potato salad, he worked on revisions of *Black Sheep*, rewriting to the specifications of Raney's superior, the managing director at Holt, Ted Amussen. He mailed the draft to Raney from Durham, and received instructions to sign a book contract when he returned to New York.

Jean's first visit as an adult to "the South land," as she referred to the officially segregated region that many blacks avoided completely if possible, was not marred by any ugly incidents, although Jean petrified her sister-in-law Estelle by drinking from a "whites only" public water fountain. At the end of their stay, Chester and Jean took the night train northbound in good spirits and arrived in New York on Friday, July 21. They booked a room at the Theresa Hotel, "relieved" to have survived their Dixie visit. Readying themselves for the advance money from the book, he and Jean splurged on a case of Irish whiskey and called up friends to produce "a celebration memorable even in the Hotel Theresa."

The festivities were premature. A hungover Chester went to the Holt office to sign his contract on the twenty-fifth, and learned that he had nothing to sign. Blaming Amussen, Bill Raney returned *Black Sheep*, declining to publish it. The rejection was a body blow. His wind knocked out of him, Chester clutched his rejected manuscript and, late in the season when the editors were on vacation, prepared himself to interest someone else in the story. In the downstairs lobby he regrouped and telephoned Margot Johnson, the agent he had been putting off for months. She had just sold Motley's *Knock on Any Door* to Hollywood for $65,000; the film would star Humphrey Bogart. Johnson agreed to represent him and would submit the prison manuscript, now under the title *Yesterday Will Make You Cry*. She discussed the possibility of film rights. But nothing happened for four long months. Her first success came when she sold the foreign rights of *Lonely Crusade* (apparently released by Lurton Blassingame) to the French publisher Editions Corréa on December 23.

Facing collapse, Chester and Jean gathered their luggage and retreated to Westford, Vermont, to Bill Smith, who had bought a ten-room hilltop dream house on 150 acres with an eastern view of the Green Mountains. The impressive brick residence had been featured in a March 1948 *Ebony* article, "Shangri-La in Vermont." Whether on account of his career setbacks or his friend's obviously flush circumstances, Chester could no longer conceal his bitter feelings of resentment and defeat. He directed his hostility at Jean. While he treated Bill's spouse, Helen, honorifically, toward Jean he was so rude as to catch the notice and disapproval of his hosts. Even the Smith children noted with discomfort Chester's abusiveness.

The unhappy Himeses went to Brooklyn again, then found a caretaker post in Craryville, New York. From October 1950 through the end of March 1951, Chester and Jean braved the weather and watched over a golf course, kept madmen in automobiles off the frozen lake, and drove around the country club in a DeSoto Town and Country. Chester was now toying with an autobiographical novel of his childhood years; at the same time, another novel began to take shape, one he had been "fooling around" with "a long time" called *The End of a Primitive*.

On November 28, five days after Thanksgiving, a hurricane lashed the northeast and caused $400 million worth of damage. Provisioned with yet another case of Irish whiskey, Chester and Jean hunkered down in a bungalow by the lake and, in the process of drinking the liquor, made such a robust fire in the chimney that they set the floor aflame and had to be rescued by fire trucks racing over downed power lines.

Chester mellowed after that, sipping from a basement cache of wine, and regained his stamina. By March he had written three hundred pages of the childhood novel. The fact that Chester was thinking about the two books, with different aims, at the same time was remarkable. The supposedly autobiographical novel *The Third Generation,* his "deliberately dishonest" book, was untrue to his life because he stressed the Oedipus complex—the sexual undertones in his relationship with his mother. In the era of the Kinsey Report and the broad popularity of psychoanalysis, he believed his audience wanted that condition. But in the other manuscript, *The End of a Primitive,* he would carry out the work begun in *If He Hollers Let Him Go* and intemperately scorch liberal beliefs about progressive race relations.

Once the Craryville job was over, he and Jean relocated to "pleasant" Bridgeport, Connecticut, easy driving to Manhattan and with a socialist mayor. With a portion of their saved winter salary they bought a used Plymouth sedan. At the beginning of the month, Chester got a speeding ticket, so he was nervous about the police. In the cool mornings, Chester would drive to a park near the seashore and sit in the car, listening to the lapping of the waves, and writing in the backseat with the typewriter on his knees. At the beginning of April, the firm of G. P. Putnam informed his agent Margot Johnson that it was turning down *Yesterday Will Make You Cry.* The comments were similar to those made in 1941: the novel was well written but too grim and it had too much homosexual content.

Toting around the unpublishable *Yesterday Will Make You Cry* manuscript seemed to invite having all of his work discounted. At a literary cocktail party in New York, rare for Chester, World Publishers' editor James Putnam told him that the early chapters of *The Third Generation* were impossible to believe on account of the improbable emphasis on black pride. As a Negro, Chester was wrong to emphasize dishonor as a problem, lectured Putnam. "You could be as much of an Uncle Tom as any Negro," Putnam told him. Expressing strong resistance to such slights seemed unwise.

As the prison manuscript was rejected over and over again, Chester grew angrier with Knopf, whom he began to consider his real enemy, because he had written *Black Sheep* and large chunks of *The Third Generation*, works they had shown no interest in. In June 1951 he approached them incautiously, asking relief from the contractual option clause and demanding to be held responsible only for the *Immortal Mammy* advance he had been paid in 1947 and 1948. "Legally I am only indebted to you for the $2,000," he snarled in a letter, trying to invalidate the entire contract after he had drunkenly ignored the May 1948 submission date, and had conveniently forgotten the money Blanche Knopf personally conveyed to Jean on his behalf a month later. Chester was burning another bridge.

The downturn in literary success was compounded by the day-to-day indignity he faced. He couldn't support a family; he couldn't find a place to live; he couldn't secure regular work commensurate with his skills. And even on the occasional payday when advance money came through, the Stork Club in Manhattan or a fancy Saratoga Springs restaurant would still reject him. Editors and agents seemed willfully to ignore the uphill struggle of a black person trying to make a living as a novelist—especially one who exposed difficult American topics— and one who was completely barred from high-paying magazines and offered only the most basic, boilerplate literary contracts when they were offered at all. It was not possible to find decent, affordable lodging in the cities where the book business was conducted, effectively network with the publishers and editors, or pick up temporary work at colleges and universities, even though these institutions were mushrooming with demobilized GIs. He felt jammed by the expectation that he should write a novel filled with platitudes extolling democracy and liberalism in the style of Fannie Cook. He refused.

After this, Chester would not hesitate to—or apologize for

attempting to—shake loose money and dodge repayment without scruple, to play the ends against the middle, in a nonstop sparring with agents, editors, and book company presidents. Some professionals considered the approach merely guile but to others it was criminally dishonest. With Lurton Blassingame and now Margot Johnson, he would press for money from his agent personally, loans that were to be "against Advances." Once the debts were piled up high and no book was sold, Chester would dart to another agent and try to wheedle money out of her or him. It was not personal. He was desperate.

Chester decided to bet his chips on selling *The Third Generation*, but he and Jean's money gave out in July, forcing them to sell the Plymouth to finance a return to New York, where Jean could find a job. The day Chester tried to sell the automobile, when Jean had gone for interviews, a Bridgeport traffic cop arrested him for denting the fender of the car of one of the town's blue bloods, on her say-so, and without any other witnesses. After thirty-six hours behind bars Chester reached Jean's younger brother Andrew in Baltimore, who wired $100 bail to the jail. By then, however, Chester had been transferred to the county prison, awaiting a trial that was then delayed a week. It took Jean twelve hours of tearful haggling and beseeching jailers, wardens, judges and court clerks, to retrieve her brother's money to have her husband released. They left immediately for New York, and once they got out of the train station there, Chester tore up the summons and never looked back.

He re-created the episode in both the 1955 novel *The Primitive* and his 1972 memoir. Being incarcerated again was deeply threatening.

> That incident shook me. It wasn't that it hurt so much. Nor was
> I surprised. I believed that the American white man—in fact
> all Americans, black or white—was capable of anything. It was
> just that it stirred up my anxiety, which had gradually settled

down somewhat. It scrambled the continuity of my memories, probably of my thoughts also. That is practically the last thing I remember about the United States in such vivid detail.

The conversation in Stamford when he planned to leave custodial work and found out precisely his employer's measure of him as a human being, followed by his arrest and jailing for a traffic offense, signaled that he might not quite escape the black dives in Cleveland or Saratoga Springs after all.

So Jean took over as the leader. They regrouped in a room in the northern Bronx until she accepted a residential job as a recreational director at the New York State Women's Reformatory near Mt. Kisco, about an hour north of the city. Following his wife in December 1951, Chester rented a bedroom in nearby White Plains. His landlady, a proud, flinty woman who reminded him of his mother, kept him on his toes and her house chilly. Jean visited him for a day and a half each weekend and paid the tab. Chester was helpless and furious at being helpless. Chester applied for work at *Reader's Digest*, presenting himself at the magazine's White Plains offices with all the charm, youthfulness, and bonhomie that he could muster. "Of course," he learned, "they had no suitable opening for a person of my capabilities." But Chester was hungry, not idealistic: he yielded to a job in the mailroom, where he remained until he proved incapable of mastering the technique to make metal stencils. He was fired before Christmas.

During the holidays in White Plains, with its flourishing black middle class (including Gordon Parks, the photographer for *Life* magazine), Chester began slowly "to lose confidence in myself." Jean's job claimed her time and energy, while he shared the boardinghouse with a young woman whose cheap clothes and hairdo seemed to reflect his own spreading poverty. Knopf kept mailing letters to get what he didn't have: the $1000 used to buy out his contract from Doubleday, and then the $1000 advance for *Immortal Mammy*, upon which he had lived during the revision of *Lonely Crusade*.

A glimmer of hope came by way of a letter from France, from a man who had begun translating *Lonely Crusade* into a French edition to be called *La Croisade de Lee Gordon*. Yves Malartic was concerned that he was misperceiving black language, so he wrote Chester: "I believe the book *is not* some sort of an exciting sexy thriller written in a queer language which would have the 'flavor of american negroes idiom'(?!) and which should be translated into rough popular French." For his perception and solicitation, Malartic won a friend. Chester wrote back, "Please, by all means, follow your first impulse and do the translation on the highest intellectual level." For that fidelity, Malartic would earn Chester's "undying gratitude."

Malartic's sense that he was dealing with a masterwork, one with profound insight into the human condition, might have been the only thing standing between Chester and psychological collapse. For his next move, Chester became the "day porter"—the janitor—at the White Plains YMCA. Three months of swinging a mop and pushing a broom, cleaning showers and latrines, togged in coveralls and cap, seemed to confirm his lowest estimate of himself. It was as if he had returned to the top bunk in an Ohio cell block. Bewildered, he no longer worked at his marriage. Too proud to take the humiliation of being marginally supported by Jean, he drank and lashed out. When they squabbled over household affairs he told her she was just a correctional officer, title or not. He blamed her for their difficult circumstances and when he couldn't blame her, he repudiated her with silence.

It is unclear whether Jean was an active or passive partner in the ending of their fifteen-year marriage. By June 1952 Chester would confide to Malartic, "My wife and I have been separated for about six months—we should have been divorced years ago." In his memoir he was more prosaic and less precise about the timing of their breakup: "Jean stopped coming to visit me and to support me and I was faced with the necessity of having to support myself." Still gripped by the puritanical views of his parents, Chester believed that his sins—"pride and arrogance"—had betokened his fall. And if Jean was the correctional officer, he was once again the prisoner, yearning for freedom.

Chapter Ten

CADILLACS TO COTTON SACKS

1952–1954

Chester quit White Plains in February 1952, taking a room in a sprawling six-story apartment building on Convent Avenue in Harlem. From his window he could see the City College gates down the street and, when the sky was clear, the tip of the Empire State Building farther downtown. But reduced to a seven-dollar-a-week room in an unsavory crowded apartment where privacy was impossible, he was not impressed by the view.

In an untimely flourish, his old buddy Ralph Ellison delivered an inscribed copy of his just published novel, *Invisible Man*. Biding his time and living off his wife's salary, Ellison had finished a career-defining masterpiece and his triumph was like a judgment against Chester. Touchy in his dealings with a friend turned rival, Chester concealed his separation from Jean, who would visit occasionally throughout the spring, and, concerning the book that would only be thought more significant with time, replied with polite banality: "Thanks greatly for the inscribed copy of your book. Jean and I are looking forward with much excitement to reading it. We feel confident it is a wonderful story." Chester had admitted to Horace Cayton, who printed it in a *Pittsburgh Courier* column, that Ellison had written "the first allegorical Negro novel," but the note was all he would ever write about a book that is routinely considered as the high mark of twentieth-century American fiction.

Instead of "beating that boy" with his now acclaimed friend and plotting further literary success of his own, Chester spent his time with Eddie Himes. His older brother now lived with his wife near Strivers Row. Less ambitious than either Joe Jr. or Chester and a product—"victim" might be a better word—of a thoroughly Jim Crow education, Eddie worked as a maître d' at a New York restaurant. The brothers ate fried chicken and biscuits and watched professional wrestling on television, which in his brief life among the literati Chester had "always considered the prime pastime of morons." But in the winter of 1952 the unhurried comfort felt good. It helped being around an older brother who couldn't reject him, even if he barely knew him. "I'm like an animal," Chester wrote later, "when I'm hurt and lonely I want to go off alone in my hole and lick my wounds."

For Christmas of 1951 Carl Van Vechten had mailed him a "devastatingly penetrating" card, one that oddly mirrored Chester's own troubles. The Negro, thought Van Vechten, was Harlequin, the acrobatic, black-masked clown of Italian Renaissance improvisational theater. Chester admitted that the assessment, comparing blacks of the western world with entertaining playthings, "hurt a little," but the "thing to do is be what we must and make it pay whatever way it might." Alone and putting off the scrounging for menial jobs he knew was inevitable, Chester squirreled away the hardest weeks of the winter at his typewriter. He told himself that the next novel, as deeply autobiographical as the prison manuscript, would make his literary reputation.

In April Margot Johnson reported the successful sale of the prison manuscript to Coward-McCann, for an advance of $1200. He believed that the book would be published under the title *Debt of Time*, but ultimately it would be called *Cast the First Stone*. Chester would finally publish the book he'd worked on for almost fifteen years. In 1998, Chester's second wife, Lesley, would publish the uncut manuscript that he drafted as *Yesterday Will Make You Cry*. That three-section book includes a middle part, "Flood of Tears," charting in detail Chester's adolescence in St. Louis and Cleveland, discussing his arrests, anxiety concerning his sexual development, and Jean's first marriage.

Yesterday Will Make You Cry and *Cast the First Stone* are quite similar, but *Cast the First Stone* benefits from the removal of the middle section, which slowed the narrative pace and slackened the development of the main character, Jimmy Monroe, in prison. *Yesterday Will Make You Cry* is considerably more sentimental and nearly apologetic. If, as Van Vechten told people, Coward-McCann insisted on changes to the manuscript they bought, those edits heightened and focused the dramatic tension and improved its quality. The other key difference is in the ending of the books: there's a suicide in *Cast the First Stone*, but Duke Dido survives in *Yesterday Will Make You Cry*. Meanwhile, Chester used the excised material in the autobiographical novel about his family, *The Third Generation*. He completed a draft of the new project in that spring of 1952.

Selling the prison novel revitalized him. Feeling reconciled with his past and confident about his future meant one direction for a black man like Chester. He rekindled his romance with fiery Vandi Haygood. In the 1970s, he downplayed what having been awarded the advance money for *Cast the First Stone* meant: "the first thing I desired now that I had money was to sleep with a white woman," he recollected. However, the classy Haygood always meant more to him than easy sex. Chester said as early as April that he would be traveling to Europe "with a friend" and, by the end of the summer, he was fantasizing about a permanent tie. It was difficult to separate Haygood's value to him both as an individual intimately familiar with his professional life and her status as a white woman. He had described to others his first kiss with Vandi as "penetrating as the moment of conception." Chester also believed that when their affair had begun, during the war, Haygood had fallen in love. Now that Vandi was divorced and had moved to New York, he had the opportunity to see whether their physical attraction had more depth.

After the Rosenwald Fund closed in 1948, Haygood had become an executive at the Institute of International Education, a private group with healthy ties to the U.S. State Department and the United Nations. The IIE promoted world peace through education and aided foreign students and scholars seeking access to American universities. Haygood orchestrated the foundation's relations with governments and funding agencies.

Notwithstanding the IIE's prestigious connections, there was an aura of scandal and political intrigue at the foundation. In the late 1940s and early 1950s, liberal efforts toward racial amity and peaceful international relations faced cruel scrutiny and accusation as part of a supposed international Communist conspiracy. In 1948 IIE president Laurence Duggan was denounced as a Communist courier by the professional anti-Communist Whittaker Chambers. A short time later, Duggan was found dead on the sidewalk, apparently having fallen from his office window. Some prominent government officials believed he had been murdered.

In spite of its hazards, the world inhabited by Haygood was one of comfortable, upper-middle-class white privilege. In 1952, when Chester began seeing her regularly, Haygood's office had just moved to the fifty-room Gould-Whitney-Vanderbilt Mansion on Fifth Avenue, with solid-marble sinks and gold plumbing. Her home life was like work. Haygood's fashionable apartment on E. Twenty-Second Street included the key to Gramercy Park, an exclusive gated garden.

Bucklin Moon came over to Vandi's apartment during the summer and, after a legendary evening at the bottle, he confirmed Chester's Doubleday nightmare by narrating the behind-the-scene circumstances hindering the publication of *If He Hollers Let Him Go*. He insisted to Chester, as the writer reported to Bill Targ, that "he did all he could for me, but there was little he could do." In the process of divorcing his wife that year, and having been unceremoniously fired by Doubleday a few months earlier, Moon was battling for his own career and falling into severe depression. The threat of being denounced as a Communist hung over his head too. In the spring of 1953 he was fired from his next job, at *Collier's*, after the magazine received threats from an advertising pressure group that charged Moon with being "subversive," one of the Red Scare words for Communist. If Moon faced this kind of pressure, Chester's portion might well be double.

Soon enough, the façade of settled life with Vandi Haygood began to mottle and blister. Haygood was brash and unpredictable and, according to Mollie Moon's friend Polly Johnson, a "nymphomaniac." To Chester, her keeping a black man meant an opportunity for a libidinal earthiness, to get vulgar without fear of losing her desirability or her standing. When the booze wore off and the allure of sex with a white society woman waned, he realized that Haygood was suspicious of his leaning on her financially and was "impatient for the money to start pouring in." He also acquired one of her vices, the over-the-counter stimulant Dexamyl, which Vandi took faithfully to increase her productivity.

In desperation, during the summer Chester returned to the New Prospect Hotel in Sullivan County to serve as a bellhop and switchboard substitute. While there, he received a telegram from William Targ, who was now working at World Publishers. For $2000, that Cleveland-based press was acquiring the hulking manuscript Chester was calling *The Cord*; it would be published as *The Third Generation*. The book presented two formal problems: the crisis of patriarchal authority in an African American family at the bottom of a caste system, and the dilemma of sexual desire in a male child growing up in such a family. *The Cord* reproduced his life in consummate detail, smoothly moving from the birth of Chester's character, Charles Taylor, in Lincoln, Missouri, to his childhood in Mississippi, fleshed out by sections featuring Pine Bluff and St. Louis and his brother's blinding. The last third concluded with Charles Taylor's young adulthood in Cleveland. However, the character based on Chester does not wind up in prison; instead, Charles Taylor's family rescues him from downfall. Chester explained the disaster of the fictionalized marriage by imagining his parents' wedding night and portraying Lillian, Estelle's surrogate, as the victim of marital rape. After that, her color complex sets in. He emphasized the conjunction between traumatic moments of violence, death, and horror on the one hand and young Charles's sensual growth away from his mother toward other sources of libidinal fulfillment. The novel shows the boy securing his erotic passion to substitutes for Lillian, light-skinned women who symbolically join violence, sexual attraction, and death. None of the mounting tragedies that occur in the narrative are connected to white oppression or economic deprivation. Chester resolved the drama by solemnly reuniting the nuclear family at the deathbed of the father and severing the "cord" between mother and son.

When he got World's telegram, he packed his bags and returned from upstate to New York City, ready to commit to Haygood as a breadwinner even as he also prepared to sail to France. He had written his Cleveland buddy Dan Levin, who was living in Paris on the GI Bill, for pointers on hotels and travel details. Chester also sent letters to Jean Chastel at his French publisher, Corréa, alerting him to his likely arrival in Paris and his hope to sell at least two new manuscripts.

The most important contact he renewed was with Richard Wright. In early October Chester broke the self-imposed silence, which he had thought necessary because of the career mishaps after *Lonely Crusade* was published. Chester thanked Wright for delivering the preface for the French edition of *Lonely Crusade,* which had praised the novel in grand language as "written with the most impeccable care" and creating "an indubitably genuine picture." Chester explained the new U.S. nadir as the House and Senate committees investigating un-American activities unleashed their force, slicing away free speech and cracking down on labor unions and alternative political forums. A "vital center" wave of conformity swept the nation. As "the only one over whom they could exert no control," and with "access to the public," Chester thought that Wright's intellectual leadership heaved "literary criticism and the liberal group" in the direction of justice. As for his own part in the public debate, Chester let Wright know that he was publishing the candid prison novel. "Maybe the boys can stand the truth about life in a state prison," Himes sounded out, referring to his critics, "better than they can stand the truth about life in the prison of being Negro in America." Wright encouraged him to try living overseas.

"Working hard" and "never happier," Chester spent the fall of 1952 revising *The Cord* and preparing for the publication of *Cast the First Stone.* Initially scheduled for release in October, *Cast the First Stone* was pushed back to January 1953; *The Cord* would have to be delayed as well. But with one book nearly published and the other in production, these were minor hurdles. In November Chester noted rosily to Van Vechten that he and Haygood would "probably be married sometime next year." He was seduced by a vision of long-lasting prosperity. None of his peers had pulled off what he was now assured to do: publish, within months of each other, two hefty novels of daring social critique—one ripping the cover off prison life in America and the other an unsparing portrait of intraracial and Oedipal conflict in a black family. Who would be able to deny that he was a marvelously successful novelist? Even sweeter, he was involved with an educated white woman living off Gramercy Park whose money he could accept without qualm—both because he wasn't financially desperate and because she was a career woman in a socially esteemed profession. Notwithstanding the dip in quality of his publishers, which he could tell himself was due to the hard-hitting subject matter, he was as ambitious as he had ever been.

Proudly, he escorted Haygood to Van Vechten's Central Park West home to see Carl's photographs and original American paintings. Chester now confided to friends that he should have divorced Jean "a long time ago, right after *Lonely Crusade* was published." Clingy, needy, and self-conscious, Jean had been unsuited to him: "Jean couldn't bear the things I wrote nor the processes of my thoughts which caused me to write them." She was appalled by Chester's willingness to mine details from the most acute tragedies of their lives, the typical practice of even the most original of writers. In contrast, Haygood seemed like a veteran of literary and cultural combat who could stand all assaults. By the time *The Cord* was submitted to World at the end of November, Chester was writing fast again, back to *The End of a Primitive*, the novel he had begun after Yaddo that would reveal the sexual intimacies of an interracial couple. He was convinced that his finger was on the pulse and he could appeal to American tastes.

But at Christmas, always an important symbolic holiday for Chester because of his pleasant childhood memories, something began to teeter. Domestic tranquility had never been his strong suit, and Haygood was rambunctious and fractious. Chester always maintained that she was also having affairs. Whether or not that was true, his lurking suspicion was a blow to his ego. "I think Vandi hurt you dreadfully," one of his closest confidantes later told him. So Chester left the apartment and on Christmas night, with the help of a bottle of King's Ransom scotch, he drank himself under the table with Jean, who had returned from a stint in California, and was lodged a few blocks away on the West Side. Before he blacked out, he tussled with the police and his wife's female roommate.

What ensued was a bad rift with Haygood. Within two days he telephoned Van Vechten asking to be hosted again, this time for cocktails, an attempt at an olive branch to Vandi. Van Vechten obliged them with a toast of mulled wine for New Year's 1953. Chester and Haygood "really 'went' for" the rarefied treatment. Nevertheless, Chester's personal life continued to unravel.

On the Sunday after the new year, he and Haygood threw a giddy celebratory party and invited Fanny and Ralph Ellison, now literary New York's most sought-after black couple. Having secured on December 31 an advance of $500 from World for a collection of short stories, tentatively titled *Black Boogie Woogie*, Chester felt prosperous enough to socialize with Ellison. It had been five years.

The men's mutual friend Horace Cayton was the other guest. Cayton's life in New York was a cautionary tale. He had been sexually intimate with Vandi Haygood in Chicago, but had been living hand to mouth in Manhattan since 1949. Cayton's world consisted of occasionally lecturing at City College, donating blood to buy cheap wine, writing a column for the *Pittsburgh Courier*, and checking himself into the psychiatric ward at Bellevue Hospital. An alcoholic art collector, Cayton liked to store valuable works of art for safekeeping with friends like Vandi Haygood and Ralph Ellison. His friends were using terms like "magnificent ruin" and "tragic" to describe him. Doubt, regret, and despair were hallmarks of any conversation with him; nonetheless, regardless of his inner trial, he always retained his outer dignity. Chester identified quite strongly with Cayton, whose high-achieving parents had come out of Mississippi, who was about Eddie's age, and who was inclined to deal with life's anguish by quoting black minstrel Bert Williams.

By contrast Ralph Ellison was fond of quoting Aristotle, his personality and point of view on life in the United States now occasionally regal. By early 1953, Ellison had ended his radical days as *New Masses* editor and left-wing critic of American commercialism and racism. To Chester, after nearly ten years of acquaintance, Ellison was now something of a mirror opposite of his earlier image: hubristically youthful (to the point of even moving his birth year forward), invincible, and full of himself.

After the miracle year of reviews, Ellison was that week hearing rumblings that he would win the National Book Award for fiction. Even *Life* seemed to bow down and scrape, when in 1952 it had, through the energetic orchestration of Gordon Parks, featured Ellison's novel photo-dramatized by Parks as "A Man Becomes Invisible." Chester, fearing "atomalypse," took this as a sign of Ellison's complete identification with right-wing power or, at the very least, his willingness to be used by it. As he wrote to William Targ a year later, he understood the buildup of Ellison in the Luce press as less an endorsement of *Invisible Man* than a repudiation of Richard Wright. In March, *Life*'s sister magazine *Time* would in fact pit Ellison, whom they termed "an abler U.S. Negro novelist," against Wright.

To Vandi Haygood, Ellison was a former needy Rosenwald applicant whom she had helped launch and who now had experienced great fortune with her nurturing and approval. She endorsed the new attitude that seemed to find unlimited possibility from American resources, and that did not dwell on racial conflict. She was also stimulated by famous, powerful men.

The small party of intimates was an awkward one, and it eventually caused Chester embarrassment. Ellison apparently bragged that he had been interviewed by Luce's deputies at *Time-Life* prior to the Parks story. Cayton and Himes joked about his covenant with the kingmakers and took sly digs at Ellison for a public comment he had made that amounted to the claim that professional success had ended his personal experience with racial discrimination. "I have joined the human race," Ellison reportedly said, referring to all that had been made possible on account of the accolades given his work. As Chester got further into his cups, he became morose and bombastic. He drunkenly bragged to Ellison that *The Cord* would be "great like Shakespeare," and Ellison mocked him, repeating, "Great. Great."

Drunken or not, Chester believed by early 1953 that *The Cord* was "the best of all" his novels and would have been deeply offended by Ellison's ridicule. Their new year's discord set the stage for yet another portrait of Ellison in the novel Chester was working on, *The Primitive.* The rivalries climaxed when, after more rounds of drunken heckling, Chester shoved or threatened Haygood, depending upon the witness. Ellison maintained that Himes picked up a butcher's cleaver and menaced Haygood, only subsiding when Ellison manhandled him. Himes and Ellison then verged on coming to blows, and Ellison liked to recall that Chester was "too chicken" to turn the weapon "on a man." Cayton remembered that Chester "was mad and acting off his nut."

Chester later called the squall between himself and Ellison "a private misunderstanding," but the sad turn of affairs in their friendship emphasized the pinhead that successful black writers tinkering away at American social problems had to stand upon. Clannish competitiveness, envy, and the burden of being deemed the only one good enough for acceptance by whites would prevent the friendship from going further. There was a shorthand way of understanding everything taken together. After the bitter night, both Cayton and Ellison concluded that Himes overregarded the effect of racism on black people.

Ellison glossed over the quarrel toward the end of the month in a letter to Richard Wright. He didn't mention that they had been at a party together, just that Chester was having a "riotous affair" with Haygood. "Recently with Horace Cayton present he became so insulting that I had to threaten to take his head off, after which he calmed down; but I am afraid he will never forgive me." Ellison here overestimated what the alcohol-sodden episode meant to Chester, while at the same time he correctly perceived the dynamic of violence unfolding between Himes and Haygood. "It gives me real agony," he concluded, "to see a man so much in the clutches of the furies." When he discussed what happened with Cayton, Ellison blamed it on Chester being "jealous." For Ellison's part, he wrote off not merely

Chester but the entire group of people he had known in conjunction with Wright in 1945.

Ellison's new gravity would grant him the last word. Within a year, William Targ of World Publishers, a genuine believer in Chester's talent, would request a blurb from Ellison for *The Cord*. "By far the most intense and compassionate probing of the psychological predicament of a middle-class Negro family yet written," Ellison would judge the novel. That comment appeared in January 1954 in a full-page advertisement in the *New York Times Book Review*. Chester knew, however, that for Ellison, "psychological" was a code word meaning that the book was artistically undistinguished.

Haygood was the most convenient and vulnerable scapegoat for Chester's torn pride. In the week following the party, he battered her to the point that a doctor was needed. Even though Chester lived during an era when many men publicly humiliated, verbally abused, and roughed up their girlfriends and wives, his smacking Haygood is one of his most disturbing encounters. At the height of the women's liberation movement in the early 1970s, he published this account: "When she went to Chicago to visit some old lover after telling me she was going to Washington, D.C. on business, I hurt her seriously. Physically, I mean. I began slapping her when she admitted the truth and all the hurts of my life seemed to come up into me and I went into a trance and kept on slapping her compulsively until suddenly the sight of her swollen face jarred me back to sanity."

One obvious source of his brutality was his insecurity that Haygood preferred other men. To make matters worse, he was also desperately in love with Vandi, who he thought was unworthy of complete trust. But the sight of this badly bruised white society woman revived the possibility of returning to prison and made him bolt to Bill Smith's in Vermont. During his escape north, Chester's father, Joseph, succumbed to kidney disease on January 16, 1953, in Oberlin. To fly to Ohio on short notice to bury his father, Chester had to eat his belligerence and fear and ask the one person he knew with ready cash to let him have the airfare: Vandi Haygood.

Cast the First Stone was published a few days after Joe Sr.'s death, on January 19. Himes's least remembered novel emerged as he returned to Vermont, spending a few weeks walking off the amphetamine jitters of Dexamyl on the frozen country roads and helping Smith on his second book, a memoir called *The Seeking*. *Cast the First Stone* did not garner rave reviews, but it was respectfully treated and Chester was acknowledged as a serious artist. One paper called "rough hewn" *Cast the First Stone* "the toughest book of the year" and added that it "expertly captures the flavor of prison speech." Chester should not have expected much more, writing candidly about incarceration and, as Gilbert Millstein discreetly observed in the *New York Times*, "relationships among men deprived of women." One obvious relief was that no one could accuse him of tearing down the race. Although the *Pittsburgh Courier* reviewer thought that Chester's portrait of Duke Dido was "perhaps one of the foulest creations in literature," he, like his counterpart in the *Chicago Defender*, gave Chester credit for the agenda of prison reform. As usual, the book was ahead of its time and quite difficult for the audience to respond to, perhaps especially for those who grasped the autobiographical seed within the story. Chester had dared to take prison life seriously and to portray situational homosexuality as something beyond pathology and sin.

A typical comment that showed the misapprehension possible in reading the book came from Ralph Ellison, who reported on the contents of the book in his last letter to Richard Wright. Ashamed of the book and apparently by what it revealed about Himes's past, Ellison understood it to be a basic admission of an inner homosexual conflict: "I am afraid it is not up to snuff. He writes mainly of homosexuality in prison but was unable to resolve it." As the more tolerant critic Richard Gibson would write, their circle of literary people and leftists, black and white, was "decidedly homophobic in the 40s and 50s."

Chester's willingness to broach the topic of homosexuality seems most strongly connected to his determination to confront the reality of lived experience, despite the penalty. Even though he was uncomfortable with its contents, he kept his files complete and never destroyed Rico's love letter to him as he was leaving the London Prison Farm.

At Smith's, Chester received the French edition of *Lonely Crusade* and several critical reviews from the French papers. Excited, he wandered the village looking for someone to translate them. On the last day of January World Publishers sent Bernard Schubert, his new literary agent, the remaining $2500 advance for *The Third Generation* and held out the possibility of $10,000 more when the paperback rights were sold. Meanwhile, Chester wrote his French publisher, Editions Corréa, trying to leverage 1 million francs (about $2000) for both *Cast the First Stone* and *The Cord*, so he could travel to Paris.

Chester booked a reservation on the boat *Ile de France* for April 3, after a flurry of letter writing. He happily received a report from Dan Levin at the Hotel Maurice, who suggested he room at 137 Boulevard St. Michel in the Latin Quarter. Fearing he would have document problems like Wright, he wrote to Ruth B. Shipley, the notorious director of the State Department's passport division, who was known to use her bureau to punish outspoken government critics. In his letter, Chester admitted his felony conviction, showed the proof of the restoration of his citizenship, and included the *New Masses* review of *Lonely Crusade*, his anti-Communist credential. His letter crossed his passport in the post office on its way back to him. For a last step, Chester secured a set of records to study French language.

In the process of renewing ties to Wright, Chester would soon learn that Wright needed him. An expatriate since 1947, Wright had not been as dazzling since going overseas. He had failed to win a commanding audience for the 1949 film version of *Native Son*, which he bankrolled and in which he himself starred as Bigger Thomas.

What's more, Wright was taking quite a few public lumps in

France and again in the States at the hands of James Baldwin, a protégé. Wright had once recommended Baldwin, as he had Ralph Ellison, for fellowships and opened his home to him. But Baldwin, once
launched, had completely dismissed the value of black literary realists
like Wright, first in a 1949 essay called "Everybody's Protest Novel,"
and then again in 1951 in "Many Thousands Gone." Both of Baldwin's
essays were published by *Partisan Review,* the powerhouse journal
of art and politics, which had also excerpted a chapter of Ellison's
Invisible Man. In 1953, *USA,* a magazine edited by the critic Lionel
Trilling for distribution from U.S. embassies around the world, recir-
culated Baldwin's article. In all of Baldwin's critiques of Wright he
could easily have inserted Chester's name; in fact, he had begun the
dismissal of black literary realism—in the process inventing the term
"social realism," a swipe at the Marxists—with his 1947 *Lonely Crusade*
review. Baldwin's critique of Wright and Himes would continue to
influence until the shift away from the nonviolent civil rights movement to black power in the mid-1960s.

So the embattled Himes and Wright were natural allies. "I suppose you received the copy of *Cast the First Stone,*" Chester began
a letter in early February. "I must say it has been very thoroughly
stoned in the press here." Sly and funny, he was endearing himself to
Wright, whom he hadn't seen in years but whose help he needed to
move abroad. Still, his message also contained a note of frustration.
As a result of the extraordinary work of Wright and Ellison (who had
in fact won the National Book Award, on January 27), the standard
for black literary success had shifted. If you did not receive dramatic
praise from the *New York Times*, a heap of publicity from Henry Luce,
and a cash payout from Book-of-the-Month Club, it was as if you
hadn't written a book. The Red Scare made the criticisms of segregation or imperial blundering un-American. Chester admitted to being
a mortal. "I am stuck with having to write about what I know about,
and prison happens to be (along with being a Negro) one of the sub-

jects on which I am an authority, having been sent to prison when I was nineteen and kept there until I was twenty-six." More pressing to him was the conversation he had not yet had with Wright, about the dismissal of his novel *Lonely Crusade*. "The critics beat it as if it was a snake and beat me as if I was a snake, and the Sams went along with their white folks as they always do, only when it comes to beating another Sam the Sams always try to outdo the white folks and quite often succeed."

When Wright's most ambitious novel, *The Outsider*, was published that March, he sent Chester a review copy. Chester took the time to read the book closely. He wrote back to Wright that the novel about the character Cross Damon, who repudiates ideology, conveyed a "really stupendous idea" and that, in the weeks after having been involved with act after act of violence toward his intimates, he was personally terrified to have such a tight identification with this socially isolated, homicidal existentialist hero: "I'm so goddamned close to that boy I don't want to talk about it," he confided. Wright believed in the outlaw as an important subject in fiction, and Chester, who had lived the outlaw life and survived the sentence, had something fundamentally in common with Wright's fictional creations.

Feeling some remorse over his behavior at the New Year's party, Chester also tried to rendezvous with Horace Cayton. Knowing that Chester considered the dramatic fight at the party Haygood's fault, Cayton now claimed he would avoid his "strange and strained" relationship to Haygood in the short term. He was, however, happy to have "a few things clear" with Chester because their friendship was "something I would pay a price for." But Cayton insisted on one point that angered Chester. Racism "does not explain everything. . . . The reality of change is upon us. It calls for the development of a new kind of person—one who is not licking his wounds but is in someway aiding and encouraging change." Chester would settle with him in *The Primitive*.

Chester repaired the love affair with Haygood by March 24, when he returned to New York and settled at her apartment. He bought a new wardrobe, splurged on an Abercrombie and Fitch kerosene stove to cook with in French hotel rooms, and retrieved electronics parts and copies of *The Outsider* for Wright. Despite the hurried week of activity, he still managed to reach the boiling point again with Haygood, breaking his own toe in an attempt to kick her the day before his ship sailed. He would leave the United States from a room at the Albert Hotel, encumbered by one trunk and a couple of pieces of luggage, his swollen foot in a felt slipper.

Chester boarded the *Ile de France* on April 3, 1953, an overcast and cold day. But things brightened considerably when William Targ sent a bottle of champagne to Chester's third-class cabin. Then, editor James Putnam, who had labeled him an Uncle Tom and who was now the secretary of the PEN Center for writers, appeared aboard and introduced him to his ex-wife, "stylish, nice-looking" Marion Putnam. A noted sculptress born in 1905, Marion Putnam had grown up in New York, the daughter of a patron of experimental musicians, and her statuesque good looks and worldliness appealed to Chester. If the relationship with Haygood had fizzled, perhaps the new freedom on the other side of the Atlantic would bring into view wealthy sophisticates like Putnam, a woman who was sometimes invited to the White House.

During the crossing Chester had moments of deep reflection, especially on the dissolution of his marriage. He imagined he would remain abroad a few months while his money lasted, and he paused over the gravity of this new choice. Attempting to recover from seasickness in the room he shared with an Austrian violinist, Chester encountered a slight, terrified woman in the lower berths. Frightened, she clung to a hallway until he escorted her to her room. Later, on deck, he exchanged introductions with Willa Thompson, a divorcée from Boston who had attended Smith College. Now the tables had turned. Heaving over the side with seasickness, Chester needed help and Willa, having made fourteen voyages, consoled him.

Thompson led Chester boldly into the exclusive second-class cabins, with better food and top-shelf drinks. While Chester had been living on the prison farm in Ohio, Willa Thompson had been winning literary prizes at her high school in Brighton, Massachusetts. A direct descendant of John Hancock, she surprised him with her frank conversation, confiding the harrowing details of her life and her reason for the voyage. She had impulsively married a Luxembourg dentist while studying abroad in 1936, been unprepared for the trauma of sexual relations, and then she had become pregnant rapidly and regularly. Thompson's "fidelity to sexual detail" when discussing her married life shocked Chester "to the core." But an innocent-looking white woman chatting about sex also aroused him.

Willa's tale was the stuff of fiction. During the war, she had sheltered downed Allied airmen and had been beaten and persecuted by her husband, a Nazi sympathizer, as a result. She left for the United States and brought a lawsuit, winning custody of two of her daughters after a scandalous 1946 trial. Unhappy with the outcome, she reconciled with her husband in Luxembourg, had another child and, after another rift, was threatened with confinement at a mental institution. She had retreated again to America and was now headed back overseas to renew her custodial fight.

Thin and dowdy, the thirty-seven-year-old Willa Thompson had survived the hardships of the war in Europe and lost a stillborn child. At forty-three, Chester conveyed the air of a more youthful person. However, Thompson was sprightly, easily literary, and from the New England upper class, at a postwar moment when it seemed as if America's elites had something to offer the world. And she was working on a novel. She told him that Edwin Seaver, an editor and the former director of the League of American Writers, the hard-left literary group that had closed in 1943, had offered to help her tidy up her book for publication; she had balked at giving him $500 for the job. Already she'd been featured in *Time* magazine and had received requests from literary agents to see her manuscript. Chester decided that "assured, distinguished" Willa was "the best of American society."

Ile de France docked at Le Havre on April 8 and late the next day Chester made his way by boat train to Paris, expecting to meet Richard Wright and his translator Yves Malartic at the station. Chester had written to Malartic that "if things work out as I hope, I shall stay a long time." Paris was the literary and intellectual capital of the West and, absent the aggravating custom of racial segregation, an attraction for blacks for many decades.

The infantry veterans among the latest crop of American novelists, like William Styron, Norman Mailer, and James Jones, were making Paris an expatriate hub. Chester's gamble to take his book advance and live in Paris for a season or two was a canny business move. It was not far-fetched at all to think that with some good connections to publishers, artists like Marion Putnam, and the literati, a far more successful career was available for Chester in Paris than in New York. All he needed was to hit the ground running before his finances gave out, to get a couple of good breaks.

Because of a mix-up at the train station with Wright and Malartic, Chester spent his first night on a small side street in a loud tourist hotel. The next morning Richard Wright found him, banged on the door, and ushered him to a nearby café for coffee and croissants. Chester relocated to the Hôtel de Scandinavie, 27 Rue de la Tournon, steps from the Luxembourg Garden. Toward the Seine, Boulevard St.-Germain was lined with cafés, nightclubs, boutiques, and medieval ruins, a friendly, cosmopolitan environment that reminded jazzy Parisians of the strip of New York's Fifty-Second Street centered around the interracial club Café Society. Paris was still recovering from the war, but the lines for necessities like meat, milk, and wine were offset for Americans by the inexpensiveness of the city. Rooms with "*eau courante*" (running water) were available for as little as thirty cents. Chester paid $1.37 a night at his hotel.

Wright hustled him over to Shakespeare and Company, an English-language bookstore, to display the copies of *The Outsider* that Chester had carried in his luggage. Two days later, Sunday, April 12, Wright hosted him more properly for lunch at his apartment at 14 Rue M.-le-Prince. Oliver Harrington, a *Pittsburgh Courier* cartoonist whom Chester had known from Mollie Moon's, joined the group. Chester noticed that Richard Wright's wife, Ellen, had transformed her style entirely. She had "gone completely French," dyeing her hair blond, cutting it short, and becoming thin. Playful Harrington, well-known for his close association with the Communist Party, and who had in turn grown stout, asked for Chester's help in securing a publisher to bring out a book of cartoons. Seeing other black writers and creative artists maintaining full lives abroad was inspirational.

Chester experienced the Paris of American tourist legend: balmy weather, chestnut trees in bloom, crowded cafés, and bookstalls and fishermen along the quays of the Seine. The customary pattern began with one of the Wrights wakening him for breakfast; then he toured the city or developed contacts such as he could. He dined with his translator Yves Malartic, whose authors included Upton Sinclair and John O'Hara, and endured the barbed wit of the French intellectual crowd. Overcharged for his daily necessities by shop owners, Chester noted the graffiti chalked on the walls throughout the Latin Quarter: "U.S. Go Home." When he broached the subject, people would embarrassedly tell him that they didn't mean him. After all, he wasn't "really American," which surprisingly doubled his feeling of rejection.

Predictably, he was preoccupied with sex. European women were reputed to have thoroughly modern sexual mores and to be fascinated by black men, some of them even possessing an "immoderate curiosity." Chester was disappointed. "I don't know exactly what I expected to get in Paris but whatever it was, I didn't get it." The well-known fleshpots on Place Pigalle had all the sensuality of a female locker room or public lavatory; the sex shows in Montmartre were gimmicky "tourist traps." He described it all as "exceedingly dull."

As it did to many Americans, classic Paris appealed to him: the Seine, Notre Dame Cathedral, the Louvre, and the sidewalk cafés of St.-Germain-des-Prés, Deux Magots in particular. His favorite person early on was Ruth Phillips, a black woman who worked at the U.S. embassy. She allowed him to purchase duty-free cigarettes and alcohol there and, when he made a pass at her, "could say no and mean it with [such] good humor." Ruth was involved with another man, but she and Chester flirted eagerly.

A bustling and confident Richard Wright dominated the American café colony. His helm for loud discussions of creative writing, the race problem in its global dimensions, and communism was the Café Monaco, just down the street from his house. At the café, Chester, who owed Wright money and gratitude for his support, was inevitably tagged as Wright's ally. But hanging out with him presented a dilemma. Chester was drawn to Wright equally for his success and his intelligent dramatization of the racial conflict and the western condition. However, Wright lacked the charm and savoir faire of a man like Ralph Ellison, even if he managed his success with less haughtiness.

In Wright, Chester sometimes observed a man who couldn't quite handle the wheel of an automobile, who overpaid for his clothes and still didn't look well attired. Chester was a suave dresser and a keen bargainer, as well as a raconteur with flair in the idiom of cotton row or a street-corner crap game. Up close in France, Chester could perceive that his panache was lost on Wright, who regarded his friend's criminal past as less a problem of circumstance and teenage impetuousness than that of a man committed to a life of "wild and raging fury." Chester took the assessment to mean that Wright also believed him a man of "adventure without responsibilities." To top it off, Wright had a fairly crude sense of humor and took pleasure in speculation on the sex lives of others, perhaps especially of Chester's.

At times Wright's friendliness seemed calculated. Chester began to suspect that Wright's grandiose show of friendship, reeling him into the café every morning, was the tactic of a competitor, preoccupying his time so that Chester would be shut off from the real literary tastemakers. Chester made a few publishers' parties, one for Henry Miller at Corréa's office near Place de l'Odéon, and another with the art set on Ile de la Cité. But he had no French and he didn't apprehend the rhythm of the packed gatherings where people gorged themselves on champagne, canapés, and caviar. Once, when Wright invited him to a literary reception, he abandoned Chester in the crowd; it wasn't until many days later that he learned that Wright himself had been throwing the party for Simone de Beauvoir. Sadly, Chester always questioned Wright's basic motives, even when Wright jockeyed on his behalf.

Nevertheless, Chester followed Wright to the "gossipy little" Café Monaco. While everyone proclaimed the wonders of the cafés, the pleasures of being acknowledged as writers, and the freedom to sleep with white women and have no thought of gangs beating them up, Chester initially considered the black retinue surrounding Wright "a lost and unhappy lot" with whom communication was strained. Of course Chester perceived something slightly infuriating about being the author of two well-received novels, with a brand-new book out, and another on the way, while getting lumped with the other black scribblers, some without any talent at all, and some entirely unproved. Chester disliked the softness of this new generation of blacks abroad, quite different from the soldiers, artists, and entertainers who had preceded them in the 1920s. The new group, "bragging about their scars, their poor upbringing, and their unhappy childhood" embarrassed him; he thought of their antics as new form of Uncle Tomming, exploiting deprivation for sympathy.

Of course a few of the men withstood his scrutiny. Ollie Harrington, in the process of making a tactical retreat that would take him eventually to live behind the Iron Curtain in East Berlin, embodied charm, storytelling prowess, success in romantic affairs, and a determination to live up to his leftist convictions. Chester liked a young black painter from Baltimore named Walter Coleman, who seemed, in his love life, to be living out the pages of *If He Hollers Let Him Go.* Between Coleman and a group of blacks who had worked at the Liberian embassy, Chester was well supplied with scotch and bourbon during his first weeks.

Most pleased to meet Chester was young William Gardner Smith, who had lavishly praised Chester's writing in the black academic journal *Phylon.* Since they both lived on the same street as the Café Tournon, Chester got to know Smith, who had landed a job translating French into English at a news agency. Dashing, chipper, and a bit full of himself, Smith maintained himself at the café, a hangout for Jewish refugees, with an interracial circle of admirers, a "smaller, less wide-eyed" group than the loungers at Wright's Monaco, but which, Chester had noticed, was "perhaps better informed." Smith had just had his second novel, *Anger at Innocence,* a book with a white cast, selected by a French book club; his third novel, *South Street,* would be out before the end of 1954. He spoke French well, and he relaxed in the evenings over drinks at the Tournon.

Probably reflecting on some of Smith's misadventures later in the decade, Chester wanted it known that he judged Smith a man whose "most outstanding characteristic" was "youth and a naïveté." But in their circle of black writers, Smith was known for his appreciation of the blues. He was also temperamentally a bit like Chester, a survivor of South Philadelphia's deadly street-gang battles who then turned in the direction of radical protest against racial discrimination. Presuming Chester to have money, that April Smith successfully persuaded Chester to spring for an evening's entertainment at the Roundhouse to see sultry Eartha Kitt, a protégée of the dancer Katherine Dunham, who would have a hit French record "C'est si Bon" that year. Smith, who had served in the occupation army in Germany, and Ollie Harrington were always on the lookout for girls. They were welcomed by northern Europeans and other Americans; the French girls typically shunned them—a palpable attitude of dissatisfaction with Americans.

Chester had barely settled in when Vandi Haygood arrived at the first-rate Hôtel des Saints-Pères. Happy to turn the tables, she telegraphed him, COME QUICKLY: FOR YOU KNOW WHAT . . . If Chester had wanted a white woman as an obvious sign of his wealth and literary success, then Haygood was equally keen to announce herself abroad as a libertine by showily consuming a black lover. In the City of Light they cavorted like young lovers, "more affectionate than we had been at any time." One evening Himes and Haygood were very nearly thrown out of Hôtel de Scandinavie for playing blues records and "being as discreet as customary in bed." The episode became a minor legend in the quarter. When they weren't in bed, they toured the city in a manner he would never duplicate. They had expensive dinners at La Tour d'Argent, La Méditerranée, Maxim's, and Chope Danton, to the envy of the black regulars at the dingy cafés.

After two weeks in Paris, Chester was invited to a Sunday afternoon reception hosted by Marion Putnam, and asked to bring his friend Richard Wright. Chester spent the morning at Wright's apartment, hanging out and listening to blues records, until Wright got a knock at the door. In came a twenty-five-year-old Harvard graduate working for the State Department and the FBI named G. David Schine. Schine assisted Roy Cohn, the chief leg man and interrogator for Wisconsin Senator Joseph McCarthy, since January the chair of the Senate's Committee on Government Operations and Red Scare architect. Schine and Cohn were harassing America's European embassies that spring, blacklisting writers and books in embassy libraries that critiqued any aspect of the American way of life, which was for them de facto evidence of a Communist conspiracy. Schine had pressured Marion Putnam to locate Wright.

Schine demanded from Wright a statement about a State Department employee, whom Schine was trying to expose as a former member of the Chicago Communist John Reed Club. Wright spurned the request peremptorily, going as far as denying his own membership in the club, which was already public knowledge. The young inquisitor was nonplussed; in spite of Chester's presence, he bragged that he could wrench and humiliate Wright, in the manner that the committee had succeeded in forcing Langston Hughes to recant his pro-socialist work just a few weeks before. But Richard Wright scoffed at Schine and ordered him out, telling Chester, "That stupid son of a bitch thinks he can threaten me."

After Schine left the apartment, the telephone rang. It was the twenty-eight-year-old literary critic and Harlem writer James Baldwin asking for a loan. Although Wright had a reputation for frugality, he agreed and at 5:00 P.M. he and Himes went to the Deux Magots terrace, to a table spilling onto the sidewalk.

Chester claimed never to have met him before, the "small, intense young man of great excitability," whom he had probably already crossed paths with at Connie's restaurant in 1945. Often destitute, Baldwin was a sharply intelligent ragamuffin who enjoyed significant prestige in New York's literary circles, only rivaled by Ralph Ellison. Baldwin understood Wright as nearly an institution, beyond the pale of criticism, and an abundant resource. Wright was used to fielding Baldwin's requests, even as Wright was surprised by the tenacity of Baldwin's scalding criticisms. Once, in December 1951, at a meeting of the black activist group Franco-American Fellowship, Wright had reprimanded Baldwin for having an "Uncle Tom attitude," and a shouting match had erupted. Now Baldwin excitedly told Wright that he was expecting any day the publication of his first novel, *Go Tell It on the Mountain*, after eight years of work. The novel reveals a tormented relationship between a black father and his son, a book that Baldwin believed exceeded Wright's artistic achievement.

For the most part, Baldwin found it "embarrassing" to be considered Wright's friend, and he understood Wright's work as Manichean, monochromatic, and wooden. He looked for avenues to assert his difference from Wright, and almost certainly because most French and American whites presumed that the men and their writings were so similar. However, none of this stood in the way of Baldwin's asking Wright for money. As he told people in the United States about his on-and-off contretemps with Wright, "We're perfectly pleasant to each other."

Over drinks they began to argue. Probably because Chester was present, Wright demanded an account for the criticisms of *Native Son* that Baldwin had published in *Partisan Review*, and would soon republish in his own book of essays. Chester, unaware of the backstory behind their feud, soon recognized the intense psychic energy each man invested in the dispute, which for Wright's part was almost certainly an acknowledgment of how genuinely gifted he believed Baldwin was. "As I listened to them talk," Chester remembered, he was surprised to discern "an exciting kind of relationship." Wright enjoyed needling Baldwin (as he had once needled Ralph Ellison), but as the conversation reached deep water, Himes had every reason to understand, however slowly, that he was not just a witness to the conflict, but Wright's codefendant, another writer whose work had been dismissed by Baldwin. Baldwin's "Many Thousands Gone" claims that the "presupposition" of *If He Hollers Let Him Go* was exactly the same as second-rate "problem" literature: "black is a terrible color with which to be born into the world." Part of the difficulty Chester would encounter in having his forthcoming novel *The Third Generation* translated and issued by Parisian publishers was because of the influence of Baldwin's critique of "protest" writing about American racial conditions, shared widely by elite American writers and critics.

As the debate wore on, Chester was embarrassed to see Marion Putnam and her clique of artists approaching them. The newcomers sided with Baldwin, who was persuasive, a native New Yorker like Putnam, and seemed the underdog. When the argument proved to have a gravitas imperceptible to the others at first, Putnam and her associates left. As Wright and Baldwin hammered away at each other, Chester grasped the real underlying tension when Baldwin stammered "the sons must slay the fathers." Baldwin would use the same term to describe Wright when he died: "my ally, my witness, and, alas!, my father." The debate had traveled from cultural politics—even their own livelihoods—onto a more intimate ground. Wright and Baldwin had each figuratively slain their fathers, in their books *Black Boy* and *Go Tell It on the Mountain*, respectively; now Baldwin was taking aim at a living man. Chester, who had lost his own father three months earlier, was unique in not having the triumph over a father or father figure as a core component of his fiction. While he was in fact inserting the father-son complex in *The Third Generation*, he did not attribute much explanatory power to it. As a boy and as a man, Chester had witnessed his father in weakness and strength, as a real person struggling, loving, and sometimes succeeding, in a manner that his black literary peers simply had not experienced. Wright had not had an adult relationship with his father; Baldwin, Ellison, and William Gardner Smith had each been the outside child in a second marriage, never knowing their biological fathers. When Baldwin delivered his cry, a slightly drunken Chester Himes thought he had "taken leave of his senses."

The three switched venues, moving down Boulevard St.-Germain to the bluesy Rhumière Martinique. Baldwin tried then to persuade Wright to accept his famous highbrow critiques, since he had "written my book and you haven't allowed any other black writer anything to write about." Himes drank and Baldwin continued to argue that to advance the artistry of black writers, Wright's achievement had to be torn down. Chester left them at one in the morning, the dispute showing no sign of easing. Chester made a joke out of the encounter. Since Baldwin had tied him and Wright together in "Many Thousands Gone," for many weeks afterward, Chester teased Wright about "our boy" and "your son." Since Baldwin bit the black hand that literally fed him, Chester wickedly renamed his book *Go Shit on the Mountain*.

More fun for Chester than the art-versus-politics debate was to resume friendship with E. Franklin Frazier, the esteemed academic, and his wife, Marie. Living in Paris as the "chief of the Tensions Project" at the Applied Social Science division of UNESCO, Frazier was working on *The Black Bourgeoisie,* a scorching critique of the black middle class that would enlarge his reputation. His wife, Marie, was a fan of Chester; coincidentally, she had just finished Baldwin's *Go Tell It on the Mountain* and concluded "it lacks force." After he gave Marie a draft of *The Third Generation,* she was ecstatic. "Wonderful to see you again and more wonderful to know you are still hitting the ball hard! Keep *it* up."

Ben Zevin, the president of World Publishers, and his wife checked in at Hôtel Meurice later in April, and asked Chester to introduce them to Richard Wright. They all went out to dinner at La Méditerranée, where the staff lined the pavement in two columns between Wright's car and the entrance in greeting. Zevin reminded Wright of their acquaintance (he had printed *Black Boy* during the war after Harper and Brothers had reached its paper-rationing quota) and didn't want to be humbled by the revered black writer. Himes found himself having to run interference, after Zevin and Wright began to disagree over the responsibility of the black artist and the white liberal. But the meeting with Zevin in Paris boded well in terms of what the company might do for Chester's new book. "*The Cord* is a hell of a book, our best novel," Chester would hear from his publisher, still using the working title, in the next weeks. "We shall promote it accordingly," Zevin promised again at Leroy Haynes's soul food restaurant in Pigalle. After Ellen Wright, who worked as a literary agent, sold Simone de Beauvoir's *The Second Sex* to Zevin, Chester engaged her to arrange the French publishing of his two recent novels, as well as a short story collection. He learned from Richard Wright, though, that he was unlikely to make a living off French publishers. "Get all you can for an advance," Wright prophetically told him, on the way to a black-market money changer one afternoon. "That's all you'll ever get."

After three weeks and a batch of correspondence, Willa Thompson arrived from Luxembourg, looking almost sexy to Chester, murmuring that she loved him and, quite penniless, that she needed him too. While her vulnerability inspired strong feelings of devotion, there were early mishaps connected to his complicated and intense feelings for Vandi Haygood, who had just left. Chester's pals, especially Wright, didn't know how to treat the new woman: an interlude? girlfriend? financial prop? Willa's formal bearing, her ill-fitting clothes, and plain looks didn't help matters. During the course of the weeks they were together she learned of—but kept to herself—the amorous nature of Haygood's visit. Two years later she would describe that tidbit of information as "soul shattering," but she did not permit it to affect her developing feelings for Chester.

Boisterous and prying, Richard Wright entertained the two of them, from the initial, uncomfortable pickup at the train station to an uncomfortable dinner at the apartment with Ellen at the beginning of May. Chester believed that Wright was self-conscious—"inferior and ill at ease"—around well-bred Americans and "furious with himself" for feeling small. The response was a kind of ricochet-shot viciousness. Chester's apparent ease at attracting the devoted attention of white women from elite American colleges who were not merely flaunting sexual taboo was intimidating to Wright. Ellen Wright, the Jewish daughter of working-class immigrants, who was probably as insecure as her husband, was rude. "Dick would have been ok if we'd met him alone on a café terrace," thought Chester's new girlfriend, but "his wife is rather evil."

Willa's combination of innocence, disciplined restraint, and courageousness also reminded Chester of his own reserved, willowy, and educated mother, Estelle. Which was unfortunate. Instead of making the break that overseas travel allowed, Chester latched on deeply to a chimera of American talent and wholesomeness from which he would extract himself only with difficulty. Three years later, he would reach a point where, reflecting on what had happened with Willa, he could write, "I have the kind of racial attitude, in general, which needs guidance." This was an admission of being lost at sea. What's more, after Willa revealed that she had been repeatedly institutionalized, he approached the relationship that would consume the next three years "as though she were my patient and I were her nurse." An old taunt of the Cleveland pimps—"Get a white woman and go from Cadillacs to cotton sacks"—was appropriate to his situation.

After the unpleasant dinner with the Wrights, Chester could understand that the tensions that emerged over the competition for black success in Paris were not so different from those in New York. One afternoon at Wright's apartment, Daniel Guérin, whom Chester once described as "the rich, French leftist authority on the brother," offered to host Chester at his artists' colony at La Ciotat on the Côte d'Azur. Chester declined, thinking it would be better to "get out from under the wing of the Wrights and act independently."

The need for this was evident, especially after one weekend with Ellen at a suburban château of a couple whom he knew slightly. French intellectuals there hounded Ellen, questioning her husband's abilities as a writer, and in terms more snide and belittling than Baldwin had used. Chester was not Wright's acolyte, but he understood the influence of Americans in France and the implications for himself. "Richard Wright is a great man and a great writer," he defensively told the crowded room at the mansion. Even though Chester believed Wright would be "foolish" to return to the United States, as a writer he hoped not to be trapped by a French public that adored him only as much as it could use his work to push the United States's massive influence and power out of France. Chafing against the role of Wright's protector, Chester had also observed elements "too subtle and complicated for explanation" that "reflected negatively on my stature as a writer and created hazards in the sale and publication of my work." The subtle tensions by the end of April had started many tears in the friendship. Wright would leave for Ghana on the same day that Chester left Paris, and the two men would never regain the camaraderie of the earlier years.

On May 11, Chester and Willa arrived at Malartic's exquisite and enchanting retreat in the fishing village of Arcachon, between Bordeaux and Biarritz. A stucco villa with a bedroom and living room facing the street, as well as a kitchen tacked on in the back garden, made Villa Madiana a cozy pied-à-terre. Willa and Chester found that, away from the "hard hurried contest of sexuality" in Paris, they could wander the seashore hand in hand, build a fire, and drink champagne, and, as special guests of Malartic, be treated amiably by the villagers. They spent time learning to sail and reading to each other on the beach. In circling back to this infatuation with Willa, Chester found himself the object of envy: as worldly Ruth Phillips promised him a carton of cigarettes, she wrote him coyly, "It must be wonderful to be in the country with nothing to do but rest, relax and make love. I really must try it sometime."

Willa was more apprehensive. She had never lived with a creative artist before and found the rhythms of work and life a bit hard to catch. "I think Mr. Himes is also happy. I don't know. I can't be sure," she wrote an acquaintance. One way that they accommodated each other's rhythms was popping pills together. Chester used the sedative Amobarbital in addition to the Dexamyl, although Willa disliked the sensation of having her hands fall asleep, feeling cold and numb, and her loss of appetite when the drug took their blood pressure down. They would both have trouble sleeping, as Chester had already experienced in Vermont.

For his part, he was satisfied with the relationship. To him, early on, it was a European fling, made better since Willa's native language was English and she could translate French. "I am living here with the wife of a Luxembourg dentist who is writing a rather interesting book . . . hoping that her husband doesn't come down here and shoot me," he joked to Van Vechten. Willa's poverty cut two ways too. Unlike Vandi Haygood, the American businesswoman of affairs whose appetites came first, Willa brought to the table her bearing, polish, education, and upbringing. She was not sexually hungry like Haygood and, since she was dependent on Chester's money, seemed materially content.

At Arcachon, Chester awaited the return of the galleys of *The Cord* from World. He steadied himself by reading Dostoyevsky's *Brothers Karamazov,* an activity that he likened to writing a book in and of itself. He admitted that he was puzzling a bit on the new book he had under way, the story of the affair with a white woman. Still wanting Wright as a friend, Chester admitted in a letter to him the agony of his composing process, confessing, "I've made so many false starts on this book of mine I'm going to begin all over and come in another door." The new direction would take him to use a first-person narrator and telescope the action into a single weekend.

But the book of his ruptured family life and the misery of the black middle class required completion. Chester locked himself into the villa's library at a rolltop desk one morning to finish the final chapter, which he rewrote completely. Chester telegraphed Bill Targ to make sure World waited for the return of Chester's galleys and did not proceed to press while he worked to resolve the plot "in one dramatic incident." In the finale Chester completely left the field of autobiography, having the hero Charles Taylor's father stabbed to death in a gin mill and Charles preparing to leave for the South to make amends with the girl he got pregnant. Regrettably, in spite of the fine overall quality of the material, the final upturned ending was abrupt and not entirely convincing. Chester had tried to resolve his story with a Freudian gloss on the family dynamic in a sensational manner, such as Ellison had already accused Chester of doing crudely with Marx and Lenin in *Lonely Crusade*. Chester had "hopes" of *The Cord* "doing fairly well," since he had been promised a paperback contract of $10,000, but his core talent as a writer was his willingness to tread uphill against the mountain of orthodox opinion, not conform to it.

But more than a melodramatic ending shaped the novel's future. Highbrow black American writers in 1953 and 1954 would not fare very well in the wake of Ellison's *Invisible Man*, and there were several underacknowledged books: John Killens's *Youngblood*, Gwendolyn Brooks's *Maud Martha*, Ann Petry's *The Narrows*, and, at least in James Baldwin's opinion, *Go Tell It on the Mountain*. These major contributions to American literature barely dented the surface of public perception, evidence of an embarrassment of riches, but a setback personally for those creative writers.

On May 25, two weeks after he had arrived at Arcachon, he mailed Targ, the editor in chief at World, the ending of the *The Cord*, writing, "I got what I wanted." Overall, the autobiographical novel was quite possibly his finest and most intense piece of fiction. Before the end of June, Targ forwarded the corrected proofs and read the concluding chapter approvingly, "with great interest and satisfaction." The press had made some minor deletions at the end of the book, in places where Chester had graphically described his hero's sex relations with a scarred moll operating a gambling dive. Targ said that while they would surmount censorship for the initial publication, the appearance of obvious "sexual matters" might greatly curtail the possibilities of paperback sales, Chester's new bread and butter. Always wanting to make a lavish gesture to a woman he had deliberately wounded, he dedicated the book to Jean.

At the end of June 1953, Chester was euphoric again. He was confident about this long project begun in 1949, his most extended piece of writing. World was betting heavily on the book, preparing considerable publicity, and anticipating its selection by a book club, as had launched both Wright's *Native Son* and *Black Boy*. The affair with Willa took on a kind of grace, not incidentally because she made it easy. Chester described her as a gallant sidekick, if without much personality: "courageous, uncomplaining, adaptable, and congenial." By the time the page proofs went back, Chester was trying out his love story between white Kriss and black Ken. The garishly sentimental "extreme hurt" of the passage when Ken "asked Kriss how she could do this to him, be unfaithful, when 'we're engaged'" convinced Thompson that he had been in love with Haygood. But the dawning success of the new book helped her affair with Chester seem worth an investment of emotion in spite of evidence for real doubt.

In early July they had to leave Arcachon and they considered the warm and inexpensive Spanish Mediterranean islands. But because the British publisher Falcon Press now owed him money and because Chester believed that his $2500 advance from World for *The Cord* was a replenishing lodestone, they decided to go to London. Regrouping briefly in Paris, they bumped into an acidly direct William Gardner Smith on the street. Like the Wrights, Smith insulted Thompson by looking her up and down and remarking, "Oh, there are lots of American white women around the Latin Quarter." Despite the snub, Chester and Willa accepted Smith's list of contacts in London. Chester also withdrew his books from Ellen Wright's agency and had her return his short story collection to World.

After a rough Channel crossing, he and Thompson arrived at Victoria Station late on the evening of July 7. At a telephone booth where he looked up numbers for a hotel, Chester's portmanteau with their passports, money, and address book was stolen. After the bell-man refused him at the Wilton Hotel, they spent the night in a fourth-floor walkup on Vauxhall Bridge Road, delighted to find a place with a clean bed after their moneyless, identityless trial. But their ordeal wasn't over. A man attempted to follow Willa into the hall bathroom and Chester had to raise a ruckus to stop him. It took several fingers of Haig & Haig to put them to sleep. It was the inaus-picious beginning of a most inauspicious sojourn.

After receiving a letter of endorsement from the office of his Eng-lish agent Innes Rose, Chester and Willa went to the housing agen-cies in London to secure a flat for a three-month stay. What he found was supremely discouraging. "Race prejudice is about the same here as in American cities like New York," Chester discovered when he went to find a house. The British practice was to write "No Col" on the advertising cards if the landlords refused black patrons outright. Housing agents liked to describe him as "slightly colored" and some-times it took several days for a landlord to discern the fact that Chester was black. They finally passed an interview with a widow on Ran-dolph Crescent and secured a four-room basement apartment in her four-story town house. With its bedroom, office, windowless galley kitchen, and sitting room filled with furniture they were implored never to use, the flat was gloomy and, at the peak of summer, ice cold. The sunken bedroom window opened on to the chained ash cans standing sentinel above them at street level. They had one bright spot: their passports were miraculously found in Hyde Park.

The overcast, damp, and chilly English summer tempered his ebullience; inside the house they had to spend a pound per day on coal to heat the rooms. Having realized that Chester was black, his landlady wanted him to move and began making it uncomfortable for them, despite the lengthy contracts he had signed and the advance money paid. Hugely disappointed by the city, he took in his first and only tourist attraction, a boat tour on the Thames to see the Tower of London, a "drab, walled prison" such as he had known from the inside. But he returned his corrected page proofs to World on July 14, feeling like a man with soaring prospects.

After the middle of July, Chester and Willa moved to a second-story flat on Glenmore Road in Hampstead, close to the Belsize Park tube station. The house was owned by the Galewska sisters, two elderly Polish Jews who accepted foreign boarders in their house. In the first weeks in the new neighborhood they walked Hampstead Heath, Parliament Hill, and Regent's Park, and took measure of the many libraries on Antrim Road, Finch Road, and Keats' Grove, where Chester was unable to locate "a single volume by an American Negro." Food at the street-corner stalls and markets was abundant and cheap. But Chester's real pastime was the quick ride to Leicester Square to hit up the American Express office, hoping for word of literary favor from America.

William Targ's letter of July 27 rendered unwelcome news. Chester could forget the Book-of-the-Month Club, with its guaranteed sales and literary stardom. "I think they are off their rockers, but what can we do?" his editor consoled him. Over the next several weeks the Literary Guild and the Book Find Club would also turn *The Cord* down. Donald Friede, one of World's most experienced editors, wrote to get him over his disappointment. "The book you have now in print—in galleys, at least—is an excellent realization of the complex story you wanted to tell. And I read it with real enthusiasm." Feeling that *The Cord* was "close to being a major achievement," Friede looked ahead "to working with you on future books." With so much of the novel set in Mississippi, World sent galleys on to William Faulkner, hoping for some kind of miracle endorsement. The press never heard back.

Downcast and unsure of himself, Chester confessed his private view of race relations in the United States and his experience in the publishing industry to his editor. A key incident for Chester was the photo-dramatization of *Invisible Man* by Gordon Parks, which, as he explained to Bill Targ in his developing paranoia, was an aggressive undermining of Richard Wright's prominence.

The situation which now exists in the US critical world, I believe, is something like this: There seems to be a sort of unspoken agreement, at this stage to keep the Negro author in his place, to keep another from getting out of control, becoming successful and world famous. One might say the reception of Ralph Ellison's *Invisible Man* disproves this. I don't think so. I know it to be a fact that the guiding source in rallying support to Ralph's book was the *Time-Life* clique. Gordon Parks, a Negro photographer on *Life* staff, who had been assigned to cover NATO in Paris for a couple of years, sold his editors on the idea of building up Ralph to beat Dick down. I know that Ralph was interviewed secretly and at great length by the top echelon of *Time-Life*, and they were satisfied by his comments on Dick. After which they assigned Parks to do a twelve-page picture story of the book at unlimited expense, and *Time* assigned a woman reporter to stick with Ralph for several weeks and do a profile for *Time*. Parks spent thousands of dollars having the sets built and photographing scenes for his story. In the meantime *Time-Life* exerted influence on as many other critics as they could. In the end only a couple of pages of the picture story were used and I don't recall whether the profile was published or not; for by that time it had become known that Ralph's book would receive the publisher's award.

All of this, I feel, was done more *against* Dick than *for* Ralph. Of course, I could be very much wrong; but Time-Life knew of Dick's forthcoming book, and knew the contents.

Now, all of this, I feel, is part of a vast propaganda campaign to silence Negro voices raised in protest, and to relegate the Negro to a place of unimportance in the literary world.

I believe it is going to be very difficult to rally support to *The Cord*. In their attempts to disparage books by Negro writers, the criticism can be vicious, brutal, and merciless and will resort to bald faced lies to make their point. You have probably already sampled some of this in the reports from [Book-of-the-Month Club].

Friendless in an overtly racist metropolis, in a nation conducting a "limited engagement" in Kenya that Chester thought was closer to mass lynching, and disappointed by the literary news from America, he tightened himself further to Willa Thompson. Since June, Chester had been courting Bill Targ to interest him in Willa's manuscript, which was called *Silver Altar*. After Targ gave some of Willa's chapters to Donald Friede to read, he rejected the book in July. At the beginning of August, Chester committed himself to helping Willa revise the book for resubmission at World and he won the firm's approval to consider freshly revised chapters. Even though Friede had been unimpressed by Willa Thompson's writing, he wrote Chester approvingly, "I shall look forward to seeing what you do with it." A novel concerned with the flight and fall of its heroine, Helen, from a Swiss ski resort to a gothic French chalet and her evil husband, Marcel, the manuscript seemed to combine draughts of Edgar Allan Poe, Patricia Highsmith, and Catholic anti-Communist pamphlets. Chester's imaginative contribution could be seen chiefly in the graphic portrait of the unpleasant sexual consummation, a climactic scene that they shuffled around until fitting it in at the manuscript's conclusion.

By the middle of August, he received news that he had been advanced another $500 from World for *The Cord*. He also tried to interest Donald Friede, editor of the anthology *New World Writing*, in a short story he'd recently finished, "The Snake." Friede turned it down, but the creation of this story, set in the summer of 1946 with

Jean, shows Chester having doubts about his relationship with Willa, as his thoughts returned to his life before *Lonely Crusade*.

On the lookout for problems down the road, Chester made a semiformal contract with Willa and secured a half-interest in the sales of her book. Then the two got to work in earnest. She drafted in a sitting room downstairs; he rewrote in the upstairs kitchen. As he worked, Chester felt a surge of pity for Willa. The story of the young American married to a sadistic European whose domination was underwritten by medieval European cultural traditions caused Chester to conclude "a nice, healthy, wholesome, innocent, and rich American white girl is as vulnerable on the Continent of Europe as a American black girl in the white South." The image that came to him was of the girl crushed under the wagon wheels at Alcorn. As he made his way through his lover's book, he found her enticing prose "hurt me as I had been hurt then."

Chester was spending emotional coin he could not spare. He had been forewarned that he needed to get out of London by November, before the genuinely foul weather set in, but instead he had worked hard from August, typing and retyping, he claimed, fifteen hundred pages. Early in September he went to the posh Dorchester Hotel to meet with New American Library paperback publisher Victor Weybright. Weybright had influenced World to change the title of *The Cord* to *The Third Generation*, a decision demonstrating the company's explicit choice that the book would sell better as a tale of black misery than as one of Freudian tragedy. It also emphasized the influence that the secondary paperback market could have on the original hardcover book run. In avuncular fashion, Weybright tried to impress Chester by talking of his own wartime journalism to advance social equality in England for black troops. He also asked about Chester's finances and plans, offering to pay out the full sum of the reprint advance. Chester hinted that he had another novel on deck, about a white woman in Europe. Weybright walked him to the elevator, telling him he would boost *Cast the First Stone* to its English publisher. Chester shielded completely the fact that he was living with Willa, fearing that it would offend the sensibilities of a white man.

The next month was disheartening. Early in October, World turned down the revised, coauthored two chapters of *Silver Altar*. "None of the readers recommends it for publication," Targ wrote him with apparent sympathy. Chester decided to regroup and complete a full manuscript before abandoning hope. As if on cue, as soon as that first rejection appeared, the August $500 advance petered out, and the three-month British visas Chester and Willa had been granted expired. On October 5 he spent five pounds to get an "aliens registration certificate," allowing them to extend their stay in London through January 7, 1954. Aided by the Dexamyl tablets, his mind started racing and the keys of his Remington portable clicking. He wrote Targ to appeal to Weybright, who had agreed to $10,000 for paperback rights to *The Third Generation*, but a "most reluctant" Targ considered the appeal presumptuous and unwise. Then Chester thought the novel should come out simultaneously in Braille. Soon it would be necessary to purchase a load of coal to fuel them through the winter; chilly August and September would be tolerable by comparison. London now struck Chester as "big, ugly, smoky and dismal."

In October he received the advertisement running in *Publishers Weekly*, two pages featuring the book jacket. In it a black man resembling Jackie Robinson in shirt sleeves and tie brooded over a desk while a defiant-looking, full-figured woman, imperceptibly black save for her ample mouth, held on to two brown boys in a doorway. The circumstance of the environment looked bleak, despite the clothes. Chester may have imagined that he had surmounted the problem of racial profiling as an artist, but World still thought that to publish the book it must emphasize both sex titillation and black despair. Always preferring the spartan Knopf cover of *Lonely Crusade* above his others, Chester described the jacket as being in "the most awful bad taste possible for adult human beings to achieve." The advertisement featuring the book cover would run in the *New York Times Book Review* the day after publication. Thousands of miles from the place where his professional career was unfolding, he began to psychologically distance himself from his effort of the last five years. "I'm keeping my fingers crossed and cooking up all the other black magic I know to make this venture a success," he wrote to Targ, as bravely as he could.

In the second week of December Chester and Willa finished their joint novel of 520 pages, and sent it back again to World. Chester began howling for money to anyone who would hear him. They spurned his request at the PEN Center, so he resigned. Margot Johnson stood up to him and refused to send anything, so he withdrew his "account," as he termed his unpublished work, from her agency. Finally Innes Rose, the London agent, agreed to advance twenty pounds to handle the couple's manuscript *Silver Altar*, which he had never seen.

Chester was in an odd place. Even to friends like Van Vechten, he did not want to admit that he and Willa were living together, apparently hoping not to embarrass himself in case of a future reunion with Haygood, and also cautious about letting anyone know the real depth of his interracial tie. He admitted to Van Vechten that he hoped his new book with Willa would "repay me well for all my effort," important now that the cupboard was truly bare. Unsure of how to pay for the next load of coal, they were miserable and "too damn cold to bathe in the heatless bathroom." Facing the expiration of their visas, Chester led a panicky rendezvous to the Home Office on January 7, where they were allowed one more additional month. Eight days later, World released $500. With *Silver Altar* no closer to finding publication, and no better prospects, Chester and Willa scampered away from London for the Spanish island of Mallorca.

Chapter Eleven

OTHELLO

1954–1955

Chester Himes and Willa Thompson purchased third-class tickets and left from Newhaven for Dieppe on January 26, 1954. Both of them were dazed and uncommunicative by the time they switched trains and headed southward in France, Chester was glazed over because the Channel crossing had been bad, and, as usual, he was violently seasick. Outside of the hardships of the war in Europe, Willa had not known what it was to travel in this fashion and was unable to grasp the pace of the chaos that had swallowed her; she withdrew "into herself like a hurt animal."

Chester had pulled off the boat ride to Mallorca by engaging World in an option ploy on the revised and completed *Silver Altar*. He asked them to reconsider the manuscript and to wire him $500. If they took the book, they could use that for the advance. If they rejected the book, then he agreed to have his account billed for the $500 and have that money taken from future royalties, such as the money owed him for the *Third Generation* paperback deal with New American Library. Chester hoped for a decision within two weeks. If the manuscript was declined, he and Willa could shop it around to other publishers.

They began their long journey through another country where "inexperienced and untraveled" Chester was unfamiliar with the language and with barely a $300 stipend to sustain them. Thankfully, the Spaniards proved entirely different from the racist Brits or the snobbish French. "I was taken up by the Spanish people because of my ignorance and my race," Chester observed with gratitude. As vulnerable and flagging as he had been after the failure of *Lonely Crusade*, he knew, "I needed all the help I could get."

From Barcelona they booked passage to the Balearic Islands. Arriving in Mallorca on January 28, they were greeted, impossibly it seemed, by wet snow. As soon as they found a hotel, Chester availed himself of a liquor store and exited clenching the necks of two bottles of brandy. After regrouping for a few days, they set out to find Calla San Vicente, which had been praised by William Haygood, Vandi's ex-husband, for its beauty and bargain prices. This quaint town was on the extreme northeastern shore of the island, across from the Bay of Pollensa. To get there they wedged aboard an ancient, wood-burning, smoke-gurgling train, sitting alongside "tearful, sinister-looking" Mallorcans, for a trip that took the entirety of the day, complicated by the fact that Chester missed their connecting point. After an afternoon-long rain-soaked ride in a broken-down taxi, they found a bar blaring jazz and English people who helped them secure lodging. Fatigued by his journey, Chester settled that afternoon on a first-floor modern apartment in the lovely house Calla Madonna, owned by Dona Catalina Rotger Amengual. The apartment had brown floor tiles, knotty-pine beams, hot water, and an American toilet, all for 750 pesetas, or about twenty dollars a month.

Escaping London eased Chester's feelings about the less than smashing response to his new novel. He hadn't been in his new place a week when he admitted to friends that he had heard little of the book's fate, "but the few New York reviews I've seen weren't too good." His dispirited attitude reflected the great expectations that he had for *The Third Generation,* though of course tempered by the reality of press responses in the past. And, unlike his other books, there was no uproar or outcry of negative criticism. No longer a young sensationalist who could shock or surprise, Chester was now a journeyman in a field crowded by writers of black American life. The *New York Times* complimented his "considerable power" and attempt to "achieve tragedy." It continued, stating that "his searing book, with its terrible pathos of the oppressed set against each other, shows how increasingly firm a position he deserves among American novelists." "Tragic power," echoed the *Chicago Tribune*. In the *Chicago Defender* critic Gertrude Martin agreed with Chester's fond ambition; he had written "his best novel to date." The others said what it was impossible to have anticipated: that by sticking as closely as he had to his own story, he had written something which seemed not a template of black life but an implausible and unending series of disasters. "The most dangerous kind of 'Momism,'" observed the *Boston Globe*, was at the center of the book, but its critic rebutted the never-ending "painful incidents" and "debaucheries" which seemed repetitious and failed to aid character development. The signal that he received loud and clear from these reviews was one he had at least considered before: his own life was completely absurd. Or, as the *New York Times* reviewer had said, "a less depressing book" would be "a more convincing one."

Worse than plodding character development was what appeared to some of his later critics as a lack of authorial development. Blyden Jackson, a black professor at Fisk, would express disappointment with both Chester ("just an exercise in horror") and Bill Smith's novel *South Street* from that year, the difference between them being that with Chester "the lesion was always there." But the condemnation was far from uniform, and Jackson, a kind of young George Schuyler with a PhD, unquestionably had the highest standards among the critics. Always a friendly reader of Chester's, Howard University professor Arthur P. Davis would chart the movement from racial protest to the "problems and conflicts within the group itself" as a decisively important shift in black writers' concerns. In fact, Chester had actually matured as a writer. He had published *Cast the First Stone,* a book he'd revised for more than ten years that ennobled not simply his experience, but *all* experience in prison. *The Third Generation* was even better, a compelling, artful tour de force of psychological revelation that bravely encountered the dissolution of his family. If it could have been said that his past was working against him, he had overcome it.

Still, he had no hit on his hands. By February the reality of the book's underwhelming reception had dawned on his editor. The best Bill Targ could say about book sales was that they were "moving along not too badly." Despite his company's fondest hope, Chester's *The Third Generation,* a book of considerable scope and power, would sell just 5146 copies in its first crucial six months. Chester had snorted to Ralph Ellison that he would outdo him; now he was eating those words. Chester took refuge in irony, blaming World's "big vulgar" advertisements in thre *New York Times.* They had overpromoted him.

The unusually cold, rainy winter at Calla San Vicente was balanced by the extraordinary natural surroundings and the Spanish food that suited his tastes. Joined now to Willa, possessing a jointly written manuscript that had not been accepted by World and alchemized into the winning formula he had hoped for, and miserable at the dwindling fortunes of *The Third Generation,* Chester returned to the writing desk. He would need another book, another fish on the hook, to remain solvent. World had the collection of short stories *Black Boogie Woogie,* but it had already advanced him $500 on this book, which was unlikely to generate dramatic interest when it was scheduled to appear in the fall of 1954. The short story collection had been a gesture to his stature as a force in American writing, an assumption that, even now with four high-quality novels under his belt, was flimsy.

In February, Chester prepared a long treatment for *Ebony* on his travels in Paris and London and took a few jabs at Richard Wright.

But the piece was too racy for the magazine. He settled in to drafting the screwball romance that had taken place with Vandi Haygood. He was still processing London's palpable racial prejudice, and contrasting that gall with Mallorca's similarly prejudiced colony of English-speaking settlers and its sizable "number of American lunatics . . . real lunatics, not play lunatics." The effect was to unstopper his rage.

Chester was "furious" at whites "feigning outrage and indignation" at the sight of an interracial couple. The flip side of the enmity directed toward him from the Mallorcan Anglos was its psychic underbelly, the "sick envy" of psychic voyeurs imagining his and Willa's "perpetual orgy." The book would demolish the notion of white innocence or a white monopoly on rational behavior. "I was trying to express my astonishment at this attitude and say that white people who still regarded the American black, burdened with all their vices, sophistries, and shams of their white enslavers, as primitives with greater morality than themselves, were themselves idiots. Not only idiots in a cretin manner, but suffering from self-induced idiocy." While he believed that, to an American, any description of nude black men and white women would automatically seem pornographic, Chester had already begun to draft "some of the most pornographic passages ever written" in his description of the sexual dynamics of his affair. "I doubt if this is going to be a particularly good book, but I'm going to throw everything, including the kitchen sink, in it in the hopes it might have a little sale and get me out of this barrel." For once, Chester, who liked to put himself beside his protagonists, felt like he had the ending right.

Even as Chester was taking charge by letting himself go—a return to the energies that he had unloosed when writing *If He Hollers Let Him Go*—his sense of himself as a man of "firm position" among American novelists was crumbling. In mid-March Chester asked World to send *Silver Altar* to literary agent Virginia Rice, who had written Willa the year before asking to see it. In a week's time, they received a note from Rice declining to even read the manuscript. His brother Joe wrote him that World was mishandling the publication of *The Third Generation*, in the same way as his previous publishers had, causing Chester to become convinced that World, like Doubleday and Knopf, did not represent him well.

He mailed a five-thousand-word letter to William Targ, unburdening himself of the fear that he had become persona non grata. "I don't want you to lose your belief in me. *And that is what I feel is happening,*" he confided. With two seasons of peremptory rejections for *Silver Altar* following very promising leads, Chester had begun to conclude that he and Willa weren't getting offers for it on account of his connection to the project. "What I'm worried about is having my name rejected, not my work." He feared his name had been added to a blacklist—perhaps one reserved for black men who seduced white women. Jewish himself, Targ knew about Anglo prejudice, and told Chester part of what he wanted to hear, but he would have to accept a strong dose of paternalism with that cheering. "Everyone here believes in you and thinks of you as a Major writer. You may not have achieved major sales, but that does not alter the dimensions of your artistic stature," Targ wrote, helping him to straighten his back. "Chin up, Chester. Everyone has problems," he chided, "you are not being ignored, conspired against, victimized."

Chester returned to his new novel, *The End of a Primitive,* a book that was as uncompromising as anything he had yet written. Confident only that he could swing a wrecking ball and was writing "one of the most profane, sacrilegious, uninhibited books on record," he doubted whether it would ever be published. Convinced that such a book would hardly pass muster with the editors at World, he included a line in his manuscript to rally his spirits. "'At least we niggers will have a chance to come into our own,'" his hero decides, "'We'll be the most uncouth sons of bitches of them all.'" The line would not be published until a second edition thirty-six years later.

The "uncouth" novel delivered the messy weekend affair between a black writer down on his luck and a modern white woman; it could perhaps be thought of as a postwar New York version of *Light in August*. But Chester hesitated to send the uncompromising outline of *The End of a Primitive* to Targ, presuming that a resumption of the sexually violent encounters between characters like Bob and Madge from *If He Hollers Let Him Go*, and Lee and Jackie Forks of *Lonely Crusade* would make people wince. He asked World for an additional advance, hoping to be kept afloat through the paperback sales of *The Third Generation*. Weybright of New American Library was no longer supportive, so Chester had little leverage at that firm. Already that winter he had urgently contacted his older brother Eddie in Harlem, putting the touch on him for $50. When Eddie sent the money to his younger brother with a note saying "every good soldier should stand on his own two feet," Chester stopped writing until 1971.

At least part of him still held out hope that *Silver Altar* would win financial reward. World agreed to stake him and it sent $50 directly back to Eddie and $150 to Chester's bank in Tangier, Morocco. It took until the end of May for the money to creep overseas. In the meantime, Chester started to describe his novel as having a "good deal of surrealism," which for him meant a competition between the third-person narrative frame and his protagonist's stream-of-consciousness interior monologue, along with dreams, flashbacks, and bursts of ditties, doggerel, and fabulist minstrel dialogue. He abandoned his naturalist concerns and lampooned and satirized American gadgetry, especially the new craze of television, and he used a talk-show chimpanzee to provide prophetic commentary about atomic bombs, Vice President Richard Nixon, Senator McCarthy, and the Cold War. However, in a book pulsating with eroticism, there wasn't, finally, any sex.

Despite his knowing publishers' restrictions on content, later made plain in the 1957 Supreme Court decision *Roth v. United States*, which excluded obscene material from First Amendment protection,

Chester was enchanted by the idea that World would support a manuscript of profanity and sexual situations. He could draw a fair clue to
their likely response from an incident in Puerto Pollensa, when, after
a long night drinking and partying, Willa fell in the bathroom, dislo-
cating her shoulder and giving herself two black eyes. Willa's bruises
were the source of local gossip, turning the couple into a cause célèbre
in the off-season colony. To the "titillated" local "American idiots and
the British die-hards," Chester was a brutal pimp, cruelly beating his
whore. To cope with the new predicament, he and Willa drank over-
proof homemade alcohol to the point where Willa was hallucinating
and Chester was blacking out.

At the end of May 1954, Chester and Willa had to leave Puerto
Pollensa as the expensive tourist season got under way. A local
painter, Roche Minué, who disbelieved the scandals about them,
suggested that they might live inexpensively in a village high in the
mountains north of Palma, Mallorca's capital. Minué, an old Spanish
Loyalist and childhood friend of Federico García Lorca, favored this
hamlet, Deya, so much that he wished to be buried there. Chester
found a home that jutted from the rocks and faced the town's main
courtyard; the locals called it the House of Bleeding Jesus. Bleeding
Jesus was affordable, but crumbling: the house oozed water between
the floor tiles. Chester sealed himself against all distractions with
Dexamyl and retreated to a backyard garden where he finished writing *The End of a Primitive*, the air redolent with the smell of the
blooming lemon trees.

The ancient village was also home to the English writer and classicist Robert Graves. When he invited Chester and Willa over for
drinks, a predictable scuffle occurred. Graves asked Chester what
musical instrument he played and Chester, hearing in the question
a typical racist dig, replied that he played the radio. "The Americans
and the English always made a point out of reminding me that I was
black, as though it were a stigma, which brought out the worst in me,"

he reflected. Then Willa and Graves conducted a hushed conversation in German, and it became evident to both Chester and Willa that Graves was trying to take her to bed. "I caught him looking at me in that funny way that night we were at his house," she recalled. Later that night, Chester angrily accused her of soliciting an affair. She feared he would become violent. He was also, in a sense, tiring of her and the toil her support required. If Willa could find "such rapport with men of her own race," he berated her, "why use up me?" He was locked into a pattern where he pursued a woman with ardor, wore himself out trying to win her, and then reverted to jealous rage once she had committed.

Chester sent *The End of a Primitive* to Targ in two sections in the third week of June, anticipating that the manuscript would be at least slightly expurgated. Although the material was as controversial as *Cast the First Stone*, he wanted a speedy decision, since he was "practically begging in the streets." By July Targ had read the entire novel. "If published it would bring down the roof on all of us," he reasoned in words of crisp rejection. "It's unthinkable for us, and I really wouldn't know who to suggest as a prospect for it in this country. Even with expurgation." Seeing Chester's personal struggle a bit too plainly, Targ psychoanalyzed him: Chester was writing not art but for "personal catharsis." Targ believed that only the Obelisk Press of Henry Miller, the bad-boy American writer who wrote about sex graphically and using four-letter words, would even consider it. The final comment in the letter signaled the end of Chester's relationship with World. Regarding the manuscript, Targ informed him, "Let's not confuse it with serious writing, such as *The Third Generation*. I'd been hoping you would adhere to that fine level of writing in your next book." Vulnerable after he had written Targ the letter asking for support, Chester felt severely rejected and foolish for being vulnerable to Targ at all. But while he could not disentangle himself from World (or from any promising financial arrangement), Chester recognized that it was useless to remain a contracted author there if they were unable to support *The End of a Primitive.*

Chester defended his book to Targ, stressing his determination to grow as writer and range beyond the thematic preoccupations and narrative style of *The Third Generation.* Denying that he wrote the novel to get over an affair, he decided that *The End of a Primitive* was "the best book written yet on the racio-sexual psychology" and a forerunner of a new kind of classic literature.

> We Negro writers seem trapped by our own development, which does not happen to other U.S. writers such as Faulkner or French writers say such as Camus, or other Europeans such as Kafka. Take Wright for instance. Obviously he can't repeat *Native Son*, he can't write another autobiography, he can't continue hammering the same approach to a many-faced problem. But he has established a precedent, and can't break out of it. Of course, he could do like Langston Hughes, just keep changing the words to the same idea, but he wants to be a writer in the world. As do I.

Chester knew that the book's sex scenes were mainly playful and not pornographic, and he presumed that the novel was dismissed because it exposed "the grim humorous attack on U.S. idiocy where it hurts the most." However, he did not discard the manuscript, deciding "I like this book better than all the others I've done put together." As if to make complete Chester's degree of American estrangement, Yves Malartic wrote him from France saying he thought the book a masterpiece, even though he considered Chester's gallivanting with Willa an ill-timed distraction. In subsequent years Chester would incorporate Targ's "catharsis" jibe of *The End of a Primitive*, although he still considered it a groundbreaking, important book.

The house in Deya proved not merely uncomfortable, but impossible. Chester confronted the landlord over the dismal conditions, refusing to pay rent until they were fixed. The spirited disagreement went on to include other townspeople, nearly resulting in blows between Chester and the town bus driver, after which he and Willa hustled out of town. At the end of July, in Terrano, a suburb of Palma, they traded away their privacy to share the house of a mechanic, his wife, and four trysting daughters. Meanwhile, the situation at World deteriorated even further. Chester's decision to have the seventy-three-year-old Carl Van Vechten write the introduction to his short story collection was part of the problem. Van Vechten thought the collected stories barely apprentice works and declined to discuss them at all, framing his remarks around Chester's masterpiece, *Lonely Crusade.* The introduction was obviously a personal favor to Chester for a book Van Vechten didn't think should be published. World took the position that Van Vechten's introduction was of little use.

When the galleys of the short stories arrived in the middle of August, Chester was legitimately frustrated. On the one hand, the editorial staff at World called him a major writer, a man at the peak of his powers. Yet they were now interested in publishing only his early work and couldn't find a place for his most stylistically complex and thematically daring ideas. Agreeing with Van Vechten, Chester finally wrote World awkwardly on August 23, "I must confess this bundle of amateurish manuscripts combined with these urgent queries have given me something of a shock." He had turned against publishing the collection, which was heavily weighted with juvenilia. Targ was out of the office and the mail was slow in being rerouted. Every two weeks he received a letter from Donald Friede asking for his corrected galleys to get the book in production. Chester didn't respond.

With the coming of fall, the French and English tourists left Mallorca, the German tourists arrived, and the rains returned. From their backyard, Chester and Willa had an excellent view of the Bay of Palma. One rainy afternoon Chester took the short story galleys, now called *My People, My People,* and chucked them into the sea. He didn't want his name attached to these short stories, and he had lost his faith in World. By September 19, Targ mailed him a curt note, canceling the spring book and reminding Chester how much money he owed, and how many more copies of *The Third Generation* were being returned every day. A week later Targ reversed himself, however, admitting that the firm actually owed Chester money. After that, neither Chester nor World would trust the other again.

The trust between Chester and Willa suffered as well. His repudiation of *My People, My People* was impractical enough to frighten her. All Chester noticed was her change to him in attitude, "distraught and intent on throwing herself away." Secretly she was trying to find a job to work her way back to the United States.

Deep in arrears, on September 11 he bounced a check for one hundred dollars from his Merchants Bank account to an English moneylender, F.G. Short and Sons. Chester and Willa slunk away from Mallorca hoping to regroup at Yves Malartic's home in Arcachon, where their romance had blossomed. They headed to Barcelona and cleared French customs on September 20. When they arrived at Arcachon, they learned that Malartic had unexpectedly sold Villa Madiana. Added to that bad news, Maurice Nedeau of Corréa declined to publish *The End of a Primitive.* In the wake of the French defeat at Dien Bien Phu in Vietnam and the demise of the colonial system, the timing for any critique of race relations was poor. Chester tried not to think about having accepted money for a collection that he had then judged was beneath his standards and literally threw away. He knew that World would take his gesture as betrayal and they would begin to accuse him of being unreliable or unable to shrug off his bitterness at racial injustice. Just before leaving Spain, he had put a typescript of *The End of a Primitive* in the mail to Victor Weybright at New American Library, begging for the novel to be published as a paperback original.

Refugees Chester and Willa took shelter with a friend of Yves Malartic named Dr. Thé; all that Chester had left to spend in Arcachon was his good name. He wrote a long imploring letter to Ben Zevin at World, pleading with him to take *The End of a Primitive* but, in the same missive, attacking World by sharing Van Vechten's privately conveyed low estimate of the press and the short story collection, word for word. Deciding that "it's better for me to stay alive, even in jail, than die forever," Chester then bounced a check to Dr. Thé at the end of a week and limped to Paris, leaving his winter clothes and trunk behind since he and Willa could not afford to have it shipped. Arriving in the chilly, drizzly dawn in Paris, they trudged from Luxembourg Gardens to the Louvre and back, searching for a hotel, Chester carrying two suitcases and Willa lugging the typewriters, and trying to keep warm. Only late in the afternoon when Willa went in alone, could they secure a room at Hotel Jeanne d'Arc on Rue Buci. The French were drawing the color line in the metropolis to keep American tourists pleased.

Attempting to maneuver, Chester ran into Slim Sunday, a Nigerian musician and one of the characters from the Latin Quarter café scene, always dressed in black, who gave him the address of a pawnshop. Chester pawned Willa's diamond engagement ring in a shop at Place de Clichy, before hurrying to another to unburden himself of his typewriter. With thirty dollars to his name, he dashed over to Yves Malartic for help on getting *The End of a Primitive* into the hands of a likely publisher. Chester and Malartic received an appointment at Gallimard, where Chester hoped for a quick decision. In a bad mood that showed, Chester gravely put *The End of a Primitive* in the hand of an editor as soon as Malartic made the introduction. "Himes, you'll never be a French writer," Malartic scolded him after this meeting. "A French writer gives his book to an editor and then takes hours to explain what his book is about so that by the time he's finished explaining the editor doesn't want to read it."

Highly cultured, long-winded Paris seemed the wrong place to be. Another overseas agent, Jean Rosenthal, wrote to him that she was unable to sell his books on account of the "puritan wave flowing around." Over the next couple of days, Chester spotted Dick and Ellen Wright in their café but since the friendship had "cooled off mightily," he said little beyond pleasantries. It was sad they had little to say to each other. In Ghana, Wright had acquired a serious illness that would be mistreated and contribute to his death six years later. Wright would soon be on his way to Bandung, Indonesia, and Chester, unknowingly, was headed back to the United States.

To keep them afloat while they tarried in Paris, Willa landed a job occasionally proofreading; they ate in their hotel room off Chester's camping stove. When she wasn't working Willa was drinking heavily to ease the pain of their circumstances (she remarked later, "I was an awful person in Paris"). She found it difficult to contribute to the household affairs. She and Chester took Dexamyl to work and phenobarbital to go to sleep, and both of them noticed blood in their urine, the effect of their too long use of the stimulant.

Struggling for survival, Chester began systematically berating all of the European literary agents who were supposed to have marketed *The Third Generation* or *Cast the First Stone*. Annoyed that Rosenthal had not attempted to sell *Lonely Crusade* to northern European countries, and pitched *Cast the First Stone* to "off-trail" publishers, Chester withdrew from the agency. He met with another agent, a woman named Jessie Boutelleau, and tried to persuade her that even though Albin Michel hadn't taken *The End of a Primitive*, she was foolish to suppose that it would dismiss *Cast the First Stone*. Another Paris agent, "Dr." Hoffman, working indirectly for World, claimed he had never even seen *The Third Generation* to take to publishers, which initiated a flurry of letters. "Sick at heart by all this mess," Chester visited Gallimard's offices in futile search of Marcel Duhamel, who had translated *If He Hollers Let Him Go*.

World's president Ben Zevin contacted him then, stunned to have heard that Chester was accusing them of shabby treatment and giving him a precise accounting of the advances he had received from late September 1952 through July 1954. Chester's books had earned the company $4,380.96, and he had been advanced $6,580.

Chester wrote again to New American Library's Victor Weybright, beseeching him a second time to take *The End of a Primitive*. He also queried magazines for work to bring in cash but found his suggestions of profiling blacks in Paris like Charles Holland were considered "too specialized." Chester summed up the fall to Carl Van Vechten: "things are now bad enough to start getting better."

Toward the end of October, Marcel Duhamel returned to his Gallimard office. Chester discussed publishing *Cast the First Stone*, since it had had a good reader's report. A hipster surrealist, Duhamel was friends with Hemingway, John Steinbeck, Henry Miller, and Erskine Caldwell, and he knew the New York jazz scene. He proposed to Chester, who seemed "rather frail" and "not at all relaxed," that he try to write for a crime-fiction series he was editing, La Série Noire. Duhamel wanted a "Negro detective story," and he dangled $700 and the promise of an initial print run of 37,000 for Chester. In the meantime, Duhamel came through with a contract for *The End of a Primitive* and 20,000 francs, about $1000.

A few days later, Chester turned in a one-page outline for a novel about an American black man framed for the murder of a white woman in Paris. Duhamel and his assistants asked Chester to fill it in, making the lead character a piano player in a jazz club. But when he fleshed out the story with details after a week or so, which contained a Bud Powell–like musician riffing off Chopin and other characters marrying white women, Duhamel informed him that he was disappointed. Chester realized that Duhamel "wanted this Negro to be a clown." He dropped the Paris story and suggested a new tale, "a detective story based in Harlem," with "plenty of comedy" and "not too much white brutality." Called *It Rained Five Days*, the novel would be held together by what Chester liked to describe as "real cops and robbers stuff."

Meanwhile, Chester had good news from the United States. On November 2, Victor Weybright agreed to publish *The End of a Primitive* as a twenty-five-cent paperback original. While it seemed a defeat at the time, an acknowledgment that the novel wasn't good enough to appear in hardcover, Chester's work was pioneering a new style: the paperback original. The advance upon signing the contract was $1000, which Chester gladly snapped up. Seeming eager to bring out his work, New American Library also contracted to reissue *Cast the First Stone* as well as *The Third Generation* in paperback. At the publication of each book, Chester was guaranteed additional money.

With this advance, Chester paid some outstanding debts, retrieved his belongings from Arcachon, and covered the check he'd floated Dr. Thé. He still hoped to outrun the debt to F. G. Short in the flight from Palma. Setting aside the Harlem detective potboiler, he turned to a new project, a first-person account of his experiences in Paris, London, and Mallorca, "and how I managed to do this and similar experiences without being frightened, upset or panicked, and in fact enjoying it." His next move was to buy a mildly resistant Willa a second-class ticket home on the Holland-America Line, leaving on December 1. The day she departed, over cognac in the train station, he told her "she shouldn't think of it as separating." He needed time alone in Paris to write and think things through, and she was heading "back to America to sell our book."

In December, Chester was interviewed by Annie Brierre, a journalist and editor at the newspaper *France-USA*, who had been wanting to meet him since his first arrival in France. She questioned Chester about contemporary writers, especially William Styron, whom she had written about in *Nouvelles Littéraires*. Chester admitted that he wasn't keeping abreast of the latest technicians of the American novel, even though Styron's book *Lie Down in Darkness* had appeared to much acclaim. Closer to his new home in Paris, Styron had also written an editorial in favor of creative work and against hyperintellectual criticism to launch the new American expatriate magazine *Paris Review*. Chester's page-long interview appeared in January 1955, by which time Brierre had read *The Third Generation,* a book she savored, "every paragraph of it, in every way." She helped him get the book to Editions Plon for consideration, admired *The End of a Primitive,* and took him out for dinner in fashionable Montmartre.

After a conversation with Yves Malartic, Chester began to realize that he was wasting his time entreating French publishers to bring out translations of his work. The gist of it was that his books were too tragic and too intellectual. The French publishers wanted a Negro Harlequin, not a Negro Hamlet. Malartic confessed that in 1952, when he had written to Himes about the density of the narrative in *Lonely Crusade,* there was actually a battle going on at Editions Corréa (a struggle made obvious by the published cover). Maurice Nedeau was convinced that Malartic had removed the comedy from the book and had turned a story of hilarious shenanigans into a cheerless funeral. Duhamel's translation of *If He Hollers Let Him Go* had in fact taken that book and transformed it into a "rough and funny story." Indeed, when French critic Jean-Claude Brisville reviewed that translation, *S'il braille lâche-le,* in 1949 for *La Nef,* he had chastised Himes for failing to provide "an art strong enough that we can tell it apart from vulgar pastiche." Arguably Brisville's comment was better directed at Duhamel.

Imagining that he would shortly have at least $3000 from New American Library, Chester decided to revisit London. He hoped to sell British editions of his books in England, especially now since he had fired all of his foreign literary agents, and to get enough peace to finish the Duhamel-inspired crime story. More practically, life in Paris had increased its challenges without Willa as translator and

white face. Despite visits to twenty-six rental agencies and fifty landlords, he was homeless again. Meanwhile service in the cafés had
grown "insolent and hostile." One time, Chester responded to slights
by hurling a table full of crockery and glassware into the street.

Before setting out for London, Chester visited Albin Michel,
which had published *If He Hollers Let Him Go,* and learned that
Wright had been correct about the duplicity of French publishers: the
accounting practices at Albin Michel were so suspect that he himself was charged the full price for books he bought, even when they
were on remainder. There were of course no royalties. He arrived in
London on December 10 and went back to Hampstead, now to 45
Glenmore Road, a neighborhood of Africans, South Asians, and East
Asians, and began contacting literary agents.

While he waited on agents and publishers, Chester looked up
Wright's friend George Padmore, a Trinidadian intellectual educated in the United States who had created the Kremlin's Africa
policy during the 1930s. Disgruntled by Soviet political waffling over
directly fighting colonialism, Padmore had left the USSR for Germany in the mid-1930s, then been deported to London, where he
founded a variety of African nationalist organizations. The mentor
of Namdi Azikwe, Nigeria's first president, and Kenyan first deputy
Tom Mboya, as well as an inspiring figure to Ghana's leader Kwame
Nkrumah, Padmore was the modern philosopher and political organizer of pan-Africanism. He was known in some circles as "the black
Prometheus cursing the white Jupiter."

Probably no writer attacked with more vitriol western colonial practices and Soviet manipulation in Africa. Padmore's most recent book
had been *Africa: Britain's Third Empire,* and he would soon bring out a
collection of essays called *Pan-Africanism or Communism?,* that, riding
the wave of favorable views of the postwar United States, advocated
an American-led Marshall Plan for Africa. Although both Padmore
and Chester believed Communists were insufficiently concerned with

black rights, Chester did not wish to be schooled in a new rhetoric of political awareness. Padmore was lecturing Chester about the achievement of Richard Wright, but Chester made the point that Wright had come to a dead end without an ideological absolute like Marxism or Christian humanism to anchor his defense of the poor. Even though an antiblack riot had occurred that November in London, the kind of topic of interest to both, the discussion with Padmore ended weakly and drove home the solitude that Chester had to accept.

But even the unsatisfying talks with Padmore were better than corresponding about the future with Willa. She was struggling in New York. Chester had imagined that Willa would have speedy success in selling *Silver Altar*. He banked on the magic of Willa's white skin and erudition to tip the scales in their favor, but she was treated like an amateur running errands. Penniless and looking ill, Willa learned that publishers weren't interested in their novel. Then, when she found Jean's name in the telephone directory under "Mrs. Chester Himes," she became disturbed. Chester had told her that he was divorced but now she knew he had lied. "Are you really divorced or just separated?" she wrote furiously to him in England. She'd had enough of New York. On Monday, December 13, Willa caught the bus to her aunt's house in Brighton, Massachusetts, taking the manuscript with her and deciding to hand-deliver *Silver Altar* to Houghton Mifflin in Boston.

Deep fissures threatening their being together were on every line of the perhaps 300 pages of letters that they exchanged between December 1954 and July 1955. Willa wrote him on December 20, "I think your writing is a gift and it is more important than whether we are together or what happens to us individually, as long as you can keep on writing . . . that's the only thing I *know* is right." For Chester's part, he had a fatalistic if plain assessment of what was under way: "We had each, from the first contact with America, gone back into our separate races."

Chester preferred to see his returning Willa "home safe" as "the only valid achievement of my entire life." Their novel itself presented the same "achievement": a Smith College heroine returning to the security of America from decadent Europe. But, at bottom, Chester was attaching to Willa emotions that emanated from his incomplete emotional life with his mother, the woman he not only couldn't make safe but could neither satisfy nor heartily repudiate.

While living on opposite sides of the Atlantic, desperate to sell the book, and mailing emotionally fraught letters, Chester and Willa fell out of sync. They wrote daily but received the garbled letters in batches, unable to respond to the shifting tide of emotions and rapidly changing circumstances. After the first glum note from Chester—"I am backing out quietly (as quietly as you will let me) and closing the door gently so as not to disturb anyone"—Willa flung back on January 5 that he was free to do with the manuscript whatever he pleased; Houghton Mifflin had also turned them down.

Giving up on London, Chester sailed for New York on January 15, 1955, aboard the *Samaria*, "broke, bitter, defeated" and "unbearably chagrined." He tried to sustain his ego with a brief affair and didn't write Willa from the boat. On January 25 his passport was stamped back into the United States and he checked in at the Albert Hotel. New York was the same as he had left it: the inconsiderate doormen declined to assist him with his trunk, and for two days it remained on the street. The day Chester docked in New York, Ken McCormick at Doubleday rejected *Silver Altar*. Chester needed a publisher and he was contacting a new agent, Kenneth Littauer, shopping books and short stories to publishers after his years at *Collier's*. But Littauer wouldn't get a manuscript until February because Willa had the wrong address, and then he would want major changes.

Willa had declined to meet Chester's boat when he was scheduled to return. Their letters had remained accusatory, and she believed she would brave ridicule from "so many [of his] friends" described to a

T in *The End of a Primitive*. She also played his game back to him: "I'd hate to have to compete with a wife and an ex-mistress." When Willa did come from Massachusetts to visit him the last weekend in January, not even physical intimacy could reconcile them. "Everything is such a terrific strain," she reasoned, while also taking him to task for inattentiveness, which signaled to her his having had affairs. He had mysteriously lost his leather-bound copy of *The Third Generation*; he had not written; he offered her cigarettes automatically, but Willa didn't smoke. Gainfully employed as a receptionist in a physician's office, she was of course in position to badger him: as usual, his finances had collapsed. Earning forty-eight dollars a week, Willa made a point of mailing a weekly stipend, tendering the patronizing relationship Chester always claimed to have abhorred. She also had learned enough with him about the business to believe she might survive as a writer. "It won't be literature, of course," she wrote to him about "the Luxembourg book," "but it might be magazine material."

Cagier by the day and disinclined to resume his old associations, Chester was rattled by Willa's presumptive questions: "Have you heard from anyone, about your EOAP [*End of a Primitive*], Weybright, have you seen [the] Ellisons? Or Carlo?" Willa had difficulty imagining that Chester—sober and with four published and well-received books and a manuscript at press and another under consideration—would not be fêted by his New York circle of Carl Van Vechten, Ralph Ellison, and Horace Cayton, as well as editors and agents. And although Chester maintained that his stay in New York in 1955 was one of unending embarrassed humiliation and isolation, he and Willa seem to have met at least with Fanny Ellison, perhaps conducting ambassadorial duty without her husband, Ralph. Willa was impressed by the finely educated, professionally accomplished wife of the famous writer. "I liked Fanny the best tho of anyone woman we've met anywhere together, the most intelligent & the kindest," she told him. Two years after his contretemps with Ralph Ellison, tempers had cooled and Chester had much to report about life in France, England, and Spain; the Ellisons themselves would move to Europe in the fall of 1955, for two years in Rome. Desiring pizzazz and contact with his cosmopolitan, celebrated friends, Willa pressed him for more than "making love to her as long as physically possible." "We might be able to go out together at sometime with the Ellisons," she suggested before packing her grip for one winter weekend, "or anywhere with Music where it's nice."

By February Chester and Willa began to have satisfying times together. They turned to the bedroom to try to resolve the disconsolate, anxious letters they had been exchanging since she left Paris. "Darling, thank you for this last weekend. It was really the nicest time I have ever had with you. The most secure, the most beautiful, the most reassuring. It is so wonderful to be sure. I never have before, of us. I am now," she cooed. He had fallen back onto the relationship and the result was unique devotion from Willa. Chester reckoned that he enjoyed "her white tiny body, her small shrinking breasts, her wild tuft of pubic hair, her strong gripping thighs, and the little spasm she would have at orgasm." She now had a pet name for his penis, "booney," a gesture so out of character for her she wrote asking him "are you shocked that I type such a word?"

While she made pleasurable sex possible, her mental and cultural endowments were the principal sources of intrigue for Chester, who never seems to have strayed too far from trying to provide the exoticism that he believed white women desired. Willa also proved useful by sending barbiturate pills in the mail, joking, "My, what a problem we have!" and observing that she now needed higher doses to remain alert.

They kept after agent Ken Littauer and tried rewriting sections of *Silver Altar*. When they finally met with Littauer, Chester was asked to conduct his part of the conversation through an open door, from another room, while Willa sat in the only available space in the agent's cramped office. During the conversation, Littauer reminisced about the "blackface" stories of the South Carolinian writer Octavus Roy Cohen. Then he suggested Chester title a story "Panther Boy." Chester concluded that the agent was rudely trying to humiliate him. Throughout the winter Chester and Willa worked up promotional material for New American Library's publication of *The End of a Primitive*; they also revised *Silver Altar* again, transforming the humorless, insipid manuscript from first person to third person and producing the copies necessary for agents and publishers. This latest draft seemed bent on heavy-handedly making the broken-leg heroine a saint, and even introduced a medical doctor who returns the protagonist to the United States, explaining Helen to herself. "God loved Eve. She was his first Woman. . . . He sent her out through the gateway of Eden into the world only when he was certain that she was fully equipped to cope with all the difficulties that life on earth presented." The novel's last line was "He said simply, as God had said, 'Go now . . .'" Showing weariness at their romance, Chester relieved himself of Willa in their novel by sanctifying and ennobling her but, in the end, casting her out.

Willa spent a few afternoons scouting apartments near Boston Common, then floated the idea of his moving to Boston, even though she was earning an education about active New England prejudice in the face of laws explicitly forbidding racial discrimination. If they tried to live together in New York they would starve and if he moved to Boston they ran the risk of defamation. "People, Americans, don't like scandals. . . . It would be foolish to mess things up now with the book so near to completion and money just around the corner because we did something foolish," Willa cautioned. In New York they were invited to have dinner with Walter Freeman, a New American Library editor, and his wife, until Chester let it slip that Willa was not his spouse but his "fiancée"; after that Mrs. Freeman steadily postponed the dinner, a tactic Willa understood. "Very few white women will accept in their homes a mixed couple, especially engaged," she explained, presenting the durable facts of life.

Her thoughts about the future with Chester were made more poignant when she also had moments to marvel at his talent. She showed the manuscript in the winter to her aunt Margaret, an English teacher, who went through the clean draft, separating Willa's sections from Chester's and highlighting his passages as examples of "magnificent" writing. Willa had moments when she exulted in him. "It is the first time I have seen you so, completely assured and mentally and physically completely at ease and strong and certain, as if you knew just where you were going and why and how you were going to get there. You looked strong, darling, in all ways."

But after a couple of months in America—Willa rooming with snobbish relatives—Chester's appeal began to lose some of its glow. The interruption to their daily lives as a couple and the new burden of conducting an interracial relationship in America worked to reduce Willa's empathy for the racism that Chester faced. Even the weekends she spent with him in New York did not alter her voicing a typical white liberal belief: the race problem would go away on its own.

In one of her most revealing letters on race in America, she mailed a gently worded reproof. Chester was a "little bit wrong" when he had previously opined that "intellectual negroes" were preoccupied by segregation and racism. Willa's point of view was limited mainly to Boston, where she worked in the Back Bay office of Dr. Henry Marble and bunked at her aunt's house in a white upper-crust neighborhood. However, she seemed to share the conclusion of Ellison and Cayton in their drunken argument with Chester in January 1953. Willa had become certain that many black writers and thinkers were not the "least bit interested in the race problem, or even aware of it."

For her counsel to Chester she claimed a venerable source of authority: a silent "old colored chauffeur." The man was in his sixties, and had been at work for Dr. Marble for thirty years. He suffered from heart disease and, according to Willa, couldn't "work hard any-more." Willa was moved particularly by the white-haired man's outer appearance of quiet dignity and self-respect. She assured Chester that her black patient looked like an academic, was "certainly not unedu-cated," and was "well-read." She observed that when the office became chaotic, the old chauffeur, the "quietest person I have ever seen," had the capacity to revive her and lend an air of tranquility, using only his grave taciturnity. Confident that the man was nearing death, Willa felt more than relief when he was around: she felt "how good it is to be alive." Because he relieved her of anxiety and tension, Willa decided that "I don't think he's aware of color at all."

Chester could glimpse what he would be in Willa's eyes in fifteen years—what his older brother was already, and what his father had been. They were servants to white people, best liked when completely silent, necessary to shore up white peoples' feelings of generosity and humanity, and to make them feel serene. And Willa saw race first: a literate, docile chauffeur was the intellectual equivalent to the man she had lived with and who had been a publishing black writer for twenty years. The portrait she had drawn was singularly dismaying.

For her part, Willa was sorely disappointed by Chester's cavalier sexual mores. He had told her that they were in their final stage of full sexual expression; as they aged further, Chester believed their sex lives might end badly if they hadn't found a compatible partner. He supported his case by referring to novels he enjoyed, like Paul Bowles's *The Sheltering Sky*, a tale of a married couple's misadventure set in North Africa and replete with sexual liaisons and doom. Once, when Willa made a brief weekend visit to New York, he casually announced that he had tried to have a prostitute come to his rooms, but she had been too expensive. He fended off Willa's obvious displeasure flip-pantly; Chester only desired "to be with a woman." Then he turned the question around, saying, "What's the difference between mastur-bating and being with a prostitute?" Willa did not agree and thought he lacked "self-discipline," which, when it came to fidelity, he regularly dismissed as an antique element of old-time Boston morality.

During another visit, on March 29, Willa's worst fears were proved. While Willa was in the bathroom, Jean Himes entered Chester's room and quickly departed, passing Willa in the hall. "Can you imagine how I felt coming to see you," she wailed, "and then to have your wife walk in, when supposedly you were divorced?" Fanny Ellison had forewarned Willa about the woman with whom Chester had begun his adult life, "a very attractive intelligent person who has had a rough time and who is most likely still very much in love." The effects of the encounter were predictably devastating. In May, after six weeks of an emotional roller coaster, Willa confessed, "I never believed it possible that a man could shatter me so." She told him that they should end their relationship.

Chester's reaction—"furious and hurt because I had been absolutely honest"—was not exclusively self-serving. The day before the romance with Willa suffered its deathblow, he had written to Carl Van Vechten with some glee, "I am hoping to get married again when finally I get together the loose ends of my life, and as a consequence I am what is coyly known as 'secretly engaged.'" Chief among the "loose ends" preventing marriage to Willa was the missing divorce from Jean.

Chester held on to the relationship both because he wanted to end the romance on his terms and Willa made him feel important and wanted. Throughout April they Scotch-taped the torn love affair. Everything of course was contingent upon a speedy exit from the United States. "I would like to go somewhere small and cheap and live quietly, with you," Willa wrote to him. "I think it would be a good idea for you to straighten out your own marital affairs too, though. Especially if you do ever have any actual intention of marrying me." She kept after this point, adding, "I am not going to pretend to be your wife, when you are all ready married."

For Willa, Chester's having led her to believe that he was divorced was the key prevarication preventing their harmony and success. She concluded that the reason they were having problems with Ken Littauer was that she had passed herself off as Mrs. Himes—thus she was "a liar," and subsequently unworthy of his "respect and friendship."

Chester considered Littauer a racist and the other book industry operatives would seem like that to him too. After a minor success finagling a reprint contract with Berkley Books, Chester ran head-on into "gratuitous insolence" from one of his old publishers. He had written Blanche Knopf a brisk business note asking for a royalty statement and received an overly blunt reply from one of her staff. "You have not received a statement from this title," William Koshland began, "because not only does the book have a sizable debit balance but also because royalties resulting from actual sales have not been enough to warrant reporting to you." Among Knopf legal staff Chester acquired the nickname "General Himes" for the useless "running battle" he was engaged in that year to regain the rights to *Lonely Crusade*.

Later in the spring he informed Willa that he had landed a menial job, a task that his girlfriend approved of so "that you finally have some money." He pressured an advance out from Berkley and wound up with $100 at the end of May, hardly enough to dent a bill for $806 he'd gotten from the Internal Revenue Service.

Then he lost more ground. Chester was forced to change the title of his new book from *The End of a Primitive* to *The Primitive*. The intellectual difference in the title was extraordinary, and in fact reversed the meaning of the book: from the black man escaping the stereotype of primitivism—his western burden—by murdering the white woman, to a black man becoming an animal through the act of murder. However, commercial transactions were no place for the nuances of philosophy. "The title," New American Library informed him, "simply will not register on the newsstands—and that is where about eighty percent of our sales will be." Chester would not recoup his advance and start receiving additional royalties until 100,000 paper-backs were sold. He consented to the title change. That same week he lost the promised job, so he was glad to have beseeched NAL's Walter Freeman for another $100 to stay afloat. At the end of May, how-ever, he returned to desperate measures: Chester wanted to persuade Doubleday to bring out a clothbound edition of *The Primitive* first. He would hold on to the idea and continue to try to place the book with other hardcover publishers, like Random House and Dial Press, but this effect would succeed only in slowing the appearance of the book: completed in 1954, it would not debut—still in paperback—until 1956.

Although Chester had pulled the plug on his foreign literary agents for lack of effort (erroneously, it turned out), in New York he was having no success on his own. He had also battered the doors of every publisher and agent on Madison Avenue, so he turned once more to Lurton Blassingame. In Chester's conciliatory note to his former agent, there were four opening paragraphs before he could write, "If you will accept my apology for my own inconsiderateness and feel we can work together again, I will be grateful if you accept me as a client." Chester enclosed four short stories and two sketches. Two of them, "Spanish Gin," and "Boomerang," he had submitted to *Esquire* that year and had received the endorsement from the fiction editor, only to be rejected later by publisher Arnold Gingrich. Another, "The Snake," had been passed over by a publication called *Manhunt* and "That Summer in Bed" was new. Chester informed Blassingame that he intended to use a European locale—France, England, Mallorca—in some future works, and that he hoped to yoke together a collec-tion of short stories. He also added the Lloyd Brown review of *Lonely Crusade* from *New Masses* to the folder of manuscripts, to demonstrate "that I have been anti-communist from the beginning." Charming and insistent when he wanted something, Chester successfully got Blassingame to work on his behalf.

He broached the idea to Willa about living together in New

York over the summer, but she refused to share his room of "horror" at the Albert Hotel, contaminated as it was for her by memories of Jean Himes. After repairing the relationship somewhat, Chester still menaced Willa over the telephone, perhaps inebriated and certainly maudlin. "What are you trying to do, threaten me?" she growled. "We should have stayed busted up the first time, in April," she wrote him. In another letter, she counseled, "Don't get a divorce on my account, because I don't want ever to marry anyone again. If I live with you again, I would like to do so openly, under my own married name." Willa had decided she would no longer "pretend." But the relationship had finally fully unwound. By mid June, Willa had bought a ticket to Luxembourg and was focused on her children. "If we're through, then let's be entirely through. No regrets or lingerings in memory." Feeling as if his presence would disconcert her aunt and uncle, she requested his absence when she boarded the ship for Europe.

Like other women in Chester's life, Willa did not wish to become fodder for his literary workshop. She asked him to return all of her letters, which she planned to destroy: "I would not like to have very intense sincere emotions that I have poured out to you, my love in words, used in another book." Chester held on to the letters, perhaps thinking of how little else he had that June, the prospects for publishing *The Silver Altar* as dim as ever, but also knowing their value in case of future legal claims.

With Willa gone he turned his attention to Vandi Haygood, who seems not to have known that Chester was in town that spring. He telephoned her for the personal items he had cached at her apartment before sailing for Europe in 1953—oddly enough, a kind of trousseau: linens, his mother's silver, and scrapbooks of his career. During the call, Haygood apparently let slip out, "Oh shit, I do so want to see you but he'll be here all weekend." Then she recovered, "I'll tell you what to do. Call me in the middle of next week and come to dinner." Chester didn't wait until the dinner and on July 13 picked up everything from Haygood's maid except for the scrapbooks. A day later, he phoned her office. In hushed tones the secretary told him that forty-year-old Vandi Haygood was dead, apparently from complications connected to taking Dexamyl. The headline in the Baltimore *Afro-American* was "Mrs. Haygood Dies in NYC: Aided Many Young, Struggling Writers." Chester had reason now to be paranoid. He had a manuscript at press in which a character like Vandi Haygood in every conceivable way was killed at the novel's conclusion by a man like Chester.

Chester pulled himself together for a welcome reprieve at Carl Van Vechten's on the Saturday night after Haygood's passing. There he met the West Indian literary sensation George Lamming, whose novel *The Castle of My Skin* was a coming-of-age experience set in Barbados written with an elegance, racial pride, and sophisticated technique that showed the successful completion of a thorough apprenticeship to James Joyce and Ernest Hemingway. Lamming, an intellectually serious man, was also completing a travel memoir called *The Emigrants* about black diasporic experiences, especially in London. The long afternoon and evening at Van Vechten's included drinks, a photo session, and dinner. Chester enjoyed the young Bajan's company enough to take him up to Harlem, to the Red Rooster for drinks, after which, with difficulty, Chester stumbled back downtown to his hotel.

The next week and with the help of Annie Brierre, the French journalist, he succeeded in landing *The Third Generation* with Editions Plon for its series Feux Croisés (Crossfire), a collection of French translations of foreign writers. Two weeks later Van Vechten had delivered two bottles of vodka for Chester's birthday; Chester drank both of them with tonic, "and the next morning I woke up with a hangover suitable for all disappointments." He was still trawling through Vandi's death and Willa's departure.

Soon afterward Lurton Blassingame, handling some of his short stories, scored a hit and got *Esquire* to accept "The Snake." Chester felt that *Esquire,* now a wealthy, established magazine, owed him since he had been involved in its early years. He telephoned editor Arnold Gingrich to ask for decisions on several other short stories and then he told Blassingame his theories of persecution. What Chester seemed unable to recognize was that he obliterated professional relationships when he squeezed through barely ajar doors in the publishing world, perhaps particularly with whites who believed they were doing him a favor to begin with, or risking their reputations by involving themselves with him. In the *Esquire* case, it would be several years before the magazine actually published this short story bought that June of 1955. Gingrich, responding to Chester's letters over the next year, would respond with comments like "I can't make a commitment at this time as we're having terrific troubles with inventory. . . . But at least I'll make an effort to try to shove the story forward." By the time "The Snake" appeared, in October 1959, Gingrich considered Chester pushy and ungrateful.

Working with him on *The Primitive* at New American Library was Walter Freeman, who positioned himself as a strong supporter of Chester's oeuvre: "I have found it a pleasure to work on *Cast the First Stone* because I greatly admire the book. The same is true of the present manuscript. Since we have become friends I have found my work even more gratifying." But in September when the galleys were prepared, shortly after Dial passed on doing a hardcover, Chester felt he had been deceived. He asked to see the original manuscript and was dismayed to find commentary from five editors in different colors, none of which had been shown to him for approval. He was fighting the same battle he had prior to the publication of *If He Hollers Let Him Go.* Freeman defended the firm, saying "practically every change was made from the viewpoint of censorship," and he was willing to restore "almost all of the deletions to which you object." But the corrections seemed ridiculous to Chester. The editors had removed references to the popular novelist Kathleen Winsor and jokes about Quakers, and he was now being asked to supply permissions to quote single lines of dialogue from Ziegfeld Follies stage shows.

To Freeman's request to revise the manuscript, Chester thundered he would seek legal redress if the version of the book published differed from "the one version, the only version" he was returning with green pencil marks restoring his exact language. Then, between outrage and acquiescence, he accepted Freeman's invitation to lunch.

That week bold *Jet* magazine published the pictures from the funeral of a Chicago eighth grader named Emmett Till. The child had whistled at a white woman in Money, Mississippi, not so far from where Chester had lived as a boy, and he had been shot and had his eye gouged out as punishment. Till had then been submerged in the local river for three days with a cotton gin fan weighing him down. Six hundred thousand people viewed his swollen, mutilated body during the funeral proceedings because his mother kept the casket open and allowed it to be photographed. "I am innately sad, a dreamer, a very lazy lonely dreamer who wishes the world were a paradise and life but an opium dream," Chester consoled himself, considering the state of American life and what needed to change for him to live there contentedly.

The dam burst by the end of September: he had to find work or be thrown out of his room. Everything, including his typewriter, was pawned. "The only jobs in New York available to a black writer without recommendations or connections were the menial jobs available to all transients and bums. Which is what I was, I suppose," he estimated. Joseph Sr., who had described his weariness of life's torture, by saying "hell is hell," had faced a similar downfall in his midforties. Chester joined the pool of men on Chambers Street looking for a day's work washing dishes or wringing a mop. He became a roving afterhours janitor for the Horn and Hardart Automat Cafeteria chain, eventually winding up as permanent staff at the branch on

Thirty-Seventh Street and Fifth Avenue. He polished stainless steel and mopped from nine in the evening until six the next morning. He did not merit the sympathy of a letter-writing Willa at all because he got to eat as much as he could hold: three quarts of orange juice in a sitting, dozens of raw eggs, feasts of steak, and whole chickens. Wolfing the food made him feel better and there were other payoffs as well. "I was storing up all the imagination and observations and absurdities which were destined to make my Harlem novels so widely read," he recounted. Of course Chester needed only to observe himself to recognize a detail of absurdity: on August 15 Berkley Books had brought out its mass-market paperback edition of *If He Hollers Let Him Go,* and he could have seen his book for sale at busy newsstands throughout New York while he weaved through crowds on his way to his custodian's job. Berkley had ninety days to pay out the rest of the advance, so he wouldn't get all of his money until mid-November.

Willa sent him a chatty note from Rotterdam, with her usual backhanded compliment. "One thing I learned from you is how to live on nothing, darling." Indeed she would return to Paris, somewhat comfortably, by September with a job as the director's assistant at the American Hospital, "way out" in the suburb of Neuilly. By then all reminders of Willa were unsatisfactory.

The problem for Chester was, actually, living on nothing. About a year after the fact, the final disposition of the empty check to Short caught up with him. He would have the judgment summarily passed against him on October 30, at which time the First District Manhattan Municipal Court could take action by garnishing his wages. He had no means to resist the suit, and had in fact been in correspondence with Milton Cooper, Short's New York attorney, throughout the year. Chester had problems with not only NAL's *The Primitive* but also Coward-McCann, which he had asked for a royalty statement and a paperback publication timetable. Of course, there had been no royalties from *Cast the First Stone* and no plans for a reprint edition with New American Library. After his letter, the accounting department contacted him for payment because "current earnings have not covered the purchases." Chester was publishing books that almost never earned royalties whatsoever.

By November 9 the final galleys of *The Primitive* were ready and Chester was counting down for Berkley to pay him the rest of his paperback advance. It took another four weeks and the assistance of a legal-aid attorney before Berkley issued him a check for $900. "I felt I had to get out of the U.S. and get out fast if I ever wanted to write again," he wrote reflectively, "because it has been rough and I am getting too old to take it like that anymore." Forty-six-year-old Chester would collect his money and secure the first ticket on a boat to France.

The only shipping line operating in December was booked solid, so he waited for a cancellation while he took care of renewing his passport. He bargained in the Bronx for a coat and splurged on a tweed blazer and charcoal brown slacks, to buttress his self-esteem for another trip to New American Library to pick up copies of *The Third Generation*. NAL had kept World's hardback cover art for the novel, but they did remove the "cheap, tenement-like effect of the background." Reinforcing his desire to leave New York, when he stopped by the automat for farewell chow with the other janitors, a drunken white policeman came upon the men, pistol drawn, and accused them of stealing his car. Chester flashed his passport, with its youthful clean-shaven picture of him wearing a tie spotted with Nefertiti cameos, and was allowed to escape from the menacing lawman. When he telephoned the shipping line on December 13 at 9:30 P.M., he learned that there had been a cancellation on SS *Ryndum* out of Hoboken. The boat would sail at midnight. He packed his gear, checked out of the Albert Hotel, wedged the big trunk into a cab, and headed for the New Jersey pier. Walking hard and feeling proud, he was the last person up the gangplank.

Chester would never again work or reside in the United States.

When he thought about the exodus, the final flight from friends, enemies, lovers, critics, and publishers, he knew that his reasons for getting out were simple enough. He left America "just to stay alive." The flip side of the coin was what he told Constance Webb: if he didn't leave he would kill someone.

Chapter Twelve

A PISTOL IN HIS HAND, AGAIN

1955–1959

On December 22, 1955, debonair in his secondhand clothes, Chester Himes arrived in France with $200 in his pocket. After two consecutive seasons of celibacy, Paris was not just a refuge but also a place for a man testing his limits in debauchery and inebriation, a contest that began as soon as he collected his bags at the Gare St.-Lazare and checked into a nearby hotel. Incurious about Willa, he instead accosted women randomly—prostitutes and students—in an alcoholic stupor. "I got America out of my mind," he reflected, "but in so doing I was rapidly destroying myself." Pulling himself together, he managed a visit to Editions Plon the day after Christmas, accompanied by Yves Malartic. He learned that Plon wished to execute a contract for *The Third Generation* for roughly $142, a lowball pitch that he thought "diminished me as an author, and my book, as a work of literature."

Annie Brierre lifted him up a few days later with a New Year's Eve invitation to her house at Square du Roule for a party of elderly, "fantastically dull bitter-enders" that included a drunken female English author and an editor from *Le Monde*. Brierre also helped him again make the rounds of publishers. He successfully negotiated up the Plon offer; on January 24 he signed an agreement with Maurice Bourdel, the firm's director general, for the translation of the book for $300. Gallimard scheduled *La Fin d'un primitif* for April; Jean-Paul Sartre requested chapters to consider for publication in the magazine *Les Temps Modernes*. Chester hammered out a short preface: "What does one expect from a culture as chaotic as ours?" he asked. His book named a new social constellation—the white sexually liberated, female executive, and the black male who "plays the role of catalyst which gives him extraordinary power."

> In the *End of a Primitive*, I take a prototype of that new kind of woman—a prototype perhaps somewhat a little exaggerated— and I show her desperately seeking from the primitives some affection and understanding that the unique position she occupies in our modern culture deprives her from receiving. Her error consists in this. She imagines that any dark-skin man is a primitive. But the black American male is a handful of psychotic entanglements such as has never before existed. He's a kind of social bastard, crushed by the vulgarity and immorality produced by our time. And there you have it, what the woman takes for a primitive.

When Gallimard's edition appeared, Chester thought Malartic's translation "excellent" and that the minimalist cover design in the postwar French style, featuring only his name and the book title in red lettering on a white background, bespoke "dignity." He dedicated the book to Willa, since she was now almost completely out of his life.

After a couple of nights at the Café Tournon he spotted William Gardner Smith, who now knew everybody on the Left Bank and directed Chester to a hotel at 14 Rue Royer-Collard, near the Luxembourg Gardens, where Chester remained through the spring.

In 1953 and 1954 he had only dabbled in Paris; now he lolled at the cafés and on the boulevards as an habitué. For the first time, Chester relied upon the languorous rhythms of the cafés to complete his work. He set up a routine of taking his morning coffee and croissant and writing at the Café au Depart, or sometimes the Monaco, working through the day and trying to pick up women. To begin with, the cafés were warm, and hotel rooms were not. And, day or night, Latin Quarter cafés hummed with a palpable intellectual and artistic energy, it being ordinary to stumble across well-known existentialist writers or internationally famous modernist painters. At the end of a strong day of writing, a pile of different-size saucers would cover Chester's table, indicating to the waiter what he had consumed and owed. Freeing himself from the flurried commerce, casual racism, and opportunism of New York, he had now begun the saga of "Maud," the minor character based on Mollie Moon whom Millen Brand, an editor at Crown, had liked in *The Primitive*. But Chester did not feel fully satisfied with the material he was drafting.

In his first month back in Paris, he wrote to the literary agent Oliver Swan, who had shopped portions of *Silver Altar* to *Harper's Bazaar*, asking him to turn over all of the sections of *Silver Altar* to Willa. She had begun using her married name, Trierweiler, and Chester claimed that he had "sold my rights back to Mrs. Trierweiler and I have no further interest, now and in the future, of any nature whatsoever, in the manuscript." By mid-March he reneged on those terms and settled an agreement with Willa through an attorney, splitting the possible proceeds of their book, now called *Garden Without Flowers*. Willa had the right to sell the volume under her own name and to conduct all negotiations. Then Chester promptly dodged the attorney's fee.

If he was stalled on new projects and brittle over the possibility of any reward from the book with Willa, he felt draped in the sexual electricity and creative brilliance of a jazz musician when

NAL shipped him fifty finished copies of *The Primitive*. He passed the books out and accepted tribute from the black expatriate contingent firmly anchored around the red-copper counter of Café Tournon. The circle had grown since he had left the year before, now including several painters like Bertel from Gary, Indiana, and Walter Coleman from Baltimore, along with students at the Sorbonne he admired such as Joshua Leslie, "with soft beautiful features and black velvet skin"; news correspondent Frank Van Bracken; Walter Bryant, who acted in the film version of Satre's *The Respectful Prostitute* and was also a nightclub manager; various piano players; Eddie Meyers, a schoolmate of Ralph Bunche now hustling newspapers on the Champs-Elysées; Ishmael Kelley, a camel-hair-coat-wearing seducer of great repute who became the subject of two novels by Richard Wright; and the ambitious writer Richard Gibson, a Philadelphian friend of William Gardner Smith. Ollie Harrington, Smith, and cynical Slim Sunday were already fixtures at the café.

Bertel, an expert artist of erotica rarely seen without his signature pedigreed dog, and who was influential in this male circle because he was understood to be conducting relations with both a mother and her daughter, theatrically declared *The Primitive* the finest book he had ever read. Even the more traditional aesthete Richard Gibson considered *The Primitive* "excellent," as would Henry Miller. The change in attitude evidenced by the acclaim from the twenty-four-year-old Gibson—who had critiqued Chester's naturalistic fiction in *Kenyon Review* in 1951, in much the same manner that James Baldwin had critiqued Richard Wright's—indicated not just Chester's new approach but also a new mood of impatience among the expatriates and their countrymen at home. As more nominal, legal freedom was gained in the United States, black Americans signaled that even more freedom was owed them. The expats' nostalgia for their birthplace was mainly reflected in jive patter, their favorite the departing salutation "Take it easy greasy, we've all got a long way to slide."

The position of the hip black artist in Paris became more conflicted during the months that the edifice of segregation cracked in
the United States. In February 1956, Authurine Lucy enrolled as the
first black student at the University of Alabama in Tuscaloosa, and a
week of rioting gave way to lawsuits. French papers like *Le Monde*,
Libération, and *L'Humanité* gave front-page coverage to Lucy's ouster,
and they considered her heroism akin to that of Rosa Parks, who
had refused in December 1955 to move from a Montgomery bus seat
reserved for whites. A new battlefront had erupted at home and it was
becoming less sporting to flitter abroad.

Chester sometimes believed that French papers liked giving space
to the American troubles to blot out the raging war in Algeria, as
the French colonial past and present threatened to topple the very
tables and chairs of the cafés themselves that winter. On February 21,
on Boulevard St.-Michel between the Luxembourg Garden and the
university classrooms, Chester witnessed thousands of students and
agitators in a counterdemonstration opposing a march led by veterans of Algeria and Vietnam. In the Algerian capital city of Algiers,
French paratroopers had been called to put down the insurgency.
Chester disliked the students and their "Hollywood type mob scene"
on the street, which to him seemed artificially contrived and point-
less. He paid closer attention to the strong response of the French
government, which deployed gendarmes and black paddy wagons in
numbers equal to the protesters. Frequently mistaken by the police
as an upstart Algerian, Dick Gibson was one of the black Americans
who identified with the Algerians, the protesters, and other victims
of French colonialism. At first, the protests and police response didn't
bother Chester.

The best-known crowd of Americans living on the Left Bank in
1956 was uninvolved in the Paris skirmishes around race and colonial
independence. Harvard and Yale blue bloods, like the *Paris Review*
founders George Plimpton and Peter Matthiessen, also enjoyed a few

seasons at Café Tournon. But Chester did not share their world of "refreshing" Paris and nighttime parties wearing capes and tails, even if they did have on staff Vilma Howard, a black female writer who had interviewed Ralph Ellison shortly after his National Book Award. The *Paris Review* founders had edited Harvard's *Lampoon,* and *Paris Review* would have been a logical venue for Chester's ribald Harlem satire that spring, an entrée to elite circles that he could have used. But although they shared pinball machines and chased the same young women from Radcliffe, none of the angry blacks at the Tournon in the "Wright" circle were considered for the *Paris Review* club.

At the tables of the Tournon or Au Depart, a maudlin and thoroughly soused Chester railed against the United States, French women who declined to share his bed, and Harlem snobs, of whom he had decided his cousins now represented the pinnacle. "He could never finish deriding the bourgeois pretensions of his relatives, the Moons," Gibson noted. Chester "detested Mollie Moon," thought Gibson, and he was expanding his "Maud" material into a novel called *Mamie Mason*; when published years later as *Pinktoes*, Gibson considered it "an act of revenge and exorcism." Of course, Chester longed for acceptance by the same cigar-chomping, white-women-crazy, Cadillac-driving crew. When Sidney Williams of the Cleveland Urban League showed up with his comfortable Midwestern black backers on their way to Ghana and invited Chester over to the hotel for drinks, Chester felt pangs of sadness: "I was the only black from their class and background and almost of the same generation who was not a financial success." In prison he had wondered whether he would ever be able to publish his book and become known as a writer; by middle age he was painfully aware of the power of the almighty dollar. The contradictions, envy, sadness, and venom toward bourgeois striving went into the new book.

Chester constructed *Mamie Mason* around a series of ramshackle joking conversations, chiefly between himself and Ollie Harrington.

The two acquaintances were becoming chummier, and they shared an irreverent ritual minstrel-show greeting. A Bronx native three years younger than Chester, son of a black father and a Hungarian mother, Harrington had completed an undergraduate degree in fine arts at Yale, played Negro League baseball in Harlem, and then worked on Adam Clayton Powell Jr.'s newspaper *The People's Voice*. As a correspondent during World War II, the stalwart Harrington had zoomed around with the black fighter pilots called the Red Tails, dodged bullets with the Ninety-Second Infantry in Italy, and landed in a glider when the South of France was taken.

Unlike the younger men grouped at the tables and bragging about their improved sex lives, Harrington had fled the United States with the government in hot pursuit. After serving as campaign manager for Ben Davis, Harlem's Communist city councilman, he had induced Orson Welles to popularize the infamous case of Isaac Woodard, a decorated war veteran blinded by police in South Carolina for resisting Jim Crow. In the course of dueling with white supremacy and as a publicist for the NAACP, Harrington had shouted down Attorney General Tom Clark, and thus exposed himself to the wrath of the congressional investigating committees. Smoking a pipe and still drawing his darkly humorous cartoon *Bootsie*, which brought out the grim detail and fierce determination behind ordinary black life in the United States, or writing about the Senegalese troops fighting for France at Dien Bien Phu, the forty-four-year-old Harrington was a favorite raconteur for good reason.

Chester concluded that the black men grouped around the Tournon table were absurd—"unique individuals, funny but not clowns, solemn but not serious, hurt but not suffering, sexualists but not whores." But Harrington, the most successful of the regulars, even owning a car, was in his own category: "Ollie was funny." His humor was prankish and puckish. Harrington invited his friends over for his specialty hare, then he stuffed the rabbit with hashish. Harrington, who married an attractive Englishwoman in 1956, had a talent for easy adaptation and winning admiration. He also had a secret weapon: "great charm."

Unbidden, Chester and Ollie Harrington could perform together. "In front of that vast white audience I could not restrain myself any more than he could," Chester remembered. Their patter was ritualistic and satiric, sometimes piffling conversations about sex across the color line, easily working the joke back to the black man's sexual equipment of legend and the black woman's strong conjugal appetite. The jokes were made more "entertaining" when they hilariously overturned the myths. In several books Chester enjoyed a line that countered the below-the-belt jest about giant black men: "'Everybody's ain't that big.'"

Because the pair had been introduced at the Moon apartment back in 1944, the escapades of the recently deceased NAACP secretary Walter White and his high-powered coterie were a natural topic for ridicule. Chester put White's affair with Poppy Cannon, the cross-racial libidinal appetites of the civil rights crowd, and Mollie's overenjoyment of people and food at the heart of *Mamie Mason*. One sentence, involving Mollie Moon and Walter White's first wife (here called Juanita), summed up the book's scope. "Mamie's one ambition was to get even with Juanita by proving to everybody it wasn't disdain that kept Juanita from her parties but shame because she had used so much alum to shrink her privacy it had dried up." While writing, Chester tried out sections of the book as he went along. One night he had the black sporting crowd up to his rooms, regaling them with the hilarity of the play on words and the language games designed to out-maneuver censorship. For some, the sexual set pieces had the potential to make the book uproariously funny. For other audiences, the jokes were stale and hard to catch, repetitive without being illuminating. Chester admitted he was "finding it difficult to keep *Mamie Mason* funny." Around the middle of spring he found himself in sight of the ending, a sadomasochistic bacchanal topped off by a costume pageant.

By the end of April 1956, Chester had mailed off the opening fifty pages of *Mamie Mason* to the Dial Press's James Silberman. He'd first met a teenage Silberman with his father, Noel, in the Moon apartment in the 1940s. Chester also might have known that Dial was gambling on James Baldwin's brilliant and tautly controlled *Giovanni's Room*, scheduled for October publication, about an American's homosexual affair in Paris. In his first pass at Chester's book, Silberman applauded the "wonderful subject" that dripped with a "good deal of the frantic flavor." He then exposed the weakness of the new style Himes was building on: "we never get a sense of where the novel is headed or even who, beyond Mamie, are the central characters." Silberman cautioned, "It seems possible that you have put too much burden on comic situation and done too little with plot and structure." Silberman's concerns made sense. Chester, nearing forty-seven, had quit Dexamyl since Vandi's death and was shucking out one-liners to titillate the hangers-on at the Tournon, now "the most notorious interracial café in Europe." He was not concentrating on a "straight narrative," and, like the new jazz musicians, he was more interested in brilliant virtuoso soloing than swinging a melody involving multiple complex parts. He was disinclined to back off from the delights of a new kind of impressionistic style, which left him feeling liberated and afforded the sense that he was hipper than his American backers. "White Americans are reading *The Search for Bridey Murphy*, searching, it seems, for another new and complete life because the present life is so dissatisfying, and Negro Americans are searching, it seems, for a present life they would not want if they had," he noted. His writing was for a new world, a new tempo, a new circumstance.

Despite not liking Silberman's editorial advice, Chester promised Silberman "a very flexible version, subject to major revisions or even a completely new approach if necessary." As always at the beginning of the dance with an editor or publisher, Chester promised to deliver whatever was asked. "Please don't feel that I am ever closed to editorial advice and suggestions. My trouble has been that when I have needed advice and suggestions, there were none forthcoming." He had often been given advice but was flattering Silberman in another difficult series of literary negotiations. *Mamie Mason* would take five years to appear, in spite of the fact that Chester had little company in the 1950s constructing satires of African American political life during the civil rights movement.

In the late spring at the Tournon Chester made a drunken date to take a German named Regine Fischer to a party at Bertel's. Thin, with pimples and a prominent nose cast in a small face, Fischer was twenty and studying acting in Paris. Having learned her American expressions from rowdy GIs, she had a dirty mouth and, at that time, she was the periodic lover of Ollie Harrington. When Chester arrived at Bertel's flat with Fischer, he was understood to be in colossally poor taste, not simply because he was escorting the lover of a friend, but because most of the black men were showing off the rich, chic, older European women who treated them in style. Among the black sports in the Latin Quarter, Himes had a reputation to uphold: he was a working black writer, reviewed and admired and who often enough took sex as his topic. His peers hoped to meet social-register-caliber Willa, whom they only knew about through William Gardner Smith and Wright and a few sightings. Chester would also have been in good stead if he had brought silver-haired Annie Brierre or Marion Putnam. Instead, he ambled to the party alongside a young waif selected at random. She would be the center of his turbulent domestic life for the next four years.

Chester believed that the national experience of defeat combined with the sinister implication of being connected to the Nazis produced in Regine a flowering of early-nineteenth-century German romantic mythological strength. "German women have extraordinary courage where their men are concerned," he wrote. "It is a courage that stems directly from their sex; when they give a man their body, their soul goes with it automatically. If they like to be loved by a man, they will die for him." Perhaps. But when he launched into this affair with a girl half his age who had been in love with Harrington, Chester was suiting up for a repeat performance of the messy love triangles that he had known with Jean, Vandi, and Willa. If the real emotional crisis in Chester's life had taken place when his brother was blinded, and he lost in the struggle for his mother Estelle's affectionate guidance and care, he seemed doomed to pursue emotional bonds and habitual sex with women whose loyalties were divided, whose estimates were adoringly generous but often enough analytically suspicious. He was compelled to win their allegiance with the tools he had at hand—sex, money, and celebrity when they were available, and promises of marriage when they were not. Then Chester would accuse his lovers of betrayal, become ashamed of his own disingenuousness, and drive them away.

Toward the end of May Chester got a note from Daniel Guérin, who had received *The Primitive* and would welcome him in June at his writers' colony La Ciotat in the South of France. Regine Fischer accompanied Chester to the train station, after spending the weekend with him, having meticulously kept track of the number of times they had "fucked," her preferred term. As she learned more about Himes, his success in America, and the reputation that he had among the French, her sexual curiosity and her ploy to make another lover jealous were replaced by admiration. Chester lodged as Guérin's personal guest in his mansion, apart from the other writers in surrounding cottages, and worked hard hours in solitude in a massive and elegantly furnished library with a commanding view of the sea. William Gardner Smith had been there in December, until he and Guérin, a regular contributor to *Présence Africain* on African American and Caribbean matters, had several sharp disagreements.

Chester, however, wrote rapidly at La Ciotat and sent Silberman a completed, revised draft of *Mamie Mason* by the middle of June, complete with a chart to understand the still fuzzy plot and characters. Chester was lonely at the writers' colony, and he kept a portrait of Regine on his desk; he also wrote a long letter to Willa, asking about *Silver Altar*, admitting how intensely he disliked Ellen Wright, and then accusing Willa of lesbian affairs. In a similar maneuver to the one with Vandi, he'd left some of his cooking utensils with her, giving him an excuse to see her again. However, tired of his indecisiveness and opportunism in the relationship, Willa retorted that "there's no point in our writing." She was through with him.

When Chester returned to Paris on June 19, Regine Fischer awaited him on the platform at Gare de Lyon. They took rooms together at 76 Rue Mazarine, near Pont Neuf. Because the hotel owner disliked having a black man in her building, after a contentious week they moved to a front room at Hôtel Jeanne d'Arc on Rue Buci, overlooking a bustling market, where he and Willa had stayed in the fall of 1954. At the Tournon, his buddies were smirking about a scuffle that had taken place between Ollie Harrington and Richard Gibson.

Chester had spent several drunken evenings with Gibson and they enjoyed each other's company. The awardee of numerous fellowships, including Yaddo, and the favorite of white American critics, the bright Gibson was an anomaly even in the black Tournon circle. An Army veteran living in Paris because he loved French writing and culture, he seemed likely to be a success in America. At sixteen he had met and impressed James Baldwin's other mentor, the painter Beauford Delaney, who also moved to Paris. By the time Gibson was nineteen, he was backed by established American critics and writers, including John Crowe Ransom, Lionel Trilling, and Eleanor Clark. Gibson had written articles for *Merlin*, the British literary magazine, and worked as a translator at Agence France-Presse; he was now drafting a novel called *A Mirror for Magistrates*, which would be published in 1958 in London. Considering Gibson's subject matter in his novel—racism and homosexuality at a boys' prep school—there was a great deal for him to discuss with Chester, as Gibson would certainly have been interested in a book like *Cast the First Stone*. And, as Gibson matured from tyro to novelist, his criticisms moved beyond critiquing black writers to faulting American writing by and large. After several years abroad, he had little good to say about U.S. novelists, who were "dedicated to the cults of sensibility without significance, style without aim" and manufacturing "escapes" and "trivialities." When Richard Wright met Gibson, who had targeted him in a dig called "A No to Nothing," Wright had said, "So you're the boy who wrote them nasty things about me," and then bought him a coffee, a rare gesture of respect.

The popular Gibson had been living in Paris for a year and a half, and after sharing a flat with Smith on Rue Tournon, he had taken over an efficiency apartment at 31 rue de Seine used by Ollie Harrington. Raymond Duncan, the eccentric, toga-wearing brother of modernist dancer Isadora Duncan, owned the apartment. Gibson and Harrington had argued about back rent and disputed belongings that spring and when Harrington returned in June, their disagreement turned unpleasant. A violent altercation would take place on the terrace of the Café Tournon itself later that summer. At that point, Harrington accused Gibson of stealing his furniture while Gibson hotly insisted that Harrington "tell the truth." Before the crowd of onlookers, Harrington thrashed the youthful Gibson, inexperienced when it came to fisticuffs. Although Chester and Harrington were sliding in different directions relative to Marxism, Ollie toward and Chester more belligerent to leftist whites of goodwill, he sided with Harrington after the fight.

If there had been a moment of easy fraternity among the expatriates at the Tournon, the combination of the racism in France spurred by the Algerian War, the successes and setbacks of the civil rights movement in the United States, and the increasingly articulate pan-African militancy of many of them was tearing it apart. Distrust and suspicion climbed seriously during the summer. French police were monitoring the conversations of colonial West African writers like Bernard Dadié, making the rounds of the cafés in July 1956, and there is every reason to believe that American and British intelligence services were keeping tabs on Americans abroad. Chester liked to say, "I've got my life almost down to fundamentals, and it's pleasant," which meant, among other things, disregard for practical political stands. "I don't even think about the 'Algerian problem,'" he decreed; that was the pastime of "true Frenchmen" like Gibson.

Chester would sidestep the problems that ensnared his friends that summer, venturing more deeply into the relationship with Regine Fischer and doing a little sly castigation of the moderate civil rights movement, while continuing work on *Mamie Mason*. Settling in with Regine inevitably meant reckoning with his past. He wrote Jean in New York, asking for a divorce, suggesting the benefits: "Why don't you marry somebody with some money and make your life easy?" he penned, basically repeating the advice he'd given in 1928. But to divorce Jean he'd need more than $1000, making it unfeasible. He had by then fallen out completely with Willa over *Silver Altar* and was sending her the same sad and angry letters he sent to his publishers, demanding the whereabouts of the manuscript and reversing himself on earlier agreements. By November, when Willa had received a contract for the book from Beacon Press, Chester threatened, "If it appears in print without my written consent, I am going to sue." Chester's reputation as a sharpie and one of the few black American novelists seems to have preceded him at Beacon. Willa's editor admitted an animus toward Chester that spilled over: "I hate him. He spoils my feelings for all negroes for some reason." The book was published by Thompson alone in 1957, under the title *Garden Without Flowers*.

A lingering fondness for Willa was not curtailed by Chester's new girlfriend. Regine had dyed her hair blond, perhaps to offset the fact that her teeth were bad and sometimes she stood in her brassiere while

she combed her hair on their Rue Buci terrace, to the catcalls of the
men working in the market on the street below. Regine had given up
Harrington, who ignored her when he bumped into the two of them
on the street, and she turned to Chester as her lifeline in Paris. He
felt "tremendous" exhaustion from sexually satisfying a twenty-year-
old, and he was also burdened as her paternal figure. In a manner
that reminded him of Jean, Regine began to speckle her conversation
with "Chet thinks." She attended acting classes four nights a week at
the ultracompetitive Théâtre du Vieux-Colombier, which admitted
few foreigners and fewer Germans. Short on money, they were tossed
from their hotel on Rue Buci and moved a couple of blocks away, to "a
front room in an old hotel on a narrow street," a road morose, dingy,
and unpleasantly aromatic. Run by a devoted, unflappable couple from
the country who believed in the arts and tolerated the idiosyncrasies
of artists, Hôtel Richou at 9 Rue Gît-le-Coeur would serve as their
on-and-off home for more than a year. After they had left, Americans
from New York and San Francisco would pour through the hotel,
among them Allen Ginsberg and William Burroughs, making this
seedy joint fashionable among the Beat Generation. But for Chester
there was little charm in the artist's poverty and suffering. After he
pawned his typewriter and Regine sold her specially bound editions
of books mailed by her father, a bookseller in Germany, the couple
was reduced to eating dog meat and having sex as their sole diver-
sion, though more frequently now Regine "had troubles" during intercourse. "Living on the goodwill of friends," Chester was at least happy
that he was in Paris, where such ambassadorships of penury could be
conducted "with a saving grace."

The summer of 1956 involved multiple fraught rendezvous. Chester believed Richard Wright was avoiding him, and when they did
sit down at the Tournon, Wright made offhand, contemptuous
remarks about Regine. Wright had seen her traipsing through the
café since May 1955 and never considered her more than a hussy.

Then, on August 24, *L'Express,* a French newsmagazine, reviewed Chester's *La Fin d'un Primitif.* In Chester's preface he had written a three-sentence synopsis of the book identifying a sexually frustrated white woman and a racially frustrated black man drenched in alcohol and sealed in an apartment for a weekend: "This results in extravagance, buffoonery, idiocy, and tragedy." The single-column review included his picture; after identifying him, the caption read, "Exercise in Buffoonery," turning Chester's words against him. To make matters worse, *L'Express* decided, "We must reread Richard Wright to understand the difference between a great black novelist and a plain lampoonist." Chester remained in Wright's shadow whether he liked it or not.

In July Ralph Ellison visited from Rome, where he was a fellow at the American Academy. He was aloof but pleasant, and Wright entertained the Ellisons and Chester at his house for dinner. By himself Chester escorted Ellison to the soul food restaurant run by massive Leroy Haynes, an overture to their conviviality from an earlier time. But ever more after the fight in Vandi's kitchen—indeed prior to that occasion—Ellison had locked Chester into a slot. For him, Chester remained "as tortured as ever," a black man "so in love with a vision of absolute hell that he can't believe . . . in the fact that the world has changed in twenty years." And the critique was personal: "Chester seems to hold me responsible," thought Ellison, considering the bitter undercurrents of any discussion between the two of them that July, "because life in the U.S. has changed in relation to his conception of it." Ellison seemed in another orbit, looking for posts at white colleges, and palling around with literary critic Alfred Kazin in Paris. When a magazine that fall published Chester's picture alongside Richard Wright's as the two exemplars of black American writers, some of the Tournon regulars grumbled that it should have been Ellison instead of Chester. Chester would continue to feel cut by Ellison's commanding stature.

One Saturday morning in August Chester was collecting his mail from the American Express office when he saw none other than his brother Joe, accompanied by his wife, Estelle, a French professor who had been taking a summer course at the Sorbonne. Chester hadn't known that they were visiting Europe; probably Joe, who maintained that he never read any of Chester's books, was still reeling from what he had heard of the psychological portrait of his family in *The Third Generation* and hadn't cared to be in touch. Doubling Chester's embarrassment, he had no money to play host. He told them he would meet them later in the day and, after he was unable to secure any money, accepted their hospitality at dinner, leaving Regine at home. On Sunday he was able to persuade Yves Malartic to invite his brother and sister-in-law to dinner. Chester felt alone in the world, in spite of the fraternal meeting. "I wonder vaguely what will happen to my body when I die," he groused in a letter to Jean. "Not that I give a damn." By September when he tallied it all up, he owed about $500 to friends in Paris alone.

Needing whatever the French publisher would offer, Chester delivered the manuscript of *Mamie Mason* on September 3 to Gallimard. Two weeks later he could have a vision of a weighty audience for what he was doing, perhaps one that hadn't existed when *If He Hollers Let Him Go* had been written. On September 19 a large conference of international black writers convened at the Sorbonne. The best of the black world's Francophone writers hit Paris, and not a few of the Anglophones as well, like Chester's drinking buddy George Lamming. Chester met with the American delegation, including James Ivy, the literary editor of *The Crisis*, the Howard University French professor Mercer Cook, and the political scientist John Davis, who had broken the color barrier and taught full-time at New York University. Wright and Baldwin also had official invitations to the conference, and Chester was mildly insulted to have been overlooked. "I didn't take any active part; in fact I wasn't invited to," he complained

TOP, LEFT: Author Richard Wright, May 1943. *(Library of Congress, Prints & Photographs Division, Gordon Parks Collection)* TOP, RIGHT: Himes, April 1946. *(Carl Van Vechten photograph © Van Vechten Trust)* BOTTOM, LEFT: Dust jacket of *If He Hollers Let Him Go*, 1945. BOTTOM, RIGHT: Photographer Carl Van Vechten, 1938. *(Library of Congress, Prints & Photographs Division, Carl Van Vechten Collection)*

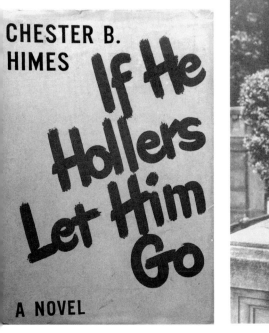

TOP, LEFT: Himes's friends. From left, sociologist Horace Cayton and writers Langston Hughes and Arna Bontemps, ca. 1946. *(Carl Van Vechten photograph © Van Vechten Trust)* TOP, RIGHT: Writer Ralph Ellison and wife-to-be Fanny McConnell, fall 1946. *(Chester Himes Papers, Amistad Research Center, New Orleans, Louisiana)*

BOTTOM, LEFT: Dust jacket of *Lonely Crusade*, 1947. BOTTOM, RIGHT: Dust jacket of *La Croisade de Lee Gordon*, 1949.

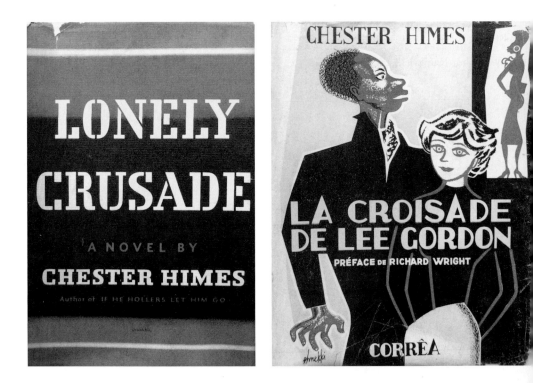

TOP, LEFT: Himes's companion Willa Thompson, ca. 1955. *(Chester Himes Papers, Amistad Research Center, New Orleans, Louisiana)*

TOP, RIGHT: Himes, June 1955. *(Carl Van Vechten photograph © Van Vechten Trust)*

BELOW: Author Ralph Ellison, 1957. *(James Whitmore / Getty Images)*

TOP, LEFT: Richard Wright, mid-1950s, at Café Tournon. *(Dominique Berretty / Getty Images)*

TOP, RIGHT: Writer Richard Gibson, ca. 1958. *(Carl Van Vechten photograph © Van Vechten Trust)*

RIGHT: Writer James Baldwin, 1955. *(Carl Van Vechten photograph © Van Vechten Trust)*

LEFT: Novelist William Gardner Smith, ca. 1952. *(Carl Van Vechten photograph © Van Vechten Trust)*

BOTTOM, LEFT: Himes and companion Regine Fischer, December 1957.

BOTTOM, RIGHT: Close-up of Himes at *Feux Croisés* book panel, spring 1957.

LEFT: Himes and Regine Fischer at bookstand, spring 1958. **RIGHT:** Himes's fiancée Elaine Lesley Packard, 1963. *(Chester Himes Papers, Amistad Research Center, New Orleans, Louisiana)*

LEFT: Elaine Lesley Packard, 1966. *(Chester Himes Papers, Amistad Research Center, New Orleans, Louisiana)* **RIGHT:** Himes, July 1962. *(Carl Van Vechten photograph © Van Vechten Trust)*

Novelist John
Williams, mid-1960s.

John Williams and
Himes, 1972.

Himes, ca. 1975. *(Chester Himes Papers, Amistad Research Center, New Orleans, Louisiana)*

Himes, ca. 1978. *(Chester Himes Papers, Amistad Research Center, New Orleans, Louisiana)*

to Carl Van Vechten, although some participants remember him padding around the seminars, "grave" and taciturn.

Although he was the most recently published black novelist in France, Chester was done a small favor by being left off the official American delegation. He wrongly presumed that Richard Wright was responsible for his omission, but in fact Wright, a conference organizer, had hoped to have Chester represent the United States, alongside Langston Hughes, William Gardner Smith, Melvin B. Tolson, E. Franklin Frazier, and Ralph Ellison. However, many forces converged to produce an American delegation of professional academics, mostly white-looking in appearance, and some of them soon to go on the dole of the Central Intelligence Agency. None other than W. E. B. Du Bois, who had been stripped of his passport and right to travel, declared himself a "socialist" who believed in "socialism for Africa." He angrily telegrammed the assembly: ANY NEGRO-AMERICAN WHO TRAVELS ABROAD TODAY MUST EITHER NOT DISCUSS RACE CONDITIONS IN THE UNITED STATES OR SAY THE SORT OF THING WHICH OUR STATE DEPARTMENT WISHES THE WORLD TO BELIEVE. Meanwhile, Ralph Ellison ignored his invitation to the Paris conference, instead attending an anti-Communist intellectual conclave in Mexico City sponsored by the Committee for Cultural Freedom. Ellison doubted Chester's ability to keep up with the conversation. When he had been in France, Ellison had observed that he could "communicate only slightly with either Chester or Dick, although Dick is so much more intelligent."

The material in Chester's novels was actually regarded well by at least a handful of those present. A thirty-three-year-old Senegalese dockworker from the rough side of Marseilles named Ousmane Sembène was in Paris attending the conference and self-publishing his first novel, *Black Docker*, which had grown specifically from Wright's *Native Son* but also sharply captured key dynamics in the recently published French version of Chester's *The Primitive*. Like Wright,

Sembène had joined the Communist Party and become a writer. His *Black Docker* rendered the demise of a working-class African novelist who murders an upper-class Parisian woman who has purloined his work. Eventually a noted filmmaker, Sembène's most formidable novel, *God's Bits of Wood*, would detail the 1948 railway strike in Senegal, a book personalizing the unions, the black peasantry, organizational politics, and French colonial forces, strongly reminiscent of Himes's work about Lee Gordon and the California aircraft industry.

More polished than the rough-and-tumble Sembène was the young Cameroonian Mongo Beti, a Sorbonne student who had begun his studies in Aix-en-Provence in 1951. A young activist who made his home in Rouen, Beti had written an article in 1955 called "Romancing Africa"; it decried the fact that "not one quality literary work inspired by Black Africa and written in French" yet existed. Beti was disgusted by the folkloric clichés he saw abounding in the black novels, "the whole gamut of the two-bit picturesque" at the expense of "all that might get him [the novelist] in trouble and particularly the colonial reality." For Beti, terms like "colonial administration" and "atrocity" belonged beside each other. He would publish that year *The Poor Christ of Bomba*, followed rapidly by *Mission to Kala*, and then a remarkable satire in 1958, *King Lazarus*.

A heroic figure to both Sembène and Beti was Frantz Fanon, the French-trained Martinique psychiatrist fond of *If He Hollers*, which he had cited in his remarkable 1952 work *Black Skins, White Masks*. (A copy of the French edition of *The Third Generation* would make its way into Fanon's library.) Fanon, of course, issued a searing lecture to the crowd. When he found supporters, Chester tended to be regarded by those on the militant, radical, or anarchic cutting edge.

Chester's active participation in the conference would have been timely and beneficial for the work he had under way that summer: character portraits of the black intellectuals then living in Paris. Chester had completed his last "intellectual" novel, set among the

Tournon crowd, and prominently featuring Wright, William Gardner Smith, Bertel, Harrington, and himself. Calling it *A Case of Rape*, Himes never found a publisher willing to stake him on this unflinching exposé of the demise of his relationship with Willa Thompson and the awe with which he and Harrington regarded upper-class white women. The novel also contained an appraisal of the international dimensions of Wright's literary reputation, especially the weird enmity that Wright seemed to have generated following *The Outsider*. Chester wrote character sketches of everyone, mixing legend, fact, and fiction to generate the rough arc of the story, which made it a kind of intellectual detective work.

His treatments of his comrades, Harrington and Wright, were the most condescending. He described Harrington's character, Sheldon Russell, as a "dilettante Uncle Tom," who "did it for free, to have the good will and personal liking of cultured and intelligent white people." Himes's depiction of Wright's character, Roger Garrison, was similarly pitiless. He appraised Wright's fame and success in the United States and in France, and also its precipitous decline.

As a yardstick for Negro intellectual capacity, he served two purposes: (1) To restrict the evaluations of college-educated culturally reared Negro intellectuals within the confines of his own mental limitations; (2) To create a Negro success story of such singular aspect as to withstand duplication, yet at the same time demonstrate it can happen. Once these ideas had been sufficiently compounded into the national race consciousness, there was no further need to be concerned about the intellectual aspirations of Negroes. . . .

On the other hand he had been used by the French, first to illustrate their freedom from racial bias and preconceptions and, secondly, to focus public attention on America's brutal persecution of its Negro minority. The French, with their vast colonial empire in Africa, sat back and laughed sly at America's discomfiture.

Consequently, his American supporters turned on Roger and denied him. This rendered him useless to the French, so they dropped him. In the United States, less talented writers were acclaimed as his superiors for the sole purpose of debasing him.

Part of the portrait plainly showed the difficulty of colliding so regularly with Wright and his reputation in the fishbowl of black Paris. As for what Wright thought of him, in the synopsis Chester created that summer, he knew that he was considered Jean Genet to Wright's Jean-Paul Sartre, "more or less a type of pimp." Ellison would go on, in the same year, to describe Chester in precisely the same language to Horace Cayton.

A few days after the September conference, Regine went to visit her family in Bielefeld, Germany. Chester loaded her with books and coached her about his most valuable work like *Lonely Crusade*; he hoped to have Regine prod her book-dealer father into helping him with German publishers. While living with her family, she tried to work hard at being his girlfriend: "I will try to be as you wish me when I am back."

But Regine returned to chaos. Their financial situation by October was of the "I don't know which way to turn" sort. Once again, Chester had a manuscript that he could not sell. Silberman rejected *Mamie Mason* for Dial on October 2 (the same week the press issued James Baldwin's *Giovanni's Room*). "I don't think *Mamie Mason* would have any great success in the trade, and would only make all of us unhappy," he wrote to Chester. Silberman partly based the rejection on New American Library's unwillingness to offer a paperback deal, frustratingly linking the hardcover edition to the possibility of a paperback reprint sale. Victor Weybright at NAL had held Chester off until he received word about the hardcover edition. Now Wey-bright was calling *Mamie Mason* "brilliant social satire," but "a little too sophisticated for the ordinary reader." It was an excruciating con-tradiction in the space of two years, to be told he was brainlessly vulgar and scatological, with *The End of a Primitive*, and now, that his new novel was beyond the capacity of the American public. As for the seventy-page synopsis of *A Case of Rape*, Silberman promised to read it quickly.

But in effect Chester had reached a genuine nadir. At the true peak of his writing ability—having been published at all levels of the Ameri-can press and been well received, with his strong talent for originality, character description, and his courageousness in examining the com-plexity of the social world and his instincts for politics—Chester would be spurned by the literary market and unable to secure other kinds of work for the necessities of life. As with the original work on *Immortal Mammy* for Knopf, his best impulses were thwarted in a marketplace that was disinterested or incredulous. He needed another path, and one that wouldn't turn him into an Uncle Tom for the French.

By the time Chester received his royalty statement from NAL that October, he could smell the stench of defeat, despite the huge paperback print run. He had believed that 225,000 copies of *The Primitive* had been distributed, but the statement indicated that only 170,000 were printed, lowering his possible royalty roughly by a quar-ter. "Please do not consider this a beef," he implored in his correspon-dence with New American Library, as he requested clarification on the terms. He was told that the print order had been reduced because the book was unacceptable for chain stores, Army bases, and the apartheid South African market. He raced to court Gallimard, but the French publisher was not interested in bringing out the satirical commentaries of a black American set in the United States. "I wish I could get away from these themes of interracial violence," he wrote to Walter Freeman, "but somehow it seems to be my destiny."

With his manuscripts rejected by friendly presses, Chester sent a note on October 16 to Marcel Duhamel, who had translated *If He Hollers Let Him Go* for Gallimard, and offered to return to the crime story he had been asked to produce for the Série Noire list back in 1954. He included a synopsis of what he proposed, warming to the project. "I like the idea. I can handle it," he wrote. Feeling pinched, he agreed to "follow your suggestions in all aspects." Chester went to work "immediately" on a book he was thinking of calling *Trouble Wears a Skirt* and assumed that he would save himself embarrassment by publishing the book under a pseudonym.

When the two of them finally met, Duhamel proclaimed Dashiell Hammett "the greatest writer who ever lived" and pushed Chester to make the story into one of action without any narration. "Make pictures," Duhamel told him, "like motion pictures." The advice wasn't an endorsement of saccharine or safe entertainment, but came from an intellectual position that located philosophical value in popular arts, especially genres relying upon representations of violence. Focusing on American film, Duhamel had written in 1955 that "the idea of death" was "eminently sane and suitable for engendering skepticism, and thus humor, and thus a certain optimism." Duhamel had been an early collaborator with André Breton, the father of surrealism in France and, as early as 1945, Duhamel had been bringing out hard-boiled crime fiction at Gallimard—mostly translations of Americans like Hammett and Raymond Chandler. It was in the spirit of American crime fiction that he had translated *If He Hollers*. Duhamel wanted Chester to open up to a new landscape of death and death-defying action in Harlem. Chester recalled Duhamel's commandment, "We don't give a damn who's thinking what—only what they're doing." And Duhamel said he would pay $1000 for this work, beginning with a $200 advance.

Chester was trying to pry money loose from Berkley's editor in chief, Charles Byrnes, whose company he had threatened to sue a year earlier, for relief from his "intolerable situation." Chester wanted to be at work on *A Case of Rape*, "a condemnation of the French racial attitude," which Yves Malartic was showing around to highly "infuriated" French editors and attorneys. Chester had the misfortune to be shopping this manuscript during the "Suez fiasco," when, to anchor their influence in the Mediterranean and oppose African nationalism, France joined with Great Britain and Israel to invade Egypt and seize the Suez Canal. The Eisenhower administration forced them out, bringing U.S.-French relations to their lowest point. French gas stations were refusing petrol to American tourists. Chester, however, was reminded of his own Egypt-like vulnerability when the U.S. embassy had him interrogated at a police station to verify his sources of income. The colonial condition was becoming difficult to ignore.

After the fallout at Café Tournon between Harrington and Gibson and the Paris black writers' conference, Chester hung out with Walter Coleman, the versatile painter who did everything from book covers to cubist abstraction. A sport who wore the "chin-strap" beard "of the cult devoted to freedom of love in the *Quartier Latin*," Coleman was living with the mother of his young child, a Swedish jewelry designer named Torun Bülow-Hübe. Chester liked visiting their Fifteenth Arrondissement home because they had central heating—the weather was cold that fall—but he was undeniably drawn to pretty Torun. Chester would sit with the couple in their bedroom until Walter fell asleep and began to snore, while Chester, imitating the younger black men at the Tournon he scoffed at, confessed the most painful experiences of his life to Torun. She listened "spellbound, silently, almost breathlessly, never taking her gaze from me." Chester won her affection, but their relationship remained platonic.

When he wasn't flirting by pathos with Torun, Chester learned something valuable from Walter, a street hustler in his own right. Walter recounted the story of the "Blow," a confidence-man scheme that he claimed he had used to steal $25,000. Chester shaped the tale into the plotline for his crime novel, which he would call *The Five Cornered Square*, meaning a square so square it has an added dimension of squareness. The novel revolved around the hapless Jackson, an undertaker's assistant, and a "banana-skin" vixen named Imabelle. Jackson's brother Goldy, a transvestite and heroin addict, was the other key character. Chester needed only 220 pages of action sequences to fulfill his contract, but the novel progressed slowly.

Then, in the middle of November, Regine failed an examination at the theater. Her examiners had been friends, some of them even former lovers, and not long afterward she and Chester stumbled into Harrington at a restaurant. She responded to the painful encounters by downing a bottle of Nembutal sleeping tablets. Chester rushed her to the American Hospital for emergency treatment. She recovered and was prescribed a diet of six "calming pills" per day. On November 25, Chester accompanied Regine to Bielefeld, which was still showing the impact of targeted Allied bombing during the war. In the odd stopover, Regine's father asked Chester his intentions with his daughter and was horrified to learn his age; a Wehrmacht veteran, Otto Fischer and Chester were born in the same year. Chester left her in Bielefeld in the care of her parents and where she would take a stenography course as a back-up career, planning to return to Paris in three months. Herr Fischer hoped that a separation would give his daughter time to reconsider. Chester took the train back to Paris on December 3; as he left, he pressed on Regine his well-traveled copy of *The Sheltering Sky*.

With twenty-five-cent paperbacks of *The Third Generation* and *The Primitive* lining shelves, Chester felt famous but destitute, a paradox no one could believe. That reality depressed him and he felt that his career seemed over. "I am pretty nearly beat on this wheel," he admitted, after a week back in Paris, in a letter to Walter Freeman. Futilely, Chester wrote *Esquire*, imploring Gingrich to publish "The Snake," the story bought eighteen months ago, to give him leverage with book publishers. He complained that he was reduced to writing "cheap" detective stories.

He found relief in Fischer, who had begun to idolize him and his work. "I am not intelligent, I am stupid," she wrote to him self-deprecatingly. "I understand perfectly how impossible it must be for you to live with some kind of animal which learned how to talk," she continued, referring to herself, and acknowledged that she could "understand too how this was making you very irritable." Lonely without him, "(even if we quarrel)," Regine plugged away in stilted English, lifting him out of his doldrums over the detective novel:

> It is no great book; but it is not cheap. Why would it be cheap? Just because you have great social ambitions? Jackson certainly takes his Imabelle for as important as Lee Gordon his place in the world. In one of your letters you said that you would cut throats, eat shit and live in sewers for the one you love. Make it the same for Jackson in his possibilities, he does so. He can still be strange and funny to the reader by the fact that the kind of "all or nothing" people exists so seldom in our days.

Perhaps—because as a German she symbolized the ruin of a particular of European righteousness—she stabilized him.

Chester waged war to keep Regine, proclaiming to her father: "I am the only person who has ever needed her," which he could maintain at least half truthfully since she was translating for him. "She feels my love for her through my need for her. And I sincerely believe, before God, that her only chance for happiness in life is with me." Otto Fischer begged Chester to leave his daughter alone, especially because Chester could be cruel to her. Tearfully inconsolable one afternoon, Regine had shown some of Chester's letters to her family, particularly ones where he had accused her of being promiscuous.

But winning the battle for impracticable Regine did not guarantee much of a future. He had heard from another American publisher before Christmas. In turning down both *Mamie Mason* and *A Case of Rape*, the editor at Crown was direct and candid: "I see no possibility of our taking either effort. *A Case of Rape*, which I much preferred, is an ingeniously devised idea which, unfortunately never really succeeds in rising above its basic design: a polemic against white supremacy." To American publishers, polemics against white supremacy were passé.

Chester had anticipated a sharp reaction by publishers against *A Case of Rape* because of the characterization of blue-blooded Mrs. Hancock, the white female victim modeled so faithfully on Willa Thompson. So, not having paid his rent in eleven weeks, he turned fully to the place where there was traction and where there were no white people and, thus, putatively, no race problem at all. He put the "Blow" story together—with its victim, Jackson, and streetwise fiancée, Imabelle, and skin-popping transvestite brother, Goldy—and showed eighty pages to Duhamel, who advanced him a couple of hundred dollars more.

In doing so, Duhamel reminded him, "You can't have a *policier* without police." After rereading his thumbed-through copy of *Sanctuary*, Faulkner's novel of backwoods bootleggers, unmanned attorneys, psychopathic gunmen, country whores, brothel madams, and debauched debutantes, Chester recalled his Los Angeles friend Jess Kimbrough, the Communist writer and policeman, and his tough-as-nails partner, Charles Broady. They became the "tall, loose-jointed, sloppily dressed, ordinary-looking dark-brown colored" Harlem detectives called Grave Digger Jones and Coffin Ed Johnson, who were the bedrock of Chester's writing for the next dozen years, the key to his international renown. Grave Digger was something of a blue-collar philosopher, while Ed served as his lethal heavy, ever-ready to apply the deadly force of his long-barreled, nickel-plated .38 caliber revolver. "It was said in Harlem," Chester wrote, "that Coffin Ed's pistol would kill a rock and that Grave Digger's would bury it."

The plain-speaking, deadly, soul-food-eating duo evoked the difficult position between black urban poverty and the white world of the middle class. But the model that Chester invented of the two Harlem detectives solving crimes enabled him to depict black urban life, with its rural slave and blues roots, with a kind of opulence and intrigue that was difficult in books with more obvious political meaning. Ishmael Reed, the ace novelist of the next generation's black avant-garde, would state Chester's influence on his own 1972 masterpiece *Mumbo Jumbo* by admitting that "[Papa] LaBas and [Black] Herman were based upon Coffin and Gravedigger."

Feeling potent with some money in his pocket, Chester found comfort with a hanger-on at the Café Tournon who occupied his bed as he wrote the book in the last week of December 1956. He was drinking two bottles of wine a day and in the home stretch pouring St. James rum on top of that. *The Five Cornered Square*, later published under the titles *For Love of Imabelle* and *A Rage in Harlem*, depicts a madcap week when Jackson is scammed by rough vagabonds from Mississippi who are trolling through Harlem for gumps to inflict the "Blow" swindle. Grave Digger and Coffin Ed, the experts on uptown crime, use their underworld connections to trap the criminals, eventually killing all of the grifters. It was "a wild, incredible story" for a French audience "that would believe anything about Americans, black or white, if it was bad enough."

Chester always maintained that the European interest in his crime novels came about because he had dropped his concern with protesting against racial oppression or writing in a realistic style. But really what he had done was to create sizzling exaggerations that amplified and telescoped his concerns. He described Harlem in the 1950s as home to "the voracious churning of millions of hungry cannibal fish." When Goldy, Jackson's brother, screams as his throat is cut, Chester

gained the distance he had been aching for from the narrow politics
of reform controlled by the stodgy middle class.

> Goldy's scream mingled with the scream of the locomotive as
> the train thundered past overhead, shaking the entire tenement
> city. Shaking the sleeping black people in their lice-ridden
> beds. Shaking the ancient bones and the aching muscles and
> the t.b. lungs and the uneasy fetuses of unwed girls. Shaking
> plaster from the ceilings, mortar from the bricks of the build-
> ing walls. Shaking the rats between the walls, cockroaches
> crawling over kitchen sinks and leftover food; shaking the
> sleeping flies hibernating in lumps like bees behind the casing
> of the windows. Shaking the fat, blood-filled bedbugs crawl-
> ing over black skin. Shaking the fleas, making them hop.
> Shaking the sleeping dogs in their filthy pallets, the sleeping
> cats, the clogged toilets, loosening the filth.

In 1969 the black radical poet Don L. Lee (Haki Madhubiti)
would publish *Don't Cry, Scream*, a collection resonant with the inad-
equacy of sentiment in favor of horror in the face of an American
corporate and carceral reaction to a nonviolent protest movement that
emphasized love. The miserable, expiring cry of Chester's outrageous
character Goldy, paired with the deft hyperboles of Harlem tenement
life, reproduced the horror of the gruesome and absurd world and
excluded the love and social justice that Chester was suspicious of. But
by shaking out the pain and tragedy, Chester had given a reader like
Marcel Duhamel the groundwork for another direction: optimism.

On January 22, 1957, Chester submitted the completed draft of
a taut *The Five Cornered Square* to Gallimard and received his final
$400. In twelve months the firm would print 40,000 copies of the
book, titled *La Reine des pommes* in French (*The Queen of Apples*) and
translated by Minnie Danzas. Although at first the books he wrote

for this series would be ignored when issued in English, now he was a French writer and had turned a corner. He was making a living, if he could not extricate himself from a familiar publishing relationship to Gallimard and Plon, which he summarized in the 1970s as "cheap, shabby and racist."

Before the money ran out, he telegrammed Regine Fischer to rejoin him in Paris. Her letters acknowledged the power of his writing and her deepening commitment; now she was reading *The Primitive*, of which she wrote, it "just makes me feel so goddamn bad." And also she had begun applying pressure. "Darling I am not coming back to you unless I can be your wife." Chester's entreaty for her return apparently signaled his willingness to do more than hear her out about matrimony. The stenography course didn't end until Easter, but in February she arrived at the hotel, having fled her parents and her confinement. Although Chester remained married to Jean, around this time he and Regine would begin telling people, including the press, that Regine was Mrs. Himes and that they had married in December 1956. She would sign letters "Regine Himes."

With his Série Noire money Chester bought her new clothes, to be worn at an evening affair at Walter Coleman's. On their way to the party, Regine went into Café Tournon and, according to Chester's version of events, asked for Ollie Harrington. Chester, in "a blind insensate fury," drew blood, beating her on a crowded street. After cleaning the blood off her clothes, Regine went with Chester to the party. He stomped through, daring his buddies to defy his open malice toward Regine. Later he apologized to her, calling himself a "dirty nigger." She remained loyal, but she was unconfused about Chester's violence. She left a message for the man who had become a mean drunk, begging him to deal with himself: "No human being can live with a man who becomes an animal as soon as he gets any acool [sic] to drink. . . . I can't continue living in the fear of getting killed one day. You are a human being so why don't you act like it. Your excuse that you are a 'dirty nigger-beast' is no excuse for me." Still, she wanted to keep him: "I love you as you generally are. . . ."

Chester took up his fists for really only one cause: the prerogative of patriarchy. In his two memoirs, *The Quality of Hurt* and *My Life of Absurdity*, he would record several confrontations and many violent, sometimes deadly situations, but he never described an instance where he fought another man. Instead, in his autobiographies he showed two key episodes of violence against white women who he believed had been unfaithful: Vandi in 1953 and Regine in 1957. In a third example, an early draft of the second volume of his memoir, using pseudonyms and written at the end of the 1950s and which originally was to have been the story of his affairs with Willa Thompson, Regine Fischer, and Lesley Packard, Chester's narrator Templeton beats up Willa's character, Wilda, for infidelity. "I couldn't stop slapping her," he wrote, having already described the beating of Vandi Haygood's character in an earlier chapter. Templeton doesn't end the punishment until "I hurt her bad enough." This passage of physical abuse also ends in his orgasm and the beating ultimately ruins the relationship between Templeton and Wilda. The rages directed against women from the top caste had some of their origins in the scenes on Everton Avenue in Cleveland, and the fury of emotions that could never keep his family together. Alcohol always made it worse. He understood at least the precipice he was on. In the weeks following the episode with Regine at Coleman's, he declared to some of his friends that his "blood pressure" was high and that while he wasn't eliminating booze, "I've cut down on the doses."

As a contrite gesture, he let Regine persuade him to enroll for classes at the Alliance Française on Boulevard Raspail, close to the southwest end of the Luxembourg Garden. "Now that you've broke into the French scene, you ought to learn the language," she insisted. Chester signed on for a beginner's course and attended the morning lectures for a couple of weeks. "I didn't learn much French," he admit-

ted, but with his clothes out from the pawnshop, he felt purpose-
ful and dignified, talented and desirable. He grew out his mustache,
which had some gray in it, accepted the distinction of age, and tried
moving on from the Tournon. In the afternoons, he claimed a table
with Regine at Café Select on Boulevard du Montparnasse, where
he would often run into Walter and stylish Torun. Chester continued there, despite his conviction that the waiters and patrons at the
Select showed their racism plainly. But he was gratified to renew his
acquaintanceship with a Danish aristocrat and jazz aficionado named
Timme Rosenkrantz. An intimate of Billie Holiday, Duke Elling-
ton, and Louis Armstrong, the "Jazz Baron" Rosenkrantz was married to the internationally famous black performer Inez Cavanaugh.
Rosenkrantz also worked as a jazz critic and journalist and he recalled
having met Chester at the Moons' festive apartment in 1944.

Distancing himself from the café crowd, Chester plowed into the
next installment for Gallimard's Série Noire, *If Trouble Was Money*,
which would be published in English as *The Real Cool Killers*, a title
chosen by the publisher without consulting him. He had ditched his
French lessons and had reread *Sanctuary*, his bible of absurdity, for
the second time in about three months and faithfully reproduced
Faulkner's scenes at the Memphis brothel with the madam. Finished
by May 1957, even before *For Love of Imabelle* was published, *The Real
Cool Killers* introduced black Islamic gangsters in Harlem, the new
fashion: its villain was a tall, light-colored Muslim who despised
whites. Chester liked to dissemble and call the book a "cesspool of
buffoonery" or "some strange shit," but *The Real Cool Killers*—with
the daughter of Coffin Ed Johnson as a member of the gang, and with
sadism and pederasty as the fountainheads of desire of the "important white man"—was, for the 1950s, a pithy and exacting account of
America's cultural malaise.

Perhaps Chester's key struggle with the composition of the books
was to show enough care for the black people of Harlem so that the

series wouldn't be labeled as racist exploitation—indistinguishable from an entertainment of crude sensationalism. With only minor distractions, he fashioned the new book of violence and murder with his two detectives, and he obtained his $800 advance from Gallimard. The new book was soon announced in the French publisher's catalog. Meanwhile, in the United States, *Duke,* a mildly erotic glossy pitched to black men, published the episode of Charles Taylor's clumsy sexual initiation from *The Third Generation,* under the title "Night of Manhood." In another layout in the same issue, the magazine offered "The Primitives," a photo-interpretation of Chester's novel, using a series of photographs simulating the sex play of a dark-skinned male dancer and a light-skinned female dancer. *Duke* promoted *The Primitive's* "frenzied boudoir adventures" of "outright debauchery and sheer sin" as without peer.

On May 21 Editions Plon held an evening panel celebrating its Feux Croisés series, and Chester accepted praise for *The Third Generation* in a group that included unbowed feminist novelist and journalist Rebecca West, author of the thousand-page Balkan study *Black Lamb and Grey Falcon,* and Nikos Kazantzakis, best known for *Zorba the Greek* and *The Last Temptation,* both later turned into successful films. The festivities had begun the night before, with a cocktail party at the elegant apartment Maurice Bourdel, the firm's director general, maintained inside the glass-domed publishing house. Regine, whom Chester dutifully introduced now as Mrs. Himes, made a "splendid appearance." Then the group of writers and spouses gathered at the home of a multimillionaire on Avenue Foch. After ascending in a private elevator to the fourth floor, Chester found himself in an enormous hall adorned with museum-quality paintings. He couldn't get his bearings and, feeling "suffocated" by the wealth, he and Regine retreated to a table at the Café Select.

The next evening at the formal ceremony, Chester concluded the program, speaking rapidly in softly spoken English his message "eulogizing Bourdel and Plon" for their work translating foreign writers. No other American had had his novels translated into the series before, which published the work of such well-known Europeans as Aldous Huxley, Erich Maria Remarque, and Somerset Maugham. In the program, the editors of Feux Croisés explained the unique merit of *The Third Generation* on account of "its insight, its violence, its structure and its style." They had chosen Chester's book because "this powerful work goes far beyond the banality of 'the Negro problem' in the USA." After very steady effort for five years, Chester had excellent reason to consider himself "free of thinking about what Americans thought about me."

Although Plon seemed quite eager to launch him and to recognize his serious accomplishment, the toll that the drinking and the hand-to-mouth existence of the last year had taken was visible. Nearly forty-eight, Chester had sharp lines around his mouth, deep circles under his eyes, and though he was still fit, the skin sagged in places on his face. He claimed that he was now getting the handle on the joke of his life, but the obvious question was how much time would he get to use the punch line.

He and Regine ducked out without being interviewed by the press, a habit Chester maintained in France, which led the newspapers to ignore him the following day, with a couple of exceptions, including the left-wing *Les Lettres Françaises*. A week later, reporter J. Claude Deven of the *Tribune de Lausaune* caught up with them, asking such questions as whether African memories or racial mixture had helped explain the rapid advance of blacks after slavery in *The Third Generation*.

But the prestigious event had asserted that his achievement in France—first the translations of his major works *If He Hollers, Lonely Crusade,* and *Third Generation,* and then the Série Noire—was consequential. Chester didn't even have problems that spring at the U.S. embassy renewing his passport. Chester had also seen, finally, the multiplying effects of his efforts. If writing serious literature kept him impecunious, the Noire series paid enough to live. Shortly after Chester was paid his second advance, Duhamel sold *The Five Cornered Square* to Fawcett, an American paperback publisher. That firm published their version under the title *For Love of Imabelle* later that year, preceding the French edition, and netting Chester another few thousand dollars. Overnight he had become affluent enough to buy a car, so he picked out a convertible Volkswagen, and prepared to begin touring Europe. "I had a German girl, a German car; I was making my living from French publishers, and I had no reason whatsoever to put foot in America," he thought.

In early June 1957 Chester worked on registering and repairing the Volkswagen and getting his driver's license. He also checked Regine into the American Hospital for four days in the middle of the month, including examinations for venereal disease. On July 1, they drove to Stuttgart, with mishaps aplenty, from wheels flying off to an engine that threatened to both melt and explode. Chester's investment was a money pit. In Stuttgart they saw an executive at a German publishers, and mainly Chester could feel well about dropping off copies of the book for consideration. Then they headed for Hamburg, stopping over at Bielefeld to see Regine's family, and her father asked pointedly about their uneven romance. Regine, however, was delighted mainly to be seen in a car.

Deciding that Copenhagen would be a fine place to summer, they looked up Timme Rosencrantz, finding him at home playing blues singers from his high-fidelity audio set. Chester and Regine secured a town house in Hoersholm, a village of lakes and woods midway between Copenhagen and Helsingør, about two miles inland from the Øresund Strait. Rosenkrantz, an aristocrat, entertained them along with his upper-class friends at fine parties. Chester found the rainy forty-eight-degree summer weather awful, which may have helped him to write ten pages a day on a new novel, *A Jealous Man*

Can't Win, building the opening off of one of Harrington's anecdotes about a man falling out of a three-story window into a container of fresh bread. The crowd at Bunch Boy's casino in Cleveland furnished the remaining characters. The third novel in the series, he made this murder mystery a love story in disguise, centered around a tough-guy Harlem gambler and his wayward young wife. Chester achieved a working balance, spurred on by his "desire to succeed without America," coupled with his "antagonism toward all white people who I thought treated me as an inferior." That summer of 1957, he claimed that he "could write like a bird sings." Swigging brandy while he hit the typewriter keys, he had carved out an angry nook of his own.

They returned to their hotel on Rue Gît-le-Coeur in Paris in mid-September. With the confidence of the car, a girlfriend, steady work, and a bit of savings, Chester hunted up Wright, Harrington, and Coleman. From his seat at the Café Tournon, Ollie had been condemning the nationalist revolt in Algeria as petit bourgeois, the basic French Communist line. It was thus perhaps a bit odd to see in the October pages of *Life* magazine his letter to the editor about France's insincere negotiations in the Algerian conflict: "Any American who thinks that France . . . will grant Algeria, if not independence, at least some liberal status . . . is mad." But Harrington had written no letter. Within a few days it became apparent that Richard Gibson was the author, at which point the French police got involved and questioned him. Harrington certainly presumed that Gibson had done it to retaliate for the beating and have him deported. To anyone who cared to ask, Gibson claimed it was a pro-Algerian prank hatched by William Gardner Smith and Jean Chandleri at Agence France-Presse, where they all worked.

Perhaps even more odd to the men at Tournon, most casting about for money and needing approval from the U.S. embassy every six months to keep their visas in good standing and every several years to have their passports renewed, was Gibson's bourgeois prosperity during the time of the scandal. Despite the cost of raising an infant daughter, he had purchased a *pavilion* in Rosny-sous-Bois outside of Paris. His novel *A Mirror for Magistrates* was published in early 1958, and shortly thereafter he left Paris for the United States. All of his moves, bundled together, seemed unusual.

Black writers and intellectuals who knew Wright believed that a postcard with Gibson's signature was sent to Wright saying, "I am sorry about what I did to O. Harrington. I am back in the USA and the FBI has promised me a job but I don't have it yet." The postcard reputedly appeared two years after the 1956 inauguration of an FBI "counterintelligence" program called COINTELPRO, designed to "disrupt, disorganize, and neutralize" subversives. COINTELPRO was ideologically similar to the work of the congressional committees investigating un-American activities, except that it operated clandestinely, concealed its punitive dimensions, and was the creation of one man, J. Edgar Hoover, an opponent of the civil rights movement. FBI director Hoover conducted infamous investigations of the Communist Party USA and the NAACP in the 1950s, but he retained special opprobrium for "racial intermarriage," wherever it might be found, and which always meant sex relations between black men and white women. Key tactics used by agents included planting stories in newspapers and magazines, sending anonymous or forged letters with derogatory information, and neutralizing a foe by creating the impression that the person was actually a paid informant of the FBI. Suspicion darted back and forth that either Gibson or his friend William Gardner Smith was a paid government informant or a spy. Chester strongly suspected Gibson.

Wary of being targeted by government forces, Chester and Richard Wright hashed out their positions on the feud and writing in France over drinks at the Rhumiére Martinique, where Chester grasped that Wright was jealous of his recent good fortune at Gallimard. The Wrights, perhaps mainly Ellen, had dismissed Chester's detective fiction even before it was released, carping that Duhamel had reported back to Chester. When they saw each other, Wright combined his awkward blend of pomp and candor, blurting out, "I've spent too much time writing political books which don't pay," implying that Chester was cashing in on lowbrow material. "I should write about a southern black man who is not poor and despised," Wright told him. He was considering a novel about one of their Tournon friends, Ishmael Kelley, and his struggle to survive small-town Marks, Mississippi, and escape to France. Wright would publish *The Long Dream*, based on Kelley's exploits, in 1958.

Once Chester submitted *A Jealous Man Can't Win*, in October 1957, to his great curiosity he found that everyone at the Gallimard office treated him oddly—including translator Minnie Danzas, who acted "as though she had a secret to hide." Young white women at the Tournon told him mysteriously that they had heard about his unpublished book, but he couldn't be sure which one. Duhamel advanced him money for yet another project, encouraged him to stick with the Harlem locale, and then offered to take him to the restaurant of his choice. The editor mentioned as an aside that *La Reine des pommes* had received high praise, but he was vague about what he meant. Chester brought Regine, Walter Coleman, and Ollie Harrington to this dinner at Haynes's soul food restaurant, where they were entertained by the white jazz musician Mezz Mezzrow, a heroin addict and a buddy of Duhamel, who had published a book written in "jive." Ollie of course entertained the table with hilarious stories of Harlem. But the hero of that evening was Walter, the streetwise, hustling rogue, who explained silk-screening to Duhamel and, after a meeting a few days later, became an artist at Gallimard. The next time Chester saw Walter at Café Select, he was ordering an Italian sports car. Stung that he had somehow missed the money pot and clutching a copy of the anthology *Negro Caravan* and some of Faulkner's novels, Chester left Paris with Regine for Mallorca, reaching Spain on October 25.

The trip to Puerto Pollensa, which he could now drive on his own as far as Barcelona, covered the same ground he'd traced with Willa in 1954. Regine had gone French, with short, dyed-blond hair. Chester talked again with Roche Minué, the painter, and rented the top floor of a house with a grand terrace overlooking the Bay of Pollensa. Once again, the weather was miserably cold, and the first of Chester's money went for wood. By the middle of December, the wind blew so forcefully that even a fire was impossible in the house. He kept warm by burning a bowl of powdered charcoal covered with ashes underneath his writing table while draping himself in blankets. With an Irish red setter named The Mike, they drove to Bielefeld for Christmas, and then back to Mallorca for New Year's. Reduced to requesting advances from Duhamel shortly after 1958 began, Chester took planes, trains, and automobiles to reach the French border to pick up a few hundred dollars of wired money. Even though he believed he could surreptitiously "lift scenes straight out of Faulkner and put them down in Harlem" to quicken his writing, he had to admit that after six months "I had accomplished nothing; I had written nothing." Living as a tourist made writing hard and haunting the locale he had shared with Willa made him relive the failed bid for literary stardom between 1953 and 1956. By the end of 1957, he was convinced that New American Library—and the paperback rider that seemed connected to his every contract in the United States—had blighted him and reduced him to being a grubber for Duhamel's pulps.

On April 25, 1958, they returned to Paris and found they had lost their cheap room at Hôtel Richou, now overrun by American Beat poets. Chester appealed to Duhamel to get him going, and was surprised again by the confidence of his editor, who, although disappointed that he hadn't completed another book, was still cheering him on. Meanwhile, Editions Plon took a $300 nibble at *Mamie Mason*, and after that, as Chester was wont to say, he had room to maneuver. After an accident on May 19, in which a truck driver deprived him of the fender to his Volkswagen, he returned to Duhamel with another concept for a book and a plan to relocate to the Côte d'Azur. On this occasion, Duhamel gave him half of the book advance up front. Duhamel also started building some publicity around Chester: he arranged a photography session at a drugstore book rack on Champs-Elysées, including Regine, and another day at the Haynes soul food restaurant. Duhamel also recommended a new destination in the South of France to complete more books, the town of Vence, between Nice and Antibes.

On the way down to the coast in June, Chester stopped in Provence to see Jean Giono, a heralded dramatist and novelist who was the champion of the French farmer. Giono had sent Duhamel a comment of praise for *La Reine des pommes* and then extended an invitation to Chester for tea at his home in Manosque. Although Giono had written epics and fables, he had also written *Un Roi sans divertissement*, something of a detective story, in 1947. The two men, about fifteen years apart in age, got on well enough that Giono invited Chester to his daughter Sylvie's wedding the next year. After reaching Duhamel's real estate agent in Vence, Chester and Regine took rooms in the lovely two-story Villa le Lavandou, on the edge of a hill in Quartier St.-Michel, sloping down to the Mediterranean, just under four miles away.

Chester had been writing swiftly in advance of the move, and completed the book *Run Man Run*, the very day that they got settled. The only one of his Gallimard's Série Noire books without Grave Digger and Coffin Ed, *Run Man Run* featured a drunken white cop who accidentally kills a black porter working at a cafeteria, then systematically murders the rest of the black janitors. Only a custodian named Jimmy escapes, and the novel follows the policeman's attempts to silence this final witness to his crime. The germ of story was of course drawn from Chester's experience in December 1955.

After only another three months, on October 9, he finished *The*

Big Gold Dream, perhaps the most formulaic of all his detective stories. The plot concerns a riddle of stolen money by a preacher confidence man named Sweet the Prophet, devoted parishioners who've
hit the numbers, and an assortment of demimonde men who meet
their demise. Chester and Regine rewarded themselves with a trip to
Switzerland and Bielefeld. From her hometown he continued north to
Frankfurt, where he discussed the possibility of a German translation
of *The Third Generation.* When they returned to France, he and Regine
stopped in Paris as Duhamel's guests for dinner. For the first time
they saw a bound edition of *La Reine des pommes,* Chester's "cheap"
story. On a special band there were endorsements from Jean Cocteau
of the Académie Française ("a prodigious masterpiece"), Jean Cau, the
novelist and secretary to Jean-Paul Sartre, and Jean Giono. Giono had
written audaciously, "I give you all of Hemingway, Dos Passos and
Steinbeck for this Chester Himes."

For a postwar French writer to imply that twentieth-century
American realists needed to have their characterizations of U.S. life
corrected by Chester's slangy, violent portraits of Harlem was not
a far-fetched claim—although when Chester told the story of the
praise, he liked to sweeten the pot by replacing John Steinbeck with
F. Scott Fitzgerald. Chester had helped the French understand themselves as not merely subordinates of the Marshall Plan of culture,
not merely existentialists reasoning through Vichy capitulation and
defeat by former colonies. He had produced the underbelly of the purportedly equitable, optimistic American society in the raw, without
any endearing vision. He presented American blacks forging ahead
in urban Harlem, in a narrative unencumbered by arguments about
civil rights or the psychological dynamics of racial oppression. Chester
enjoyed knowing that his books, filled with blues ditties and vernacular toasts, and featuring violent murders and rough characters, were in
essence blues tales, "out of the American black's secret mind." Additionally, the French had a concept of style and black entertainment

performance that avidly consumed the sharp pepper in his novels. After all, France was the kind of place where people liked to predict the outcome of Sugar Ray Robinson's fights on the basis of his robe, his trunks, and his hairdo. The French combination of presuming blacks as the acme of chic and being grossly paternalistic angered some white American expatriates, who thought it showed "the super-ignorant sentimentality Europe and England have about the Negro."

And thus, Chester understood immediately two things: that the fulsome praise would make him a target of ridicule in American literary circles, and that Duhamel had protected him from his rising celebrity for many months and that in the process he had basically written an entire oeuvre, five books for La Série Noire.

Chester had hit a lead-off home run: *La Reine des pommes* would be published in the United States as *A Rage in Harlem* in 1959, and be produced as a film in 1991. With the novel he had recaptured the energy of "To What Red Hell" from 1934 and by that June the reviewer for *Mystère* was claiming the book "the most extraordinary detective story since I started writing this review." He and Regine had hardly returned to Vence after seeing the book than he was summoned back to Paris in November 1958 to receive Le Grand Prix de la Littérature Policière, an award for best detective fiction in French, for *La Reine des pommes*. In an instant, Chester had achieved French and European recognition, and on Franco-European terms. The French coronet was considerably more than what he could have expected from the United States. And if it was not the official respect accorded Ralph Ellison for *Invisible Man*, he had surpassed the notice that James Baldwin had received from the critics for his fiction. It might also be said that in France Chester had surpassed Richard Wright. What's more, from then on, the reluctant American newspaper critics begrudgingly gave him his due.

His personal life immediately tipped after the boon. In Paris, he stopped being seen with Regine as he made the rounds of interviews.

Paris-Match caught up with him and Jean Giono together in a book-filled room at Chez Boleniou, and Chester took a room at 23 Boulevard Brune in the Fourteenth Arrondissement. When Chester appeared at Café Tournon now, accompanied everywhere by his big dog, he "caused a sensation." Partly the sensation was due to his manner of rounding corners on two wheels in the pale-blue Volkswagen before sauntering over with The Mike.

In the winter of 1959 Chester spotted William Gardner Smith at a table, accompanied by an attractive young British journalist from the *Herald-Tribune*. Lesley Packard introduced herself saying, "Congratulations, I hear you have won the prize." An assistant editor at the paper, she had seen Chester's picture and story come across her desk the day before. The three of them went out for drinks, dinner, and jazz clubs. "Beautiful and chic," smartly employed, and fashionably attired, Lesley Packard contrasted strongly with the neurotic Regine Fischer. Lesley seemed like the sort of grown-up woman appropriate to Chester as he saw himself now, a sexy, globally recognized literary man-about-town. She even knew the Tournon crowd—but not intimately like Regine. Richard Wright enjoyed noticing Lesley by teasing her, calling her "that dangerous Packard woman," a line from a novel he had enjoyed as a youth.

From then on, whenever Chester turned up in Paris and could free himself from Regine, he looked up Lesley Packard; in turn she "took a personal interest" in his welfare. In reality she had looked out for his welfare before she had even known him. The *Herald Tribune* editor was "a little bit of a racist" and Lesley had to push aggressively to include the story about Chester's prize in the English-language news. Born in 1927, Lesley had grown up on a farm in Suffolk, England, and attended boarding schools. She had settled in France after the war, working as a secretary for the U.S. Army in Orléans, an experience that also introduced her to jazz and the jitterbug. Although several of his friends believed that she was racist, by July 1959 Chester was sleeping with Lesley and scribbling to Regine perfunctory notes to keep her content in Vence.

Chester's growing fame seems to have been the impetus for an article the previous fall in *Time* explaining black expatriates, titled "Amid the Alien Corn." Using a quote from Jean Giono that called his work "extraordinary," *Time* flattered Chester as having done "impressively well" abroad. The magazine interviewed him as happy to live in a climate where he was accepted not merely as a black man, but as an artist. "In America you have this personal problem, of course. But that's not what I mean about France. I like France, and can work here because everybody, and I mean everybody—the concierge as well as the intellectual—respects creative work. They understand writers and help them." The article also quoted William Gardner Smith, Ollie Harrington, Richard Gibson, and Richard Wright. (Except that Wright had not actually been interviewed, although *Time* refused to admit it, even after receiving a letter from Wright's attorney.) Gibson's position in the article as the clean-up batter, disgusted with the narrow possibilities in the United States, was also odd: when it appeared, he had already moved back to America, was working as a news correspondent for CBS, and he soon would become an organizer for the Fair Play for Cuba Committee.

Chester was living mostly in the South of France now; he had new value becoming "a person in Vence not to be thrown away." After a mild new year's accident Chester was without a car and stranded in Vence, despite the hopes of Parisian reporters at *L'Express* and *Paris-Match* for interviews. He stayed there revising *The Big Gold Dream*, while the biggest bookstore in the capital devoted an exclusive section of the window display to his work. In the early spring, Regine's mother arrived to spend some time with them; probably she hoped to accomplish, at least, his engagement to her daughter. Instead, after an argument at dinner, Chester encouraged Regine to return to Germany and complete a diploma in translation studies. A likely drunken Chester then attempted to get a switch from a tree to tame their dog and injured his eye. Conflicted about his relationship with Regine, Chester had hoped to see his twenty-three-year-old girlfriend stand up to her mother. But when she did not, he was also of a mind to put as much distance between the two of them as possible, possibly forever. After seeing her mother aboard the train back to Bielefeld, Regine drove with him to La Ciotat, where he would recover from the eye injury. The following morning, she took a train to Germany. He stuffed francs into her hand through the window as the train pulled off, promising his support, part of him wishing for her to stay at home.

After Chester recuperated at La Ciotat, he went to Paris, where the proprietors, waiters, young French girls, and even the gendarmes accorded him recognition and respect. He ran into Harrington and, after a revealing conversation, Chester realized, "I was a real celebrity." Feeling confident, he went to Lesley Packard's house at 5 Rue Grégoire-de-Tours, anxious to get off a nighttime street where he might be mistaken for a North African, fair game during the Algerian war tensions. Their affair was not exclusive and Chester courted her with sophistication and persistence. Harrington had to go to Moscow for work, so Chester agreed to take over his apartment on Rue de Seine. He met with Duhamel and negotiated an advance of 5000 francs (a bit more than $1000), for a book called *Don't Play with Death*. One of the strongest in the series, it would be published in English in 1960 as *All Shot Up*.

Chester totaled the Volkswagen in May, and a few weeks later purchased an English roadster. He drove to Hamburg to see Regine Fischer, by now a sort of condolence visit, which he contrived to keep her attached but remaining in Germany. He was demoting her from the position of wife to consort; once he returned to France, he sent her crisp business letters that downplayed the personal dimensions of their tie. He spent July with Regine in Hamburg, making arrangements with a literary agent handling foreign-language rights named Ruth Liepman to sell his books to German publishers. After a visit with George Ramseger, the editor of the newspaper *Die Welt*, Chester and Regine were allowed the use of Ramseger's villa for the month. Drinking too much wine, Chester still managed to send wooing letters to Lesley Packard in Paris. While he sometimes referred to Regine as his "wife," he was determined finally to end their connection. "I confess it is a relationship that is absolutely dead," he wrote to Lesley.

In the middle of August he developed severe stomach pains and was diagnosed with ulcers. Chester returned to Paris and was put on a strict diet that excluded alcohol for three months. The day the doctor announced him recovered from the ulcers, Chester returned to old habit and drank a bottle of French gin. When Regine visited, she stayed with him, and when she returned to Germany, he raced after Lesley Packard. Regine wished badly to be in Paris, and she warned him that she was coming and would not be put off: "I am going to Paris with or without a job." Now that a modicum of success had arrived, she intended to share it too.

In a sign of Chester's increasing visibility, Christian Millau and Serge Bourge, two *Paris-Match* journalists, sought him out to make a Harlem film treatment. Chester created a fifty-four-page scenario about a preacher on a white horse kidnapped to perform a miracle by the mob, which was good enough to secure $100 from a producer named Louis Dolivet. Chester had a celebratory dinner on Boulevard Brune with friends of William Gardner Smith and Ollie Harrington, which turned into a drunken debacle, with Chester falling down the stairs and sideswiping several cars on his way to the Mars Club, where bebop pianist Art Simmons was playing. Lesley gamely jumped in the swerving car to try to protect him. Chester's mishaps with cars, regular and increasingly dangerous, are strong evidence that his drinking had reached the stage of a deadly condition.

Now there was a restrained hum of applause from American critics. They ignored the prize-winning *La Reine des pommes/A Rage in Harlem*, but daubed his lesser subsequent books with the brush of approval. "The French," wrote *New York Times* critic Anthony Boucher, "have gone mad over the work of Chester Himes, an American Negro now resident in Paris." Boucher blamed the French for wanting a tawdry portrait of the United States and sniped at Chester, observing that "Himes writes about the America that a European likes to believe in . . . a lurid world of squalor and oppression and hatred and meaningless violence." Still, Boucher supplied tantalizing adjectives to describe the new books: "fascinating and not uncomic" and "shocking, grotesque."

A week later, thre *New York Times* again gibbered him into its fold, in a kind of replay of the Doubleday advertisements in 1945 and 1946. "The question arose as to just who Mr. Himes is," wrote critic Lewis Nichols with mock folksiness, then calling Chester "an old friend who was around these parts a decade back." Chester never forgave what came next, as Nichols categorized all of his books as "thrillers," putting *If He Hollers Let Him Go* in the Série Noire and describing him as "forty or so, with a small mustache and a large red setter dog." The notice continued incorrectly, "He last visited the United States in 1958," before ending that Chester had an easy, carefree life in Paris or touring Europe. Chester, whose story "The Snake" was finally published in October's *Esquire,* now basked in the same lukewarm applause in which the ultrapopular African American novelist Frank Yerby was drenched. But Chester clung to his bitterness, regarding all comments about him in the U.S. press as negative. "I dread reading any reference to me in the American press," he wrote, depressed that the "calculated ill will" would ruin the chances of placing books like *Lonely Crusade* and *The Third Generation* with German and Scandinavian publishers. "It hurt more than I care to admit to be rejected by the American press," he explained in 1976, quite similar to the suggestion he made in 1959: "The *New York Times* could not have chosen a more unfortunate time for such misinformation."

More accurately, Chester was rejected and embraced simultaneously. "I haven't seen anything of my compatriot writers in many months," he had written to Van Vechten in the spring of 1959 from Vence. By that fall, he was back in the mix. In November 1959, shortly after Chester was in newspapers in Paris and New York, U.S. Army Communications Zone Europe officers were in contact with their operative at the Tournon. The operative informed the military that Oliver Harrington belonged to "a group of negro residents in Paris who are disciples" of Richard Wright, still considered a thorn in the side of the United States, and featured in a report called "Possible Subversives Among US Personnel in France." Chester, too, was fingered as a Wright acolyte. After a hiatus of twenty years, his public opinions had resurfaced as an interest of the American government.

The one other "disciple" in the report was Jamaican mathematician Joshua Leslie. Tall, dashing, and married to a white American, Leslie introduced young African colonials, like Abiola Irele from Nigeria, to their first taste of Marxism, to the Chameleon Jazz Club, with its cellar playing space, and to Chester Himes. Irele, studying French and living on Rue des Ecoles across from the offices of *Présence Africain*, was brought to Café Tournon in 1960 as a part of his education. Irele saw the author of *La Reine des pommes* "lots of times," and remembered Chester as, "very quiet, suave in a reassuring way, not a clever suave, and he got on well with the black people at the Tournon." Noted for his hostility toward white supremacy, his suspicion of Marxism, but also for his versatility in international western capitals, Chester was a necessary component of a young intellectual's education in Paris during the era of decolonization. He was chiefly known to the African crowd for *If He Hollers*, but his body of work, in diverse genres, was widely available in English and French by 1959.

He exposed the depravity and racism of urban America, countering
the promise of Eisenhower and then Kennedy's "New Frontier" world
leadership. African writers in France, particularly Cameroonians Fer-
dinand Oyono, a sharp satirist, as well as Mongo Beti, had written
books on traditional African societies invaded by a colonial power and
the rupture created by modernity. Beti had read *La Reine des pommes*
and then met Himes, whose spending for drinks was appropriately
"flamboyant" and whose attitude toward Europeans and Communists
"truculent." Chester's anger and his survival skills were necessary for
the younger writer, so devastated by the French army's assassination
of Cameroonian socialist politician Ruben Um Nyobé in September
1958 that he stopped writing fiction for more than a decade. Chester's
novels, his attitude, and his sensibility defied the notion that Europe
was the only appropriate passageway to civilization.

Chapter Thirteen

FIVE CORNERED SQUARE

1959–1962

Shortly before Christmas 1959, a thin, aggrieved Regine Fischer arrived unannounced at Chester Himes's apartment at the southern edge of Paris. A few days later Chester arranged to meet Lesley Packard at the Time-International office near Place de la Concorde. Before he reached the glass door of the building, Fischer surprised him, smashing him in the face with her handbag, and in the process breaking the glasses that Chester had now begun to use to drive. She accused him of indiscretions, and he responded by wrestling Fischer into the car and driving home, where they struggled over the ringing telephone in the apartment—obviously a call from a mystified Lesley. He slapped Regine and she dashed into the bathroom, took his razor blade, and slit her wrists. It had taken half a century, but Chester recognized it for what it was, "the worst moment in my life."

He had to telephone the police because he could not stop her from fighting him, despite nearly bleeding to death. The concierge and the policemen arrived and took Fischer to jail. Chester reached Christian Millau to help with the translating and had Fischer released to the American Hospital and then to Maison de Santé, a clinic in Nogentsur-Marne. She underwent psychiatric sessions and shock treatments. Chester admitted some responsibility for Regine's woes, but that feeling was typically overcome by a core obdurateness which enabled him to feel entitled to take advantage of people when it was convenient. He was also conscious of the manner in which using people added to the misery he was experiencing himself, what he disgustedly called "this veritable ocean of motherraping goddamned self-torture I've lived in for all my goddamned life."

Chester agreed to stop seeing Regine but characteristically battled with her father about who was to blame and how soon or in what manner he ought to break off contact. Shortly after the crisis had passed, he resumed his position of disregard. "This is me, Chester Himes," he rebutted Otto Fischer's prayer to abandon ties to Regine in early 1960, "you don't expect you and I to agree." Fischer arranged for his daughter's admission to a mental health facility in Austria. For her part, Regine downplayed the significance of the bloody episode. "You know that I really did not intend any harm at Christmas," she wrote from a room with barred windows. "Tell those people that I did not intend to kill myself this time."

Despite the distance between them (it was twenty-four hours by car), Chester now lived warily in fear of Regine's rages. In fact, he became convinced that she was planning a cruel reunion in Paris to splash acid on Lesley's face, a dreadful retribution lifted from the pages of *A Rage in Harlem*. When Regine did reappear in Paris, at the beginning of spring, a rueful Chester scurried back to the South of France. Regine expressed deep ambivalence about the two of them, saluting Chester as "my only love" but looking critically at the three years: "For you I have never been but a toy. You plaid [sic] with it until it broke." Partly to keep her at bay, and partly because he was compelled by her devotion and felt responsible for her, Chester would write back, make veiled insincere promises about the future, and send her a few dollars, but always shield his whereabouts. "I don't have your address down on the coast," she wrote to him, trying to find a way to belong in his life. After a couple of weeks, Regine circled back to Hamburg, where she still had a few credentials in publishing circles as Mrs. Himes.

During the winter Chester completed a detective novel now called *All Shot Up*, the story of a double-crossed, bisexual machine politician. With money from this book, he purchased a 1934 Fiat two-seater and in March went with Lesley to Nice. Afterward, they took a train to Milan to see the publisher Longanesi about bringing out *For Love of Imabelle*. The four-day trip to Italy went so well that Chester and Lesley decided to move in with each other. He was still avoiding Regine, who made occasional, sudden appearances in Paris, one time phoning Lesley to say that she had her head in the oven with all of the windows closed. Chester retreated to his most preferred terrain, the pastoral and calm South of France, typically within a twenty-mile coastal arc including St.-Tropez, Antibes, and Nice. Close to the shore, about five miles from Antibes ("a village of poor, gangster-like Italians"), was the Biot home of Walter Coleman and Torun Bülow-Hübe. Hiding from Regine that spring, he made a refuge in their storeroom.

In spite of the fact that he was drinking a fifth of Pernod every other day to manage his personal life, his stay was almost pleasant. Chester was captivated by gorgeous Torun and he marveled at Walter's stories in the way he had enjoyed the banter with Harrington. Still sporting his beard, Coleman liked to entertain white women with the complete panoply of sexual mythology, telling them he was twelve before he knew he was making babies. Chester had his own advice to dole out, privately, to his younger friend. He told Coleman that when it came to business with whites, "Never stop giving them hell. The moment you let up, they'll slap you down." Walter was struggling to make a living on his art. When his cubist paintings of Billie Holiday didn't pay the bills, Walter had found a niche moving narcotics. But even living with working artists (Torun was a silver-smith), Chester was unable to do any writing in early 1960, shuttling back and forth to Paris to see Lesley, and dodging Regine.

The only project showing signs of life was the Harlem screenplay project with Christian Millau. Chester had begun the preparatory work, which included some documentary filming to fill in produc-tion, and he had unashamedly reestablished contact with his cousins the Moons to obtain the permission of Urban League honcho Lester Granger to film portions of Harlem's Beaux Arts Ball. Meanwhile, the crisis in Algeria was threatening to spill out into the streets of Paris: "Everyone here, even the most level-headed and responsible Frenchmen, were [sic] so shaken by the Algerian uprising that they thought any minute there would be civil war and fighting in the streets of Paris," Chester wrote back home. In the political confusion, Millau had mistaken the dates of the ball and didn't get to the United States to film it.

Probably seeing more wisdom in living with Regine briefly than running from her, Chester decided "suddenly" to meet his old girl-friend in Germany that June. While this was a quicksilver impulse helped by alcohol, the decision to live with Regine always worked magic for the detective series. The battling couple rented an attic in Hahenhof, Austria, where he successfully finished another novel. *The Heat's On* introduced memorable characters like Pinky, an albino giant, and Sister Heavenly, an elderly Bronx drug pusher, as well as underworld delicacies like "speedball"—injected cocktails of cocaine and heroin.

By mid-September he submitted the manuscript for the book and with the income, returned to Lesley Packard in Paris. Uncomfort-able in France, the couple went as far as securing visas to Yugosla-via, a trip they ultimately did not make. Angry that he left her once again, Regine wrote him threatening, sarcastic letters from Austria. "It's so sweet of you to wish me well after you did everything to make me sick," she complained. "I am not well at all and if nothing happens I shall be back in the hospital soon enough." Ignoring both her determination to marry and the threats of suicide, but seeing the wisdom of independence in his new and preferred relationship, Chester drove down to the Côte d'Azur, with Lesley following in another car; they then proceeded east to Italy, taking writing implements and their assortment of cats and dogs along the way. They passed through Genoa, Livorno, Civitavécchia, Naples, and Salerno, stopping to see the Isle of Capri from the hills north of Naples. Along the way, they made a short obligatory trip to Rome to take in the Via Veneto, which they knew from Fellini's new film *La Dolce Vita*, and settled in a little burg called Acciaroli on the Gulf of Salerno.

With the sound of the pounding surf from the nearby beach in the background and ample markets at his doorstep, Chester found it easier to concentrate. He was hoping to push onto Tunisia, then meander south to Ghana, in the process conducting "an extemporaneous journey through the more settled of the new nations." It was a trip that Frantz Fanon had just taken, under harder circumstances. Like Richard Wright and William Gardner Smith, he was smitten by African independence and sentimentally curious about the land of his ancestors, but he ran low on money. Early in November, he heard favorable news—a payment of 1000 francs and a publication date for *Mamie Mason*—from Suzanne Blum, an attorney he had engaged to force Editions Plon to finally publish the book. He hurried to Paris to pick up his money, barely avoiding Regine, who was haunting the Hôtel Richou—escorting Madame Richou to the theater, chatting up William Gardner Smith on the street, and waiting for Chester. He decided to go with Lesley to the South of France.

On Tuesday morning, November 29, Chester was in St.-Tropez with Lesley, where they had traveled to visit her friends. Their landlady told them she had heard a radio broadcast reporting that Richard Wright was dead. Newspapers that week were filled with headlines about the capture of Patrice Lumumba and the discussion of Algeria at the United Nations. Alarmed, Chester turned to Lesley and told her, "Get the cat and the dog. We must go to Paris," then headed for his room to pack. In an hour they were on the road, hurtling over five hundred miles like pilgrims to a sacred altar of black literary affairs. Chester, like Langston Hughes (who had visited with Wright on November 25), had not known that Wright was ill or in any danger. They had become suspicious of each other after *A Case of Rape*, where Wright had the chance to see himself through Chester's eyes "as a failure." Wright had organized a "Paris Club" of black expats and kept Chester out. But Wright had also fallen upon tough times. He had had to sell the grand apartment on Rue M.-le-Prince for smaller quarters on Rue Régis, and his farmhouse retreat in Normandy had also been sold. The final time Chester had seen the Wrights together, Ellen had accused him of dragging Richard back into the world of deprived black sharecroppers and ghetto dwellers in his writing. She may also have held Chester, a man known for his unkempt personal affairs, as a contributor to the couple's marital difficulties. Ellen had reportedly shouted at Chester, "I don't want him to wallow in the gutter like you."

Since the fall of 1958, Ellen had been living in London with their daughter Julia, who studied at Cambridge; Wright had tried to settle in Britain but had been turned down for permanent residency by the British Home Office, which, apparently, declared him an undesirable. And though Chester sometimes squelched rumors that Ellen and Richard Wright were separated, at the end Wright had been closest to his girlfriend, Cecilia Hornung, and to Ollie Harrington, whom he telephoned every morning. Another recent girlfriend had been Japanese.

Chester and Lesley took a room in a hotel off Boulevard St.-Germain and made arrangements to see Ellen Wright, who they learned planned to cremate her husband and bury his remains without a funeral. Chester was appalled that a figure of such international stature would have no ceremony of benediction. "How dare she do this?" he sulked to Lesley before reaching Ellen on the telephone and arranging dinner along with Ollie Harrington, who was back from the USSR. To persuade her to hold a more formal memorial service, Chester built up his fallen friend. "Dick was the greatest black writer in the world," he found himself repeating. At the meal Ellen acceded to the request and they scrambled to assemble a program, agreeing that the gentle Senegalese journal editor Alioune Diop should deliver the principal eulogy.

After Diop's words, on the morning of December 3, a coffin holding Wright with a copy of *Black Boy* on his chest was cremated at Père Lachaise cemetery in Paris. Despite the success of the formal ceremony, Chester concluded that most of the guests were Wright's "enemies," precluding much socializing after. (Meanwhile, the rumor mill declared that Wright had been poisoned by an elusive female CIA agent.) Although Chester made amends and conducted himself amiably with Ellen on several subsequent occasions, he was also angrily suspicious of her and he relieved his feelings by habitually circulating rumors that Ellen had in some manner participated in a conspiracy—like the one surrounding the demise of Congo's Patrice Lumumba—to murder her husband. Wright's champion George Padmore had also died unexpectedly in 1959, as had the Cameroonian politician Félix Moumié, who had been poisoned in early November 1960, elevating the sense of panic among the vocal black critics of western colonial power. Harrington apparently took the conspiracy so seriously that, despite the military standoff between the Americans and the Soviets during a visit to Berlin in October 1961, he would decide to live in East Germany.

"I had never realized before how much influence Dick had over me," reflected Chester after the funeral, for the first time wrestling seriously with Baldwin's heartfelt remarks over drinks eight years earlier. That black men one generation removed from slavery had taken it upon themselves to write fiction about blacks murdering whites and lusting after white women, while defiantly blaming whites—from the Negrophobes to the Negrophiles alike—was unprecedented. "The realest thing about Dick was his absurdity," Chester wrote, also rationalizing his own course against conventional piety and ideologically driven politics. Chester's closeness to Wright also had the effect of a kind of passing of the torch; people who knew the men involved understood that Himes was responsible for carrying over hard-earned wisdom about literary affairs and the black writer's life to the next generation. He was the senior black international writer for younger blacks to seek out and, even though Chester was private and easily irritated, he didn't discourage their fond attachment to him. Harvard graduate William Melvin Kelley, author of the Faulkneresque *A Different Drummer* (1962), visited Paris in 1965. Ten years later, he was still berating himself for not having the wisdom to seek Chester out. But, once the two men established contact, Kelley, by then a well-received artist in his own right, wrote ebulliently, "DChief call d'young Proofessor tcome t'd'golden Stool."

Stepping into his role as the royal patriarch was not without obvious pitfalls. After the impromptu funeral it was not difficult to see that Wright would not be immortalized in the United States; his death was commented on in slender notices in the black press, along with a few other terse statements. *Ebony* presented the richest portrait of Wright's last years in Paris, along with a photograph of Ellen and Julia consoling each other as three Frenchmen carried Wright's ashes in a catafalque. That elegiac essay, nominally written by Ollie Harrington, was actually orchestrated by Chester. Harrington's obituary presented the details of "the Gibson affair," the *Life* magazine predicament from 1958, hinting that Wright had met with foul play.

With Wright dead and Himes an heir apparent for some of the slings and arrows Wright had received, Chester morosely tried to prepare his new girlfriend for what was in store. "If you want me," he wrote to Lesley, "this world is going to crucify you."

She was not deterred. They drove to Biot in December, arriving to relentless feuding between Walter and Torun. On Christmas Day 1960, Torun packed the children into the car and drove to Sweden, leaving Walter, Lesley, and Chester to feast on a liquor-soaked turkey that made Lesley ill. Torun and Lesley never got on well; in the fall of the next year Lesley would admit to Chester that she liked speaking to Torun "as much as I would want to speak to the devil." But as an interracial couple themselves, Chester and Lesley had to accept overtures of friendship where they occurred. Chester and Lesley hopped around St.-Tropez for the next several months while Chester stewed, disappointed that Walter did not intellectually admire him as much as he did Wright and Harrington. In an attempt to punish his friend, Chester ignored Walter's opening gala in March at Karin Moutet's Parisian gallery. The combination of being slighted by his friend and still having some financial miscues left Chester feeling "broke, outcast, put down by American publishers, ignored by English publishers, nibbled on by German publishers, only honored by the French, for almost free."

Lesley and Chester drifted apart in the spring and at one point Chester returned to the Latin Quarter and its cheap rooms. At the Blue Note jazz club he observed his expatriate twin Bud Powell, the genius architect of bebop, dragging behind his dope-pushing girlfriend. In a dismal episode, Powell, wracked by alcoholism, begged Chester for a beer.

To complete *Mamie Mason* for the Plon contract, Chester realized that he would need one of his original copies; the only one he knew of had already been deposited in the collection at Yale established by Van Vechten. He requested it and it was mailed to him. Playing with fire, he took a room in the Nineteenth Arrondissement on Rue Botzaris, in a section of Paris distant from his friends, and invited Regine to type the manuscript.

Chester and Regine shared a bond with each other in the way that prizefighters need deadly rivals for their careers. While no steadier than usual, Regine proved her value immediately by retyping the manuscript and then helping arrange for a German book contract and advance through agent Ruth Liepman for *A Rage in Harlem*. For two print runs, he was promised $2000. On the French scene, the "very pleasant" Maurice Girodias, director of Olympia Press, telephoned Chester and made overtures about a book contract. Chester decided to sell him *Mamie Mason,* which he renamed *Pinktoes,* a black male slang term for desirable white women. Although Chester was only capable of selling Girodias the rights to the English-language version of this novel, since he had already agreed to publish it with Plon, he preferred to think of the arrangements as two separate and completely distinct literary deals. On April 28 Chester signed a contract with Olympia, a press noted for its taste for pornography (Girodias had also made a small fortune issuing Vladimir Nabokov's *Lolita* when no one else would). Chester agreed to add some racy sex scenes and accepted 5000 francs, similar to what the German press had promised. He would learn shortly that the bawdy Girodias, when it came to literary business, was a hawk. *Pinktoes* was Chester's first book written and published originally in French that was not a detective story.

At a cocktail party given by New York *Herald Tribune* columnist Naomi Barry, Chester, accompanied by William Gardner Smith, was introduced to NAACP labor secretary Herbert Hill, a hard-charging thirty-seven-year-old Jewish American. Studious and tenacious, Hill had a contract from Knopf for an anthology of black writers. He presented himself as if he had all of the answers to the race problem. A former member of the Harlem branch of the Socialist Workers Party, Hill also traveled with Congressman Adam Clayton Powell Jr. as his labor advisor, and of course in New York he worked alongside Henry Lee Moon, who was now the NAACP national publicity secretary. Unmindful of the bitterness between Chester and his cousin Henry,

Hill talked affably with Chester about the projected anthology, which would be published in 1963 and called *Soon, One Morning*.

For Hill's new project, Chester fished out an excerpt from *Pinktoes*, "A Mamie Mason Party." The day after meeting Hill, Chester took him over to Girodias's office to get the chapter. Chester knew that it was unorthodox, even insulting, to offer a critique of black civil rights elites, no matter how mild or farcical, but something about Hill's style—like Mezz Mezzrow at Leroy Haynes's restaurant—indicated he would appreciate the material. When Hill returned to the United States, the NAACP man wrote Chester "absolutely delighted with the piece and certainly plan to use it." However, Hill was two-faced and cultivated Chester primarily to secure an essay from Richard Wright's estate. "I hope I am not imposing too much," he began a request, before asking Chester to intervene with Ollie Harrington and Ellen Wright for the essay. Harrington, perhaps aware of some of the other dynamics at play, had evaded Hill.

Chester also agreed to help Hill track down black writers in Europe. In exchange, he hoped for Hill's assistance in New York gathering paperback copies of his books to send to a new agent. After agreeing, the labor secretary neglected Chester's not inconsiderable request, then declined it outright. To assist with the anthology project, Chester delivered a letter from Richard Wright to his editor Edward Aswell, but Ollie Harrington, in Corsica with a girlfriend, couldn't be reached. Chester marveled at how Harrington seemed able to hold it all in balance: the Communists and the liberals, his work, his personal finances and his romances.

Planning ahead for the summer of 1961, Regine engaged the home of the vacationing Dr. Ramseger in Hamburg, where they had spent time in 1959. Chester and Regine bumped into Ellen and Rachel, the Wrights' younger daughter, and invited them to a celebratory dinner with Girodias at his restaurant La Grande Séverine. The meal, complete with house-band jazz musicians offering Ellen condolences, went so well that Chester and Regine made available to the widow and her younger daughter a summer month in Hamburg. Wright's family decided to go in August, relieving some of the antagonism in Chester's relationship with Ellen.

Chester and Regine's summertime visit to Germany was topped off by an entertaining August evening near Frankfurt with Dean Dixon, a black New York conductor who had chucked the United States to earn a living at his craft. A genius who had graduated Juilliard, finished a Columbia PhD, and been directing interracial orchestras since he was a teenager, Dixon had been told that to break into conducting in America he should try performing in white face and with white gloves. Equally outspoken about racism, Dean and Chester always had plenty to talk about. The Dixon family was celebrating Dean's appointment as conductor of the Hesse Radio Orchestra in Frankfurt. At the party Chester got so drunk that when he drove away, after the inevitable argument with Regine, he got her out of the car, turned himself over to the police, and spent the night in jail.

The drunken episode, complete with a permanent demerit on his driver's license, made for a convenient excuse to leave Regine in Germany and to return to the Côte d'Azur. In the interim Girodias had brought out *Pinktoes* and the Gallimard edition of *The Heat's On*, under the title *Ne nous énervons pas!*, had become a hit. He wrote Duhamel asking for a $500 advance on a new book and was invited to the editor's vacation home in Mouans-Sartoux, about fifteen miles from Biot. He was surprised to find a village of houses that looked rustic but contained modern plumbing, heating, and electric conveniences. Chester toured an engineering marvel, a seventeenth-century castle that had been completely disassembled, refurbished, transported to a new site, and rebuilt. The luxury of the surroundings alerted him as he approached Duhamel's modest-appearing two-story house. Although the home looked simple from the outside, Chester realized the real effort had gone into the design; there were elaborate open interior spaces, three bedrooms each with its own bath, and an open wall facing a rear patio along with a delicious vista of the surrounding countryside. Among Duhamel's trophies of modernist art was a heavy lead-coated door at the back of the house with all the titles from La Série Noire inscribed on it. In magnificent size *La Reine des pommes* began horizontally at the top corner and stretched to the bottom, "like a mighty river taking all its tributaries to the sea." Chester's heart stood "utterly still" as he shockingly recognized the small fortune that his book had generated for Gallimard and Duhamel personally. Chester would keep appealing to Duhamel throughout the fall, thoroughly convinced now that Gallimard had enslaved him.

In September Chester got a place in Mougins, near Biot. "I find that to get down to work alone in a strange city is rather terrifying," he wrote, hungover, to Lesley. Part of his new problem was notoriety, recognition in "almost every bar or café where I go" and where well-wishers plied him with whiskey and then launched into lengthy orations in incomprehensible French. He usually lunched with Walter and Torun, who was breaking under the stress of marriage and recently had deliberately driven her car into a ditch. But before Chester could get any writing under way, he became involved with Marianne Greenwood, an attractive Swedish photographer. Greenwood had photographed Pablo Picasso's art and was at work on a book called *Picasso at Antibes*. On Sunday, September 10, Chester had had a long leisurely lunch with Picasso and Duhamel on the beach in Cannes and then was treated to a tour of Picasso's formal gallery, studio, and ceramics workshop at his château in Antibes. Chester told Lesley that he had to remain in the South to protect Greenwood from a gangster boyfriend.

Chester anguished over his competing attraction to the two women. A tall, sought-after professional artist, Marianne enticed him, but Lesley was a more practical companion. He borrowed $200 from Gallimard and on October 14 dashed over to London with Greenwood for a frolic, "very much in love." Three days later they returned to Paris. Greenwood was preparing to depart for South America to take photographs for a book on the United Fruit Company with the writer Everet Taube. Chester left at three in the morning for Antibes. On his drive south, Chester, likely inebriated, hit a tree at 50 mph and "sailed over the crushed steering wheel through the windshield."

At a public hospital in Sens, Chester was told he had no significant injuries, but that he should remain a couple of days for observation. He got along so imbibingly well there that they called him "the barkeeper." News of his accident made the press. A concerned visitor was French filmmaker Dominique-Pierre Gaisseau, ushered into his room by Marianne Greenwood, who had postponed her trip to be with him. Gaisseau claimed he had been looking for Chester since he had seen the premiere of the American film *A Raisin in the Sun*, based on Lorraine Hansberry's play, at the Cannes Film Festival in May, where it won a specially created award for "outstanding human values." A quick-witted, high-strung, and risk-prone artist, Gaisseau was convinced Chester could write a screenplay more faithful to black American life than Hansberry's safe melodrama. Once, when Gaisseau had been prohibited from making a new film, he had turned his adventures in French West Africa into a book called *The Sacred Forest*. Frustrated that others on La Série Noire were making a mint with the cinematic version of their novels, Chester made an appointment to see the film director when he left the hospital. He and Greenwood cut a side deal about making a book with Harlem photographs illustrating the screenplay. Harrington drove down to Sens and brought Chester back to Paris.

Chester checked into the Hôtel Aviatic on Rue de Vaugirard. He collected $500 from Girodias on *Pinktoes* and some more money from Gallimard. Walking near Gare Montparnasse, Chester fell down in the street and had to be rushed to the American Hospital. After examining X-rays, bone specialists noticed a hairline fracture in his pelvis and confined him to bed for two weeks. Concerned about how he would pay for it all, Chester wrote Lesley asking her to request further assistance from Gallimard. Toward the end of October, Duhamel wrote, promising "I'll do what I can," but "you must understand that this is my personal money." Duhamel had heard rumors of Chester's intentions to visit the firm personally with a representative to inspect the accounts, which he believed in error. Fearing that Chester's strong sense of recrimination would irretrievably damage their publishing relationship, Duhamel sighed that, destructive as such a gesture might be, he might as well go ahead. "Once an author has got it in his head that he is gypped or something—no argument, not even proof—will make him listen to reason." Reminding fifty-two-year-old Chester of the "favors, help and friendship" which he had shown, Duhamel hoped it would turn out well, after the hospital bill was paid. His advice was more hard work. "If I show Gallimard another good book soon I might be able to convince them to make a *full* reprint of *La Reine des P.* which is the only way to settle the matter of your advance," he cautioned. Chester thought Duhamel was concerned only about "defending the honor and integrity of Gallimard's accounting department."

Gaisseau visited Chester again in the Parisian hospital, and this time he was accompanied by an American from Switzerland, six-foot-two Arthur Cohn. The president of Michael Arthur Films and brother to Harry Cohn, president of Columbia Pictures, Cohn had produced Gaisseau's recently released film *The Sky Above, the Mud Below*, a documentary of tribal life in Papua, New Guinea. The producer liked projects "out of the ordinary, enriching, and apt to be remembered for a long time." Reaching a formal agreement with Chester, Cohn and coproducer René Lafuite paid him 12,000 francs (more than $4000) to write a film scenario. Chester finally got his big-time payday. "I was beginning to feel rich."

Out of the hospital, Chester pursued his amorous connection to

Marianne Greenwood. Still on crutches, he flew to Stockholm on November 21 to spend a week with Greenwood before she sailed for South America on December 5. Back in Paris, his downhill relationship with Gallimard hit bottom. He believed that *Ne nous énervons pas!* was a "runaway best-seller," but there had been no royalties. By Christmas Chester was seeing new Swiss book-club editions of *La Reine des pommes* that seemed mysteriously absent from the statements he received from Gallimard. As a result, although he contracted with the firm to publish the French translation of *Blind Man with a Pistol* in 1970 (the first of the detective fictions to initially appear in English), he never published another original book with Gallimard again.

In order to write the screenplay, Chester took over Greenwood's apartment in Antibes. In rooms overlooking the Mediterranean, with the Italian coast sometimes in view, and an occasional hurricane forcefully lashing the shore, he lost himself in the story. Chester gave up drinking for a time to channel his energy and found his mind "so lucid and active it is overloaded with every imaginable type of thought and imagery." He told friends he was working "very-very hard" as he neared finishing the screenplay, tentatively called *Baby Sister*. He knew how dicey it was to try to write about black life and appeal to popular American tastes. "We are trying to begin it in utter secrecy," he told Carl Van Vechten, "otherwise it might destroy it." During the last days of 1961 he completed *Baby Sister*, "a Greek tragedy in blackface." Writing the play's concluding line, Chester broke into tears. Cohn and Gaisseau were impressed and wanted to rush forward, hoping to start production in the United States in March.

In the film scenario, Chester had indeed seemed to utterly reverse the story of the striving black family of *A Raisin in the Sun*. He had written a script that might be applauded by a hip audience. However, he was vulnerable to accusations from the prim blacks and whites connected to the American civil rights movement that he had created a drama of carnally fixated black depravity. One element of his

Harlem-set passion play directly appealed to the instincts of a man like Gaisseau: cannibalism. What Harlemites succumb to "when you have no food is to eat your baby sister," he wrote. Bookended by funerals, the plot featured the maneuverings of Susie, a violently cruel older brother, and Pigmeat, his protective younger brother, to keep the white police detective Fischer from continuing his affair with Baby Sister, their wanton seventeen-year-old sibling. Chester took a character like Lorraine Hansberry's Beneatha Younger or Ann Petry's Lutie Johnson and gave her a taste for skintight clothes, sex, cocktails, and nightclubs. To survive, Baby Sister must destroy the patriarchal order of Harlem—killing father, brother, and her detective lover in order to achieve freedom. In the process Baby Sister makes love to strangers, has an abortion, and is about to be sold to a pimp by her incest-fueled brother Susie, who refers to her as a "natural-born call girl." Switchblades glint in five different scenes of the drama.

Back in Paris in a stylish gray flannel suit and cashmere overcoat, Chester enjoyed the parties following New Year 1962 with his new friend the film director. He learned that during the filming of *The Sky Above, the Mud Below*, Gaisseau had become lost in the jungle but, in spite of inadequate supplies, had refused to abandon the project. Three of Gaisseau's crew died due to the director's resolve. Some professionals in the arts world wouldn't speak to Gaisseau, and often enough it was Chester's name that got them past the doormen at the clubs. Another evening—which would end with Chester, drunk and high, passing out, and Gaisseau, in the same condition, parking his car in the middle of the street and breaking the axle—they listened to Bud Powell, now fully "on the downgrade," at the Blue Note. Angry, Chester despised the cruel exploitation of this jazz giant, which seemed like tolerance. The French public didn't condemn addiction to drugs or alcohol in the same manner as Americans, but Chester saw Powell "making the white Frenchman rich and paying for it with his life." Powell, whose famous psychiatric problems and alcoholism had begun when he was viciously beaten by New York City policemen as a teenager, would be dead within a year. Three years earlier, Chester had listened to Lester Young, another supreme black musician whose music he loved but whose spirit had been shattered by the U.S. Army, school a younger saxophonist in front of Club St.-Germain: "To play jazz you must suffer," Young counseled. Young's suffering had ended in 1959, but Chester, who likened Young's saxophone to "someone laughing their way toward death," would be damned if he would let it happen to him. It also seemed unlikely. Editions Plon's French translation of *Mamie Mason* was released that winter and for several months Chester received favorable notices, sometimes being compared to Rabelais, from *Le Figaro* to *Le Revue de Paris*.

After putting Chester on a monthly salary, Arthur Cohn left for the United States in early 1962 to secure additional studio help to finance and develop *Baby Sister*. Chester returned to Antibes and worked on a new screenplay called *Back to Africa* (unfortunately, there is no trace of it). The momentum increased in April, when Gaisseau's film won the Academy Award for best documentary, although Cohn, in Hollywood, somehow managed to have the name of the prize converted to "Best Achievement in Documentary Production" so the Oscar was given to himself and René Lafuite and not to the director. The situation precipitated some distrust and bad blood with Gaisseau and thus with his friend Chester. By the end of April, Chester was writing Cohn requesting the return of his rights, terminating the contract, and agreeing to repay the 12,000 francs if he sold the scenario elsewhere.

In late spring, French producer Pierre Lazareff of the news show *Cinq Colonnes à la Une*, broadcast by the ORTF station, asked Chester to assist a French crew that would be making a short documentary film in Harlem that summer. Chester was needed to arrange the locales for the shots and, since he could understand French somewhat, help in rough translations to set up the show. Lazareff funded Chester to make it possible. Gaisseau, whose photograph adorned the cover of several major United States magazines that summer, would go at the same time to the United States to try to sell Chester's film scenario to a producer.

Brother Joe and sister-in-law Estelle visited Chester in June, on their way back to the United States after Joe's year as a Fulbright fellow in Helsinki. Joe had stepped beyond the segregated college network to take a permanent job at the University of North Carolina's Greensboro campus. Joe saw a Chester different from the threadbare outcast in 1956, when he had last visited his brother. Chester proudly ushered them over to Plon, where an editor gushed about how well *Mamie Mason* was selling. Joe praised him in a manner Chester had always badly needed to hear from his brother, whose suffering, discipline, and success he was never sure he had matched.

Chester and Gaisseau flew to the United States on June 22, 1962, Chester's first return since December 1955. They stopped by the French consulate, then went to Harlem, where Chester helped Lazareff's crew settle and make their arrangements. They stayed at the Theresa Hotel on their split mission. First, the ORTF crew would, with Chester's help, make preparations to film the documentary on Harlem life. Next, Chester and Gaisseau hoped to secure a new producer and funding to make *Baby Sister*. Gaisseau wanted to take a "semidocumentary" approach to the feature film. They would shoot exclusively on location and, even with principal characters, use an "unprofessional" cast of actors. "The important thing to me," Gaisseau told the press in July, " is that we not follow our script exactly and allow leeway to develop natural, lifelike situations and dialogue."

Chester arranged for the *Cinq Colonnes* crew to shoot scenes at Small's Paradise, now owned by the basketball star Wilt Chamberlain, as well as at the Palm Café, a 125th Street bank, a motorcycle club, and a fashion show. He was most interested in the lengthy interview conducted with Malcolm X, the dynamic, youthful Nation of Islam

minister and rising political star who had received nationwide notoriety in a 1959 CBS news broadcast called *The Hate That Hate Produced.*
Chester gravitated to the gangly, red-haired, clean-shaven minister
who roped an evangelist's fire-and-brimstone style into the service
of a street-corner, pan-Africanist theology. While members of the
Lost-Found Nation of Islam declined to participate in the civil rights
struggles of the integrationist groups SNCC, CORE, and NAACP,
they were ultraradical in a way that aligned them with avant-garde
artists who were making symbolic militant gestures. Malcolm and his
colleagues were publicly antiwhite, railing that whites were diabolical
and merited dire punishment for their crimes against blacks. When
a jetliner of Atlanta's elite had crashed taking off from Paris's Orly
Airport that spring, Malcolm X had welcomed the news at a Muslim
rally, telling his faithful that divine intervention had struck the white
race for the death a few weeks earlier of Ronald Stokes, a Muslim
man shot in the back by the Los Angeles police. Although denounced
by civil rights leaders, Malcolm X's unkind remark only proved the
axiom that all press is good press. By the middle of the summer, Malcolm X was a national force.

Impressed by his skillful manipulation of the news media and the
loud black-nationalist philosophy, Chester "got to know" Malcolm
X "well" during his summer in Harlem. Lewis Michaux, a friend of
Chester who owned the National Memorial Bookstore at 125th Street
and Seventh Avenue, introduced the two men at his shop. Malcolm
X excitedly recalled having read *If He Hollers Let Him Go* in prison.
Chester made Michaux's bookstore the headquarters for the film, and
Malcolm X enjoyed holding informal tribunals condemning western society on the street outside. Wearing his sunglasses, Malcolm X
shared the gory pictures of the slain Ronald Stokes with Chester and
Gaisseau. Malcolm X and Chester discussed and agreed upon a new
phenomenon uptown: syndicated drug sales, different from the prostitution and gambling that they both had known when they were

young. "White syndicates control, encourage, and distribute" the drugs, Malcolm X said. To the generation coming of age, which Malcolm X led, Chester appeared to be a "tough, honest, hip" man in the know and disinclined to overvalue civil rights victories. Separated by sixteen years, the two ex-cons from Midwestern, middle-class homes of light-skinned mothers and dark-skinned fathers understood each other perfectly.

While Chester did not admire the Islamized religion espoused by Malcolm X, he was delighted to find someone persuasively booming his pet beliefs: "distrusting white people" and the "only means of achieving equality is armed rebellion." A photograph of Chester, Gaisseau, and Malcolm X appeared at the end of July in the Nation of Islam's flagship newspaper, *Muhammad Speaks*. On cue, the FBI added Chester's contact with Malcolm X to the writer's briefly reopened file.

Michaux and Malcolm X belonged to the A. Philip Randolph–led Emergency Committee, which addressed Harlem's problems, and they were drawing strength from their similar nationalist messages and impulses that July. A plain-spoken, diminutive man in his late seventies, Michaux was Harlem's everyday pan-Africanist, organizing the local "Back to Africa" and "Buy Black" movements. Michaux organized protesters against the opening of a white-owned steakhouse on 125th Street. Baseball legend Jackie Robinson denounced the picketers as anti-Semitic in his weekly newspaper column, and was verbally throttled by Michaux in return. The dispute later brought intervention from Governor Nelson Rockefeller's New York State Commission for Human Rights.

The summertime grievances were topics for Malcolm X at a 2500-person rally on July 21 in Harlem Square, the locale of Michaux's bookstore and Chester's hotel. Because he addressed the audience in language foreseeing bloody Armageddon—"The fuse has already been lit, the crisis been reached and if something is not done immediately there will be an explosive situation in the Negro community more dangerous and destructive than a hundred megaton bombs"—Malcolm X both startled and provoked. Inflected by Islam, Malcolm X's pitch was not very different from Cleveland's Future Outlook League or the Los Angeles Communist Party, which Chester had grown impatient with. But what was new was the sight of educated blacks—people who worked with the NAACP or SCLC like attorney Percy Sutton, civil rights organizer Anna Arnold Hedgeman, and Gandhian pacifist Bayard Rustin—seated on the platform alongside an ex-convict as obviously ferocious as Malcolm X. The next week at the Waldorf-Astoria, Malcolm X caught the public off-guard again by loudly denouncing Los Angeles mayor Samuel Yorty on the issue of police brutality against blacks in L.A. during a question-and-answer session following the mayor's address. Was Malcolm X a confidence man, draped in the flamboyant garb of a religious cult? Or had he harnessed an organization to broadcast more effectively the observations available from the ghetto street corners, where exploitation was naked? Or was he what he claimed to be, the organic messiah, ready to lead the poor blacks in the cities to rightful reparations? Whichever one, he became ever more important to the solid citizens of the northern black civil rights movement, who increasingly sought to debate him, be seen with him, and court his favor. Chester was right in the middle and where he would remain, compelled by the idea of militantly achieving black freedom, but incredulous at the possibility of its execution.

Chester had already rendered a gangster treatment of the Muslim vogue in *The Real Cool Killers*, giving the Sheik, the key character, Malcolm's physical qualities. Even so, the nationalist militants would preoccupy his thoughts for the rest of the 1960s. He was nearly alone among his contemporaries in recognizing them at all. In the novel he was to begin once back in France, published in 1965 as *Cotton Comes to Harlem*, Chester would prepare a critique of the Garveyite back-to-Africa position, and show how a putatively black nationalist Christian

minister exploited Harlemites on the basis of black nationalist yearn-
ings. But the essence of that novel, arguably the finest treatment of
the soul-food-eating detectives Grave Digger Jones and Coffin Ed
Johnson he created, reflected his understanding of the serious but
quixotic impulse of African return for ordinary black Americans.

During his summer in the United States, striking Marianne
Greenwood made a guest appearance. Chester introduced her to his
mildly amused brothers at lunch in Harlem (Joe Jr. had just met him
with Lesley in Paris). When Chester visited Van Vechten's new apartment on Central Park West to have his photograph taken, he brought
along Greenwood as well. She recognized in Van Vechten's professional voyeurism a kindred spirit and immediately saw how he might
aid her career and began writing him. In Chester's parlance, Van
Vechten had made "an intense impression on her and she loves you."
But Greenwood was still wavering toward Chester. He had finally
met his match in terms of a woman capable of exhausting everything
that he could provide and who still yearned for more.

Van Vechten engineered a crucial meeting between Chester and
someone who was a bit more generous, the thirty-six-year-old writer
John A. Williams. A Navy veteran born in Mississippi but raised in
upstate New York, Williams had returned from the war, attended
Syracuse University, gone into the publishing industry, and, seemingly
by dint of will, forged himself into a serious novelist. Reserved and
charming but also cool and unbending when it called for it, Williams
had taken the craft of the intense, personal novel about black middle-
class life to a new height with his 1960 work *The Angry Ones*. This was
followed a year later by a novel about a heroin-addicted jazz musician
and his white friend, *Night Song*.

The year Williams met Chester was unforgettable for all of the
wrong reasons. In January the American Academy of Arts and Letters had notified his publisher that Williams had been awarded the
academy's Rome Prize, the same fellowship held by Ralph Ellison

between 1955 and 1957. Then a week later he was written that the award was subject to the approval of the academy's office in Rome. Following a perfunctory interview in February with academy director Richard Kimball, the offer was withdrawn. Williams understood that he had been disallowed because of rumors that he was married to a white woman. After receiving pressure from Williams's editor, Roger Straus of Farrar, Straus, and Giroux, the American Academy of Arts and Letters jury, which included John Hersey and John Cheever, voted to award Williams $2000 for travel, but Williams rejected the face-saving bribe. Publicly shamed by the obvious racism, the academy would suspend its funding for the Rome Prize in October.

No other serious black novelist in 1962 held as deep a suspicion of the American literary establishment as Himes, whose grim view of the publishing world and the highly selective promotion of black talent easily confirmed the painful, publicly humiliating experience Williams had suffered. Williams became convinced of the importance of Chester's work and his struggle for integrity, and took it upon himself to keep Chester's books alive.

After the French film crew finished capturing shots of churches, beauty parlors, and Eighth Avenue bars, Himes took up residence at the Albert Hotel near Washington Square and attempted to help Gaisseau sell *Baby Sister* and draft a budget for an interested producer named Joseph E. Levine of Embassy Pictures. While Gaisseau hoped to have the project as a French nationality film to cut costs, in New York the labor union laws would require him to employ a local crew. To use both a French and American crew would make the film too costly, but everyone connected to the project recognized the importance of shooting the movie in Harlem. Before arriving in the United States, Chester had been counting on Herbert Hill, whom he presumed to be an ally, to secure a low-cost, racially integrated film crew.

By then, Hill had reversed himself on Chester's chapter from *Pinktoes*, but he did wrangle a few pages of *Lonely Crusade* from

Knopf for the anthology, showing Lee Gordon's party with Communists. He was anything but an ally by the summer. In fact, he had begun strangling the film project in April. Not long after Hill had returned to the United States, on April 16, he wrote to Arthur Cohn's production company, throwing the NAACP's weight around to scuttle the project. "*Baby Sister* consists almost entirely of banal caricatures, unrelieved violence and endlessly repeated eroticism," Hill intoned. Calling the screenplay "a travesty on Negro life in Harlem," Hill charged, "It has no relationship to reality and is not redeemed by any literary values." He insisted, "This opinion is shared by all my colleagues in the Association." His activities obstructing Chester and Gaisseau were complicated by the fact that, by the middle of 1962, Hill had become an FBI informant, interested in blocking leftists from participating in the Monroe movement in North Carolina, an effort to organize armed blacks to resist the Ku Klux Klan, which had been led by former NAACP bureau chief Robert F. Williams before he'd exiled himself to Cuba. In August FBI director J. Edgar Hoover himself attempted to block *Baby Sister* by contacting the French government and asking for scrutiny and disavowal of Gaisseau because he had been in touch with Malcolm X, the leader of a "fanatical" "antiwhite organization."

Chester fell prey to an odd confluence of pressing issues. Hill cooperated with the FBI, but he did so knowing that, as a former member of the Socialist Workers Party, he himself could be exposed and have his career destroyed. At precisely the same time Hill was emerging as the national gatekeeper for black actors and workers in Hollywood. By June of 1963 Hill would make national headlines at a press conference where he stated his intentions to file formal complaints with the National Labor Relations Board to have Hollywood's craft guilds decertified for excluding black members. Continuing Walter White's fight, Hill also demanded that "the Negro" be depicted "more honestly" by screenwriters and directors in their films. The NAACP promised mass street demonstrations, and the next month more than one hundred executives convened at the Motion Pictures Producers headquarters in Los Angeles to negotiate the particulars with him. In this climate, Hill's activities had an unusual impact on the production of films like *Baby Sister*, though presenting raw material about black life—at least when written by whites—was not impossible. White writer Warren Miller's 1958 novel *The Cool World* went to Broadway (and introduced to audiences actors Billy Dee Williams, Calvin Lockhart, and Raymond St. Jacques) then was turned into a film by Shirley Clarke in 1963. That book and film made Himes appear, by comparison, a squeamish sentimentalist in his depiction of black ghetto life. By 1964 Clarke would begin discussions with Chester about filming *For Love of Imabelle*, and Lockhart and St. Jacques would be standout actors in the 1970 film of *Cotton Comes to Harlem*.

The problem with Hill helped to cement Chester's quick bond to John A. Williams. Williams had also fallen out with Herbert Hill and his anthology of black cultural stewardship. When *Soon, One Morning* was published in 1963, more than one newspaper touched on the flaw that "such important new writers as John Williams" were "somehow overlooked." In August 1963, when Hill spotted Williams in the crowd during the March on Washington and rushed over to greet him, happy to acknowledge and be acknowledged by a dark-skinned black American on that historic day, Williams told Hill that he would not "shake his motherfucking hand for nothing in the world." Card-carrying members in the brotherhood of frank talkers, Williams and Himes responded quickly and aggressively to racist slights, especially of the paternalistic sort, a common ground that brought them together.

Despite the friendship that developed with Williams, the summer visit to the United States bore little fruit. Chester, still in the habit of drinking heavily during the day and popping "blue boys" to sleep at night, was overwhelmed by the prospect of a Hollywood success.

In turn, he disturbed Gaisseau. "I suppose I offered too many suggestions for the essential necessities," Chester wrote guardedly in his memoir. In the attempt to deal with the excitement of his Harlem room at the Theresa Hotel, his face on the cover of American magazines, and Chester's persistence for "necessities," Gaisseau suffered a "nervous breakdown" and returned to Paris. Deflated by the failure to get a producer for his screenplay, and miffed at Berkley Books for not snapping up reprint rights for *The Primitive* and *Cast the First Stone*, Himes too flew back to France on August 14, retreating to Antibes.

When a rough edit of the Cinq Colonnes film premiered to an audience of influential French studio officials and celebrities on September 7, 1962, Chester walked out of the screening, displeased probably by the film's exotic view of Harlem, showcasing the dancers doing the twist and lingering scenes emphasizing "primitive" black religion at a storefront church. The footage of Malcolm X at the rally, the simmering discontent, the compulsive consumption of the bourgeoisie, were all lost. "I did not like at all the documentary film they made on Harlem," he wrote Van Vechten. But he believed that by walking out of the screening, he had "cut off" his career in Paris. He had a reputation now only with "the nobodies of the Latin Quarter."

To relieve his disgust, Chester sat down and wrote out his major objections in response to the aestheticization of blackness in the film. Himes called the essay, his first return to critical work since 1948, "Harlem, or, an American Cancer." In this thirty-five-page article he offered a richly detailed political and ethnic history of black life in New York, leading to the formation of a black Harlem. Pierre Lazareff had promised him a couple hundred dollars for the "reportage" work.

The rebuttal grew to about ten thousand words, in order to offer a succinct and accurate historical overview of Harlem, but one that would also contain startling facts, like the "$10K Cadillac driving by while poor are crawling on sidewalk." In a work that should have prepared his audience for the disaster of rioting in urban American cities that would start in July 1964, he asked the rhetorical question, "How can a negro love Harlem"? He tripped up his readers completely when he suggested that Depression-era public welfare programs like the Works Progress Administration only accented the precariousness of black life, alienating black Americans from their segregated neighborhoods, where they were always renters, always exploited by businesses. And he quoted E. Franklin Frazier ("the black bourgeoisie is a bastard class that lives in a state of nothingness") and comedian Dick Gregory ("you are a nigger, no matter what your social class") to attack the stuffed black entrepreneurs. When it was published, the essay would introduce the French-language audience to Malcolm X, whom he quoted saying gently and scholastically, "Our primary objective is to teach Negroes about their race so that they don't feel inferior to whites." After describing Harlem's origins in black migrants fleeing the Ku Klux Klan, Chester included a full discussion of "*les stupefiants*"—narcotics. There were a few other writers who had recorded what he saw—such as, perhaps unsurprisingly, two jazz-loving Jewish New Yorkers, Seymour Krim and Norman Mailer—but Chester's intellectually sharp and detailed reportage, which doubled down on what he had revealed in the detective fictions, was scabrous, lacerating news. The U.S. ghettos would not be relieved by civil rights legislation.

Believing that Pierre Lazareff could appreciate a full-blown critique, Chester was surprised and furious that the television producer sat on his hands with his Harlem essay. Chester was also uniquely disturbed by the slack pace of change in the United States, emblematized by a besieged student named James Meredith requiring 250 federal marshals to attend class at the University of Mississippi. On October 1, Chester banged out a sharply worded editorial for the magazine *Candide*. "James Meredith: It Will Take 450 Years," compared "the racists in Mississippi to the OAS," referring to the Organisation de l'Armée Secrète, the French right-wing terrorist sect, which hoped to retain white control in Algeria. Although Chester, as he wrote to John Williams, had zingers in the piece like "U.S. racists were going to win and the French racists lose," really he was still battling against the people who believed that America was swiftly changing. "It will happen, in the near future, some blacks will attend all of the schools of the U.S.," he concluded in the published editorial, "but they will be a small number that can't change the problem of education for blacks in its entirety. . . . At this rate, it must be 450 years before segregation disappears in its entirety in the South." When he hit at racist whites, Chester was in rare form. Comparing them and their OAS compatriots with Christian martyrs who preferred death to accepting the rights of blacks, he answered his rhetorical question of how the problem could be solved: "The solution is to let them [bigoted whites] die."

Chester sounded exactly like Malcolm X when the article predicted a "rain of blood" that would soothe "the poor black American exile," and his interviews and reportage work did not endear him to his neighbors in the South of France. "In trouble with the OAS," he wrote Van Vechten. "I will have to leave France for a time." While the OAS threat had to be taken quite seriously—that August, the group had tried to assassinate the French President Charles de Gaulle—Chester simply shuttled up to Paris.

The last major writing of the year was more personal. In the final days of October, Chester set down a frank five-thousand-word narrative of his life and publishing career in a letter to John Williams, such as had not been exchanged between black writers who belonged to different generations. The account, nearly a father's legacy to his son, wearied him. He also needed Williams to believe him because he was at odds with his latest U.S. agent, James Reach, who refused to release any manuscripts or books until he had been paid $500. Chester believed it possible that he might have owed his agent the money, but he also knew that it was a fantasy he would be able to pay such an amount. Instead, ever pursuing the American literary market, Chester tried to see if John Williams's agent, Carl Brandt, would take him on, and for that, he needed Williams to act as his broker. The heartfelt letter worked. When he wrote Arnold Gingrich of *Esquire* with fresh stories in "a European locale," he asked, if they were rejected, for them to be sent to his confidant John Williams in lower Manhattan.

Since Lazareff seemed disinclined to make a media event of Himes's contrasting Harlem article, with resignation and defiance Chester gave "Harlem: An American Cancer" to *Présence Africain*. The editors, Alioune Diop and Martinican poet Aimé Césaire, released it in the spring of 1963, probably seeing not a little of Richard Wright in Chester's work. Impressed by the response to the article and understanding its significance, they republished it as a stand-alone pamphlet of forty pages, complete with the story of the protest involving Malcolm X, Michaux, and Jackie Robinson. Dr. Ramseger's *Die Welt* also agreed to publish a portion in early 1964.

Chester had made up his mind to get on with the book about his affairs with Willa, Regine, and Lesley, but he was unsure whether he should fictionalize the account or write straight autobiography. He appears to have begun drafting a long piece on the romance with Fischer, which became the foundation of the second volume of his autobiography, *My Life of Absurdity*. But would Americans be interested in reading a blunt discussion about a black man's love affairs with white women? "I don't know how this will take with the American public—and this is what I must come to New York to talk about," he decided.

All roads seemed to lead back to America. He needed a new literary agent to sell the detective stories to a large firm and continue the parlay with the film industry; it didn't make any sense that he had best sellers in France and duds in the United States—everybody was twisting to the same dance craze, absorbing the same mass culture. He was also excited about the possibilities of getting further along in his romance with Greenwood, who was living in Mexico. But the move was dependent on Gaisseau making *Baby Sister* and well before Christmas Chester stopped hearing from him. The film project was dead in its tracks.

Back in Paris, he stowed his gear at 39 Rue de la Harpe, Lesley's apartment on the tourist-jammed streets between St.-Germain-des-Prés and the Seine, all the while trying to plan an encounter with Greenwood on another continent. Meanwhile, as had happened with Doubleday, Knopf, Coward-McCann, and World, Gallimard claimed that fall that Chester was indebted to them, for more than 11,000 francs. When Chester identified the misstatements on the ledgers given him by the accounting department, Duhamel wrote back a letter half-pleading that "I did my best." But the other half of Duhamel's letter threatened that if Chester's explanations did not hold up to an attorney's scrutiny, Gallimard "won't let you publish the books elsewhere." Chester fell silent with Duhamel for the next five years. He took his next detective story to Editions Plon, getting a contract for the book on December 17, 1962. Stipulating that the typescript was due by March 31, 1963, Plon paid 7500 francs for a book called *Back to Africa*. It was just enough for a flight to New York.

Chapter Fourteen

COTTON COMES TO HARLEM
1963–1965

C lean-shaven and accentuating his youth, Chester flew back to the United States on January 2, 1963, and checked into the Albert Hotel in Greenwich Village. He looked up a friend named Emile Caddoo and became mildly distracted by Emile's pretty sister, Joyce, an artist and teacher of troubled youth. At Joyce's St. Mark's Place apartment, Chester met twenty-nine-year-old LeRoi Jones, the stirring jazz critic, poet, and playwright whose string of award-winning off-Broadway plays would begin the next year. Chester was familiar with Jones from his essays on jazz, which had appeared in the magazine *Revolution* and would be collected that May in the book *Blues People*. By this time, Jones had traveled to Cuba and taken over Richard Gibson's job as chairman of the Fair Play for Cuba Committee, and he was experiencing the same sort of magnetic attraction to Malcolm X as Chester had felt in the previous summer. Jones reminded him of his younger self and the reason he'd gotten out of the United States. Jones's eye was swollen shut because he had just been poleaxed by three drunk, off-duty policemen.

During that week, Chester took Joyce with him to visit Constance Pearlstein. Formerly Constance Webb, she had briefly married C. L. R. James, had a son, and then remarried Edward Pearlstein. He emptied bottles of scotch at John Williams's place and when friends asked about other Yank writers around Paris, Chester sizzled, "What the hell do I want to see James Jones for?" (Jones was said to have made "disparaging remarks" about Chester's detective novels.) Chester insisted to Williams that Paris offered little to blacks. As Himes was hoping, an obliging Williams introduced him to literary agent Carl Brandt at a good Italian restaurant. The meeting went well and Chester, who wrote Lesley that Brandt was "considered the best in New York," forwarded all of his materials for consideration.

Feeling good, Chester gave Williams the speech he had delivered at the University of Chicago in 1948 for publication in *The Angry Black*, an anthology the younger writer was editing. After having read Williams's third novel, a black family drama called *Sissie*, in manuscript that fall, Chester believed him "at the very top of all Negro writers who have lived."

Chester even included Williams in some of his publicity efforts. Editor Allan Morrison of *Jet*, the glossy pocket-size weekly, interviewed Chester in his Sixth Avenue office and photographed him and Williams. Hoping to secure an agent to sell *Pinktoes* in the United States, Chester used the interview to sell himself. He reported having sold 480,000 copies of his books in France and he sang the tune of progress as it was then known. "One day people might cease to think of books by Negroes as Negro books but as books period." He also claimed that "Negro" writers of the day were "more fashionable" than before, and he attributed some of their success to James Baldwin, though he managed to drive home that, unlike himself, Baldwin was "practically unknown in Europe." But by the end of the short interview Chester was "very disappointed" and at odds with an American audience, black or white. "At this rate," he observed, "it will be a long time before segregation is banished."

Involuntarily he lingered in New York, waiting for decisions about paperback reprints and trying to sell a long story describing his travels in his Volkswagen in France and Germany. Admitting to himself that "my nerves are on the point of explosion," Chester produced one of his classic axioms of the American scene. The publishers "just want brothers to keep on writing about our difficulties and persecutions," he decided, "and they feel insulted by anything but our complaining about our racial injustices." He mailed an entreaty to Knopf, requesting the reprint rights to *Lonely Crusade*, and then slipped out of town.

Chester flew to Mexico's Yucatán peninsula and on January 19 made his way to the village of Sisal, outside Mérida, to reunite with the ravishing Marianne Greenwood. She was renting a cottage— really a hut with a high palm-thatched roof, although it had running water and a toilet. A Mayan Indian family next door cleaned the rooms and brought over plates of corn tortillas, fish, beans, vegetables, and chilis. Initially Chester felt guilty about stringing Lesley along, as well as anxious over the condition of his literary estate. However, he wrote competently and steadily as Greenwood struggled with her own book. Before long he would be forced to admit that "it isn't easy for two people to write in the same house." His other company besides Greenwood was a potent local brew called *pisa*, a kind of tequila. Instead of conducting a sensual love affair, he sat alone in his room and wrote his book.

As for Greenwood, she was working on a travelog, which would be published in 1965 as *The Tattooed Heart of Livingstone*. It discussed her adventures and romances in Europe and Guatemala. She admired the natural beauty of Mérida and thought Chester, with his long hair and his bushy mustache, was looking attractive and manly. Tempted to stray from an "elaborate and sometimes difficult" book, Greenwood yearned for the bedroom, the "nicer ways to pass one's time."

Their friction, compounded by jealousy, began quickly. Always excessively possessive, but this time probably right, Chester believed

Greenwood had first gone to Sisal accompanied by a Guatemalan boyfriend. She left his love life in France alone and marveled at Chester's discipline, but his formidable concentration was a source of envy. Chester himself had to confess that "things did not go well." Part of the problem stemmed from being two late-middle-aged people still aching for recognition, but nearly destitute in Mexico, constantly reminded of how near they were to success without truly having it.

During eight weeks in Sisal, Himes wrote a draft of the book he was calling *Back to Africa*, which would ultimately be published in English as *Cotton Comes to Harlem*. For the first time he deliberately revised a draft of one of the detective fictions, and the book worried him in a new way, coming as it did "sometimes well; sometimes poorly; sometimes rapidly; sometimes slowly." In the caper that would characterize the entire series, Grave Digger and Coffin Ed pursue two con men, one black and one white, to rescue the money stolen from "our poor colored people." The novel identified Chester's friend Lewis Michaux as a contemporary Back to Africa proponent, carrying forward the ideas of Marcus Garvey, and featured as its most colorful antagonist Deke O'Malley, an ex-con-turned-minister who exploits Harlemites' Back to Africa nostalgia. Chester considered "the Back to Africa program in the U.S. . . . one of the most absurd things the black people of America had ever supported," but that did not mean that he dismissed it. In the novel that offered speculative riffs on the dense meaning of jazz and introduced the competing "Back-to-the-Southland" movement organized by white con men, Chester strongly sympathized with common black people enamored of the African repatriation scheme, "seeking a home—just the same as the Pilgrim Fathers." Chester romantically portrayed the fierce feelings of ethnic pride and longing for an ancestral homeland away from the strife of racism and the history of enslavement. The pensive partner of the duo, Grave Digger, who notices the antique map upon which the bogus repatriation scheme had been based, explains his commitment to recover the lost money in similarly nostalgic terms: "'I wouldn't do this for nobody but my own black people.'" Chester's portrait in *Cotton Comes to Harlem* of sentimental longing, absurd violence, urban slang, and droll country humor would captivate swathes of black America for many decades.

One night near the end of February 1963, Chester was making love to Greenwood, when he rolled over and felt pins and needles scoring the right side of his body. The pain increased until half his body was unable to move; his face was contorted into a grimace. Shivering irrepressibly, he presumed that he had been stung by a scorpion. After a while control of his body returned and he likely understood himself to be suffering physical exhaustion and alcoholic or narcotic tremors. Headed into his fifty-fourth year, Chester was sleeping with a woman who was not petite like Willa Thompson or Regine Fischer. The next morning he struggled out of bed and tramped down the beach past the yellow Coca-Cola stands, but his strides became heavier and slower. He and Greenwood cobbled together bus fare to Mérida, to seek medical assistance. On March 1 he saw a doctor who said he had suffered "a brain spasm" and checked him into the local Catholic hospital, a group of ramshackle one-story buildings. Doctors told him never to smoke again and drink only occasionally.

Once he was admitted to the hospital he had a new problem: getting out. He was there for two weeks trying to raise money to pay the bills. He shared the narrow ward with a single other patient, one slowly dying of cancer. Although Chester limped on his right side, he rallied and managed to type out the final chapter of the novel; he mailed it to Editions Plon the week before the contractual deadline, begging for the balance of his advance. He telegraphed Carl Brandt, asking for $200, and Brandt, who by then had already sent him $50 and learned of Chester's habit of borrowing from his agents, declined to take Chester on as a client, sending a letter that frightened Chester by referring to heavy "'financial obligations.'" In a hot, ragged barracks, with an electric fan, a single sheet, and hospital food, Chester was feeling hard-pressed again, and describing his ordeal as life "on the tip of a needle." Finally, the German publisher Buchergilde Gutenberg came through, cabling $250. Chester returned to Sisal, collected his bags, and flew to New York on March 24. Greenwood wrote that she would visit New York as soon as she got some money, but they had already come to a "parting of the ways." Chester wrote to John Williams, "Marianne and I have decided that we can't possibly live together with our separate careers and our egos and without money."

In New York, Chester returned to the Albert Hotel and was soon seen by a doctor, who directed him to the Neurological Institute on 168th Street. He wrote a hasty letter that was hand-delivered to Carl Van Vechten, requesting $50 to pay the room rent at the hotel and to help him distinguish the health of his body from the health of his finances. Another letter, this one mailed to Paris, was even more unguarded and sincere. Aware that his romance with Marianne had no future, and hoping that the stable, business-oriented Lesley had not chosen another man, Chester blurted out to her, "If you are involved with someone please for Christ's sake say so." His flailing about his health and finances made Lesley more attached to him. The eldest girl in her family, Lesley had lost her adored mother, who was considered the angel of her village, as a teenager. The role of nurturer came to her quite naturally. Packard's compassionate instincts were put to the test at once because Marianne Greenwood did not give Chester up. She had learned of his relationship with Lesley and wrote to her, graphically exposing the details of their romance and, in spite of their differences making a future impossible, laying claim to Chester. While the letter caused a dramatic moment between Chester and Lesley, her rival's strong pursuit also made Chester ever more desirable.

On April 2, he checked in for tests at the Neurological Institute, including early methods of brain tissue examination, a spinal tap, and multiple X-rays. He was diagnosed as having had a stroke, and he was also suffering from hypertension, a dangerous and prevalent ailment, especially among adult African American men. Adding to the pressure, he received a letter from Knopf scotching the possibility of a release of *Lonely Crusade* in paperback unless he repaid the $2000 advance from 1947. When the tests concluded, he wound up with a prescription to treat high blood pressure and advice to reduce salt and fat in his diet. "I feel much better, almost normal. Perhaps the feeling of security in being here helps," he wrote to Van Vechten. By the afternoon of April 13, he was back at the Albert Hotel with a "clean bill of health," although after that he walked with a slight, permanent limp. *Jet* magazine reported he had experienced "partial paralysis," alerting Joe, who dropped him a mildly consoling line about his "slight indisposition."

Feeling guilty about his agent's rebuff, a devoted John Williams visited Chester daily while the money began to trickle in. A young director named Larry Kostroff decided to risk a slender stake on him, in the hopes of making a film of one of the detective stories. Chester had a short lunchtime conference with Bucklin Moon, their grievances patched up. Moon was now an editor at Pocket Books and, up to his old tricks, promised Chester a hefty $5000 for three chapters of a new book. Fifty dollars dribbled in from *Nugget* magazine for a story, and he wrote Lesley asking for money, which she sent. When Plon sent what was owed upon delivery of the manuscript, Chester selected a better room. Marianne, having scraped together the resources to fly out of Mexico, visited him briefly at the hotel. But although she showed some affectionate feeling by the gesture, Chester was disinclined to reverse himself about their affair. He resumed his visits with such friends as John Williams, Carl Van Vechten, and Joyce Caddoo.

Chester left for France, "where I am safe," on April 26. "I have discovered," he noted with some wincing, "that there is absolutely nothing for me here in the U.S." He was not convinced that life in a busy European capital was a final refuge either. After having written his story of "the lost and hungry black people from black Harlem . . . dreaming of the day when they could also go back home in triumph and contentment," he yearned to see Ghana. "I want to go to Africa," he wrote to friends, but not to work on an African book: "I just want to go to Accra and live while I am writing."

Upon his return to chilly, overcast Paris, Chester moved into Lesley's apartment. As before, having been reduced to desperate measures in his relationship with the New York publishing world meant he would have to write without the security of an American publisher's advance. In contrast, two publications strengthened his position in France, once again making him the heir apparent to Richard Wright. The *Présence Africain* pamphlet "Harlem, or, an American Cancer" was making the rounds of intellectual circles interested in the African diaspora and decolonization that spring. In May, *A Case of Rape*, Chester's playful but most concisely intellectual book, was released as *Une Affaire de viol* by a small French press sympathetic to the Algerian liberation movement, Editions Les Yeux Ouverts; translated by André Mathieu, a Café Tournon pal, it featured an afterword by the French feminist writer Christiane Rochfort. The book brought him a new audience that started to connect him more to the *Présence Africain* article than the detective fiction and *If He Hollers Let Him Go*.

A Case of Rape, his foray into France and its touchy racial politics, produced a swirling controversy. "I became very much disliked," Chester recalled. By suggesting that African Americans couldn't get a fair trial in France, the book indirectly jabbed at French racism and strong anti-Algerian bias. "All the Parisian press claimed that I was calling the French racists," he remembered. But he was helping them understand the world. *Paris-Presse* ran a headline "In Harlem This Summer It's Going to Be Hot," above an interview with him.

Toward the latter part of 1963, he noticed "a number of articles in the French press about the growing racism in France (and how un-French it is)," and his work and words contributed to "a sort of soul searching." If he did not get a best seller out of it, his publicizing the problem of racism in France during the epochal American summer of the March on Washington and the bombing of the Sixteenth Street Baptist Church in Birmingham brought him visitors by the score. By now, when he heard a knock on his door, he protected his time, shouting, "Go away!"

"People are crowding in on me and I am hoping to get somewhere relaxed and warm," he told Van Vechten. As usual, he would hustle down to Torun and Walter Coleman's home in the South of France. Before leaving, he had a visit with Thierry de Clermont-Tonnerra, the head of Editions Plon, and the marketing staff about the manuscript he had finished in Mexico. Chester insisted on a share of the royalties, "not like my other books that Plon had published" (*La Troisième Génération* and *Mamie Mason*). Like their American colleagues before them, the French publishers were unused to having an author call them dishonest; de Clermont-Tonnerra's "face fell" and the head of publicity walked out.

Chester took solace in his friendship with Walter Coleman. The two chauvinists went to the Cannes Film Festival that spring, where Christiane Rochfort was secretary, and attended some of the champagne-fueled parties on the terrace at the Bleu Bar. When Rochfort called American directors over to shake Chester's hand, and they instinctively snubbed Walter, Chester roared hysterically. Americans, he thought, would never change.

On his return to Paris, his notoriety had intensified. It struck him that he was "more famous in Paris than any black American who had ever lived." What it meant was a nonstop parade of the trivially curious, and an end to his serenity. He balanced the superficiality of the celebrity by attending the talks at the *Présence Africain* lecture halls, where the elite of African writers held discussions. Guy de Bosscheres reviewed *Une Affaire de viol* in that magazine and decided, "The purpose of this work is precisely to denounce the odious mechanism of the racist conspiracy that irresistibly leads the black man in the infernal circuit from where he will be unable to escape henceforth only by forfeiture and death."

One perk of fame was a radio broadcast that led to an invitation to tea with Clara Malraux, wife of France's culture minister, the novelist André Malraux. Chester received a note the next day from the writer "asking me what had happened," or if he and Clara had had sex. (They had not.) Meanwhile, a professor named Jacques Panijel enticingly dangled another potential film project; he wanted to bring *Une Affaire de viol* to the screen. Over drinks, Panijel, who had scored a hit with the controversial film *October in Paris*, concocted a plan to prepare a screenplay with Chester, enter a government-sponsored contest, and split the prize money for best film scenario. Chester thought it through while spending a month with Lesley on vacation in Antibes and Corsica, writing, seeing friends, and eating well.

He was getting to a comfortable place now. When Chester's friend Dean Dixon, now sought-after, returned to Paris in November for concerts, Chester took the maestro out afterward to meet the saxophone sensation Roland Kirk. With Dixon and his old buddy tenor Charles Holland, Chester was sure of himself as an uncompromising professional, a black expatriate artist. After all, he wasn't alone in his sacrifice or persecution, gargantuan as it appeared to him. Their expatriate choice seemed wise at the end of the month, when the assassination of President Kennedy exposed an instability in their country that had seemed reserved for the likes of Cameroon and Congo. Also, like France, America seemed vulnerable to being toppled by the grasping right.

In December 1963, Chester went back to his retreat in the South of France for thoroughgoing revisions of the *Back to Africa* novel, which he was now calling *The Cops and the Cotton*. From Christmas through January 7, he saw and spoke to no one, concentrating on his manuscript. Like the original in the series, *La Reine des pommes*, this book was not a potboiler. Philippe Daudy of Plon had asked for rewrites and Chester was surprised at the level of grammatical mistakes as he reworked and tightened the book. The added diligence allowed him "time to sharpen it and make the points." The detectives "express just how they, and other black people, feel in Harlem," he wrote in his regular update to Van Vechten. "It's been so long since I've worked at my occupation," he reflected, "that I am surprised to find out how well I like doing it, and how well I can write." He had hit another stride. "I am a writer and a writer writes."

Away from his desk, he dropped in on Walter and Torun, and dashed over to Nice for provisions, where fresh fish, chicken, oranges, tomatoes, and good quality typing paper were abundant and cheap. Falling into his old habit, on New Year's Day Chester drank by himself a bottle of vodka with tomato juice, until his face swelled. "Holidays always bother me," he philosophized, trying to figure out the emptiness that drove him so deeply into alcohol. Then, in a message to Lesley, he said simply, "I am a mean and evil man." But for his next project, the mature rascal had a clear vision. "I am anxious to get to work on my projected book about my life and experiences in Europe—*and that will shock* EVERYBODY."

At the end of 1963 Lesley Packard rented a duplex at 3 Rue de Bourbon-le-Château, a "fantastic location" with good markets nearby and where they could see St.-Germain-des-Prés and Place de Furstemberg underneath the window. She took over the apartment from a Smith College graduate. Chester admonished Lesley for having shared his books with the young American preppie, convinced that she represented precisely the type who had sought to demolish his career. "My books drive these people crazy," he warned his lover. "She'll make you suffer just a little, hoping it's me." He didn't complain about the apartment, with its expansive red-carpeted living room, a built-in dining room table, large bath, and an upstairs bed-room with a grand balcony. The only downside was that it was seven flights up from the street.

The apartment he would enjoy with Lesley boded good things for the coming year. In 1964 Chester would be fortunate with his many publishers. Plon got behind *Cotton Comes to Harlem* (published in France as *Retour en Afrique*), issuing such a large print run that Chester was autographing books for two days. In the spring he would learn that, following the reissue of *If He Hollers Let Him Go*, NAL would reprint new paperback editions of *The Third Generation* and *The Primitive*, and Avon would reissue *For Love of Imabelle* under its most enduring title, *A Rage in Harlem*. Also back in the States, negotia-tions got under way with Stein and Day for *Pinktoes*, and Putnam promised a hardcover of *Cotton Comes to Harlem* in 1965. The angry, bluesy humor of these unflinching books had increased their value by explaining Americans to themselves as the sharp teeth of a cruel decade were bared.

One of his visitors from the French press was a young black American reporter with a Dutch surname. Melvin Van Peebles was a self-confident novelist and filmmaker in his early thirties from Chi-cago who had landed in France in 1960. Van Peebles was capable of surviving on his own. He didn't flock to the Tournon and isolate him-self among the soul brothers, but he wasn't an opportunist mimick-ing Europeans. He was in the midst of preparing a tense, surreal screenplay about a black GI and his French girlfriend, called *Story of a Three-Day Pass*. In sync with Chester to explore the erotic energy from black-and-white pairings, Van Peebles's cinematic oeuvre would bring the legendary black sexuality and its full implications—erotic, folkloric, and militantly revolutionary—to the big screen. When *Story of a Three-Day Pass* was released in 1968, it would mark the first time a U.S. motion picture directed by a black American was distributed by a major Hollywood studio.

But in February 1964, Van Peebles climbed to the top of the stairs and, after a little impolite confusion during which Chester initially told him to shove off, the two men delighted each other in long conversation. Lesley had marching orders from Chester to interrupt a discussion after twenty minutes to free him from the legion of visitors but, recognizing a friend, Chester waved her off. Go-getters with sympathetic artistic visions, Van Peebles and Himes had independently achieved their radical political goals.

Settling down to tall glasses of *vin ordinaire* to fortify themselves against the winter wind, the Midwesterners talked about black life in Paris. When Van Peebles asked about Richard Wright, Chester called him "the greatest black American writer who ever lived." When he was asked about Baldwin, whose full color portrait had adorned a May 1963 issue of *Time* magazine, Chester used a long anecdote about the great bebop drummer Max Roach, the most political of the jazz musicians. After a show, a white man, a music producer who owed Roach's son money, stood in a line to congratulate the musician. When the producer approached the drummer, Roach hit the man in the mouth with his fist, knocked him to the ground, and kicked him with his feet. He extracted the white man's wallet and exactingly pocketed the money in question. He turned to his child. "Let that be a lesson to you, sonny," Roach was heard to say. "He must be made to see that you exist." Baldwin's two breakaway best sellers in the United States, *Another Country* of 1962 and *The Fire Next Time* of the following year, had both explicitly chosen love as the best method to transform the country into a multiracial democracy. The eloquent Baptist preacher Martin Luther King Jr. said much the same thing in his national addresses that year, but especially in his "Letter from a Birmingham Jail," touting a "more excellent way of love and non-violent protest." Theirs was a path to social reform that Chester did not share. He told Van Peebles that what he had to say to Baldwin was that he needed to prepare himself for confrontational violence, akin to Roach. Van Peebles called the interview, "Chester Himes, the Unvanquished."

Despite the fact that his detective series and satires finally seemed to be catching on in American markets, Chester ached to write what he called "a good book I suppose." A "good book" meant a long, direct narrative drawn unflinchingly from his life. But when the left-wing French press asked what he was working on, he admitted to a change of heart about the value of his detective fictions. He told them he was writing in the spirit of Dostoyevsky's *Brothers Karamazov*, Dashiell Hammett, and *Macbeth*, a "very bloody book." "I write novels, that's all," he told a reporter for Louis Aragon's highbrow Communist-y literary sheet *Les Lettres Françaises*. "There's no difference between the genres. There isn't one side so to speak, the 'detective stories,' and the other the ordinary novels. . . . I simply describe the social conditions of poor people who need to win money."

Chester and Lesley traveled to London, where he saw the film *Dr. Strangelove*, which satirized American military commanders bent on winning a nuclear war against the Soviet Union, and Chester had an epiphany to surrender to the autobiographical book he'd been wanting to write. He decided to continue the "long journey" that he had begun, fictionalizing the relationship between himself and Willa, and show the shift in the man's affection, "the love goes into pity, the pity into sacrifice."

His ambition was cooled at the end of May, when his health failed him again and he had to be hospitalized and reprioritize his physical well-being, taking the blood pressure medicines Ismelin and Hygroten. Soon to turn fifty-five, he had outlived Wright by three years. But when *Arche* magazine placed him on the cover of the June issue, with the tagline "Jews and Blacks: A Discussion with Chester Himes," he looked "handsome" and "full of life" as an admirer recalled.

In July, Harlem cracked apart, as Chester had already indicated that it must, and deadly battles with the police, looting, and arson swept the neighborhood that he had introduced to the postwar French public as the most significant and subtle hive of black people on the globe. Chester noted the black revolutionary Jesse Gray speaking of almost the same strategy that he had advocated in 1945 in the *Afro-American* newspaper: fifty thousand well-organized black men ready to die could change the nature of U.S. race relations.

Van Peebles came to him again for another article for *France-Observateur*. In "Harlem on Fire," Van Peebles compared remarks by New York police and the FBI to the effect that the rioters were simply criminals and hoodlums with "the same terms used by French authorities about 1954," referring to the Algerian uprising. The article included a short fable by Chester called "The Mice and the Cheese," his way of explaining the insincere liberal sops thrown at American blacks in pursuit of dignity in the north. Undeterred by the casualties that mounted in the violent unrest in the United States, Van Peebles and Himes considered the bloody riots a signal that "the black revolution is irreversible." Chester's views, which had trod vigorously against the opinions of both friends and enemies, would be vindicated in 1964 and made prophetic after 1967.

Chester was an offstage director of the extraordinary events unfolding in the United States, his work a conduit for the blistering attitudes of young black Americans, who were demanding either immediate full participation in the nation or their right to tear it apart. Congressional committees of inquiry would summon writers like Ralph Ellison and Claude Brown to Washington to explain the riotous summer, and soon enough politicians were waving studies declaring that black matriarchal households and emasculated patriarchs were the root cause of American racial inequality. The rage leading to violence and the crisis of black domesticity, much of it due to prejudice and economic inequality, had been Chester's bailiwick in the 1940s and 1950s—even if the anomalous robust employment years of the Second

World War, the massive suburban expansion aided by the GI Bill educating veterans and guaranteeing mortgages, and the subsequent interstate highway system had collectively made it difficult for his observations to take hold. Whites puzzling through televised images of escalating racial unrest and increasing reports exposing crushing economic inequity were wondering how the literary tradition and its custodians had been so inept at shining a light on these hidden nooks of U.S. life. Admitting that the media industry he worked for had never effectively published or distributed Chester's writing, editor Don Preston wrote to him, "I'm sure you have not really had your say, and that recent turmoils and tensions have not left you entirely unmoved, even from a distance." America was turning, somewhat, to Chester.

After the Harlem eruption, Chester gave in to his impatience to see Africa and be inspired. Needing a destination that was convenient and easy to secure entry to, he skedaddled with Lesley to Egypt for two weeks of bedbugs, nausea, and diarrhea. Most appalling to him was the obvious racism of the Arabs toward Africans. "Not only is there indefinable poverty shrouding Alexandria and Cairo, but the Arabs haven't gotten over their tradition of slave trading. In fact, the black Africans and their descendants are still slaves in Egypt," he fumed. Despite the squalor, the prejudice, and the bloody, fly-covered meat carted through the street, Chester was glad he had gotten to visit the ancient artifacts at the Egyptian Museum in Cairo, "which I consider the best museum in the world."

While Chester had convincing firsthand evidence discounting any racial panacea in parts of Africa itself, by October he had discovered in Paris "that racism has greatly increased her [sic], like the number of automobiles and the standard of living." He mused, "I'm wondering where I can go now." He found himself unsatisfied with his visits to the Côte d'Azur and dissatisfied with his homeboy Walter Coleman. Walter held Torun, a talented, pretty, successful woman greatly attractive to Chester, in a trance it seemed. But now Walter acted "as bad as those Egyptians, but in a different way." Chester began to think of Walter as "a French uncle tom," a black man who praised whites without the idea of a reward. As for the way Chester saw himself at the same time: "I'm an evil, highly sensitive, unsuccessful old man—but I am not an American Negro in the usual connotation of the word . . . unless there might be some resemblance to Malcolm X." Publishers were recognizing that fact. On the recommendation of John Williams, Seymour Lawrence, vice president at Knopf—the same firm he was still disputing charges and the copyright to *Lonely Crusade* with—wrote a friendly letter to see whether he had written his memoirs, the project that Chester admitted to having held "in the back of my mind for some time."

Replacing some of his longer standing friendships, Chester met that October a vibrant young black man fresh to Paris and with an accent and a manner that were difficult to place. Cosmopolitan and sure of himself, he spoke English like an American, Spanish like a South American, and French with ease. Carlos Moore was a Cuban, born to Jamaican parents, who had gone to high school in New York, and been introduced to the Harlem Writers Guild by the singer and poet Maya Angelou. In high school he had helped to organize a small insurrection of February 15, 1961, at the United Nations, protesting the organization's involvement in the capture and murder of Patrice Lumumba. Daring, bright, and impatient with world affairs, Moore had returned to Cuba in 1961 and joined the Castro government, until his cries of racism within revolutionary Cuba caused him to become an object of persecution. By late 1963, he was forced to flee Cuba for his personal safety, finding refuge first in Guinea's embassy before making his way to Egypt.

In Egypt Moore had befriended David Du Bois, the stepson of W. E. B. Du Bois, and Elijah Muhammad's son Akbar Muhammad, who shared the work of their hero, William Gardner Smith. Then Moore made his way to Paris and started working on an article

about Fidel Castro's racist policies, particularly the suppression of
the Yoruba religion, an important cultural force in Cuba and Brazil,
where numbers of Yoruba had been enslaved. In Paris, he was welcomed by Ellen Wright and introduced to Smith. Impressed by the
young expatriate, Smith ushered Moore to meet Chester Himes, the
writer Smith believed the most talented in France, profoundly anti-
Communist, and an arch advocate for black freedom. Moore recognized the name. As a boy in Havana he had rescued a paperback book
from the trash purely on account of its intriguing cover, which seemed
to feature a black man twisting the arm of a white woman. He proceeded to read *If He Hollers Let Him Go.*

Chester welcomed Smith and Moore during a time of crisis, surprise, and excitement. *Retour en Afrique* had become a best seller in
France. The OAS kept threatening to topple de Gaulle's government,
causing a heightened military presence in Paris. And because of the
flood of people still disturbing him as well as the threats from the
OAS, Chester's friends used a special combination knock on the door,
so he'd let them in. At first, to Moore, Himes was "unfriendly, very
savage, dangerous" and "viscerally anti-Communist." But Himes liked
Moore at once, partly because, Moore was a dark-skinned man proud
of his heritage and that instinctive pride reminded Chester of his own
father's attempt to manage in a world of strong skin-color bias, from
blacks as well as whites. He read the "wonderful" essay Moore was
working on and determined to help him publish it.

True to their politics, Chester and Trotskyite William Gardner Smith quickly got into an argument about the appropriateness
of socialism for blacks. "Chester had this thing about communism
wouldn't work for black people, so he and Bill Smith were always
arguing on this issue," Moore remembered. "Chester was explaining
the manipulative attitude of Marxists and Communists," and Smith
dissented, although there was a high degree of affection between the
two men. The year before Smith had published *The Stone Face,* a novel

expressing deep solidarity with the struggle for Algerian independence and featuring a "bitter and hermetic" character based on Chester who would emerge "from his apartment now and then to drink heavily and launch an ironic tirade against the United States and the white world in general." In an autumn that included discussion of the far-right militarist Senator Barry Goldwater, the Republican Party presidential nominee, Moore observed that "Chester was a very bitter, bitter, bitter person." When the conversation shifted away from politics, Chester told young Carlos that if he wanted to write, he had to stick to his artistry in the same manner in which a boxer boxes or a professional athlete trains. To make his point, Chester described the afternoon he took *The Third Generation* to a publisher and was turned down because the book was "too sad." Rejection and punishment were a part of a writer's training regimen.

That fall Chester was in his best position to laugh at the difficulties of the past. On November 4, after its French success, U.S. publishers Putnam (hardcover) and Dell (paperback) split the rights to *Cotton Comes to Harlem*, offering Chester $7500 on signing and another $7500 on publication in February 1965. It was his biggest payday ever. In January 1965 he would conclude a deal on *Pinktoes* with Stein and Day for $10,000. After publication it would become his first novel to earn royalties beyond its initial advance, and, as a Dell paperback, it would climb onto the best-seller list. He wrote to Van Vechten, quite happy that "the American publishers have forgiven me." On American bookstands he now had the paperback reprints of *If He Hollers Let Him Go*, *The Third Generation*, *A Rage in Harlem*, *Cotton Comes to Harlem*, and *The Primitive*. Most sensationally, *Adam*, a French men's magazine published by the creators of *Vogue*, focused their November 1964 issue on race in America and the riots in Harlem. A full-color photograph of Chester, his chin down and his penetrating eyes slanting in fury, was on the cover of the magazine, "displayed in the place of prominence on every newsstand in Paris, north, east, south and west." Vainly in love with his magazine cover, which made him look like a sex symbol as much as a man of mystery, and which casual observers at first assumed to be Egyptian president Gamal Nasser, Chester knew a heightened level of fame. "After that everybody knew me by sight." He framed the cover and hung it in his study.

Chester's affinity to Nasser of Egypt or Malcolm X of Harlem became more apparent in late fall. In early 1964 Malcolm X had left the Nation of Islam and since July he had been traveling through Africa and the Islamic Middle East as a kind of minister without portfolio of black revolutionary nationalism. In November, from Ghana, Malcolm X contacted Ellen Wright to prepare for his visit to France, which was his final stop before returning to the United States. Ellen Wright contacted Carlos Moore, who had attended the Nation of Islam's Harlem mosque and seen Malcolm X speak in New York. Moore went to Himes and the Frenchman Robert Sine, a cartoonist who had helped hide Algerian freedom fighters in safe houses, to strategize about the best way to defend Malcolm X from violent attack while in Paris. The black nationalist would be defended by half a dozen bodyguards from Guadeloupe and Martinique and, Chester suggested, hidden at the villa of the jazz singer Hazel Scott.

On November 22, Malcolm X arrived in Paris and went to Ellen Wright's house, where he met Carlos Moore for the first time. Moore took him to the Café Realis, switching his orange juice with Malcolm X's, worried that it might have been poisoned. Needing to discuss the security he had planned, Moore casually remarked to Malcolm X that they do so at Chester Himes's home. Malcolm X replied, "Chester Himes is here?" surprising Moore, both that he knew the writer and was delighted to visit. After Malcolm and one of his young bodyguards climbed the seven flights of steps and made the secret knock and Chester opened the door, the two friends fell into each other's arms laughing. Moore was suddenly in the presence of a Malcolm X "that few people had known," a man who started swapping uproarious Harlem tales with Chester.

Their discussion swiftly reached a serious vein. Malcolm fell silent for twenty minutes while Chester, glass in hand, described his experience in Cairo and Alexandria and the antiblack racism of the Arabs. Chester emphasized his points about unreliable Arab partners saying, "Carlos knows this. These are slave traders." Committing himself to establishing a chapter of Malcolm's new group, the Organization of Afro-American Unity, in Paris and prepared to give his life for Malcolm X, Moore was surprised by the unreserved barbs. To Moore, Chester's mocking disbelief in the legends of ethnic, religious, or social-class solidarity was "way out . . . he was so anti-Arab, anti-Communist, anti-Muslim." Chester continued to underscore the perfidy of Arab Muslims and professional Marxists alike, pointing to his young comrade Moore, who had to leave both Cuba and Egypt on account of his color and respect for African culture. "Carlos lived it," Chester said over and over, referring to the racism of the Cuban Marxists and the Arabs.

Chester's chorus to Malcolm X was "You're being gullible . . . totally gullible." Part of their discussion dealt with left-wing allies in armed revolutionary struggles where Malcolm X was trying to organize assistance, such as in the Congo. But Chester kept belittling the possibility of alliance with the Communists. "It won't work," he badgered the minister, "These people are no good." Years after these meetings, Moore would write to Chester in praise of the "beautiful things" that the younger militants gleaned from Chester's worldly tutorials: "a refusal to be caged in by epithets, ideologies, useless "isms," and the constant search for truth, even at the cost of personal solitude." For people born during the 1940s like Moore, Chester represented a unique form of independence and defiance, a life that in its own way was political art. As one of his admirers would say in 1970, "we are where we are because you and other cultural independents . . . you all had the integrity to give us a book of records."

When they adjourned, Malcolm X was more at ease, but also somber. "They're going to get me, Chester," he confessed wearily. After they had departed, Malcolm X asked Moore about Chester's diatribe, deeply impressed. "I talked to him and said that Chester was correct." For Malcolm X, his trip abroad—meeting with black expatriate writers working in the Nkrumah government in Ghana like Julian Mayfield and Maya Angelou, then Himes and Moore, followed by a meeting with Aimé Césaire and Alioune Diop—was a turning point. Moore and Himes proved accurate in their predictions for Malcolm X. An hour after Malcolm X left the apartment, someone mounted the seven flights of stairs and rapped hard on the door several times. Chester and Lesley silently hunkered into the couch, waiting for the unannounced visitor to leave. It was thirty minutes before they heard footsteps going back down the stairs.

The next evening, Chester and Lesley attended Malcolm X's lecture at the Sorbonne, with Moore translating him simultaneously into French. The lecture was partly arranged by *Présence Africain,* and Malcolm X presented himself as the leader of Organization of Afro-American Unity, working as a "bridge between the peoples on the African continent and their African descendants in the Americas." Malcolm X held out the possibility of French exceptionalism—France was praiseworthy because she refused to be an American "satellite." He suggested that Americans were merely carrying out the imperialist mandate put in place by Britain more than a century ago. The U.S. government, he advised his audience, was incapable of world leadership. "She's morally bankrupt," he insisted, "especially those at the helm." He warned his listeners against the notion that somehow a new dawn had arisen concerning the issue of racism; instead he reminded them of the pressures of World War II and British and

French decolonization that had led to legal change in the United States. The overtures made by administrators like John F. Kennedy and Lyndon Johnson were strategic. "They want to Americanize us for fear that now we might become Africanized," he said.

When asked how he felt about black and white romance, probably with friends like Chester in mind, Malcolm X said, "Whoever a person wants to love, that's their business . . . their personal affair." Even closer to home for Chester, Malcolm X scoffed at the African American obsession with their European ancestry, saying "it's not a status symbol anymore to be running around talking about your Scotch blood." And Carlos Moore, who continued to serve as Malcolm's lieutenant in France for the next three months, observed that Malcolm was convinced by the conversation with Himes the day before. "In no country has the Black man ever come to the top, even in your so-called socialist and Marxist and other type societies."

Three days before Christmas, Chester sadly learned that Carl Van Vechten had died in his sleep. He was eighty-four. If Chester typically felt like a fervent, uncompromising Malcolm X, in his personal life he had needed to know that it was possible to have sustaining friendships with white people like Van Vechten. Solicitously courteous until the end, Van Vechten had written him in the first week of December, congratulating him on completing *Cotton Comes to Harlem*. Chester had written back that he hoped the legal wrangling over *Pinktoes* would end soon and an American edition would be brought out, but certainly the hard years seemed past. Chester telegrammed Van Vechten's spouse, Fania Marinoff, in earnest: I AM DREADFULLY SORRY. MAY I HELP?

The new year of 1965 brought little ease. Malcolm X was correct: Chester would not get a chance to see him again. Malcolm attempted to return to France on February 9, to another gathering held by the OAAU-Paris group. At the airport, the police detained him for two hours before declaring him an "undesirable" who would cause violent demonstrations and sending him back to London. The authorities referred to his November 23 lecture as evidence. Moore talked by telephone to Malcolm X, who was stranded in England, and read the speech that Malcolm X had planned to make at the gathering.

Chester believed that the French police prevented Malcolm X from entering to avoid the scandal of having him killed on French soil. Malcolm X concurred that he was being targeted for death by American governmental agents, telling the journalist Alex Haley, "the more I keep thinking about what happened to me in France. I'm going to quit saying it's the muslims." Back in the United States, Malcolm X's house in Queens, New York, was firebombed on February 14, nearly killing his children. A week later, on February 21, Malcolm X was shot dead in front of his family by Nation of Islam gunmen at the Audubon Ballroom in New York, with several undercover police agents on hand. For several years Chester had believed that the climate in France was becoming more racist, and the public turning away of the younger man whom he admired and whose background reminded him so much of his own would prove to him that France was no western exception. He was ever more determined to leave.

Chapter Fifteen

A MOOR IN SPAIN
1965–1972

The horrifying assassination of Malcolm X caught Chester up with his biological age and years of hand-to-mouth living. Graying at the temples and in his mustache, slurring words, and struggling a bit more in his gait, he couldn't dodge the look now of an elder statesman of black literary affairs. Chester too had cried out against racial oppression, and if he had not quite created the menacing enemies of Malcolm X and Richard Wright, certainly he had stimulated fear. But something changed, as he no longer casually sought political enemies, even as he felt chased more ardently than ever by admirers. The man who tirelessly pursued a fling, ordered his liquor by the case, and battled every taunt had retired.

In the early months of 1965, Chester's main problem was unconnected to the demise of the militant leader. He had to resolve a legal problem brought on by his having somewhat knavishly signed contracts for *Pinktoes* with the American publishers Putnam and Dell after Maurice Girodias's Olympia Press published an English-language edition in France. Complicating matters further, the American press Stein and Day bought Olympia's list and planned to bring *Pinktoes* out in the United States. Chester reached a signed agreement with Girodias and Putnam and Stein and Day on January 29, 1965: Putnam would publish the trade hardcover edition of *Pinktoes* in the United States, and Stein and Day would handle all subsidiary rights. Dell would produce a *Pinktoes* paperback a year later. Although Chester and Girodias were each paid $10,000, he could not have anticipated that the book, about ten years after its drafting, would become a top seller. The New York publishers took out advertisements with impish slogans like "All that most middle-class Negroes want is status and white women."

Since he had the money to live wherever he liked to, Chester took a studio in Cannes at the Palais Rouaze and settled into work on his latest Harlem thriller, *Blind Man with a Pistol*. Once he had described his writing process to Melvin Van Peebles as putting 220 sheets of paper on the left side of the typewriter and then concluding the story as the pile dwindled. Success had raised the bar. "My novel moves all right," he wrote Lesley, "but it is not swinging. I like to both read and write novels that swing." Finally he swung into eight pages of the new work and he could see that the typical anatomy of the detective story was inadequate to address his needs. *Blind Man* read "like a cross between *La Reine des pommes* and *Pinktoes*," or a book that was moving away from a mysterious killing followed by a resolution to a book featuring a sequence of roughly connected episodes. He would "let it go and see what happens." *Blind Man*, a roundabout murder mystery satirizing the militant power movement and the exotic power of black sexuality, was completely unlike the other novels featuring the detectives Grave Digger and Coffin Ed.

Always requiring heavy reassurance by mail that he was on the mind of any current girlfriend, Chester was dealing with a new sort of loneliness too. He now pressed for a permanent tie. "You should marry me, Lesley," he wrote, knowing he had not yet been able to afford to pay for the divorce from Jean he had proposed in 1956, but wanting to ensure her caring for him. He also did not want to be made a fool of by rumors that she was having other lovers in Paris.

In February he saw a *Les Temps Modernes* article he liked that had been written by René Micha. "The Parishioners of Chester Himes" praised Chester's detective books as a technical achievement beyond his earlier fiction. Complimenting Duhamel's thought concerning the power of the absurd, Micha recommended the books because they were unconcerned with bitter resentment and nineteenth-century moralizing:

> a humorous catalog of Harlem painted one could say by a Flemish or a Dutch: which shows in turn the garden of delicacies, the triumph of death, the miracles, the proverbs, the games: not to make horror but to make laughter. More satisfying from the aesthetic point of view than from the moral view: allowing illumination which is not at all from grace, which is from the *pittura brillante.*

Chester was now officially addressed by the French left intellectual scene, at roughly the same time that he had the economic wherewithal to become something more than a prole. Undeniably on the ascent with his Putnam advance, the largest single payment he had ever received, he started scanning car advertisements, determined finally to purchase the most exclusive of English automobiles, a Jaguar. Now, as he neared completion of the new novel, he rewarded himself with a Greek holiday. Draped in a shantung silk suit and Italian leather shoes, Chester took Lesley to Rhodes on May 1 and then to Crete, where they spent two weeks feasting on roast kid and honey-covered yogurt and puttering around at the excavation of a Heraklean temple. He had his brief moment of luxury appropriate to an Achillean hero.

In the Athens airport, Chester left a manuscript on a seat in the lounge and forgot it while boarding. He never saw it again, although Lesley tried to bolt from the plane to retrieve it. The man known for sending a table load of dishes to the sidewalk when he wasn't seated quickly enough at a café had become uninspired by physical activity. Lesley would double up on tasks. As Van Peebles would crisply report, there was a strong functional element to the deepening relationship with Lesley: "Chester needed a fucking nurse."

Chester and Lesley returned to Nice to find Walter and Torun separated and, when they did stumble across the couple, the pair were engaging in bitter, sometimes violent fights. Although Torun had visited Chester at his studio apartment alone, they had remained chaste friends. While at fifty-five he had better control over his sexual impulse, she gave him one final seductive taste: Chester, Lesley, and Torun together sunbathed nude on her terrace. "I hated to give up the pleasure of looking at her," he wrote after the neighbors complained. Torun left Walter in Nice and drove to Paris with Chester and Lesley, where she planned to return to Sweden. Always fond of the underdog, in Paris Torun met and quickly took up with a young black guitarist from Detroit named Charles who had gone tone-deaf. Meanwhile, Chester and Lesley took another apartment, on Rue d'Assas.

Before the end of winter, Chester could also see that he had something of a hit on his hands with the U.S. publication of *Cotton Comes to Harlem*. The detective series, which he had considered in the beginning as "cheap," had won over the critics. The *New York Times* now decided he had an "extraordinary series." In Los Angeles, where there would be a catastrophic explosion of violence that summer in Watts, the work was considered beyond simple genre fiction, and likened to the edgy intellectual humor of black comedian and civil rights star Dick Gregory, who also had had a hand in instructing Malcolm X. "More important in this book than its entertainment value is the social comment it makes throughout," wrote the *Los Angeles Times*. "In this picaresque novel of crime and violence, Himes has employed a plot that enables him to speak out in an oblique way on some of the Negro problems current in this country." The only problem was that *Cotton Comes to Harlem*—like the reissued *The Heat's On* after it, as well as *Run Man Run* several years before—sputtered in hardcover sales; what kept him in good graces at Putnam were the paperback deals for these three books, which turned "losses into a modest profit." Genre fiction aimed at a mass market was destined for paperbacks.

Back in Paris, he and Lesley made themselves comfortable. He was contacted by Bill Targ, his old editor from World, who was now the editor in chief at Putnam, and learned that Targ was marrying a young literary agent. Rosalyn Siegel came to Paris and she and Chester went to dinner, where Chester marveled at the "quick, sharp, sexy" and "good looking blond businesswoman." He thought that Rosalyn would be fiercely loyal and tireless on his behalf, "just the type of agent I needed." Almost as surely, she created the terms for a renewed friendship between Chester and Bill Targ, after the *Third Generation* misfire and the aborted story collection *My People, My People* in 1954.

Chester traveled to London to pick up his sand-colored 1966 Jaguar MK10. The car cost more than £2000. Within a few days of returning to France he had dinged it up, but this swift ("faster than any car I had ever driven") large auto that stopped traffic made his point. Success was at hand. Chester and Lesley turned over the new Rue d'Assas apartment to Melvin Van Peebles, who had just won a French award for an original screenplay, the same prize for which Jacques Panijel had tried to submit *Une Affaire de viol*. Van Peebles would also write a graphic adaptation of *La Reine des pommes* for the French satirical magazine *Hara Kiri*, published in June 1966.

Piling their belongings into the luxury car that fall, Chester and Lesley drove to Copenhagen. They rented a town house in Holte, an outpost eighteen miles north of Copenhagen. With his new common-law wife, beautiful car, and cash, Chester succumbed to the more boorish element of his personality. At a succulent meal with a painter named Herb Gentry and his circle of friends, Chester told the crowd that he had not even a dilettante's concern about the quality of his art or its political dimensions. "I don't write for money accidentally," he lectured, "it's my main purpose." Continuing, he said that he wrote "just for money, to buy a Jaguar." His guests had expected a more delicate inspiration, and Chester continued to exalt wealth until everyone felt uncomfortable and left. After so many years with so little to show for it, he refused to apologize for good fortune.

He was also more comfortable with his crude parts. When he and Lesley proudly received a work of art from their friend Romare Bearden, the Harlem-based painter famous for his collages, Chester drowned it in varnish. He similarly ruined a bottle of prime champagne at a party by dumping it into a punch. There was a gauche quality about him, a streak of unsophistication, linked to having been bred in the rural South, and come to adult maturity in prison.

The same ragged edges enabled him to maintain the salacious fawning after Torun, whom Lesley heartily disliked. Nonetheless, he and Lesley took off for a "rugged" Christmas in Sweden with Torun and Charles at Torun's family's farm, southeast of Malmö.

When Putnam brought out the novel *The Heat's On* in January 1966, Chester received applause. Name recognition, book sales, and the tensions before a summer that would bring more rioting would make this story of a speedball-shooting albino giant appeal to a wider readership than ever before. "In its wild funhouse-mirror way a powerfully contemptuous picture of a venal and vicious world," clucked Anthony Boucher. Chester's writing hadn't gotten better, but the *New York Times* critic of crime and suspense tales no longer ribbed him for creating hyperboles for European audiences. Back in 1959, unable to ignore Chester, Boucher had erected a special category of disdain for him. "I have a feeling [Chester's characters] would be denounced as chauvinistic stereotypes if they were written by a white," he had suggested about *The Crazy Kill*. In America, if there was no higher praise for a writer born Negro than to claim they had transcended their race, there was no stronger criticism than to claim a black person was demanding the right to do something from which whites were excluded. Typically Boucher had liked to give Himes a slight brace of adjectives: "perverse blend of sordid realism and macabre fantasy-humor"; "shocking, grotesque"; "turbulent, nightmarish, sometimes harshly comic." But by 1966 Chester's naturalistic arguments of black bitterness in standard English had pierced white literary circles. Now they began to see Chester as "underrated and underpublicized," and they were willing to understand something else about his work that had been there all along, the point that he "tempers anger with humor." So Boucher had espied the new land for Himes when he called *Cotton Comes to Harlem* "the wildest of camps—grotesque, macabre, black humor (using 'black' in a quite nonracial sense)."

One of the people reading Boucher's assessment was the film producer Samuel Goldwyn Jr., son of one of the founders of M-G-M. In 1944 Chester's fortunes had nosedived when Jack Warner determined that "niggers" didn't belong at his film studio. More than twenty years later, in late fall of 1966, Goldwyn took an option to film *Cotton Comes to Harlem*. Goldwyn had first come across Chester's name in a biography of Ian Fleming, the creator of the James Bond novels, who died in 1964 and had admired Chester Himes. Then Boucher's swirling adjectives in the *New York Times* caught his attention, and Goldwyn plucked a few books from the shelves. "I'm convinced they will make superb, unusual thrillers that also will be gallows humor at its best," Goldwyn told the press after inking the deal in December. Chester was delighted and wrote back to Goldwyn suggesting that he secure Claude Brown, author of *Manchild in the Promised Land,* America's angry young black memoirist, to write the screenplay. Although the film industry was notoriously labyrinthine and fickle, especially concerning financial arrangements, if the deal went through, Chester would reap a considerable financial reward.

Lasting fame and financial success had arrived later in life. By now Chester was achy. He checked into a hospital when he got a cold that winter, only to discover that he was really bothered by arthritis. He was hobbling around, unable to carry anything heavier than the groceries, and relying more than ever on Lesley for the necessities of daily life. In 1966 they would go down to La Ciotat, taking a ferry from Sweden and driving through East Germany on their way to Switzerland and France. Chester reunited with Daniel Guérin, rented the main house, Rustique Olivette, where the artists' colony formerly had been housed, and hosted a "sumptuous feast." In a warm house with a roaring coal furnace and plenty of bouillabaisse to eat, Chester turned seriously to his latest project, his autobiography; he would poach from what he had already attempted in *The Way It Was*, the novel describing his relationships with three white women.

Patricia Highsmith wrote him from London, letting him know that she had reviewed *Cotton Comes to Harlem* for the *Times Literary Supplement*. Surprisingly to Chester, she began the review by admitting the fact of racism. As an "American Negro, one can understand why he chose to live in France," she allowed, while noting that he was no longer wielding the "hatred" of *If He Hollers Let Him Go* days. Now that he was "mellowed," making money with the detective stories and poking fun at Harlem high society in *Pinktoes*, Highsmith felt that he had become an artist. While Chester was yet "concerned with the Negro's plight," and although "Mr. Himes's underlying violence is still with him," he had reached a new plateau for her and those she represented: he was a "novelist." "It is his value as a writer, and it makes this book a novel, that he jests at all of it, makes stiletto social comments, and keeps his story running at the speed of his Buick 'Roadmasters' in the days of yore." Nearly twenty years later, she wanted to let people know that she knew the kind of car Chester had once driven. In 1965 and 1966, Chester would make almost $50,000, his best earnings ever for a two-year period. Now he was a member of the club, and the independently wealthy Highsmith was solicitous, as she would continue to be for the rest of the decade.

The spring at La Ciotat was pleasant, with trips to see a jazz band led by Roger Luccioni and slurp *crème de cassis* cocktails on a yacht owned by Roger's father, the proprietor of a large Bandol estate. Chester was visited by Alan Albert, a Jewish French writer who had published critiques in *Présence Africain* and masqueraded as a black person, apparently a ploy to help him publish a novel. Daniel Guérin took Chester and Lesley to swank restaurants along the coast and Chester was "beginning to enjoy France for the first time." New followers took inspiration from his work. A young black New Yorker named Kristin Hunter wrote a novel about housing exploitation called *The Landlord* and dedicated it to Chester. Closer to the urban turmoil that would engulf America shortly, the young black Chicago poet Don L. Lee, a legend in the making, published a poem "Understanding but Not Forgetting," that was "about my mother whom I didn't understand but / She read Richard Wright and Chester Himes and / I thought they were bad books." Chester's years priming the pump for black activist-artists had begun to yield results as he moved ever further from the fray. Later in 1966, he and Lesley rented a mud-walled two-story farmhouse in Aix-en-Provence, where they were surrounded by the lush French countryside and a town teeming with cafés and well-stocked food stores plentiful with wine. "It was the first time I had really lived as I wanted," he remembered.

Living as he wanted and dealing with the arthritis and tooth troubles made him more cantankerous. Chester could be generous from time to time, like when the old-timer Jay Clifford stopped by for a drink, but was mean with everybody else. Carl Van Vechten had warned John Williams back in 1962 that "people say bad things about [Chester] because he doesn't like most people and he shows it," but Chester was living up to his reputation and the friendship with Williams, who had been slated to visit Chester in Paris in late October 1965 but had a travel mix-up, would soon suffer. Walter Coleman came by for the big catered feast of New Year's 1966 with his new Polish wife, but Chester's attitude showed brittle disappointment. Now he feared his creativity and work ethic were lost. After the days of writing with his typewriter on his knees in a car, or in longhand at a café, he now brooded listlessly in his ample studio, trying to compose, but "nothing jelled." He found that the thrill of writing the racially explosive work had waned once he had landed better deals and had domestic tranquility. "Once upon a time I could run across a sentence in *If He Hollers Let Him Go,* or *For Love of Imabelle* that would thrill me like writing them had. But no more. I was thrilled by driving my Jaguar 125 miles per hour."

Chester's anxiety extended to the screenplay he was sweating over for the film version of *Cotton Comes to Harlem.* Goldwyn had written him that he wanted more from the novel's villain Deke O'Malley, "a wonderful character." "As I'm sure you know," the producer advised Chester, "this kind of melo-dramatic movie is often as good as the villains in it are." Goldwyn also felt strongly drawn to the commingling "quality of violence and wacky humor with its underlying seriousness." If Chester didn't want to botch the possibility of making the film, with its possible payday and acclaim, he would have to continue to work on the screenplay.

Taking a break from his obligations, Chester plotted a speedy trip to Spain, where he sought relief from the French winter. It was also an excuse to get into the Jaguar and drive. In a journey of notable scenic beauty, he and Lesley sped down the Spanish coast, walked into Gibraltar, and then hurried back to Aix. Chester seemed on the verge of living the life of a successful tourist. But in April 1967 he had a characteristic experience in France that sweetened his thoughts about the Spanish countryside. He went to the dentist, who, before making any inquiries, pulled his front tooth, which had had serious and costly recuperative work. When he learned that the patient was the famous writer Chester Himes, the dentist apologized for resorting to methods reserved for the indigent. Chester felt the sting of being a black man in France. "That was my entire life in France; I was treated like a nigger until the natives recognized me and then I became a celebrity and the natives tried to make up for the damage they had inflicted."

As before, he needed the resources of home. He arrived alone in New York on May 2 for dental work and business. Chester had all of his teeth pulled after the dentist confirmed their poor condition. Looking as if he had gone a few rounds in a boxing ring, Chester awaited his dentures and stared into the utter erosion of his youth and vitality. When the false teeth arrived in June, they cut into his gums for a couple of days, but he was pleased with the job.

Also that spring, the *New York Times Book Review,* which he considered his nemesis, solicited a couple of paragraphs describing which of his books he would most enjoy rereading. Always eager for U.S. press, Chester had responded with alacrity. His reply was in the June 4 edition, along with others from Kurt Vonnegut Jr., Isaac Bashevis Singer, and John Updike. In what was Chester's last essay for the highly literate American public, who saw little of the social critiques he had published in France in the early part of the decade, he would claim, "It has always been my opinion that we American Negroes are one of the most sophisticated people in the history of mankind." He defined his terms: sophisticated as in deprived of original simplicity, complicated, refined, subtle. Chester boosted his new favorite among his works, *The Primitive,* and punished Willa and her class in the process. He had written the book "while living with an American woman socialite, graduate of Smith College, descendant of the Pilgrims, in a state of near destitution . . . on the hot, dirty square at the foot of the steps in Deya, Mallorca." If *The Primitive* had not fully reached an American audience, he would yet find a way to drag America's best and brightest through his own brand of blackjack mud.

Chester had reversed the stereotype. "Believing that this cultured woman with whom I lived and this other white woman of whom I wrote were more primitive than I, it amused me to write this book, and it still amuses me to read it," he offered. He gloated about having the affair in 1954, the year of the *Brown v. Board of Education* Supreme Court decision. He cast whites like Willa Thompson and Vandi Haygood as primitives. "Being largely autobiographical (I did not kill the white woman, however gladly I might have), the book acted as a catharsis, purging me of all mental and emotional inhibitions that restricted my writing." But with the climate in the United States boiling—urban riots that summer of 1967 would be put down by Vietnam-hardened paratroopers in a situation like the French in the Algerian capital in 1956—Chester's representation of black frustration leading to homicide now made perfect sense. The junior staffer who solicited his reply wrote him back delighted by the "superb" comment. As America swiveled toward its year of public death and conflagration, Chester's previously considered outrageous observations on American culture were becoming practical common sense.

Now the denture-wearing literary militant, remarkably enough, was flush. Samuel Goldwyn extended the movie option and seemed to retain his excitement about the film of *Cotton Comes to Harlem.* And with Chester's *Times* appearance and his hustling new agent Rosalyn Targ, he had cachet in New York, in spite of his age. Constance Pearlstein, the lover of C. L. R. James, brought him soup while his gums healed. Dramatist Shirley Clarke welcomed him and Joyce Caddoo over to her penthouse at the Chelsea Hotel for a party. Chester's royalties from *Pinktoes* since publication amounted to $3999. He cabled Lesley to take a flight over in the middle of June: "expense is no matter."

Lesley arrived on June 17 at his room in the graffiti-dappled hallways of the Hotel Albert. Chester felt relief at her being there. The next day, a tall man wearing tortoiseshell glasses and conservative clothes knocked at the door: Samuel Goldwyn Jr. in the flesh. Chester prepared strong French coffee and they discussed *Cotton Comes to Harlem*. After disapproving of Chester's work on the screenplay, Goldwyn had engaged a professional television writer to produce a new script. Chester looked it over with distaste. Goldwyn did not feel that the detectives were distinct enough and he hoped to develop two more characters, the villain Deke O'Malley and Lieutenant Anderson, to broaden the dramatic appeal. Chester bristled, as he did at all criticism, and certainly because Lieutenant Anderson, Grave Digger and Coffin Ed's boss, was mainly a foil to reveal the plot. Goldwyn's determination to change the script became harder to deal with when he insisted that Chester collapse the detectives solely into Grave Digger, whom Goldwyn believed more compelling than the acid-splashed Coffin Ed. Goldwyn had a commanding personality and was the film professional. He was also a multimillionaire. Chester agreed to shift the characterization and to devote himself to writing the screenplay for a retainer of $750 per month.

Chester spent the ensuing several days visiting friends and shopping with Lesley on Fifth Avenue, in the throes of a "buying jag." He felt elegant, well heeled, and frivolous; he bought beach clothes that he would give away before ever wearing. Toward the end of the New York holiday, they had a party, inviting Rosalyn and Bill Targ; Constance and Edward Pearlstein; Joyce Caddoo; his typist Helen; and Charles, Torun's new but already estranged husband, who had returned to the United States. Chester expressed his fury on occasion, like a time when Leslie accidentally spilled oranges on the floor, and when white barbers refused to cut his hair. But although Chester still drank, he remained under control. Mostly, he was reformed.

Chester left America in July, just before pitched battles between militant blacks and police erupted in Newark, New Jersey, on the twelfth; over five days, twenty-six people were killed and a thousand injured. On July 14 New Jersey's governor ordered National Guard units into the city, including armored personnel carriers, machine-gun units, and tanks, which opened fire on a public housing project. The same day playwright LeRoi Jones was arrested, charged with carrying concealed revolvers, and photographed in a police station with a head wound. In the white sections of the city, crowds gathered in support of martial law, shouting, "Shoot the niggers." The newspapers carried passages that called to mind the same terms as used for slave rebellions: "there were so many Negroes it was impossible to control them."

Deeply moved, Chester sat down and set aside the work with Goldwyn, the book on his love affairs, and his latest detective story in order to produce an extended treatment of the Newark revolt, "On the Use of Force." Newark blacks looting stores, burning buildings, and sniping at police were "invisible," he wrote for his French readers. Unlike the trendy black American tourists seen in the shops along the Champs-Elysées, the majority of black American citizens were "never seen until they lie bloody and dead from a policeman's bullet on the hot dirty pavement of a Ghetto street." That ghetto, Chester decided, was "shockingly similar to that in large cities in South Africa" and he insisted that the police manhandled African American citizens with the same techniques as the apartheid regime. "Police brutality toward black people in the United States is of such common usage and longstanding as to have attained acceptance of proper behavior," Chester wrote. "The theory has always been that the way to treat black people is like children; that they have to be punished when they misbehave and make a nuisance of themselves such as asking for their civil rights."

If the police believed in force, many blacks considered resistance to physical assault by whites as "noble," their principal right since the abolition of slavery. Chester made an observation that needed to be heard:

"Every race riot in the United States has stemmed from the one single fact that a white law enforcement officer has committed a brutality against a black citizen." Chester then correctly predicted that a United States capable of electing a black president was thirty or forty years in the future, when Americans then under twenty "assume control of all aspects of American life."

Chester and Lesley found a short-term rental on Rue de L'Estrapade near Rue Mouffetard, where Chester went back to work, mainly on his detective story, the bread and butter of his European career. He continued drafting his book on Regine Fischer, whom he had renamed "Marlene," and he hoped to sell the book through a short treatment, similar to *Une Affaire de viol.* The portrait pursued sexuality as the sole preoccupation of the main characters. When Bill Targ asked him about his narrator's "thoughts on writing, writers, books, publishers . . . political scandals . . . Bardot? Camus? De Beauvoir? The War?" he found Chester unresponsive. Chester was having more fun with Leroy Haynes at the soul food restaurant, gawking at the nude photographs of Haynes and his wife at French beaches, and stopping by the jazz club Living Room to hear Art Simmons, who was writing a column for *Jet* magazine on blacks in Europe. In August Chester and Lesley left town for the Netherlands, where they rented a dilapidated mansion in a tony Amsterdam suburb called Blaricum; there they regularly visited Charles Holland, who was taking a break from his marriage. In Amsterdam, Chester was treated well by his Dutch publisher, who arranged for extensive press and news coverage, including television programs. The Dutch were fascinated by *Pinktoes.*

While enjoying the Netherlands, Chester met with Phil Lomax, a buddy Melvin Van Peebles had introduced to him in Paris. Lomax told Chester a story about a blind man on the subway train in Brooklyn, responding to a physical insult by wildly shooting a pistol in the direction of his foe. Naturally (though black blind men had been known to shoot robbers), the blind man missed his assailant and shot wildly.

Chester enjoyed this anecdote well enough to work it into the new novel, *Blind Man with a Pistol*. He regarded this book "not [as] a detective story," but rather "a wild sort of 'psychodelic,'—if that is how it is spelled—novel about Harlem in the grip of crime, riots, fantasies, and such,—in fact a number of wild scenes held together only by the ambience." That "ambience" was not enough to keep the book at Putnam, where Editor in Chief Bill Targ decided the manuscript was "not up to the standard you set in the other Harlem novels." Amicably—and in a sea change of difference from the 1940s—Chester's agent Rosalyn Targ (Bill's wife) quickly found another home for the book, at William Morrow. Chester's new publisher did not quite think the "ambience" held the book together enough either, but his editor there, James Landis, agreed with Chester to "let the book stand as it is, with all its confusions, because it's a very confusing, and confused, world you're writing about." The book satirized the often internecine, bloody, fiery, disconcerting urban conflagrations. While Chester believed the violence was therapeutic and necessary and, of course, supremely vindicating, he called it mistaken, analogizing its probable success to a blind man wielding a firearm. However, the novel concludes with his blind man shooting a racist police officer in the head. Chester would later say about his fiction to *Newsweek*, "Shooting people in the head generates power."

Chester returned to tinkering on the script of *Cotton Comes to Harlem*, but in October a "most unhappy" Goldwyn chastised him for his efforts. Goldwyn only conceded, "I had expected too much for a first try." Feeling beloved after a long interview for Dutch television, Chester blew up at the letter, having turned the screenplay into a battle between Grave Digger and Deke O'Malley. Goldwyn still felt that he had only a "loose construction of a movie. . . . We must still find a way to prolong the search to give us this kaleidoscopic view of Harlem as Grave Digger unravels the crime." Chester believed that Goldwyn "with all the screenwriters in Hollywood at his disposal . . . wanted [me] to do the impossible." Goldwyn suggested bringing Himes to Hollywood for a series of discussions about the script, but never did.

Chester's friend John Williams published his major work, *The Man Who Cried I Am*, in November of 1967 and, at first, Chester read the book avidly and with delight. Telling Williams that he had written "the only milestone produced (legitimate milestone) since *Native Son*," Chester called *The Man Who Cried I Am*, "the greatest book, the most compelling book, ever written about the scene." Williams visited Himes in Spain a few months after publication. There was one problem: the brilliant, powerfully written book about a black American writer was partly a roman à clef, drawing amply from the stories that Chester had bubbled with over the years about himself and his friendship with Richard Wright. Williams had reproduced G. David Schine's visit to Wright's apartment in April 1953, as well as the subsequent discussion with James Baldwin (called Marion Dawes in Williams's novel) a few hours later. The entire book hinged around a plot by American intelligence agencies to silence black writers who have stumbled upon a conspiracy for black genocide carried out by western governments, the legend a favorite tale of Chester's and Harrington's. When Chester shared his confidential stories with Williams, he could not have imagined that another writer would do so much with them. Chester had been ignored and shut out for so long that when someone saw the value in what he had to say, he became affronted. Williams had used the information to create a compelling suspense plot, and then given the novel the emotional depth of Himes's *Lonely Crusade*. He had done so by taking Chester seriously as an historical actor in a way that Chester did not allow much of his own later work to reflect. Chester could also see in the fully developed treatment that Williams was expert at the missed chance for

A Case of Rape which, in its abbreviated form, never achieved the high seriousness of Williams's book.

The depth of friendship between the two men was difficult to measure. In a complimentary review essay at the end of 1964 that had some prickly lines, Williams had described Chester as "a nervous, wretched man." Chester didn't forget that, adding the cutting remark to his increased petulance in 1967, and would avoid Williams for the rest of the year. "Angered," Williams would wonder why Chester had turned cold and shut him out. "More than you could ever know I shared your misfortunes and grief," he wrote sadly to Chester before the end of the year. Asking forgiveness for the "seeming indifference," and admitting "I have been passing time on the outskirts of life," Chester reheated the friendship, which helped him conduct business in the United States. Nevertheless, with *The Man Who Cried I Am,* Williams was a rare late-twentieth-century African American novelist who perceived a genuine richness in the postwar black literary tradition, and who went to pains to articulate his historical moment and recover its creative black expatriate actors.

Feeling his creative gifts waning, Chester began to perceive the same exploitation from other blacks like Williams as he had from publishers. And he was not always being paranoid or bitter. In Amsterdam in 1968, Phil Lomax confessed shamefully to publishing Chester's written material under his own name. "It's all right, man, relax. Nothing is hurt," Chester soothingly told him, as the two huddled behind closed doors. The next year though, Chester went out of his way to acknowledge Lomax's contribution to the plot of *Blind Man with a Pistol.* "A friend of mine, Phil Lomax, told me this story about a blind man with a pistol," he began on the book's first page, in a "Preface," something he'd never used before. He wanted to send a message to the younger men about integrity.

In other encounters he was less forgiving. His anger and feelings of persecution flared more openly when Richard Gibson tried to

contact him after more than ten years. Gibson had just left southern
Africa and was now an expert on that region's anti-imperialist struggles. His experiences would produce a book called *African Liberation
Movements: Contemporary Struggles Against White Minority Rule*. Like
Chester, Lesley was convinced that Gibson worked for the American
intelligence services and was conducting FBI-like "pretext" calls to
track Chester's whereabouts. When he telephoned the house, Chester
angrily shouted from the bathroom for Lesley to hang up. He never
spoke to Gibson again.

The cold of northern Europe was increasingly difficult to toler-
ate, but there was little doubt that Chester had his best success as
a black American author writing and living in Europe. In addition
money stretched further in the Old World than in New York, to him
the most habitable American metropolis. Chester required the ano-
nymity and historical complexity of European cities, but the South
of France, where he preferred living, was still too pricey. He looked
farther south, to Spain, a place with traditionally warm weather and
excellent food.

When Chester and Lesley headed south of Barcelona in December 1967, testing the waters for the possibility of buying a house, they
saw on the sides of walls "Deutsche Haus," a welcome sign in German
to Nazis in hiding. A bulwark against communism since the Spanish
Civil War, Spain in the late 1960s was nearing the end of the Franco
dictatorship, and becoming more attractive for permanent residency.
Despite its tightly controlled state and cowed public (constitutional
rights would be suspended in 1968), Spain would miss some of the
painful public turmoil that marked France and America, especially
in the next year. Chester had not voted regularly when he lived in
the United States, so the thought of moving to a country without
democratic elections and where the Communist Party was outlawed
did not discourage him. As in France, he assumed that if he avoided
touchy issues, such as the number of people executed by the Nation-

alist government during the civil war of 1936–1939 and afterward (the estimates were 200,000), the state police would not pursue him. Although Chester told people that his books could not be sold in Spain, *The Primitive* had been translated and made available there; perhaps the more strongly pro-union *If He Hollers Let Him Go* and *Lonely Crusade* would have made the authorities less comfortable.

Chester and Lesley inched southward along the coast, until they reached the province of Alicante, with its Moorish terraced landscapes and alcazar watchtowers designed to counter the invasions from Africa. Chester's early impression of the town where he would spend the remainder of his life was swift and disapproving: "Moraira was as racist as the American South," he wrote to his agent. Rosalyn Targ advised him, "Spain is not a place where you feel comfortable, and I think the best thing would be for you to leave as soon as possible." But swiftly a kind of fatalism set in. Spain had been a kind of sanctuary since 1954. Was the racism there any worse than the other varieties he had so painstakingly observed? At the end of the month, in Moraira, the Arabic-named town with Spanish people darker in skin color than Chester, he impulsively bought two plots of land overlooking the sea and initiated plans to build a house.

Duplicating an earlier trip, Chester and Lesley walked over to Gibraltar and left the Jaguar for mechanical repair; the roads in Spain had been spottily maintained and Chester had not eased up on his speed to accommodate them. They went north in early 1968 and took an apartment in Sitges, about twenty minutes south of the Barcelona airport. Again, Chester "divorced the United States from my mind." He was returned there when the news of the assassination of Martin Luther King Jr. on April 4, and the resulting widespread rioting and arson throughout the black sections of urban America reached them.

The day after the announcements of King's death headlined papers around the world, Chester began to appear in the headlines himself. "Comic Suspense Film of Negro Detectives to Be Made in Harlem" reported the *Philadelphia Tribune*. It had not been an easy path getting to the point of filming. Not three weeks after King's death, Chester and Lesley went to the Lancaster Gate Hotel in London to celebrate. Chester was delighted that, after three years, Samuel Goldwyn Jr. had finally purchased the film rights for *Cotton Comes to Harlem*, which was going into production. Good money and publicity for the series would now be at hand.

When Goldwyn finally decided to make the film with United Artists, to write the screenplay he hired Arnold Perl, best known for one-act plays on Russian Jews, but probably selected on account of his *Who Do You Kill?*, a 1963 televised play about race and economic discrimination. The first thing that Perl did was to reinsert Coffin Ed into the script. Goldwyn admitted his imperfections: "Perhaps that was one of the mistakes which I made before." Despite the putative liberalism of Perl, Chester found what had been done to the story "offensive." In a candid discussion with Hoyt Fuller, the editor of *Negro Digest*, Chester would resentfully accuse Perl of gimmicky exploitation, which he resented more because Chester surmised that Perl believed "the Jews had a right to do so." As a counterproposal, Chester suggested LeRoi Jones, who had, in the wake of the Newark riots, changed his name to Amiri Baraka. However, Baraka refused to accept anything less than the scale for Hollywood screenwriters, which Goldwyn was unwilling to pay. In the second half of 1968, Ossie Davis, the actor and activist who had delivered the funeral eulogy for Malcolm X, was brought on board to deliver a script; Davis would also direct the film.

Returning from London to Paris, Chester and Lesley moved to a third-floor apartment on Rue Abel Ferry in the Sixteenth Arrondissement, a distant post from his usual haunts, but where he found a mood remarkably similar to that of the United States. The students had barricaded themselves inside the Sorbonne and fought off the police. No public services were available and garbage piled up in the street; the trains were not running, and the din of protests and looming battle were a regular part of life. When Rosalyn and Bill Targ visited for a series of meetings and a holiday in July, Paris had become dangerous. Orly Airport was closed. Chester volunteered to drive them to Brussels so they could return to the United States. He drove the Jaguar like an airplane, at 115 miles an hour, a trip that the couples never forgot and served as Chester's final act of muscular tenacity and nerve. Spain seemed perpetually serene by comparison.

That summer of 1968 Chester went to Darmstadt, Germany, for quiet refuge. He spent time with Janheinz Jahn, one of his European friends and a man who also had considerable impact on black intellectuals. Jahn had become the German ambassador to Nigeria and Senegal, and his wife had become a practitioner of an African religion, where Jahn himself had considerable scholarly expertise. Jahn had written about the life-force concept of Muntu, which came from the Bantu peoples, the ancestral race of much of western, southern, and central Africa.

Chester and Lesley returned briefly to Paris during the summer. In September they left for Spain and Chester began to plot a novel called *Plan B*, which would conclude his detective series with the black revolution. "I am trying to show . . . how the violence would be if the blacks resorted to this," he would inform John Williams. This last book was about real revolt, when the militant's "objective is not to stand up and talk," but "to blow out [the enemy's] brains." The novel opened with a chapter called "Tang," about a poor, middle-aged black couple, T-Bone and Tang. A lazy minstrel of a man, T-Bone embraces the stereotypes afforded blacks by white society; his wife, Tang, less contentedly accepts life as a cheap prostitute in Central Park. A mysterious box is delivered to them containing an automatic rifle and a note to begin the war of black liberation. T-Bone wishes to betray the cause while Tang cheers. "'It's the uprising, nigger!'" and "'We gonna be free!'" Ideologically opposed, the couple struggles over the gun and T-Bone kills Tang. When Coffin Ed and Grave Digger show up, Digger kills T-Bone, setting up the final action in the drama.

In a series of set pieces showing comic grotesque violence between blacks and whites, and with a backstory of the revolutionary hero whom Chester had hatched in the 1950s, the novel had at its core the question of nationalism and racial belonging. It evolved into a final confrontation between Grave Digger and Coffin Ed, in which Digger kills his partner, who threatens the revolution. "'You can't kill, Black, man,'" Grave Digger tells his partner. "He might be our last chance, despite the risk. I'd rather be dead than a subhuman in this world." Chester was racing through the novel, referring to the Sharpeville massacre of 1960 in South Africa and foreshadowing Philadelphia mayor Wilson Goode's explosive response in 1985 to MOVE. The gore and bald rhetoric made *Plan B* one of his least artistically interesting novels, even if he did presage the bloody blaxploitation films, slasher horror movies, and Quentin Tarantino films like *Pulp Fiction* and *Django Unchained,* which would eventually delight American audiences. The possibility that the book was lightweight didn't bother him. "The main thing in this game," he told Williams, "is to keep putting books out. Even if you have to put out a lot of fillers—who knows but that they might become classics in time. Look at Hemingway." Chester's book might have become a kind of classic, if he could have gotten it out in the 1960s or early 1970s, during the strong periods of black revolutionary militancy in the United States. However, *Plan B* would not be released until 1986.

Chester worked more diligently on his autobiography and determined, after he had written several hundred pages and had not quite begun his second round in Europe in late 1955, that he would write another volume. The book of his life covering 1954 to 1970, substantially filled with epistles he had collected from over the years, his long essay for *The New Yorker* about his car troubles (in the context of his work, a fascinating rejoinder to the idea of western industrial supremacy), infused with sex and modern profanity, would be an intertextual effort, quite different from the first volume. He liked the new possibilities available in language with the decline of censorship, one of his long-standing wars, and in *Blind Man with a Pistol* he had added a one-line "Foreword" from a "Harlem Intellectual": "Motherfucking right, it's confusing," he purportedly quoted, "it's a gas baby, you dig."

Blind Man with a Pistol did get a push from William Morrow (whose other strong books written by African Americans included the LeRoi Jones anthology *Black Fire* and Harold Cruse's *The Crisis of the Negro Intellectual*) and, unlike his other detective fiction, received a solo review in the *New York Times*. Perhaps because it eschewed the tight plot of the other books in the detective series and prevented, in its finale, the detectives from resolving or explaining away the crime, the book was understood, finally, as literature. "Reading *Blind Man with a Pistol* is like reading Ralph Ellison's *Invisible Man*," considered one reviewer, "without the spiritual progress that alleviates the horrors of that novel." Again the reviewer detrained at the question of Chester's authentic representations of black life. "His Harlem blacks look and sound like the kind of idiots and psychopaths and punks a white man of similar background might think them all to be." But the next year, when the Mystery Writers of America awards banquet was held in New York on May 1, Chester's *Blind Man with a Pistol* was announced as runner-up for best mystery of the year. Chester's buddy Phil Lomax described the dynamic of reading it: "I got my standard two laughs and a wince per page," calling Chester's "hack and slash" scene involving Dr. Mubuta, Mr. Sam, Viola, Van Raff, and Johnson X "*a tour de force.*" Chester had written the series for ten years, without becoming jaded or bored. The *Times* reviewer had proposed that a white man of "similar background" to Chester was around. In his forthcoming autobiography, he would remind the public that such a white person did not exist.

Chester mailed off a nearly four-hundred-page draft of the first

half of his autobiography to Rosalyn Targ in March 1969, hoping
for a windfall from a good press. After an angry and disheartening
exchange with the paperback house Dell over the cover of *Run Man
Run*, which featured a lascivious Harlem belle (Dell editorial staff
making the decision about the book's cover declined to read the book
itself, about a white detective killing unarmed black men), May was
busy and filled with visitors. John Williams proved his devotion by
trooping out to the city of Alicante for a five-day visit at Chester and
Lesley's apartment on Calle Duque de Zaragoza. The lengthy interview Williams conducted would have talismanic qualities for the next
generation when it anchored *Amistad 1*, the Random House project
conceived by Williams in 1970. But the rub between the two was evident. Williams would introduce the interview, which some reviewers
thought "the highlight of the issue," with what people reading the
article recognized as a "self-indulgent" opening. For the second time
he described Chester as decrepit, "almost sixty now" and "not well,"
a description that no working writer would have liked. To introduce
a long interview that was so revelatory as to be nearly shocking, Williams mainly emphasized the vulnerability and weakness of his older
buddy: "Himes' life has been filled with so many disasters, large and
small, that I lived in dread that one of these would carry him away."
By noting Chester's frailty, Williams nearly reproduced the oedipal
struggle that Baldwin had confessed to Wright.

The day after Williams left, May 15, Hoyt Fuller of *Negro Digest*
(later *Black World*) arrived to interview him. Chester set out much of
the same material again in another long conversation, but this time
he settled his score with Ralph Ellison. Chester detailed the needling
by Ellison at Vandi Haygood's apartment in 1953 about Ellison's *Time*
magazine contacts as "the thing that cooled our relationship." Ellison
had chilled the relationship with Chester by 1948, given his embarrassment about *Lonely Crusade*. By 1968 he was becoming known as
the antagonist to the young black novelists. In a book jacket blurb

for James Alan McPherson's *Hue and Cry* (1969), Ellison proposed that younger black writers were overpraised and "take being black as a privilege for being obscenely second-rate." Chester endeared himself to blacks coming of age in the 1960s and '70s himself by taking the opposite position: the American publishing industry itself represented the prime indecency and stupidity. And then he went further: Chester suggested that "the white press and writers" had introduced a canard by elevating Ellison. "They say [he] took time to learn his craft," Chester fumed, considering the squabble in the winter of 1945 when Wright had huffed to them both that Ellison's early chapters of *Invisible Man* were too similar to *Native Son* and *Black Boy*. Perhaps thinking of what he himself had accomplished in terms of storytelling in *The End of a Primitive*, Chester made a point of saying that he didn't believe that Ellison "introduced any new techniques."

With his unfiltered disdain for established literary conventions and his immutable underdog credentials, Chester became the doyen of the black writers whose aesthetic values were formed in the maelstrom of the 1960s. For these talented writers on the margins, Chester's retreat to Europe made principled sense. The bunch included novelists like Williams, Clarence Major, Arnold Kemp, Steve Cannon, Sam Greenlee, Ishmael Reed, Kristin Hunter, and Ronald Fair; memoirist Eldridge Cleaver; poets Nikki Giovanni, Haki Madhubuti, and Maya Angelou; and critics Julius Lester, Hoyt Fuller, and Addison Gayle. As Williams wrote Chester in a letter in 1969, "the younger writers know of and have read Chester Himes. They want to know where he is, what he's up to. This 'black revolution' or whatever it is has shocked them into life. They missed Wright and Hughes, and Ellison gives them nothing but platitudes from what I hear, and they are reaching desperately for roots—which means you."

By the end of the decade, James Baldwin started boosting Chester too. When Hollywood cribbed the title *If He Hollers Let Him Go* for one of the movies cashing in black misery in 1969, Baldwin was indignant on Chester's behalf. Calling *If He Hollers Let Him Go* a "fine novel," whose very title should never have been purloined by Hollywood, Baldwin found himself spouting Himesian lyrics about Americans not only "far from being able to abandon the doctrine of white supremacy" but being "prepared to blow up the globe to maintain it." For the final twenty years of his career, Baldwin would find himself held in decreasing esteem as he pointed out the chronic ulcers of American life.

Quite different from Chester's formative literary years in the 1940s, the shift in American cultural space at the dawn of 1970 presented a wholesale transformation. Chester was a necessary antenna for perspicuity. *Chicago Tribune* reviewer Shane Stevens called him "the best black American novelist writing today." The proof of the new acceptance was in celluloid, as *Cotton Comes to Harlem* neared completion. The film was shot on location in Harlem with the paramilitary Black Citizens Patrol guarding the props and the actor Godfrey Cambridge defending Chester's vision on set against producer Samuel Goldwyn Jr. When Roz Targ visited in July 1969, she reported that Cambridge was unafraid "to speak up if he feels Sam is going in any wrong direction."

Chester's recognition as a writer and one with a novel being turned into a movie did not heal an old wound; even the bubbly Targ was struggling to find a taker for his autobiography. At Random House, a black editor named Charles Harris failed to persuade the senior staff to acquire the book. "White folks won't know what Chester's talking about," he declared to John Williams, "they want a black autobiography, not one by a human being." Harris would be fired in a year, eventually publishing the English-language version of Chester's *A Case of Rape* at Howard University Press. Chester chalked up the failure at Random House to another source. "I can imagine," he wrote to John Williams about the difficulties preventing a contract, "that most of them stem from Random House regarding Ralph Ellison as the oracle of black writing and all black thought, and anything that doesn't follow the path of his platitudes is regarded as unmentionable."

Chester could add the dismissal to his other worries. By August 1969, he was trying to have a home built on the Moraira lots he'd bought in 1967. To construct the small villa on a hillside overlooking the Mediterranean would be an all-consuming, drawn-out task, filled with the delay and difficulty he had come to expect in Spain. By late fall he had decided that the work on his home "looked like an imbecile child playing with mud." In mid-1970, he remained strongly dissatisfied. He was annoyed by the tardy progress when his brother Joe wrote about visiting at the end of the summer. Chester discouraged him, describing the Costa Blanca retreat as "physically difficult" and possessing "uneven streets (I have had three different exhaust systems knocked from the bottom of my car by unseen rocks and protusions [sic]), heat, flies, crowds, and indifferent food." Then he received an oddly cheery notice from Ken McCormick at Doubleday ("Nice to hear from you again via our legal department"), after Chester had made some boilerplate inquiries about the sales and rights of *If He Hollers Let Him Go*. Since he was reputably famous, Doubleday as well as Knopf responded now with speed and politesse. McCormick's slight rapprochement betokened the source of Chester's final major writings. Fickle Doubleday would bring out his personal annals in two volumes, beginning in 1972.

The relationship was wobbly from the start. After Sandy Richardson, the company's recently appointed editorial director, read the memoirs in April 1970, he offered $10,000 for the autobiography's first volume; for the second volume, due the following year, Doubleday promised only $5,000. "I'm not very happy to be back with Doubleday, but beggars can't be choosers" was how Chester summed up the situation to John Williams. One bright spot, Chester was working with a black editor, a young woman named Helen Jackson who adored him and his work. (Blacks were showing signs of some leverage in publishing. That summer Williams successfully demanded that a white Doubleday editorial staffer be fired for calling his book editor a "nigger-lover.") Some of the earliest discussions with Doubleday were aimed at publishing both volumes of the autobiography within a year. Chester also seconded a contract to publish a revamped version of his abandoned short story collection of 1954, with the robust *Baby Sister* at its center, to be called *Black on Black*.

With greetings from Amiri Baraka and the novelist Cecil Brown (of *The Life and Loves of Mr. Jiveass Nigger* fame), Chester felt better about traveling to New York. He reached the United States on August 26, 1970, to ink the deal with Doubleday and to enjoy the film success of *Cotton Comes to Harlem*. His no-holds-barred interview with Williams in *Amistad 1* had "got a lot of things cracking." In it, Chester had proved his uncanny ability to truthfully render the multiracial complexity of American writing while demolishing the myths of white superiority. Chester said repeatedly how much he admired William Faulkner, but then he told Williams, "Look, I have talked to black sharecroppers and convicts and various black people who could tell, without stopping, better stories than Faulkner could write." His old editorial sparring partner Bill Targ, soon to be promoted to president at Putnam, admitted that Chester's raw candor was "impressive as an overall, much needed commentary" and would contribute to "your long overdue recognition."

Back in June, *Cotton Comes to Harlem*—in director Ossie Davis's words, featuring Harlem's "colorful, exciting life-style and wit," with a score by the creator of the hit Broadway musical *Hair*—had opened and delivered a knockout punch at the box office. In Philadelphia, theaters kept doors open twenty-four hours a day to handle overflow crowds, and *Cotton* broke the opening-day box-office records in New York, Chicago, Washington, D.C., and Detroit, finally grossing $5.1 million. Despite the young Chicago film critic Gene Siskel's sour estimate—"the best way to handle ethnic humor is to leave it alone"—

black audiences especially seemed to express relief at a comedy, featuring underground talent like Redd Foxx, that placed serious political matters as the context and not the center. Remembering Chester fondly, the New York black newspaper the *Amsterdam News* had his back: "P.S." its article concluded, "Chester Himes has been writing and getting published for too long without due recognition."

The *New York Times* greeted the film with "a sense of liberation, for here is a film by a new black director (Ossie Davis, otherwise the actor and author), based on the work of a black novelist (Chester Himes), shot in Harlem with a large and talented black cast." While Davis couldn't help from sputtering that "concessions" he made might have "cut the gut and heart out of what we are trying to say to black people," the strong box-office appeal for the quirky humor indicated the emergence of a new genre.

About six months later, Melvin Van Peebles started screening his independently produced revolutionary film *Sweet Sweetback's Baadasssss Song*, which would be distributed broadly in the spring of 1971. Himes's old friend, whom Chester believed had "tapped [his] literary vault," used guerrilla advertising methods, like handbills with the slogan "Rated X by an all-white jury," to promote his unyielding film. Van Peebles directed and starred in the movie, which eventually grossed more than $10 million.

The same year, Gordon Parks released *Shaft*, whose $12 million at the box office rescued parent company M-G-M from bankruptcy. Together, the three films proved the sound economic value of black-cast movies also written and directed by African Americans. After *Shaft*'s success was duplicated by the 1972 film *Super Fly* by Gordon Parks's son, Gordon Parks Jr. (who had earned credentials filmmaking with Dominic-Pierre Gaisseau), a film featuring a criminal as its hero, the NAACP generated the term "black exploitation" (soon shortened to "blaxploitation") to describe the trend of financially successful studio films, sometimes in the crime genre and sometimes

"B movies," with majority black actors. It was amusing to Chester that his old antagonists at the NAACP would point to *Cotton Comes to Harlem* as the originator of the trend.

Chester, who did not earn a percentage of the film gross, considered himself the primary person exploited. He told the Hollywood studios who came after *Cotton*'s success that he wanted $100,000 for the rights to use the other novels featuring his gun-toting detectives. In New York he spent some time with the latest black artist to achieve a national audience, six-foot-tall Maya Angelou. He made a "big hit" with Angelou, who was in turn later "duly pleased" to hear that Chester had liked her. Then Chester broke a denture eating a rabbit's leg and had to be rescued by his dentist. He went to Los Angeles to discuss future projects with Goldwyn, to whom he sold *The Heat's On*, which became the film *Come Back Charleston Blue*, the sequel to *Cotton Comes to Harlem*. During the negotiations, in light of the inconsiderate "general American attitude toward the value of my work," Chester backed down to $25,000, but he would receive 5 percent of the studio's net profit.

The U.S. visit also allowed him to be in New York on September 20, 1970, for the inaugural award ceremony of the Black American Academy of Arts and Letters, an organization that grew out of the black cultural nationalist explosion of the period; the idea was to create a permanent institution somewhat parallel to the American Academy of Arts and Letters. Someone burglarized his hotel room while he stayed in New York, but Chester was more happily distracted by appearing on television shows and the rising tide of approval from younger black writers. Ishmael Reed dedicated his new book *19 Necromancers from Now* to Chester, and Donald Goines, a cult favorite of black readers, went on to call the protagonist of his novel *White Man's Justice, Black Man's Grief,* "Chester Hines," the same name from the 1930 Ohio penitentiary census report.

Chester returned to his new but poorly constructed home in

Spain. He welcomed his editor Helen Jackson to Moraira in October and they worked hard to get *The Quality of Hurt*, his autobiography, ready for publication in the fall of 1971. The book he published differed from the graphic manuscript he had submitted. "As you know," his editor told him after a few months of work on the project, "there were deletions and occasional rewrites of sections dealing with subsidiary characters and major revisions of the references to Willa. These were mandatory—not based on editorial considerations but on legal grounds—and are not subject to reinstatement." By May 1971 Helen Jackson had taken the unusual step of traveling to Spain again to see him because of difficulties at the publisher. Jackson told him that the editorial director Sandy Richardson "has shirked all responsibility" and that Chester's agent, Rosalyn Targ, was "so busy playing the 'grand dame'" that she had become "frankly impossible." With all the corrections, Jackson worried that Chester would understand himself to be reliving the censorship crisis he had faced with Doubleday in 1945 with *If He Hollers*.

Doubleday asked Chester to tone down the sexual references to get the book into municipal libraries. Fearing that the autobiography would suffer in the process, at one point in the summer Jackson turned the entire project over to Sandy Richardson, insisting that he devote expertise to the manuscript. Jackson wrote Himes clarifying the racial terrain in a way he could clearly understand and for the first time in his publishing career. "Major authors are not given to junior editors—major white authors are not." So, instead of appearing in the fall of 1971, the book was released in the spring of 1972 and Helen Jackson left Doubleday to open up a bookshop in the Caribbean.

When the galleys were sent out, Chester got raves from his latest group of admirers, the black artists drawing direct inspiration from the U.S. counterculture and revolutionary black politics. Maya Angelou put plainly the case for his esteem from younger black artists. "For those who wonder what to do with and about the young black radicals of 1972, it is incumbent upon them to read Mr. Himes' book." She insisted, "I admire the writer and after reading *The Quality of Hurt* I love the man." The echo was heard overseas. Lindsey Barrett wrote from the University of Ibadan in Nigeria that his new collection of poems *Lip Skybound* was "influenced by your work and personality" and acknowledging that "many of us have only now begun to know your strength." Howard University English professor Addison Gayle sent Chester a copy of his new work, *The Black Aesthetic.* Clarence Major, another significant talent as a poet and novelist, wrote to Chester that he enjoyed best the portraits of Spanish landscape and the train ride in Mallorca. Chester had written a relievedly humanist document for the black writers coming out of the deadly 1960s, "a very lasting and important human record for human beings who care about the individual pain and struggle of other human beings." But the highlight of the year, beyond being embraced by a new bunch of glamorous and seemingly fearless young writers, came in December when he wrote to Bill Targ to have Putnam forward his share of the purchase price of the dramatic rights for *Cotton Comes to Harlem.* It was a check for $25,000. The sum was the rough equivalent of what he might have hoped to have gotten on the snowy November night in 1928 when he went to rob the Samuel Millers at their house in Cleveland.

The Quality of Hurt: The Autobiography of Chester Himes, Volume I was fairly well received in American newspapers, caught now between roaring militants quick to accuse them of racist gatekeeping and the old tradition of expecting gratitude from black writers for any notice at all. Arnold Gingrich tried to have it both ways, in a widely serialized review, by claiming credit for having launched Chester, while also complaining of Chester's "son-of-a-bitchery." A weirder, more openly negative critique appeared in the *New York Times Book Review.* The reviewer was Nathan Huggins, a black Columbia professor who had just published *The Harlem Renaissance,* a history of black writers of the 1920s. Proclaiming that Alex Haley's portrait of Malcolm X and Eldridge Cleaver's *Soul on Ice* (both men mentioned by name in the prison sequence of *The Quality of Hurt*) had achieved "direct, straightforward, honest, self-critical, socially critical, and proud black self-expression," Huggins accused Himes of writing a book that was "vacuous and unimportant." And Huggins's comment that the book was "perhaps directed to American readers of the early 1950s, who might have found something daring in interracial sex," showed the formidable amnesia that had already set in. Chester had been unable to sell his novels in the 1950s precisely because they broached sex, as he had struggled in the 1940s when they broached politics.

Activist and writer Julius Lester wrote to the *Times* to correct the "unfair" review, "so unkind and cruel." Lester, who sent Chester a note saying "I feel that it is the job of some of us younger black writers to deal with a review like that," was a Himes fan. "Because this book tells me of a world I could know no other way, it is an extremely valuable addition to my life and the lives of other young blacks." The *Los Angeles Times* called the book "raw" and "penetrating," and the *Amsterdam News*'s Myra Bain admired the "truthful" portrait of the writer and his milieu. Given that white literary critics like Christopher Lehmann-Haupt judged Chester first and foremost "an angry, alienated black who feels that his considerable body of writing has suffered because of bigotry," the notices were not bad.

Chester returned to the United States with Lesley in early February 1972 for, considering his health, a whirlwind series of interviews, book parties, signings, and readings, mainly in New York. A portion of the book came out in *Contact* magazine and on the twenty-seventh he was interviewed for the television show *Soul* by Nikki Giovanni, the twenty-six-year-old member of the radical black aesthetic vanguard. Giovanni threw a party for him at her apartment downtown and old friends like Melvin Van Peebles stopped by. A core group of irreverent black artists appointed him their hero.

On March 12, after Chester traveled in New York and to North Carolina to see Joe, the Harlem Writers Guild, under the direction of Rosa Guy, held a book signing for him at the United Nations Plaza Hotel. There were seven hundred guests, most of them young and black, and they were unapologetically outspoken. Critics like Addison Gayle, Larry Neale, Mel Watkins, and John Henrik Clarke, novelist Toni Cade Bambara, playwrights Loften Mitchell and Ed Bullins, and uncompromising jazz musician Max Roach were on hand to cheer him, along with five hundred copies of the book. Ossie Davis opened the program and his wife, Ruby Dee, read from *The Quality of Hurt*. Then John Williams introduced Chester, who gave a short speech.

Another day the young black literary lions Steve Cannon, Ishmael Reed, Quincy Troupe, and Clarence Major partied with Chester in his suite at the Park Lane Hotel. Chester served so much scotch that when Cannon got to the Fifty-Seventh Street subway station, he fell down an entire flight of stairs and was bedridden for a week. Reed, an uncompromising high priest of his artistic generation, seconded the assessment of the event that produced some memorable photographs: "all of us really enjoyed being with you and Leslie [sic] and the cat that wonderful afternoon at the Park Lane."

Thankful for being largely left out of Chester's autobiography, Ralph and Fanny Ellison got back in touch with him. (Ellison, who sparred throughout the 1970s with this same group, told Steve Cannon that Chester had stabbed him at Vandi Haygood's New Year's party in 1953.) In his account Chester had not removed them from his memoir, but he had quietly glossed the action, boiling down the sequence of rich events between the fall of 1944 and the summer of 1947 until he had reduced them to less than two pages. Both volumes of the memoir would show his life with two women: Willa Thompson in volume one and Regine Fischer in volume two. Jean Himes and Lesley Packard, respectively, would obliquely balance it out with their understated roles in each volume. In effect, Chester had fleshed out a bit the material he had wanted to write on a black man's love affairs abroad.

Despite the memoir's preoccupation with interracial sex (and avoiding the backlash that John Williams feared from the reviewers "who are proponents of the every white chick is a tramp theory"), Chester continued to get a lift from black-run publishers and magazines and the younger generation. Melba Boyd, an assistant editor at Dudley Randall's radical Broadside Press, wrote to him, enthralled by his corpus. Henry Louis Gates Jr., a twenty-two-year-old black graduate student at Oxford University who would become a famous academic in the 1980s and '90s, was among those clamoring to talk to Chester. Writing an article on black expatriates for *Time*, and having succeeded in interviewing James Baldwin and Josephine Baker, he hurriedly telegrammed Chester, sending greetings from Baker, and imploring, STOPRY [sic] INCOMPLETE UNTIL I SEE YOU. Chester's buddy Nikki Giovanni told him the story he knew, but which she was reckoning with at the age he had just gotten out of prison. "I think fame," she wrote to him about celebrity in the United States, "is more trouble than it is generally stated to be." Chester knew she was right. After the large parties and interviews in New York, he and Lesley went back to Spain at the end of spring 1972. There, Chester felt the telltale tingling and numbness. It was another stroke.

Chapter Sixteen

AFRO-AMERICAN PEOPLE'S NOVELIST

1972–1984

The new stroke in Spain left Chester feeling completely worn out, and it took even more time than before for recovery. After a long convalescence, he was requesting medical help from the American Hospital in Madrid for maladies that were serious and threatening. "I still suffer from my stroke all along my right side in addition to my hernia in my right groin, and my arthritis in left shoulder and chest," he wrote to the staff physician. "I cough a lot and am continually in pain seemingly all over my body." Meanwhile, a valetudinarian Chester was working on the second volume of his autobiography in what he felt was a drive against time.

In early 1973, *Black on Black*, the "admittedly chauvinistic" salvage of the collection of short work he had chucked into the Mediterranean in 1954 and for which Doubleday had paid only $3000, was published to minor notice. He tried to stir up interest and protect himself from obvious critiques in his preface. "You will conclude if you read them," he wrote about these early short stories, "that BLACK PROTEST and BLACK HETEROSEXUALITY are my two chief obsessions." Since most of the book was from an earlier era, he was cast as the antidote to the black militants, "no jive or rage; just real talk and real people." Chester's exceptional gift as a black novelist ultimately resided with his interior portrait of black life and black speech, the topic of his work when the white overlord was absent. The offbeat, funny, uncanny, always erotically charged scenes he created—between Bob and Ella Mae in *If He Hollers Let Him Go*; among Susie, Johnson and Play Safe, Lee and Luther in *Lonely Crusade*; and during the television-set delivery scene in *Blind Man with a Pistol*—all kept paramount the tapestry of ordinary organic black life, rich and fructifying on its own. By comparison, the less robust material in the short stories justified the "briefly noted" epigraph-length reviews, even if the screenplay *Baby Sister* was still fascinating.

Perhaps the brightest news of that year came from Chester's older brother. Joe wrote to him in the summer, saying that he was scheduled for a cornea transplant on his less damaged eye, which might then restore his sight on the left. With the successful landing on the moon, technology seemed poised to remedy the most severe of injuries. After the surgery, in May 1973, Joe reported "substantially improved sight, not enough to read, but very useful improvement." Joe's first graft was not a success, but the next year, surgeons implanted a living graft and he reported, "I can see more than I have for over half a century." Joe's increased eyesight, after so many years, cheered Chester. Indeed, it seemed to reverse the great symbol of the downfall of his family.

Chester and Lesley came to the United States in the late fall of 1973 and they spent the holidays in Harlem and Durham, North Carolina, with his brothers. Eddie, a high-ranking mason and official with the service workers union, told Chester that his detective fictions had attained veracity, particularly *Run Man Run,* the story of the white cop on a murderous rampage. Joe had received an honorary doctorate of science degree at Ohio State in the football stadium where, forty-eight years earlier, Chester had helped pulled down the goalposts after the fall games. It was possible to accept some closure, some measure of redemption for the lives they had lived and what they had accomplished. Chester tried to return to active writing, now with the gambit that the detective fiction contained "the best of my writing and the best of my thinking and I am willing to stake my reputation on them."

Pushing himself physically for a journey, Chester traveled to Germany to appear on an NAACP-sponsored "Black Literature Night" inaugural dinner in Stuttgart on February 11, 1974. There, a bearded Chester shared the dais with James Baldwin. Twenty years after the two men had first met each other through Richard Wright, they found mutual comfort side by side; their professional achievements and public stands were, in the end, self-sustaining. Baldwin was gracious and charming to him, a kindness to which the obviously ailing Chester responded warmly. Baldwin, fifteen years younger than Chester, would outlive him by barely three years.

Perhaps inspired by his brother's medical gains, in July 1974 Chester went to London for a hernia and prostate operation. At first, the prospects seemed bright. "My health has improved (I hope) at great expense and I hope this will be my year. I am desperately trying to get part II of my autobiography finished for summer." Chester would be at work on the volume until he eked it out at the tail end of 1976.

Chester, correctly it turned out, anticipated a turn in the reviews for the second volume: his praise as a pop star. He had tried, in mid-1974, to inch Doubleday into bringing out a collection of the eight Harlem detective stories. "The Harlem detective stories featuring Grave Digger Jones and Coffin Ed Johnson is [sic] my biggest contribution to literature," he wrote to Sandy Richardson. "I have been brainwashed into thinking otherwise by American book reviewers, which I know now and have always known was a mistake." But getting Doubleday to take such action at this point in his American career was like turning an aircraft carrier around, and no offer was made to lasso the various copyrights and contracts and bring out the collection of detective fiction in a single volume as he had hoped.

So he labored on, but with increasing difficulty, even after the modest physical improvement from his surgery. By the end of 1974, Chester was at work "desperately" trying to make the publisher's deadline for volume two of the autobiography. Also concerned about releasing *Une Affaire de viol* in English, he asked Michel Fabre, a professor of American literature at the Sorbonne, who had written the first comprehensive biography of Richard Wright, to help translate it. "I have great hopes for this little book," Chester confessed to the French scholar. Then Chester's rheumatoid arthritis acted up so badly he couldn't stand up straight. To compound matters, his Spanish bank temporarily refused to let him withdraw $40,000 of his money, starting a flurry of letters of complaint to the U.S. embassy. Mixed in, there were occasional moments of good news, such as when Ishmael Reed sent him a message, noting that he had published an article in popular urban magazines giving credit to "Gravedigger [sic] and Coffin Ed for being seminal ideas for my two occult detectives."

My Life of Absurdity contained at least one instance of calculated revenge. Chester alleged, apparently because of an emphasis in articles by John Williams during the 1960s on Chester's frailty, that the younger man was a frivolous opportunist. Williams, understandably upset, stopped speaking to Himes. After Chester's death, when Williams was asked privately about his relationship with Chester, he praised Chester's writing and reflected on their camaraderie—that is, after he had warned Chester about homosexual-seeming overtures and excessive gophering, "punk shit."

But Chester's sniping at friends occurred in the context of his own diminishing lucidity. By 1976 he had found that "my mind is getting very erratic." Concentration was a problem too. After he had submitted his draft of the second volume of the autobiography to his publisher, he was beyond physical exhaustion. "My health has deteriorated so completely I need help of all kinds and at all times." When Jean replied to another request for divorce from Chester, there was a note of pity for how much he was suffering. Chester deflected her concern, just noting, "My sins are catching up to me." That same year he wrote miserably to Marcel Duhamel, "I will probably be dead soon but things will go on the same."

His friends continued to support his work in the United States. At a New York party in October 1976, attended by William Demby, Toni Cade Bambara, Maya Angelou, Steve Cannon, and Quincy Troupe, Ishmael Reed asked a white professor named Edward Margolies why he had dismissed Chester's detective fiction as "potboilers." Satisfied by Margolies's beating a hasty retreat, Reed wrote Chester, "How does it feel to see your critics eat crow in your lifetime." It felt good to Chester, but the physical collapse that John Williams had been writing of since the mid-1960s opened the door to being haunted by other feelings. Chester and Lesley trooped back to New York in November for the publication of *My Life of Absurdity*. Before he made the trip, he wrote to his brother Joe, with *The Third Generation* and his memoirs and their representation of his family in the back of his mind, "I hope that I haven't offended you by my 'literature.'"

In a country swarming with discotheques and the latest fitness craze, *My Life of Absurdity*'s reviewers wrote about Chester as the creator of a detective series, not as a pioneer choosing a sometimes stylish, sometimes desperate self-exile to resolve the dilemma of racial and social injustice. Even so, Chester was now receiving the most serious praise of his lifetime and in the best places. The *Los Angeles Times* declared that "taken together, the two volumes are a satisfying, fascinating work by an important novelist." Chester was now considered a man who had written the detective series "very successfully," won prizes, and made popular movies. In one of the most thoughtful, generous, and incisive examinations of his work, the novelist Al Young tackled the autobiography for the *New York Times Book Review*.

Young's review was a turnabout play, since he had had a 1972 review of *The Quality of Hurt* changed by a "knuckleheaded" editor, without his consent, to be realigned with Nathan Huggins's blast. Reminding readers that the first volume was "a singularly poignant autobiography," Young then agreeably dealt with the second part: "The controlled intensity and lucid sense of focus that distinguished the earlier volume are missing. But this lack is more than made up for by the sheer passion, thoroughness and candor with which [Himes] writes about and, at the same time, deromanticizes the artistic expatriate life in which outrage, loneliness and frivolity abound."

My Life of Absurdity opens with unforgettable chapters showing Chester polishing the stainless steel fixtures of a Times Square cafeteria and saying "I got you beat now, motherfuckers," to New American Library editors in an elevator. The heart of the book was his journey with Regine in the ignoble Volkswagen lemon. He changes style then and moves in an intertextual direction, pioneered by Reed (whom he had directly queried about his method in *Mumbo Jumbo*), mixing portions of mildly emended letters to Carl Van Vechten and Lesley to flesh out the narrative of café life in Europe between roughly 1956 and 1970. He illustrated some pages with photographs of his mother and father and his early life, followed by photos of his life abroad with his white girlfriends. The book was out in the world only a few months when Chester learned that Marcel Duhamel, thought by Chester to be the honest man among the thieves at Gallimard, died suddenly of a heart attack. Mortality was at his doorstep.

He was also wrongly despairing at having missed the admiration of both the reading public and his intimates. Instead his reputation was climbing. Critics were saying that he had written four "classic" books before leaving the United States. In fact, full-length critical studies by James Lunquist and Stephen Milliken were at hand. Chester feared missteps, nonetheless. "I should not have written autobiography. It seems to have embarrassed everyone," he moaned in a letter to

Rosalyn Targ in 1977. Some of the resentment toward the book should have been anticipated, since he made casual, belittling remarks about friends like John Williams and Walter Coleman that he declined to make about other writers or publishers powerful enough to hurt his reputation. Walter Coleman, who had housed Chester regularly in the 1950s and '60s and enabled him to retreat from Paris, wrote Chester that he was free to write whatever he liked, fiction or nonfiction, so long as he spelled his name right. "I've made a lot of enemies," he told Chester, "but I'm still fucking with everybody." Generously, Walter uplifted his older friend, regardless of his continuing to publish: "You have already made a big contribution to the human race."

Chester tried to keep going. Raunchy *Players* magazine published five pages of his autobiography early in 1977, but by fall he would come to grips with the change of life, "sex doesn't delight me anymore."

That summer, he had feared illness would overtake him and that Jean, as his wife, would have legal right to his copyrights. He sued for divorce in a Paris court. Jean, living in Chicago and the well-regarded director of city recreation programs, and Chester became officially divorced on May 2, 1978. He and Lesley were married soon after. Chester remained depressed, mostly because of his ill health. Lesley wrote Joe that "his moral being is not so great and he feels very bad about not being able to do more around the house, studio, etc." They decided to sell the house in Spain, and retire in either Brazil or the United States, where they might have medical care nearby and Chester could be more comfortable.

To do so, by early 1980, Chester and Lesley were hoping to settle in California and have a single-level house. They visited the Bay Area in the spring, and were regally treated by Ishmael Reed and others belonging to the Before Columbus Foundation. Chester had roughly $50,000 in savings, and with the combination of a strong sale of the Moraira house and a few royalties, he could relocate and live his final years in modest contentment. Joe would counter their dream by describing the situation in 1980, known for the resurgence of the right in American politics and vigorous race-baiting, as "things are a mess here and getting worse."

That September Chester and Lesley seemed to have a buyer for their small villa, a British Petroleum consultant, who settled on a purchase price of £53,800. Then a global recession shocked the stock market, and the consultant backed out of the deal. The window on spending his final years in California closed firmly. Over seventy years old, Chester spent most of his time in bed now and labored to put on his clothes. He often used a wheelchair to get around, since he couldn't walk farther than the living room. That had its own risks, as he learned one afternoon when they had car trouble and Lesley had set him up in the chair on the side of the road. The wheels turned and he tumbled onto the ground, although Chester smiled about the mishap when she helped him back into the chair. His doctors were really surprised he could maneuver himself at all. But most difficult of all, as Lesley wrote to Joe, "his memory is terrible." Unable to attend even to correspondence, Chester found the idea of writing in his studio insufferable. Lesley felt the need to look into where he should be buried and proposed having him cremated and flown to Paris. "Depressing . . . but has to be thought of," she wrote wearily to Joe.

The Before Columbus Foundation, Ishmael Reed's brainchild, bestowed on Chester the American Book Award for Lifetime Achievement in 1982. Reed undoubtedly warmed Chester's heart more than he could have known by informing him that the American director Francis Ford Coppola wanted to make a film of *Lonely Crusade*. Perhaps the novel awaited rediscovery by another generation. For Chester, the physical end was near. By 1983 he was totally bedridden and listless. Roz Targ visited and confirmed the inevitable: "It saddened me enormously to see Chester looking so wan but there is a certain look in his eyes which shows his indomitable spirit." Joe wrote his younger brother in August 1984, asking whether Chester wanted to send his papers to the place that Joe had made arrangements for his own documents of a professional life, the Amistad Research Center at Tulane University in New Orleans, where Lesley thoughtfully agreed to deposit them. Lesley's friends, however, commented on the hurtful and bitter remarks that she had begun using as commonplaces, as she wore down under the strain of caretaking. While not perfect, Lesley had cared dutifully for Chester and she would continue to handle Chester's literary affairs on her own for decades after his death. On Monday, November 13, 1984, Chester died in the early afternoon in Moraira, where he was buried.

As soon as he heard the news, John Williams wrote to Lesley with a sincere and heartfelt eulogy. He had refused to speak or write to Chester after the chiseling knives in *My Life of Absurdity*. As much as anyone, Williams had felt the contradictory generosity and wrath of Chester's great gifts, his spirited realism from the bottom that defied fear and always cut hard enough to draw blood. But Williams saluted him appropriately: "When Chester was Chester I loved him."

Notes

ABOUT SOURCES

The notes that follow include full bibliographic information for all books, interviews, and periodicals that are cited. The more frequently cited archival collections are given in the list of abbreviations below.

Chester Himes's papers, beginning about 1954, are available at the Amistad Research Center of Tulane University. The collection was mostly transferred by Lesley Himes in the 1990s; she added some materials in the 2000s, which are indicated by the number 180. Another collection, containing some of Chester Himes's early manuscripts, is at Yale University's Beinecke Research Library.

In addition, the following archives were valuable: Alcorn State College Archives; James Baldwin Mss., Lilly Library, Indiana University, Bloomington; Charlotta Bass Papers, Southern California Library, Los Angeles; John Earle Bomar Memoirs, South Caroliniana Library, University of South Carolina, Columbia; Arna Bontemps Papers, Special Collections Research Center, Syracuse University Library, Syracuse, New York; Alice Browning Papers and Horace Cayton Papers, both at the Vivian Harsh Collection, Carter G. Woodson Branch, Chicago Public Library; John Henrik Clarke Papers, Schomburg Center for Research in Black Culture, New York Public Library, New York City; Cleveland Public Library,

Cleveland; Fannie Cook Papers, Missouri History Museum Library and Research Center, St. Louis; Malcolm Cowley Papers/Midwest Writers Collection and Maxim Lieber Papers, both at Newberry Library, Chicago; Matt and Evelyn Crawford Papers and John Oliver Killen Papers, both at Stuart A. Rose Library, Emory University, Atlanta; Crowell-Collier Publishing Company Records and Yaddo Papers Collection, both at Manuscripts and Archives Division, New York Public Library, New York City; Cuyahoga County Archives, Cleveland; E. Franklin Frazier Papers, Moorland-Spingarn Research Center, Howard University, Washington, D.C.; Georgia State Archives, Morrow, Georgia; Lincoln University Archives/Ethnic Studies Center, Jefferson City, Missouri; Ken McCormick/Doubleday Papers, Library of Congress, Washington, D.C.; Bucklin Moon Papers, Manuscripts and Archives, Rollins College, Winter Park, Florida; Ohio History Connection (formerly Ohio Historical Society), Columbus; Ohio State University Archives, Columbus; Jo Sinclair Papers, Howard Gotlieb Archival Research Center, Boston University, Boston; South Carolina Department of Archives and History, Columbia; and Spartanburg County Court Records, Spartanburg, South Carolina.

ABBREVIATIONS

Abbreviations are used throughout the notes that follow for frequently cited archives, people, and published works.

Archives

AAK Alfred A. Knopf Papers, box 30, folder 11, Harry Ransom Humanities Research Center, University of Texas, Austin

AG Arnold Gingrich Papers, Special Collections Library, University of Michigan, Ann Arbor

CH-FBI Chester B. Himes, File No. 105-2502, Federal Bureau of Investigation

CH-RF Chester Himes Application, Julius Rosenwald Papers, box 421, folder "Chester Himes," John Hope and Aurelia E. Franklin Library, Fisk University, Nashville, Tennessee

CHP-T Chester Himes Papers, Amistad Research Center, Tulane University, New Orleans, Louisiana

CHP-Y Chester Himes Papers, Beinecke Library, Yale University, New Haven, Connecticut

CUY Cuyahoga County Court Records, Cleveland, Ohio

CVVP Carl Van Vechten Papers, Beinecke Library, Yale University, New Haven, Connecticut

HLM Henry Lee Moon Papers, Western Reserve Historical Society, Cleveland, Ohio

JC Jack Conroy Papers, Newberry Library, Chicago

JSH Joseph S. Himes Papers, Amistad Research Center, Tulane University, New Orleans, Louisiana

LH Langston Hughes Papers, Beinecke Library, Yale University, New Haven, Connecticut

LM Loren Miller Papers, Huntington Library, San Marino, California

LPH Lesley Packard Himes Papers, Amistad Research Center, Tulane University, New Orleans, Louisiana

MF Michel Fabre Papers, Stuart A. Rose Manuscript Archives and Rare Book Library, Emory University, Atlanta, Georgia

MHLM Mollie and Henry Lee Moon Papers, Manuscripts, Archives and Rare Books Division, Schomburg Center for Research in Black Culture, New York Public Library, Astor, Lenox and Tilden Foundations, New York City

ODH Ohio Department of Health, Columbus

RE Ralph Ellison Papers, Manuscript Division, Library of Congress, Washington, D.C.

RW Richard Wright Papers, Beinecke Library, Yale University, New Haven, Connecticut

SAB Sterling A. Brown Papers, Moorland-Spingarn Research Center, Howard University, Washington, D.C.

People

CH Chester B. Himes

CVV Carl Van Vechten

JAW John Williams

WT Willa Thompson

Published Works

ATB-MF *As the Twig Is Bent* by Joseph Himes, Michel Fabre Papers, box 8, folder 27, Stuart A. Rose Manuscript, Archives, and Rare Book Library, Emory University, Atlanta, Georgia

CFS Chester Himes. *Cast the First Stone.* New York: Coward-McCann, 1952

CH-*CSS* Chester Himes. *The Collected Short Stories of Chester Himes.* New York: Thunder's Mouth Press, 1990

DCDJ *Dear Chester, Dear John: Letters Between Chester Himes and John A. Williams.* Edited by John and Lori Williams. Detroit: Wayne State University Press, 2008

HF Hoyt Fuller, "Chester Himes: Traveler on the Long, Rough, Lonely Old Road" [interview], *Black World,* March 1972, pp. 4–22, 87–98

MLA My Life of Absurdity: The Later Years, the Autobiography of Chester Himes by Chester Himes. 1977. Reprint, New York: Paragon House, 1990

MMH-*DCDJ* "My Man Himes: An Interview with Chester Himes." Pp. 179–232 of *Dear Chester, Dear John* (see above entry)

QH The Quality of Hurt: The Early Years, the Autobiography of Chester Himes by Chester Himes. 1972. Reprint, New York: Paragon House, 1990

TG The Third Generation by Chester Himes. 1954. Reprint, New York: Thunder's Mouth Press, 1989

PROLOGUE

xi **"the problem of the Twentieth Century"**: W. E. B. Du Bois, "The Forethought," in *The Souls of Black Folks*, ed. Henry Louis Gates Jr. and Terri Hume Oliver (New York: W. W. Norton, 1999), 5.

xii **"jingle in a broken tongue"**: Paul Laurence Dunbar, "The Poet," in *The Complete Poems of Paul Laurence Dunbar* (New York: Dodd, Mead, 1913); Benjamin Brawley, *Paul Laurence Dunbar: Poet of His People* (Chapel Hill: University of North Carolina Press, 1936), 76–77.

xii **"a fighter fights, and a writer writes"**: *QH*, 117.

xiii **"if he is not the greatest"**: CVV, "Letters of Reference—Chester B. Himes," CH-RF.

xiii **"for sheer intensity of feeling"**: M.R., October 25, 1946, AAK.

xiii **"nauseated her"**: *QH*, 77.

xiii **"We are not accustomed"**: Ken McCormick to CH, April 1, 1953, Ken McCormick/Doubleday Papers, box 51, folder "Chester Himes," Library of Congress, Washington, D.C.

1: OLD SCHOOL NEGRO

1 **by his middle name, Chester:** In a second case of Estelle and Joseph naming their children after relatives whose names of official record differed substantially from their colloquial ones, Estelle named her son Chester Bomar after her own father, who never had any name recorded on an official document, whether census or property deed, other than Elias Bomar. But the real irony lay in the fact that she delivered her son on the birthday of John Earle Bomar, the man who had owned her father during much of his twenty-seven years of slavery.

2 **using the terms "turks" and "brass ankles":** Richard B. Morris, "White Bondage in Ante-Bellum South Carolina," *South Carolina Historical and Genealogical Magazine*, October 1948, 194.

2 **"pedigreed Englishman":** "Estelle's Notes," transcribed by Joseph Himes Jr., MF box 8, folder 26.

2 **a prosperous Spartanburg merchant:** Jesse Cleveland, Estate Inventory, December 3, 1851, Deed Book, Spartanburg County, Spartanburg, South Carolina.

2 **much of the original land:** Dr. J. B. O. Landrum, *History of Spartanburg County: Embracing an Account of Many Important Events and Biographical Sketches of Statesmen, Divines and Other Public Men and the Names of Many Others Worthy of Record in the History of Their County* (Atlanta: Franklin Publishing, 1900), 55, 60.

2 **valued at $700:** Cleveland, Estate Inventory.

3 **$39,000 worth of "personal property"**: "Robt E. Cleveland," 1860 U.S. Census, South Carolina, Spartanburg District, p. 17.

3 **the last Cleveland child:** "Estelle's Notes."

3 **estimated value was $550:** "Theron Earle," 1840 U.S. Census, South Carolina, Spartanburg County, p. 158; Last Will and Testament of Theron Earle, November 12, 1841, Spartanburg, South Carolina, File 2351, South Carolina Department of Archives and History, Columbia.

3 **an "octoroon":** "Estelle's Notes."

4 **granddaughter of Elisha Bomar:** *QH*, 5.

4 **"no one ever wielded a more graceful pen":** Landrum, *History of Spartanburg*, 362.

4 **stocked with works by Alexander Pope:** John Earle Bomar, Inventory, Book J, p. 68, Probate Court Spartanburg County, Spartanburg, South Carolina.

5 **"white looking":** *QH*, 4–5.

5 **"a worse heart-broken":** Tom Moore Craig, *Upcountry South Carolina Goes to War* (Columbia: University of South Carolina Press, 2011), 147.

5 **$125 for a lot:** Melinda Bomar Grantee, A. J. Marshall Grantor, CL #2 E. Morris Street, August 12, 1871, Book G, Deed Book, Dalton County, Georgia, p. 211.

5 **born on February 23, 1874:** Estelle B. Himes, Death Certificate #53275, ODH.

6 **accepted $103 from Elias:** Elias Bomar, Book DDD, Deed Book, Spartanburg County, pp. 552, 554, 574.

6 **own twenty-seven shares:** Petition for the Estate of Thomas Bomar, "Inventory and Appraisement of the Estate of Thos. M. Bomar, Deceased," Book D, Probate Court, Spartanburg County.

6 **"We must make this institution":** Leland S. Cozart, *A Venture of Faith: Barber-Scotia College, 1867–1967* (Charlotte, N.C.: Heritage Printers, 1976), 12.

7 **three-fifths—of black teachers:** James M. McPherson, *The Abolitionist Legacy: From Reconstruction to the NAACP* (Princeton, N.J.: Princeton University Press, 1975), 274.

7 **"know the Book":** Catherine Owen Peare, *Mary McLeod Bethune* (New York: Vanguard, 1951), 58.

7 **"gave me my very first vision":** Mary McLeod Bethune, interviewed by Charles Johnson, summer 1946, Daniel Mortimer Williams Collection, M95-2, State Library and Archives of Florida.

8 **"the greater part of the [Negro] race":** Frenise Logan, *The Negro in North Carolina, 1876–1894* (Chapel Hill: University of North Carolina Press, 1964), 140, quoting from Albert Bushnell Hart, *The Nation*, March 17, 1892, 208.

8 **earned a first-class certificate:** Spartanburg Board of Examiners, Book SSS 1891–1892, South Carolina Department of Archives and History.

8 **Joseph Sandy Himes:** Joseph S. Himes, Death Certificate #3825, ODH. The death certificate, completed by G. B. Forbes, gives the birth date as 1874; however, the 1880 U.S. Census, conducted in June of that year, has him as already being seven years old.

9 **Sandy Neely:** "Sandy Neally," 1870 U.S. Census, Georgia, Washington County, Tennille Township; *QH*, 5; Fannie Wiggins, Death Certificate #57902, ODH.

9 **Samuel Robinson:** "Samuel Robinson," 1860 U.S. Census, Georgia, Washington County, Schedule 2, Slave Schedule.

9 **Elizabeth Hines:** "Elizabeth Hines," Personal Property Tax Records, Washington County, 1872–1877, Tanner's District 93, Georgia State Archives, Morrow, Georgia.

9 **came from Londonderry, Ireland:** William Neale Hurley, "John William Hines: His Descendants Principally of North Carolina and Virginia and Their Associated Families" [pamphlet] (Bowie, Md.: Heritage, 1995), iii.

9 **O'Heyne, or O'hEidhin:** Ibid., 7. This seems to be the most plausible origin of the Himes surname, particularly since there were numerous people named Hines in the antebellum American South, but only a handful named Heinz. In the United States, there came to be no appreciable distinction between the pronunciation of "Heinz" and "Hines," and in the South, by African American speakers to white Americans, there were only fairly slight distinctions between "Hines" and "Himes." Between 1880 and 1920, a variety of public and official documents recorded the family name of Chester Himes's father as "Hines," "Hinds," "Hynes," "Hymes," and "Himes." The 1920 U.S. Census uses "Hinds," the 1889 Claflin University catalog uses "Hines," and the 1906 Spartanburg State Court record uses "Hynes."

9 **an "ungovernable temper":** *TG*, 34–35. I have decided to selectively use *The Third Generation*, particularly the descriptions of the Taylor family in the Deep South, as autobiography. In a letter written in 1973, following the publication of CH's memoir *The Quality of Hurt*, a professor from England wrote to him and compared *Third Generation* with *Quality of Hurt*, specifically the overlapping passages. CH replied in a rare case of an author unguardedly reflecting on the autobiographical dimensions in fiction and the fictional dimensions of memoir in works written decades apart. He claimed that *Third Generation* was, with the obvious exception of the conclusion, a more faithful example of autobiography, mainly because he was temporally closer to the first twenty years of his life and able to recall them with more precision when he was writing the novel in 1952 and 1953.

Most of *3rd Gen* is true as I remembered my life at the time I was writing it. The last chapter is entirely fictional. . . . The "green paint episode" as you term it, is more likely true in the novel, as are many other things (true to my memory at that time), because the novel was written twenty years before my autobiography which was written after the sharp reality of memory begins to fail. . . . Even now I remember the wrecking of aunt Bee's (Fannie Wiggins') car as pure fact. . . .

In the *3rd Gen* I was trying to use some of the essential truths of my life, as I remembered them, to write a work of fiction; in my autobiography I was trying to state the unvarnished truth of my life as I remembered it and my publisher would publish it.

CH to Mr. Julie, September 5, 1973, MF.

9 **racially charged event:** Tad Evans, compiler, "Washington County, Georgia, Newspaper Clippings," vol. 2, 1867–1880, Genealogical Room, Washington County Museum, Sandersville, Georgia, pp. 66–67, 68, 262. The newspaper digests at this historical society show regular evidence of homicidal racial violence in the aftermath of the Civil War.

10 **owned personal goods:** "Sandy Neely," Personal Property Tax Records, Washington County, 1872–1877, McBride's District 88, Georgia State Archives.

10 **Anna Himes died:** "Funeral Notice [Mrs. Himes]," box 3, folder 33, HLM.

10 **a child named Fannie in 1886:** Fannie Wiggins, Death Certificate #57902, ODH. The certificate, filled out by Leah, lists Annie Robinson as Fannie's mother. However, the death notice for "Mrs. Joseph Himes" was retained among Leah's effects. In 1892, all of the Himes children, led by Leah, were involved in a court petition against Mary Himes to redistribute the estate.

10 **"well known and highly honored":** Henry Lee Moon, English IIC Composition, March 23, 1917, MHLM, box 6, folder "Glenville High School."

11 **On February 4, 1891:** Leah Himes and Roddy K. Moon, certificate of marriage, February 4, 1891, box 3, folder 2, HLM.

11 **Himes entered the first-year normal school:** Claflin University catalog, 1889–1890, courtesy of Jennifer Squire.

11 **"a good moral character":** Blinzy L. Gore, *On Hilltop High: The Origin and History of Claflin* (Spartanburg, S.C.: Reprint Publishers, 1994), 44.

11 **a "magnificent actor":** *TG*, 35.

11 **"fully committed to Industrial Education":** Gore, *On Hilltop High*, p. 112.

12 **"not one in 1,000":** McPherson, *The Abolitionist Legacy*, 281.

12 **finished the three-year course:** Claflin University catalog, 1893, p. 14; Claflin University Archives, miscellany (typescript list of students in 1893), Orangeburg, South Carolina.

12 **a standard curriculum:** Clyde W. Hall, *One Hundred Years of Educating at Savannah State College 1890–1990* (East Peoria, Ill.: Versa Press, 1991), 14.

12 **Savannah's 55,268 residents:** 1900 U.S. Census, Georgia, Chatham County, Savannah Township.

13 **"Massa, tell 'em we are rising":** Richard R. Wright Jr., *87 Years Behind the Curtain* (Philadelphia: Rare Books, 1965), 17.

14 **Among Wright's prized volumes:** Ibid., 53.

14 **"I do not believe in educating":** Ibid., 35.

14 **"Get up and go!":** Gore, *On Hilltop High,* 110.

15 **He ran a commercial blacksmithing:** "J.S. Himes, Blacksmith and Wheelwright," advertisement, *Savannah Tribune,* 18 November 18, 1905, 2.

16 **married on June 27, 1901:** "A Spartanburg Wedding," *Savannah Tribune,* July 6, 1901, 2.

16 **"popular" young couple:** Ibid.

17 **his *Savannah Tribune* columns:** Linda O. Hines and Allen Jones, "A Voice of Black Protest: The Savannah Men's Sunday Club, 1905–1911," *Phylon* (2d quarter 1973): 195.

17 **the court granted Estelle one-tenth, $752.04:** "Sale Bill," Estate of Thomas Bomar, Probate Court, Spartanburg County.

17 **"promptly and satisfactorily done":** "J.S. Himes, Blacksmith" ad.

18 **"ignorant and narrow-minded":** Booker T. Washington, "One Other Lesson," *Savannah Tribune,* July 15, 1905, 2.

18 **"chased negroes, stoned and shot":** "Orgie of Bloodshed," *Savannah Tribune,* September 29, 1906, 1.

18 **twenty-five African Americans:** Charles Crowe, "Racial Massacre in Atlanta, September 22, 1906," *Journal of Negro History* (April 1969): 168.

18 **had to shoulder a rifle:** Walter White, *A Man Called White* (1948; repr., New York: Arno Press, 1969), 5–12.

18 **paraphrase of the song "Dixie":** Hines and Jones, "A Voice of Black Protest," 199.

18 **Black Savannah citizens boycotted:** "Separate Seats for Negroes," *Savannah Tribune,* September 15, 1906, 1.

19 **"the Negro was emotional":** Wright, *87 Years Behind,* 72.

20 **parties, which were noticed:** "In a Social Way," *Atlanta Tribune,* February 8, 1902, 2.

20 **on August 27, 1907:** Minutes of the Board of Trustees, Lincoln Institute, p. 77, Lincoln University Archives/Ethnic Studies Center, Jefferson City, Missouri.

20 **they agreed to name him Joseph Sandy:** Joseph Himes understood his second son to be junior, and either did not know his father's first name or didn't acknowledge the custom. Of course, the second son, Joseph Sandy, was properly Joseph Sandy Himes III.

20 **the strongest college preparatory curriculum:** W. Sherman Savage, *The History of Lincoln University* (Jefferson City, Mo.: Lincoln University, 1939), 124.

21 **"fundamental idea shall be to combine":** Ibid., 3.

21 **By 1879 the state had taken over:** Henry Sullivan Williams, "The Development of the Negro Public School in Missouri," *Journal of Negro History* (April 1920): 154.

22 **An "artist at the forge":** *TG*, 29.

22 **"fresh and vigorous":** Anna Julia Cooper, *A Voice from the South* (1892; repr., New York: Oxford University Press, 1988), 11.

23 **"Here in America":** Ibid.

23 **patrolled the dormitories:** Louise Hutchinson, *Anna J. Cooper: A Voice from the South* (Washington, D.C.: Smithsonian Institute, 1981), 83.

23 **"to be a first class American":** Olin P. Wells, "What It Means to Be an American," 1914 Senior Class Yearbook, "The Gate to Success," Lincoln University Archives/Ethnic Studies Center.

23 **"bad English":** Joseph Himes, taped interview with Michel Fabre, November 15, 1985, MF, box 35.

24 **open can of paint:** CH to Julie, September 5, 1973.

25 **"All the leading Negroes":** Roddy Moon to Leah Moon, May 1, 1904, HLM, box 3, folder 33.

25 **Allen fired his old friend:** Minutes of the Board of Trustees, Lincoln Institute, p. 188, Lincoln University Archives/Ethnic Studies Center; *TG*, 42.

25 **"The automobile has replaced the wagon":** Lincoln University, Fifty-First Annual Catalog, 1922–23, p. 45, Lincoln University Archives/Ethnic Studies Center.

2. THE SOUTHERN CROSSES THE YELLOW DOG

27 **"lazy Missouri accent":** CH to Yves Malartic, February 26, 1953, MF, box 7, folder 4.

28 **"protected in all their rights":** "General Alcorn Had a Tough Job," *Mississippi Democrat*, December 29, 1965, in "Alcorn, James L.," clipping file, Vicksburg Public Library, Vicksburg, Mississippi.

28 **"shielded" the boys:** ATB, 4.

28 **Alcorn had only a quarter:** "Catalogue of the Officers and Students of Alcorn Agricultural and Mechanical College, 1914–1915," Alcorn A&M (Natchez, 1915), p. 35.

29 **turned away a hundred:** "Report of the Board of Trustees," Alcorn State College Archives, RG1, box 1, folder 5 "1912–1913," Lorman, Mississippi.

29 **"give the students a thorough mastery":** "Catalogue 1914–1915," p. 57.

29 **"the negro dialect"**: "Clipping File," *Woodville Republican*, June 5, 1918, p. 1, Port Gibson Public Library, Port Gibson, Mississippi.

29 **"ain't" was "absolutely prohibited"**: ATB, 4.

29 **fifty male students**: "Catalogue 1914–1915," p. 47.

30 **"to train practical blacksmiths"**: "Catalogue of the Officers and Students of Alcorn Agricultural and Mechanical College, 1916–1917," Alcorn A&M (Natchez, 1917), p. 30.

30 **one graduate annually**: Ibid., pp. 74–75.

30 **"a comedown"**: *TG*, 49.

31 **"had been hurt"**: *QH*, 265.

31 **"escape safari"**: ATB, 4.

31 **"very fair girls"**: *TG*, 116.

31 **for her ability to translate**: Gloria T. Williams-May, "Lucy Craft Laney— The Mother of the Children of the People: Educator, Reformer, Social Activist," PhD diss., University of South Carolina, 1998, 44–48.

32 **"shocked by the sight"**: *TG*, 115.

32 **a state that did not provide**: James Anderson, lecture, Emory University, November 2009.

32 **"de goat done dead"**: *TG*, p. 122.

32 **three thousand people were left homeless**: "Fire Sweeps Through Augusta: Flames Cut Red Swath to the Boundary of the City; Put Loss at $8,000,000," *Atlanta Constitution*, March 23, 1916: 1–2; Craig Britt, "Undaunted by Great Disaster, Citizens of Augusta Prepare for Building a Better City," *Atlanta Constitution*, March 24, 1916, 1, 5, 12.

33 **"Alcorn Ode"**: Mrs. E. B. Himes, "Alcorn Ode," Alcorn Centennial Yearbook, 1928, p. 28, Alcorn A&M College, Alcorn, Mississippi.

33 **"These were the moments"**: *TG*, 70.

34 **"Forget our special grievances"**: W. E. B. Du Bois, "Close Ranks," *The Crisis*, July 1918, 111.

34 **dismissed for reading northern periodicals**: *TG*, 67.

34 **"Women were standing"**: Ibid., 104.

35 **"high levels of expectation"**: ATB, 4.

35 **"We were a small"**: Ibid.

35 **the word "damn"**: Ibid.; *TG*, 86.

35 **playing Chopin's "Fantaisie Impromptu"**: *TG*, 94.

36 **"You mustn't think of yourself as colored"**: Ibid., 99; *QH*, 5.

36 **he apparently withdrew**: Edward Harry Himes, Pine Bluff, Ark., *Atlanta University Bulletin*, series 2, no. 43, April 1921, p. 33; Edward Harry Himes, Pine Bluff, Ark., *Atlanta University Bulletin*, series 2, no. 47, April 1922, p. 33. None of the subsequent bulletins in the 1920s carry the name of Edward Himes as a student.

36 **a regular visitor to the school**: Bobby Wade Saucier, "The Public Career

of Theodore G. Bilbo," PhD diss., Tulane University, 1971, 21; Stephen Cresswell, *Rednecks, Redeemers, and Race: Mississippi After Reconstruction, 1877–1917* (Jackson: University of Mississippi Press, 2006), 209–10. Between 1916 and 1920 when he was governor, Bilbo himself often needed a retreat; the sparring with his political rivals regularly became violent and he was assaulted and knocked unconscious by his constituents on more than one occasion between 1911 and 1920.

36 **Joseph Himes joked with him:** The Bilbo Papers at the University of
· Southern Mississippi in Hattiesburg offer nothing to verify Bilbo's trips to Alcorn during his first term as populist governor of the state (1916–1920). According to Bilbo scholar Chester Morgan, Bilbo at least argued unsuccessfully for a higher appropriation for Alcorn during his second term as governor (1928–1932).

37 **"my father was born and raised":** *QH*, 22.

37 **"Mother kept chopping":** Joseph Himes, taped interview with Michel Fabre, November 15, 1985, MF, box 35.

37 **"a quarrelsome nature":** Estelle B. Himes Plaintiff, Joseph S. Himes Defendant, "Decree," December 20, 1927, Court of Common Pleas, CUY.

37 **the Greek and Roman myths:** Michael J. Bandler, "Portrait of a Man Reading: Chester Himes, Author of *The Quality of Hurt*," *Washington Post*, April 9, 1972, BW2.

38 **thirty-two people were dead:** Joyce Bridges, "Looking Back," *Port Gibson Reveille*, December 15, 1988; Joyce Bridges, "Looking Back," *Port Gibson Reveille*, November 10, 1998.

38 **4525 Garfield Avenue:** St. Louis City Directory; Joseph Himes to Michel Fabre, March 7, 1986, MF, box 8, folder 26.

38 **wartime surge of blacks:** Randy Finley, "Black Arkansans and World War One," *Arkansas Historical Quarterly* (Autumn 1990): 250.

38 **Hundreds of African Americans:** Grif Stockley and Jeannie M. Whayne, "Federal Troops and the Elaine Massacres," *Arkansas Historical Quarterly* (Autumn 2002): 272–83; Walter F. White, "'Massacring Whites' in Arkansas," *The Nation*, December 6, 1919, 715–16.

39 **none of the graduates:** Elizabeth Wheeler, "Isaac Fisher: The Frustrations of a Negro Educator at Branch Normal College, 1902–1911," *Arkansas Historical Quarterly* (Spring 1982): 40.

39 **Himes family boarded downtown:** "Pine Bluff, Arkansas," Sanborn Fire Insurance Map, 1908, Pine Bluff Public Library; "Lillie Grotia," 1920 U.S. Census, Arkansas, Jefferson County, Pine Bluff, Ward 2.

40 **Himes boys were placed:** "Annual Catalogue, 1920–21," Agricultural, Mechanical and Normal School, Branch of the University of Arkansas, pp. 46–47.

41 **"gone to Memphis":** *QH*, 9.

41 **"sentimentality and hypocrisy":** H. W. Boynton, "Book Reviews: Yellow Is Black," *The Independent*, May 13, 1922, 108.

41 **By 1923 she had provided:** "Annual Catalogue, 1920–21," p. 15.

42 **"ate that stuff up!":** Joseph Himes, taped interview.

42 **"acquaint the student with the facts":** "Annual Catalogue, 1920–21," p. 17.

42 **"a number of textbooks":** *QH*, 10.

42 **"a thrilling and eye-opening experience":** ATB, 5.

42 **"I could read blueprints":** *QH*, 74–75.

43 **"A delicate and dangerous":** Ibid., 11.

43 **"naughty":** Ibid.

43 **Joseph maintained that Chester:** Joseph Himes, taped interview.

44 **"Penelope and I was Ulysses":** *TG*, 155.

45 **city of nearly 800,000:** Joseph Heathcott, "Black Archipelago: Politics and Social Life in the Jim Crow City," *Journal of Social Life and History* (Spring 2005): 707.

45 **eventually settling on Belle Glade Avenue:** Joseph S. Himes and Estelle B. Himes indenture to Abraham and Bettie Davis, December 24, 1923, St. Louis Deed Book, microfilm, St. Louis City Hall, p. 380, St. Louis, Missouri.

45 **fifty people dead:** Robert Asher, "Documents of the East St. Louis Riot," *Journal of Illinois Historical Society* (Autumn 1972): 327.

45 **"He was a pathetic figure":** *TG*, 159.

46 **For a full year he specialized:** CH, transcript, Charles Sumner High School, St. Louis, Missouri, 1925.

46 **"hated" Sumner:** *TG*, 160.

3. BANQUETS AND COCAINE BALLS

49 **Joseph Sr. and Chester came first:** Estelle B. Himes Plaintiff v. Joseph S. Himes Defendant, November 16, 1927, "Petition for Alimony and Equitable Relief," Court of Common Pleas, CUY.

50 **By 1930, Seventy-Ninth Street:** Todd Michney, "Changing Neighborhoods: Race and Upward Mobility in Southeast Cleveland, 1930–1980," PhD diss., University of Minnesota, 2004, 93.

51 **also a friend of Mary:** Henry Lee Moon to Mary McLeod Bethune, November 5, 1937, HLM, box 1, folder 2.

51 **"My father's people":** *QH*, 16.

52 **"'You don't like black people'":** *TG*, 155–56.

52 **"infantilized":** Joseph Himes, taped interview with Michel Fabre, November 15, 1985, MF, box 35.

52 **Chester began his scholastic year:** CH, transcript, Charles Sumner High School, St. Louis, Missouri, 1925. The record was mailed on March 2, 1925.

53 **"anxious to prove":** Chester B. Himes, "Spring Day of 1925 in Cleveland," *Cleveland News*, December 5, 1945, Chester Himes Clipping File, Cleveland Public Library, Ohio.

54 **kept a 90 average:** "Brooks Friebolin Leads Honor Roll," *Blue and Gold*, October 29, 1925, 3, Cleveland Public Library.

54 **On October 8, 1925:** Joseph S. and Estelle B. Himes, CUY, Deeds Book, V. 3330 p. 74.

54 **"the nicest house":** Joseph Himes, taped interview.

54 **the shouts of "colored boy":** Henry Lee Moon, "Encounter with the C.P.," p. 4, MHLM, box 14, folder "Memoirs."

55 **had written "86":** *QH*, 17.

55 **along with dozens of other members:** "College Is Goal of Majority of Students," *Blue and Gold*, January 22, 1926, 1, Cleveland Public Library.

55 **"Our people need more doctors":** Henry Lee Moon, "The Closed Door," MHLM, box 14, folder "Memoirs."

56 **"No matter what your aim":** *TG*, 200.

56 **"ruined" after a season:** Moon, "The Closed Door."

56 **"to an old fat ugly whore":** *QH*, 18.

57 **"spattering open":** Ibid., 20.

58 **"incontinent vanity":** *TG*, 236.

58 **"will you please-please-please shut up!":** Ibid., 243.

61 **"a brief survey":** Ohio State University Catalogue, 1926, p. 102.

61 **"permanently excused":** CH, transcript, Ohio State University, CHP-T, box 40, folder 6.

61 **successfully petitioned:** Pamela Pritchard, "The Negro Experience at The Ohio State University in the First Sixty-Five Years 1873–1938 with Special Emphasis on Negroes in the College of Education," PhD diss., Ohio State University, 1982, 62; Ohio State University Yearbook, 1926.

62 **1389 Summit Street:** Ohio State University Student Directory, 1926.

62 **"He dreaded the classes":** *TG*, 261.

62 **"colored people should not":** Pritchard, "The Negro Experience," 78.

63 **"slightly hysterical":** *TG*, 264.

63 **"Light-complexioned blacks":** *QH*, 29.

64 **"You got an awful lot":** Ibid., 25.

65 **"leaped atop tables":** Ibid., 28.

65 **"I fixed your little red wagon":** Ibid., 30.

66 **"ill health and failing":** CH, transcript, Ohio State University.

66 **"one of those soft":** *QH*, 37.

67 **"small, dried up looking":** Ibid., 32.

67 **"soft-spoken, handsome":** Ibid.

67 **"that peculiar, almost virgin":** CH, *Lonely Crusade* (1947; repr., New York: Thunder's Mouth, 1993), 325.

68 **one hundred bootleggers:** Rick Porello, *The Rise and Fall of the Cleveland Mafia* (New York: Barricade, 1995), 28.

69 **he featured in his first detective fiction:** CH, *A Rage in Harlem* (1957 as *For the Love of Imabelle*; repr., New York: Vintage, 1991), 21.

69 **"'Unchain 'em in the big corral'":** CH, *If He Hollers Let Him Go* (1945; repr., New York: Thunder's Mouth, 1986), 37.

69 **"a big-framed":** *QH*, 38.

69 **"But where he got":** CH, "Prison Mass," CH-CSS, 162.

70 **proclaimed Joe a "genius":** Lester A. Walton, "Pupils Win Honor Despite Handicaps," *Pittsburgh Courier*, March 12, 1927, 5.

70 **"hearty congratulations":** Ernest Wilkins to Joseph Himes, February 21, 1928, JSH, box 1, folder 2.

70 **on September 26, 1927:** *State of Ohio v. Chester Hines*, No. 16313, "Indictment for Forgery and Uttering a Forged Check," Chester Hines, Court of Common Pleas, Franklin County, Ohio.

71 **"failed and willfully neglected":** Estelle B. Himes Plaintiff v. Joseph S. Himes Defendant, "Petition for Alimony and Equitable Relief," Court of Common Pleas, CUY.

71 **summon Joseph to court:** *Estelle B. Himes Plaintiff, Joseph S. Himes Defendant*, "Decree," December 20, 1927, Court of Common Pleas, CUY.

71 **On December 20, 1927:** Joseph S. and Estelle B. Himes, CUY Deeds Book, V. 3330, p. 74.

71 **Chester changed his plea to guilty:** *State of Ohio v. Chester Hines*, No. 16313. CH provides a completely different chronology of events in his memoir *The Quality of Hurt*, which he wrote forty-three years later and without any of the legal records.

72 **"a congested area of vice":** *TG*, 276.

72 **hoped to take Jean to Detroit:** *QH*, 39.

73 **"She told him she thought":** CH, *Yesterday Will Make You Cry* (New York: W. W. Norton, 1998), 150.

74 **arrested them on October 9:** "Two Held in Firearms Theft," *Cleveland Plain Dealer*, October 6, 1928; Chester Himes, No. 35051, Criminal Record Department, Cuyahoga County Archives, Cleveland.

74 **"not likely to engage":** *State of Ohio v. Chester Hines*, Case No. 16313, Court of Common Pleas, Franklin County, January 28, 1928, Columbus, Ohio.

74 **"over the vehement protests":** *QH*, 42.

76 **requiring an examination:** *State of Ohio v. Chester Himes*, Case No. 35052, Cuyahoga County Common Pleas Court, December 6, 1928, p. 327.

76 **McMahon sentenced:** Chester Himes, Case No. 35051, December 19, 1928, Judge McMahon Presiding, *Record of Convictions January Term 1926 to & September Term 1931 Cuyahoga County*, p. 190. A dozen years later

McMahon, no friend to African Americans, would uphold the foreclosure of a home purchased by a black couple attempting to integrate a white neighborhood—see "The Right to Own a Home," *Cleveland Call and Post*, February 29, 1940, 6.

76 **bout for local headlines:** "Robber Gets 20 Years: Youth Sent in Pen for Holdup in Heights," *Cleveland Plain Dealer*, December 20, 1928, 2.

4. GRAY CITY OF EXILED MEN

77 **He entered the prison two days:** "#59623 Himes, Chester," *Ohio Penitentiary Register of Prisoners*, Ohio History Connection, microfilm 1536, pp. 111–12, Columbus, Ohio.

78 **forty-two hundred convicts:** D. J. Bonzo, "Statistical Report with Movement of Population of the Ohio Penitentiary, June 1931," Ohio State Historical Society, box 51, 593, series 1796, p. 7; P. E. Thomas, "The Ohio Penitentiary," *State of Ohio Eighth Annual Report of the Department of Public Welfare* (December 1930), 503.

78 **stood at the end of lines:** "Ohio Penitentiary Fades into History," *Cleveland Call and Post*, May 24, 1973, 4A.

79 **more than a quarter of:** D. J. Bonzo, "Balance Sheet of Color of Men for Year Ending December 31, 1931"; "Annual Statistical Report with Movement of Population of the Ohio Penitentiary January 1, 1931, to December 31, 1931," Ohio History Connection, box 51, 593, series 1796, p. 50.

79 **forty-six-year-old Kentuckian:** "Flo Wallace," 1930 U.S. Census, Ohio, Franklin County, Columbus City, p. 228.

80 **Only about fifty:** P. E. Thomas, "Education of Men Entering and Leaving the Institution," *State of Ohio Eighth Annual Report of the Department of Public Welfare* (December 1930), 509.

80 **"He hadn't ever had":** Chester Himes, "I Don't Want to Die," CH-*CSS*, 205.

80 **"Every one of them looked":** *CFS*, 4; CH to CVV, February 18, 1948, CVVP, box He–Hols, folder "Himes, Chester B. 1948–1956." CH described major portions of the novel *Cast the First Stone* as "more or less autobiographical."

81 **"treacherous" lot:** *QH*, 62.

81 **"free to roam the city":** David Myers and Elise Myers *Central Ohio's Historic Prisons* (Charleston, S.C.: Arcadia Publishing, 2009), 43.

81 **"half afraid that every big":** *CFS*, 110.

82 **Pat McDermott:** "Bloody Crew Is Loosed on State," *Cleveland Plain Dealer*, February 20, 1929, 1.

82 **on February 28, 1930:** Myers and Myers, *Central Ohio's Historic Prisons*, 55–57.

83 **"in these hands I hold":** CH, *Yesterday Will Make You Cry* (New York: W. W. Norton, 1998), 75.

83 **he claimed ignorance:** "Chester Hines," 1930 U.S. Census, Ohio, Franklin County, Columbus City, p. 228.

83 **"I didn't get anything but":** *CFS*, 124.

84 **"loaded stick and the concrete":** *QH*, 69.

85 **he received a check:** "Ohio Convict Rewarded," *New York Times*, April 23, 1930, 3.

85 **the 166th Regiment:** "Pen Ex-Warden's Rites Tomorrow," *Cleveland Plain Dealer*, October 7, 1952, 7. "Convict Charges Pen Dope Traffic," *Cleveland Plain Dealer*, January 25, 1935, 8.

85 **"bitchery and abomination":** *CFS*, 167.

85 **"passive resistance" campaign:** "Ohio Penitentiary 1930 Fire," *Columbus and Central Ohio Historian* (November 1984): 17.

85 **On April 28:** F. Raymond Daniell, "Ohio Prison Quiet, 300 Resume Work," *New York Times*, May 2, 1930, 5.

86 **commandant of the 166th:** "Machine Gun Kills Two Ohio Convicts," *New York Times*, May 9, 1930, 15.

86 **"small rebellious army":** Thomas, "The Ohio Penitentiary," 562.

87 **Negro inmates were the recognized:** "Negroes Are Fire Heroes," *Cleveland Plain Dealer*, April 22, 1930, 1, 3.

88 **"grotesque fantasy":** *CFS*, 137.

88 **"I want you for my woman":** Ibid., 137, 107.

88 **"no one tried to rape me":** *QH*, 61.

89 **Ohio legislature passed three laws:** N. R. Howard, "Ohio Adopts Plan for Prison Reform," *New York Times*, April 19, 1931, 57.

89 **"Under the provisions":** J. C. Woodard, "The Ohio Board of Parole," *State of Ohio Thirteenth Annual Report of the Department of Public Welfare* (December 1935), 275.

89 **"take it easy":** "Local Items," *Ohio Penitentiary News*, September 12, 1931, 2.

89 **September 17, 1931:** "#59623 Himes, Chester" file.

90 **"having stared so long":** *CFS*, 178.

90 **"if I just had my life":** CH, *Yesterday Will Make You Cry*, 219; *QH*, 60.

90 **In May 1932:** Joseph Himes and Agnes Rowe, May 26, 1932, Marriage Record #A4776, CUY.

90 ***Chicago Defender* carry news:** Alexander O. Taylor, "Ohio State News: Cleveland News," *Chicago Defender*, June 25, 1932, 12.

91 **to work toward a master's degree:** "Blind Student to Return to Oberlin Studies Soon," New York *Amsterdam News*, September 23, 1931, 3.

91 **"There is one rule":** "Writing," *Ohio Penitentiary News*, July 5, 1930, 2.

91 **"'I asked him was there'":** *CFS*, 106.

92 **"black murderer of great intelligence"**: *QH*, 64.

92 **"'I'm going to take you up'"**: *CFS*, 138–39.

92 *The Maltese Falcon*: Michael J. Bandler, "Portrait of a Man Reading: Chester Himes, Author of *The Quality of Hurt*," *Washington Post*, April 9, 1972, BW2.

92 **"Most of the black convicts"**: *QH*, 64.

93 a **"dark brown skin" man**: CH, "His Last Day," CH-CSS, 291, 303.

93 **"crying softly"**: CH, "The Night's for Crying," *Esquire*, January 1937, 148.

93 **1400 African American prisoners**: Bonzo, "Balance Sheet of Color of Men for Year Ending December 31, 1931"; "Balance Sheet of Life Men for Year Ending December 31, 1935"; "Annual Statistical Report with Movement of Population of the Ohio Penitentiary January 1, 1935, to December 31, 1935," Ohio History Connection, box 51, 593, series 1796, p. 42.

94 **Merrill Chandler**: The data in this paragraph on prisoner executions comes from an archives of photographed prisoners, "Photographs of Executed Prisoners," State Properties, Ohio History Connection, box 3, folder Ohio Penitentiary.

94 **circulation of around 100,000**: Donald Joyce, "Magazines of Afro-American Thought on the Mass Market: Can They Survive?," *American Libraries* (December 1976): 680–81; Abby Johnson and Ronald Johnson, *Propaganda and Aesthetics: The Literary Politics of African-American Magazines in the Twentieth Century* (Amherst: University of Massachusetts Press, 1990), 109–11.

95 **"put in the 'cripple' company"**: CH, "Prison Mass," CH-CSS, 152, 163.

95 **"I might not have believed**: Ibid., 186.

96 **"the whiteness of Swiss cheese"**: Ibid., 152, 170.

96 **"He wanted to do"**: Ibid., 191.

97 **"What right had a 'nigger'"**: CH, "A Black Man Has Red Blood," *Chicago Defender*, June 2, 1934, 9.

97 **"we ate our good-doin' bread"**: *CFS*, 188.

97 **Sentenced to ten years**: "#67175 Rico, Prince," *Ohio Penitentiary Register of Prisoners*, Ohio History Connection, microfilm 1536, pp. 293–94.

98 **"was the boy in the story"**: CH to CVV, March 11, 1952, CVVP, box He–Hols, folder "Himes, Chester B. 1952–1955."

98 **"I think Mother talked"**: Joseph Himes to Robert E. Skinner, September 23, 1988, MF, box 8, folder 26.

100 *Esquire* **had a newsstand circulation**: Arnold Gingrich, *Nothing but People: The Early Days at Esquire; A Personal History 1928–1958* (New York: Crown, 1971), 107.

100 **"ample hair on its chest"**: Arnold Gingrich to Ernest Hemingway, Febru-

ary 24, 1933, quoted in Michael Reynolds, *Hemingway: The 1930s* (New York: W. W. Norton, 1997), 123.

100 **"any trace of any kind of accent"**: Gingrich, *Nothing but People*, 95.

100 **"compulsory and universal"**: *Esquire*, February 1934, contents page.

100 **"If you print the story"**: "The Sound and the Fury: Foul Blow from Philly," *Esquire*, February 1934, 12.

101 **"Don't you think having"**: "The Sound and the Fury: Citation from Oklahoma History," *Esquire*, February 1934, 12.

101 **"By all means shoot"**: "The Sound and the Fury: A Lift from Voltaire," *Esquire*, February 1934, 12.

101 **"your readers would appreciate"**: "The Sound and the Fury: Some Like It Hot," *Esquire*, February 1934, 12.

101 **"one of these golden"**: Langston Hughes, "A Good Job Gone," *Esquire*, April 1934, 142.

101 **"through correspondence"**: CH to JAW, October 31, 1962, DJDC, 17.

101 **seventy-five dollars**: Ibid., 18.

101 **"a long-term prisoner"**: CH, "Crazy in Stir," *Esquire*, August 1934, 28.

102 **a sample of 862 men**: W. F. Armine, "London Prison Farm: Unstable Character of Population," *State of Ohio Thirteenth Annual Report of the Department of Public Welfare* (December 1935), 286–87.

102 **"He would see what"**: CH, "Crazy in Stir," 114.

102 **powerful short story**: "Along the Literary Front," New York *Amsterdam News*, October 6, 1934, 8.

103 **Blackie has a "queer feeling"**: CH, "To What Red Hell," *Esquire*, October 1934, 100.

103 **"big blonde guy kissing"**: Ibid., 101, 122.

104 **"White faces, gleaming"**: Ibid., 100, 122.

104 **"received the greatest"**: *MLA*, 26.

105 **On August 2, 1934**: "#59623 Himes, Chester" and "#67175 Rico, Prince" files.

105 **"had a full and complete"**: CH to CVV, March 11, 1952.

105 **"the farm was the way"**: *CFS*, 346; "#59623 Himes, Chester" file.

105 **the population fluctuated**: T. C. Jenkins, "The London Prison Farm," *State of Ohio Fifteenth Annual Report of the Department of Public Welfare* (December 1934), 514.

106 **"so many upbraidings"**: Chester B. Himes #59623 to Miss Armine Mail Censor, n.d. [c. 1934], MF.

106 **"Glad you're through"**: Prince Rico to CH, March 13, 1936, CHP-Y, box 3, folder 9.

107 **lauded in the press**: "Prisoner's Songs Go into His Opera," clipping from unknown periodical, January 20, 1935, CHP-Y, box 3, folder 9.

108 **parole was finally granted**: "#59623 Himes, Chester" file.

5. WHITE FOLKS AND THE DAYS

109 "'This can't be *my* home'": CH, "On Dreams and Reality," CH-CSS, 217.

110 "We'll put the big pot": Joseph Himes to CH, November 24, 1973, JSH, box 6, folder 4.

110 the director of research: "Blind Student Awarded Ph.D. by Ohio State," *Atlanta Daily World*, July 5, 1938, 1.

110 Chester served out the maximum sentence: Polly Johnson, interview with Michel Fabre, n.d., MF, box 6, folder 31.

110 "more hysterical": *QH*, 66.

111 "Several times": Ibid.

112 "with the past kind of living": Roddy Moon to Henry Lee Moon, July 2, 1936, HLM, box 3, folder 33.

112 Chester met Cleveland's most famous: MMH-*DCDJ*, 200; Bud Douglass, "Langston Hughes Safe in Cleveland; Denies That He Is Lost in Spain," *Cleveland Call and Post*, August 6, 1936, 3.

112 living with his mother: "Dates Changed on Little Ham; Opens June 9," *Cleveland Call and Post*, June 4, 1936, 7.

112 "because I am both a Negro": "Langston Hughes at Paris Conference," *Cleveland Call and Post*, August 5, 1937, 2.

112 giving lectures at middle-class teas: "Alpha Art Club," *Cleveland Call and Post*, July 2, 1936, 4.

113 "America's principal servant": CH, "A Salute to The Passing," *Opportunity*, March 1939, 75–76.

114 "I had it hard": CH to JAW, October 31, 1962, *DCDJ*, 17.

114 increased his fee: Ibid., 18.

114 Jean was living: *Jean Plater v. Harry Plater*, "Affidavit for Service by Publication," No. 453701, January 20, 1937, Court of Common Pleas, CUY.

115 "I grew to love her too": *QH*, 70.

115 "gross neglect of duty": *Jean Plater v. Harry Plater*, "Petition for Divorce," No. 453701, March 15, 1937, Court of Common Pleas, CUY.

115 on Tuesday, July 13, 1937: CH and Jean L. Plater, Marriage License, No. A43102, CUY.

116 "just be a nigger": CH, "All God's Chilluns Got Pride," *The Crisis*, June 1944, 189.

116 "Until then there had been": *QH*, 70.

116 "They have all admired": CH to Henry Lee Moon, September 15, 1937, MHLM, box 3, folder "Henry Moon and Chester Himes 1937–1942."

117 "the leading American teacher": Advertisement, "Fiction Writing," Thomas H. Uzzell, *New York Times Book Review*, September 24, 1933, 27;

advertisement, "Ten Talks on Fiction Writing," Thomas H. Uzzell, *New York Times Book Review*, September 13, 1936, 31.

117 **"Did You Ever Catch a Moon":** CH, "A Nigger," typescript with handscript revisions [fragment], CHP-T, box 26, folder 5.

117 **"outlined in my mind":** CH to CVV, November 23, 1952, CVVP, box He–Hols, folder "Himes, Chester B. 1952–1955."

117 **"discerning cosmopolite":** "A New Magazine for Men," *Bachelor*, May 31, 1937, 134–135; editorial page, *Bachelor*, February 1938, 25.

117 **"You call out to the Negro":** CH, "Scram!" *Bachelor*, February 1938, 27.

118 **"enjoy[ed] the recognition":** ATB, 12.

118 **a career liftoff:** Henry Lee Moon, "Liberia Recovers Under New Regime," *New York Times*, August 30, 1936, E7; Henry Lee Moon, "Law on Lynching Is Pressed Again," *New York Times*, April 18, 1937, 71; Henry Lee Moon, "Housing Problem Is Still Acute," *New York Times*, June 20, 1937, 63; Henry Lee Moon, "Policy Game Thrives in Spite of Attacks," *New York Times*, July 25, 1937, 56.

118 **"I could not hire you":** *QH*, 71.

118 **"pile of manuscripts":** Henry Lee Moon to Mollie Moon, May 20, 1938, MHLM, box 1, folder "Correspondence."

119 **"rather depressing":** Virginia Bird to Gideon Kishur, March 10, 1938, Crowell-Collier Publishing Company Records, box 134, folder 382–401, Manuscript and Archives Division, New York Public Library, New York City.

119 **"I hope I am not presumptuous":** CH to "Editor *American Magazine*," May 22, 1938, ibid.

119 **"We were very much interested":** *American Magazine* to CH, May 31, 1938, ibid.

119 **"It does not occur":** CH, "Statement of Plan of Work" (1944), p. 3, CH-RF.

120 **"bitterly resentful [of] that fate":** Ibid., p. 5.

120 **"I am happy to know":** CH to Sterling Brown, May 30, 1938, SAB, box 8, folder "H."

121 **"the first clear, pointed":** CH to Brown, November 25, 1938, ibid.

121 **"What seems 'tragically desperate'":** Ibid.

122 **"packing in a maze of essentials":** CH to Henry Lee Moon, June 29, 1938, MHLM, box 1, folder "Correspondence."

122 **78,000 WPA workers:** "Works Progress Administration," Encyclopedia of Cleveland History, http://ech.case.edu/cgi/article.pl?id=WPA1; "15.2% of All WPA Workers Are Colored," *Cleveland Call and Post*, March 17, 1938, 6.

122 **white-collar work:** "Are We to Have a WPA Scandal?," *Cleveland Call and Post*, March 24, 1938, 6.

122 **Chester wrote letters:** CH to JAW, October 31, 1962, 18.

122 **demand the inclusion:** "'Colonel Alexander Has Insulted Our Entire Race,' Says Payne," *Cleveland Call and Post*, May 26, 1938, 1.

123 **"He filled with a recurrence":** CH, "With Malice Toward None," *Crossroad*, April 1939. The story is reprinted in CH-CSS; quotation at 51.

124 **the practice of demoting foremen:** "WPA Discrimination," *Cleveland Call and Post*, June 30, 1938, 6; "Supervisors, Foremen Using Layoff 'Authority' to Prune WPA Rolls of Negro Workers," *Cleveland Call and Post*, April 27, 1939, 1; "Harrington Promises Probe of Discrimination in Cleveland WPA Projects," *Cleveland Call and Post* May 4, 1939, 1; "18 Month Rule Resurrects a Wave of Discrimination," *Cleveland Call and Post*, September 14, 1939, 1.

124 **Charles Dickinson being appointed:** "Ohio WPA Administrator Appoints Negro as Employment Investigator," *Cleveland Call and Post*, September 29, 1938, 2.

124 **"favorable impression":** CH to Henry Lee Moon, June 29, 1938.

124 **pay jumped to $95:** CH to JAW, October 31, 1962, 18.

125 **"Most of Cleveland's Negroes":** Ohio Writers' Project, *Ohio: The Ohio Guide* (New York: Oxford University Press, 1940), 218.

125 **"While on the Writers' Project":** *QH*, 72.

126 **She told him about a new book:** CH to Richard Wright, n.d. [Christmas 1945] RW, box 99, folder 1393.

126 **"This'll be good for you":** Ruth Seid to Michel Fabre, June 23, 1988, MF, box 6, folder 31.

127 **"an effective campaign for jobs":** Henry Lee Moon, "Negroes Win Help in Fight for Jobs," *New York Times*, August 28, 1938, E10.

127 **"Sam Katz opened a wine store":** Jo Sinclair, "Cleveland's Negro Problem," *Ken*, December 15, 1938, 76, 79.

127 **"insidious Jewish chauvinism":** CH to Jo Sinclair, December 21, 1945, Jo Sinclair Papers, box 36, folder 14, Boston University, Boston.

127 **using Chester's life:** Alan Wald, *Trinity of Passion: The Literary Left and the Anti-Fascist Crusade* (Chapel Hill: University of North Carolina Press, 2007), 242.

128 **"to catch up on financially":** CH to Henry Lee Moon, August 10, 1938, MHLM, box 1, folder "Correspondence."

128 **his $900 annual salary:** "Chester Himes," 1940 U.S. Census, Ohio, Cuyahoga County, April 5, 1940, sheet no. 3A.

128 **Ohio governor John Bricker:** *QH*, 72.

128 **"medium for creative talent":** "'Crossroad,' New Art Magazine Makes Bid for Negro Works," *Cleveland Call and Post*, February 16, 1939, 11.

129 **"My God, politics isn't fatal"**: CH, "A Modern Fable—Of Mr. Slaughter, Mr. McDull, and the American Scene," *Crossroad* (summer 1939): np.

130 **"which would inspire Negro art"**: CH to Henry Lee Moon, September 16, 1939, MHLM, box 1, folder "Correspondence."

130 **sales of $15 million**: "Plane Parts, Tools: Many Companies Gear Operations for Share of Business," *Wall Street Journal*, May 18, 1940, 1.

130 **"what racial prejudice is like"**: *QH*, 72.

130 **"shunted away"**: "Cleveland Plants Ignoring President's Order, But Are Careful to Make Excuses," *Cleveland Call and Post*, August 9, 1941, 1A.

131 **conversation like a "tonic"**: CH to Henry Lee Moon, February 23, 1940, MHLM, box 1, folder "Correspondence."

131 **He also wrote the text**: CH to Henry Lee Moon, June 30, 1940.

132 **"Looking Down the Street"**: CH, "Looking Down the Street: A Story of Import and Bitterness," *Crossroad*, Spring 1940, 85.

132 **90 percent**: Todd Michney, "Changing Neighborhoods: Race and Upward Mobility in Southeast Cleveland 1930–1980," PhD diss., University of Minnesota, 2004, 93–94.

132 **mutual friend Langston Hughes**: "Langston Hughes Speaks Here Sunday," *Cleveland Call and Post*, April 25, 1940, 3; Arnold Rampersad, *The Life of Langston Hughes, vol. I, 1902–1941, I, Too, Sing America* (New York: Oxford University Press, 1986), 383.

132 **"attacking *Esquire*"**: C. Himes to Henry Lee Moon, June 1, 1940, MHLM, box 1, folder "Correspondence."

133 **"felt called" to enter**: Ibid.

133 **"Bigger Thomas came alive"**: CH, "Review and Comment: 'Native Son': Pros and Cons," *New Masses*, May 21, 1940, 23.

134 **she was "quite swept away"**: C. Himes to Henry Lee Moon, June 22, 1940, MHLM, box 1, folder "Correspondence"; "Karamu Dancers to Show at Worlds Fair: Group to Give Tune Up Performance on June 21st," *Cleveland Call and Post*, June 22, 1940, 7.

134 **saluted with two asterisks**: Edward J. O'Brien, ed., *The Best Short Stories 1940* (Boston: Houghton Mifflin, 1940), 519.

134 **"what with Hitler looking westward"**: CH to Henry Lee Moon, June 30, 1940.

135 **Chester began to note her personal traits**: Mollie Moon to Henry Lee Moon, July 10, 1940, MLHM, box 1, folder "Correspondence."

135 **"big fat mannish woman"**: CH to JAW, October 31, 1962, 19.

135 **he might begin collecting material**: CH to Henry Lee Moon, June 1, 1940.

135 **"I found the job of editing"**: CH to Henry Lee Moon, November 19, 1940, MLHM, box 1, folder "Correspondence."

136 **"Chester, you have paid"**: *QH*, 71.

137 **"People coming from"**: CH, "This Cleveland: E. 55th–Central," *Cleveland News*, November 8, 1940, 12.

137 **"boys down there blew"**: CH to Henry Lee Moon, November 19, 1940.

137 **steel mill sprawl**: CH, "This Cleveland: Broadway at Central at Woodland," *Cleveland News*, November 22, 1940, 6.

137 **"is there not a little of disappointment"**: CH, "This Cleveland: Shaker Square," *Cleveland News*, November 20, 1940, 10.

138 **"struggling to inject continuity"**: Editorial note, "Face in the Moonlight," *Coronet*, February 1941, 63.

138 **Jellifes entertained a man**: Russell Jellife to Zell Ingram, December 17, 1940, Karamu House Papers, box 8, folder 120, Western Reserve Historical Society, Cleveland, Ohio.

139 **"poor man's [Somerset] Maugham"**: Charles Poore, "Books of the Times," *New York Times*, November 15, 1945, 17.

139 **Booming and profane**: Robert Van Gelder, "An Interview with Mr. Louis Bromfield," *New York Times Book Review*, March 29, 1942, 2.

139 **crammed their apartment**: CH to CVV, September 13, 1946, CVVP, box He–Hols, folder "Himes, Chester B. 1946–1947."

140 **"queer nonsense"**: CH, "Face in the Moonlight," *Coronet*, February 1941, 63.

140 **"Chester B. Himes writes"**: Editorial note, "Face in the Moonlight," 63.

140 **"one of those periods"**: CH to CVV, February 18, 1947, CVVP, box He–Hols, folder "Himes, Chester B. 1946–1947."

140 **"I'd hate to see mother"**: CH to H. Moon, November 19, 1940.

141 **"I had the story"**: CH to CVV, February 18, 1947.

6. RUIN OF THE GOLDEN DREAM

142 **on June 5, 1941**: CH to Henry Lee Moon, June 27, 1941, MHLM, box 1, folder "Correspondence."

142 **"I had to give up"**: Ibid.

142 **"I would be content"**: CH to Carl Van Vechten, September 13, 1946, CVV, box He–Hols, folder "Himes, Chester 1946–1947."

143 **they were paid $120**: Ibid.

143 **"until I'm numb"**: Ivan Scott, *Louis Bromfield, Novelist and Agrarian Reformer* (Lewiston, U.K.: Edwin Mellen Press, 1998), 356.

143 **"Them that works, eats"**: Ellen Bromfield Geld, *The Heritage* (1962; repr., Athens: Ohio University Press, 1999), 105.

143 **"exceedingly hard"**: CH to CVV, September 13, 1946.

143 **"The main reason"**: CH to Henry Lee Moon, June 27, 1941.

144 **"extremely well and vividly"**: Ibid.

144 **"write so well I'd hate":** Ibid.

144 **three trips from Ohio to Los Angeles:** Frederick C. Othman, "Noted Author Has System All His Own," *Washington Post*, August 19, 1941, 8; Thomas Brady, "Hollywood Strikes a New 'Bell,'" *New York Times*, August 24, 1941, 142.

144 **promised his new butler:** CH to Langston Hughes, October 20, 1941, LH, box 30, folder 1531.

144 **Urging Chester to go west:** MMH-*DCDJ*, 203.

145 **"tall, gangling man":** CH, *Lonely Crusade* (1947; repr., New York: Thunder's Mouth Press, 1997), 168; *QH*, 98.

145 **"'There is no place like America'":** CH, *Lonely Crusade*, 174–75.

146 **"compulsion to agree":** Ibid., 175.

147 **"I hope that they will":** Leah Moon to Henry Lee Moon, October 17, 1941, HLM, box 3, folder 33.

147 **by 1944 that figure would jump:** Rick Moss, "Not Quite Paradise: The Development of the African American Community in Los Angeles Through 1950," *California History* (Fall 1996): 224.

147 **"a drab panorama":** CH, *Lonely Crusade*, 15.

147 **"remote districts":** Langston Hughes to Maxim Lieber, December 17, 1940, *Selected Letters of Langston Hughes*, ed. Arnold Rampersad and David Roessel (New York: Knopf, 2015), 216.

148 **so dubbed "Rochester Lane":** Donald Bogle, *Bright Boulevards, Bold Dreams: The Story of Black Hollywood* (New York: Ballantine, 2006), 269.

148 **"was in those days ten or fifteen years":** Dizzy Gillespie with Al Frazier, *To Be or Not to Bop* (Garden City, N.Y.: Doubleday, 1979), 248, 243.

148 **"ten, fifteen, or twenty" cars:** CH, "Zoot Riots Are Race Riots," *The Crisis*, July 1943, 201.

148 **California Sanitary Canning Company:** "Chester Himes Paints Local Scene in Novel," *Los Angeles Tribune*, January 7, 1946; CH-RF.

148 **"the city a little better":** CH to Hughes, October 20, 1941.

149 **remembered by the foreman:** "Report," November 25, 1944, pp. 3–4, CH-FBI; "Report," January 8, 1945, CH-FBI.

149 **"black people were treated":** *QH*, 73.

149 **put Chester's name first:** Langston Hughes to Maurice Murphy, October 11, 1941, LM, box 3, folder "Langston Hughes."

149 **An orator and former track star:** Walter Gordon, interview with author, April 30, 2010; Welford Wilson, "We White Americans," *Pittsburgh Courier*, January 20, 1940, 7; "Athlete Lands City College Office Job," New York *Amsterdam News*, September 21, 1935, 1.

149 **"I was given the works":** CH to JAW, October 31, 1962, *DCDJ*, 21.

150 **"a great influence":** Ibid.

150 **more than a quarter:** Gerald Horne, *The Final Victim of the Blacklist: John*

Howard Lawson, Dean of the Hollywood Ten (Berkeley: University of California Press, 2006), 132.

150 **"Are you anti-Semitic?":** Dalton Trumbo, "Rough Draft of Letter to FBI Agents," [c. 1944], in *Additional Dialogue: Letters of Dalton Trumbo, 1942–1963*, ed. Helen Marshall (New York: M. Evans, 1970), 31.

151 **an African American film production company:** John Kinloch to father, September 29, 1941, Charlotta Bass Papers, box 2, folder "John Kinloch," Southern California Research Library, Los Angeles.

151 **the word "duplicity":** Henry Lee Moon, "Memoirs: Encounters with the CP," p. 24, MHLM, box 14, folder "Memoirs."

151 **offered analyses:** Ella Winter to Loren Miller, March 5, 1939, LM, box 5, folder "Correspondence 1944–1946."

151 **"realistically" . . . "social history":** Loren Miller, "Blood Won't Tell," LM, box 33, folder 19.

151 **"burn holes in the toughest skin":** Amina Hassan, *Loren Miller: Civil Rights Attorney and Journalist* (Norman: University of Oklahoma Press, 2015), 11–12.

152 **"I don't know when":** CH to CVV, September 13, 1946.

152 **Kenneth Littauer:** CH to Henry Lee Moon, December 8, 1941, MHLM, box 1, folder "Correspondence."

152 **"got to feeling funny about it":** Ibid.

153 **"things are getting a little pressing":** CH to Henry Lee Moon, December 2, 1941, MHLM, box 1, folder "Correspondence."

153 **"This town is getting too hot":** CH to Henry Lee Moon, December 8, 1941.

153 **apprenticed as a shipfitter trainee:** *QH*, 74–75.

153 **"I think the suggestion":** Arthur Huff Fausett, "I Write as I See," *Pittsburgh Courier*, February 7, 1942, 4; "Suspect in Attack on Woman Lynched by Mob in Missouri," *Los Angeles Times*, January 26, 1942, 1; "The Courier's Double 'V' for a Double Victory," *Pittsburgh Courier*, February 14, 1942, 1; Lee Finkle, "The Conservative Aims of Militant Rhetoric: Black Protest During World War II," *Journal of American History* (December 1973): 694.

154 **Holland had wowed radio audiences:** Frank Daugherty, "'Ninotchka' Influence Noted; New Negro Tenor for Screen," *Christian Science Monitor*, September 13, 1940, 8; Langston Hughes to Arna Bontemps, May 26, 1941, in *Selected Letters of Langston Hughes*, 82.

154 **pressure to build black morale:** Clayton Koppes and Gregory Black, "Blacks, Loyalty, and Motion Picture Propaganda in World War Two," *Journal of American History* (September 1986): 384, 392–93.

155 **"restriction of Negroes":** Herman Hill, "Change of Attitude Observed," *Pittsburgh Courier*, August 8, 1942, 20.

155 **Hollywood Writers Mobilization:** "Chester Himes Paints Local Scene in Novel."

155 **"We've been discriminating":** "Native Sons," *Communiqué: Hollywood Writers Mobilization for Defense*, April 10, 1942, 6, Southern California Library, Los Angeles.

155 **"I don't believe we":** Herman Hill, "Change of Attitude Observed," *Pittsburgh Courier*, August 8, 1942, 20.

156 **"I don't want no niggers":** MMH-*DCDJ*, 207.

156 **heralded the appointment:** "Phil Carter, Harlem Scribe, in Film Job," *Chicago Defender*, October 31, 1942, 21.

156 **"degrading":** Quoted in Hill, "Change of Attitude Observed," 20.

157 **80,000 blacks:** Errol Wayne Stevens, *Radical L.A.: From Coxey's Army to the Watts Riots, 1894–1965* (Norman: University of Oklahoma Press, 2009), 259.

157 **"unforgettable" May 9:** Mary Oyama, "A Nisei Report from Home," *Common Ground*, Winter 1946, 26, "Mary Mittwer," 1940 U.S. Census, California, Los Angeles, sheet no. 7A.

157 **a similarly committed writer:** CH to Henry Lee Moon, May 25, 1942, MHLM, box 1, folder "Correspondence."

158 **his unforgiving manner:** Brad Pye Jr., "Washington, Johnson, Bradley Hold Rank of Lieutenant," *Los Angeles Times*, June 25, 1959, B17.

158 **notorious for shooting:** R. J. Smith, *The Great Black Way: Los Angeles in the 1940s and the Lost African American Renaissance* (New York: PublicAffairs, 2006), 114–15; Nat Freedland, "A Black Cop in Old L.A. Tells Story," *Los Angeles Times*, March 29, 1970, P14; "Bring No Proof: Delegation Complains About Conduct of Policeman," *Los Angeles Times*, February 20, 1916, I10; "Vindication for Negro Patrolman," *Los Angeles Times*, March 28, 1916, I12; "Ten Policemen Now Awaiting Hearings," *Los Angeles Times*, May 4, 1920, I14; "May Be First to Die in New Gas Chamber," *Pittsburgh Courier*, April 23, 1938, 12.

158 **"pitiless bastards":** "Chester Himes" [interview with Michael Mok], in *Conversations with Chester Himes*, ed. Michel Fabre and Robert Skinner (Jackson: University of Mississippi Press, 1995), 107.

158 **"how I managed":** Jess Kimbrough, *Defender of Angels* (New York: Macmillan, 1969), 15; J. Kimbrough, "Georgia Sundown," *Water: A Play in One Act / Georgia Sundown: A Drama in One Act* (Los Angeles: Theater Journal Publishing, 1940).

158 **"much better writer":** CH to Henry Lee Moon, May 25, 1942.

158 **wrote to Sterling Brown:** CH to Sterling Brown, March 15, 1942, SAB, box 8, folder 1930–1949.

159 **"I have just about come":** CH to Henry Lee Moon, May 25, 1942.

159 **fifteen hundred or so members:** Horne, *Final Victim of the Blacklist*, 115.

According to New York literary Communist Lloyd Brown, Perry claimed that CH actually joined the Party during this period, but was expelled for sexually assaulting white women: Alan Wald, "Narrating Nationalisms: Black Marxism and Jewish Communists Through the Eyes of Harold Cruse," in *Left of the Color Line: Race, Radicalisms, and Twentieth-Century Literature*, ed. Bill V. Mullen and James Smethurst (Chapel Hill: University of North Carolina Press, 2003), 156.

160 **activists like Dorothy Healey:** Dorothy Healey and Maurice Isserman, *Dorothy Healey Remembers: A Life in the American Communist Party* (New York: Oxford University Press, 1990), 91.

160 **"as Jim-Crowed":** CH to JAW, October 31, 1962, 21.

160 **"mental corrosion of race prejudice":** *QH*, 76.

160 **thirty-year-old Eluard McDaniel:** Alan Wald, *Exiles from a Future Time: The Forging of the Mid-Twentieth Century Left* (Chapel Hill: University of North Carolina Press, 2002), 285; Adrienne Ruggiero, *American Voices from the Great Depression* (Tarrytown, N.Y.: Benchmark, 2005), 73–74; Eluard Luchell McDaniel, *Bumming in California* (New York: Viking, 1937), 112–18.

161 **"regardless of the capitalist politics":** CH to editor, *People's Daily World*, August 14, 1942, 4.

161 **"Now, in the year 1942":** CH, "Now Is the Time! Here Is the Place!" *Opportunity*, September 1942, 271.

161 **"the character of this writer":** Ibid.

162 **"fight to preserve and make strong":** Ibid., 273–74.

162 **"qualified white mechanics":** Stevens, *Radical L.A.*, 266.

162 **"she would mother":** CH, "In the Night," *Opportunity*, November 1942, 335, 334.

163 **"I can revert":** Ibid., 349, 335.

164 **"Led by Uncle Tom's son":** CH, "Heaven Has Changed," *The Crisis*, March 1943, 83.

164 **ceramics class:** "Los Angeles Defense Workers Learn the Art of Ceramics from U.S.C. Professor," *Pittsburgh Courier*, September 11, 1943, 9.

164 **"respected and included":** *QH*, 75.

165 **"When the war is over":** Clore Warne to Fletcher Bowron, May 25, 1943, LM, box 5, folder 1.

165 **nightsticks on disabled Latino men:** Luis Alvarez, *The Power of the Zoot: Youth Culture and Resistance During World War II* (Berkeley: University of California Press, 2008), 174.

165 **"eye-witness of the recent riots":** CH, "Zoot Riots Are Race Riots," *The Crisis*, July 1943, 201.

166 **delinquency suitably corrected:** Lawrence E. Davies, "Zoot Suits Become Issue on the Coast," *New York Times*, June 13, 1943, E10.

166 **"the birth of the storm troopers"**: CH, "Zoot Riots Are Race Riots," 201.

166 **"aimless bridge games"**: Smith, *The Great Black Way*, 100.

166 **"the compulsion making"**: CH to JAW, October 31, 1962, 22.

167 **"the ruin of a golden dream"**: Will Thomas [Bill Smith], *The Seeking* (New York: A. A. Wyn, 1953), 114, 122.

168 **"he was that type of mulatto black"**: *QH*, 127.

168 **"I—I don't know just when"**: CH, "So Softly Smiling," *The Crisis*, October 1943, 315.

169 **"Here I sit"**: Mollie Moon to Henry Lee Moon, August 28, 1943, MHLM, box 1, folder "Correspondence."

169 **"During the past couple of years"**: CH, "Statement of Plan of Work" (1944), p. 1, CH-RF.

170 **"success as an individual"**: Ibid.

170 **"the hard way"**: Ibid., p. 16.

170 **"dangerous, explosive"**: Ibid., p. 18.

170 **"He knows that the Negro"**: Ibid., p. 19.

170 **"strong and shrewd"**: Mr. N. R. Howard, "Letters of Reference—Chester B. Himes," p. 3, CH-RF.

170 **"dynamic and comprehensive"**: Mr. Henry Lee Moon, "Letters of Reference—Chester B. Himes," p. 1, CH-RF.

171 **telegraph the fund:** Henry Lee Moon, telegram to Vandi Haygood, February 9, 1944, CH-RF; Alfred Perkins, *Edwin Rogers Embree: The Julius Rosenwald Fund, Foundation Philanthropy and American Race Relations* (Bloomington: Indiana University Press, 2011), 189.

171 **"consideration of his own"**: Howard, "Letters of Reference," p. 4.

171 **"We have never met him"**: Mr. Roy Wilkins, "Letters of Reference—Chester B. Himes," p. 4, CH-RF.

171 **"The Negro has been"**: Patrick Washburn, *A Question of Sedition: The Federal Government's Investigation of the Black Press During World War II* (New York: Oxford University Press, 1986), 101.

171 **"Hitler ought to get you"**: "Singer Charges Police Beating in Georgia City," *Chicago Daily Tribune*, July 17, 1942, 5; "Beaten in Georgia, Says Roland Hayes," *New York Times*, July 17, 1942, 9.

172 **taking advantage of every contact:** "The People We Know," *The War Worker*, November 1943, 6.

172 **The participants included:** "Sproul Welcomes Writers Congress," *Los Angeles Times*, October 2, 1943, A1; "Racial Tolerance Needed in Laws Writers Told," *Los Angeles Times*, October 3, 1943, A1.

172 **"tarts of the Negro's daughters"**: Koppes and Black, "Blacks, Loyalty, and Motion Picture Propaganda," 392.

172 **"Here I am—exhibit A"**: Walter White, "People and Places: Writers Congress," *Chicago Defender*, October 23, 1943, 15.

172 **In December, Trumbo would officially:** Trumbo, *Letters of Dalton Trumbo*, 146.

172 **Rex Ingram had too:** Horne, *Final Victim of the Blacklist*, 159.

173 **"who have never been permitted":** CH, "The People We Know," 6.

173 **"If, after reading":** Ibid., 7.

173 **The Army called him up:** "Report," February 3, 1945, p. 2, CH-FBI.

173 **"appeal to carnality":** "Himes Doesn't Like Musical *Sweet 'N' Hot*," *California Eagle*, February 17, 1944, 109.

174 **"Those that are on the other side":** Ibid.

174 **"domestic reasons":** *QH*, 75.

175 **"It is difficult to express":** CH to Vandi Haygood, April 24, 1944, CH-RF.

175 **"our author argues brilliantly":** CH, "Negro Martyrs Are Needed," *The Crisis*, May 1944, 159.

175 **"the enforcement of the Constitution":** Ibid., 159.

176 **"We have not achieved":** Ibid., 174.

176 **"You will note":** "CHESTER B. HIMES" and "Report," July 10, 1944, pp. 3–4, CH-FBI; "Report," January 8, 1945, p. 11, CH-FBI.

176 **"every morning":** CH, "All God's Chillun Got Pride," *The Crisis*, June 1944, 188, 189.

177 **"He is proud of their independence":** CH, "Statement of Plan" (1944), p. 17.

177 **"complexion was black":** CH, "All God's Chillun," 189.

178 **Jean now worked closely with:** Christy Fox, "Caravan Programs Outlined," *Los Angeles Times*, June 21, 1944, A5.

178 **"I gave up my good":** Michael Carter, "This Story Had to Be Told," *Afro-American*, January 5, 1946, 10.

178 **"It hurt for my wife":** *QH*, 75.

178 **"Shattered" by the "mental corrosion":** Ibid., 76.

179 **"defiantly" and "without thought":** CH to CVV, February 18, 1948, CVVP, box He–Hols, folder "Himes, Chester B. 1948–1951."

7. TRYING TO WIN A HOME

180 **"Harlem's most talked":** Jervis Anderson, *This Was Harlem: 1900–1950* (New York: Farrar, Straus and Giroux, 1982), 341, 343.

180 **"Was Chester drunk?":** *QH*, 178.

181 **"tallest and best kept":** CH, "New York 1944" [introduction to 1972 CBS news program and interview], CHP-T, box 29, folder 8.

181 ***Race, Sex and War*:** "Chester Himes Writes Three Novels, Wins Award," *Chicago Defender*, October 14, 1944, 16.

181 **Henry had left his federal job:** "CIO Political Action Committee Names Ex-Clevelander to Staff," *Cleveland Call and Post*, April 8, 1944, 1B.

181 **Sidney Hillman:** Bill Cunningham, "On Sidney Hillman and the Political Action Committee," *Atlanta Constitution*, July 20, 1944, 9.

182 **"all of labor's gains":** "CIO Political Action Committee Names Ex-Clevelander," 1B.

182 **he advocated a permanent:** "CIO Political Action Committee Supports Negro Rights Action," *Cleveland Call and Post*, July 8, 1944, 11A; Henry Lee Moon, "The Truth About PAC," *Chicago Defender*, October 21, 1944, 1–2.

182 **Hastie resigned:** "Hastie Threat to Bolt PAC Gets Little Support," *Chicago Defender*, August 26, 1944, 1.

182 **prominent black Communist artists:** "Seven Negroes on New Political Action Unit," New York *Amsterdam News*, July 22, 1944, A12.

183 **"strangely religious" elements:** *QH*, 76.

183 **"This is social equality":** CH to CVV, February 2, 1949, CVVP, box He–Hols, folder "Himes, Chester B. 1948–1951."

183 **Women's Division:** "Anne Mason Opens Western Tour of Political Action Committee," *Cleveland Call and Post*, August 19, 1944, 5A.

183 **"Brilliant and charming":** Polly Johnson, interview with Michel Fabre, n.d. MF, box 6, folder 31.

183 **"I lost myself":** *QH*, 76.

184 **"had been a charade":** Kenneth Robert Janken, *White: The Biography of Walter White, Mr. NAACP* (New York: New Press, 2003), 328; CH, *Pinktoes* (1961; repr., New York: Dell, 1966). The subplot of the 1961 novel *Pinktoes* is the furious machinations of the nominal protagonist Mamie Mason to force Juanita Wright, wife of Wallace Wright, "the great Negro race leader of one sixty-fourth Negro blood" who is "a small blond man with a small blond mustache" (pp. 68–69), and who "looked so much like a white man" (82), to attend a party at Mamie's home.

184 **"the decadent, rotten sense":** CH, *Lonely Crusade* (1947; repr., New York: Thunder's Mouth, 1997), 48.

184 **"sometimes one of frustration":** Bucklin Moon, "Memoir," Bucklin Moon Papers, box 1, folder 16, Manuscripts and Archives, Rollins College, Winter Park, Florida.

184 **worked his way up:** "Bucklin Moon," *Publishers Weekly*, June 19, 1943, 2309.

184 **"with a feeling akin":** Bucklin Moon, "On Black Causes/Colleges," Bucklin Moon Papers, box 1, folder 35.

185 **"one of the greatest":** Bucklin Moon to Maxim Lieber, November 3, 1944, Maxim Lieber Papers, box 20, folder 1075, Newberry Library, Chicago.

185 **"strong feeling[s]":** Ibid.

185 **"too many negative novels":** Bucklin Moon, "The Race Novel," *New Republic*, November 16, 1946, 830.

185 **"that deals with American Negroes"**: "Doubleday, Doran Makes First George Washington Carver Award," *Publishers Weekly*, June 9, 1945, 2287.

185 **on October 19, 1944:** Robert Smith to CH, August 4, 1969, CHP-T, box 1, folder 8.

186 **"What frightens me most"**: CH, "Democracy Is for the Unafraid," in *Primer for White Folks*, ed. Bucklin Moon (New York: Doubleday, 1945), 479.

186 **"the white man's sudden consciousness"**: Ibid., 482.

186 **"famed get-togethers"**: "Socially Speaking: Last Thursday," New York *Amsterdam News*, November 4, 1944, 12A.

186 **"for the debasement"**: "Rev. Grant Reynolds' Crusade," *Cleveland Call and Post*, October 14, 1944, 8B.

187 **"career from medicine"**: "Chester Himes Writes Three Novels," 16.

187 **he missed voting:** *QH*, 76.

187 **"a puritan all my life"**: Ibid., 13.

188 **"not known to be"**: SAC Los Angeles, office memorandum, to Director FBI, November 25, 1944, CH-FBI.

188 **confidential parties:** CH to JAW, October 31, 1962, *DCDJ*, 23.

188 **"deal with life"**: Constance H. Curtis, "About Books: What Is Obscenity," New York *Amsterdam News*, April 29, 1944, 10A.

188 **"a real literature"**: Constance H. Curtis, "About Books: Shortage of Negro Authors," New York *Amsterdam News*, June 17, 1944, 10A.

188 **man originally from Oklahoma City:** *HF*, 13.

189 **Ralph speaking at an event:** Arnold Rampersad, *Ralph Ellison* (New York: Knopf, 2008), 182.

189 **Ellison had secured a deal:** Lawrence Jackson, *Ralph Ellison: Emergence of Genius* (New York: Wiley, 2002), 299.

190 **"congenial and attentive"**: HF, 14.

190 **The guests included Cuban writer:** "Langston Hughes Gives an International Party Here," New York *Amsterdam News*, December 16, 1944, 13A; Langston Hughes to Arna Bontemps, December 8, 1944, in *Arna Bontemps/Langston Hughes Letters, 1925–1967*, ed. Charles H. Nichols (New York: Paragon, 1990), 176.

190 **L.A. was his "home town"**: Loren Miller to CH, December 27, 1944, LM, box 3, folder 1.

190 **"reigning in the place"**: CH to JAW, October 31, 1962, 23.

191 **a "very small and prejudiced minority"**: Michel Fabre, *The Unfinished Quest of Richard Wright*, 2nd ed. (Urbana: University of Illinois Press, 1993), 255–56, 264.

191 **"found me deeply involved"**: *QH*, 76.

191 **Friends remembered a drunk Chester:** Johnson interview.

191 **"I spent half my time"**: CH, "A Night of New Roses," *Negro Story*, December 1945–January 1946, 10.

193 **"there was no way out"**: B. Moon, "The Race Novel," 831.

193 **the word "fuck"**: CH, manuscript of *If He Hollers Let Him Go*, p. 4, CHP-Y, box 7, folder 71.

193 **"'I'm gonna have you'"**: Ibid.

194 **rape of Mrs. Taylor:** "Blueprint Fight to Nab Rapists of Negro Woman," *Chicago Defender*, December 2, 1944, 5.

194 **"'You can't insult me'"**: Chester Himes, manuscript of *If He Hollers Let Him Go*, pp. 209–10.

196 **"Her blonde hair"**: CH, *If He Hollers Let Him Go* (1945; repr., New York: Thunder's Mouth, 1986), 145, 146, 147.

197 **"so industrialized"**: CH, "Make with a Shape," *Negro Story*, August–September 1945, 4.

197 **"a tour of inspection"**: "Calif. USO Worker Lauds Local Club," *Philadelphia Tribune*, February 24, 1945, 14.

197 **"roughly in the middle"**: CH to Vandi Haygood, March 15, 1945, CH-RF.

197 **"many social obligations"**: "Chester Himes to Finish Second Novel in California," *Los Angeles Tribune*, May 5, 1946, clipping in CH-FBI.

198 **"like Himes' project much"**: Vandi Haygood to Arna Bontemps, March 6, 1944, Arna Bontemps Papers, box 24, folder "Julius Rosenwald Fund, 1938–1949," Special Collections Research Center, Syracuse University Library, Syracuse, New York.

198 **"a wild, drunken week"**: *QH*, 135.

198 **"very put together"**: Constance Webb, *Not Without Love* (Lebanon, N.H.: University Press of New England, 2003), 146.

198 **"meek mannered"**: Michael Carter, "This Story Had to Be Told: Author of *If He Hollers*, in Exclusive Interview, Describes West Coast Shipyard Conditions," *Afro-American*, January 5, 1946, 5.

198 **"very progressive"**: Donald Bogle, *Bright Boulevards, Bold Dreams: The Story of Black Hollywood* (New York: Ballantine, 2006), 318–19.

198 **"dancing between Whites"**: Hedda Hopper, "Goldwyn Preparing Annapolis Feature: Out of Character," *Los Angeles Times*, September 13, 1948, B6.

199 **"summoned" to Los Angeles:** Arna Bontemps to Vandi Haygood, May 8, 1945, Arna Bontemps Papers, box 11, folder "Haygood, William C."

199 **Lena Horne:** Arna Bontemps to Langston Hughes, n.d. [before June 3, 1945], in *Bontemps/Hughes Letters*, 182.

199 **had been promised the Carver Award:** Arna Bontemps to Jack Conroy, September 25, 1945, JC, box 3, folder 151.

199 **"Dr. Carver was"**: MMH-*DCDJ*, 206.

199 **"I think he is too excited"**: Arna Bontemps to Bucklin Moon, June 18, 1945, Arna Bontemps Papers, box 7, folder "Doubleday & Company Inc."

200 **announced on June 9:** "Doubleday, Doran Makes First George Washington Carver Award," *Publishers Weekly*, June 9, 1945, 2287.

200 **"it seems a little grotesque"**: Orville Prescott, "Books of the Times: Review of *Mrs. Palmer's Honey* by Fannie Cook," *New York Times*, February 8, 1946, 26.

200 **"One of the women executives"**: CH to CVV, September 13, 1946. CH uses nearly the same wording in the novel *The End of a Primitive*: "Suddenly he thought of the woman editor who, upon reading the galley proofs of his first novel that had been submitted for a prize, said it made her sick, nauseated her" (p. 95) and in the autobiography *The Quality of Hurt*: "it was rejected because one of the women editors said it nauseated her" (77).

200 **Clara Claasen:** "Doubleday, Doran Gave a Cocktail Party," *Publisher's Weekly*, November 3, 1945, 2051; Al Silverman, *The Time of Their Lives* (New York: St. Martin's, 2008), 205.

201 **on July 19:** CH to Dorothy Elvidge, July 19, 1945, CH-RF.

202 **telephoned Vandi Haygood:** Vandi Haygood to Bucklin Moon, July 30, 1945, Julius Rosenwald Papers, box 436, folder 12, John Hope and Aurelia E. Franklin Library, Fisk University, Nashville, Tennessee.

202 **vice president and the legal department:** CH to CVV, September 13, 1946.

202 **"crazy cousins"**: Mollie Moon to Henry Lee Moon, September 17, 1945, MHLM, box 1, folder "Correspondence."

203 **died of a cerebral hemorrhage:** Estelle B. Himes, Death Certificate #53275, ODH.

203 **cried hysterically:** Johnson interview.

203 **on October 2:** Fannie Wiggins, Death Certificate #57902, ODH.

203 **"a woman of iron will"**: *QH*, 161.

204 **"a tough, controversial"**: "Doubleday, Doran Books for a Big Autumn," *Publishers Weekly*, September 22, 1945.

204 **"A Real Shocker!"**: Advertisement, *If He Hollers Let Him Go* by Chester Himes, *Publishers Weekly*, September 29, 1945.

204 a **"surprised" Chester:** CH to CVV, September 13, 1946.

204 **"remember me kindly"**: Henry Lee Moon to Mollie Moon, October 22, 1945, MHLM, box 1, folder "Correspondence."

205 **threw parties for white authors:** "Doubleday, Doran Gave a Cocktail Party," 2051; "Doubleday, Doran Gave a Party," *Publishers Weekly*, March 3, 1945, 1016.

205 **"I don't like it one bit"**: Henry Lee Moon to Mollie Moon, October 31, 1945, MHLM, box 1, folder "Correspondence."

205 **"a mixture of polemics"**: Charles Poore, "Books of the Times: *If He Hollers Let Him Go," New York Times*, November 1, 1945, 21.

205 **"amid the clinking"**: Dan Burley, "Dan Burley's Back Door Stuff: Modern Mose on Sugar Hill," New York *Amsterdam News*, November 10, 1945, 14.

206 **"I consented to go"**: CH to CVV, September 13, 1946.

206 **"nerve-wracking" tension**: Henry Lee Moon to Mollie Moon, November 5, 1945, MHLM, box 1, folder "Correspondence."

206 **"presenting a true picture"**: Earl Conrad, "A Lady Laughs at Fate," *Chicago Defender*, January 5, 1946, 9.

206 **"Chester Himes, author"**: "George Washington Carver School: Meet the Author" [flyer], Countee Cullen—Harold Jackman Memorial Collection, box 2, folder 13, Atlanta University, Atlanta.

206 **"fan letter"**: Ruth Seid to CH, November 15, 1945, RW, box 99, folder 1393.

207 **"very much excited"**: Horace Cayton to Richard Wright, October 29, 1945, RW, box 95, folder 1255.

207 **"the paralyzing fear"**: Horace Cayton, "'*If He Hollers*': Los Angeles Writer Has Produced Powerful Novel of American Life," *Pittsburgh Courier*, November 3, 1945, 7.

207 **"the ticket-of-admission"**: "Ohioan Joins Nation's Top-Flight Novelists," *Cleveland Call and Post*, December 1, 1945, 9A.

207 **"the calculated castration of prejudice"**: Constance Curtis, "About Books and Authors: *If He Hollers Let Him Go*," New York *Amsterdam News*, November 17, 1945, 23.

207 **"tells so accurately"**: Roy Wilkins, "Book Reviews: 'Blind Revolt: *If He Hollers Let Him Go*,'" *The Crisis*, November 1945, 362.

208 **"Jerky in pace"**: Richard Wright, "Two Novels of the Crushing of Men, One White, One Black," *PM*, November 25, 1945, M8.

208 **Wright received Chester**: Richard Wright, December 14, 1945, "Diary 1945," RW, box 113, folder 1812.

209 **"Nothing can hurt me"**: Michel Fabre, "Interview with Chester Himes" [1963], in *Conversations with Chester Himes*, ed. Michel Fabre and Robert Skinner (Jackson: University of Mississippi Press, 1995), 7.

209 **"The manner in which"**: CH to Richard Wright, n.d. [December 1945], RW, box 99, folder 1393.

209 **"a wonderful time"**: CH to Richard Wright, n.d. [December 25, 1945], ibid.

209 **Joseph Himes Jr. came to town**: "Afro Visitors," *Afro-American*, January 5, 1946, 12; CH to Richard and Ellen Wright, December 27, 1945, RW, box 99, folder 1393.

210 **according to Webb**: Constance Webb Pearlstein to Lesley Himes, May 12, 1997, and December 1, 1998, LPH, box 1, folder 16.

210 **"used to pump frustration"**: CH to Jo Sinclair, December 21, 1945, Jo Sinclair Papers, box 36, folder 14, Boston University, Boston.

210 **"blues school of writers"**: Earl Conrad, "American Viewpoint: Blues School of Literature," *Chicago Defender*, December 22, 1945, 11.

210 **"I developed a hatred"**: Ibid.

211 **requested that the director:** SAC Los Angeles, memorandum to F.B.I. Director, December 5, 1945, CH-FBI.

8. MONKEY AN' THE LION

213 **"crazy racialist"**: E. Franklin Frazier, Federal Bureau of Investigation File # 138-825, Section 4.

213 **"It is not a question"**: E. Franklin Frazier, *"Black Metropolis: A Study of Negro Life in a Northern City,* by St. Clair Drake and Horace Cayton," *Social Forces* (March 1946): 362.

213 **He received $2000:** CH to CVV, September 13, 1946, CVVP, box He–Hols, folder "Himes, Chester B. 1946–1947."

213 **"limited opportunities"**: Isaac Rosenfeld, "Best Intentions," *New Republic*, December 31, 1945, 910.

213 **"the one clouded spot"**: "Ohioan Joins Nation's Top-Flight Novelists," *Cleveland Call and Post*, December 1, 1945, 9A.

213 **"If he asked me"**: CH, *If He Hollers Let Him Go* (1945; repr., New York: Thunder's Mouth, 1986), 81.

213 **"contribution to American literature"**: Walter White, "People, Politics and Places," *Chicago Defender*, December 22, 1945, 13.

214 **"stout weapon"**: Arthur P. Davis, "With a Grain of Salt: Rev. of *If He Hollers Let Him Go," Norfolk Journal and Guide*, February 9, 1946, 6.

214 **"see the progress made"**: Ruth Jett, review of *If He Hollers Let Him Go*, by Chester Himes, *Congress View*, December 1945, 8.

214 **"there is a hell of a lot"**: Eugene Gordon, "Powerful Novel of Negro Life," *Daily Worker*, December 30, 1945, 9.

214 **a time of "self-flagellation"**: Alan Wald, *Trinity of Passion: The Literary Left and the Anti-Fascist Crusade* (Chapel Hill: University of North Carolina Press, 2007), 72.

214 **to warn about "maneuvering"**: CH to Richard Wright, n.d. [Monday], RW, box 99, folder 1393.

215 **"*Mrs. Palmer's Honey* is a book"**: Advertisement for *Mrs. Palmer's Honey*, *Publishers Weekly*, January 5, 1946, 1.

215 **"[*Mrs. Palmer's Honey*] is a novel"**: "From Where I Sit," advertisement for *Mrs. Palmer's Honey*, *Saturday Review*, February 9, 1946.

216 **"unreasonable" complaints:** CH to William Targ, April 4, 1954, CHP-T, box 9, folder 12.

216 **"the veiled references":** CH to CVV, September 13, 1946.

216 **"black corner":** MMH-*DCDJ*, 187.

216 **"someone in the firm":** CH to William Targ, April 4, 1954.

216 **"I believe conclusively":** CH to Wright, n.d. [Monday].

217 **"treated us like stepchildren":** Arna Bontemps to Jack Conroy, September 25, 1945, JC, box 3, folder 151.

217 **"the only change I would consider":** CH, "Second Guesses for First Novelists: Chester B. Himes *If He Hollers Let Him Go*," *Saturday Review of Literature*, February 26, 1946, 9.

217 **"New York Critics have never":** CH to William Targ, April 6, 1954, CHP-T, box 6, folder 1.

217 **"the bitter cries":** Walter White, "Negro Heroes in Fiction," *Chicago Defender*, February 23, 1946, 15.

218 **sold 13,211 hardcovers:** Robert A. Smith to CH, August 4, 1969, CHP-T, box 1, folder 8.

218 **gathered to "beat that boy":** CH to Wright, n.d. [Monday].

219 **"the important people to himself":** CH to JAW, October 31, 1962, in *DCDJ*, 24.

219 **"invariably taken for a coon":** Edward White, *The Tastemaker: Carl Van Vechten and the Making of Modern America* (New York: Farrar, Straus and Giroux, 2014), 48.

219 **"it is the only hope":** Ibid., 164.

220 **"the undisputed downtown authority":** Emily Bernard, *Remember Me to Harlem: The Letters of Langston Hughes and Carl Van Vechten, 1925–1964* (New York: Knopf, 2001), xvii.

220 **"pompous" . . . "hysterical":** MMH-*DCDJ*, 188.

220 **his own series of photographs:** CH to CVV, n.d. [March 22, 1946], CVVP, box He–Hols, folder "Himes, Chester B. 1946–1947."

220 **"calm and serene":** CH to CVV, June 25, 1946, ibid.

220 **"The Boiling Point":** CH and Joseph Himes, "The Boiling Point," *Afro-American*, March 9, 1946, 4.

220 **New York Public Library:** "Books—Authors," *New York Times*, March 16, 1946, 11.

221 **"citizens of the communist-dominated":** CH, "Negro Martyrs Are Needed," *The Crisis*, May 1944, 159.

222 **"other Negroes own":** CH, "Journey Out of Fear," *Tomorrow*, June 1949, 38.

222 **blamed the cuts to the book:** CH to Richard Wright, May 7, 1946, RW, box 99, folder 1393.

223 **"chatted with us":** CH to CVV, September 13, 1946.

223 **"sit down to a table":** *QH*, 78.

223 **"brutal and vicious":** Ibid.

223 **"I hope to be following"**: CH to CVV, May 12, 1946, CVVP, box He–Hols, folder "Himes Chester B. 1946–1947."

223 **arriving on May 7**: CH to Wright, May 7, 1946.

224 **"modern version of a sharecropper's shanty"**: Ibid.

224 **"I remember that summer"**: *QH*, 93.

224 **"no publisher would"**: Bucklin Moon, "Book Boom," *Negro Digest*, April 1946, 79.

224 **"a better relationship"**: CH to CVV, June 10, 1946, CVVP, box He–Hols, folder "Himes Chester B. 1946–1947."

225 **"blemishes, marks, scars"**: Ibid.

225 **reputedly sent him a long saga**: CH to CVV, September 13, 1946.

225 **Doubleday agreed**: CH to CVV, December 4, 1946, CVVP, box He–Hols, folder "Himes Chester B. 1946–1947."

225 **"as it nears the end"**: CH to CVV, July 19, 1946, ibid.

225 **"absolute exhaustion"**: CH to CVV, August 12, 1946, ibid.

225 **his father's costly operation**: Statement of Charges, Mr. Joseph S. Himes, Cleveland Clinic Foundation, August 6, 1946, and January 25, 1947, CHP-T, box 5, folder 15.

226 **"Few things that ever happened"**: CH to CVV, August 12, 1946.

226 **Chester airmailed**: CH to CVV, August 30, 1946, CVVP, box He–Hols, folder "Himes, Chester B. 1946–1947."

226 **"quick-tempered but charming"**: CVV to CH, September 4, 1946, CHP-T, box 6, folder 11.

226 **"tremendous and powerful"**: CH to CVV, September 4, 1946, CVVP, box He–Hols, folder "Himes, Chester B. 1946–1947."

226 **"felt a sense of inferiority"**: CH, *Lonely Crusade* (1947; repr., New York: Thunder's Mouth, 1997), 294.

226 **"that beaten, whorish look"**: Ibid., 7.

227 **she "hated" the novel**: *QH*, 93.

227 **"I often wondered"**: Ibid.

227 **They checked in**: CH to CVV, October 14, 1946, CVVP, box He–Hols, folder "Himes, Chester B. 1946–1947."

227 **"no great shakes as a success"**: "Angry Author from Brooklyn," *Ebony*, July 1946, 48.

227 **"too well-heeled"**: *QH*, 96; Constance Webb, *Not Without Love* (Lebanon, N.H.: University Press of New England, 2003), 174.

227 **"finishing touches"**: CH to Langston Hughes, October 28, 1946, LH, box 80, folder 1531.

228 **"become a free man"**: C.S., "Report on LONELY CRUSADE by Chester Himes," AAK.

228 **"raw and fiery"**: M.R., "Second Report on *A Lonely Crusade* by Chester Himes," AAK.

228 **"one of the most dramatic":** Mrs. Blanche Knopf, "Letters of Reference—Chester B. Himes," p. 3, CH-RF.

228 **"southern liberals":** Bucklin Moon, "The Race Novel," *New Republic*, November 16, 1946, 831.

229 **"travel abroad for a year":** CH to William C. Haygood, November 7, 1946, CH-RF.

229 **"the immediate influence":** Chester Himes, "Statement of Plan of Work" (1946), CH-RF.

229 **"the good food":** Ralph and Fanny Ellison to CH, February 11, 1972, CHP-T, box 3, folder 10.

229 **"Lenin's Principles of Marxism":** CH to Ralph Ellison, November 12, 1946, RE, box 52, folder "Hi" miscellaneous.

230 **"certain general aspects":** Ralph Ellison, draft letter to Horace Cayton, n.d., RE, box 41, folder "Cayton, Horace"; Ralph Ellison, "Richard Wright's Blues" (1945), in *Shadow and Act* (New York: Random House, 1964), 78; Lawrence Jackson, *Ralph Ellison: Emergence of Genius* (New York: Wiley, 2002), 342.

231 **"the certainty of a crushing fate":** Albert Camus, *The Myth of Sisyphus*, trans. Justin O'Brien (New York: Knopf, 1955), 54.

231 **"not by consolation":** Ellison, "Richard Wright's Blues," 90.

231 **"learnedly and vehemently":** CH, *Lonely Crusade*, 61.

231 **"one of our best times":** Ralph and Fanny Ellison to CH, February 11, 1972.

232 **"Hope it didn't":** Jean Himes to Fanny Ellison, December 12, 1946, RE, box 52, folder "Hi" miscellaneous.

232 **"I am intolerant":** CH to CVV, May 23, 1947, CVVP, box He–Hols, folder "Himes Chester B. 1946–1947."

232 **"long and steadily":** CH to William C. Haygood, December 30, 1946, CH-RF.

232 **On December 21:** "Jilted, He Shoots Girl, Kills Self: E. Side Businessman Dies of Self-Inflicted Wounds in Daylight Murder Attempt," *Cleveland Call and Post*, December 21, 1946, 1A.

232 **"I want to go to Europe":** CH, "Statement of Plan of Work" (1946), p. 2, CH-RF.

232 **"I wish that I could have been more convincing":** CH to William C. Haygood, December 30, 1946.

232 **Chester resubmitted:** "Himes, Chester: Manuscript Record," AAK.

232 **"Himes has done everything":** C. S., "Report on Revision of Chester Himes' LONELY CRUSADE," AAK.

233 **"experiencing a sense of letdown":** CH to William C. Haygood, n.d. [c. February 2, 1947], CH-RF.

233 **"the circle of restraint":** CH to CVV, February 18, 1947, CVVP, box He–Hols, folder "Himes, Chester B. 1946–1947."

233 **"Waldorf of Harlem"**: "The Waldorf of Harlem," *Ebony*, April 1946, 8.

233 **"secret understanding"**: *QH*, 116.

234 **"No publisher is likely"**: CVV to CH, February 19, 1947, CVVP, box He–Hols, folder "Himes, Chester B. 1946–1947."

234 **"artistic flow of language"**: CH to William C. Haygood, n.d. [c. February 2, 1947].

234 **small photography exhibit:** Jean Himes to CVV, March 19, 1947, CVVP, box He–Hols, folder "Himes, Chester B. 1948–1951."

234 **Blassingame requested a $2000 advance:** Lurton Blassingame to Clinton Simpson, April 14, 1947, AAK.

235 **"We simply must get away"**: CH to CVV, June 10, 1947, CVVP, box He–Hols, folder "Himes, Chester B. 1946–1947."

235 **"riding out another"**: Will Thomas [Bill Smith], *The Seeking* (New York: A. A. Wyn, 1953), 130.

236 **"I do not see a very"**: Ibid.

236 **In Smith's kitchen:** Ibid., 191.

236 **"You know: give us"**: CVV to Langston Hughes, May 9, 1947, in Bernard, *Remember Me to Harlem*, 245.

236 **"I expect by now"**: Langston Hughes to CVV, May 13, 1947, ibid., 246.

236 **"Most of the people"**: Langston Hughes to Blanche Knopf, August 26, 1947, LH, box 97, folder 1823–1830.

237 **"What he has to say"**: Richard Wright, "If I had the power," June 5, 1947, AAK.

237 **"this fine statement"**: CH to Richard Wright, June 14, 1947, RW, box 99, folder 1393.

237 **"beautifully written"**: Langston Hughes, "Here to Yonder: One Old One New," *Chicago Defender*, May 17, 1947, 14; Horace Cayton, "A Terrifying Cross Section of Chicago," *Chicago Tribune*, May 4, 1947, B3.

237 **"marital conflict"**: CH to Richard Wright, n.d. [c. June 16, 1947], RW, box 99, folder 1393.

237 **"Chester Himes' *Lonely Crusade*"**: Richard Wright, "COPY OF BLURB FROM 'RICHARD WRIGHT,'" June 24, 1947, AAK.

238 **"Honestly, it is rather nice"**: CH to CVV, n.d. [c. August 8, 1947], box He–Hols, folder "Himes, Chester B. 1946–1947."

238 **"a great work of art"**: Horace Cayton to William Cole, August 18, 1947, AAK.

238 **"this novel boasts"**: CVV to William Cole, n.d., AAK.

239 **"happy memories"**: "People Who Read and Write," the *New York Times Book Review*, August 10, 1947, 8.

239 **"among the most promising"**: "Books: 'A Negro's Bitter Pen,'" *Newsweek*, September 8, 1947, 82.

240 **"fustle and bustle"**: CH to CVV, September 10, 1947, CVVP, box He–Hols, folder "Himes, Chester B. 1946–1947."

240 **"Remember, son, New York"**: *QH*, 100.

240 **"tightly constructed"**: Constance Curtis, "About Books and Authors: Rev. of *Lonely Crusade* by Chester Himes," New York *Amsterdam News*, September 13, 1947, 11.

240 **"the story has power"**: Arna Bontemps, review of *Lonely Crusade* by Chester Himes, *New York Herald Tribune*, September 7, 1947, 8.

240 **"terrible and tragic"**: Marian Sims, "A Life Scarred by Fear: Rev. of *Lonely Crusade* by Chester Himes," *Atlanta Journal*, September 7, 1947, clipping in AAK.

240 **"The victim is the classic"**: John Farrelly, review of *Lonely Crusade* by Chester Himes, *New Republic*, October 6, 1947, 550.

240 **"I didn't like *Lonely Crusade*"**: Willard Motley to CH, September 3, 1947, in James R. Giles and Jerome Klinkowitz, "The Emergence of Willard Motley in Black American Literature," *Negro American Literature Forum* 6 (Summer 1972): 32

241 **"regret exceedingly"**: CH to Willard Motley, n.d. [c. mid-September 1947], MF, box 2, folder 2.

241 **"We learn early that Lee"**: Williard [sic] Motley, "Book Day: Rev. of *Lonely Crusade* by Chester Himes," *Chicago Sun*, October 1, 1947, clipping in AAK.

241 **"some white people"**: CH, *Lonely Crusade*, 361.

242 **"closer to the ofays"**: Ed Reeves to CH, n.d. [c. January 1972], CHP-T, box 5, folder 12.

242 **"Gordon—and his creator Himes"**: "Time to Count Your Blessings," *Ebony*, November 1947, 44.

242 **"It has been rumored"**: "Books of the Day: Rev. of *Lonely Crusade* by Chester Himes," *The People's Voice*, September 20, 1947.

242 **"a Negro intellectual"**: Martin Harvey, "Worker's Bookshelf: Rev. of *Lonely Crusade* by Chester Himes," *The Militant*, November 24, 1947, clipping in AAK.

242 **"It was not that the Communist Party"**: CH, *Lonely Crusade*, 255.

243 **"I cannot recall"**: Lloyd L. Brown, "White Flag," *New Masses*, September 9, 1947, 18.

243 **"extreme leftists"**: Emerson Price, "New Book by Ex-Clevelander Arouses Controversy Among Critics," *Cleveland Press*, November 15, 1947, clipping in AAK.

243 **"Hatred reeks through"**: Stoyan Christowe, review of *Lonely Crusade* by Chester Himes, *Atlantic Monthly*, October 1947, 650.

243 **"bound to stir up"**: "Books in Brief," *Forum*, October 1947, 249.

243 **"Such writing"**: Milton Klonsky, "The Writing on the Wall: Rev. of *Lonely Crusade* by Chester Himes," *Commentary*, February 1948, 190.

244 **"sub conscious disturbances"**: Chester Himes, "Author's Protest," *Commentary*, March 1948, 474.

244 **"is one colored person"**: J. Saunders Redding, "Book Review: 'Dear Editor' by Chester Himes," *Afro-American*, January 3, 1948, 4.

244 **"For the most part"**: Ralph Ellison to Ida Guggenheimer, October 8, 1947, RE, box 49, folder "Guggenheimer, Ida."

245 **"very poor stuff"**: Ida Guggenheimer to Ralph Ellison, October 22, 1947, RE, box 49, folder "Guggenheimer, Ida."

245 **"I read the old Himes book"**: Stanley Edgar Hyman to Ralph Ellison, October 1, 1947, RE, box 51, folder "Hyman, Stanley Edgar."

245 **"Personally I was disappointed"**: Ralph Ellison to Richard Wright, February 1, 1948, RW, box 97, folder 1314.

245 **"Could he fear"**: Ibid.

245 **"It was then"**: *QH*, 102.

246 **"I will never change"**: CH to Richard Wright, October 19, 1952, RW, box 99, folder 1393.

9. INFLICTING A WOUND UPON HIMSELF

247 **The hardcover sales petered out**: CH to CVV, n.d. [c. May 1948], CVVP, box He–Hols, folder "Himes, Chester B. 1948–1951."

247 **earned only $1701.89**: Ray Meyer, memorandum to Mr. [J. C.] Lesser, November 26, 1947, AAK.

247 **"a debit balance"**: J. C. Lesser, memorandum to Mr. Braunstein and Mr. Meyer, February 27, 1948, AAK.

247 **"Advances against royalties"**: Lurton Blassingame to J. C. Lesser, December 9, 1947, AAK.

248 **"needed support badly"**: *QH*, 102.

248 **"It is a great self punishment"**: CH to CVV ("Just a line"), n.d. [c. February 1948], CVVP, box He–Hols, folder "Himes, Chester B. 1948–1951."

248 **"psychological processes"**: CH to Elizabeth Ames, n.d. [c. late February 1948], Yaddo Papers Collection, box 254, folder "Chester Himes," Manuscripts and Archives Division, New York Public Library, New York City.

249 **"won't take me long"**: CH to CVV ("Just a line") [c. February 1948].

249 **"a siege of virus X"**: CH to CVV ("Thank you for writing"), n.d. [c. April 1948], CVVP, box He–Hols, folder "Himes, Chester B. 1948–1951."

249 **Randolph and Reynolds conveyed**: "Civil Disobedience Campaign Outlined," New York *Amsterdam News*, April 3, 1948, 1; C. P. Trussell, "Congress Told UMT Racial Bars Would Unleash Civil Disobedience," *New York Times*, April 1, 1948, 1.

249 **"mass civil disobedience"**: CH, letter to the editor, *Cleveland Call and Post*, April 24, 1948, 4B; CH, "Likes Randolph Plan," *Chicago Defender*, June 12, 1948, 14.

249 **"sugar boy"**: CH, "These People Never Die," New York *Amsterdam News*, May 29, 1948, 24.

249 **"I don't have any"**: CH to CVV ("Thank you for writing"), n.d. [c. April 1948].

250 **a nefarious and significant character:** James Baldwin, "History as Nightmare: Review of *Lonely Crusade* by Chester Himes," *New Leader*, October 25, 1947, 11.

250 **"misinformation trimmed with insults"**: W. A. Swanberg, *Luce and His Empire* (New York: Scribner's, 1972), 399. For a useful assessment of MacArthur, see Richard Halberstam, *The Coldest Winter: America and the Korean War* (New York: Hyperion, 2007), 102–37.

250 **"guest list"**: Elizabeth Ames to CH, April 5, 1948, Yaddo Papers, box 254, folder "Chester Himes."

251 **had been slave quarters:** Marjory Peabody Waite, *Yaddo: Yesterday and Today* (Saratoga Springs, N.Y.: Yaddo, 1933), 13.

251 **typed admonitory notes:** John Cheever, "John Cheever," in Eleanor Clark, John Cheever, Malcolm Cowley, Alfred Kazin, Hortense Calisher, and Gail Godwin, *Six Decades at Yaddo* (1986; repr., Ann Arbor: University of Michigan Press, 2008), 2–3.

251 **"should have come before"**: Elizabeth Ames to Malcolm Cowley, May 23, 1942, Malcolm Cowley Papers, box 2, folder 86, Midwest Writers Collection, Newberry Library, Chicago.

251 **"one or two weird things"**: Elizabeth Ames to Malcolm Cowley, September 5, 1947.

252 **"the formal integration"**: Micki McGee, "Creative Power: Yaddo and the Making of American Culture," in *Yaddo: Making American Culture* (New York: New York Public Library and Columbia University, 2008), 10.

252 **"I do not object"**: Edward Sweeney to Elizabeth Ames, June 18, 1942, Yaddo Papers, box 255, folder 29.

252 **"we have decided"**: "Anonymous note in Horace Cayton's Yaddo file," April 9, 1962, Yaddo Papers, box 234, folder 23.

252 **"It is an ideal place"**: CH to CVV, May 12, 1948, CVVP, box He–Hols, folder "Himes, Chester B. 1948–1951."

252 **"beaming Sybarites"**: Clark et al., *Six Decades at Yaddo*, 21.

252 **"thirteenth century" Catholic girl:** Brad Gooch, *Flannery: A Life of Flannery O'Connor* (Boston: Little, Brown, 2009), 156.

253 **"a coiled Spring"**: Joan Schenkar, *The Talented Miss Highsmith: The Secret Life and Serious Art of Patricia Highsmith* (New York: St. Martin's, 2009), 255.

253 **Highsmith followed Chester:** "Notebook/Cahier," 11–30 May 1948, A-05/17, January 1948 to July 1948, Patricia Highsmith Papers, Swiss Literary Archives, Bern, Switzerland. Schenkar prefers to have Himes attempt to kiss Highsmith in *her* room, and slightly mistranslates the passage. The word in question is "*sienem.*"

253 **"Maybe you remember":** Patricia Highsmith to CH, January 10, 1966, CHP-T, box 4, folder 1.

253 **"I feel I have":** Schenkar, *Talented Miss Highsmith*, 257.

254 **"I was sitting here":** CH to Patricia Highsmith, n.d. [c. April 1965], CHP-T, box 4, folder 1.

254 **"the boy's development of homosexuality":** CH to CVV, n.d. [c. May 12, 1948].

254 **"The Individual in":** "*Lonely Crusade* Author Speaks at Mandel Hall," *Chicago Defender*, May 8, 1948, clipping in AAK.

255 **"the essential necessity":** CH, "The Dilemma of the Negro Novelist in the U.S.," in *Beyond the Angry Black*, ed. John Williams (New York: Cooper Square, 1969), 52.

255 **"be like inflicting":** Ibid., 53.

255 **"Any American Negro's":** Ibid., 54, 56, 57.

255 **"a dead silence":** *QH*, 104.

255 **"Until the period":** Ibid.

255 **"although I might":** CH to Yves Malartic, May 27, 1952, MF, box 7, folder 4.

256 **"there has been a lot":** Ames to Cowley, July 26, 1948, Malcolm Cowley Papers, box 2, folder 86, Midwest Writers Collection, Newberry Library, Chicago.

256 **"a man going home":** CH, "Da-Da-Dee," CH-CSS, 370.

256 **"Some day he'd have to":** CH, *The Primitive* (New York: Signet, 1955), 55.

256 **"a famous writer":** CH, "Da-Da-Dee," CH-CSS, 367, 370.

257 **"felt more like just lying":** CH, *The Primitive*, 60.

257 **"desperate need":** CH to CVV, June 9, 1948, CVVP, box He–Hols, folder "Himes, Chester B. 1948–1951."

257 **"ill and our need urgent":** CH to Blanche Knopf, June 11, 1948, AAK.

257 **"This is a rather unusual request":** Blanche Knopf to CH, June 14, 1948, AAK.

257 the term **"atomalypse":** CH to Blanche Knopf, June 17, 1948, AAK.

258 **"a good many now":** Ames to Cowley, July 26, 1948.

258 **"felt truly sorry":** *QH*, 104.

258 **"The support of the family":** *QH*, 104–5.

258 **"If I can spend this winter":** CH to CVV, n.d. ("It has really been a source"), n.d. [c. late summer 1948], CVVP, box He–Hols, folder "Himes, Chester B. 1948–1951."

259 **Cayton had tried to get off alcohol:** Will Thomas [Bill Smith], *The Seeking* (New York: A. A. Wyn, 1953), 236.

259 **"moment of lucidity":** CH to CVV, December 22, 1948, CVVP, box He–Hols, folder "Himes, Chester B. 1948–1951."

259 **"I think in many ways":** Ibid.

260 **"an autobiographical novel til":** CH to CVV, October 15, 1948, CVVP, box He–Hols, folder "Himes, Chester B. 1948–1951."

260 **"smutty and profane":** CH to CVV, February 2, 1949, ibid.

260 **"I know what I have":** CH to CVV, March 24, 1949, ibid.

260 **the fight to have Norman Mailer's:** Mary Dearborn, *Mailer* (Boston: Houghton Mifflin, 1999), 53.

261 **New studies by researchers:** While Kinsey began breaking taboos about sexuality early in the 1940s, especially with "Criteria for a Hormonal Explanation of the Homosexual," *Journal of Clinical Endocrinology* (May 1941): 424–28, it was at the end of 1947 that popular magazines began to showcase the research, in such articles as Albert Deutsch's "The Sex Habits of American Men," *Harper's Magazine*, December 1947, 493, and Harold Clemenko, "Toward a Saner Sex Life," *Look*, December 9, 1947, 106–7.

261 **37 percent of American men:** Alfred Kinsey et al., *Sexual Behavior in the Human Male* (Philadelphia: W. B. Saunders, 1948), 656.

261 **"I had done it":** *CFS*, 337.

262 **"'Everyone else seems'":** Ibid., 290–91.

263 **"inclusion in the social":** CH, "Journey Out of Fear," *Tomorrow*, June 1949, 42.

263 **"a subtly dishonest book":** CH to JAW, October 31, 1962, *DCDJ*, 26.

263 **after *Collier's* accepted:** CH, "A Short History of a Story," *The Crisis*, November 1949, 307–8.

263 **"like the Bronx set down":** *QH*, 108.

264 **"Life there was like":** Ibid., 119.

264 **"there was a bit of unpleasantness":** Ibid., 120.

265 **"Believers in democracy":** "Chester B. Himes Delivers Address to N.C.C. Group," *Durham Morning Herald*, July 10, 1950, 2:4; "Negro Novelist Slated to Speak at N.C.C. Today: Chester B. Himes Serves as Adviser to Writing Class," *Durham Morning Herald*, July 9, 1950, 1:4

265 **"no good book":** Herbert A. Weinstock to CH, June 27, 1950, AAK; Langston Hughes, "Some Practical Observations: A Colloquy" *Phylon* (4th quarter 1950): 307–11.

266 **deciding to drop the Epps case:** "Local Negroes Drop Plan to Challenge State Law," *Durham Morning Herald*, July 13, 1950, 2:1. CH misleadingly characterized the paper's portrait of the case and the coverage given him in his memoir, perhaps a backhanded slap at the prominence of the newspaper in his lecture series.

266 **"the South land":** Jean Himes to CVV, July 19, 1950, CVVP, box He–Hols, folder "Himes, Chester B. 1948–1951"; *QH*, 124.

266 **"a celebration memorable":** *QH*, 125.

266 **declining to publish it:** CH to CVV, July 25, 1950, CVVP, box He–Hols, folder "Himes, Chester B. 1948–1951."

266 **telephoned Margot Johnson:** CH to CVV, April 4, 1951, CVVP, box He–Hols, folder "Himes, Chester B. 1948–1951."

267 **she sold the foreign rights:** CH, contract, La Page International for Editions Corréa, December 23, 1950, CHP-T, box 20, folder 1.

267 **he was so rude:** Anne Smith, interview with author, June 3, 2013.

267 **"fooling around":** CH to CVV, August 1, 1950, CVVP, box He–Hols, folder "Himes, Chester B. 1948–1951."

268 **"deliberately dishonest":** CH to JAW, October 3, 1962, *DCDJ*, 26.

268 **"pleasant" Bridgeport:** *QH*, 111.

268 **speeding ticket:** CH, speeding ticket, March 3, 1951, MF, box 7, folder 13.

268 **"You could be as much":** CH to William Targ, April 6, 1954, CHP-T, box 6, folder 1.

269 **"Legally I am only indebted":** Memo to B[lanche] W K[nopf] from JCL[esser], "re Chester Himes," February 8, 1963, AAK. CH's letter from June 24, 1951, referred to in the memorandum, is missing.

270 **he would press for money:** Ruth Seid to Michel Fabre, June 1, 1988, MF, CHP-T, box 6, folder 31; CH to Lurton Blassingame, n.d. [c. May 1955], CHP-T, box 1, folder 9.

270 **"That incident shook":** *QH*, 115.

271 **"Of course, . . . they had no suitable opening":** Ibid., 131.

271 **"to lose confidence in myself":** Ibid., 132.

272 **"I believe the book":** Yves Malartic to CH, December 6, 1951, MF, box 7, folder 4.

272 **"Please, by all means":** CH to Yves Malartic, December 29, 1951, ibid.

272 **"My wife and I":** CH to Yves Malartic, n.d. [c. June 1952], ibid.

273 **"Jean stopped coming":** *QH*, 132.

10. CADILLACS TO COTTON SACKS

274 **"Thanks greatly":** CH to Ralph Ellison, March 25, 1952, RE, box 52, folder "Hi Miscellaneous."

275 **"the first allegorical Negro novel":** Horace Cayton, "Newest 'Hit' Author Ralph Ellison Gives Literary World New Form, Writing Style," *Pittsburgh Courier*, May 10, 1952, 9.

275 **"always considered":** *QH*, 132.

275 **"I'm like an animal":** CH to CVV, February 15, 1952, CVVP, box He–Hols, folder "Himes, Chester B. 1952–1955."

275 **"devastatingly penetrating"**: Ibid.

276 **as Van Vechten told people:** CVV to JAW, August 2, 1962, *DCDJ*, 1.

276 **"the first thing I desired"**: *QH*, 135.

276 **to Europe "with a friend"**: CH to Yves Malartic, April 14, 1952, MF, box 7, folder 4.

277 **"penetrating as the moment"**: WT to CH ("Darling: I have your special here"), n.d. Thursday noontime [c. summer 1955], CHP-T, box 6, folder 5.

277 **Duggan was found dead on the sidewalk:** "Police Seek Cause of Duggan's Plunge," *Christian Science Monitor*, December 22, 1948, 11.

277 **solid-marble sinks:** "Fifth Avenue Mansion Gets New Role," *New York Times*, December 16, 1951, 49.

278 **"he did all he could"**: CH to William Targ, April 4, 1954, CHP-T, box 2, folder 20.

278 **charged Moon with being "subversive"**: "Editor Loses Job, Charges a 'Smear,'" *New York Times*, April 18, 1953, 9.

278 **"nymphomaniac"**: Polly Johnson, interview with Michel Fabre, n.d., MF, box 6, folder 31.

278 **"impatient for the money"**: CH to Yves Malartic, n.d. [c. June 1952], MF, box 7, folder 4.

278 **For $2000:** Ben Zevin to CH, October 16, 1954, CHP-T, box 2, folder 20, *QH*, 135.

279 **delivering the preface:** Richard Wright, preface, *La Croisade de Lee Gordon* (Paris: Editions Corréa, 1952), 8.

280 **"the only one over whom"**: CH to Richard Wright, October 19, 1952, RW, box 99, folder 1393.

280 **"Working hard"**: CH to CVV, November 11, 1952. CVVP, box He–Hols, folder "Himes, Chester B. 1952–1956."

281 **"a long time ago"**: CH to CVV, November 23, 1952, ibid.

281 **"I think Vandi hurt"**: WT to CH, August 25, 1955, CHP-T, box 6, folder 4.

282 **"really 'went' for"**: CH to CVV, n.d. [c. January 1953], CVVP, box He–Hols, folder "Himes, Chester B. 1952–1956."

282 **Having secured on December 31:** Zevin to CH, October 16, 1954.

282 **"magnificent ruin" and "tragic"**: Horace Cayton to CH, March 18, 1953, MF, box 2, folder 8.

283 **photo-dramatized by Parks:** Gordon Parks, "A Man Becomes Invisible," *Life*, August 25, 1952, 8–11.

283 **"an abler U.S. Negro novelist"**: "Native Doesn't Live Here Anymore: Rev. of *The Outsider* by Richard Wright," *Time*, March 30, 1953, 92.

283 **"I have joined"**: HF, 14.

283 **"great like Shakespeare"**: Horace Cayton and Ralph Ellison, interview notes, September 8, 1968, MF, box 46, folder 56.

284 **"the best of all"**: CH to Yves Malartic, February 26, 1953, MF, box 7, folder 4.

284 **"too chicken"**: Ralph Ellison to Horace Cayton, n.d. [winter 1957], RE, box 41, folder "Cayton, Horace."

284 **"was mad and acting"**: Cayton and Ellison, interview notes.

284 **"a private misunderstanding"**: *MLA*, 124.

284 **"riotous affair"**: Ralph Ellison to Richard Wright, January 21, 1953, RW, box 97, folder 1314.

285 **"By far the most intense"**: Advertisement for *The Third Generation*, *New York Times Book Review*, January 10, 1954, 9.

285 **"When she went to Chicago"**: *QH*, 136.

286 **"rough hewn"**: Gertrude Martin, "Book Reviews: Rev. of *Cast the First Stone* by Chester Himes," *Chicago Defender*, January 24, 1953, 11; Paul Sampson, "Prison Story Misses Its Mark," *Washington Post*, February 8, 1953, B6.

286 **"relationships among men"**: Gilbert Millstein, "Life in a Cell-Block," *New York Times Book Review*, January 18, 1953, 24.

286 **"perhaps one of the foulest"**: Henry F. Winslow, "Book of the Week: Rev. of *Cast the First Stone* by Chester Himes," *Pittsburgh Courier*, April 18, 1953, 9.

286 **"I am afraid"**: Ellison to Wright, January 21, 1953.

286 **"decidedly homophobic"**: Richard Gibson to Michel Fabre, June 6, 1988, MF, box 6 folder, 18.

287 **Even though he was uncomfortable**: CH to CVV, December 11, 1952, CVVP, box He–Hols, folder "Himes, Chester B. 1952–1956."

287 **the remaining $2500 advance**: Zevin to CH, October 16, 1954.

288 **"social realism"**: James Baldwin, "History as Nightmare," review of *Lonely Crusade* by Chester Himes, *New Leader*, October 25, 1947, 11.

288 **"I suppose you received"**: CH to Wright, February 19, 1953, RW, box 99, folder 1393.

289 **"I'm so goddamned close"**: CH to Wright, March 18, 1953, ibid.

289 **"strange and strained"**: Cayton to CH, March 18, 1953.

290 **"stylish, nice-looking"**: *QH*, 150.

291 **"fidelity to sexual detail"**: Ibid., 157.

291 **sheltered downed Allied airmen**: "Husband Beat Her for Aiding Allies," *Daily Boston Globe*, December 10, 1946, 12.

292 **featured in *Time***: "Untitled," *Time*, February 2, 1953, 11.

292 **"assured, distinguished"**: *QH*, 297.

292 **"if things work out"**: CH to Malartic, March 11, 1953, MF, box 7, folder 4.

292 **reminded jazzy Parisians of the strip**: Marcel Duhamel, *Raconte pas ta vie* (Paris: Mercure de France, 1972), 527.

293 **"gone completely French"**: *QH*, 180.

293 **"immoderate curiosity"**: Ibid., 183.

293 **"I don't know exactly":** CH to CVV, May 12, 1953, CVVP, box He–Hols, folder "Himes, Chester B. 1952–1956."

294 **"exceedingly dull":** *QH*, 185.

294 **"could say no":** Ibid., 189.

294 **"wild and raging fury":** Ibid., 178.

294 **"adventure without responsibilities":** CH, *A Case of Rape* (Washington, D.C.: Howard University Press, 1984), 94.

295 **Wright himself had been throwing:** CH to JAW, October 31, 1962, *DCDJ*, 24.

295 **"gossipy little" Café Monaco:** CH, "Impressions of Europe," p. 2, CHP-T, box 7, folder 82.

295 **"a lost and unhappy lot":** CH to CVV, May 12, 1953.

295 **"bragging about their scars":** *QH*, 224.

296 **"smaller, less wide-eyed":** CH, "Impressions of Europe," p. 2.

296 **"most outstanding characteristic":** *QH*, 185.

297 **"COME QUICKLY":** Ibid., p. 190.

298 **Schine demanded from Wright:** HF, p. 93.

298 **already public knowledge:** Richard Wright, "I Tried to Be a Communist," *Atlantic Monthly*, September 1944, 48–56.

298 **"That stupid son of a bitch":** *QH*, 199.

298 **"small, intense young man":** Ibid., 200.

298 **Franco-American Fellowship:** Lawrence Jackson, *The Indignant Generation: A Narrative History of Black Writers and Critics, 1934–1960* (Princeton, N.J.: Princeton University Press, 2010), 386.

299 **Baldwin found it "embarrassing":** James Baldwin to William Cole, n.d. [c. August 1953], James Baldwin Mss. Lilly Library, Indiana University, Bloomington.

299 **"We're perfectly pleasant":** James Baldwin to William Cole, n.d. [c. November 1952], ibid.

299 **"As I listened":** HF, 94.

299 **"black is a terrible color":** James Baldwin, "Many Thousands Gone," in *Notes of a Native Son* (1955; repr., Boston: Beacon, 1984), 30. This influential essay was originally published in 1951 in *Partisan Review* and reprinted in 1953 in the journal *Perspectives USA*.

300 **"the sons must slay the fathers":** *QH*, 201.

300 **"my ally, my witness":** James Baldwin, "Richard Wright," *Encounter*, April 1961, 58.

300 **"taken leave of his senses":** *QH*, 201.

300 **"written my book":** HF, 7.

301 **"our boy" and "your son":** CH to Wright, June 1, 1953.

301 **"it lacks force":** Marie Frazier to CH, n.d. [c. May–June 1953], CHP-T, box 7, folder 9.

301 **"We shall promote"**: William Targ to CH, June 2, 1953, CHP-T, box 2, folder 20.

302 **"Get all you can"**: *QH*, 208.

302 **"soul shattering"**: WT to CH ("Darling I was very glad"), n.d. Friday night, [c. late June 1955], CHP-T, box 6, folder 5.

302 **"inferior and ill at ease"**: CH, *A Case of Rape*, 70.

302 **"furious with himself"**: *QH*, 208.

302 **"Dick would have been"**: WT to CH, ("Darling: I was glad to hear"), n.d. Monday morning [c. January 1955], CHP-T, box 6, folder 4.

303 **"I have the kind"**: CH to Walter Freeman, December 10, 1956, CHP-T, box 3, folder 14.

303 **"as though she were my patient"**: *QH*, 163.

303 **"the rich, French leftist"**: CH to William Targ, July 14, 1953, CHP-T, box 2, folder 20.

303 **"Richard Wright is a great man"**: *QH*, 211.

304 **"too subtle and complicated"**: CH to Targ, July 14, 1953.

304 **"hard hurried contest"**: CH to Malartic, May 11, 1953, MF, box 7, folder 4.

304 **"It must be wonderful"**: Ruth Phillips to CH, June 3, 1953, CHP-T, box 7, folder 3.

304 **"I think Mr. Himes"**: WT to Yvonne Malartic, May 14, 1953, CHP-T, box 6, folder 4.

304 **Willa disliked the sensation**: WT to CH, ("Chester: You asked me"), n.d. Tuesday night [c. April 1955], CHP-T, box 6, folder 4.

305 **"I am living here"**: CH to CVV, June 1, 1953, CVVP, box He–Hols, folder "Himes, Chester B. 1952–1955."

305 **"I've made so many"**: CH to Wright, June 1, 1953.

305 **"in one dramatic incident"**: CH to Malartic, n.d. ["Thursday," c. June 1953], MF, box 7, folder 4.

306 **"hopes" of *The Cord* "doing fairly well"**: CH to Malartic, February 18, 1953, ibid.

306 **"I got what I wanted"**: CH to Targ, May 25, 1953, CHP-T, box 2, folder 20.

306 **"with great interest and satisfaction"**: Targ to CH, June 2, 1953, ibid.

307 **"courageous, uncomplaining"**: *QH*, 211.

307 **"asked Kriss how she could"**: WT to CH, ("Darling: I have your special"), n.d. Thursday noontime [December 1954], CHP-T, box 6, folder 5.

307 **"Oh, there are lots of American white women"**: *QH*, 247.

308 **"Race prejudice is about"**: CH to Malartic, July 11, 1953.

309 **"drab, walled prison"**: CH, "Impressions of Europe," 9.

309 **"a single volume"**: Ibid.

309 **"I think they are off"**: Targ to CH, July 27, 1953, CHP-T, box 6, folder 1.

309 **"The book you have"**: Donald Friede to CH, August 1, 1953, CHP-T, box 2, folder 20.

310 **"The situation which now exists"**: CH to Targ, August 13, 1953, CHP-T, box 2, folder 20.

311 **"limited engagement"**: *QH*, 261.

311 **Since June, Chester has been courting**: Targ to CH, June 10, 1953, CHP-T, box 2, folder 20.

311 **"I shall look forward"**: Donald Friede to CH, August 10, 1953, CHP-T, box 2, folder 20.

312 **"a nice, healthy, wholesome"**: *QH*, 264, 265.

313 **Early in October**: Targ to CH, October 2, 1953, CHP-T, box 2, folder 20.

313 **"None of the readers"**: Ibid.

313 **"most reluctant" Targ**: Targ to CH, October 9, 1953, CHP-T, box 2, folder 20.

313 **"big, ugly, smoky and dismal"**: CH to Malartic, October 21, 1953, MF, box 7, folder 4.

313 **"the most awful"**: CH to CVV, August 17, 1954, CVVP, box He–Hols, folder "Himes, Chester B. 1952–1955."

314 **"I'm keeping my fingers"**: CH to Targ, December 3, 1953, CHP-T, box 2, folder 20.

314 **"repay me well"**: CH to CVV, January 19, 1954, CVVP, box He–Hols, folder "Himes, Chester B. 1952–1955."

314 **"too damn cold to bathe"**: *QH*, 269.

11. OTHELLO

315 **"into herself like a hurt animal"**: *QH*, 271.

315 **engaging World in an option ploy**: Ben Zevin to CH, October 16, 1954, CHP-T, box 2, folder 20; CH to CVV, April 15, 1954, CVVP, box He–Hols, folder "Himes, Chester B. 1952–1955."

316 **"inexperienced and untraveled"**: *QH*, 271.

316 **"tearful, sinister-looking"**: Ibid., 274.

316 **"but the few New York reviews"**: CH to CVV, February 5, 1954, CVVP, box He–Hols, folder "Himes, Chester B. 1952–1955."

317 **"considerable power"**: John Brooks, "Tragedy in Sepia," *New York Times Book Review*, January 10, 1954, 29.

317 **"Tragic power"**: Edmund Fuller, "A Moving Novel of Negro Life," *Chicago Tribune*, January 10, 1954, B5.

317 **"his best novel to date"**: Gertrude Martin, "Book Reviews," *Chicago Defender*, January 16, 1954, 7.

317 **"The most dangerous"**: Marion L. Starkey, "Most Dangerous Kind of 'Momism,'" *Boston Globe*, January 31, 1954, C71.

317 **"a less depressing book"**: Brooks, "Tragedy in Sepia."

317 **"just an exercise"**: Blyden Jackson, "The Blithe Newcomers: Resume of Negro Literature in 1954: Part I," *Phylon* (1st quarter 1955): 9.

318 **"problems and conflicts"**: Arthur P. Davis, "Integration and Race Literature," *Phylon* (2nd quarter 1956): 143.

318 **"moving along not too badly"**: William Targ to CH, February 9, 1954, CHP-T, box 2, folder 20.

318 **5146 copies:** Royalty Statement, The Third Generation by Chester Himes, World Publishing Company, September 25, 1954, CHP-T, box 2, folder 20.

318 **"big vulgar" advertisements**: CH to CVV, August 17, 1954, CVVP, box He–Hols, folder "Himes, Chester B. 1952–1955."

319 **"number of American lunatics"**: CH to Yves Malartic, May 29, 1954, MF, box 7, folder 4.

319 **"I was trying to express"**: *QH*, 285.

319 **"some of the most pornographic"**: CH to CVV, April 15, 1954, CVVP, box He–Hols, folder "Himes, Chester B. 1952–1955.".

320 **"I don't want you"**: CH to William Targ, April 6, 1954, CHP-T, box 2, folder 20.

320 **"Everyone here believes"**: Targ to CH, April 13, 1954, ibid.

320 **"one of the most profane"**: CH to CVV, May 25, 1954, CVVP, box He–Hols, folder "Himes, Chester B. 1952–1955."

321 **"every good soldier"**: CH to Edward Himes, November 20, 1971, JSH, box 2, folder 11; *QH*, 290.

321 **sent $50 directly:** CH to Targ, April 25, 1954, CHP-T, box 2, folder 20.

321 **"good deal of surrealism"**: CH to CVV, July 7, 1954, CVVP, box He–Hols, folder "Himes, Chester B. 1952–1955."

322 **"American idiots"**: CH to Malartic, February 16, 1954, MF, box 7, folder 4.

322 **"The Americans and the English"**: *QH*, 306.

323 **"I caught him looking"**: WT to CH ("Darling: I have your special") n.d. Thursday noontime [April 1955], CHP-T, box 6, folder 5.

323 **"such rapport with men"**: *QH*, 307.

323 **"practically begging in the streets"**: CH to Malartic, June 7, 1954, MF, box 7, folder 4.

323 **"If published it would"**: Targ to CH, July 1, 1954, CHP-T, box 2, folder 20.

324 **"We Negro writers"**: CH to Targ, July 6, 1954, CHP, box 2, folder 20.

324 **"the grim humorous attack"**: CH to Malartic, July 7, 1954, MF, box 7, folder 4.

324 **"I like this book"**: CH to Yves Malartic, July 29, 1954, ibid.

324 **he thought the book a masterpiece:** CH to CVV, July 29, 1954, CVVP, box He–Hols, folder "Himes, Chester B. 1952–1955."

325 **"I must confess this bundle"**: CH to Targ, August 23, 1954, CHP-T, box 2, folder 20.

326 **"distraught and intent"**: *QH*, 323.

327 **"it's better for me"**: CH to Ben Zevin, n.d. [c. September 1954], CHP-T, box 6, folder 15.

327 **"Himes, you'll never"**: *QH*, 347.

328 **"puritan wave flowing around"**: Jean Rosenthal to CH, September 30, 1954, CHP-T, box 1, folder 6.

328 **"cooled off mightily"**: CH to CVV, October 16, 1954, CVVP, box He–Hols, folder "Himes, Chester B. 1952–1955."

328 **"I was an awful person in Paris"**: WT to CH, n.d. [c. December 12, 1954], CHP-T, box 6, folder 4.

328 **Chester withdrew from the agency**: CH to Jean Rosenthal, October 15, 1954, CHP-T, box 1, folder 6.

328 **she was foolish to suppose**: CH to Mrs. Boutelleau, October 14, 1954, CHP-T, box 3, folder 3.

328 **"Sick at heart"**: CH to Targ, October 11, 1954, CHP-T, box 2, folder 20.

329 **earned the company $4,380.96**: Ben Zevin to CH, October 16, 1954, ibid.

329 **"too specialized"**: J. Laughlin to CH, November 9, 1954, CHP-T, box 1, folder 17.

329 **"things are now bad enough"**: CH to CVV, October 16, 1954.

329 **"rather frail"**: Marcel Duhamel, *Raconte pas ta vie* (Paris: Mercure de France, 1972), 589.

329 **a contract for *The End of a Primitive***: CH to Marcel Duhamel, July 19, 1955, CHP-T, box 1, folder 11.

329 **"wanted this Negro"**: CH to CVV, December 16, 1954, CVVP, box He–Hols, folder "Himes, Chester B. 1952–1955."

329 **"a detective story"**: CH to CVV, November 29, 1954, ibid.

330 **"and how I managed"**: CH to Victor Weybright, November 3, 1954, CHP-T, box 1, folder 24.

330 **"she shouldn't think of it"**: *QH*, 350.

330 **He needed time alone**: WT to CH ("Darling, I don't quite know how"), n.d. Friday [c. June 1955], CHP-T, box 6, folder 4.

331 **"every paragraph of it"**: Annie Brierre to CH, n.d. [c. 1954–1955], CHP-T, box 3, folder 3.

331 **"an art strong enough"**: Jean-Claude Brisville, review of *S'il braille, lâche-le*, by CH, *La Nef* (December 1949–January 1950): 130, quoted in Grégory Pierrot, "Chester Himes, Boris Vian, and the Transatlantic Politics of Racial Representation," *African American Review* (Summer–Fall 2009): 256.

332 **"insolent and hostile"**: CH to CVV, November 29, 1954.

332 **"the black Prometheus"**: Leonard Barnes, review of *How Britain Rules Africa*, by George Padmore, *International Affairs* (September 1937): 797.

333 **"Are you really divorced"**: WT to CH ("trouble in Paris"), n.d. [c. April

1955], CHP-T, box 6, folder 4; WT to CH ("Darling: I have your special"), n.d. Thursday noontime [c. April 1955].

333 **"I think your writing"**: WT to CH, December 20, 1954, CHP-T, box 6, folder 4.

333 **"We had each"**: *MLA*, 11.

334 **"I am backing out"**: Ibid., 10.

334 **free to do**: WT to CH, January 5, 1955, CHP-T, box 6, folder 4.

334 **on January 15, 1955**: WT to CH, January 20, 1955, ibid.

334 **"broke, bitter, defeated"**: *MLA*, 11.

335 **"Everything is such"**: WT to CH ("Monday morning, This will be"), n.d. [c. late February 1955], CHP-T, box 6, folder 4.

335 **mailing a weekly stipend**: WT to CH ("Here's your check") n.d. Friday noon [c. late February 1955], ibid.

335 **"Have you heard"**: WT to CH ("Wednesday at home 2pm, This is just"), n.d. [c. early February 1955], ibid.

335 **"I liked Fanny"**: Ibid.

336 **"making love to her"**: *MLA*, 14.

336 **"We might be able"**: WT to CH ("Friday night, Just before I left"), n.d. [c. late February 1955], CHP-T, box 6, folder 4.

336 **"Darling, thank you"**: WT to CH ("It is finally my lunch hour"), n.d. [c. late February 1955], ibid.

336 **"her white tiny body"**: *MLA*, 25.

336 **"booney"**: WT to CH ("Well I finally did get home") n.d. Monday morning [c. late February 1955], CHP-T, box 6, folder 4.

336 **"My, what a problem we have!"**: WT to CH, ("Darling: I came in anyway"), n.d. Wednesday [winter 1955], ibid.

336 **through an open door**: CH to JAW, October 31, 1962, *DCDJ*, 27.

337 **"God loved Eve"**: CH and WT, *Silver Altar*, typescript, LPH, collection 690, box 3 (8), folder 9, pp. 608, 609.

337 **"People, Americans"**: WT to CH ("Darling I am so weary"), n.d. Monday, [c. late February 1955], CHP-T, box 6, folder 4.

337 **"Very few white women"**: WT to CH ("Chester: You asked me to write"), n.d. Tuesday night [April 1955], ibid.

338 **"magnificent" writing**: WT to CH ("Darling: Now I shall write you a nice long letter"), n.d. Wednesday afternoon [late spring 1955], ibid.

338 **"It is the first time"**: WT to CH ("It is finally my lunch hour") n.d. [c. late February 1955].

338 **"little bit wrong"**: WT to CH ("Friday night, Just before I left") n.d. [c. late February 1955].

339 **"What's the difference"**: WT to CH ("Darling I was very glad"), n.d. Friday night, [c. late June 1955], CHP-T, box 6, folder 4.

340 **"Can you imagine"**: WT to CH ("Now that I have recovered") n.d. Thursday night, [c. June 1955], ibid.

340 **"a very attractive intelligent person"**: WT to CH ("Chester: You asked me to write"), n.d. Tuesday night [April 1955].

340 **"I never believed it possible"**: WT to CH ("Darling I received your long letter"), n.d. Saturday [c. May 1955], CHP-T, box 6, folder 4.

340 **"furious and hurt"**: *MLA*, 19.

340 **"I am hoping"**: CH to CVV, March 28, 1955, CVVP, box He–Hols, folder "Himes, Chester B. 1952–1955."

340 **"I would like to go somewhere"**: WT to CH ("Darling I have your Wednesday letter"), n.d. Thursday [c. May 1955], CHP-T, box 6, folder 4.

341 **"a liar"**: Ibid.

341 **finagling a reprint contract**: Charles Byrnes to CH, March 16, 1955, CHP-T, box 1, folder 2.

341 **"You have not received"**: William Koshland to CH, March 16, 1955, AAK.

341 **"General Himes"**: Harry Buchman to William Koshland, March 29, 1955, AAK; William Koshland, memorandum to Mrs. Knopf, February 4, 1963, AAK.

341 **"that you finally have some money"**: WT to CH ("Darling: I said I'd write"), n.d. Thursday [c. late April 1955], CHP-T, box 6, folder 4.

341 **$100 at the end of May:** Byrnes to CH, May 31, 1955, CHP-T, box 1, folder 2.

341 **a bill for $806:** CH to Charles Byrnes, May 25, 1955, ibid.

341 **"simply will not register"**: Walter Freeman to CH, May 3, 1955, CHP-T, box 1, folder 24.

342 **beseeched NAL's Walter Freeman:** CH to Walter Freeman, May 9, 1955, ibid.; Freeman to CH, May 11, 1955, ibid.

342 **"If you will accept my apology"**: CH to Lurton Blassingame, n.d. [c. May 1955], CHP-T, box 3, folder 3.

343 **his room of "horror":** WT to CH ("Chester: I'll only have time"), n.d. Friday afternoon [May 1955], CHP-T, box 6, folder 4.

343 **"We should have stayed busted up"**: WT to CH ("Thanks for sending the stuff"), n.d. Friday [c. late June 1955], ibid.

343 **"Don't get a divorce"**: WT to CH ("I have received your long letter"), n.d. Saturday [May 1955], ibid.

343 **"If we're through"**: WT to CH ("Chester: You asked me"), n.d. Tuesday night [c. April 1955], ibid.

343 **"I would not like"**: Ibid.

343 **"Oh shit, I do so want"**: *MLA*, 17.

344 **Vandi Haygood was dead:** "Mrs. Haygood Dies in NYC: Aided Many Young, Struggling Writers," *Afro-American*, July 30, 1955, 21.

344 **landing *The Third Generation*:** Annie Brierre to CH, n.d. [c. 1954–1955], CHP-T, box 3, folder 3; CH to Targ, July 19, 1955, CHP-T, box 2, folder 20.

344 **"and the next morning":** *MLA*, 24.

345 **he told Blassingame his theories:** Lurton Blassingame to CH, August 30, 1955, CHP-T, box 3, folder 3.

345 **"I can't make a commitment":** Arnold Gingrich to CH, December 17, 1956, AG, box 12, folder "H #2."

345 **"I have found it a pleasure":** Freeman to CH, May 3, 1955.

345 **"practically every change":** Freeman to CH, September 12, 1955, CHP-T, box 3, folder 14.

346 **Emmett Till:** "Nation Horrified by Murder of Kidnapped Chicago Youth," *Jet*, September 15, 1955, 6–9.

346 **"I am innately sad":** CH to CVV, September 27, 1955, CVVP, box He–Hols, folder "Himes, Chester B. 1952–1955."

346 **"The only jobs in New York":** *MLA*, 27.

346 **"hell is hell":** CH to Duhamel, July 19, 1955.

347 **"I was storing up":** *MLA*, 29.

347 **"One thing I learned":** WT to CH, August 23, 1955, CHP-T, box 6, folder 5.

347 **"way out":** WT to CH, September 2, 1955, ibid.

347 **the judgment summarily passed:** F. G. Short and Sons, Plaintiff, against Chester Himes, Defendant, Index No. 33154/55, CHP-T, box 20, folder 4.

348 **"current earnings have not covered":** Frank Vogel to CH, September 29, 1955, CHP-T, box 1, folder 5.

348 **"I felt I had to get out":** CH to CVV, December 20, 1955, CVVP, box He–Hols, folder "Himes, Chester B. 1952–1955."

348 **"cheap, tenement-like effect":** Freeman to CH, November 9, 1955, CHP-T, box 3, folder 17.

349 **"just to stay alive":** CH to JAW, July 9, 1969, *DCDJ*, 92.

349 **he would kill someone:** Constance Webb Pearlstein to Lesley Himes, September 19, 1995, LPH, box 1, folder 15.

12. A PISTOL IN HIS HAND, AGAIN

350 **On December 22, 1955:** Chester Himes, no. 39540, U.S. Passport, issued March 1953, CHP-T, box 12. CH writes in *MLA* that he arrived on December 26, but his passport was stamped on the twenty-second.

350 **"I got America":** *MLA*, 36.

350 **"diminished me":** CH to Charles Orengo, January 12, 1956, CHP-T, box 1, folder 20.

350 **"fantastically dull bitter-enders":** CH to Walter Freeman, January 4, 1956, CHP-T, box 1, folder 7.

351 **on January 24:** Contrat d'Édition: La traduction francaise de *The third generation*, Monsieur Chester Himes et la Librairie Plon, January 24, 1956, CHP-T, box 19, folder 2.

351 **"What does one":** CH, "Chester Himes," *La Fin d'un primitif,* trans. Yves Malartic (Paris: Gallimard, 1956), 9.

351 **bespoke "dignity":** CH to CVV, April 26, 1956, CVVP, box He–Hols, folder "Himes, Chester B. 1956–1961."

352 **ordinary to stumble across:** Lesley Packard Himes, interview with author, May 2009.

352 **"sold my rights":** CH to Oliver Swan, January 21, 1956, CHP-T, box 5, folder 15.

352 **Willa had the right:** Affidavit "Know All Persons by These Present," March 15, 1956, CHP-T, box 19, folder 1.

353 **"with soft beautiful features":** *MLA*, 107.

353 **theatrically declared:** Ibid., 38.

353 **considered *The Primitive* "excellent":** Richard Gibson to Michel Fabre, May 26, 1988, MF, box 6, folder 18.

353 **as would Henry Miller:** Walter Freeman to CH, April 20, 1956, CHP-T, box 3, folder 17.

353 **"Take it easy greasy":** Walter Coleman to CH, October 18, 1973, CHP-T, box 3, folder 5.

354 **French papers:** "La Resistance des Noirs: Devient chaque jour de plus en plus puissante," *Le Monde,* February 28, 1956, 1.

354 **On February 21:** J. P. Chabrol, "Le Quartier Latin a l'heure antifasciste," *L'Humanité,* February 24, 1956, 7F.

354 **"Hollywood type mob scene":** CH to Freeman, March 5, 1956, CHP-T, box 3, folder 17.

355 **their world of "refreshing" Paris:** David Remnick, "George Plimpton's Good Life," *Washington Post,* November 4, 1984, H2.

355 **"He could never finish deriding":** Gibson to Fabre, May 26, 1988.

355 **"I was the only black":** *MLA*, 124.

356 **Attorney General Tom Clark:** Mel Tarpley, "Is Ollie Harrington, Battling Cartoonist, Returning?," New York *Amsterdam News,* June 29, 1991, 30; Wil Haygood, "Expatriate Artist Looks Homeward: Oliver Harrington, Who Fled U.S. in McCarthy Era, Is Wistful but Devoted 'My Life to My Beliefs,'" *Boston Globe,* March 20, 1988, 83.

356 **"unique individuals":** *MLA*, 36.

357 **"great charm":** Ibid., 57.

357 **"In front of that vast white audience":** Ibid., 37.

357 **"'Everybody's ain't that big'":** CH, *Pinktoes* (1961; repr., New York: Dell, 1966), 81.

357 **"Mamie's one ambition":** Ibid., 35.

357 **"finding it difficult"**: CH to CVV, April 26, 1956.

358 **first met a teenage Silberman:** HF, 12.

358 **"wonderful subject"**: James Silberman to CH, May 6, 1956, CHP-T, box 1, folder 7.

358 **"the most notorious"**: *MLA*, 72.

358 **"straight narrative"**: CH to CVV, August 28, 1956, CVVP, box He–Hols, folder "Himes, Chester B. 1956–1961."

358 **"White Americans are reading"**: CH to CVV, April 26, 1956.

358 **"a very flexible version"**: CH to James Silberman, May 9, 1956, CHP-T, box 1, folder 7.

359 **"German women"**: *MLA*, 78.

360 **worked hard hours in solitude:** CH to Walter Freeman, December 12, 1956. CHP-T, box 3, folder 17.

361 **"there's no point"**: WT to CH ("Dear Chester: Thanks for your letter"), n.d. [June 1956], CHP-T, box 6, folder 5.

361 **several drunken evenings:** Gibson to Fabre, May 26, 1988.

362 **"dedicated to the cults"**: Richard Gibson, "Curzio Malaparte: The Vision of Defeat," *Merlin* (December 1954): 307.

362 **"So you're the boy"**: Richard Gibson, "A No to Nothing," *Kenyon Review* (Spring 1951): 252–55; Richard Gibson, "Richard Wright's 'Island of Hallucination' and the 'Gibson Affair,'" *Modern Fiction Studies* (Winter 1995): 907.

362 **argued about back rent:** Gibson, "Richard Wright's," 910.

362 **"tell the truth"**: Gibson to Fabre, November 18, 1987, MF, box 6, folder 8.

362 **he sided with Harrington after the fight:** *MLA*, 34, 73; Lesley Himes interview; Gibson to Fabre, May 26, 1988.

363 **French police:** Bernard Dadié, *An African in Paris*, trans. Karen C. Hatch (Urbana: University of Illinois Press, 1994), 146–47.

363 **"I've got my life"**: CH to CVV, April 26, 1956.

363 **"Why don't you marry"**: CH to Jean Himes, July 30, 1956, CHP-T, box 5, folder 8.

363 **reversing himself on earlier:** WT to CH, June 19, 1956, CHP-T, box 6, folder 5.

363 **"If it appears in print"**: CH to Mr. Bledsoe, December 8, 1956, CHP-T, box 3, folder 3.

363 **"I hate him"**: Edward Darling to WT, April 17, 1958, Beacon Press Records, box 123, folder "Thompson, Willa/Garden Without Flowers," Andover-Harvard Library, Harvard Divinity School, Harvard University, Cambridge, Massachusetts. For a full exploration of the literary relationship between Himes and Thompson see Guy Conn, "The Racio-Sexual Psychology of Inter-Racial Relationships: Recovering Chester Himes' *Garden Without Flowers*," PhD diss., Emory University, forthcoming.

364 **"Chet thinks"**: *MLA*, 76.

364 **"a front room"**: CH to CVV, October 8, 1956, CVVP, box He–Hols, folder "Himes, Chester B. 1956–1961"; Paul Zweig, "Departures," in *Americans in Paris: A Literary Anthology*, ed. Adam Gopnick (New York: Library of America, 2004), 513.

364 **Regine "had troubles"**: Regine Fischer to CH, December 6, 1956, CHP-T, box 3, folder 15.

364 **"Living on the goodwill"**: CH to CVV, August 28, 1956.

365 **"This results in extravagance"**: "Noir et blanc," *L'Express*, August 24, 1956, 16.

365 **Chester escorted Ellison:** *MLA*, 35.

365 **"as tortured as ever"**: Ralph Ellison to Horace Cayton, n.d. [c. April 1957], RE, box 41, folder Horace Cayton.

365 **literary critic Alfred Kazin:** Ralph Ellison to Saul Bellow, August 15, 1956, Saul Bellow Papers, box 2, folder 8, Regenstein Library, University of Chicago.

366 **"I wonder vaguely"**: CH to Jean Himes, October 11, 1956, CHP-T, box 5, folder 8.

366 **he owed about $500:** CH to Freeman, September 23, 1956, CHP-T, box 3, folder 17.

366 **"I didn't take any active"**: CH to CVV, October 6, 1956, CVVP, box He–Hols, folder "Himes, Chester B. 1956–1961."

367 **"grave" and taciturn:** Davidson Nicol, "Alioune Diop and the African Renaissance," *African Affairs* (January 1979): 7.

367 **Wright, a conference organizer:** Michel Fabre, *The World of Richard Wright* (Jackson: University of Mississippi Press, 1985), 199.

367 **the dole of the Central Intelligence Agency:** Lawrence P. Jackson, *The Indignant Generation* (Princeton, N.J.: Princeton University Press, 2010), 462–63.

367 **"socialism for Africa"**: W. E. B. Du Bois, "To the Congres des Ecrivains et Artistes Noirs," *Le 1er Congrès International des Écrivains et Artistes Noirs:* Présence Africaine, numéro spécial (June–November 1956), p. 383. See Guirdex Masse, "A Black Diasporic Encounter: The First International Congress of Black Writers and Artists and the Politics of Race and Culture," PhD diss., Emory University, 2014.

367 **"communicate only slightly"**: Ellison to Cayton, n.d. [c. April 1957].

368 **"not one quality literary work"**: Mongo Beti, "Romancing Africa," in *Cruel City*, trans. Pim Higginson (Bloomington: Indiana University Press, 2013), xi, xiv.

368 **which he had cited:** Frantz Fanon, *Black Skin, White Masks*, trans. Charles Markmann (1952; repr., New York: Grove Press, 1967), 140.

368 **A copy of the French edition:** Frantz Fanon, *Ecrits sur l'aliénation et la liberté*, ed. Jean Khalfa and Robert Young (Paris: Editions la Découverte, 2015), 608.

369 **"dilettante Uncle Tom":** CH, *A Case of Rape* (1980; repr., New York: Carroll and Graf, 1994), 47.

369 **"As a yardstick":** Ibid., 33–34.

370 **"more or less a type":** Ibid., 94.

370 **"I will try to be":** Regine Fischer to CH, September 25, 1956, CHP-T, box 3, folder 15.

370 **"I don't know":** CH to Victor Weybright, October 12, 1956, CHP-T, box 1, folder 24.

370 **"I don't think *Mamie Mason*":** Silberman to CH, October 2, 1956, CHP-T, box 1, folder 7.

371 **"brilliant social satire":** Victor Weybright to CH, October 11, 1956, CHP-T, box 1, folder 24.

371 **"Please do not consider":** CH to Freeman, September 23, 1956.

371 **He raced to court Gallimard:** CH to P. D. Mascolo, October 14, 1956, CHP-T, box 1, folder 11.

371 **"I wish I could":** CH to Freeman, September 23, 1956.

372 **"I like the idea":** CH to Marcel Duhamel, October 16, 1956, CHP-T, box 1, folder 11.

372 **"follow your suggestions":** Ibid.; CH to CVV, November 18, 1956, CVVP, box He–Hols, folder "Himes, Chester B. 1956–1961."

372 **"the greatest writer":** *MLA*, 102.

372 **"the idea of death":** Jonathan P. Eburne, "The Transatlantic Mysteries of Paris: Chester Himes, Surrealism, and the Serie Noir," *PMLA* 120, no. 3 (2005): 810; Marcel Duhamel, "Préface," *Panorama du film noir américain*, ed. Raymonde Borde and Emil Chaumenton (Paris: Minuit, 1955), vii–x.

372 **"We don't give a damn":** *MLA*, 102.

373 **"intolerable situation":** CH to Charles Byrnes, November 2, 1956, CHP-T, box 1, folder 2.

373 **"a condemnation":** CH to Freeman, December 10, 1956, CHP-T, box 3, folder 14.

373 **U.S. embassy had him interrogated:** *MLA*, 123.

373 **"of the cult devoted":** CH, *A Case of Rape*, 36.

373 **"spellbound, silently":** Walter Coleman to CH, October 18, 1973, CHP-T, box 3, folder 5.

374 **"I am pretty nearly beat":** CH to Freeman, December 12, 1956.

375 **"I am not intelligent":** R. Fischer to CH, December 6, 1956.

375 **"I am the only person":** CH to Otto Fischer, December 16, 1956, CHP-T, box 6, folder 15.

376 **"I see no possibility"**: Arthur Fields to CH, December 18, 1956, CHP-T, box 1, folder 5.

376 **"You can't have a *policier*"**: *MLA*, 105.

376 **"tall, loose-jointed, sloppily dressed"**: CH, *A Rage in Harlem* (1957; repr., New York: Vintage, 1991), 44.

376 **"It was said in Harlem"**: Ibid., 49.

377 **"[Papa] LaBas and [Black] Herman"**: Ishmael Reed to CH, July 27, 1972, CHP-T, box 5, folder 13.

377 **"a wild, incredible story"**: *MLA*, 109.

377 **"the voracious churning"**: CH, *A Rage in Harlem*, 93.

378 **"Goldy's scream mingled"**: Ibid., 105.

379 **"cheap, shabby and racist"**: Lawrence Jordan to CH, January 22, 1976, CHP-T, box 1, folder 9.

379 **"just makes me feel"**: Fischer to CH, January 10, 1957, CHP-T, box 3, folder 15.

379 **"Darling I am not coming"**: Fischer to CH, December 15, 1956, ibid.

379 **She would sign letters:** Regine Himes to "Chere Madame," n.d. [from Vence Villa Lavadou], CHP-T, box 3, folder 16; CH to CVV, December 19, 1957, CVVP, box He–Hols, folder "Himes, Chester B. 1956–1961."

379 **"a blind insensate fury"**: *MLA*, 118.

379 **"dirty nigger"**: Fischer to CH, n.d. [c. March–April 1957], CHP-T, box 3, folder 15.

379 **"No human being"**: Ibid.

380 **"I couldn't stop slapping"**: CH, "The Way It Was," typescript with hand-written revisions, p. 42, CHP-T 180, box 6.

380 **"I've cut down"**: CH to CVV, April 23, 1957, CVVP, box He–Hols, folder "Himes, Chester B. 1956–1961."

380 **"Now that you've broke"**: *MLA*, 121.

381 **"cesspool of buffoonery"**: Ibid., 126.

382 **"frenzied boudoir adventures"**: "The Primitives," *Duke*, June 1957, 63.

382 **"suffocated" by the wealth**: *MLA*, 165.

383 **"its insight, its violence"**: *Feux Croisés: Ames et Terres Étrangères*, May 21, 1957, Théatre de l'Alliance Français, CHP-T, box 23, folder 253.

383 **"free of thinking about"**: *MLA*, 144.

383 **African memories or racial mixture:** J. Claude Deven, "Chester Himes: Les Noirs d'Amérique à la troisième génération," *Tribune de Lausaune*, May 26, 1957, clipping in CHP-T, box 34, folder 3.

384 **"I had a German girl"**: *MLA*, 144.

385 **"desire to succeed"**: Ibid., 155.

385 **"could write like"**: Ibid.

385 **Ollie had been condemning:** Gibson, "Richard Wright's," 911–12.

385 **"Any American who thinks"**: Ollie Harrington, letter to the editor, *Life*, October 21, 1957, 10.

385 **Gibson claimed:** Richard Gibson, letter to Michel Fabre, November 10, 1987, MF, box 6, folder 18.

386 **"I am sorry about what"**: Horace Cayton, interview notes with St. Clair Drake, September 1968, MF, box 46, folder 56.

386 **"disrupt, disorganize, and neutralize"**: Curt Gentry, *J. Edgar Hoover: The Man and the Secrets* (New York: W. W. Norton, 1992), 442–45.

386 **Chester strongly suspected Gibson:** *MLA*, 34, 73; Lesley Himes interview; Gibson to Fabre, May 26, 1988.

387 **"I've spent too much"**: CH, "Richard Wright hadn't much to say to me," typescript fragment, MF, box 8, folder 16.

388 **burning a bowl:** CH to CVV, December 17, 1957, CVVP, box He–Hols, folder "Himes, Chester B. 1956–1961."

388 **"lift scenes straight"**: *MLA*, 169.

388 **"I had accomplished nothing"**: Ibid., 177.

388 **being a grubber:** CH to CVV, December 19, 1957.

390 **"I give you all"**: Anthony Boucher, "Criminals at Large," *New York Times Book Review*, September 9, 1959, 13.

390 **replacing John Steinbeck:** *MLA*, 181.

390 **"out of the American black's secret mind"**: Ibid.

391 **"the superignorant sentimentality"**: Dawn Powell to Joseph Gousha, n.d. [c. December 1950], "Three Letters," in Gopnick, *Americans in Paris*, 459.

391 **"the most extraordinary"**: Igor Maslowski, "Ma Selection du mois: *La Reine des pommes*," *Mystère*, June 1958, 117.

392 **"caused a sensation"**: *MLA*, 185.

392 **"Congratulations, I hear"**: Lesley Himes interview.

392 **"Beautiful and chic"**: *MLA*, 186.

392 **believed that she was racist:** Carlos Moore, interview with author, May 2010.

393 **"In America you have"**: "Amid the Alien Corn," *Time*, November 17, 1958, 30.

393 **"a person in Vence"**: *MLA*, 181.

394 **"I was a real celebrity"**: Ibid., 185.

395 **"I confess it is"**: CH to Lesley Packard, July 28, 1959, CHP-T, box 6, folder 5.

395 **"I am going to Paris"**: Fischer to CH, September 10, 1959, CHP-T, box 3, folder 15.

395 **drunken debacle:** CH to Lorraine Williams, October 22, 1965, *DCDJ*, 47.

396 **"The French . . . have gone mad"**: Boucher, "Criminals at Large," 13.

396 **"The question arose"**: Lewis Nichols, "In and Out of Books," *New York Times Book Review*, September 27, 1959, 8.

396 **"I dread reading"**: CH to CVV, October 5, 1959, CVVP, box He–Hols, folder "Himes, Chester B. 1956–1961."

396 **"It hurt more"**: *MLA*, 196.

397 **"The *New York Times* could not have chosen"**: CH to editor, *New York Times*, October 10, 1959, CHP-T, box 5, folder 15.

397 **"I haven't seen anything"**: CH to CVV, March 30, 1959, CVVP, box He–Hols, folder "Himes, Chester B. 1956–1961."

397 **"a group of negro residents in Paris"**: Legat Paris to Director FBI, February 11, 1960, Oliver Wendell Harrington, FBI File #100-379980, Federal Bureau of Investigation.

397 **"Possible Subversives Among US Personnel"**: Legat Paris to Director FBI, February 11, 1960, Richard Nathaniel Wright, FBI File #100-157464, p. 169, Federal Bureau of Investigation.

397 **Irle saw the author . . . "lots of times"**: Abiola Irele, interview with author, September 2013.

398 **"flamboyant" . . . "truculent"**: Mongo Beti, "Le Pauvre Christ de Bomba Explique!," *Peuple Noirs, Peuples Africains* 19 (1981): 116–17.

13. FIVE CORNERED SQUARE

399 **"the worst moment"**: *MLA*, 198.

400 **"this veritable ocean"**: CH to Lesley Packard, n.d. [c. 1961], CHP-T, box 5, folder 6.

400 **"This is me, Chester Himes"**: *MLA*, p. 200.

400 **"You know that I"**: Regine Fischer to CH, March 1, 1959 [mistaken date], CHP-T, box 3, folder 16.

400 **"For you I have never"**: Fischer to CH, March 15, 1960, ibid.

400 **"I don't have"**: Fischer to CH, January 2, 1960, CHP-T, box 6, folder 16.

401 **"a village of poor"**: CH to JAW, October 11, 1962, *DCDJ*, 2.

401 **"Never stop giving"**: Walter Coleman to CH, May 26, 1970, CHP-T, box 3, folder 5.

402 **"Everyone here"**: CH to Lester Granger, February 14, 1960, CHP-T, box 3, folder 18.

402 **"It's so sweet"**: Fischer to CH, September 30, 1960, CHP-T, box 6, folder 16.

403 **"an extemporaneous journey"**: *MLA*, 211.

404 **"Get the cat and the dog"**: Lesley Packard Himes, interview with author, May 2009.

404 **"as a failure"**: CH, *A Case of Rape* (1980; repr., New York: Carroll and Graf, 1994), 34.

404 **"I don't want him to wallow"**: *MLA*, 216.

404 **Wright had been closest to his girlfriend:** Ollie Harrington, "The Last Days of Richard Wright," *Ebony*, February 1961, 86.

405 **"How dare she do this?":** Lesley Himes interview.

405 **"Dick was the greatest":** *MLA*, 214.

405 **Wright's "enemies":** Ibid., 215.

405 **"I had never realized before":** Ibid., 217.

406 **"DChief call d'young":** William Melvin Kelley to CH, December 14, 1970, CHP-T, box 4, folder 12.

407 **"If you want me":** CH to Packard ("Monday afternoon Lesley darling"), n.d. [c. winter–spring 1961], CHP-T, box 4, folder 7.

407 **"as much as I would":** Packard to CH, ("Thursday evening Chester darling"), n.d. [c. late fall 1961] CHP-T, box 4, folder 7.

407 **"broke, outcast, put down":** *MLA*, 220.

408 **"very pleasant" Maurice Girodias:** : Fischer to CH, May 16, 1961, CHP-T, box 6, folder 16.

408 **On April 28:** Contract between CH and the Olympia Press, April 28, 1961, CHP-T, box 19, folder 2.

409 **"absolutely delighted with the piece":** Herbert Hill to CH, June 17, 1961, CHP-T, box 4, folder 1.

410 **performing in white face:** "Dean Dixon, 61, Dies, Conductor in Exile," and Ronald Smothers, "His 'Maestro' Was Hard Won," both in *New York Times*, November 5, 1976, 18.

411 **"like a mighty river":** *MLA*, 227.

411 **"I find that":** CH to Packard, September 18, 1961.

412 **"very much in love":** CH to CVV, December 16, 1961, CVVP, box He–Hols, folder "Himes, Chester B. 1956–1961."

412 **"sailed over the crushed steering wheel":** *MLA*, 237.

412 **"outstanding human values":** "*Exodus* Opens Cannes Festival," *Chicago Daily Tribune*, May 4, 1961, C3; "2 Movies Share Top Cannes Prizes," *New York Times*, May 19, 1961, 23.

413 **"I'll do what I can":** Marcel Duhamel to CH, October 27, 1961, CHP-T, box 1, folder 11.

413 **"defending the honor and integrity":** CH to Packard ("Friday Lesley darling—my own darling"), n.d. [c. fall 1961], CHP-T, box 4, folder 7.

413 **"out of the ordinary":** Annette Insdorf, "Cohn Makes the Right Move Towards Success," *Los Angeles Times*, March 13, 1985, SD-D7.

413 **"I was beginning to feel rich":** *MLA*, 238.

414 **"runaway best-seller":** Ibid., 226.

414 **"so lucid and active":** CH to Packard ("Friday afternoon . . . Your letter"), n.d. [c. December 1961], CHP-T, box 4, folder 7.

414 **"very-very hard":** CH to CVV, December 16, 1961.

415 **"when you have no food"**: CH, "Baby Sister," in *Black on Black: Baby Sister and Selected Writings* (Garden City, N.Y.: Doubleday, 1973), 12.

415 **"natural-born call girl"**: Ibid., 66.

415 **"on the downgrade"**: *MLA*, 241.

416 **"To play jazz you must suffer"**: CH, "Harlem, ou le cancer de l'Amérique," *Présence Africain*, Spring 1963, 81.

416 **"someone laughing their way"**: CH, *The Heat's On* (1966; repr., New York: Vintage, 1988), 146.

416 **"Best Achievement in Documentary Production"**: "Winner of Film Academy Awards," *Los Angeles Times*, April 10, 1962, A2.

416 **terminating the contract:** CH to Arthur Cohn, April 29 and May 1, 1962, CHP-T, box 3, folder 5.

417 **a "semidocumentary" approach:** Howard Thompson, "French Filmmaker to Direct Semidocumentary in Harlem," *New York Times*, July 7, 1962, 9.

417 **the lengthy interview conducted:** Jesse H. Walker, "Theatricals," New York *Amsterdam News*, July 21, 1962, 17.

418 **"got to know" Malcolm X "well":** *MLA*, 247.

418 **Malcolm X excitedly recalled:** CH and François Bott, "Chester Himes: Il n'y a dans aucune autre ville du monde," *Adam*, November 1964, 75.

418 **Malcolm X shared the gory pictures:** "French Film Producer Sees Results," *Muhammad Speaks*, July 31, 1962, 22.

419 **"White syndicates control":** CH, "Harlem, ou le cancer de l'Amérique," 77.

419 **"tough, honest, hip":** Lebert Bethune, "Malcolm X in Europe," in *Malcolm X: The Man and His Times*, ed. John Henrik Clarke (New York: Collier, 1969), 228.

419 **"distrusting white people":** *MLA*, 247.

419 **briefly reopened file:** "Letter to Paris RE: Nation of Islam," August 8, 1962, CH-FBI.

419 **dispute later brought intervention:** "Harlem Business Yields in Dispute," *New York Times*, June 13, 1962, 9.

419 **"The fuse has already":** "2,500 at Moslem Rally," New York *Amsterdam News*, July 28, 1962, 33.

420 **loudly denouncing Los Angeles mayor:** "Mayor Yorty Says Cult Backs 'Hate,'" *New York Times*, July 27, 1962, 8.

421 **She recognized in Van Vechten's:** Marianne Greenwood to CVV, July 27, 1962, CVVP, box He–Hols, folder "Himes, Chester B. 1962–1964."

421 **"an intense impression":** CH to CVV, October 9, 1962, ibid.

422 **the offer was withdrawn:** Robert Cromie, "The Bystander," *Chicago Tribune*, April 8, 1962, D8.

422 **voted to award Williams $2000:** "Novelist Rejects Award; Lays Earlier Loss to Race Bias," *Afro-American*, June 2, 1962, 20.

422 **a few pages of *Lonely Crusade*:** CH, "From *Lonely Crusade*," in *Soon, One Morning*, ed. Herbet Hill (New York: Knopf, 1963), 210–30.

423 **"*Baby Sister* consists":** Herbert Hill, memo to Arthur Cohn, April 16, 1962, MF, box 46, folder 56; JAW, "Chester Himes Is Getting On," *New York Herald Tribune*, October 11, 1964, 2.

423 **Hill had become an FBI informant:** Christopher Phelps, "Herbert Hill and the Federal Bureau of Investigation," *Journal of Labor History* (November 2012): 561–70.

423 **"fanatical" "antiwhite organization":** Legat Paris to Director FBI, August 8, 1962, CH-FBI; Manning Marable, *Malcolm X: A Life of Reinvention* (New York: Viking, 2011), 212.

423 **"the Negro" be depicted "more honestly":** John C. Waugh, "NAACP Scolds Hollywood on Race," *Christian Science Monitor*, June 27, 1963, 1.

424 **"such important new writers":** Robert Kirsch, "Art of Negro Poets and Authors Transcends Race," *Los Angeles Times*, June 24, 1963, D6; L. M. Meriwether, "From Cover to Cover," *Los Angeles Sentinel*, May 30, 1963, A6.

424 **"shake his motherfucking hand":** JAW to CH, March 20, 1966, *DCDJ*, 48.

425 **"I suppose I offered":** *MLA*, 248.

425 **"I did not like":** CH to CVV, October 9, 1962.

425 **"cut off" his career:** *MLA*, 248.

425 **"$10K Cadillac driving":** CH, "Harlem, ou le cancer de l'Amérique," 51.

426 **"the black bourgeoisie":** Ibid., 64.

426 **"Our primary objective":** Ibid., 60.

426 **"the racists in Mississippi":** CH to CVV, October 9, 1962.

427 **"U.S. racists were":** CH to JAW, October 11, 1962, 2.

427 **"It will happen":** CH, "James Meredith: Il y en a pour 450 ans," *Candide*, October 8–10, 1962, 6.

427 **"rain of blood":** Ibid.

427 **"In trouble with the OAS":** CH to CVV, October 9, 1962.

428 **"a European locale":** CH to Arnold Gingrich, November 14, 1962, AG, box 12, folder "H #2."

428 ***Die Welt* also agreed:** Dr. Ramseger to CH, December 30, 1962, CHP-T, box 5, folder 13.

428 **"I don't know how":** CH to CVV, n.d. [November 29, 1962], CVVP, box He–Hols, folder "Himes, Chester B. 1962–1964."

429 **Gallimard claimed:** Marcel Duhamel to CH, September 12, 1962, CHP-T, box 1, folder 11.

429 **Chester identified the misstatements:** CH to Duhamel, December 17, 1962, ibid.

429 **"I did my best":** Duhamel to CH, December 28, 1962, ibid.

429 **paid 7500 francs:** CH, contract with Libraire Plon, December 17, 1962, CHP-T, box 19, folder 2.

14. COTTON COMES TO HARLEM

431 **"What the hell":** MMH-*DCDJ*, 219.

431 **"disparaging remarks":** *MLA*, 201.

431 **"considered the best in New York":** CH to Lesley Packard ("Friday: Lesley darling, in one"), n.d. [c. early 1963], CHP-T, box 4, folder 7.

431 **"at the very top":** CH to JAW, November 1962, *DCDJ*, 30.

431 **"One day people":** Allan Morrison, "Expatriate Novelist Himes," *Jet*, January 31, 1963, 22–23.

432 **"my nerves are on the point":** CH to Packard, n.d. "Wednesday" [c. January 9, 1963], CHP-T, box 4, folder 7.

432 **"it isn't easy":** CH to JAW, Friday, February 1963, *DCDJ*, 38.

432 **"elaborate and sometimes difficult":** Marianne Greenwood to CVV, n.d. [c. January 29, 1963], CVVP, box He–Hols, folder "Himes, Chester B. 1962–1964."

433 **"things did not go well":** CH to CVV, March 29, 1963, ibid.

433 **"sometimes well; sometimes poorly":** CH to JAW, February 6, 1963, *DCDJ*, 39.

433 **"our poor colored people":** CH, *Cotton Comes to Harlem* (1965; repr., New York: Vintage, 1988), 53.

433 **"the Back to Africa program":** *MLA*, 258.

433 **"seeking a home":** CH, *Cotton Comes to Harlem*, 26.

434 **"'I wouldn't do this'":** Ibid., 122.

434 **"a brain spasm":** *MLA*, p. 260.

434 **"'financial obligations'":** CH to JAW, March 6, 1963, *DCDJ*, 41.

435 **"on the tip of a needle":** CH to Packard, April 15, 1963, CHP-T, box 4, folder 7.

435 **"parting of the ways":** CH to JAW, February 25, 1963, *DCDJ*, 40.

435 **"If you are involved":** CH to Packard, April 1, 1963, CHP-T, box 4, folder 7.

435 **wrote to her, graphically exposing:** CH to Lesley Packard, April 3, 1963, ibid.

436 **"I feel much better":** CH to CVV, April 12, 1963, CVVP, box He–Hols, folder "Himes Chester B. 1962–1964."

436 **"clean bill of health":** CH to CVV, January 15, 1964, ibid.

436 **"partial paralysis":** "New York Beat," *Jet*, May 23, 1963, 63–64.

436 **"slight indisposition":** Joseph Himes to CH, June 8, 1963, CHP-T, box 4, folder 5.

436 **"where I am safe":** CH to JAW, March 6, 1963, *DCDJ*, 41.

436 **"I have discovered":** CH to CVV, March 29, 1963, CVVP, box He–Hols, folder "Himes Chester B. 1962–1964."

437 **"the lost and hungry black people":** CH, *Cotton Comes to Harlem*, 7.

437 **"I want to go to Africa":** CH to CVV, April 5, 1963, CVVP, box He–Hols, folder "Himes Chester B. 1962–1964."

437 **"I became very much disliked":** *MLA*, 269.

438 **"a number of articles":** CH to CVV, January 15, 1964.

438 **"Go away!":** Melvin Van Peebles, interview with author, February 2010.

438 **"People are crowding":** CH to CVV, January 15, 1964.

438 **"not like my other books":** *MLA*, 269.

438 **"more famous in Paris":** Ibid., 270.

439 **"The purpose of this work":** Guy de Bosscheres, review of *Une Affaire de viol* by Chester Himes, *Présence Africain*, Fall 1963, 240.

439 **"asking me what had happened":** *MLA*, 271.

440 **"time to sharpen it":** CH to CVV, January 15, 1964.

440 **"I am a writer":** CH to Packard ("Thursday morning, Lesley darling, I got your"), n.d. [c. early 1964], CHP-T, box 4, folder 7.

440 **"Holidays always bother me":** Ibid.

440 **"I am anxious to get":** CH to CVV, January 15, 1964.

440 **"My books drive":** CH to Packard ("Thursday morning, Lesley darling, I got your"), n.d. [c. early 1964].

441 **the first time a U.S. motion picture:** Renata Adler, "Screen: A Black G.I. and a French Girl," *New York Times*, July 9, 1968, 9.

442 **"the greatest black American":** Melvin Van Peebles, "Chester Himes, l'invaincu," *France-Observateur*, February 20, 1964, 14.

442 **"more excellent way":** Martin Luther King Jr., "Letter from a Birmingham Jail," in *Why We Can't Wait* (1964; repr., New York: Signet, 2000), 100.

443 **"a good book I suppose":** CH to CVV, April 6, 1964, CVVP, box He–Hols, folder "Himes Chester B. 1962–1964."

443 **"very bloody book":** Tristan Renaud, "Chester Himes: 'Homeless,'" *Les Lettres Francaises*, March 12, 1964, 5.

443 **the "long journey":** CH to CVV, n.d. [May 12, 1964], CVVP, box He–Hols, folder "Himes Chester B. 1962–1964."

443 **"handsome" and "full of life":** Van Peebles, "Chester Himes, l'invaincu," 13.

444 **"the same terms used":** Van Peebles, "Harlem en Feu," *France-Observateur*, July 23, 1964, 9.

445 **"I'm sure you have":** Don Preston to CH, September 18, 1964, CHP-T, box 1, folder 1.

445 **"Not only is there indefinable poverty":** CH to CVV, October 23, 1964, CVVP, box He–Hols, folder "Himes, Chester B. 1962–1964."

445 **"which I consider"**: *MLA*, 289.

445 **"that racism has greatly"**: CH to CVV, October 23, 1964.

446 **"I'm an evil, highly sensitive"**: *MLA*, 278.

446 **"in the back of my mind"**: CH to Seymour Lawrence, November 4, 1964, AAK.

446 **organize a small insurrection**: Peniel Joseph, *Waiting 'Til the Midnight Hour: A Narrative History of Black Power in America* (New York: Henry Holt, 2006), 313.

447 **Fidel Castro's racist policies**: Carlos Moore, "Le People noir a-t-il sa place dans la revolution cubaine?," *Présence Africain*, Summer 1964, 177–230.

447 **"unfriendly, very savage"**: Carlos Moore, interview with author, May 2010.

447 **the "wonderful" essay**: *MLA*, 268.

447 **"Chester had this thing"**: Moore interview.

448 **"bitter and hermetic"**: William Gardner Smith, *The Stone Face* (New York: Farrar, Straus Giroux, 1963), 176.

448 **"Chester was a very bitter"**: Moore interview.

448 **$7500 on signing**: CH, contract with Dell and Putnam for *Cotton Comes to Harlem*, November 4, 1964, CHP-T, box 14, folder 1.

448 **Stein and Day for $10,000**: CH, contract with Stein and Day, January 29, 1965, CHP-T, box 14, folder 1.

448 **"the American publishers"**: CH to CVV, October 23, 1964.

448 **"displayed in the place of prominence"**: *MLA*, 290.

449 **"After that everybody"**: Ibid., 290–91.

449 **On November 22**: The most accurate biography of Malcolm X, Manning Marable's *Malcolm X: A Life of Reinvention* (New York: Viking, 2011), suggests that Malcolm X arrived in Paris on November 18, 1964, and checked into the Hotel Dêlavine, where he is to have remained for five days until the lecture (p. 386). Marable cites as evidence Nicol Davidson, "Alioune Diop and the African Renaissance," which does not mention Malcolm X or his visit to Paris. Malcolm X's travel diary, located in the Schomburg Center for Research in Black Culture, appears to have its final entry on November 16, 1964, and his FBI file picks him up in the United States on November 24, 1964. In this case, I find Carlos Moore's representation of the events and the timetable more credible than Marable's account.

449 **took him to the Café Realis**: Carlos Moore, "Malcolm, je me souviens," *Présence Africain*, Spring 1967, 85.

449 **"Chester Himes is here?"**: Moore interview.

450 **"that few people had known"**: Moore, "Malcolm, je me souviens," 88.

450 **"Carlos knows this"**: Moore, interview.

450 **"You're being gullible"**: Ibid.

450 **"beautiful things"**: Carlos Moore to CH, May 19, 1975, CHP-T, box 4, folder 19.

451 **"we are where we are"**: Ishmael Reed to CH, November 23, 1970, CHP-T, box 5, folder 13.

451 **"They're going to get me"**: Moore interview.

451 **Chester and Lesley silently hunkered:** Lesley Packard Himes, interview with author, May 2009.

451 **"bridge between the peoples"**: Malcolm X, "The Afro-American in the Face of the African Revolution," p. 1, Carlos Moore Papers, box 6, folder "1964–1965," Ralph Bunche Center, University of California at Los Angeles.

452 **"Whoever a person"**: Ibid, pp. 8, 9.

452 I AM DREADFULLY SORRY: CH, telegram to Mrs. Carl Van Vechten, December 23, 1964, CVVP, box He–Hols, folder "Himes, Chester B. 1962–1964."

452 **declaring him an "undesirable"**: Malcolm X and Alex Haley, *The Autobiography of Malcolm X* (New York: Ballantine, 1965), 434.

453 **"the more I keep thinking"**: Ibid., 438.

15. A MOOR IN SPAIN

455 **Putnam would publish:** Lewis Nichols, "In and Out of Books: Collaboration," *New York Times Book Review*, April 4, 1965, 8; Publishing agreement, G.P. Putnam, Stein and Day, and Maurice Girodias, June 15, 1965, CHP-T, box 19, folder 2.

455 **"All that most middle-class Negroes"**: *Pinktoes*, advertisement, *New York Times Book Review*, July 11, 1965, 11.

455 **described his writing process:** Melvin Van Peebles, interview with author, February 2010.

455 **"My novel moves"**: *MLA*, 295.

455 **"like a cross"**: Ibid., 297.

455 **"You should marry"**: Ibid., 301.

456 **"a humorous catalog"**: René Micha, "Les Paroissiens de Chester Himes," *Les Temps Modernes*, February 1965, 1517.

456 **left a manuscript:** Lesley Packard Himes, interview with author, May 2009.

457 **"Chester needed a fucking nurse"**: Van Peebles interview.

457 **"I hated to give up"**: *MLA*, 301.

457 **"extraordinary series"**: Anthony Boucher, "Criminals at Large" (review of *Cotton Comes to Harlem* by CH), *New York Times Book Review*, February 7, 1965, 43.

457 **"More important in this book"**: Jory Sherman, "Crime and Social Comment" (review of *Cotton Comes to Harlem* by CH), *Los Angeles Times*, February 14, 1965, B16.

458 **"losses into a modest profit"**: William Targ to CH, November 28, 1967, CHP-T, box 2, folder 4.

458 **"quick, sharp, sexy"**: *MLA*, 302.

458 **"faster than any car"**: Ibid., 303.

458 **write a graphic novel adaptation**: CH, "La Reine des pommes," adapted and realized by Melvin Van Peebles, drawings by George Wolinski, *Hara Kiri*, June 1966, 9–53.

459 **"I don't write for money"**: *MLA*, 310.

459 **"In its wild funhouse-mirror way"**: Anthony Boucher, "Criminals at Large" (review of *The Heat's On* by CH), *New York Times*, January 16, 1966, 18.

459 **"I have a feeling"**: Anthony Boucher, "Criminals at Large" (review of *The Crazy Kill* by CH), *New York Times Book Review*, December 6, 1959, 42.

460 **"perverse blend"**: Anthony Boucher, "Criminals at Large" (review of *The Real Cool Killers* by CH), *New York Times Book Review*, September 6, 1959, 13.

460 **"turbulent, nightmarish"**: Anthony Boucher, "Criminals at Large" (review of *The Big Gold Dream* by CH), *New York Times Book Review*, March 6, 1960, 43.

460 **"underrated and underpublicized"**: Andrew Sarris, "Good Intentions," *New York Times Book Review*, April 24, 1966, 20.

460 **"the wildest of camps"**: Boucher, "Criminals at Large" (review of *Cotton Comes to Harlem*), February 7, 1965, 43.

460 **One of the people reading**: A. H. Weiler, "Success Spangled Simon," *New York Times*, December 4, 1966, 14.

460 **a biography of Ian Fleming**: "Movie Call Sheet: Role for Shelley Winters," *Los Angeles Times*, December 6, 1966, D25.

460 **"I'm convinced they"**: Weiler, "Success Spangled Simon," 14.

461 **"sumptuous feast"**: *MLA*, 315.

461 **"American Negro"**: Anonymous [Patricia Highsmith], "Balefull of Laughs: Review of *Cotton Comes to Harlem* by Chester Himes," *Times Literary Supplement*, January 20, 1966, 37.

462 **"beginning to enjoy"**: *MLA*, 319.

462 **"about my mother"**: Don L. Lee, *Think Black!* (Chicago: Nuace Printers, 1967), 21.

462 **"people say bad things"**: CVV to JAW, August 2, 1962, *DCDJ*, 1.

463 **"nothing jelled"**: *MLA*, 327.

463 **"As I'm sure you know"**: Samuel Goldwyn Jr. to CH, December 12, 1966, CHP-T, box 3, folder 20.

464 **"That was my entire life"**: *MLA*, 337.

464 **"It has always been my opinion"**: CH, "Reading on Your Own," *New York Times Book Review*, June 4, 1967, 4.

465 **"Believing that this cultured":** Ibid.

465 **"superb" comment:** Erik Wensberg to CH, May 19, 1967, CHP-T, box 6, folder 13.

465 **"expense is no matter":** *MLA*, 339.

466 **Chester expressed his fury:** Constance Pearlstein to James Sallis, December 10, 1998, *LPH*, box 1, folder 16.

467 **LeRoi Jones was arrested:** "LeRoi Jones Seized in Newark After Being Hurt," *New York Times*, July 15, 1967, 11.

467 **"Shoot the niggers":** Martin Arnold, "Negroes Battle with Guardsmen," *New York Times*, July 15, 1967, 11.

467 **"never seen until they lie bloody":** CH, "On the Use of Force," p. 1, CHP-T, box 23, folder "'On the Use of Force' Photocopy Typescript."

467 **"Police brutality toward":** Ibid., p. 7.

468 **"Every race riot":** Ibid., p. 9.

468 **"thoughts on writing, writers":** Targ to CH, November 28, 1967.

469 **"not [as] a detective story":** CH to Marcel Duhamel, April 20, 1968, CHP-T, box 1, folder 11.

469 **"not up to the standard":** Targ to CH, November 28, 1967.

469 **"let the book stand":** James Landis to CH, June 28, 1968, CHP-T, box 2, folder 18.

469 **"Shooting people":** "Ship of Rebels," *Newsweek*, April 6, 1970, 15.

469 **a "most unhappy" Goldwyn:** Goldwyn to CH, October 24, 1967, CHP-T, box 3, folder 20.

469 **"loose construction of a movie":** Goldwyn to CH, November 13, 1967, ibid.

470 **"with all the screenwriters":** Rosalyn Targ to CH, December 12, 1967, CHP-T, box 1, folder 12.

470 **"the only milestone":** CH to JAW, June 13, 1969, *DCDJ*, 83.

471 **"a nervous, wretched man":** JAW, "Chester Himes Is Getting On," *New York Herald Tribune*, October 11, 1964, 21.

471 **"More than you could":** JAW to CH, December 12, 1968, *DCDJ*, 52.

471 **"seeming indifference":** CH to JAW, December 28, 1968, ibid., 54.

471 **"It's all right, man":** *MLA*, 347.

471 **"A friend of mine":** CH, "Preface," *Blind Man with a Pistol* (1969; repr., New York: Vintage, 1989), 5.

472 **Chester angrily shouted:** Richard Gibson to Michel Fabre, May 26, 1988, MF, box 6, folder 18.

472 **"Deutsche Haus":** Donna Rothraud Meindorfer, interview with author, May 2009.

473 **estimates were 200,000:** Julius Ruiz, "Seventy Years On: Historians and Repressions After the Spanish Civil War," *Journal of Contemporary History* (July 2009): 451.

473 **"Moraira was as racist":** *MLA*, 369.

473 **"Spain is not a place"**: Rosalyn Targ to CH, December 12, 1967.

473 **"divorced the United States"**: *MLA*, 355.

473 **"Comic Suspense Film"**: "Comic Suspense Film of Negro Detectives to be Made in Harlem," *Philadelphia Tribune*, April 6, 1968, 19.

474 **"Perhaps that was one"**: Goldwyn to Himes, April 24, 1968, CHP-T, box 3, folder 20.

474 **"offensive"**: HF, 87.

474 **"the Jews had a right"**: Ibid.

475 **"I am trying to show"**: HF, 195.

475 **"'It's the uprising, nigger!'"**: CH, *Plan B* (Jackson: University of Mississippi Press, 1993), 8.

476 **"'You can't kill, Black, man'"**: Ibid., 202.

476 **"The main thing"**: CH to JAW, December 18, 1968, *DCDJ*, 56.

477 **"Motherfucking right"**: CH to JAW, "Foreword," *Blind Man with a Pistol*, 5.

477 **"Reading *Blind Man*"**: Richard Rhodes, "Blind Man with a Pistol," *New York Times Book Review*, February 23, 1969, 32.

477 **Mystery Writers of America**: Allen J. Hubin, "Criminals at Large," *New York Times Book Review*, May 10, 1970.

477 **"I got my standard"**: Phil Lomax to CH, August 8, 1969, CHP-T, box 4, folder 17.

478 **"the highlight of the issue"**: Julius Lester, "The First Magazine of Black Writing: *Amistad 1*," *New York Times Book Review*, May 3, 1970, 36.

478 **"almost sixty now" and "not well"**: *MLA*, 364.

478 **"the thing that cooled our relationship"**: *DCDJ*-MMH, p. 14.

479 **"take being black"**: Ralph Ellison, dust jacket, *Hue and Cry* by James A. McPherson (Boston: Little, Brown, 1969).

479 **"the white press"**: HF, 14, 15.

479 **"the younger writers"**: JAW to CH, July 14, 1969, *DCDJ*, 93.

480 **"far from being"**: James Baldwin, "The Price May Be Too High," *New York Times*, February 2, 1969, D9.

480 **"the best black American"**: Shane Stevens, "'The Best Black American Novelist Writing Today,'" *Chicago Tribune*, April 27, 1969, L4.

480 **"to speak up if he"**: Rosalyn Targ to CH, July 30, 1969, CHP-T, box 1, folder 12.

480 **"White folks won't know"**: JAW to CH, July 14, 1969, 93.

480 **"I can imagine"**: CH to JAW, July 19, 1969, *DCDJ*, 95.

481 **"looked like an imbecile child"**: CH to JAW, November 2, 1969, ibid., 107.

481 **"physically difficult"**: CH to Joseph Himes, May 9, 1970, *TSH*, 181, folder "Correspondence Chester Himes."

481 **"Nice to hear from"**: Ken McCormick to CH, August 18, 1969, CHP-T, box 1, folder 8.

481 **he offered $10,000:** Rosalyn Targ to CH, April 13, 1970, CHP-T, box 1, folder 12; Chester Himes, contract for *My Life of Absurdity*, Doubleday, July 16, 1975, CHP-T, box 14, folder 1. CH received a $5000 advance on April 29, 1971.

481 **"I'm not very happy":** CH to JAW, July 27, 1970, *DCDJ*, 133.

482 **"nigger-lover":** JAW to CH, June 30, 1969, ibid., 89.

482 **"got a lot of things cracking":** JAW to CH, April 15, 1970, ibid., 123.

482 **"Look, I have talked":** MMH-*DCDJ*, 214.

482 **"impressive as an overall":** William Targ to CH, April 7, 1970, CHP-T, box 2, folder 4.

482 **"colorful, exciting life-style and wit":** Vincent Canby, "Ossie Davis' *Cotton Comes to Harlem*," *New York Times*, June 11, 1970, 50.

482 ***Cotton* broke the opening-day box-office records:** "Theaters to Remain Open 24 Hours Daily for *Cotton Comes to Harlem*," *Philadelphia Tribune*, July 18, 1970, 21; Eithne Quinn, "'Tryin' to Get Over': Super Fly, Black Politics, and Post Civil Rights Film Enterprise," *Cinema Journal* 49, no. 2 (Winter 2010): 86–87.

482 **"the best way":** Gene Siskel, "Trying Too Hard," *Chicago Tribune*, May 28, 1970, C17.

483 **"Chester Himes has been writing":** Carole Lyles, "A Movie About Blacks Without Social Comment," New York *Amsterdam News*, June 13, 1970, 20.

483 **"a sense of liberation":** Canby, "Ossie Davis' *Cotton Comes to Harlem*," 50.

483 **"cut the gut and heart":** Lindsay Paterson, "In Harlem, a James Bond with Soul," *New York Times*, June 15, 1969, D15.

483 **"tapped [his] literary vault":** JAW to CH, May 13, 1970, *DCDJ*, 127.

483 **parent company M-G-M:** Jon Hartman, "The Trope of Blaxploitation in Critical Responses to *Sweetback*," *Film History* 6, no. 3 (Autumn 1994): 391.

483 **the sound economic value:** They were assessed by the industry in the following rank: *Shaft* ($7 million), *Cotton* ($5.1 million), and *Sweetback* ($4.1 million). See Lawrence Cohn, "All-Time Film Rental Champs," *Variety*, May 10, 1993, C76–106, 108; Quinn, "'Tryin' to Get Over.'"

483 **the NAACP generated the term:** Quinn, "'Tryin' to Get Over,'" 87.

483 **"blaxploitation":** Junius Griffin quoted in "NAACP Takes Militant Stand on Black Exploitation Films," *Hollywood Reporter*, August 10, 1972.

484 **"big hit":** Helen Jackson to CH, September 30, 1970, CHP-T, box 4, folder 13.

484 **"general American attitude":** CH to William Targ, January 3, 1971, CHP-T, box 6, folder 1.

485 **"As you know":** Jackson to CH, May 14, 1971, CHP-T, box 4, folder 13.

485 **"Major authors are not":** Jackson to CH, June 10, 1971, ibid.

485 **"For those who wonder":** Maya Angelou to Helen Jackson, December 27, 1971, CHP-T, box 6, folder 1.

486 **"influenced by your work and personality"**: Lindsey Barrett to CH, n.d., CHP-T, box 3, folder 3.

486 **"a very lasting and important"**: Clarence Major to CH, December 31, 1971, CHP-T, box 4, folder 19.

486 **"son-of-a-bitchery"**: Arnold Gingrich, "A Writer Writes," *Chicago Tribune*, March 26, 1972, I-12.

487 **"direct, straightforward, honest"**: Nathan Irvin Huggins, "The Helpless Victim" (review of *The Quality of Hurt* by Chester Himes), *New York Times Book Review*, March 12, 1972, 5.

487 **"I feel that it is"**: Julius Lester to CH, n.d. [Spring 1972], CHP-T, box 4, folder 17.

487 **"Because this book tells"**: Julius Lester, "Letter to the Editor: *The Quality of Hurt*," *New York Times Book Review*, April 30, 1972, 39.

487 **"raw" and "penetrating"**: Michael J. Bandler, "Travails of a Black Author" (review of *The Quality of Hurt* by Chester Himes), *Los Angeles Times*, July 14, 1972, F6.

487 **the "truthful" portrait**: Myra D. Bain, "Himes Tells a Special Tale: Rev. of *The Quality of Hurt* by Chester Himes," New York *Amsterdam News*, March 25, 1972, D7.

487 **"an angry, alienated black"**: Christopher Lehmann-Haupt, "Another Quality Not Strain'd" (review of *The Quality of Hurt* by Chester Himes), *New York Times*, March 8, 1972, 41.

488 **seven hundred guests:** "Chester Himes Book Party," *Black World*, March 1972, 92.

488 **"all of us really enjoyed"**: Ishmael Reed to CH, May 11, 1972, CHP-T, box 5, folder 13; see also Steve Cannon to CH, May 9, 1972, CHP-T, box 3, folder 5.

488 **Chester had stabbed:** Keith Gilyard, interview with author, January 2013.

489 **"who are proponents"**: JAW to CH, January 12, 1972, *DCDJ*, 152.

489 STOPRY **[sic]** INCOMPLETE: Skip Gates, telegram to CH, August 20, 1973, CHP-T, box 3, folder 14.

489 **"I think fame"**: Nikki Giovanni to CH, November 13, 1973, CHP-T, box 3, folder 18.

16. AFRO-AMERICAN PEOPLE'S NOVELIST

490 **"I still suffer"**: CH to Director General, American Hospital, Madrid, January 9, 1973, CHP-T, box 18, folder 1.

490 **"admittedly chauvinistic"**: CH, *Black on Black: Baby Sister and Selected Writings* (Garden City, N.Y.: Doubleday, 1973), 7.

491 **"no jive or rage"**: "Black on Black," *Chicago Tribune*, February 11, 1973, F3.

491 **"substantially improved sight"**: Joseph Himes Jr. to CH, May 28, 1973, CHP-T, box 4, folder 5.

491 **"I can see":** Joseph Himes Jr. to CH, May 27, 1974, ibid.

491 **attained veracity:** CH to Marcel Duhamel, February 25, 1974, CHP-T, box 3, folder 8.

492 **"the best of my writing":** CH to Sandy Richardson, May 2, 1974, CHP-T 180, box 1, folder 9.

492 **in July 1974 Chester went:** CH to Ishmael Reed, July 23, 1974, CHP-T, box 5, folder 13.

492 **"My health has improved":** CH to Michel Fabre, January 13, 1975, MF, box 41, folder 4.

492 **"The Harlem detective stories":** CH to Richardson, May 2, 1974.

493 **"I have great hopes":** CH to Fabre, January 13, 1975.

493 **"Gravedigger [sic] and Coffin Ed":** Ishmael Reed to CH, January 24, 1974, CHP-T, box 5, folder 13.

493 **"punk shit":** Robert Adams, interview with author, April 2003. This assertion is lent validity by a short aside Willa Thompson once made in 1955, suggesting that when they lived together in 1954 she had suspected CH of having had a liaison with a boy—see WT to CH ("Darling: I have your special here"), n.d. [c. June 1955], CHP-T, box 5, folder 6. Thompson wrote, "You never mentioned that you saw this strange boy who gave you the book in London around that time. You never mentioned the girl whose name is on the French edition of If He Hollers. . . ."

493 **"my mind is getting":** CH to Rosalyn Targ, March 1, 1976, CHP-T, box 8, folder 10.

493 **"My health has deteriorated":** CH to Rosalyn Targ, November 11, 1976, ibid.

494 **"My sins are catching":** CH to Jean Himes, February 25, 1976, CHP-T, box 4, folder 11.

494 **"I will probably be dead":** CH to Duhamel, May 11, 1976, CHP-T, box 3, folder 8.

494 **"How does it feel":** Reed to CH, October 22, 1976, CHP-T, box 5, folder 13.

494 **"I hope that I haven't:** CH to Joseph Himes Jr., November 25, 1976, CHP-T, box 4, folder 7.

494 **"taken together, the two volumes":** Don Bredes, "The Purgative Thoughts of Chester Himes," *Los Angeles Times*, March 20, 1977, U7.

495 **"knuckleheaded" editor:** Al Young to CH, May 7, 1972, CHP-T, box 6, folder 18.

495 **"a singularly poignant autobiography":** Al Young, "Rev. *My Life of Absurdity: The Autobiography of Chester Himes, Volume II* by Chester Himes," *New York Times Book Review*, February 13, 1977, 7. Online.

495 **"I got you beat":** *MLA*, 30.

495 **"I should not have"**: CH to Rosalyn Targ, February 12, 1977, CHP-T, box 1, folder 12.

496 **"I've made a lot"**: Walter Coleman to CH, October 18, 1972, CHP-T, box 7, folder 5.

496 **"sex doesn't delight me anymore"**: CH to Rosalyn Targ, September 22, 1977, CHP-T, box 1, folder 12.

496 **divorced on May 2**: "Le Chambre Matrimoniale, Section 13 du Tribunal de Grande Instance de Paris, I6 II8/77 No. 7703417, Divorce, Sieur Himes contre Dame Plater-Johnson; No. 2734 Divorce de Himes, Chester Bomar et Plater-Johnson, Jean L., 30 Novembre 1978, Ministère des Affaires Etrangères, Nantes," CHP-T, box 20, folder 8.

496 **"his moral being is not so great"**: Lesley Packard to Joseph Himes Jr., March 3, 1978, CHP-T, box 4, folder 7.

497 **"things are a mess here"**: Joseph Himes Jr. to CH, October 12, 1980, CHP-T, box 4, folder 5.

497 **the consultant backed out**: George Rolfe to CH, September 26, 1980, CHP-T, box 20, folder 4.

497 **he tumbled onto the ground**: Lesley Himes, interview with author, May 2009.

497 **"his memory is terrible"**: Packard to J. Himes Jr., March 3, 1978.

497 **the American Book Award**: Gundar Strads to CH, March 29, 1982, CHP-T, box 5, folder 13.

497 **"It saddened me enormously"**: Rosalyn Targ to Lesley Himes, January 27, 1984, CHP-T, box 2, folder 13.

498 **hurtful and bitter remarks**: Helen Chapparal to Lesley Himes, LPH, box 1, folder 5.

498 **chiseling knives**: *MLA*, p. 254.

498 **"When Chester was Chester"**: JAW to Lesley Himes, November 28, 1984, *DCDJ*, 162.

Acknowledgments

I began this project in 2002 after a long conversation with my friend and teacher Horace Porter. The next year I was fortunate to spend the afternoon with Michel Fabre at his home in Mt. Royal and to be the recipient of much of his generosity in the form of copies of the materials he had collected when he coauthored a biography of Chester Himes in 1997. I have endeavored to write the "big book" that Michel and I thought Chester Himes deserved.

I would like to thank the College of Emory University and in particular Robin Foreman, the dean of the college, who has supported my career at crucial stages. My fellow biographer of black writers Keith Gilyard has lent great support and genuine brotherhood to me and been an uncle to my children. Dean Beverly Wendland and Vice Dean Chris Celenza at Johns Hopkins University have also been unusually helpful and supportive of this project. At Johns Hopkins, I also appreciate the welcome and support of colleagues Hollis Robbins, Chris Nealon, Mark Thompson, John Marshall, Cheryl Holcombe-McCoy, and Kathryn Edin.

There are always a series of mischances and odd occasions in the course of writing a biography, but I would like to thank three people who have made a powerful impression on my understanding of Chester Himes. One year before her death, an ill Lesley Himes welcomed me into her home in Spain. She was a gracious and considerate hostess, in spite of the fact that she was rushed to the hospital during my brief stay in Moraira. Melvin Van Peebles also was very generous with his time. Finally, Carlos Moore, whom I regard highly as a complex committed man of literary and intellectual affairs, made himself available on multiple occasions and contributed a valuable portrait of two world-class figures whom he knew intimately.

Dr. Preston King has graciously taken his time to help me develop my reflections on this period and shared his knowledge, wisdom, and personal recollections of several key twentieth-century transatlantic black figures. It has been my privilege to have him as a friend.

I would also like to thank James A. Miller and Jerry G. Watts, who joined the ancestors in 2015. My friends David Miller, Dr. Leroy Reese, Nathan McCall, and James Ezelio have helped me to see the brighter side of life. My mother and my sons have been unusually supportive and understanding of the odd life of the writer.

My agent, Regina Brooks; my editor, Amy Cherry; her assistant, Remy Cawley; and my expert copy editor, Trent Duffy, have contributed a great deal to this project.

Evelyn Crawford and Mary Louise Patterson are exemplary women I have been so very fortunate to know. I would also like to thank colleagues Michael D. Hill, Alan Wald, Vanessa Siddle-Walker, Isabel Wilkerson, Richard Yarborough, Jonathan Eburne, Dianne Stewart, James Sallis, Michelle Gordon, Shana Redmond, Lena Hill, Valerie Loichot, François Furstenberg, James West, William Maxwell, Dolan Hubbard, Kevin Bell, Elizabeth Alexander, Manthia Diawara, Ike Newsum, Ayesha Hardison, and Beverly Moss. Several people shared their knowledge of World War II–era California: Alden Kimbrough, Walter Gordon, and William Beverly.

Molly Lewis, Rosylin Meindorfer, and Marylin Mobeley hospitably contributed to my understanding of New York, Spain, and Cleveland.

I am especially grateful for the insights and hard work of students Gloria Jirsairaie, Olivia Young, Nicole Morris, Adam Newman, Joshua Coen, Jimmy Worthy, Guy Conn, Guirdex Masse, Toni Jones, and Rebekah Ramsay.

I would like to express my gratitude for the help of multiple librarians and the libraries who serve the public: Amistad Library, Tulane University: Christopher Harter and Lee Hampton; Ralph Bunche Center, UCLA: Susan Anderson, Dalena Hunter, and Darnel Hunt; Southern California Library for Social Studies Research: Yusef Omowale, Michele Wesling, Julie Grigsby, and Racquel Chavez; Huntington Library; Missouri Historical Society; the Stuart A. Rose Library at Emory University: especially Randall Burkett and Pellom McDaniels; Emory University library staff, Marie Hansen, Jerrold Brantley and Erica Brucho; St. Louis Public Library; Alcorn State College Library: Professor J. Janice Williams; Yale University: Jacqueline Goldsby, Robert Stepto, and the staff at the Beinecke Rare Book Library; University of Arkansas, Pine Bluff Special Collections; Cleveland Public Library; Western Reserve Historical Society; Cuyahoga County Archives; Ohio State Historical Society, Columbus; Schomburg Center for Research in Black Culture; Moorland-Spingarn Research Center, Howard University.

Enfin, je voudrais dire "merci" aux mes amis et frères le plus generieux qui habitant en Bouake et Abidjan, Côte d'Ivoire: Eugene N'Guessen, Daouda Coulibaly, Vamara Koné, Herman Camara, Pierre Kramoko, Toh Zorobi, Zie Outtara, *et* Azouma Outtara. *Amities.*

Index